Beaches and Coasts

Beaches and Coasts

second edition

Cuchlaine A. M. King
Professor of Physical Geography, University of Nottingham

New York · St. Martin's Press

AFFILIATED PUBLISHERS: Macmillan & Company, Limited, London
— also at Bombay, Calcutta, Madras and Melbourne — The Macmillan
Company of Canada, Limited, Toronto

Preface to the second edition

The rewriting of the second edition was started about ten years after the publication of the first edition. During this decade knowledge and techniques have advanced rapidly, but much of the basic work remains of value. In the new edition, therefore, relatively little of the old has been discarded, but it has been abbreviated and rearranged in what it is hoped is a more logical way. The increase of material has necessitated further subdivision and some chapters are entirely new; others are expanded sections of the first edition.

The present volume is arranged in four parts. The first one introduces the forms and the techniques for studying them. The second deals with the processes operating to give the beach and coast their character. A new chapter on sea level fluctuations is included. The third part is devoted to beaches. It deals with beach material, its movement and the forms it produces, concluding with a new chapter on minor forms and features related to the special climatic conditions of the tropics and polar regions. The fourth part is devoted to the coast.

The basic division between beaches and coasts is their scale and the tempo at which they change and evolve. This matter is considered in the concluding chapter. The importance of the beach to coastal development is stressed and the great variety and variability of coastal phenomena are shown to be due to the unusual conditions of the present time. The cause of the unique coastal situation in geological time is the recent, large and geologically very rapid fluctuations of sea level. The sea has only been relatively stable in level during the last 3000 years, following a very rapid rise during the preceding millennia.

C. A. M. King
UNIVERSITY OF NOTTINGHAM

Preface to the first edition

Since D. W. Johnson's book on *Shore processes and shoreline development* was published in 1919 much work has been done on the processes at work on the coast and on the evolution of different coastal areas. A number of books have appeared, such as Shepard's *Submarine geology*, Steers' *Coastline of England and Wales* and Guilcher's *Morphologie littorale et sous-marine*, which deal with coastal features. This work approaches the subject from a rather different aspect, and is an attempt to gather together some of the recent work on coastal problems, especially those associated with the character of the beach.

For most people the seashore is an area for relaxation, but some, such as Civil Engineers concerned with coastal processes, must look more critically at the forces at work on the coast. It is hoped that this book may contain information of use to them and to other workers engaged in research or planning on the beach and coast. Of the forces acting upon the shore, waves are the most important in the development of the beach and coast, but they are also one of the most difficult to analyse, especially near the coast.

My thanks are due to all who have assisted in many ways. I would like to acknowledge gratefully, the help and advice kindly given by Dr G. E. R. Deacon, F.R.S., and other members of the staff of the National Institute of Oceanography, particularly Mr Darbyshire, in the preparation of the chapter on waves. However, any errors in this and other chapters are solely my responsibility. Acknowledgement is also made to all who have kindly permitted figures from their published work to be reproduced and especially to the Beach Erosion Board, Washington, whose Technical Memoranda provide a valuable source of data on current research.

C. A. M. King
UNIVERSITY OF NOTTINGHAM
April 1959

Contents

Acknowledgements

The author and publisher gratefully acknowledge permission given by the following to reprint or to modify copyright material:

The American Geophysical Union for a figure from *Transactions* 33, 855–65 (paper by R. S. Arthur, W. H. Munk and J. D. Isaacs) [Figure 2-7D],[1] 3 figures from *Transactions* 33, 381–9 (paper by C. L. Bretschneider) [Figures 3-11A & B, 3-12], a figure from *Transactions* 30, 337–45 (paper by J. A. Putnam, W. H. Munk and M. A. Traylor) [Figure 4-17], 3 figures from *Transactions* 31, 196–212 (paper by F. P. Shepherd and D. L. Inman) [Figures 4-19A–C], 2 figures from *Transactions* 31, 555–65 (paper by T. Saville) [Figures 10-4A & B], and 2 figures from *Transactions* 32, 868–74 (paper by W. N. Bascom) [Figures 11-6, 12-11]; the Editor and Andhra University for a figure from *Andhra University, Memoranda in Oceanography* 62, 69–74 (paper by C. Mahaderson and R. Prasada Rao) [Figure 19-10]; the Editor for a figure from *Journal of Applied Ecology* 4, 239–53 (paper by D. S. Ranwell) [Figure 16-6B]; the Editor and the author for a figure from *Australian Journal of Applied Science* 6, 261–6 (paper by R. Silvester) [Figure 3-14]; University of Wisconsin, Department of Meteorology, the Editor and the author for a figure from *Arctic and Alpine Research* 1, 67–68 (paper by J. T. Andrews) [Figure 7-7]; the Editor and the authors for a figure from *Australian Geographer* 8, 42–4 (paper by J. L. Davies) [Figure 13-1], and for a figure from *Australian Geographer* 6, 76–90 (paper by J. N. Jennings) [Figure 19-13A]; the U.S. Army, Corps of Engineers, Beach Erosion Board for the following from *Beach Erosion Board Technical Memoranda*: 4 figures from no. 43 (by G. Neumann) [Figures 3-13A–D], 3 figures from no. 55 (by T. Saville) [Figures 4-6A–C], 2 figures from no. 79 (by D. L. Inman and N. Nasu) [Figures 4-11, 4-12], a figure from no. 63 (by A. T. Ippen and P. S. Eagleson) [Figure 9-5], a figure from no. 82 (by D. L. Inman and G. A. Rusnak) [Figure 9-6], a figure from no. 34 (by G. M. Watts) [Figure 9-9], a figure from no. 68 (by J. M. Caldwell) [Figure 10-7], a figure from no. 126 (by P. S. Eagleson, B. Glenne and J. A. Dracup) [Figure 11-1], a figure from no. 65 (by P. D. Trask and C. A. Johnson) [Figure 11-3], a figure from no. 76 (by P. D. Trask) [Figure 11-5], 2 figures from no. 15 (by F. P. Shepherd) [Figures 12-17, 12-30], and a figure from no. 44 (by P. Bruun) [Figure 17-5]; the Editor and the U.S. Army, Corps of Engineers, Beach Erosion Board for a figure from *Bulletin* 9, 5–13 (paper by R. F. Dearduff) [Figure 3-18]; the Beach Erosion Board, Washington, D.C., for a figure from *Interim Report*, 1933 [Figure 9-8]; the Syndics of Cambridge University Press, the Editor and the author for a figure from *Biological Reviews* 44, 433–98 (paper by D. R. Stoddart) [Figure 14-3]; the Editor and the Biological Society of the British Isles for a figure from *Bulletin* 7, 1–7 (paper by J. C. E. Hubbard and R. E. Stubbings) [Figure 16-6A]; the University of California Institute of Engineering Research, Wave Research Laboratory for 2 figures from *Sand movement by waves* by T. Scott [Figures 11-2, 12-10]; the Syndics of Cambridge University Press for a figure from *The dynamics of the upper ocean* by O. M. Phillips [Figure 3-6]; the American Society of Engineers and the

---

[1] Figure numbers enclosed in square brackets refer to those in this book.

Editor for 2 figures from *Proceedings of the Tenth Conference of Coastal Engineers*, Tokyo, 217–33 (paper by K. Horikawa and Chin-Tong Kuo) [Figures 4-2A & B], 3 figures from *Proceedings of the Tenth Conference of Coastal Engineers*, Tokyo, 236–48 (paper by T. Edelman) [Figures 12-31A–C], and 3 figures from *Proceedings of the Tenth Conference of Coastal Engineers*, Tokyo, 1331–59 (paper by K. P. Blumenthal) [Figures 16-12, 16-13, 16-14]; the U.S. Army, Corps of Engineers, Coastal Erosion Research Center for 5 figures from *Technical Report* 4, third edition (by C. L. Bretschneider) [Figures 3-11C, 4-7A–D], a figure from *Technical Memo* 26 (by B. R. Bodine) [Figure 4-20], a figure from *Technical Memo* 18 (by J. C. Fairchild) [Figure 10-5B], a figure from *Technical Memo* 14 (by J. A. Cherry) [Figure 10-11], a figure from *Technical Memo* 19 (by A. J. Bowen and D. L. Inman) [Figure 10-12], and a figure from *Technical Memo* 28 (by M. A. Carstens, F. M. Neilson and H. D. Altenbilek) [Figure 14-1]; the Editor for 7 figures from the *Dock and Harbour Authority Journal* 37, 31–4 (paper by J. Darbyshire) [Figures 3-4A–E, 3-15, 3-16]; John C. Doornkamp for 2 figures from *Numerical analysis in geomorphology* by John C. Doornkamp and Cuchlaine A. M. King, Edward Arnold, 1971 [Figures 13-2, 16-7]; the Editor for a figure from *Die Erde* 6, 296–315 (paper by H. Valentin) [Figure 17-8]; the Editor and the authors for a figure from *East Midland Geographer* 22, 307–21 (paper by A. H. W. Robinson) [Figure 5-10], and for a figure from *East Midland Geographer* 15, 20–31 (paper by F. A. Barnes and C. A. M. King) [Figure 16-5]; The Elsevier Publishing Company, Amsterdam, the Editor and the authors for a figure from *Marine Geology* 5, 133–40 (paper by L. Draper) [Figure 4-15], 3 figures from *Marine Geology* 4, 119–48 (paper by K. Volbrecht) [Figures 10-1, 10-2, 10-3], a figure from *Marine Geology* 7, 529–51 (paper by W. Harrison) [Figure 12-27], a figure from *Marine Geology* 4, 187–206 (paper by G. S. Gorsline) [Figure 12-29], and 2 figures from *Developments in Sedimentology* 5 (by J. C. Ingle) [Figures 10-9, 10-10]; the Editor and J. A. Dixon, Engineering, Ltd for 2 figures from *Engineering* 195, 482–4 (paper by M. Derbyshire and L. Draper) [Figures 3-17A & B]; the Editor for a figure from *Journal of Fluid Mechanics* 2, 417–45 (paper by O. M. Phillips) [Figure 3-5]; the author and the Editor for 3 figures from *Annales de géographie* 72, 13–31 (paper by J. Pinot) [Figures 16-3A–C]; the Editor, the author and the Association de Géographes français for a figure from *Bulletin* 303/4, 53–65 (paper by A. Guilcher) [Figure 19-6]; the Editor for a figure from *Geografiska Annäler*, Series A, 51, 207–18 (paper by C. A. M. King) [Figure 14-2]; the Royal Geographical Society and the Editor for 2 figures from *Geographical Journal* 122, 176–89 (paper by S. Y. Landsberg) [Figures 6-10, 6-11], a figure from *Geographical Journal* 123, 474–80 (paper by J. N. Jennings) [Figure 6-12], and a figure from *Geographical Journal* 119, 299–305 (paper by H. Valentin) [Figure 7-4]; the Editor, the authors and the University of Chicago Press for a figure from *Journal of Geology* 55, 1–26 (paper by W. H. Munk and M. A. Traylor) [Figure 2-8]; the Geological Society of America and the Editor for a figure from *Bulletin* 78, 1125–36 (paper by J. H. Hoyt) [Figure 20-6]; the Geological Society of London for a figure from *Quarterly Journal* 119, 175–99 (paper by A. H. Stride) [Figure 5-11], and a figure from *Quarterly Journal* 87, 360–75 (paper by H. H. Swinnerton) [part of Figure 18-1]; the Editor, the American Geophysical Union and the author for a figure from *Journal of Geophysical Research* 73, 6929–36 (paper by W. Harrison) [Figure 4-18]; Hutchinson & Co. Ltd and the authors for 2 figures from *Waves and Tides* by R. C. H. Russell and H. Macmillan [Figures 4-3, 4-4]; the Hydrographer of the Navy and Her Majesty's Stationery Office: Hydrographical Department of the Admiralty for 8 figures from *Admiralty Manual of Tides* (A. T. Doodson and R. D. Warburg, 1941) [Figures 5-1, 5-2, 5-3, 5-4, 5-5, 5-6, 5-7, 5-8], and for information from *Admiralty Chart 5058* [Figure 5-5]; the Royal Irish Academy and the authors for 2 figures from *Proceedings* 61B17, 283–338 (paper by A. Guilcher and C. A. M. King) [Figures 19-9, 19-11]; the Lincolnshire National Trust for a figure from *Transactions* (1936) (Presidential Address by H. H. Swinnerton) [Part of Figure 18-1];

Acknowledgements

Collier-Macmillan Inc. and the Editor for 3 figures from *Papers in Marine Geology* edited by R. L. Miller (paper by J. R. Curray) [Figures 21A–C]; the Editor for a figure from *The Marine Observer* 25, 114–18 (paper by J. Darbyshire) [Figure 3-3]; the Coastal Research Group of the Department of Geology, University of Massachusetts for a figure from *Coastal Environments: Northeast Massachusetts and New Hampshire* (paper by P. S. Anan) [Figure 6-7]; the editor for 2 figures from *Mededelingen Van de Geologische Stichting*, series C, VI (by S. Jelgersma) [Figures 7-2, 7-3], and a figure from *Mededelingen Van de Geologische Stichting*, new series, 17, 41–75 (paper by L. M. J. U. Van Straaten) [Figure 20-4]; the Superintendent of Documents, Washington, D.C. and the National Bureau of Standards for 2 figures from *Circular* no. 521, 9–32 (paper by H. W. Iverson) [Figures 4-13, 4-14]; Massey & Son, Ltd, the Editor and the author for 3 figures from *The Naturalist* 87, 113–20 (paper by G. De Boer) [Figures 18-4A–C]; the U.S. National Engineering Science Council for 2 figures from 'On the breaking of waves arriving at an angle to the shore' by E. Mehauté and R. C. Y. Koh, ONR task no. S134–10 [Figures 4-8A & B], and for a figure from 'On tides and longshore currents over the continental shelf' by C. L. Bretschneider, ONR task no. SN 134–6 [Figure 4-16]; the author for a figure from 'Geometry and development of spit-bar formation at Horseshoe Cove, New Jersey' by W. E. Yasso, ONR task no. 388–057, Geography Branch, Technical Report 5 [Figure 13-6]; the *Institute of Navigation*, the Editor and the authors for a figure from *Journal* 18, 180–87 (paper by L. Draper and H. S. Fricker) [Figure 3-2]; Oliver & Boyd Ltd (the Longman Group) for a figure from *Processes of coastal development* by V. P. Zenkovitch edited by J. A. Steers [Figure 19-4]; the Editor and VEB Hermann Haach, Gotha, for a figure from *Petermanns Mitteilungen* Erg 246 (paper by H. Valentin) [Figure 15-1], and for a figure from *Petermanns Mitteilungen* 105, 81–92 (paper by H. G. Gierloff-Emden) [Figure 20-1]; the Royal Society for 4 figures from *Philosophical Transactions* A240, 527–60 (paper by N. F. Barber and F. Ursell) [Figures 3-7A & B, 3-8, 3-9], a figure from *Philosophical Transactions* A255, 5065–84 (paper by W. H. Munk and others) [Figure 3-10], and for a figure from *Philosophical Transactions* A246, 371–99 (paper by J. R. Rossiter) [Figure 4-22]; the Society of Economic Paleontologists and Mineralogists and the Editor for a figure from *Journal of Sedimentary Petrology* 38, 238–40 (paper by W. F. Tanner) [Figure 8-1], for a figure from *Journal of Sedimentary Petrology* 11, 64–72 (paper by W. C. Krumbein) [Figure 8-2A], a figure from *Journal of Sedimentary Petrology* 34, 156–64 (paper by R. Moberly) [Figure 8-3], and a figure from *Journal of Sedimentary Petrology* 36, 200–214 (paper by J. E. Kloran) [Figure 8-4]; the University of South California Press for a figure from *Essays in Marine Geology in honour of K. O. Emery*, 1–10 (paper by F. P. Shepperd) [Figure 7-1]; the Editor and the Royal Society of Victoria for a figure from *Proceedings* 79, 75–88 (paper by E. C. F. Bird) [Figure 20-5]; the Editor and the Yorkshire Geological Society for a figure from *Proceedings* 32, 407–27 (paper by R. Agar) [Figure 17-6]; Gebrüder Borntraeger for a figure from *Zeitschrift für Geomorphologie* 9, 422–36 (paper by A. L. Bloom) [Figure 15-2], a figure from *Zeitschrift für Geomorphologie* 8, 127*-42* (paper by J. L. Davies) [Figure 15-3], and for a figure from *Zeitschrift für Geomorphologie* NF 11, 34–46 (paper by L. W. Wright) [Figure 17-3].

Part I
Introduction

1 Introduction

1 The variables and their relationships

A beach is one of the most variable of land forms. It can be there one day and gone the next. This variability provides both opportunity and difficulty for those engaged in a study of beach problems—opportunity, because beach changes can be measured over an interval of relatively short duration, unlike many other geomorphological processes; and difficulty, because the observations, under the conditions in which the changes are most rapid, are by no means easy to make. The complexity of the forces causing the beach changes is another major difficulty. It is this that makes the mechanism of the detailed processes causing beach movement so little understood. Knowledge of these processes and their effects on the beach is, however, growing steadily.

A beach is an accumulation of loose material around the limit of wave action. For this book the beach may be taken to extend from the extreme upper limit of wave action to the zone where the waves, approaching from deep water, first cause appreciable movement of the bottom material. The first factor on which the character of the beach depends is the nature of the material of which it is composed. Its size, sorting and quantity are all significant factors determining its final form. In considering the material of which the beach is formed it is important to differentiate between sand and shingle, as the responses of these materials differ in some very significant respects. The characteristics of beach material are considered in chapter 8. The character of the foundation on which the incoherent material rests must also be considered. Its gradient, height in relation to mean sea level and its permeability are important, while its resistance to erosion is significant in the general rate of development of the coastline.

The waves are the fundamental force operative on the beach. They themselves depend on the winds that generate them in the ocean. The character of wind waves has been studied theoretically by mathematicians, experimentally in model tanks and by direct observation and measurement in the sea. Waves at sea are always complex owing to the variation of the wind and the amalgamation of numerous wave trains. An analysis of their effect on the beach is inevitably not straightforward. It has, however, been established that particular characteristics of the dominant waves are of great significance in their effect on the beach material. The size of the waves is partly determined by the distance of water over which the wind can blow, known as the fetch of the waves. This factor is closely related to the exposure of the beach, and an exposed beach will differ from an otherwise similar one in a sheltered area. Waves in deep water are considered in chapter 3 and the effects of shallow water on waves are discussed in chapter 4.

The wind is also important in explaining beach changes. Its effects are considered in chapter 6. It can work with or against the wave action to produce very different results. The height of the water level can be vitally affected at times by variations in wind and pressure. One of the main causes of the disastrous North Sea flooding in 1953 was the generation of a surge that raised water level to exceptional heights. The generation of surges is considered in chapter 4.

The tide, considered in chapter 5, is another important factor affecting beaches. Although in the past the importance of tidal streams tended to be exaggerated, the tide must nevertheless not be ignored, and in some areas is very significant. Changes of sea level are also important in the long term, but in the short term they can usually be ignored. They are considered in chapter 7.

Human interference can also have a marked effect on the beach. The building of structures, sea-walls, groynes, harbours and piers all disturb the natural movement of beach material and may cause profound changes in their immediate vicinity and adjoining areas, some of which may be starved of material while others receive an unusually large supply, resulting in problems of siltation.

The factors enumerated above determine the nature of the beach and coast. They are referred to as the process variables because they constitute the dynamic elements of the beach system. They operate together to form the characteristics of the beach at any point and these characteristics constitute the response variables. The beach in profile and in plan may, therefore, be referred to as the response variables.

A great deal of work has been devoted during the last decade to a study of the interrelationships between the process and the response variables. Methods have been developed to deal with the very complex multivariate systems that result when the relationships between the two types of variables are analysed. The analysis has been greatly facilitated by the rapidly growing availability of computers to process the large amounts of data that are being collected. In the next chapter some of the more recent methods of analysis and study will be mentioned. Great stress is now laid on the model approach in the analysis of complex natural phenomena. The main aim of this approach is to simplify the natural situation so that meaningful relationships can be established.

The multivariate nature of the problems of beach analysis is further complicated by the mutual interaction of many of the variables. This two-way relationship is known as feedback. It can be exemplified by the relationship between beach slope and wave steepness. The wave steepness affects the beach slope, but is in turn affected by the beach slope so that a feedback relationship exists between the two variables. Feedback is positive when the change in one variable is intensified by a change in the second. It is negative when the change in the second variable results in the first being modified in such a way that it tends to return to its original state. The positive feedback loop results in self-generation of processes, while the negative leads to self-regulation. The fact that equilibrium conditions can be established on beaches suggests that negative feedback, with its self-regulating influence, is important in beach changes. There are, however, situations in which changes are continuous in one direction. Under these circumstances, either feedback does not occur, as in a situation where longshore drift is continuous in one direction, or feedback relationships are positive. The lack of feedback appears to be the most common, and is responsible for many coastal features.

The establishment of a state of dynamic equilibrium is dependent upon time, which is an important factor. The speed with which the response variable reacts to changes in the process variables is known as the relaxation time. It is defined as the time required for the change to reach a value of $1/e$ ($e = 2.718$) of the total variation involved.

A simpler definition is the time required for equilibrium to be established. Equilibrium is the state in which little change is taking place. W. C. Krumbein (1961) has carried out observations to determine the time required for a beach profile to reach equilibrium under changing wave conditions. The relaxation time for such changes on a steep, coarse beach is a matter of hours. On the other hand, the relaxation time for changes in hard rock cliffs must be measured in hundreds of thousands if not millions of years. It is very unlikely that the controlling process variables, which include sea level, will remain static for this length of time, and hence the cyclic concept of coastal development, which implies a constant sea level for long enough for the cycle to run its course, must be doubtful (this topic is considered in the last chapter). Two very different relaxation times thus apply to beaches and to coasts: this difference provides the basis for the subdivision of the book.

The process variables are considered in part II, and their effect on the beach form in profile and plan, through the movement of beach material, is dealt with in part III. The longer-term changes that lead to characteristic coastal forms are considered in part IV. The remaining chapter in part I is devoted to methods of research into beach and coastal phenomena. Work in this field has been particularly productive during the last decade: new methods have been devised and older ones applied more widely. At the same time there have been considerable developments in the methods of analysing the data obtained in the field, as well as the use of other methods of analysis.

2 Nomenclature

The term 'beach' will be used to include the backshore, foreshore and offshore zones as defined in figure 1-1. The term 'backshore' is used for the zone above the limit of the swash of normal high spring tide, and is, therefore, only exceptionally under the direct influence of the waves. On a rocky coast it includes the cliffs and on a low coast may consist of sand dunes or mature salt marsh. The 'foreshore' zone includes all that part of the beach which is regularly covered and uncovered by the tide. On a tideless beach this zone will be very narrow, only covering the distance between the limit of the swash and backwash of the larger waves. The 'offshore' zone extends from the uppermost point always covered by water to a depth at which substantial movement of beach material ceases under normal circumstances, or becomes very small. This depth is called the 'surf-base', and is discussed in section 9-4. Ripple formation and minor changes of level take place in greater depths.

Figure 1-1 shows diagrammatic composite-sand and shingle-beach profiles. The 'berm' is a terrace formed in the backshore zone above the limit of the swash at high tide to form a flat terrace, or a ridge with a reverse slope. It is sometimes double. Sand ridges may be found exposed on tidal beaches at low water. The term 'ridge' is used only for features which are, for part of the time at least, above water level. Below low water the positive features on the sandy floor in the offshore zone are called 'submarine bars'. The term 'bar' implies that the feature is never exposed above the water level, a property which is emphasized by the adjective 'submarine'. Such features have in the past been referred to by other names, including 'offshore bars' and 'low and ball'. The latter term is ambiguous, having been used for both sand ridges and submarine bars by different authors. The features described by V. Cornish (1898) seem to be sand ridges, while those discussed by O. F. Evans (1940) under the title 'low and ball' are found in Lake Michigan, which is tideless. These features must, therefore, be submarine bars.

The hollows found on the landward side of the ridges and submarine bars of sandy beaches are termed respectively 'runnels' and 'troughs'. The runnel on a tidal beach carries the water draining off the beach as the tide falls and is flooded first by the rising tide. The trough of a sub-marine bar is always underwater.

A larger feature which is built permanently above the limit of high tide, and which is separated from the shore by a lagoon or channel, is referred to as a 'barrier island', following F. P. Shepard

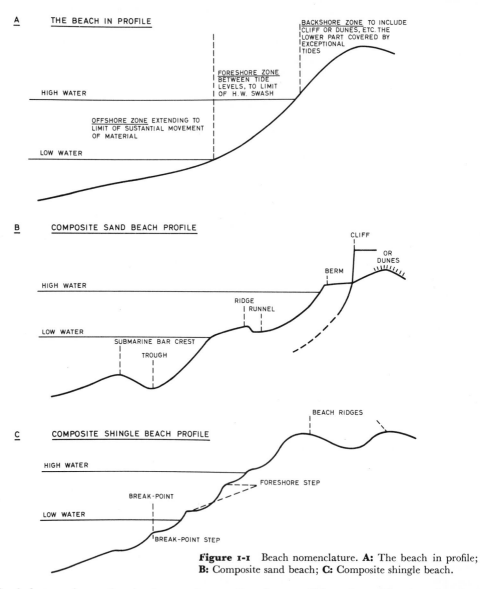

Figure 1-1 Beach nomenclature. **A:** The beach in profile; **B:** Composite sand beach; **C:** Composite shingle beach.

(1952). Such features have often in the past been referred to as offshore bars. The term barrier, however, appears appropriate as the feature separates the land from the open sea and is thus a barrier to movement on and offshore.

The features typical of a shingle beach differ from those found on a sand beach, and confusion is therefore avoided if they are referred to by different terms. The features built considerably above the limit of the storm waves may be called 'backshore beach ridges', while the term 'swale' is suitable for the generally shallow depressions which separate such ridges. The smaller features built up between the tide marks may be called 'foreshore steps', indicating the part of the beach where they are found. Another step is often found at the break-point of the waves and to differentiate it from the former may be referred to as a 'break-point step'.

The terms for the constructional features of the beach zone in plan are discussed in chapter 19 (table 19-1 lists some of them). 'Down-drift' and 'up-drift' will be used when discussing the longshore movement of material to indicate the dominant direction towards which and from which beach material is moved respectively.

Table 1-1 gives the equivalent terms in other languages as far as possible.

Table 1-1   Nomenclature

Terms used	French	German	Dutch	Swedish
Beach	Plage	Strand		Strand
Berm	Terrasse de plage	Strandterraßen		
Beach ridge (shingle)	Leveés de plage, bancs de galet	Strandwälle	Strandrug	Strandvellar
Barrier beach or island	Cordon littoral	Nehrung, Lido Kustendammwall	Shoorwall vrije losse strandwall	
Lagoon	Lagune, étang (littoraux)	Lagune, Haff		Laguner
Ridge (sand) exposed at low water	Crêtes prelittoraux	Schwellen	Aangroeiinsrug	
Runnel (exposed at low water)	Sillons prelittoraux	Zwin		
Submarine bar (never exposed)	Barre	Sandriff, Barre	Strandbank	Revel
Submarine bar trough	Creux		Rifftalen	Träg

References

CORNISH, V. 1898: On sea beaches and sand banks. *Geog. J.* **11,** 628–51.

EVANS, O. F. 1940: The low and ball of the eastern shore of Lake Michigan. *J. Geol.* **48,** 476–511.

KRUMBEIN, W. C. 1961: The analysis of observational data from natural beaches. *Beach Erosion Board. Tech. Memo.* **130.** (59 pp.)

SHEPARD, F. P. 1952: Revised nomenclature for depositional coastal features. *Bull. Am. Assoc. of Petrol. Geol.* **36**(10), 1902–12.

2 Methods of research

1 **Models:** a) Conceptual or theoretical; b) Physical or mathematical-deterministic; c) Statistical; d) Simulation; e) Hardware scale: (*i*) *Scale problems*; (*ii*) *Model laws*; (*iii*) *Model apparatus.*

2 **Field observations:** a) Observing beach and coast characteristics: (*i*) *Sediment sampling,* (*ii*) *Beach surveys*; (*iii*) *Accuracy of surveys*; (*iv*) *Amount of change in successive profiles*; b) Measurement of dynamic processes: (*i*) *Waves*; (*ii*) *Tidal streams*; (*iii*) *Experiments with tracers.*

3 **Laboratory methods:** a) Sediment analysis; b) Wave refraction diagrams: (*i*) *Construction*; (*ii*) *Results of wave refraction and other methods of presentation.*

4 **Search procedures:** a) Historical records; b) Air photographs.

Summary

The development of different types of model approaches has provided a valuable framework in which beach and coastal studies may be set. In this chapter some of the types of model are mentioned first, and then field techniques are considered by which data are collected for further analysis by one or other of the model approaches. Laboratory analysis is next discussed and finally search procedures, which provide historical data.

1 Models

Beach studies can be carried out within the framework of a number of different types of model.

a Conceptual or theoretical models

The conceptual or theoretical model provides a broad framework that gives coherence to a study, especially when this is concerned with a complex multivariate situation, as is common in beach studies. The process-response models, discussed by W. C. Krumbein (1961), W. Harrison and Krumbein (1964) and E. H. T. Whitten (1964), exemplify the application of this type of model to beach studies.

The process variables that affect beach character have already been enumerated (section 1-2): these are the dynamic elements of the situation that can be measured in the field. They vary rapidly over time in many instances, and therefore must be measured repeatedly. The response variables are the slope of the beach, the distribution of different types of sediment on the beach and the form of the beach in plan. The process variables affect the response variables and vice versa to provide feedback loops (section 1-2).

The process variables can be further subdivided into immediate or proximal variables and regional or ultimate variables. The former provide the small day-to-day variations, the latter control the general setting and change more slowly. In the same way the response variables can be divided into those that vary over the short term and are local in their response and those that vary over a longer period. The former are those that normally can reach an equilibrium state via negative feedback loops, while the latter often show a continuous development over a longer period of time, a development that may be cyclic or continuous (C. A. M. King, 1970).

In this type of process-response model the process variables are independent, while the response variables are dependent in that they are largely controlled by the varying processes. The model provides a framework into which various statistical analyses may conveniently be fitted. This is particularly necessary when dealing with natural beach data in which the variables cannot be controlled by direct means and where as a result many variables must be considered simultaneously. Each variable in the model may be expressed as a vector that includes all its possible range of values. The variables may themselves form another vector. These two vectors may then be expressed as a matrix in which one forms the rows and the other the columns. The matrix then provides the whole range of possible combinations of the process variables, each of which may produce a different value in the response variables.

If the numbers of variables are large, as they mostly are in nature, and their ranges are great, then a very complex situation arises, with a great many possible values for the response variables. The response variables are, however, constrained by certain physical limits, such as the angle of stability of loose sediments in water, and not all possible combinations of the process variables will necessarily occur. Nevertheless the situation is demonstrably so complex that it must be simplified and made amenable to analysis. The other models to be considered provide possible methods of approaching this complex natural situation.

b Physical or mathematical-deterministic models

These are essential to a fuller understanding of beach phenomena. Good examples are provided by the contributions of D. L. Inman (1963) and R. A. Bagnold (1963), who show how it is possible to use basic principles of physics, dealing with the known laws concerning the movement of solid particles in a moving medium, in order to understand the processes operating on the beach. This type of model takes an ideal situation, such as the movement of a single particle, or particles of uniform size, on a plane beach under constant and uniform waves. Only such a simplified situation is amenable to study in this way, and it is not yet possible to study theoretically the movement in the turbulent area of the breaking wave—where most important changes are taking place—owing to the complexity of flow in this area.

In order to analyse the movement of sediment by a method involving this type of model it is necessary to know certain properties of the sediment and the water movement. The properties of significance in the sediment include their packing, porosity and dilatation, which are all interconnected. The importance of these properties lies in their effect on the speed with which water can be transmitted through the beach. Another related property is the permeability of the sediment. All these properties exert a marked effect on the slope of the beach.

Other necessary physical principles are concerned with the nature of fluid motion, which can be either laminar or turbulent. The fluid stress and eddy viscosity determine the nature of the fluid flow. As far as the beach processes are concerned, however, the important aspects of the model are the processes that link the nature of the material with that of the fluid flow. The settling velocity of the particles through the water plays a part in their movement and again depends on their size and shape. These attributes also determine in part the threshold fluid velocity required to initiate movement of the particles. This aspect is particularly important and equations have been developed by Bagnold to relate the threshold velocity at which movement is started with the character of the sediment. The velocity required reaches a minimum value for material of about 0·18 mm diameter when the bed is smooth. When the bed is rippled the generalized friction coefficient is much higher, owing to the increased drag over the rippled bed.

The way in which the particles move can also be studied theoretically, as for example by Bagnold (1963). The movement may be as bed load or as suspension load. The total transport varies with the nature of the bed, which in turn depends on the character and velocity of flow. At low flow the movement is laminar and only the uppermost grains move over a smooth bed. At higher velocities the bed becomes rippled, and with still greater speeds the sediment moves as a sheet over a smooth bed in a semi-suspension form. The flow is turbulent when ripples develop. At the highest speeds anti-dunes form and the water surface takes on an undulating surface parallel to the bottom forms, which move upstream. Equations have been developed for both bed load and suspended load transport in terms of the sediment and flow characteristics. The situation on a beach is more complex than in a stream owing to the reversing nature of the flow in wave action.

Certain generalizations must be made to make analysis possible, but it is by applying basic physical principles to the movement of sediment that the fundamental causes of beach phenomena can be best understood. Such studies provide theoretical models of beach behaviour which can be tested against observations in the field or the laboratory. The mathematical-deterministic model provides an ideal situation which is considerably less complex than reality. Other models must, therefore, be developed to simplify reality so that the natural observations can be used to check the results of the theoretical models and assess their applicability and reliability.

It is partly the large number of variables involved in beach problems that makes their solution difficult. One mathematical technique which has been used to deal with the numerous variables is dimensional analysis: here a complex series of variables can be reduced to dimensionless ratios, which are functions on which the particular feature under consideration depends. Take, for example, the beach slope and the factors on which it depends. These are given in the following list, using the symbols:

$$i \quad h \quad l \quad p \quad v \quad d \quad u \quad s \quad E \quad g$$

i = beach slope	dimensionless	
h = wave height	L	m
l = wave length	L	m
p = wave period	T	sec
v = sand settling velocity	LT^{-1}	m/sec
d = density	ML^{-3}	kg/m^3
u = viscosity	$ML^{-1}T^{-1}$	kg/m/sec
s = sand median diameter	L	mm
E = wave energy	ML^2T^{-2}	$kg\ m^2/sec^2$
g = acceleration of gravity	LT^{-2}	m/sec^2

E, l and v are taken as three variables because they include all three quantities of mass, time and length. Dimensionless equations can be solved for all the other variables in turn, giving the following six dimensionless ratios:

$$i = f\left(\frac{h}{l}, \frac{vp}{l}, \frac{v^2 l^3 d}{E}, \frac{l^2 vu}{E}, \frac{s}{l}, \frac{lg}{v^2}\right)$$

The beach slope is a function of these dimensionless ratios, and clearly dependent upon the wave steepness h/l. The sand size, itself a function of the settling velocity, is also a significant factor as shown by the second ratio, vp/l, since p and l are dependent on each other. The wave length, as shown by the ratio s/l, is important too. It will be shown in chapter 12 that these are in fact the variables that determine the gradient of the beach.

c Statistical models

The many statistical models that can be used to analyse beach data may be divided into descriptive and inferential models.

The descriptive models enable the variability of the beach variables, both process and response, to be expressed in meaningful statistical terms. In nearly all beach problems it is necessary to sample the data available. It is, therefore, also important to be able to infer from the sample to the total population, which is the subject of interest.

An example of the application of sampling is seen in the description of the size and shape of beach sediment. The beach is made up of a vast number of small sand grains or pebbles. These cannot possibly all be measured, so that sampling is essential. Considerable work has been done to establish the optimum sampling plan, for example by W. C. Krumbein and H. A. Slack (1956). The plan should allow all the environments to be represented. The number of samples taken should be dependent on the variability of the material. Thus a proper sampling plan of truly random samples is a prerequisite of most beach studies that involve a study of the material.

When the samples have been collected their moment measures can be established by methods reviewed in chapter 8. These measures provide valuable data concerning the characteristics of the size distribution within each sample which can be related to other variables.

Similar sampling and description is necessary in the analysis of wave data. Wave heights vary continuously so that records over a given period of time must be analysed to provide a measure of the wave height and period which will be most useful in the analysis of the beach changes. The significant wave height is often used: this is the mean height of the highest one third of the waves recorded. The significant period is the period of these waves. Such generalization is essential if the multiplicity of data is to be rendered usable.

Inferential statistics provide many methods of analysis that give greater precision to statements of relationships among the variables. Some of these methods are considered and exemplified in part IV of *Numerical analysis in geomorphology: an introduction* (J. C. Doornkamp and C. A. M. King, 1971). There are the simple two-variable situations, for instance, which can be successfully analysed in those cases where the two variables can be isolated from the many that are operating simultaneously. An example is the study of the relationship between the height of ridges on the beach of Lincolnshire and the amount of accretion on the foreshore.

The relationship between the gradient of the beach and the length of the waves provides an example of a rather more complex situation. Another statistical technique is applicable to this situation. Although the wave length can be shown to influence the beach gradient, it is not the only factor at work. The other variables, of which beach material size is one and wave steepness another, cannot be directly controlled. The observations can be made on only one beach, and this will limit the range of beach material size present, but the wave steepness cannot be controlled in this way. It can, however, be controlled by the statistical method of partial correlation. This allows the variation of one variable to be controlled while two others are correlated. Thus the principle of control and simplification characteristic of the model approach can be achieved.

In the more complex situations, where many variables are being considered together, other statistical methods can be used to simplify the situation. W. C. Krumbein (1961) has shown how multiple correlation and regression can be applied to several beach process variables to determine their individual and combined effects on the response variable. In his study of the effect of wave height, period, direction of approach and shore current velocity on beach slope, he has shown that wave height is the single most important variable, but that the explanation is increased when a number of variables are combined. He also introduces the time element into the analysis. His study was concerned with variations on one beach over a period of time. Another somewhat similar study of a wide range of beaches indicates that material size is the dominant factor in determining beach gradient. The results are discussed in section 12-2(d).

There are various other multivariate techniques that can be used to simplify the very complex natural situations. Principle component and factor analysis provide a useful means of sorting out a large number of variables into a smaller number of composite factors, which best accounts for the variability in the original data. These methods have been used increasingly as computers have become more readily available. There are other useful techniques, such as multiple discriminant analysis, that allow numerical classification to be based on sound statistical principles. Statistical models have played an important part in making coastal studies more rigorous and quantitative so that results can be expressed within the framework of probability theory.

d   Simulation models

A new method of research has been developed with the advent of computers. It also provides a means of controlling and simplifying the problem, and can, therefore, be called a model. The aim of the method is to simulate the formation of a particular feature by means of a series of steps, the order of which is usually random to a certain extent. This type of model can thus be called a stochastic simulation model. In establishing the model it must be assumed that the effects on the response variable of the different process variables built into the model are known. The relative frequency of the action of the different process variables can be set at the beginning of the program and varied with each run. The order in which they operate is made random by the use of a random number generator in the program, so that the natural variability of the operation of the different processes and their relative intensity is simulated.

If the simulation model reproduces the natural situation, then it may be suggested that the processes operating in the model are those important in reality and that the selected frequency is appropriate. It is also possible by changing the frequency to indicate which variables are most important in building up the prototype. When the prototype development can be accurately simulated, then it is possible to extrapolate the development into the future and thus use the model for prediction. The success of the model depends on the degree of correspondence between the simulated processes and the real ones; it is this that provides the positive element in the model. If some vital process is omitted from the model then it will be unlikely to simulate the real feature accurately and must be modified accordingly until it does.

The simulation of a specific spit formation provides an example of the application of this method. Hurst Castle spit on the coast of Hampshire is formed by a number of different wave types coming from different directions. It prolongs the northwest to southeast coastline and then swings round to an east–west direction as a result of wave refraction. There are a number of recurves built up by waves coming from the northeast down the Solent. The bulk of the shingle that reaches the spit comes from the west under the influence of oblique westerly waves, and is built up into the main ridge by storm waves. As the spit lengthens eastwards its rate of growth is slowed down by increasing water depth offshore, since a greater amount of material is required to build the spit up to the water level as it grows into deeper water. All these elements of the situation are built into the model (McCullagh and King, 1970). They are allowed for by a series of subroutines in the main computer program. The subroutine *west* allows material to elongate the spit whenever the appropriate range of values comes up in the random number generator. The subroutine *storm* makes the material brought by the *west* subroutine form a ridge on the next higher row of the matrix on which the spit is built. There are also subroutines that build up perpendicular recurves and laterals, simulating the action of waves from the south and northeast.

The effect of refraction is allowed for by making the westerly waves operate on higher rows of the matrix when certain values of the random numbers are called. The effect increases at an exponential rate as the spit elongates. The rate of growth eastwards is controlled by the opera-

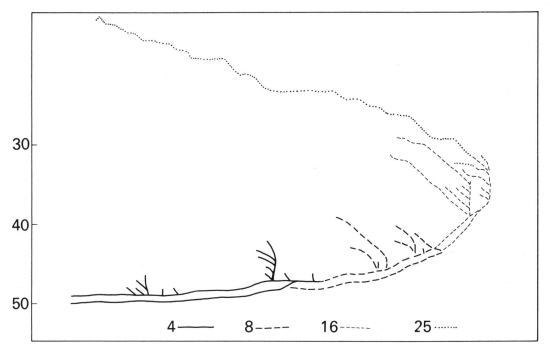

Figure 2-1 Outline of computer-simulated Hurst Castle spit. Stage 16 is the best fit stage and stage 25 suggests possible future development. The outline should be compared with the map of Hurst Castle spit shown in figure 13-4.

tion of a depth factor that acts slowly at first and then at an increasing rate to prevent the placing of material by the westerly waves as the spit becomes longer.

The simulated spit bears a very close resemblance to the real spit as shown in figure 2-1. The simulation model suggests that the processes simulated are those operating to form the natural feature. The range of values allocated to the different subroutines can be changed and the depth and refraction values modified to assess the effect of changes of wave pattern and off-shore relief (King and McCullagh, 1971).

One of the main advantages of the simulation model is the speed with which the results can be obtained and different combinations of variables tested. In these qualities it is superior to the hardware scale model, but scale models also have a valuable part to play in coastal research.

e   Hardware scale models

(*i*) *Scale problems:*   Because of the large number of variables involved both theoretical and full-scale observations of beach processes are difficult. The experimental approach to the problems is all the more attractive because the variables can be controlled and isolated in the model wave tank. Observations of beach changes and measurement of wave characteristics are also greatly facilitated. The range of problems that can be investigated by means of scale models is large. They can be used to study how closely waves follow the theoretical pattern and motion calculated mathematically, both in deep water and as the waves move into shallow water and break. The movement of beach material and the form of the beach may be studied in profile and in plan, while the effect of different waves and the wind on a variety of beach types can be measured.

Unless these experimental results can be applied to their full-scale counterparts, however, they are of relatively little value, especially from a practical point of view. It is relevant, therefore, to consider the problem of scale in the application of the results of model experiments to beaches in nature.

Various aspects of ideal waves in deep water, including wave form, orbital radii and mass transport, can be reproduced in a model wave tank with a very good correlation to the theoretical values. As the waves move into shallow water the degree of correlation with theoretical values often decreases considerably, although this does not necessarily mean that the model behaves differently to the natural counterpart. Some studies, however, such as that by J. W. Johnson (1949), show a close correlation with empirical relationships derived from observations on a particular beach. A 1 : 40 model of the Scripps beach in California shows that model values of the relationship between wave steepness and depth of breaking agree closely with the empirical curve. Model results indicate, however, that there may be some discrepancy between the theoretical figures and the actual ones, and so far model experiments have not contributed substantially to solving the problem of wave generation.

Models can be used to study the movement of beach material and the character of beach profiles in general, or to study particular problems of a specific area. In either instance the material forming the beach is a vital factor in the analysis. The conversion of the size of beach material from model to nature and vice versa is difficult and has led to considerable difference of opinion. One argument is put forward by R. A. Bagnold (1940) and is based on the requirements of geometrical similarity. He considers that the beach profile should be similar if the ratio, R, equals H/d, where H is the wave height and d is the diameter of the material, is constant for the model and the prototype. The ratio R increases as the material becomes finer and as the waves increase in height: thus for a fine sand beach, where the median diameter of the sand is 0·20 mm, R would be 6000 for a wave of only 1·2 m in height. In order to imitate these conditions in a model wave tank, if the wave height were 12 cm, the diameter of the material would have to be 0·02 mm, which is below the limit of fine sand. To imitate high storm waves the material would have to be even finer in grade. When sand is used in the model tank it would simulate shingle on a natural beach if the scale were considered in this way. There are, however, many respects in which sand and shingle beaches differ in nature. Their profiles are different and they affect and are affected differently by the waves. It appears unlikely that sand in a model tank would give reliable data concerning a shingle beach in nature. On the other hand sand in nature is not likely to be simulated correctly by silt or clay in the tank, as geometrical similarity would suggest it should.

One relevant factor in this discussion is the velocity required to initiate movement of material on the bottom. It has been shown by P. Hjulstrøm *et al.* (1935) that this velocity for a bed of uniform material depends on the size of the particles. The most easily eroded particles are those with a diameter between 0·1 and 0·5 mm. Particles both smaller and larger than this size require a considerably higher velocity to initiate movement. Once the material is in suspension, however, different laws come into force. The finer material is not deposited until the velocities are very much lower than those which would allow coarser material to settle on the bed. Other properties of the sediments are also important: the cohesion of the finer particles will affect their movement, while the different rate of percolation through sediments of different size is very significant.

The factors mentioned above have led some workers, notably R. D. Meyers (1933), to go to the opposite extreme. He considers that the same material should be used in the tank as that on the natural beach, if comparable gradients are to be obtained. At the steeper limits of the experimental and natural gradients his results agreed well, but for the flatter natural slopes the differences became considerable. The flatter natural gradients were about 1 in 100 for fine sand, while his comparable experimental slopes were only 1 in 11·6. These results indicate that this solution to the problem is also unsatisfactory.

The value of model results would be greatly increased if it were possible to formulate exact laws connecting the model beach results to their natural counterparts. An attempt to assess the reliability of model results has been made by the Beach Erosion Board (1933), who compared the results obtained in a large wave tank with those obtained in a smaller one. All the dimensions including the sand size were reduced to scale for the models in ratio 1 to 2. The sand size in the larger model was 0·56 mm and in the smaller it was 0·28 mm. There was a close agreement in the beach profiles for the three wave lengths used. The gradients of the swash slope did not agree exactly. For linear scales smaller than 1 in 2 the sand diameter was kept at 0·28 mm, but good agreement with the larger model was maintained up to a scale of 1 in 3·5. When the scale between the models was 1 in 4·5 there was still a general similarity of profile, although the smaller model reacted less quickly to the waves than the larger one. J. W. Johnson (1949) mentions a similar set of experiments made by the United States Waterways Experimental Station (1940) when wave tanks on the scale 1 : 2 : 3 were used for the tests. With a beach slope of 1 in 5 similar waves produced very similar results and there was a close agreement of the stable slopes.

The results of these model experiments suggest that there is a reasonable agreement between models and natural beaches under similar conditions. One type of wave will produce a storm profile in both model and natural beach, while the opposite type will build up a summer profile. The critical wave characteristic that determines which type of beach profile will form appears to differ slightly from model to prototype, and indeed, from one natural beach to another. The similarity noted by W. V. Lewis (1943) between features formed in a small lake in Iceland—where the greatest fetch was less than 500 m—and larger features, shows that the same processes can produce similar results on widely differing scales. One of the features formed in a small lake in some respects closely resembled the great shingle structure of Chesil beach in Dorset. Both on their very different scales turn to face the dominant storm waves.

Another scale problem associated with wave action in a model tank has been discussed by R. A. Bagnold (1946). He notes that the ripples which form in the sandy bed of the scale model are very much greater in proportion to other features than their full-scale counterparts. The large model ripples exert too great a drag between the water and the bed thereby exhausting the waves too soon. In order to overcome some of the scale difficulties concerning the character and behaviour of the bed material, Bagnold (1947) carried out experiments with material of much smaller density than normal quartz sand, in the hope that it might react to the smaller tank waves in a way more similar to natural sand and full size waves. The material he used was ground perspex with a density of 1·18. His conclusions, however, suggest that the low-density material does not give helpful results in the study of beach profiles, although it is useful in studying the action of waves in deeper water where the velocities are lower. It can also be used with advantage in experiments with wind when the currents generated are too slow to move quartz sand (see chapter 6).

(*ii*) *Model laws:*   Model laws have been developed by Froude to enable different parameters to be converted to scale. His derivation of the model laws has shown that the model must be undistorted, and that geometrical, kinematic and dynamic similarity must be maintained between model and nature. Figure 2-2 shows the relations between model and prototype in an undistorted model. The coordinates of point C in the prototype are a and b, while those of the model point C′ are a′ and b′. Therefore b/b′ = a/a′ = A, where A is a constant defined as the length ratio, assuming geometrical similarity between the model and the prototype.

The kinematic similarity between the model and the prototype depends upon the time ratio.

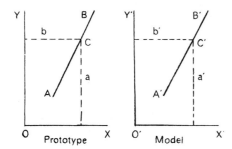

Figure 2-2   Diagram to illustrate the derivation of model laws.

The time taken for a point to travel from B to C (figure 2-2) is equal to t, and from B′ to C′ is equal to t′. This gives the ratio of velocities, C, as

$$\frac{V}{V'} = \frac{CB}{t} \bigg/ \frac{B'C'}{t'} = \frac{At'}{t}.$$

Now if t/t′ = B (where V is the velocity in the prototype and V′ is the velocity in the model, and B is a constant defined as the time ratio), V/V′ is now equal to A/B. The acceleration ratio is similarly A/B^2.

A ratio of forces must be considered in discussing dynamic similarity. The forces of inertia and gravity only will be considered. The inertia in nature on a particle of volume Q is Qra (where r is the density and a is the acceleration). The inertia on a model particle is Q′r′a′. Therefore the ratio of forces, Fi, is Qra/Q′r′a′, and Q/Q′ = A^3 and a/a′ = A/B^2. If the ratio of densities is R, then

$$Fi = \frac{RA^3 \times A}{B^2} = \frac{RA^4}{B^2}$$

R = 1 if the same fluids are used in the model as those in nature. The ratio of the gravity forces, Fg, is Qra/Q′r′a′ and Fg = $RA^3 \times 1$, as gravity is the same in nature as in the scale model. The same ratio of forces must hold for gravity and inertia, and therefore Fi = Fg; if R = 1, then $A^4/B^2 = A^3$, $A/B^2 = 1$, so A = B^2. The ratio of velocity, C, is given by C = A/B; therefore C = B. From these relationships Froude's law follows. It is A = B^2 = C^2. The law states that the time and velocity scales are equal to the square-root of the linear scale. Froude has also shown that it is impossible to use a geometrically distorted model in the study of gravity waves.

For any model in which wave action is an important aspect, the model must not be distorted. When constructing models of particular areas, however, good results are usually obtained by using a vertical exaggeration of scale. This applies particularly to models of harbours and river mouths in which tides and currents are of prime importance. For most areas the range of the tide in the model would be negligible without vertical exaggeration.

(*iii*) *Model apparatus:* There are two different types of model apparatus each of which serves a different function. One is designed for a specific area and usually aims to solve a particular engineering problem. It is usually related to such features as harbours and breakwaters, and used for problems of coastal defence or in the tidal reaches of rivers. As this type of model is associated largely with specific engineering problems and has been described in detail by J. Allen (1947), it is not necessary to consider it here in detail. There is nearly always a vertical exaggeration of scale, chosen so that the behaviour of the model can be made to simulate known changes in the prototype: future changes can hence be extrapolated and the effect of structures on the regime examined. The effect of the tide is also included. The models of the Mersey estuary, described by W. A. Price and M. P. Kendrick (1963), are good examples of this type.

The second type of model is one designed to establish fundamental relationships between the different factors which affect the character of beaches under wave action. Such models provide empirical data that can then be checked against either full-scale phenomena or theoretical results. Many examples of the use of models for both these purposes will be considered in the following chapters. The apparatus used by workers for different problems varies but can be divided into two main groups. In the three-dimensional type studies of movement both normal to the shore and parallel to it can be made. The two-dimensional type is narrow and used to study the processes which operate normal to the shore.

As an example of a long, narrow wave tank the one in the Geography Department at Cambridge may be described (figure 2-3). This is nearly 10 m long, 24 cm wide and about 60 cm deep. In one experimental situation the waves were generated by a curved paddle fitted to a 0·25 horse-power engine. The wave heights could be adjusted by varying the eccentricity of the arm attaching the paddle to the motor, giving a range in deep water from 2 to 10 cm. The wave length was varied by use of a system of gears, giving periods of 0·75 seconds, 1·5 seconds and 2·2 seconds. Variations between these values could be obtained by use of electric resistance. Wave heights were measured with a point and hook gauge at the required depth and the period of the waves was timed by stop-watch. The wave length in deep water was calculated from the period. The wave height does not begin to increase rapidly till d/L, the depth to wave length ratio, is about 0·05. For most purposes, therefore, the wave height measured in the deeper part of the tank gives an adequate value for the deep-water wave height.

In addition to the paddle for generating waves a fan, to simulate the effect of an onshore wind, was set up over the wave generator, as shown in figure 2-3. The fan produced winds of up to 35 mph (56 km/hr). The wind speed could be varied and was measured with a small anemometer over the beach area or where required. The results of experiments with the fan in operation are discussed in section 6-1. A baffle was placed behind the wave paddle to absorb any effect of disturbance in the water behind the paddle. At the other end of the tank a sand beach was built. The profile could be recorded easily by reference to a grid stretched across the glass window in the tank. The beach extended over a distance of about 3 m from the top of the tank and was built of quartz sand of fairly uniform size. It was passed through a sieve of 20 meshes to the inch and had a median diameter of 0·41 mm.

Many of the experiments in this tank were concerned with the measurement of the volume of material moved along the beach under varying conditions. (Some of the results are described in chapter 9.) The experiments were made by collecting sand in a trap designed to measure the sand moving both onshore and offshore. The trap, which extended across the full width of the tank, was divided into two portions by a central division running the length of the trap as shown in the inset in figure 2-3. Sand travelling onshore fell into the part nearest the sea, while sand moving offshore fell into the other half. The difference between the two amounts gave the net quantity of sand moved and the direction in which it was moving. The width of the half trap, which was 2·5 cm, appeared to be enough to prevent sand from by-passing the

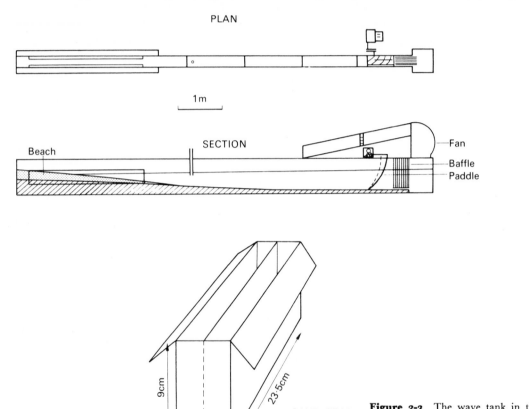

PLAN

1m

SECTION

Beach

Fan
Baffle
Paddle

9cm

23·5cm

5cm

SAND TRAP

Figure 2-3 The wave tank in the Geography Department at Cambridge University. The trap used to determine the direction and amount of sand transport is shown.

trap nearest to it, except perhaps, under the largest waves near their break-point, where the turbulence was greatest. Up to 400 gm of sand was caught in the traps during the normal run of 5 minutes.

An example of the large type of three-dimensional tank is that used by T. Saville (1950) to study the character of longshore currents and the transport of material alongshore. The results of his studies are considered in chapter 4. The lay-out of the tank is shown in figure 2-4, which gives its dimensions and the alignment of the beach at an angle to the wave generating flap. Various precautions were taken to ensure that the movement of sand along the beach simulated conditions in which no interference of sand drift occurred.

A considerably larger three-dimensional model reproducing the shore in the Dunwich area of Suffolk on a horizontal scale of 1 in 30 has been built by the Hydraulics Research Board, and is described in the report for 1956. The model reproduces 915 m width of beach, extending 550 m offshore. There is a slight vertical exaggeration, giving a vertical scale ratio of 1 in 20. The waves were made with a new type of pneumatic generator. The aim of the experiments was partly to test the effectiveness of various types of groynes in stabilizing the beach under the action of oblique waves. The waves approached the shore at 30° to normal. The wave height was

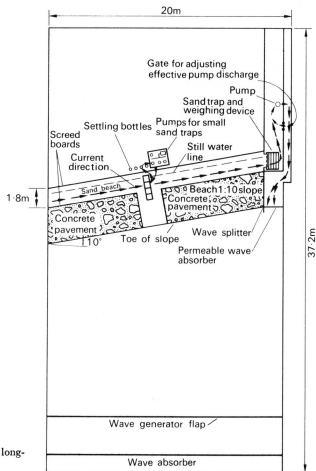

Figure 2-4 Plan of wave tank used to study longshore transport. (*After Savelle: 1950.*)

60 cm on the prototype in deep water. The sand used in the model had a diameter of 0·15 mm compared to 0·45 mm in the prototype. The results of the experiments are mentioned in chapter 10.

Experiments have been made by oscillating a carrier containing sand through still water for studying the formation of ripples. By this method longer accelerations, similar to those occurring in nature, can be more easily simulated than in a normal wave tank. Experiments of this type were carried out by R. A. Bagnold (1964) and are described in chapter 14. A rather different type of apparatus has been used by M. R. Carstens *et al.* (1969) to study various types of bed features including ripples. The apparatus was U-shaped and the method of operation eliminated initial and final transients from the water motion. They studied incipient motion, evolution of a rippled bed, the geometry of equilibrium ripples and energy dissipation in the flow over a rippled bed. The experimental results were interpreted in the light of physical relationships. The test section used for the observations was 3·05 m long, 0·305 m high and 1·22 m wide. Transparent sides allowed the bed form to be recorded photographically. Three types of sand were tested to establish the effect of bed material on bottom character.

2 Field observations

Although much useful information both on the general nature of wave action on the beach and on specific problems of coastal engineering can be gained from models, the final aim of coastal studies is to understand the forces at work on the beaches in nature. For this purpose it is essential to make full-scale observations of the many different processes and features in the field. These vary from the generation of waves in the open ocean to the movement and character of the beach material and a study of the backshore zone. Field observations can be broadly divided into those studies concerned with recording the characteristics of the beach and coast, and those that observe the processes that are operating upon them—the response and the process variables respectively.

a   Observing beach and coast characteristics

(*i*) *Sediment sampling:*   The nature of the sediment is an important aspect of the beach. The necessity for sampling to obtain a valid estimate of the character of the beach material has already been mentioned. The most satisfactory sampling plan is usually the stratified random one advocated by W. C. Krumbein and H. A. Slack (1956), in which samples are taken from each of the different environments within the area being studied in proportion to their sizes. These environments may include the backshore zone, in which dune sand may be an essential element, the upper foreshore at and above the swash limit, the swash zone, the breaker zone, the shallow offshore zone just behind the breakers, the zone where wave movement first starts to affect the bottom and the deeper water offshore.

The number of samples required from each zone can be established by taking a small preliminary sample, with which the degree of variability of the material may be assessed. Where the material is very variable more samples will be required, but where it is homogeneous a few samples will suffice to give the estimated value of the population characteristics to the required degree of confidence. The relationship

$$n = \frac{[st_{\alpha/2}(m)]}{d}$$

may be used to assess the correct sample size, where n is the number of values required, s is the sample standard deviation, $t_{\alpha/2}(m)$ is the upper Student's t value at the required confidence level, m is the number in the sample less 1, and d is the required degree of accuracy in units from the true population mean.

Instead of being randomly selected in each different zone the sample may be taken along a series of profiles across the zones. Krumbein and Slack suggest that if six profiles are used, each with five samples, an estimate of the population mean with a relative error of about 10% at 95% confidence level will be achieved. To halve the possible error would require four samples to be taken at each sampling point.

Sediments are not only sampled for their size distribution and other size characteristics; several further important attributes may be observed. These include the density of the material, its organic content, its mineralogical character and, especially for the larger particles, its shape. Interesting studies on the heavy mineral content of beach sands have been made, and these provide evidence for the source of the material and its longshore movement. The shape of the larger particles also gives some indication of the intensity of wave action and the source of the beach material.

The variation of the characteristics of the beach material must be considered both in an areal distribution and in depth. The former type of analysis provides a measure of the variability in the different beach environments at any one time, the other useful information of the beach changes over time. In studying the latter aspect of sedimentation the stratigraphical relationships are important as they give data concerning the processes of sedimentation. The firmness of the deposit, its bedding and thickness are also all relevant. It has already been suggested that the permeability of the material is important in an analysis of the behaviour of the material in a moving fluid medium, and so too is the water level in the sediment. The nature of the surface beneath the beach and the character of the backshore should also be investigated.

(*ii*) *Beach surveys:* One advantage of model beach profiles in a wave tank is that changes in the profile can be easily measured to any required depth of water. Similar observations in nature are much more difficult to make. Where there is a considerable tidal range the wide foreshore may be surveyed at low water. Levelling along a straight line at right-angles to the coast from some fixed datum is the usual method. An Ordnance Survey bench mark, for example, gives an accurate height which can be related to the tide levels by means of the tide tables. This measurement is necessary as it is important to be able to mark the mean tide levels on the profile. The distances along the profile can usually be measured best by tacheometry, which avoids the actual measurement of distance along the beach. Instruments have been developed to record the profile directly as they are wheeled over the surface of the beach, but these have the disadvantage that they will only operate effectively on a firm surface unless special precautions are taken.

In order to be able to relate change in sand level and profile to the relevant wave and wind characteristics it is necessary to repeat surveys of the same beach profiles at intervals. The shorter the intervals the better the changes can be correlated with the frequently changing pattern of wave action. It is not necessary, however, to survey the profile by levelling each time observations are made, if these are required at fairly short intervals, such as daily or weekly. On beaches which are not too frequented the variations in level on the beach from day to day can easily be measured by placing thin pegs in the sand along the surveyed profile at appropriate places. The length of peg standing above the sand can be noted at the required intervals of time. The pegs are not disturbed by the waves and accurate changes in level can be recorded. If changes are required over a longer period more substantial markers must be fixed in the beach. 5 cm scaffolding poles buried deeply in the beach can withstand considerable changes of beach level and wave attack. They were used successfully on a beach near Blackpool for observations between 1943 and 1945 for daily measurement of the beach levels. Forty poles were fixed in the beach at significant points on the profile extending over a distance of 1220 m horizontally and about 7·32 m vertically, as this is a very flat beach with a considerable tidal range. Clamps were fixed on each pole at a known height to facilitate the measurements, which were made daily for a period and thereafter weekly.

Techniques were devised during World War II to establish the profiles of beaches that could not be surveyed directly. Some of these techniques have been described by W. W. Williams

(1947). There are three main methods: the water-line method is only applicable to tidal beaches as far as the low-water level; the wave-transparency method is only applicable to beaches covered by very clear water with little or no wave action; while the third is based on the changes in wave length and velocity in shallow water. The last is only applicable under suitable wave conditions, when long, clearly defined swell is reaching the beach. All three require conditions under which good aerial photographs of the beach can be taken at suitable intervals.

If an aerial photograph contains part of the offshore region where the water depth is more than half the wave length, the deep-water wave length can be measured on the photograph and converted into distance by reference to the scale of the photograph. The period of the waves can be ascertained from this value and their length in any depth can be found by reference to the set of curves shown in figure 4-1. The lengths of the waves as they move into shallow water are measured on the photographs and the equivalent water depth can be established. A plot of these depths gives a reasonably accurate profile of the beach. This method can only be used when waves with long even crest-lines are reaching the beach.

It has been found increasingly necessary to extend surveys into the offshore zone because changes here are related to changes on the foreshore, and offshore surveys are essential in estimating the amount of longshore transport of material. The straightness of the offshore survey line can be maintained by keeping two beacons on shore in line. The distance can be measured by horizontal sextant angles to fixed beacons on shore. An alternative method is to fix the position of the boat from which soundings are being made by plane-table angles from the shore. If the profile is only required to extend to a depth of about 4 m it may be obtained by levelling from the shore provided the gradient is not very flat. Distances may be obtained tacheometrically.

One of the disadvantages of the sounding method is that only spot depths are recorded and unless these are made very frequently some of the irregularities of the bottom may be missed. This problem is overcome by using echo-sounding. Modern instruments are specially designed for use in shallow water and these give depths accurate to 7·5 cm. A continuous profile is also traced out on the recording drum.

Tests have been made with other devices designed to give the underwater profile directly or in the form of changing gradients, and other instruments have been designed for observations of rapid beach changes on steep shingle beaches. For example, in tests made on Chesil beach to record changes around the break-point over short time intervals, the instrument used consisted of a long pole to which a marker was fixed. The marker could be manipulated from the shore, and recorded the level of the shingle at the position of the pole. The method could only be used on shingle beaches where the gradient is very steep. A similar device has also been used in the U.S.S.R. (Zenkovich, 1962).

D. L. Inman and G. A. Rusnak (1956) using another device tested the accuracy of positioning for sounding. They found that in a depth of 9·15 m 50% of the observations fell within a radius of 1·52 m of the required point out of 45 tests, while 80% fell within a 3·05 m radius. Their method of positioning was to keep the boat on line by aligning two markers on shore and fixing the distance by horizontal sextant angles to a third fixed point. Observations were made by the fixing of reference rods in the sea floor at the points tested. Brass rods, 9·5 mm by 1·22 m long, were fixed in the sand at depths of up to 22·8 m by observers wearing breathing apparatus. They were buried 0·915 m deep in the sand, leaving 30·5 cm exposed above the sand surface. The rods only caused slight scour. At each reference point six rods were placed in the form of a T, and their mean length above the sand surface provided a measure of the change of beach level.

A more elaborate system has been developed to measure beach profiles. It makes use of a helicopter. A sledge on which slope recording machinery is fitted is dropped at the seaward end of the profile by the helicopter. It is then dragged to the shore, recording the profile as it is moved landwards. This provides a rapid method of carrying out a series of profiles along a stretch of coastline. It has the advantage that it can be operated in stormy weather when the greatest beach changes are taking place.

Another method that also allows observations in stormy conditions has been developed in the U.S.S.R. An overhead rail system running out through the surf zone along the Black Sea coast allows profiles to be measured in any weather conditions (Zenkovich, 1967). They have also developed the vibrocorer to obtain samples of bottom material along the profile.

The development of the aqualung has brought the shallow submarine zone into much more direct reach. The use of aqualungs allows the stake method of measuring changing sand levels to be observed directly to depths up to about 30.5 m. The character of the bottom can also be examined. These methods can only be applied effectively in areas where the shallow-water zone is clear. Problems of location and visibility are severe in the sediment-laden waters around the coast of Britain, though C. Kidson et al. (1962) consider that, even in the relatively unfavoured British coastal waters, the aqualung has potentialities worth developing for underwater survey work.

(iii) *Accuracy of surveys:* The most accurate method of underwater measurement is the direct recording of changes on rods, followed by echo-sounding. The standard error of observation of rod measurements, for example, was 1·525 cm for four stations in depths varying between 5·5 m and 21·3 m. The error became less further from the shore. Sonic sounding was carried out at the same time to test the relative accuracy of the two methods. Five runs were made and these agreed closely, giving a range of 9·1 cm. The experimental accuracy of the echo-sounding was about ± 15 cm in depths of 9·15, 15·8 and 21·3 m (D. L. Inman and G. A. Rusnak, 1956).

The relative accuracy of lead-line sounding and echo-sounding has been discussed by T. Saville and J. M. Caldwell (1953) for surveys carried out on Mission Beach, California. The probable error of the two methods was $0·6745\sigma$, where σ is the standard deviation. The echo-sounder used under favourable conditions gave a probable error of 2·13 cm, while that for the lead-line was 3·36 cm in shallow water for the deviation from the average profile, or 6·1 cm between successive profiles.

Beach profiles may be used for calculating the amount of material transported alongshore. The volumetric change in beach material can be established from a series of profiles. Several profiles are surveyed across the area in question at different times. It is assumed that the beach changes along the measured profiles are representative of the changes between the profiles. Thus the closer the spacing of the profiles the more accurate will be the assessment of the volume of material added to or eroded from the beach. There are two sources of error—the sounding and spacing errors—inherent in the use of profiles for the calculation of longshore movement or other volumetric changes of beach material. The double error is equal to the square-root of the sum of the squares of the two separate errors. The error, E, in cubic yards is given by

$$E = \sqrt{\frac{e_a{}^2 e_s{}^2 LL'}{27}}$$

where L and L' are the length of beach between surveys and the length of profile, both in feet. The curves shown in figure 2-5 give the probable error for both lead-line sounding and echo-sounding (Saville and Caldwell, 1953). An example shows that on a stretch of beach 3050 m wide, with a profile 1370 m long, of which the outer 1220 m are sounded by echo-sounding and the inner 150 m by lead-line, the error varies as follows for differing distances between surveys:

1 If the spacing is 305 m apart, which would entail 10 surveys, the probable error would be 54,100 m³
2 If the profiles were surveyed every 61 m the error would be reduced to 30,400 m³
3 These errors would be decreased by about 5% if all the profiles were surveyed by echo-sounding.

Thus for fairly small amounts of volumetric change the error due to inaccuracy of the surveyed beach profiles may lead to very misleading results, even if the surveying is done with accurate instruments. The errors might be even larger than suggested as the sounding error may have been underestimated.

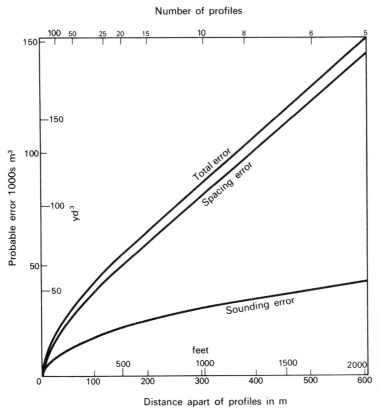

Figure 2-5 Probable error of volume of sediment moved for 3050 m (10,000 feet) of beach on profiiles 1370 m (4500 feet) long. The first 153 m (500 feet) were sounded by lead-line, the remainder by echo-sounder. (*After Saville and Caldwell, 1953.*)

(*iv*) *Amount of change in successive profiles:* Beaches vary considerably in their relative mobility, and a method for assessing the variability of the beach profile is useful. The superimposition of a long series of beach profiles gives an indication of the variability of the beach. Smooth beaches will tend to have profiles that cover a smaller range than beaches with ridges and runnels.

The line joining the highest points on all the profiles indicates the height above which the beach is unlikely to extend. Similarly the lowest points indicate the level below which material is unlikely to be removed. The zone between the upper and lower curves is called the 'sweep'

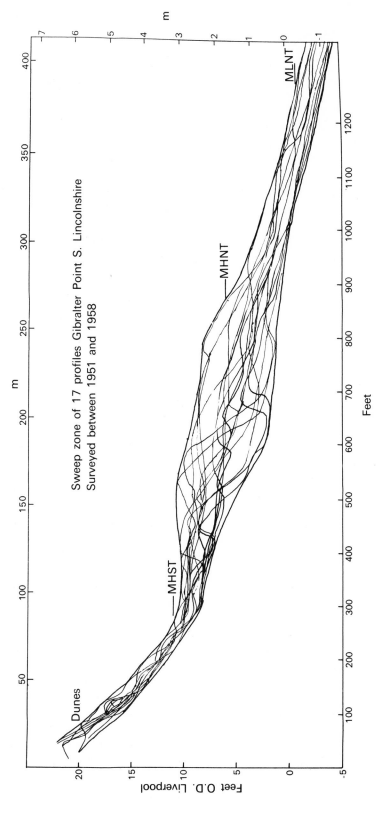

Figure 2-6 Sweep zone profiles at Gibraltar Point, Lincolnshire.

zone, and defined as the vertical envelope within which movement of beach material may take place by wave action.

In some instances the lower sweep-zone profile will be the foundation of the beach. In other areas it may lie entirely in mobile beach material. Where a beach is ridged or barred the profile at any one time will not lie entirely along the upper sweep-zone profile, as indicated in figure 2-6. On a smooth beach, however, the profile may lie along the upper sweep-zone profile.

Over a relatively short period of time the sweep zone indicates the maximum and minimum possible conditions of the beach profile. The comparison of sweep zones over a considerable period is a useful method of assessing the longer-term beach changes—the rate, for example, at which the coast is advancing or retreating—in that it eliminates the effect of temporary variations due to the operation of different types of waves. The displacement of the whole sweep zone indicates longer-term changes and can probably be attributed to longshore movement, rather than movement normal to the shore. The latter usually accounts for the day-to-day short-term changes in the beach profile (C. A. M. King and F. A. Barnes, 1964; C. A. M. King, 1968).

b   Measurement of dynamic processes

Much effort has been expended in the development of methods of measuring different elements of the process variables. A number have been devised. The processes include waves, tides, wind and the movement of beach material.

(*i*) *Waves:*   W. A. Koontz and D. L. Inman (1967) describe an elaborate modern system of measuring several of the process variables, including wave dimensions, currents, bottom pressure and suspended sediment density.

A digital staff has been developed to record the wave height accurately in the surf zone and a series of these staffs can be used to measure the direction of wave approach. The staff provides a continuous analysis of the water height, spectral analysis giving the significant wave dimensions. Both the changing water elevations as the waves pass and the wave currents are measured. A Savonius current meter has been specially designed to use digital logic similar to that of the wave recording system: pulses are produced for each revolution of the rotor, providing a digital record of the current flow, which is recorded on a chart. The varying pressures on the bottom as the waves pass over can be measured by a vibrating-wire pressure sensor: this provides a very accurate record, as it is sensitive to very small variations in pressure in a high-pressure environment, such as that of the surf zone. Underwater photography may also be used to estimate the amount of material in suspension and to record the character of the bottom. These intruments are very elaborate and make use of recently developed electronic devices and computer facilities. Their main disadvantage is their expense and the elaborate mounting they require.

An instrument, based on ultrasonic flow, to measure the direction of wave approach is described by L. C. Williams (1965). It has been tested in the laboratory wave tank and in the field with satisfactory results. A meter measures the bi-directional flow of water past a pair of sensing elements. The direction of flow is in line with the sensing elements. It is only necessary to rotate the meter, when it is in place, in order to determine the direction from which the flow is at a maximum and this will indicate the direction of wave approach. The instrument responds almost instantaneously to changes in flow under the crest and trough of the waves.

A ducted impellor flowmeter for measuring water velocities in breaking waves is described by W. L. Wood (1968). This has a velocity range from zero to 4·757 m/sec, a hyperbolic response to axial flow and a cosine response to off-axis flow. Tests of the meter show that its response to orbital flow, such as occurs in shallow-water waves, is excellent in relation to the axial calibration of the meter. It reacts to bi-directional flow, but only records accurately for flow in one direction. This can be allowed for by placing two meters side by side facing in opposite directions.

J. C. Ingle (1966) recorded waves and currents by simpler means for his study of beach material movement. He measured waves either by means of a graduated pole held in the breaker zone, or with a graduated pole held at the still-water level against which the level of the horizon was measured. Maximum wave heights recorded were 3 m. The angle of wave incidence at the break-point was measured with a compass. Wave-induced currents were measured by timing the movement of dye inserted in the waves at the required points. Wind speeds were measured with a hand anemometer.

Wave measuring devices for deep-water waves are mentioned in chapter 3.

(*ii*) *Tidal streams:* Tidal streams are important in some coastal areas, and methods of measuring them in the short term and over longer periods have been developed.

Short-term measurements may be made by means of J. N. Carruthers's (1962; 1967) jelly bottles. The bottles, partly filled with hot liquid jelly in which a compass card is enclosed, are lowered and fixed close to the bottom. The angle of the bottle is a measure of the current velocity and the compass shows the direction of the current. These values are fixed when the jelly cools and sets. Results of observations with this instrument are discussed in chapter 5.

A longer-term method of estimating the net direction of tidal stream flow—the residual tidal stream—uses neutrally buoyant floats, called Woodhead sea-bed drifters, which move close to the bottom. These are released at a specific point and then travel close to the bottom until they are washed up on a beach. Their place and date of recovery is recorded by the finder on a card attached to the float. The card is then returned. The method cannot provide an accurate estimate of the residual current velocity, but it does give useful data for studies of supply of sediment and general water movement in regions of strong tidal streams (A. W. Phillips, 1970). This method and some of its results are considered in more detail in chapter 5.

(*iii*) *Experiments with tracers:* One of the most important and most difficult variables to record accurately in the field is the longshore movement of material. Estimates have been made by repeated surveys of areas affected by coastal engineering works that trap the sediment moving alongshore. This method can provide a value of the mean annual movement between the years of survey.

Shorter-term observations of longshore movement are being increasingly made by use of marked material similar to the normal beach material. Uusally either the material is made radio-active so that it can be traced by means of geiger or scintillation counters, or else fluorescent material is used which can be traced in very low concentrations with an ultra-violet lamp.

These methods of measuring longshore movement of material suffer from the disadvantage that they only cover short time intervals. It is difficult to ensure that conditions during the experiment are representative of the long-term conditions on the particular beach being studied. There is the advantage, however, that the short-term observations can more readily be related to the process variables that are operating to cause the longshore transport of material.

One difficulty is exemplified by the work carried out by C. Kidson, A. P. Carr and D. B. Smith (1958) on Orfordness in Suffolk. The shingle, marked with radio-active tracer using the isotope barium-140–lanthanum-140, was placed close to the low-water level. The marked shingle moved slowly northwards during the first month of tracing, an abnormal direction on this spit which has grown southwards. Rapid southerly movement then took place when the uncommon southeasterly waves were replaced by the more usual northeasterly ones during the later part of the experiment. Had the experiment only lasted for a month, however, a completely misleading result would have been obtained, because the first month was atypical. In this experiment the marked shingle was traced by means of a scintillation counter towed behind a boat in the offshore zone. Finds of marked stones were fixed by horizontal sextant angles to fixed points on shore. The marked pebbles above water level were located with a geiger counter dragged over the shingle. The marked shingle in this experiment was traced over a period of 6 weeks.

An example of the use of marked sand, traced over much shorter periods, is provided by the observations of J. C. Ingle (1966). His observations were made in the surf zone on a series of beaches in California. Sand was collected from the beach and marked with fluorescent dyes. Samples weighing between 1·36 and 18·2 kg were released at each test site, several different colours of dyed sand being released simultaneously at different points along one beach profile. Samples were then collected at specific grid points on either side of the release points at specific intervals of time depending on the intensity of wave action. The longest periods of time were between two to three hours, and samples were collected at about three intervals with a maximum of four during the whole run. Over these relatively short periods wave conditions were recorded. Sampling was carried out by pressing a greased card into the beach at the correct grid point. The samples collected in this way were then later analysed in the laboratory under ultra-violet light, and the concentration of marked sand grains counted on the card, which was 7·5 cm by 7·5 cm.

Experiments of this type allow estimates to be made of the effect of different intensities and directions of wave approach. It is also possible to estimate the total volume of longshore transport. The marked material must, however, have the same characteristics of the material where it is released, and this may be difficult, because even if sand is taken from a specific point on the beach, by the time it is dyed and returned to the beach for injection, the size of the sand at that point may have changed. It can be shown that material differing in size from the surrounding material will not move at the same speed or perhaps even in the same direction. Thus the movement of the marked sand may not be representative of the sand where it is injected. This difficulty is particularly great on a beach with variable sized material, and may account for some of the rather anomalous results and the scatter of points obtained from these observations. Another disadvantage of this type of experiment is the very rapid spread of sand from any one point under vigorous wave action. This limits the period over which the experiment can be continued.

When fluorescent sand is used it is possible to use several colours at different points on one profile, and in this way the movement at different positions can be recorded simultaneously. The results of Ingle's observations were presented on maps of the experimental area, showing contours of equal tracer concentration.

Some deep-water experiments were also carried out in the course of Ingle's work. The marked sand was released by skin divers or SCUBA-equipped divers working from a boat at depths of up to 46 m. In deeper water, however, mechanical devices become necessary. A variety of devices has been used, such as passing the marked sand down a tube or fixing a knife above the bag containing the sand in such a way that it cuts the bag open when the latter touches the bottom. A false-bottomed drum has also been used successfully. Recovery can be made by means of greased sampling cards, which are collected by SCUBA divers in relatively shallow water. A weighted device can be used in deeper water where it is allowed to sink onto the bottom. A considerable number of studies using these and similar techniques have now been made and some of the results will be discussed in chapters 9 and 10.

3 Laboratory methods

a Sediment analysis

Laboratory methods concerned with the analysis of beach material are important in beach studies, and are an essential part of nearly all beach work. Details of the results of analysis of beach sediments will be considered in chapter 8. The normal method of analysing beach sand consists of mechanical dry sieving. Very fine material is rare on beaches, but it is sometimes necessary to analyse finer sediment, and this cannot be done by sieving. It must be done by pipette or settling tube analysis.

A problem associated with these methods is that they measure different properties of the sediment. Sieving measures the geometrical properties of shape and size, while pipette and similar methods measure the hydraulic properties of the sediment. There is some advantage, however, in measuring the hydraulic properties because of their importance in sediment that is mostly being moved in water. For this reason settling tube analysis is advocated for all sizes of sediment by the Coastal Engineering Research Center (1966, 145). A sample of 5 to 7 gm is sufficient for analysis by this method, and the visual-accumulation tube described by B. C. Colby *et al.* (1957) is suggested as a suitable instrument.

Interesting results have also been obtained by means of an electron microscope (E. W. Biederman, 1962). The surface character of individual sand grains can be studied and their detailed shape characteristics considered. Shape studies can, however, be more easily carried out on larger particles, such as shingle.

A number of different measures of shape have been devised. The visual system of dividing sand grains seen under a low-power microscope into one of six shape classes of increasing angularity is advocated by F. P. Shepard and R. Young (1961). P. H. Kuenen (1963) has developed an instrument for measuring the pivotability of sand grains: this divides them into 12 categories according to the time they take to cover the length of a trough that is being rocked to and fro. Kuenen showed that high pivotability increased the rate of transport by traction, but decreased the movement in suspension.

Another useful shape measure is the roundness index devised by A. Cailleux (1945). This is given by $2r/a \times 1000$, where r is the minimum radius of curvature in the principal plane and a is the maximum length of the pebble. For a completely spherical pebble the value reaches 1000. Beach pebbles normally show a fairly high roundness value. Cailleux's measures provide a satisfactory measure of roundness according to M. Blenk (1960) and V. Tonnard (1963).

Cailleux has also devised a flatness measure, given by $(a + b)/2c \times 100$, where a is the length, b is the width and c the thickness of the pebble. This measure is not so useful as the roundness. Measurements show that there is a strong negative correlation between it and Krumbein's sphericity measure, which is given by $\sqrt[3]{bc/a^2}$.

Zingg (W. C. Krumbein, 1941) has defined four shape classes according to the b/a and c/b axes, namely discs, spheres, blades and rods. These and Krumbein's sphericity measures are shown in figure 8-2. Zingg's classes only provide a nominal grouping and there is thus an advantage in using the ratio data provided by Cailleux's index or Krumbein's sphericity measure, as parametric statistics can then be applied to the results of the study if the data are normally distributed.

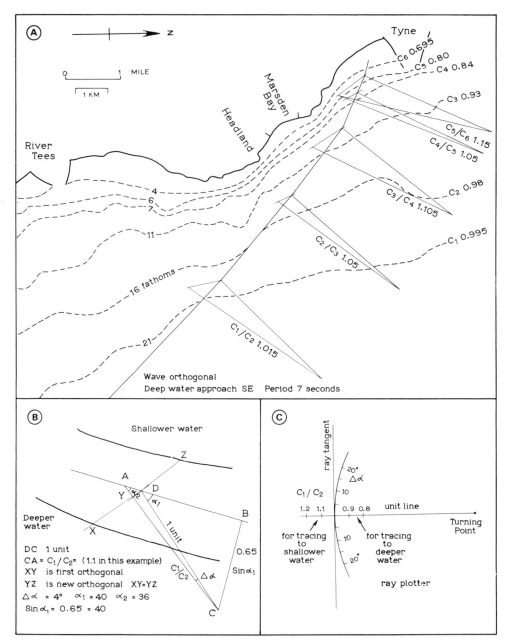

Figure 2-7A, B, C Diagrams to illustrate the construction of wave rays.

b Wave refraction diagrams

(*i*) *Construction:* Another useful technique that can be carried out in the laboratory is the construction of wave refraction diagrams. Wave refraction depends on the length of the waves in deep water, on their direction of approach and on the offshore relief. The last control means that each area must be treated individually, and the analysis depends on the availability of

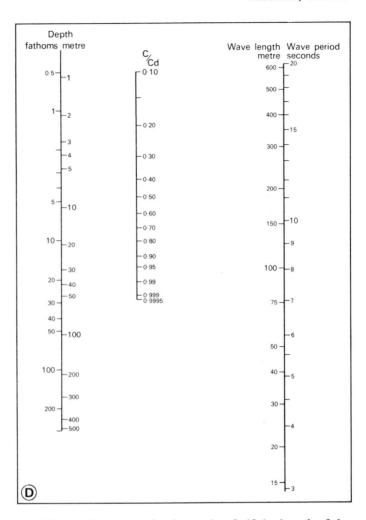

Depth
fathoms metre

C/Cd

Wave length Wave period
metre   seconds

Figure 2-7D Diagram to relate wave period, length and velocity for varying depths. (*D after Arthur, Munk and Isaacs, 1952.*)

(D)

good submarine charts. The charts should extend out to a depth equal to half the length of the longest wave for which refraction diagrams are to be drawn.

The refraction diagram shows the wave crests and the orthogonals, which run at right-angles to them. If the orthogonals are equally spaced in deep water it is assumed that the energy between any two of them remains equal. As they are traced towards the shore they diverge or converge as the wave crests bend, and the distribution of energy at the coast becomes uneven. The pattern of orthogonals or wave rays, as they are often called, is the important part of the diagram, and the wave crests can be omitted.

The older method of drawing refraction diagrams first traced successive wave crests from deep into shallow water, and then, as a second step, the orthogonals were drawn in at right-angles to the wave crests. More recent methods, which are more accurate, draw the wave rays directly.

The orthogonals can be constructed towards either the deep or shallow water. The ratio of the wave velocity at two successive contours is calculated relative to the deep-water value. As shown in figure 2-7B the mean contour between two depth contours is drawn by eye. The orthogonal cutting contour 1 is produced to cut the mean contour at D. Then DC is drawn perpendicular to XD and equal to unity on any convenient scale. Next c_1/c_2 is drawn on the same scale from C to cut BD produced at A. YZ, the new direction of the orthogonal, is drawn perpendicular to AC so that YZ = XD.

For reasonable accuracy the angle α_1 should be less than 15° and $\Delta c/c_1$ should be less than 0·2. The orthogonals can be traced continuously in this way. A diagram such as that shown in figure 2-7D facilitates the calculation of the wave velocity for any depth in relation to the deep-water velocity, and hence c_1/c_2 can easily be found. Figure 2-7C illustrates the ray plotter, which can be drawn on tracing paper. It is used to fix the position of the point A from which the new wave ray YZ is drawn. Figure 2-7A exemplifies the construction of one wave ray from a depth of 21 fathoms, off the coast of County Durham, to a depth of 4 fathoms for a wave of 7 second period approaching from the south-east.

J. W. Dunham (1951) has compared the value of the old and the new methods and comes to the conclusion that the latter, crestless, method is more likely to be accurate. In fact the earlier method is considered obsolete by W. J. Pierson et al. (1955), who also advocate the crestless method just described.

The construction of wave refraction diagrams is a mechanical process that can be carried out with reasonable efficiency by computer provided that the offshore relief is not too complex. W. Harrison and W. S. Wilson (1964) and W. S. Wilson (1966) have discussed the application of computer techniques to the construction of wave refraction diagrams.

Wilson (1966) describes how a digital computer and incremental plotter can be used to calculate and plot wave rays. The area to be used must first be defined, bearing in mind both the depth at which refraction starts and the bending of the wave rays as they approach the land. Once the appropriate area has been determined a grid is set up over it with the Y axis parallel to the greatest depth contour. The grid size is chosen so that the total number of grid intersections does not exceed 20,000 and that, as far as possible, each section can be considered a plane surface. The depth value is needed for each coordinate point and the direction of approach of the wave rays into the area under consideration must be established. It is possible to trace rays both onshore and offshore from a specific point.

The computer starts with the origin and direction of the wave ray and works out each successive point. Water depths and gradients are obtained from a plane 'fitted' to the nearest four depth points by the method of least-squares, and the ray curvatures are calculated by reference to these values. The coordinates of the points reached by each ray, as it is traced to the shore or the edge of the grid, are recorded on magnetic tape. The plotter can enter selected soundings on the ray diagram as well as the coastline. It can also show the position of every stated wave crest along the ray. Unless the relief is very simple this system is much quicker than the hand method. A grid of depths must, however, be constructed before the program can operate.

(ii) *Results of wave refraction and other methods of presentation:*   From refraction diagrams the zones of convergence and divergence of wave energy become apparent. The variation of energy causes reduction of wave height in areas of divergence and an increase in areas of convergence. The former will occur, for example, opposite submarine canyons or in bays, while the latter occur opposite submarine ridges or on headlands. The variation of wave height sets up significant longshore currents. The effect of wave refraction on the wave energy and characteristics along the coast is thus very important in considering beach processes, the movement of beach material, and coastal alignment.

The refraction diagrams so far discussed show the detailed conditions that occur for one wave length, coming from one direction, along a considerable stretch of coast. It is also possible to

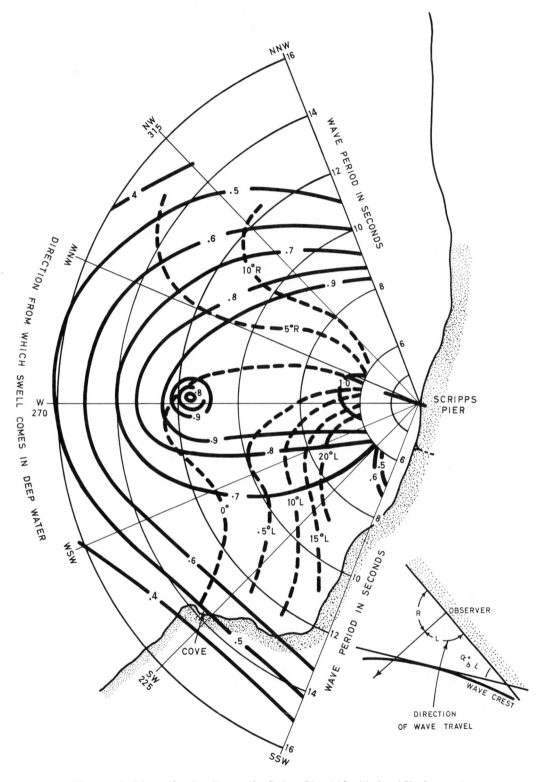

Figure 2-8 Wave refraction diagram for Scripps Pier. (*After Munk and Traylor, 1947.*)

construct a diagram in which data for a number of different wave directions and periods are considered together for one locality. An example of such a diagram, constructed by W. H. Munk and M. A. Traylor (1947) for the Scripps pier in California, is shown in figure 2-8. Refraction is given in terms of K_b and α_b for wave periods between 6 and 16 seconds and for direction from south-southeast to north-northeast. The factor K_b approaches unity as the waves become shorter and as their direction of approach becomes more normal to the coast. K_b is the refraction factor and refers to conditions at the break-point. It is related to the wave energy and is apparent in changes of wave height. These are given by the equations $H/H_0 = \gamma K$, $H_b/H_0 = \gamma_b K_b$. The value of K_b equals $\sqrt[3]{S_0/S_b}$, where S is the distance apart of the orthogonals on the refraction diagram, the suffixes $_0$ and $_b$ referring to deep water and the break-point respectively. K_b in terms of wave velocity and angle of approach for a straight beach with parallel depth contours is given by

$$\left[\frac{\cos 2\alpha_0}{1 - (c_b/c_0)\sin \alpha_0{}^2} \right]^{1/6}$$

The constants are only applicable to one depth and are intended to allow for the effects of friction and diffraction, the latter permitting energy to flow across the orthogonals. It appears from the good agreement between forecast and observed wave heights that both these factors are relatively unimportant in areas where refraction is great. The angle α_b determines the angle between the wave crest and the shoreline, as explained on the figure. Diagrams of this type therefore provide very useful evidence concerning the relative effectiveness of waves approaching from different directions.

In a mathematical treatment, M. S. Longuet-Higgins (1956) discusses the modification of certain wave characteristics as the waves are refracted on entering shallow water, with particular reference to changes in crest length. The observed increase of crest length can be explained by the refraction of the waves. The length of crest relative to wave length depends on the angular deviation of the wave components: the smaller the deviation the greater will be the crest length to wave length ratio. The length of the wave crest is affected by refraction in two ways. Firstly, if the waves are of the same length but vary in direction, they are collimated to become more parallel to the coast, their angular deviation is reduced and their crest length is increased. Secondly, if the waves come from the same direction but vary in length, they are refracted by differing amounts. Their angular difference increases and they become shorter-crested. In deep water the second type would be long-crested, but the crest would split up in shallower water as refraction takes effect.

In general Longuet-Higgins found that an increase of crest length appears to be more common than a decrease. The former sometimes takes place as the result of a combination of longer swell with shorter waves. The longer waves, which are usually longer-crested, are amplified more than the shorter, leading to an increase of crest length. The analysis does not apply to high waves nor to waves which steepen at their crests and break. In considering the changes in amplitude Longuet-Higgins showed mathematically that waves approaching a coast obliquely increase less than those approaching normally. He provides a graph to facilitate numerical calculation of this effect.

4 Search procedures

a Historical records

In some coastal problems valuable material can be found by searching the historical records and examining early maps and photographs. Specific examples of the results of this type of research are considered in chapter 18. It is only in particularly favourable circumstances that useful historical data are available for a reasonable period of time. Maps made before the beginning of the nineteenth century are generally not trustworthy. This conclusion was reached by G. de Boer (1969), who has made a very detailed study of the historical evidence for the earlier stages of development of Spurn Head in east Yorkshire. He considers that the first fully satisfactory map of this area is the first edition of the Ordnance Survey six-inch map published in 1852.

The earliest maps to show the headland of Ravenser Odd, as it was called at that time, were the Portolan charts of the early fourteenth century. These charts then became standardized and did not change throughout the three centuries they were used. They are wildly inaccurate and hence can be of little historical value as evidence of coastal change. Ravenser is shown at the northern end of the Wash, at the site of Gibraltar Point in Lincolnshire, rather than in the Humber, which is not even marked. The only point of value is that it is shown as a headland and not as an island. No map of the fifteenth century provides any evidence. The first map of the Humber to show any detail is dated about 1540. On this Spurn Head is shown with a narrow neck and bulbous head, labelled Ravens Spurn. Saxton's map of 1577 is the next to show the feature in detail. From this date the maps become somewhat more detailed and reliable, but it is not until the Ordnance Survey maps that accuracy is such as to allow measurements to be made in quantitative terms.

The study of the cartographic evidence for this particular feature shows that the earliest maps can rarely be used as evidence on their own merits, but used in conjunction with written records and other evidence they may provide valuable supporting material of a qualitative type. Provided adequate caution is used in the interpretation of this evidence it can be used effectively.

A. P. Carr (1969) has made a similar study of the cartographic data on Orfordness in Suffolk and its growth. He also counsels caution in the use of cartographic data for quantitative assessments. He argues that rates of growth of the spit based on the early maps may well be unreliable for two main reasons. Firstly, the maps may well not be sufficiently accurate to warrant such measurements. Secondly, the maps are not necessarily produced when the spit reached turning points in its growth. Its growth appears to be erratic, at times grows fast when a submarine foundation has been prepared earlier. At other times its growth is slow, while occasionally it becomes truncated in times of severe storm.

b Air photographs

Air photographs may provide a valuable source of information concerning the development of shore forms. They are particularly valuable in revealing the pattern of beach ridges, which usually show very clearly on air photographs and are difficult to interpret from a ground view, especially when they have become vegetated. The pattern of growth of complex features can often be interpreted by means of air photographs. An example is discussed in section 19-5(a)(iii).

Colour photographs can also be used with advantage in the study of both underwater and shoreline features, such as salt marsh and dunes. The complex pattern of submarine bars and troughs shows up very clearly on air photographs and their movement can be traced on successive photographs. In fact some types of submarine bars, such as the crescentic bars found in parts of the Mediterranean Sea, were not recognized until they were revealed on air photographs. The shallower water over the bar crests is shown as a lighter strip on the photograph, owing to the greater reflection of light from the sand under the shallow water over the crest compared with the deeper water in the trough. Air photographs were also used during World War II to determine the profiles of enemy-held beaches.

Summary

Beaches and coasts can be studied in many different ways. The natural beach environment is very complex so that model studies are valuable. The main aim of the many different types of models is to control the many variables and to simplify the complex natural situation. Model studies include the conceptual framework, the mathematical deterministic model, statistical methods, simulation by computer program and the use of hardware scale models. Many different types of problems can be studied in a model wave tank, including two-dimensional processes, three-dimensional situations and models of specific areas built to solve specific problems.

All model studies must be related sooner or later to relevant field observations. These include a study of the characteristics of the beach material and the profile and plan of the beach. Such field studies may be termed static studies to differentiate them from the study of the processes —for example, the action of waves and tides—that modify beaches. Recent field studies have been devoted to the measurement of longshore movement of material by means of experiments with tracers, such as radio-activated or fluorescent material.

Laboratory methods of analysis include the study of the character of the beach sediment, for example its size distribution and shape. Such studies require careful sampling plans, but can reveal valuable information concerning the beach processes. The construction of wave refraction diagrams is useful in considering the distribution of energy along the shore and in accounting for the alignment of some beach features. The best method of constructing wave refraction diagrams is by drawing orthogonals either from deep water towards the shore or in the reverse direction.

The historical development of the coast can be studied by means of suitable early maps and charts where these are available, although great caution is required in their use. Quantitative measurements can rarely be made prior to the Ordnance Survey maps in the nineteenth century. Locally other historical information may be relevant to coastal studies. Air photographs reveal many features that are not easily appreciated by other means. They sometimes provide evidence of earlier stages of development and include much more relevant detail than most maps.

References

ALLEN, J. 1947: Scale models in hydraulic engineering. London.

ARTHUR, R. S., MUNK, W. H. and ISAACS, J. D. 1952: The direct construction of wave rays. *Trans. Am. Geophys. Un.* **33**(6), 855–65.

BAGNOLD, R. A. 1940: Beach formation by waves—some model experiments in a wave tank. *J. Inst. Civ. Eng.* **15**, 27–52.

BAGNOLD, R. A. 1946: Motion of waves in shallow water, interaction between waves and sand bottoms. *Proc. Roy. Soc.* A **187**(1008), 1–18.

BAGNOLD, R. A. 1947: Sand movement by waves: some small-scale experiments with sand of very low density. *J. Inst. Civ. Eng.* Paper **5554,** 447–69.

BAGNOLD, R. A. 1963: Beach and nearshore processes: Part I, Mechanics of marine sedimentation. In M. N. Hill (Editor), *The sea,* **III,** New York: Wiley, 507–28.

BEACH EROSION BOARD 1933: *Interim Report.* U.S. Army, Corps of Engineers.

BIEDERMAN, E. W. 1962: Distinction of shoreline environments in New Jersey. *J. Sed. Petrol* **32,** 181–200.

BLENK, M. 1960: Ein Beitrag zur morphometrischen Schotteranalyse. *Zeits. für Geomorph.* NF **4,** 202–42.

BOER, G. DE and CARR, A. P. 1969: Early maps as historical evidence for coastal change. *Geog. J.* **135**(1), 17–39.

CAILLEUX, A. 1945: Distinctions des galets marins et fluviatiles. *Bull. Geol. Soc. France.* **5,** XV, 375–404.

CARRUTHERS, J. N. 1962: The easy measurement of bottom currents at modest depths. *Civ. Eng.* 57, 484–86.

CARRUTHERS, J. N. 1967: An improved simple current measuring bottle for fishermen. *Nat. Inst. Oceanog.*

CARSTENS, M. R., NEILSON, F. M. and ALTINBILEK, H. D. 1969: Bedforms generated in the laboratory under an oscillatory flow: an analytical and experimental study. *C.E.R.C. Tech. Memo.* **28.** (39 pp.)

COASTAL ENGINEERING RESEARCH CENTER 1966: Shore protection, planning and design. *C.E.R.C. Tech. Rep.* **4,** 3rd Edition. (401 pp.)

COLBY, B. C., JOHNSON, C. O. and WATTS, G. M. 1957: *The development and calibration of the visual accumulation tube.* Subcommittee on Sediment, Intra-agency Comm. on water resources, Anthony Falls Lab., Minneapolis, Minn.

DOORNKAMP, J. C. and KING, C. A. M. 1971: *Numerical analysis in geomorphology: an introduction.* London: Arnold; New York: St Martin's Press.

DUNHAM, F. W. 1951: Refraction and diffraction diagrams. Chap. 4 in *Proc. 1st Conf. on Coastal Eng.* 1950, Council of wave research, 33–49.

HARRISON, W. and KRUMBEIN, W. C. 1964: Interaction of the beach–ocean–atmosphere system at Virginia Beach, Virginia. *C.E.R.C. Tech. Memo.* **7.**

HARRISON, W. and WILSON, W. S. 1964: Development of a method of numerical calculation of wave refraction. *C.E.R.C. Tech. Memo.* **6.**

HJULSTRØM, F. 1935: Studies of the morphological activity of rivers as illustrated by the river Fyris. *Bull. Geol. Inst. Uppsala* **25.**

INGLE, J. C. 1966: The movement of beach sand. *Developments Sediment.* **5.** Amsterdam: Elsevier.

INMAN, D. L. 1963: Chapter 5 in F. P. Shepard, *Submarine geology,* 2nd Edition, 101–51.

INMAN, D. L. and BAGNOLD, R. A. 1963: Littoral processes—Part II. In M. N. Hill (Editor), *The sea,* **III,** New York: Wiley, 529–53.

INMAN, D. L. and RUSNAK, G. A. 1956: Changes in sand level on the beach and shelf at La Jolla, California. *B.E.B. Tech. Memo.* **82.**

INMAN, D. L. and BOWEN, J. 1962: Flume experiments on sand transport by waves. *Proc. 8th Conf. on Coast. Eng.* 137–50.

JOHNSON, J. W. 1949: Scale effects in hydraulic models involving wave motion. *Trans. Am. Geophys. Un.* **30**(4), 517–25.

JOHNSON, J. W., O'BRIEN, M. P. and ISAACS, J. D. 1948: Graphical construction of wave refraction diagrams. *U.S. Hydrog. Off. Pub.* **605.**

KIDSON, C., CARR, A. P. and SMITH, D. B. 1958: Further experiments using radioactive methods to detect the movement of shingle over the sea bed and alongshore. *Geog. J.* **124,** 210–18.

KIDSON, C., STEERS, J. A. and FLEMMING, N. C. 1962: A trial of the potential value of Aqualung diving to coastal physiography on British Coasts. *Geog. J.* **128**(1), 49–53.

KING, C. A. M. 1964: The characteristics of the offshore zone and its relationship to the foreshore near Gibraltar Point, Lincolnshire. *East. Mid. Geogr.* **3**(5), 230–43.

KING, C. A. M. 1966: *Techniques in geomorphology.* London: Arnold. (342 pp.)

KING, C. A. M. 1968: Beach measurements at Gibraltar Point, Lincolnshire. *East Mid. Geogr.* **4**(5), 295–300.

KING, C. A. M. 1970: Feedback relationships in Geomorphology. *Geogr. Ann.* **52**A (3–4), 145–59.

KING, C. A. M. and BARNES, F. A. 1964: Changes in the configuration of the inter-tidal beach zone off part of the Lincolnshire coast since 1951. *Zeits. für Geomorph.* NF **8,** 105–26*.

KING, C. A. M. and MCCULLACH, M. J. 1971: A simulation model of a complex recurved spit. *J. Geol.* **79**(1), 22–36.

KOONTZ, W. A. and INMAN, D. L. 1967: A multipurpose data acquisition system for instrumentation of the nearshore environment. *C.E.R.C. Tech. Memo.* **21.**

KRUMBEIN, W. C. 1941: Measurements and geological significance of shape and roundness of sedimentary particles. *J. Sed. Petrol* **11,** 64–72.

KRUMBEIN, W. C. 1961: The analysis of observational data from natural beaches. *B.E.B. Tech. Memo.* **130.** (59 pp.)

KRUMBEIN, W. C. 1964: A geological process-response model for analysis of beach phenomena. *Ann. Bull. B.E.B.* **17,** 1–15.

KRUMBEIN, W. C. and SLACK, H. A. 1956: Relative efficiency of beach sampling methods. *B.E.B. Tech. Memo.* **90.**

KUENEN, P. H. 1963: Pivotability studies of sand in a shape sorter. In van Straaten (Editor), *Developments Sediment.* **1,** 207–15.

LEWIS, W. V. 1943: Miniature spits and embankments on a lake shore in Iceland. *Geog. J.* **102,** 175–9.

LONGUET-HIGGINS, M. S. 1956: The refraction of sea waves in shallow water. *J. Fluid Mech.* **1**(2), 163–76.

MCCULLAGH, M. J. and KING, C. A. M. 1970: Spitsym—A spit simulated by synthetic methods. *University of Kansas, Computer Contributions* **50.**

MEYERS, R. D. 1933: *A model of wave action on beaches.* Thesis for M.Sc., Univ. of Calif., Doc. **91.**

MUNK, W. H. and TRAYLOR, M. A. 1947: Refraction of ocean waves: a process linking underwater topography to beach erosion. *J. Geol.* **55,** 1–26.

PHILLIPS, A. W. 1970: The use of the Woodhead seabed drifter. *Brit. Geomorph. Res. Gr. Tech. Bull.* **4.** (29 pp.)

PIERSON, W. J. 1951: The interpretation of crossed orthogonals in wave refraction phenomena. *B.E.B. Tech. Memo.* **21.**

PIERSON, W. J., NEUMANN, G. and JAMES, R. W. 1955: Practical methods for observing and forecasting ocean waves by means of wave spectra and statistics. *U.S. Navy, Hydrog. Off. Pub.* **603.**

PRICE, W. A. and KENDRICK, M. P. 1963: Field and model investigation into the reasons for siltation in the Mersey Estuary. *J. Inst. Civ. Eng.* 473–517.

SAVILLE, T. 1950: Model study of sand transport along an infinitely long straight beach. *Trans. Am. Geophys. Un.* **31**(4), 555–65.

SAVILLE, T. and CALDWELL, J. M. 1953: Accuracy of hydrographic surveying in and near the surf zone. *B.E.B. Tech. Memo.* **32.**

SHEPARD, F. P. and YOUNG, R. 1961: Distinguishing between beach and dune sands. *J. Sed. Petrol.* **31,** 196–214.

TONNARD, V. 1963: Critères de sensibilité appliques aux indice de formes des grains de sables. In van Straaten (Editor), *Developments Sediment.* **I,** 410–16.

WHITTEN, E. H. T. 1964: Process-response models in Geology. *Bull. Geol. Soc. Am.* **75,** 455–63.

WILLIAMS, L. C. 1965: An ocean wave direction gage. *Marine Sci. Instrum.* **3,** 257–71.

WILLIAMS, W. W. 1947: The determination of the gradient of enemy held beaches. *Geog. J.* **109,** 76–93.

WILSON, W. S. 1966: A method of calculating and plotting surface wave rays. *C.E.R.C. Tech. Memo.* **17.**

WOOD, W. L. 1968: A ducted impellor flowmeter for shallow-water measurement of internal velocities in breaking waves. *Tech. Rep.* 1, Off. Nav. Res. Con. No. N 000 14–68 A 0109 0002 Nr. **388–089.** (57 pp.)

ZENKOVICH, V. P. 1962: Some problems and methods of shore dynamics investigations in the USSR. *De Ingenieur* **15,** Bouw- en Waterbouwkunde 8, B95–B107.

ZENKOVICH, V. P. 1967: *Processes of coastal development.* Edinburgh: Oliver and Boyd.

Part II

Processes

3 Waves in deep water

1 **Ideal waves:** a) Wave length, velocity and period; b) Wave height; c) Wave steepness; d) Wave form; e) Wave energy; f) Orbital velocity and mass transport.

2 **Wave description and measurement:** a) Sea; b) Swell; c) Wave measurement and analysis.

3 **Wave generation:** a) H. Jeffreys; b) H. U. Sverdrup and W. H. Munk; c) C. Eckart; d) O. M. Phillips; e) J. W. Miles; f) Conclusions.

4 **Wave propagation and decay**

5 **Microseisms**

6 **Wave forecasting:** a) The Sverdrup–Munk–Bretschneider method: (*i*) *Generation*; (*ii*) *Attenuation*; b) Pierson–Neumann–James; c) Darbyshire: (*i*) *Generation*; (*ii*) *Attenuation*; d) Comparison of the different methods of wave forecasting.

Summary

1 Ideal waves

The equations which relate ideal wave velocity, length and period were developed by G. B. Airy (1845). A few years later G. G. Stokes (1847) extended the theory to waves of finite height. His solution required that the velocity should depend to some extent on the wave height and that the orbital movement was in the form of open circles, indicating the existence of mass transport. Stokes did not obtain a rigorous solution, although he worked out the equations to a fifth approximation. T. Levi-Civita (1925), however, proved that the series was convergent for deep-water waves, while D. J. Struik (1926) obtained an exact solution for finite depths. The form of the waves in Airy's analysis is sinusoidal, but for waves of finite height the form approximates to a trochoid.

Another theory of wave motion has been developed on the assumption that the waves are exactly trochoidal. The theory was developed independently by F. Gerstner (1802) and W. J. H. Rankine (1863). The orbits of the particles are said to be exactly circular, and hence the theory does not allow for mass transport, which has been shown to exist, for example by C. F. Mitchim (1940). The results of this theory are very similar to those of Airy for low waves in deep water. It also has the advantage that the equations are much simpler than those of Stokes's theory and provide exact solutions for the motion of particles, and for the wave form, energy and velocity. The theory was extended for shallow water by D. D. Gaillard (1904).

The two wave theories outlined above require different forms of motion in the water. It appears that the theory of Stokes, which requires both irrotational flow and mass transport, is closer to reality than the simpler theory of Gerstner and Rankine, in which the flow is rotational and no mass transport is allowed.

Mass transport is one of the most important properties of Stokes's irrotational theory. Its velocity at the surface, which is proportional to the square of the wave steepness, is very small compared with the wave velocity. It becomes very small for low waves and is negligible for very low waves. The volume of mass transport is given by

$$H^2 \sqrt{\frac{g\pi}{32L}}$$

where H is the wave height and L is the wave length per unit of wave crest. This value has been checked experimentally by C. F. Mitchim.

The trochoidal waves of Gerstner's theory require rotational water motion and can be defined simply. The wave form in deep water is given by $x = R\theta - r \sin \theta$ and $y = R - r \cos \theta$, where L is 2R and H is 2r. The height of the crest above still-water level is given by

$$\frac{H}{2} + 0 \cdot 7854 \frac{H^2}{L}$$

and the depth of the trough below still-water level is given by

$$\frac{H}{2} - 0 \cdot 7854 \frac{H^2}{L}$$

Thus the crest height is greater than the trough depth. The energy of the wave is given by

$$E = \frac{wLH^2}{8}\left(1 - 4 \cdot 93\frac{H^2}{L^2}\right)$$

which is the total kinetic and potential energy per wave length. For flat waves the equation is the same as that for the low sinusoidal waves.

a   Wave length, velocity and period

The three properties of wave length, velocity and period are closely associated. In deep water their relationship is given by $L = CT$, where L is the wave length, C is the velocity and T is the period. The length is the distance between two successive crests; C is the speed of movement of the wave form; and the period is the time taken for the wave form to move the distance of one wave length. In the more recent wave research the wave frequency, defined as $1/T$, is used instead of the wave period. Frequency, f, is given in cycles/kilosecond. For a period of 10 seconds, $f = 100$ c/ks, for a 20 second period f is 50 c/ks, and for a 5 second period f is 200 c/ks.

If the wave period is measured in deep water, and this can be done relatively easily, the wave length and velocity—which cannot be easily measured in the open sea—can be obtained from it. The relationship between the wave length and period is given by $L = 5 \cdot 12T^2$, where L is in feet and T is in seconds ($Lm' = 1 \cdot 56T^2$). The velocity and length are related by

$$C = \sqrt{\frac{gL}{2\pi}}$$

which is derived from the equation

$$C = \sqrt{\frac{gL}{2\pi} \tanh \frac{2\pi d}{L}}$$

where g is the force of gravity and d is the depth of water. In deep water d/L is large and tanh $(2\pi d/L)$ approaches 1, giving the first equation. If d/L is 0·5, tanh $(2\pi d/L)$ is 0·9963. For most purposes, therefore, the water may be considered to be deep if the ratio of d to L is more than 0·5. These equations apply strictly only to waves of very low amplitude, but can be used in fact for waves of finite height without too much error. To a closer order of accuracy

$$C = \sqrt{\frac{gL}{2\pi}\left(1 + \frac{\pi^2 H^2}{2L^2}\right)}$$

showing that steeper waves travel rather faster than flat ones. At the maximum steepness $(H/L = 1/7)$, however, the increase is only about 10%.

b   Wave height
The height of the wave, measured vertically from trough to crest, is an important wave characteristic, but it is on its relationship to the other fundamental dimension of the waves, length, that its effect on the beach largely depends.

c   Wave steepness
The wave steepness is the ratio, H/L, the height divided by the length. It has been known for some time that this variable is fundamental in the constructive and destructive effect of the waves on the foreshore. The steepness cannot exceed 1/7 or the wave becomes unstable and breaks. This value is rarely reached in nature. Another limiting dimension is the crest angle, which cannot exceed 120°. Waves in the open ocean are often below 0·02 steepness, although exceptionally they may attain a steepness of 0·055. This steepness corresponds to a wave 10 feet (3·05 m) high and 6 seconds period, with a length of 184 feet (56·1 m).

d   Wave form
The form of ideal low waves is sinusoidal or trochoidal, according to the two theories already mentioned. A trochoid is the curve swept out by a point within a circle that is rolled along a straight line. The trochoidal wave has a flatter trough and sharper crest than the smooth profile of a sinusoidal wave, which has symmetrical troughs and crests. The asymmetry of the trochoidal wave increases and the crest becomes sharper as the wave steepness increases. Waves in the generating area are even more irregular owing to the effect of the wind.

e   Wave energy
The energy of the wave, another important characteristic, also depends on the length and height. The energy determines the amount of work a wave can do on the beach, but not whether this will be destructive or constructive, a result which depends primarily on the wave steepness. Waves of great energy can do very much more work in a given time than low-energy waves, hence the importance of this characteristic.

   The energy in a deep-water wave is half potential, due to the height of the wave crest above still-water level, and half kinetic, due to the velocity of the water particles within the wave form. The kinetic energy remains still, but the potential energy moves at the wave velocity: thus the total energy of a wave train moves at half the velocity of the wave form. A train of waves of limited number travelling through still water appears to move at half the speed of the individual waves, which appear to travel through the whole train, forming in the rear and dying out in the front.

The actual amount of energy, E, in foot-pounds per foot of wave crest per wave length is given by

$$E = \frac{wLH^2}{8}$$

where w is the weight of 1 cubic foot of sea-water (64 lbs). The energy depends on the square of the wave height and one power of the wave length. It increases rapidly, therefore, as the wave height increases. The equation may be expressed as $E = 0.64wH^2T^2$, or $E = 41H^2T^2$, where T is the wave period. The wave energy may be calculated from the wave height and period. These equations apply strictly only to waves of low amplitude and sinusoidal form, but can in fact be applied to waves of finite height within the accuracy of observation. The equation for waves of finite height is

$$E = \frac{wLH^2}{8}\left(1 - 4.93\frac{H^2}{L^2}\right)$$

f   Orbital velocity and mass transport

Although the wave form advances with a speed dependent on its length the actual particles of water normally move at a much lower velocity. At the surface their velocity depends on the wave period and height. They must complete one orbit, the diameter of which is equal to the height of the wave, during the wave period. Water in high, short waves will therefore move faster than that in low, long waves. It is only in breaking waves that the water at the crest of the wave moves with the wave form. The movement of the particles on the surface is in very nearly circular orbits, but with each period the particle advances slightly in the direction of wave advance. The circles are called open, and the slight forward movement of the water is known as the mass transport. The velocity of mass transport is very small compared with the wave velocity and the orbital velocity, especially when the waves are low.

Beneath the surface the orbits of the particles remain almost circular, but they decrease very rapidly in diameter. For every 1/9 of the wave length in depth the orbit is approximately halved. At a depth equal to the wave length the orbit is 1/535 of its surface value and it is 1/12,400 at 1·5L: in other words the water is almost still at a depth equal to about one wave length.

2 Wave description and measurement

a   Sea

The size of wind waves depends on three variables, the wind speed, the wind duration and the fetch and any one of the three can set a limit independently. Thus however long the wind blew at great speed, it could not generate large waves if the fetch were limited. This limit could be imposed either by the meteorological situation, which determines the distance over which a wind is blowing in a constant direction, or by the configuration of the water body, which in some areas determines the fetch available for wave generation. The exposure of a coast, determined by the available fetch, is a very important element in considering its type of beach.

Waves in the open sea are more complex in form than the ideal waves that can be treated theoretically. In the open ocean there are nearly always a large number of waves superimposed on each other, giving the water surface a confused appearance. This characteristic is more marked in the area where the wind is actively generating waves at the time. Waves of different lengths and heights are superimposed on one another to form the wave spectrum. Variations in the direction of the wind and waves cause still greater confusion. The waves in the area in which they are being generated are known as 'sea'.

b Swell

When the waves move out of the generating area into an area of calm they change from sea to swell. They cease to grow in size and to gain energy as they start to decay. In this process they slowly change form. In estimating the wave pattern in any coastal area it must be borne in mind that swell travels a very long distance without losing its identity. If it has been generated by strong winds of long duration, giving it a low steepness value, it will have a slow rate of attenuation. R. L. Wiegel and H. L. Kimberley (1950), for example, drew attention to the presence of swell on the coast of California during the summer months which had originated in the south Pacific Ocean between 40° and 65° south and 120° to 160° west. This swell normally had a significant breaker height of 60 cm to 2 m, but reached a maximum of 3–3·7 m; it had a very long period of 12 to 18 seconds, sometimes reaching 22 seconds; it had probably travelled up to 11,200 km. It would not have been considered if only the relatively local weather situation had been taken into account. Swell is, nevertheless, very important in a consideration of the

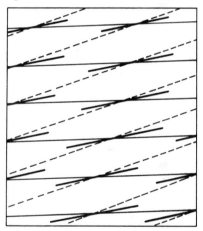

Figure 3-1 The interference of two wave trains from different directions, giving a short-crested wave pattern.

beach processes. Waves generated during storms off Cape Horn have been recorded on the Cornish coast, after travelling 9600 km.

In the area of attenuation the wave pattern and form assumes some measure of order. The shorter, slower-travelling waves are left behind and the longer ones dominate the spectrum. Where there is only one major set of waves travelling as a swell they are usually long-crested. Their crests are continuous over considerable distances at right-angles to their direction of movement. These waves may be contrasted with the short-crested waves that occur when two wave trains are travelling in different directions so that their respective crests only occasionally coincide to make a particularly high wave. Neither set of waves has continuous crests, owing to the interference of the other set. Their interaction is shown in figure 3-1.

The sharp crests typical of the storm area become rounded and the swell becomes almost sinusoidal. Swell waves may not be conspicuous, owing to their great length, if smaller local waves are superimposed upon them. Such long swells, however, are rejuvenated as they approach a shore and will become the dominant waves on the beach because of their great energy, which is due to their great length and moderate height.

c Wave measurement and analysis

In order to test the accuracy of wave generation theories and wave forecasting techniques it is necessary to obtain reliable information concerning the size and frequency distributions of waves in the ocean. There are nearly always a large number of different wave heights and periods present at any one time, so that the waves must be interpreted in terms of the wave spectrum.

Wave recording devices can be placed in a number of classes. There are those that record waves as undulating lines with respect to time, the line referring to the variations in water level. Instruments that fall into this class include pressure-sensing devices fixed below the surface, wave poles, wave wires, shipborne wave recorders and pulsed sound beams pointing upwards from the bottom (inverted echo-sounder). All these record changes of level at a fixed point over time. Probably the most successful of these is the shipborne recorder. It has the added advantage that no fixed installation is required, as is the case for wave wires, for example.

The second class of wave recording methods covers an area of the sea surface in three dimensions at one instant in time. Stereo-photogrammetric techniques are used for this purpose, so that a contour map of the sea surface at a point in time can be obtained. Low-flying aircraft can provide maps covering areas of 813 m by 540 m, as shown in the work of L. J. Coté *et al.* (1960) in connection with the project S.W.O.P. (Stereo Wave Observation Project).

The third class of wave measuring device records further properties of the waves. The splashnik records wave accelerations, while the wave buoys, developed by the National Institute of Oceanography (N.I.O.), record heave, surface slope and slope differences, giving the curvature of the wave form.

The interpretation of the results of these measurements depends on the development of statistical theory, and especially that by Tukey and M. S. Longuet-Higgins (1952). They have studied the analysis of the heights and periods of the complex combination of waves that make up the recorded wave spectrum. In these analyses the earlier analogue devices are now being superseded by digital computer devices. Time series analysis is used in conjunction with other statistical methods to establish the wave spectra and to obtain data concerning the significant heights and periods of the waves.

The measurement of the spectrum in the open ocean can be made with a shipborne wave recorder. The wave buoy developed recently by the N.I.O. is described by M. S. Longuet-Higgins, D. E. Cartwright and N. D. Smith (1963). The buoy floats freely in the open ocean. Its vertical acceleration combined with the two angles of pitching and rolling can provide the first five Fourier coefficients of the angular distribution of energy in each wave frequency band. These values can then be used to calculate the weighted average of the directional spectrum with respect to the horizontal azimuth. The buoy also provides other useful data including the total spectral energy, the mean direction of energy, the angular spread of the energy and an indication of the shape of the energy distribution. Measurements of this type can be used to test the validity of different theories of wave generation. The instrument provides a two-dimensional wave spectrum, rather than the one-dimensional spectrum normally yielded by earlier types of observation.

The one-dimensional spectrum can be analysed by Fourier analysis to give the frequencies in the spectrum and their relative amount of energy. For some purposes, however, it is more convenient to obtain only a height and period from each record, the results then being analysed statistically. The development of prediction formulae may require the energy spectrum of a non-directional recording, but for yet other purposes, where directional spectra are needed, the cross-power spectra must be obtained.

For the simplest requirement the mean wave height and period may be obtained with a suitable attachment to an electrical wave meter. The full wave record is needed for spectral analysis, and the photoelectric analogue analyser is a satisfactory means of analysis. Newer digital methods, however, are rather more accurate, and are used to analyse the cross-spectral records (M. J. Tucker, 1963). Another method of recording wave spectra is described by P. S. de Leonibus (1963): here a stationary submerged submarine used an inverted echo-sounder to record fluctuations of the sea surface; power spectra were then provided by digital methods.

R. Bonnefille *et al.* (1967) describe an ultrasonic inverse wave recorder, which consists of a piezoelectric transducer. The instrument is set vertically and is connected by cable to the land, where the recorder is located. The results consist of punched paper tape in a state suitable for computer analysis. Each record consists of 20 minutes of observation and can be programmed to give the statistical distribution of crests, the period of the swell, the spectral energy, the significant and maximum values of both wave height and period, and a graphical output showing the percentage energy in each height and period band.

The difficulties of wave measurement in the ocean stem from both sampling problems and the problem of calibration (B. Kinsman, 1965). The latter arise owing to the lack of a method of measurement at least an order more accurate for comparative purposes. Each instrument tends to distort the profile, which is not itself accurately known, in a different way. A considerable variety of instruments has been developed lately. The splashnik invented by W. Marks and R. G. Tuckerman (1961) is a telemetering accelerometer buoy, which can be dropped from a ship and which records while in range. Other instruments can be fixed to the sea bed for considerable periods, such as the Mark X strain gauge wave pressure transducer, designed by F. E. Snodgrass *et al.* (1966). This transmits signals by cable to the shore. Resistance wires can be fixed to rigs sited offshore, and these can provide directional wave energy spectra provided the wires are suitably spaced.

The lack of calibration from which all the instruments suffer may mean that spurious Fourier components emerge in the spectral analysis. The problem is intensified by the short length of the record that is available for analysis in most instances. These considerations must be borne in mind when wave prediction and wave generation are considered and compared with wave records. Further uncertainty is added during spectral analysis.

Despite the uncertainty that surrounds wave recording and analysis, some record is better than no record, and useful records have been obtained in various ways, for instance from weather-ship and lightship records. Some examples will be given. J. Darbyshire (1955b) described wave observations made on the O.W.S. *Weather Explorer* in the North Atlantic at the positions 61° N, 15° 20′ W and 52° 30′ N, 20° W between January 1947 and February 1953, and compared them with records taken at Perranporth on the coast of Cornwall. The results were shown by plotting the percentage time the wave height fell between two limits for each month. The mean wave period of each group was also shown, and the significant wave periods were analysed similarly. The results demonstrated that the wave heights in the open ocean are very much greater than in coastal waters. Waves 12·2 m to 15·25 m high were not uncommon in the winter months in the open ocean, but waves over 6·1 m rarely occurred in coastal waters. On the other hand the significant period of the waves was found to be much longer on the coast, where periods over 15 seconds were much more common than in mid-ocean. On the coast they occurred for up to 45% of the time in some months, but they never exceeded 5% in mid-ocean in winter. It must be remembered that the two years compared are not the same at both places (figure 3-2).

It does appear that the process of wave generation is not so efficient in shallow water. Further-more the shorter-period waves are probably attenuated by the time they reach the coast. Figure

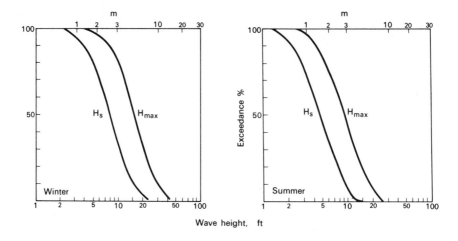

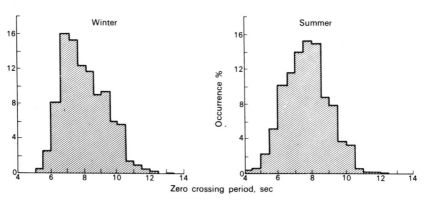

Figure 3-2 Waves off Land's End at Sevenstones. The significant and maximum wave heights are shown for winter and summer. (*After Draper and Fricker, 1965.*)

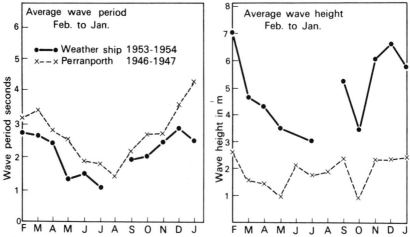

Figure 3-3 Average monthly wave period and height for Perranporth and mid-Atlantic weather ship. (*After Darbyshire, 1955b.*)

3-3 shows the average monthly significant period and wave height at the two stations. In general the longer and higher waves occurred during the winter months.

The statistical distribution of wave height has been calculated by N. H. Jasper (1955). He used 12,000 observations from U.S. weather-ships and expressed the results in the form

$$y = A \exp - (\log x - \log a)^2/b^2,$$

where y is the probability density, x the significant wave height and a the most probable value of x. J. Darbyshire (1956) has fitted this equation to three years' observations of the O.W.S. *Weather Explorer* in three positions in mid-Atlantic, including the two already given and 59° N, 19° W. The y axis (see figure 3.4) is the time percentage that any given height is exceeded and the x axis is the maximum wave height. The points fall on a straight line if the logarithmic normal law holds. This was found to be true for values between 1·37 m and 13·7 m, but not outside these limits. The logarithmic normal distribution can be plotted by dividing the waves into one foot groups and plotting the percentage in each group (see figure 3-4b). The points plotted fall almost on the curve given by $y = 6\cdot6 \exp -(\log x/9)^2/0\cdot126$. This curve fits the observations for the three separate years plotted independently, showing that there is a significant variation in the pattern from year to year. Plots for different seasons also show some variation in pattern with the time of year. The following curves fit each seasonal group:

December–March $\quad y = 6\cdot6 \exp -(\log x/14)^2/0\cdot065$
April–July $\qquad\quad y = 9\cdot2 \exp -(\log x/8)^2/0\cdot104$
August–November $\quad y = 6\cdot1 \exp -(\log x/8)^2/0\cdot137$

Wave data for Casablanca and Perranporth have been analysed in a similar way and the following relationships hold for these areas. Casablanca for 1952–5 gives $y = 18 \exp - (\log x/3\cdot5)^2/0\cdot137$; Perranporth for 1946, $y = 13 \exp -(\log x/4)^2/0\cdot199$.

L. Draper and H. S. Fricker (1965) have recorded waves in 61 m of water on the Sevenstones lightship 32 km southwest of Land's End. 12 minute records were taken every three hours with a shipborne wave recorder. The analysis of the data gives H_1, the sum of the distances of the highest crest and lowest trough from the mean water level; T_z, the mean zero-crossing period; T_c, the mean crest period; H_s, the significant height; H_{max}, the most probable height of the highest wave in the period; and ε, the spectral width parameter, $(\varepsilon^2 = 1 - (T_c/T_z)^2)$. The graphs in figure 3-4 show the results for some of the measures. Wave heights were considerably greater in winter and wave period was lower in summer, while the spectral width parameter did not change markedly with the seasons. Wave steepness values are also shown.

Further wave records have been published from data obtained by the weather-ship *India*, stationed at 59° N, 19° W in the Atlantic Ocean (L. Draper and E. M. Squire, 1967). These results are presented in the same form as those given above for Land's End. 2,000 records have been analysed spread over a period of 13 years, and together they may be considered to represent an average year. The wave heights are again presented in terms of percentage exceedance. The results show that the Atlantic in winter has a high percentage of large waves. Heights exceeded 4·58 m for 41% of the time in winter, and the heights and number of zero-crossing periods were significantly greater than in any other season. The most common wave conditions were a significant height of about 2 m combined with a zero-crossing period of about 9 seconds. The pressure unit was placed at a distance below the surface that effectively eliminated waves of periods less than 5 seconds. The higher waves were almost always associated with the longer periods, but some long periods had small heights, when the waves came from a distant storm. Wave steepness values rarely were lower than 0·056, and the steepest wave recorded was 0·115,

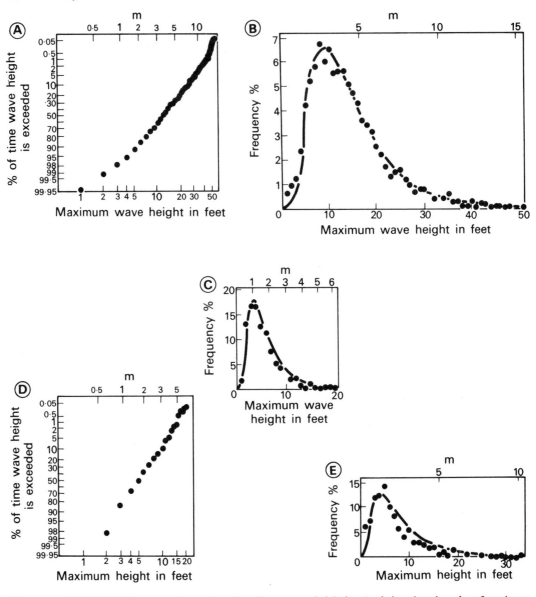

Figure 3-4 **A:** Graph of percentage time a value of maximum wave height is exceeded against the value of maximum wave height for all weather ship data. **B:** Frequency occurrence of value of maximum wave height against the value of maximum wave height for all weather ship data. **C:** The same data for Casablanca. **D:** Graph of percentage time a value of maximum wave height is exceeded against the value of maximum wave height for Casablanca. **E:** Frequency of occurrence of value of maximum height against the value of maximum wave height for Perranporth in 1946.
(A, B, C, D, E, after Darbyshire, 1956.)

compared with the theoretical maximum of 0·14. This wave had a height of 10·7 m and a period of 7·65 seconds. The highest wave recorded during the period was 20·4 m, although one of 24·4 m may have been experienced.

This analysis of waves recorded over a long period provides a valuable indication of the dimensions of waves generated in the stormy conditions of the North Atlantic Ocean. Other wave observations will be considered in connection with the generation and propagation of waves in deep water. The measurement of waves in shallow water will be reconsidered in the next chapter.

3 Wave generation

The generation of waves depends on the transference of energy from the wind to the sea. Some of the theories put forward to explain this will be discussed briefly.

a   H. Jeffreys

The sheltering theory of Jeffreys (1925) assumes that the air flow is laminar over the windward slope of the wave and turbulent on the lee slope, that the lee side of the wave form is sheltered by the crest and that low velocities are found there. The normal pressure is thus said to differ between the windward and lee faces. If the wind velocity exceeds the wave velocity, energy is transferred from the air to the water. Tangential friction is ignored in the theory. One important parameter in the analysis is the 'sheltering coefficient', s, which is related to that proportion of the windward slope of the wave which offers resistance to the wind. The value of s is given as 0·27.

Jeffreys's theory accounts reasonably satisfactorily for the initial generation of waves, when their steepness is very low, but as the waves increase in steepness his value of s appears too great. Experiments by T. E. Stanton *et al.* (1932) showed that the sheltering coefficient was only $\frac{1}{10}$ of Jeffreys's value, and it becomes clear that drag must be taken into account to explain the growth of waves, as the observed sheltering coefficient is much smaller than the theoretical one.

b   H. U. Sverdrup and W. H. Munk

The theory developed by Sverdrup and Munk (1947) is based on rough turbulent flow, which occurs when the wind speed exceeds 7 m/sec (force 4 Beaufort scale). Above this velocity ripples of small dimensions are formed on the wave surface and these alter the type of surface from hydrodynamically smooth to hydrodynamically rough. The concept of a critical speed has since been criticized by Munk (1957), who originally put it forward. It now appears that there is no critical wind speed. The air flow is considered to be similar to that suggested by Jeffreys, as eddies form in the lee of the wave. The sheltering coefficient used is about $\frac{1}{20}$ of Jeffreys's, s being 0·013.

It is suggested that the tangential stress of the wind, which is an important factor in this theory, varies with the square of the wind velocity above a certain figure. The waves acquire energy from the wind by tangential stress when the water particles move in the same direction as the wind, and lose energy when the particles move against the wind, but because of mass transport, there is a net gain of energy. The wave velocity is much greater than the velocity of the particles within the wave, and it is thus possible for the wave velocity to exceed that of the generating wind. The limit would be reached when the particle velocity equalled the wind speed. When the waves are moving faster than the generating wind the energy transfer is in two directions. The waves are gaining energy by tangential stress, but are losing it by the pressure of the wave form on the wind. Energy is also converted into heat by turbulence. The wave will continue to grow until the loss of energy equals the gain. The whole energy of the tangential and normal stress of the wind goes into the wave and causes an increase of height and length. The increase in height is more important when the wave is moving slower than the wind, but when the wave speed exceeds the wind velocity most of the energy goes to increase the wave velocity. The proportion of energy increasing the height and length is determined by the relation between the wave steepness and the wave age. Observations fit fairly well with the theoretical curve and provide a basis for the forecasting of wave height.

c C. Eckart

Eckart's theory (1953) of wave generation applies to fully turbulent flow in the open ocean. Gusts are said to provide a random pattern of normal pressure distribution independent of the waves already formed. One disadvantage of the theory is that sheltering is ignored. The gusts producing the waves are assumed to be similar, moving over the water with the speed of the wind, which is assumed constant. Owing to the lack of observations of the wind pressure it is not possible to check the results of calculations using the theory. It does, however, appear that the simplest model, which does not take sheltering into account and considers only the normal pressure, is not sufficiently accurate.

d O. M. Phillips

One of the most promising theories has been put forward by O. M. Phillips (1957). He assumes that a turbulent wind at a given moment starts to blow over a surface previously at rest. The pressure on the surface fluctuates in a distribution which is a stationary random function of position and time. The study aims to discover the properties of the surface displacement at subsequent periods. Eckart has already attempted to solve a similar problem, but his assumption of the pressure distribution was not sufficiently random to give accurate results, his predicted waves being too small.

The random distribution assumed by Phillips is an important part of his analysis, which involves a type of resonance. The turbulent nature of the wind is an essential factor in the growth of waves and causes random stresses on the water surface. These include both normal stress or pressure and tangential shear stress. Eddies, in the air stream, are carried by the wind and change as they move, so that the stress distribution moves across the surface with a certain velocity dependent on the wind speed. This convection velocity of the stress fluctuations is defined as the velocity of the frame of reference, U_c, in which their frequency scale is least, or their time scale is greatest. This velocity is nearly equal to the wind velocity as measured from a ship.

The fluctuating pressure upon the water surface is held responsible for the birth and early growth of waves, and an analysis of the surface should show a wide variety of wave numbers and frequencies in both two-dimensional space and time. The component of the pressure fluctuations acting on the surface generate small forced oscillations. These fluctuations affect the amplitude components on the surface. If the pressure distribution includes components whose wave numbers and frequencies coincide with possible dimensions of free surface waves a type of resonance is set up, and the continued presence of these particular frequencies in the pressure distribution will generate surface waves whose amplitude will increase. Thus, it is asserted that the frame of reference is not changing in character but is moving with the convection velocity, and if one of the wave frequencies generated is moving with the same velocity, then the two move together and growth can continue. This, however, ignores the evolution of the stress pattern and so is an over-simplification: if the pressure pattern is changing slowly the growth of the wavelets is reduced.

At first the surface may be assumed to have no effect on the pressure distribution, but this will not last for long. Small ripples will soon form and these have a considerable effect on the vertical velocity distribution. The long gravity waves do not appear to influence the pressure distribution. The viscosity of the water is ignored, which is probably justified for all but the shortest waves. The motion is then irrotational. The results apply when the mean square slope is small so that the surface boundary conditions can be considered linear. At later stages of growth the non-linear effects may become important.

In the initial generation of waves the minimum velocity is given by the equation

$$C_{min} = (4gT_s/\varrho)^{1/4}$$

where ϱ is the water density, T_s is the surface tension at the interface, and C_{min} is the minimum velocity. The wave length of the critical waves is about

$$L_{cr} = 2\pi(T_s/\varrho g)^{1/2}.$$

For water $\varrho = 1$ gm cm^{-3}, T_s is 73 gm sec^2, and g is 980 cm sec^{-2}, in which case C_{min} is 23 cm sec^{-1} and the critical wave length $L_{cr} = 2\pi/n_{cr}$ is 1·7 cm. The initial waves generated may travel at directions almost perpendicular to that of the generating wind as this increases in force, and some observational evidence supports this view. The minimum wind velocity which will generate resonance waves is 23 cm sec^{-1}, but a lower wind velocity will disturb the surface although the waves will not continue to grow. The most probable value for U_{min} appears to be zero, although values up to 790 cm sec^{-1} have been proposed by different workers.

It can be shown that, after the initial stage of growth, the mean square wave height is directly proportional to time. The wave spectrum is independent of time until the mean square slope increases beyond a certain point, when non-linear factors become significant. This point is reached first for the shorter waves. It appears, therefore, that the direct proportionality of wave height to time does not change until the largest waves reach the limiting value of the mean square slope. The spectrum is narrower for light winds and the waves appear more regular. The wave spectrum can be defined by

$$\bar{\xi}^2 \sim \frac{\bar{p}^2 t}{2\sqrt{2}\, p^2 U_c g}$$

where $\bar{\xi}^2$ is the mean square surface displacement, t the time elapsed, U_c the convection speed of the surface pressure fluctuations, and $\bar{p}^2$ is the mean square turbulent pressure on the water surface. The terms cannot be directly applied to observations made in the oceans, but the equation can be expressed in different terms with reasonable accuracy. The relationship between the mean square turbulent pressure and the recorded wind velocity is one of the more difficult to define. M. S. Longuet-Higgins (1952) has shown that the significant height, H, is related to the mean square surface displacement by the equation $H^2 = 8\bar{\xi}^2$ approximately. This equation can now be given as

$$\frac{gH}{U^2} \sim 6 \times 10^{-4} \left(\frac{gT}{U}\right)^{1/2}$$

The accuracy of the constant is quite low as the value of $\bar{p}^2$ is not certain. The equation gives results that agree well with observations given by Sverdrup and Munk over a restricted range of duration. The wave heights observed are close to the computed values as shown in figure 3-5.

According to Phillips's theory (1957) the main problem of wave generation is related to the distribution of pressure on the moving, random water surface under the influence of a turbulent wind. The pressure fluctuations are of two kinds. One is produced by the turbulent eddies in the wind and the other is induced by the air flow over the irregular surface. The total pressure pattern is the sum of these two. The first, the turbulent pressures, provide energy input over a

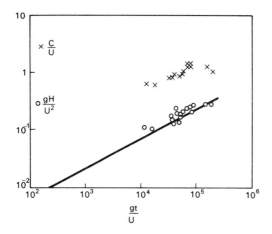

Figure 3-5 The relationship between wave height and wind speed and duration. (*After Phillips 1966.*)

wide spectral range, while the second, the directly induced pressure, provides a selective feedback which allows certain components to grow rapidly. The influence of vorticity in the water can be neglected and the motion can be taken to be irrotational. O. M. Phillips (1966) in a more recent study again showed the importance of resonance in the relationship between the free surface waves and the turbulent pressures that cause them.

e   J. W. Miles

J. W. Miles (1965; 1967) deals with an alternative process of wave generation. His theory considers the flow of air over a fluid boundary with a small sinusoidal displacement. Another aspect he includes is the pressure on the water surface resulting from the perturbation of the original flow. M. S. Longuet-Higgins (1962) states that 'the component of the pressure in phase with the surface elevation imparts no energy to the waves, but the component in quadrature generally results in work being done on the water, which, if it exceeds the loss due to molecular or eddy viscosity, causes the wave amplitude to grow'. The wind profile must be non-uniform. The input of energy into a wave of phase velocity, C, is related to the curvature of the wind velocity profile, where U = C. The wind velocity profile is logarithmic.

Miles has combined two theories of wave generation, firstly turbulent pressure fluctuations and, secondly, shear-flow instability. The second component multiplies Phillips's results in the main stage of wave growth by

$$e\frac{MT_{-1}}{MT} = f$$

$$T = \frac{gt}{U}$$

and

$$M = \frac{\varrho_a}{\varrho_w}\left(\frac{U_1 \cos \phi}{C}\right)^2 \frac{U_1}{C}\beta$$

In the early stages Phillips's value still holds, but as t grows MT $\geqslant$ 1, f increases and the instability factor becomes dominant. f can vary between 1 and 10^6. The effect of instability is to increase those components that are travelling in directions nearest to the wind, thus narrowing the directional spread.

The pressure fluctuations at the surface are the aerodynamical pressure changes due to the flow of air over the undulating surface. The initial disturbance of the water surface may be due to turbulent pressure as described by Phillips at the lower frequencies, although pressure fluctuations are weaker than first estimated.

In the main stage of wave growth Miles's shearing flow is effective, leading to the observed reduction of angular spread. At highest frequencies the spectrum is controlled by the breaking of waves, as the spectrum depends on the fifth power of the frequency, σ. The wind profile and amplitude, and the scale of turbulent pressure fluctuations are fundamental. Model studies in which the wind profile and pressure fluctuations cannot be reproduced accurately are useless.

Miles (1965) has shown that the transfer of momentum to the surface waves from the wind blowing over the water must affect the wind velocity profile. The mean shear should be reduced by this transfer through a reduction of the curvature and of the Reynolds stress, which is responsible for the momentum transfer. These reductions are probably small for normal wind speeds. The surface wave form, however, does affect the wind velocity profile. The analysis is based on the Neumann spectrum, which may not be accurate, and hence the results may not be either.

According to Miles (1967) the mean momentum transfer consists of, first, a singular part proportional to the product of the velocity profile curvature and the mean square of the wave-induced vertical velocity in the critical layer, where the wind speed equals the wave speed; secondly of a vertical integral of the mean product of the vertical velocity and the vorticity, ω; and thirdly of the perturbation in the mean turbulent shear stress at the air–water interface. The turbulent Reynolds stress must be specified for further progress in theoretical analysis.

The inviscid laminar model underestimates the energy transfer from wind to wave over a significant part of the spectrum. The resonance mechanism probably plays an important part in early stages of wave growth, and may play a dominant role in very long wave generation. Earlier opinions of M. J. Lighthill (1962) and M. S. Longuet-Higgins (1962) are considered by Miles to be possibly too optimistic. Miles's model is, however, supported qualitatively by the model experiments of D. H. Shemdin and E. Y. Hsu (1966) in a wind-wave tunnel 35·1 m long, though phase-shifts in the wave-induced aerodynamic pressures are significantly larger than theoretical prediction suggests. One difficulty is that the mean velocity profile is difficult to measure in the laboratory and impossible to measure at sea. R. L. Snyder and C. S. Cox (1966) state that the energy transfer to 17 m waves from a 10 to 20 knot wind at 6 m is 8 times the calculated value for the laminar model with an assumed logarithmic profile. The statement is based on field observations and is supported by other field data. It is likely that wave-induced turbulent Reynolds stresses are not negligible over a significant proportion of the gravity wave spectrum, and increase in importance as the scale increases.

f Conclusion

The assumption of quasi-laminar conditions in the air flow allows theoretical analysis and solution, but the neglect of the effects of turbulence does not provide realistic solutions. Turbulence does appear to have a profound effect on the induced pressure distribution, particularly when the wave speed is comparable with the wind speed (O. M. Phillips, 1966).

As the waves grow in amplitude they become distorted and their crests become sharper than their troughs. If the spectrum has a sharp maximum, secondary peaks may sometimes be found at multiples of the frequency of the primary peak. There is also energy transfer among the different wave components, a process involving resonances among particular groups of wave components. The result causes a gradual spread of energy beyond the high spectral region. There is a trend towards a more uniform directional distribution of spectral density as a result of resonant interactions in gravity waves, but this effect is sometimes obscured by the influence of other factors.

The growth of waves under the influence of the wind cannot continue indefinitely according to O. M. Phillips (1966). The interaction among the waves is not capable of transferring energy from a given wave-number band as rapidly as it is supplied by the wind. The size of the waves is limited by the requirement of stability of the water surface. Instability results in the breaking of the waves locally. Energy is lost and stability is restored. Breaking will often occur when two wave crests run together. When waves are generated by a uniform and steady wind, the typical spectrum has a steep forward face, which rises to a sharp maximum where the frequencies are low, and falls at higher frequencies in the equilibrium part of the spectrum. At frequencies above the spectral peak the values of many observations fall into a straight line on a logarithmic scale as shown in figure 3-6. These results occur regardless of wind speed and fetch. The results provide a numerical value of β of 1.17×10^{-2}, where β is the wave frequency. As time passes the spectral peak occurs at lower frequencies.

It seems likely that Miles's mechanism operates as a primary means of wave growth in conditions of relatively short wind duration or short fetch. For the longer waves, when the wave velocity divided by the wind velocity (C/U_*) is greater than 20, other processes operate. The resonance mechanism operates effectively when the convection velocity, U_c, is large, as it is in large-scale atmospheric pressure systems, being about $25U_*$. The amplification factor has then become almost independent of C/U_*, and is the result of the undulatory turbulent flow over the waves, so that all the components growing by resonance are increased at about the same rate. The low-frequency waves that are excited by turbulent pressure fluctuations moving at about the convection velocity of the large-scale atmospheric turbulence, are generated in conditions of very long wind durations and fetches. Waves that move still more rapidly only grow very slowly. This gives support to the usefulness of the concept of a fully aroused sea. The very low-frequency waves will continue to grow slowly, but they will have a low spectral density. The directional spread of the spectra increases as the frequency bands become fully saturated.

C. L. Bretschneider (1965) has given a useful summary of the state of knowledge of wave generation. The random velocity fluctuations of the air flow over the sea surface provide the mechanism for Phillips's theory of wave generation. The stresses are both normal and tangential. The unstable eddies are carried forward in the wind stream at the mean wind velocity (the convection velocity), developing and interacting as they move. These pressure fluctuations are responsible for the early phases of wave generation. Phillips does not consider the tangential stresses. As C/U approaches unity other processes come into operation, including sheltering effect and the variations of shear stresses. Phillips has shown that for high-frequency waves the energy varies as f^{-5}.

Miles has developed a model for wave generation based on the instability of the interface between the air flow and the water. Whereas Phillips's theory predicts the growth of waves as porportional to time, Miles's theory, which takes over as the waves grow, shows an exponential growth rate. Phillips's model is uncoupled in that the air flow is assumed independent of the feedback; Miles's theory is coupled, in that the coupling can lead to instability and rapid wave growth.

It seems very likely that both mechanisms occur in the ocean, with the different models being dominant at different frequencies. The advantages of both Phillips's and Miles's theories are that no unknown constants enter into the equations and both yield theoretical wave spectra that can be compared with measured ones. Phillips's theory gives both the frequency and direction of travel. There is still, however, much to be learnt concerning the dissipation of

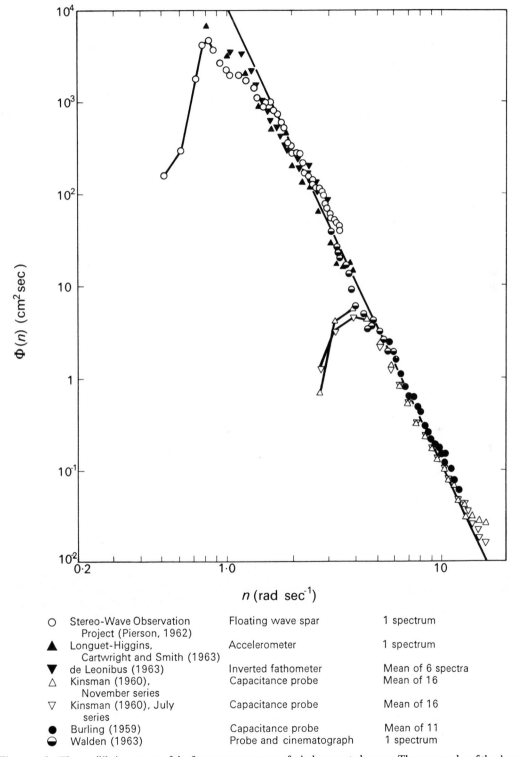

○	Stereo-Wave Observation Project (Pierson, 1962)	Floating wave spar	1 spectrum
▲	Longuet-Higgins, Cartwright and Smith (1963)	Accelerometer	1 spectrum
▼	de Leonibus (1963)	Inverted fathometer	Mean of 6 spectra
△	Kinsman (1960), November series	Capacitance probe	Mean of 16
▽	Kinsman (1960), July series	Capacitance probe	Mean of 16
●	Burling (1959)	Capacitance probe	Mean of 11
◒	Walden (1963)	Probe and cinematograph	1 spectrum

Figure 3-6   The equilibrium range of the frequency spectrum of wind-generated waves. Three examples of the shape of the spectral peak are shown, otherwise only the saturated part of the spectrum is shown. (*After Phillips, 1966.*)

energy in growing waves before accurate predictions can be made. The loss of energy is seen in the 'white horses' that accompany storms at sea where waves are being actively generated.

4 Wave propagation and decay

Section 3-3 was concerned with the generation of waves, but many of the waves reaching the shore were generated at a great distance and have travelled perhaps thousands of miles across the oceans. N. F. Barber and F. Ursell (1948) have developed a useful method of analysing swell records. The basic assumption of their analysis is that the wave trains travel at a speed equal to half the wave velocity. The wave records provided a wave spectrum by Fourier analysis. A typical wave record and spectrum are shown in figure 3-7. The series of spectra cover a $2\frac{1}{2}$ day period from 30 June to 2 July 1945, when the swell from a small intense depression reached the coast of Cornwall, where the wave recorder was situated. The tropical hurricane could be followed on the synoptic charts as it moved northwards along the east coast of the U.S.A., reaching its greatest intensity on 26–27 June, off the coast between Cape Hatteras in North Carolina and Nantucket, Mass., about 2700 to 3000 nautical miles from the Cornish coast.

The spectra shown in the figure indicate that the first effects of the storm arrived at 1900 on 30 June, the waves having a period of about 18 seconds. Subsequently the wave period band increased in width as the periods became shorter, decreasing to 13 to 15 seconds by 2 July. There was some irregularity in the decrease, indicated in figure 3-8, due to the interference effect of tidal streams near the wave recorder. From the time of arrival and period of the waves a propagation diagram can be drawn, as shown in figure 3-9. The time is plotted against the distance from Cornwall. On the diagram the position of the storm centre is shown at different times. The full straight lines refer to the minimum period and the dashed to the maximum at any one time of arrival. The lines indicate that the shortest waves are generated first and the longest when the wind reaches its maximum. The crossing of the lines shows that the shorter waves are nearly all overtaken by the longer ones before they reach the coast. The conclusions drawn from this study strongly suggest that wave trains of different periods can be propagated independently with a speed equal to half their velocity. It also appears that there is an upper limit to the wave period which can be generated by a given wind, but that this increases with increasing wind strength.

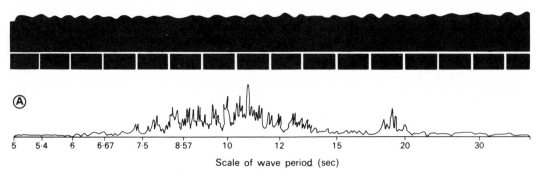

Figure 3-7 **A:** Typical wave record and spectrum. **B:** Wave spectra at Pendeen, Cornwall, 30 June to 2 July 1945. (*A, B, after Barber and Ursell, 1948.*)

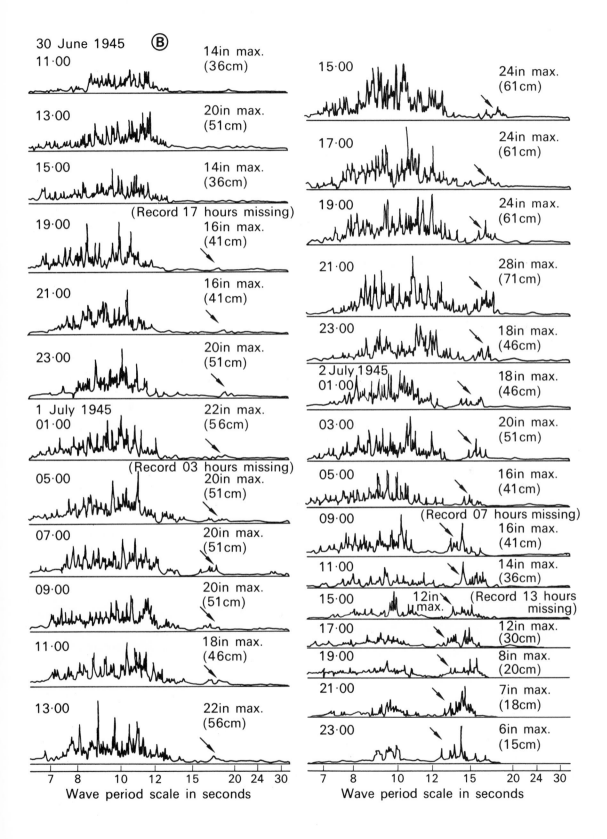

30 June 1945 Ⓑ
11·00   14in max. (36cm)

13·00   20in max. (51cm)

15·00   14in max. (36cm)

(Record 17 hours missing)
19·00   16in max. (41cm)

21·00   16in max. (41cm)

23·00   20in max. (51cm)

1 July 1945
01·00   22in max. (56cm)

(Record 03 hours missing)
05·00   20in max. (51cm)

07·00   20in max. (51cm)

09·00   20in max. (51cm)

11·00   18in max. (46cm)

13·00   22in max. (56cm)

7   8   10   12   15   20   24   30
Wave period scale in seconds

15·00   24in max. (61cm)

17·00   24in max. (61cm)

19·00   24in max. (61cm)

21·00   28in max. (71cm)

23·00   18in max. (46cm)

2 July 1945
01·00   18in max. (46cm)

03·00   20in max. (51cm)

05·00   16in max. (41cm)

(Record 07 hours missing)
09·00   16in max. (41cm)

11·00   14in max. (36cm)

15·00   12in max. (Record 13 hours missing)

17·00   12in max. (30cm)

19·00   8in max. (20cm)

21·00   7in max. (18cm)

23·00   6in max. (15cm)

7   8   10   12   15   20   24   30
Wave period scale in seconds

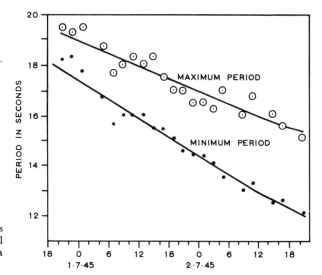

Figure 3-8 Maximum and minimum periods limiting the frequency band from the tropical storm of 26 to 28 June 1945, in the wave spectra of 1 and 2 July. (*After Barber and Ursell, 1948.*)

Since the early and very valuable work of Barber and Ursell more records of distant travel of swell waves have been collected. Analysis is now made mainly by digital computer rather than by analogue machines, such as that used by Barber and Ursell. D. E. Cartwright (1967) has discussed some of the work carried out in this field. He shows that water waves are dispersive, their speed of travel depending on their period. A 24 second wave propagates at 19 m/sec or 14.5° latitude/day.

W. H. Munk *et al.* (1963) studied swell propagated across the Pacific Ocean towards the coast of California. The swell was recorded by Vibroton, which supplies data suitable for digital computer analysis by means of a vibrating wire in a vacuum capsule. Three vibrotons were placed in a triangle in 100 m of water so that the direction of wave approach could also be determined. The spectra are illustrated in the form shown in figure 3-10, which shows equal energy density contours plotted against time for different wave frequencies. The figure shows the gradual increase of the frequency of waves with time for any one set, the direction of which is indicated by the straight lines. Each main set of waves is represented by a ridge on the diagram. The time and origin of the linear events can be given accurately in terms of bearing and angular distance.

Swells from the Antipodes can reach the west coast of the U.S.A. through a window south of New Zealand, the travel distance being 165 to 176° from their source between Kerguelen and Madagascar. The higher frequencies, about 50 c/ks, are heavily attenuated. In the generating area in deep water there is much energy in the 100 c/ks (10 second period) region. The loss of energy in this band could be due to opposing winds in the Trade Wind belt, causing breaking of smaller waves on the swell and thus a loss of energy. Scattering of the waves due to non-linear interaction within the spectrum itself could also cause attenuation. Munk set up six recording stations on a great circle between New Zealand and Alaska. The records were obtained by FLIP (Floating Instrument Platform) in the gap between Honolulu and Yakutat. Spectral plots were obtained for 12 major storms. There was no evidence of loss of energy in the Trade Wind belt, indeed at times the energy increased. The attenuation of waves with frequencies about 50 c/ks in the first 20° from the generating area was much greater than that over the whole of the rest of the distance, probably as a result of scattering.

The wave motion is predominantly linear and a resonance situation can appear whereby

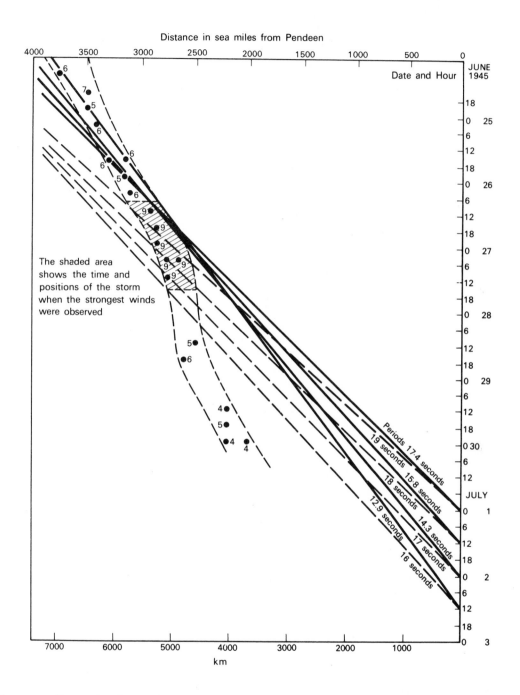

Figure 3-9 Propagation diagram for waves reaching Pendeen between 24 June and 2 July 1945. (*After Barber and Ursell, 1948.*)

BC—D

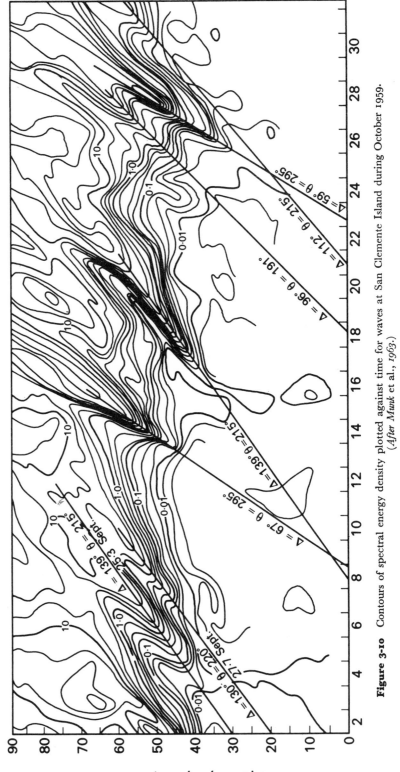

Figure 3-10 Contours of spectral energy density plotted against time for waves at San Clemente Island during October 1959. (*After Munk et al., 1963.*)

Frequency cycles/kilosecond

a new wave is formed and gains energy linearly with time. The new wave can be a tertiary wave formed from three primary waves and is a free wave in its own right. This wave gains energy from the primary waves, which are scattered. After the initial area of scattering the swell becomes a fairly narrow beam. In the north Atlantic the generating sources are nearer to the coasts and the waves are often still in the strong scattering zone when they reach the coast. They have a wide angle source, and secondary and tertiary waves are less common than in the Pacific. Further reference is made to wave attenuation in connection with wave forecasting, considered in section 3-6.

5 Microseisms

Swell waves as they travel over the ocean sometimes give rise to secondary waves of a different type which have been called microseisms, as their energy is transmitted to the bottom of the sea. They then travel as waves through the earth's crust and are recorded on seismographs.

The reason why microseisms can penetrate to the bottom, unlike normal wind waves, is that they are generated by standing waves. The standing waves result from the interference of two trains of swell moving in opposite directions. This pattern can occur where swell waves are reflected from a steep coast or where, in a small intense storm, waves are generated moving in opposite directions on either side of the storm. Observations have established that microseisms have periods equal to half that of the generating waves. They are the result of pressure fluctuations on the bottom caused by the interference of two wave trains of the same frequency. The crests and troughs change places twice for each complete cycle and this causes the centre of gravity to change slightly in phase. This change accounts for the microseism having a period half that of the sea waves from which they are derived. The fluctuations are in phase and therefore build up. A secondary type of microseism has been identified near the coast, but this only contains 1/100 of the energy of the main microseisms. The waves that travel along the ocean floor through the earth's crust are of both Rayleigh and Love types (M. H. P. Bott, 1971, p. 4), the former generating the latter as they move (B. J. Hinde and D. I. Gaunt, 1967).

Microseisms are long waves and so do not travel along great circle paths, but are affected by depth and geological structures, which cause some refraction. The rays by which they travel can be constructed as refraction diagrams. It is found that the rays converge and diverge at different points and that there are some barriers across which microseisms are not propagated. These are the result of geological shadow zones or refraction, and make the recording and interpretation of microseisms complex. Hence they are not of much practical assistance in wave forecasting, although at times they can give warning of approaching storm swells.

6 Wave forecasting

The knowledge of wave generation is not yet sufficiently advanced to allow accurate prediction of the wave spectrum from theory. There is also considerable difficulty in measuring the wave spectrum at sea, especially in storm conditions when the waves are being actively generated. Wave forecasting is nevertheless of considerable value in relation to beach and coastal analysis and wave hindcasting can also be used to relate known beach changes to wave type.

Wave forecasting can be divided into three stages. Firstly, the wave spectrum as generated by any particular wind velocity, duration and fetch can be predicted. Secondly, the effect of

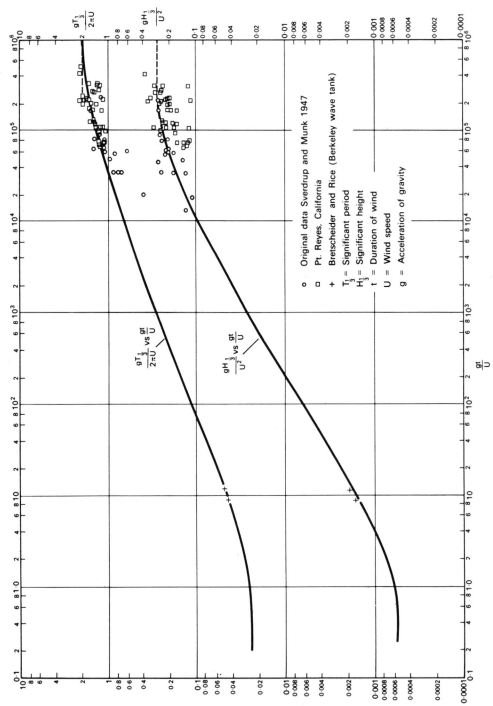

Figure 3-11 A: Duration graph.

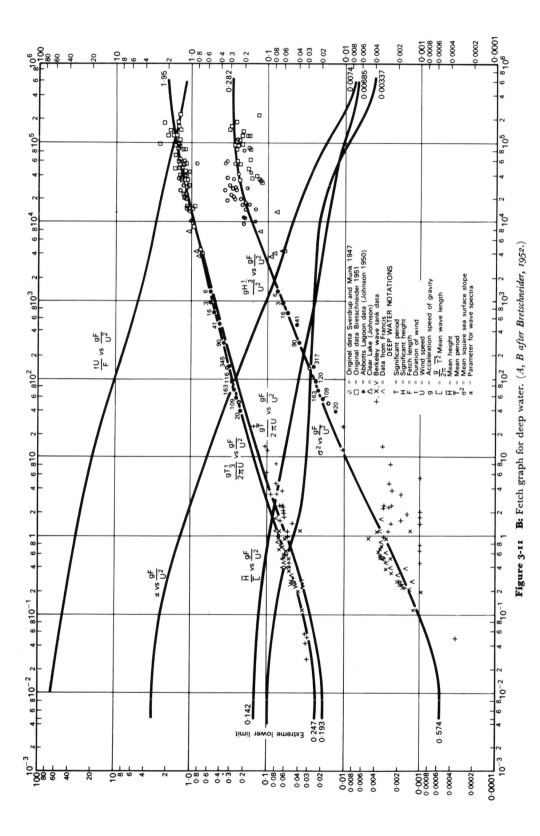

Figure 3-11 B: Fetch graph for deep water. (*A, B after Bretschneider, 1952.*)

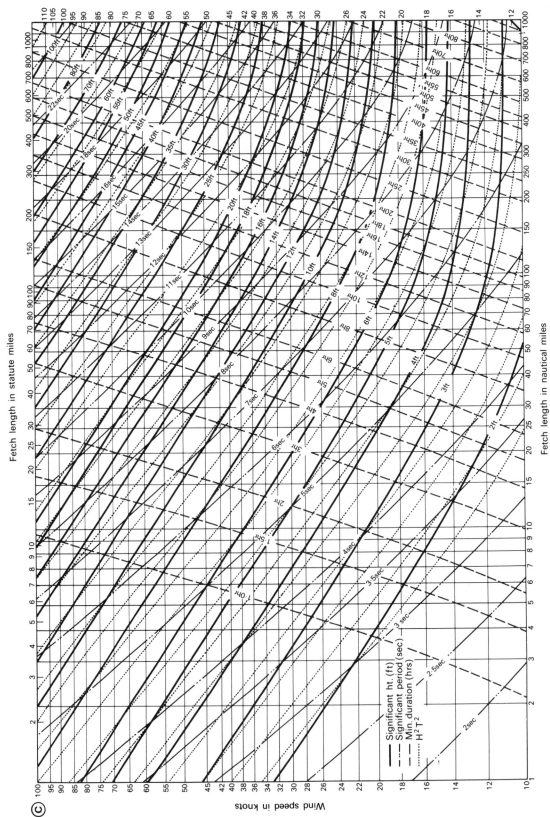

Wind speed in miles per hour

Fetch length in statute miles

Wind speed in knots

Fetch length in nautical miles

Significant ht. (ft)
Significant period (sec)
Min. duration (hrs)
$H^2 T^2$

Figure 3-11 C: Deep water wave forecasting curves as a function of wind speed, fetch length and wind duration. (C *after Bretschneider, Coastal Engineering Research Centre, 1966.*)

wave attenuation must be considered as the sea changes into swell. Thirdly, there are the shallow-water effects that influence the waves before they arrive at the coast. The first two aspects will be considered in this chapter and the third in the next.

The methods that are now being used for wave forecasting are semi-empirical and semi-theoretical. They can be broadly divided into two classes. The first method considers the significant height and period of the predicted waves. It was originally devised by H. U. Sverdrup and W. H. Munk (1947) and was extended and brought up to date by C. L. Bretschneider (1952). It is often referred to as the SMB method. The second is based on the wave spectrum and was first developed by W. J. Pierson, G. Neumann and R. W. James (1955). It is generally referred to as the PNJ method. Useful relationships have also been put forward by J. Darrebyshi (1952; 1955a; 1955b), and by M. Darbyshire and L. Draper (1963).

a   The Sverdrup–Munk–Bretschneider method

(*i*) *Generation:* Sverdrup and Munk (1947) collected many wave observations in order to establish the empirical relationships between the variables affecting the growth and character of waves. A later analysis of the same data with all available subsequent material was made by Bretschneider (1952). The curves he has drawn use dimensionless parameters similar to those used by Sverdrup and Munk. $T_{1/3}$ is the deep water significant period in seconds; U is the average surface wind speed; F is the length of fetch; $H_{1/3}$ is the significant wave height and L is the wave length; t is the wind duration. Bretschneider's curves are drawn in figure 3-11. Figure 3-11A shows the relationship between the significant wave period, which is directly related to the wave length and velocity in deep water, and the ratio of wind duration to wind speed. The relationship between the significant wave height and the generating wind is shown also on this graph. Figure 3-11B shows a number of wave characteristics in relation to the ratio of wind fetch to wind velocity. The characteristics include mean square sea surface slope, a measure of wave steepness, and steepness in the form of wave height over wave length. The variation of wave height and period is also shown in relation to the wind characteristics. The curve for tU/F gives the time required for the generation of waves of maximum energy for that particular fetch and wind velocity. In these two figures the parameters used are dimensionless, while in figure 3-11C actual values of the fetch and wind speed can be entered in the graph to estimate the significant wave heights and periods to be expected.

(*ii*) *Attenuation:* When the generating wind dies down or the waves move out of the generating area they cease to grow and gradually attenuate with time and distance. Their velocity does not vary but their height is reduced. The modification of the wave height as the waves decay in moving across the ocean is important from the point of view of the beach. The attenuation of swell is the chief cause of the different effect of sea and swell on the beach. Hence it is one of the main reasons for the importance of beach exposure.

Bretschneider (1952) has drawn a series of empirical graphs, shown in figure 3-12, from which the change in wave height and period as the waves decay may be found. The graph relates decay length and fetch length, D/F, and dimensionless ratios of height and period to decay distance. The higher and steeper the waves as they leave the generating area, the more rapid will be their reduction in height. For a wave period of 10 seconds, a fetch distance of 100 nautical miles and an initial height of 6·1 m, after travelling 200 nautical miles the wave height will be less than 3·05 m, while after 1600 nautical miles it will be only 1·22 m. According to the curves given by Bretschneider the period, during the same distance of 1600 nautical miles, would have increased to nearly 12 seconds. The apparent increase in wave period is due mainly to the

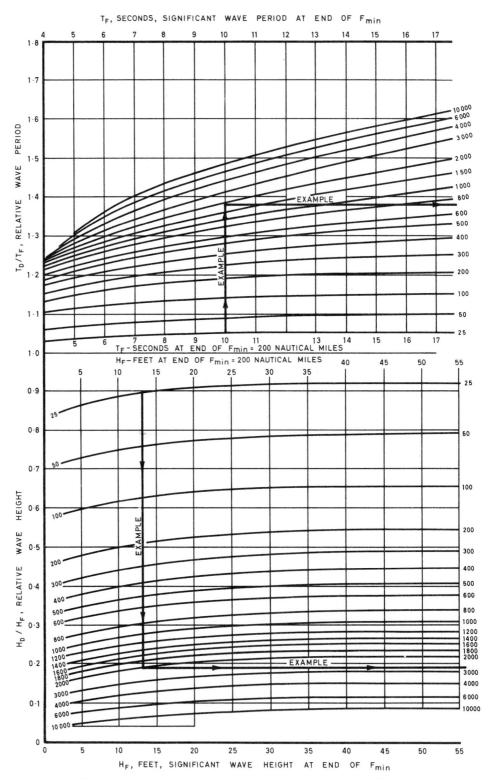

Figure 3-12 Forecasting curves for wave decay. (*After Bretschneider, 1952.*)

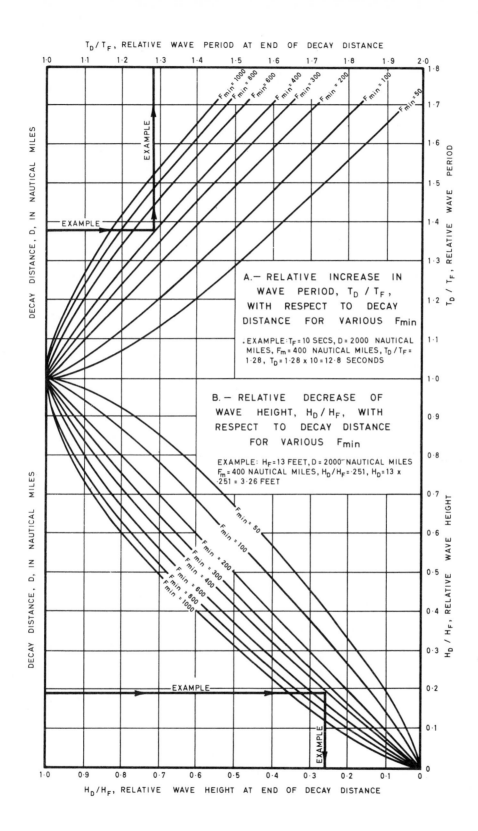

T_D/T_F, RELATIVE WAVE PERIOD AT END OF DECAY DISTANCE

A.— RELATIVE INCREASE IN WAVE PERIOD, T_D / T_F, WITH RESPECT TO DECAY DISTANCE FOR VARIOUS F_{min}

EXAMPLE: T_F = 10 SECS, D = 2000 NAUTICAL MILES, F_m = 400 NAUTICAL MILES, T_D / T_F = 1·28, T_D = 1·28 x 10 = 12·8 SECONDS

B.— RELATIVE DECREASE OF WAVE HEIGHT, H_D / H_F, WITH RESPECT TO DECAY DISTANCE FOR VARIOUS F_{min}

EXAMPLE: H_F = 13 FEET, D = 2000 NAUTICAL MILES F_m = 400 NAUTICAL MILES, H_D / H_F = ·251, H_D = 13 x ·251 = 3·26 FEET

H_D/H_F, RELATIVE WAVE HEIGHT AT END OF DECAY DISTANCE

dispersion of the wave spectrum, which naturally follows from the concept of travel at the appropriate group velocity. The wave heights which are made up of the superimposition of many different wave trains to form the wave spectrum are also affected.

b   Pierson–Neumann–James

The data are presented in another form in the second method of wave forecasting. The results are based on the complete wave spectrum. Examination of the wave spectrum shows that the wave energy is concentrated in a relatively narrow band. The range of periods within this band determines the actual wave pattern. Pierson, Neumann and James made use of visual observations owing to the limited instrumental data available at that time. The most easily observed dimensions of the waves is the length of time between successive crests passing a fixed point. This value is called the apparent period of the waves, and can be related empirically to the speed of the generating wind. Each wind velocity produces a certain range of periods with a well-defined maximum, which increases with the wind velocity. The empirical relationships can be supported theoretically.

In the spectrum the wave components with a significant amount of energy cover a well-defined band of frequency, f, where $f = 1/T$. A 20 knot wind, for example, produces a range of f between 0·083 and 0·30, or 12 to 3 seconds, with a maximum period at 8·1 seconds or $f_{max} = 0·124$. There is a very rapid increase of energy, which is proportional to the square of the spectral wave height, as the wind increases. The frequency of the optimum band is given by $f_{max} = 2·475/U$ knots, and $T_{max} = 0·405U$. The total energy is shown to be proportional to the fifth power of the wind speed in a fully developed sea with composite wave motion.

The wave heights can be considered in terms of the average height, the height of highest $\frac{1}{3}$ of the waves (the significant height), or the highest $\frac{1}{10}$ of the waves. The relationship between these values has been found from wave records and from theory by M. S. Longuet-Higgins (1952). He gives the following results:

$$H_{av}/H_{1/3} = 0·65 \text{ from wave records,} \quad 0·625 \text{ from theory}$$
$$H_{1/10}/H_{1/3} = 1·29 \text{ from wave records,} \quad 1·27 \text{ from theory}$$

These values can be related to the computed wave energy. The wave height can also be related to the wind velocity by the equation:

$$H \text{ (cm)} = 0·9 \times 10^{-5}U \text{ (cm/sec)}^{2·5}$$

This fits closely the observed upper limit of the wave height, but further data are desirable. The figure, however, agrees with the relationship already given for the total energy, which depends on U^5, as the wave height depends on $U^{2·5}$.

Neumann (1953) has developed a graphical representation of the wave spectrum in a diagram he calls the co-cumulative power spectrum. Figure 3-13 shows the curves for winds of speeds between 20 and 36 knots. The ordinate scale is in units of E, which, as it is a function of wave energy, can be converted into wave height. The abscissa is in f, the frequency, or T units, the wave period, so that the wave height and period for the whole range of the spectrum can be found. From the graph the significant range of periods can be found by ignoring the upper 5% and the lower 3% of the curve. Table 3-1 gives the resulting upper and lower limits of the wave periods, and table 3-2 gives the period of the most energetic wave, the average period and various wave heights.

Neumann (1953) has also presented curves and tables showing the effect of fetch and wind duration on the generation of waves. He has superimposed lines of constant duration and fetch

Table 3-1 Significant range of periods in a fully arisen sea at different velocities

U knots	km/hour	T_1 sec	T_u sec	U knots	km/hour	T_1 sec	T_u sec
10	18·5	1·0	6·0	34	62·2	5·5	18·5
12	22·2	1·0	7·0	36	66·8	5·8	19·7
14	26·0	1·5	7·8	38	70·6	6·2	20·8
16	29·7	2·0	8·8	40	74·3	6·5	21·7
18	33·4	2·5	10·0	42	78·0	6·8	23·0
20	37·5	3·0	11·1	44	81·7	7·0	24·0
22	40·9	3·4	12·2	46	85·5	7·2	25·0
24	44·5	3·7	13·5	48	89·2	7·5	26·0
26	48·2	4·1	14·5	50	92·8	7·7	27·0
28	52·0	4·5	15·5	52	96·6	8·0	28·5
30	55·6	4·7	16·7	54	100·3	8·2	29·5
32	59·4	5·0	17·5	56	104·0	8·5	31·0

Table 3-2 Characteristics of a fully arisen sea

U knots	km/hour	$\hat{T}$ sec	T_{max} sec	H_{av} feet	H_{av} m	$H_{1/3}$ feet	$H_{1/3}$ m	$H_{1/10}$ feet	$H_{1/10}$ m
10	18·5	2·8	4·0	0·88	0·27	1·41	0·43	1·79	0·55
12	22·2	3·4	4·8	1·39	0·42	2·22	0·65	2·82	0·86
14	26·0	4·0	5·6	2·04	0·62	3·26	0·99	4·15	1·27
16	29·7	4·6	6·5	2·85	0·82	4·56	1·39	5·80	1·77
18	33·4	5·1	7·2	3·80	1·16	6·10	1·86	7·8	2·38
20	37·5	5·7	8·1	5·0	1·25	8·0	2·44	10·2	3·12
22	40·9	6·3	8·9	6·4	1·95	10·2	3·12	12·8	3·91
24	44·5	6·8	9·7	7·9	2·41	12·5	3·82	16·0	4·88
26	48·2	7·4	10·5	9·6	2·93	15·4	4·70	19·6	5·98
28	52·0	8·0	11·3	11·3	3·45	18·2	5·56	23·1	7·06
30	55·6	8·5	12·1	13·5	4·12	21·6	6·59	27·6	8·44
32	59·4	9·1	12·9	16·1	4·91	25·8	7·88	32·8	10·00
34	62·2	9·7	13·6	18·6	5·68	29·8	9·10	38·0	11·60
36	66·8	10·2	14·5	21·6	6·60	34·5	10·51	43·8	13·40
38	70·6	10·8	15·4	24·7	7·55	39·5	12·50	50·2	15·30
40	74·3	11·4	16·1	28·2	8·61	45·2	13·77	57·5	17·55
42	78·0	12·0	17·0	31·4	9·60	50·1	15·30	63·9	19·50
44	81·7	12·5	17·7	36·0	10·98	57·7	17·60	73·4	22·40
46	85·5	13·1	18·6	39·7	12·10	63·5	19·38	80·6	24·60
48	89·2	13·7	19·4	44·4	13·52	71·0	21·67	90·4	27·60
50	92·8	14·2	20·2	48·9	14·90	78·0	23·80	99·4	30·30
52	96·6	14·8	21·0	54·0	16·47	87·0	26·50	110·0	33·60
54	100·2	15·4	21·8	59·0	18·00	95·0	29·00	121·0	37·00
56	104·0	15·9	22·6	64·0	19·52	103·0	31·40	130·0	39·85

T_{max} is the period of the most energetic wave spectrum.
$\hat{T}$ is the average period.

on the curves of wave generation already mentioned. The limiting effect of these variables can easily be assessed in terms of wave period and height. Figures 3-14C and D show that as the wind speed increases, so the fetch and duration required for the generation of a fully developed sea also increases.

Further refinements in the actual process of preparing a forecast are described in H.O. Publication 603, (Pierson, Neumann, and James, 1955). The character and position of the storm

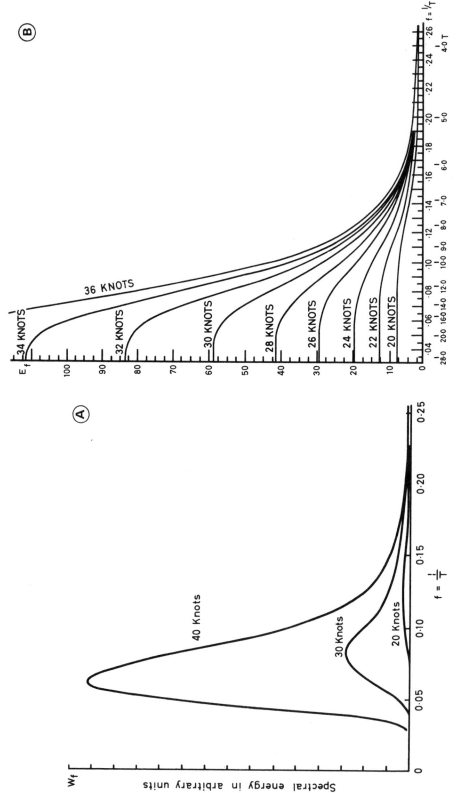

Figure 3-13 **A:** Wave spectra for fully arisen sea at a wind speed 0, 20, 30 and 40 knots. **B:** Co-cumulative power spectra for ocean waves at wind velocities between 20 and 36 knots.

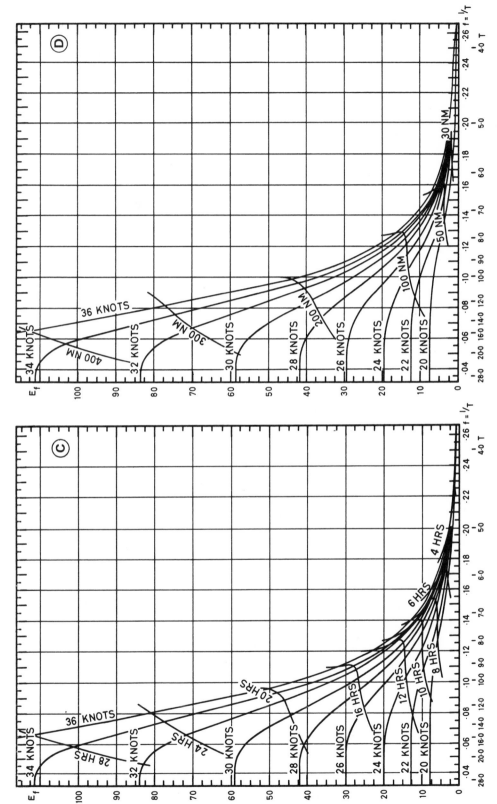

Figure 3-13 **C:** Co-cumulative spectra or wind speeds from 20 to 36 knots as a function of duration. **D:** Co-cumulative spectra for wind speeds from 20 to 36 knots as a function of fetch. (*A, B, C, D after Neumann, 1953.*)

in relation to the point for which a forecast is required are taken into account by the use of filters, which considers the angular spreading of the waves that results from the variation in direction of wave travel within the storm area. Filter I examines a line source of waves, and determines which wave directions and periods will affect any point not in the direct path of the generating storm. Filter II takes into account the effect of the fetch over which the storm winds are blowing and calculates the arrival of waves generated near the rear of the storm. Filter III considers the situation in which the storm area is moving at about the speed of the generating waves when the storm and waves would arrive almost together. Filter IV estimates the result of a rapid cessation of storm winds and the resulting reduction in height of the waves generated by them. All synoptic situations must be simplified for analytical purposes, but the importance of the width of the fetch is made clear: it affects the wave height and the width of the wave front.

A modification of the wave spectrum method of forecasting has been put forward by H. U. Roll and G. Fischer (1956). They point out that two empirical equations provided by Neumann (1953) for the mean wave energy in a small frequency band give different values for the period of the wave of maximum energy, T_{max}. One equation uses the wave period and the other the frequency. The first equation gives T_{max} as $0.641U$ and the second as $0.785U$. The discrepancy is due to the different powers of T which enter the equation, and can be resolved if the period and frequency relationship is taken logarithmically and not, as Neumann does, linearly. With this modification the second equation gives the same result as the first.

The expression derived for the increment of energy can be integrated to give the total wave energy from the frequency equation, if it is extended to all frequencies. The total energy is given in terms of the wind speed as follows:

$$E = \frac{cp\pi^2}{16g}U^4 \text{ (ergs cm}^{-2}) \tag{1}$$

where p is the density and c is a constant. This equation relates the wave energy to the fourth power of the wind speed and not the fifth as given in Neumann's equation. The wave energy is proportional to the square of the wave height, which Sverdrup and Munk have shown to be proportional to the square of the wind speed. The fourth power is, therefore, more likely to be correct than the fifth.

Roll and Fischer (1956) derive the constant c in the equation above by two methods, both of which give the value of 1.96×10^{-2}. Neumann give the value of c as 8.27×10^{-4} (sec^{-1}), derived from observations. A direct comparison of the two values is not possible because they relate to different forms of the energy equation and have different dimensions.

The constant given by Roll and Fischer can be tested by relating the wave energy to the mean height of the apparent sea, $\tilde{H}$. Taking the value of $\tilde{H}$, given by Longuet-Higgins (1952), of $1.772\sqrt{E}$, and using the equation (1) in which c is taken as 1.96×10^{-2}, they give

$$\tilde{H} = \frac{0.275}{g}U^2$$

This value agrees satisfactorily with 0.26 given by Sverdrup and Munk (1947) and 0.30 by C. G. Rossby and R. B. Montgomery (1935). There is, however, doubt about the derivation of the values, as these are based on visual observations of the significant wave height. The correlation of this value with the mean height of the apparent sea, $\tilde{H}$, is uncertain. According to the present analysis for a fully developed sea, $\tilde{H}_{1/3} = 2.832\sqrt{E}$, which according to the relation given by Longuet-Higgins and equation (1) gives

$$\tilde{\tilde{H}}_{1/3} = \frac{0{\cdot}44}{g}U^2.$$

This value is very high and casts some doubt on the value of c, which does not yet appear to be satisfactory. The constant c depends on whether the relationships described by Neumann (1953), which have been used in research so far, do in fact correctly relate the apparent add the true wave size. The value of c may be too great.

H. Walden (1956) has suggested a new value for the constant c of $0{\cdot}48 \times 10^{-2}$. This gives the equation for $\tilde{\tilde{H}}_{1/3}$ as $(0{\cdot}22/g)U^2$. The value of $0{\cdot}22$ is lower than those of Sverdrup and Munk, and Rossby and Montgomery, but it appears to give satisfactory results.

c Darbyshire

(i) *Generation:* J. Darbyshire (1952) has analysed experimentally the generation of waves by storms in fetches of varying length. Some measurements were made in the open ocean for fetches of 100 to 1000 miles (160 to 1600 km), some in the Irish Sea for fetches of 40 to 100 miles (64 to 160 km), and others for the shorter fetches of 1 to 10 miles (1·6 to 16 km) in Lough Neagh. The aim of the analysis was to establish the spectral distribution of wave energy in the storm area. The wave spectrum was analysed to give a series of sine waves, the periods of which are submultiples of the duration of the record, and the heights of which are proportional to the heights of the peaks in the spectrum.

The wave energy is given by $\frac{1}{8}g\rho H^2$ for a wave height H. The total energy is, therefore, $\frac{1}{8}g\rho\Sigma H_n^2$, where H_n is the height of the nth peak in the spectrum. The equivalent height of a hypothetical wave which has the same energy as the complicated wave train can be calculated from this value and related to the maximum observed height. The equivalent height, H_T, can be found in the same way for any given wave period band of one second, T, i.e. $T - \frac{1}{2}$ to $T + \frac{1}{2}$. The heights may then be related to the strength of the generating winds and the length of fetch.

It was found from the analysis that the maximum wave period in seconds is about 1/3 of the maximum gradient wind in knots. The period of the highest waves was found to be about $\frac{1}{4}$ of the mean gradient wind speed in knots, U_g. This value held for fetches of considerable length. The value of the equivalent height, H, is given by $H = 0{\cdot}027U_g^{3/2}$ (H in feet and U_g in knots).

All the relationships given by Darbyshire were derived from observations in fetches greater than 160 km. They indicate that for waves of 13 second period, which was the maximum considered, an increase of fetch would not significantly change the relations H_T/T and T/U_g. The rather surprising conclusion was reached that the wave characteristics became more or less independent of the fetch after 320 to 480 km.

R. Silvester (1955) has drawn graphs for Darbyshire's equations and these are shown in figure 3-14. They relate the fetch and wave height for different wind speeds, and the fetch to the wave period. The wave height is given in terms of the mean wave height, H_{mean}, which is the average of all waves. If H_{mean} is taken as 1·0, then the equivalent height, H, is $1{\cdot}2H_{mean}$, the significant height is $1{\cdot}6H_{mean}$ and the maximum height is $2{\cdot}4H_{mean}$. The significant period can also be related to the wind velocity and fetch, F, by the equation:

$$T_s = 0{\cdot}24U_g(1 + 1{\cdot}25 \times 10^{-4}F)\left\{1 - \frac{1}{e}0{\cdot}23F^{1/2}\right\}$$

where T is in seconds, U_g in knots and F in nautical miles. Computation of these data from the observed heights and periods of Sverdrup and Munk (1947) gives a satisfactory agreement.

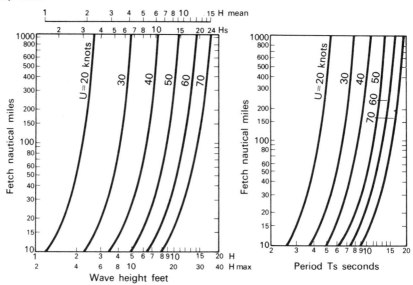

Figure 3-14 Graph relating wave height and fetch for varying wind speeds and wave periods and fetch for varying wind speeds for the equations of Darbyshire. (*After Silvester, 1955.*)

The steepness of the waves is important and is given by $0.149/U^{1/2}$ or $0.091/U_g^{1/2}$, (where U is the surface wind) for a fully developed sea. The steepness depends on the square-root of the wind velocity, and on the stage of development of the waves if they are not yet fully developed. The latter can be given in terms of the ratio of wave speed to wind speed (C/U according to Sverdrup and Munk). The steepness of the highest waves is equal to

$$\frac{0.163}{U^{1/2}}\left(\frac{C}{U}\right)$$

The work of Darbyshire (1952), which has just been discussed, was based on observations made largely at Perranporth, in the Irish Sea and Lough Neagh. More recently Darbyshire (1955a) has analysed wave data recorded in deep water by the Ocean Weather Ship situated at 61° N, 15° 20' W and 52° 20' N, 20° W. These observations were carried out with a shipborne wave recorder between February 1953 and January 1954. It was found that the equations already given, which apply to waves generated in relatively shallow water over the continental shelf, cannot be applied accurately to waves generated in deep water. Empirical results of the analysis indicate that the effect of fetch is small after 160 km in deep water as well as shallow water. The period of the longest waves was found to depend on $2.3U_g^{1/2}$ instead of $U_g/3$, while the period of the highest waves was $1.64U_g^{1/2}$ instead of $U_g/4$. The value of the equivalent height is thus now $H = 0.0038U_g^2$.

The results show that in deep water lower wave heights were generated with winds under 50 knots, but that at higher speeds greater heights occurred. The ratio of wave steepness to wind speed for a fully developed sea for deep water equalled 0.00028 and while for deep water, there was a linear increase in wave steepness with wind speed, in shallow water there was a decrease. The plotted points, however, show a large scatter. In both shallow and deep water the steepness of the waves was found to increase as the fetch increased until the equilibrium value was attained.

J. Darbyshire (1956) has re-analysed observations made on Lough Neagh in fetches between

1 and 100 miles (1·6 km and 160 km) in the light of the results obtained from the analysis of the deep ocean records. Two wave recorders were used on Lough Neagh, one of which was movable. The gradient wind was obtained by multiplying the surface wind by $\frac{3}{2}$. A relationship between the maximum wave height and the wind speed was given by H_{max} (feet) $= 0.0032U_g^2$ (knots) and T_s (sec) $= 0.67U_g^{1/2}$ (knots), where T_s is the significant period. For the open sea the relations were $H_{max} = 0.0076U_g^2$ and $T_s = 1.64U_g^{1/2}$. The same ratio of 0·41 holds between the short-fetch wave heights and the large-fetch wave heights, and between the short- and long-fetch wave periods. If the ratio of the wave height in any fetch to that in infinite fetch is termed

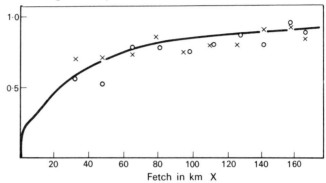

o Ratio of wave height to wave height at infinite fetch

× Ratio of wave period to wave period at infinite fetch

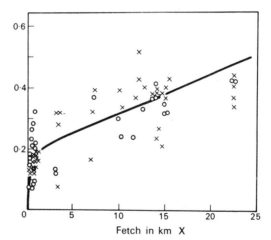

Figure 3-15 Relationship between wave characteristics and fetch related to infinite fetch. (*After Darbyshire, 1956.*)

y, its value can be given in terms of x, the length of fetch in nautical miles. Darbyshire gives the best fit equation for y as $y = (x^3 + 3x^2 + 65x)/(x^3 + 12x^2 + 260x + 80)$. This relationship provides a good fit for fetches between $\frac{1}{4}$ mile (0·4 km) and 100 miles (160 km), the curves being shown in figure 3-15.

(*ii*) *Attenuation:* Since so many waves reach the coast after a long period of decay, the changes which take place after the waves cease to be generated are very important. The problem of the attenuation of swell has been considered by Darbyshire (1957a). He analysed the wave records of the *Weather Explorer*, considering decay distances of 400 miles (640 km) to 1600 miles (2560 km). The square-root of the peaks for each 1 second period interval, H_T, was used. This is the height of the simple sine wave that has the same energy as the total energy of the spectrum for that period interval. The values of H_T for each wave period tend to reach a maximum value at a particular time, and the wave propagation lines for these points meet at the centre of the storm. The value of T_{max}, the maximum wave period with a measurable H_T value, and T_s, the period with the highest H_T value, could be determined. T_{max} was found to depend on the gradient wind, equalling $2 \cdot 30 U_g^{1/2}$, while $T_s = 1 \cdot 64 U_g^{1/2}$, with U_g in knots and T in seconds. The ratio $H_T/H°_T$ ($H°_T$ being the value of H_T for the generating area) does not vary with the wave period or with the velocity of the following winds. These values are shown in figure 3-16 where it can

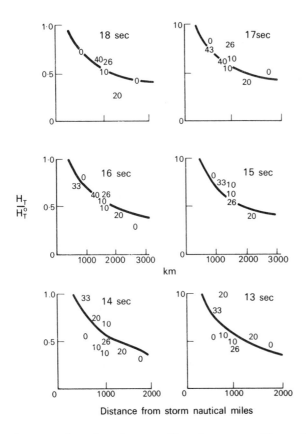

Figure 3-16 Reduction of wave height in relation to distance from storm centre and strength of following winds. (*After Darbyshire, 1957a.*)

be seen that they do not affect the curves. The reduction in wave height appears to depend largely on the decay distance, D, according to the equation $H_T/H°_T = (300/D)^{1/2}$, where D is in nautical miles. This is a simpler relation than that proposed by Bretschneider (1952), but it also gives a very considerable reduction in wave height with decay distance.

The reduction in height may be due to three possible causes. The first is dispersion, although the effect of this is reduced by the use of only a narrow frequency band for the analysis. The second is loss of energy due to air resistance and turbulence, but since both these factors depend on the wave period, which has been shown to be insignificant in this respect, they are not important. The third factor is divergence, and this probably causes the observed effect. Computed and observed values of wave height and period for swell at Casablanca agreed to within 25% using the relation given by Darbyshire (1957), most of the results being considerably better.

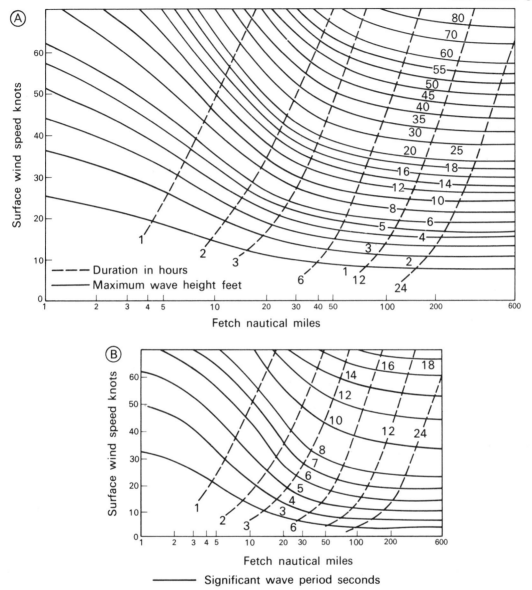

Figure 3-17 **A:** Graph relating wave height to wind speed and duration, and to fetch for oceanic waters. **B:** Graph relating wave period to wind speed, duration and fetch for oceanic waters. (*A, B after Darbyshire and Draper, 1955.*)

A convenient set of graphs for forecasting wind-generated sea waves has been prepared by M. Darbyshire and L. Draper (1963). The curves, shown in figure 3-17 are derived empirically, but they are based on more wave records than some of the earlier sets of curves—ten years of records from weather ships in the central Atlantic, as well as observations made from light vessels in coastal waters including Morecambe Bay, the Irish Sea area and Smith's Knoll in the North Sea. The records from these two coastal areas agree well with each other, but there is a significant difference between them and the records for the open ocean. The prediction charts are, therefore, prepared for two types of area, the open ocean and coastal waters. The former refers to water depths greater than about 183 m (600 feet), while the coastal waters refer to areas with a depth between 30 and 45 m.

The data required to determine the wave dimensions are the wind speed in knots, the wind duration in hours and the fetch in nautical miles in the appropriate wind direction. Darbyshire and Draper used the mean wind over the generating period. The graphs give a maximum wave height and significant period. The significant period is what would be obtained from a typical record of 100 waves. All the graphs are based on instrumentally recorded wave dimensions. Significant height may be obtained from the maximum height by the relationship $H_{max} = 1 \cdot 60 \, H_s$, where H_s is the significant height.

The accuracy of the forecast depends to a considerable extent on the accuracy with which the wind data are measured. They may be obtained either from wind observations or the analysis of the synoptic weather charts. The highest wave of the storm can be estimated statistically from the data. Its magnitude depends partly on the duration of the storm, increasing as the storm duration increases, because the statistical probability of a large number of wave crests coinciding increases the longer the storm lasts.

No allowance can be made in this type of prediction graph for the presence of swell waves. The swell waves do not add simply with the sea waves in a linear manner. For practical purposes the relationship between the two waves combined can be given by $H = \sqrt{h_1{}^2 + h_2{}^2}$, where h_1 and h_2 are the heights of the two separate waves and H is their joint height. Swell waves are more liable to affect the heights of waves in deeper water and more exposed coastal areas. They are not a problem in the Irish Sea or the southern North Sea.

The results given by the graphs show that there is a considerable difference in period of the predicted waves in the open sea, particularly when the winds are strong. Close to the shore, wave prediction becomes considerably more complex than it is in the open ocean. Any one of the three variables on which the wave size depends can set a limit to the growth of the waves, so all three must be taken into account in forecasting.

d   Comparison of the different methods of wave forecasting

The state of wave forecasting from meteorological data is such that it is not yet possible to choose definitely between the different methods. One may give better results in one area, while another may suit another place. It is likely that in many areas local conditions will have to be taken into account.

Sverdrup and Munk's (1947) and Bretschneider's (1952) curves are entirely empirical and only attempt to give a value for the significant wave heights and lengths. The PNJ method, with the later modification of Roll and Fischer (1956), is largely theoretical, although the whole spectrum of the waves is considered. J. Darbyshire's (1957) results are based on more precise measurements than the other methods, and adopt a more experimental approach.

A comparison of the three methods of forecasting wave heights has been recorded by R. F. Dearduff (1955) for a storm off California. The particular storm considered occurred in October 1950 and the various wave heights recorded and forecast, using the same fetch pattern, are shown in figure 3-18. It shows that the PNJ technique gives waves much higher than the other methods, and twice as high as the observed waves. One reason may have been due to the comparative difficulty of using the curves. Another point which applies to all methods of forecasting waves is the difficulty of analysing the synoptic chart correctly to give an accurate value for the length of fetch, its width and the wind direction and force. The same fetch and wind force were used for the different forecasting methods. J. Darbyshire has pointed out that the decay of the waves appears to be largely due to divergence—the width of the fetch, therefore, is an important

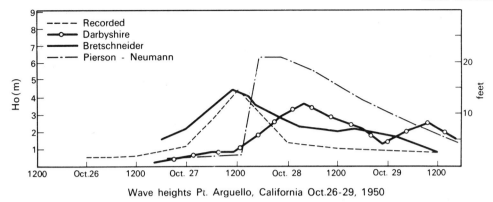

3-18 Correlation of three different techniques of forecasting waves with observed wave heights. (*After Dearduff, 1955.*)

factor. For example, if one fetch is twice as wide as another it will, for the same decay conditions, produce waves $\sqrt{2}$ higher than the other.

In the example discussed by Dearduff the SMB method gives the most reliable estimate of the wave height. Until the methods have been tested more thoroughly, however, it is premature to be dogmatic about the relative merits of the different techniques. Neumann's curves, to make their application easier, have been redrawn, in the form of distorted co-cumulative spectra graphs. The problem of obtaining the correct synoptic situation will be lessened when satellite observations of weather conditions are readily available for the oceanic areas.

R. W. James (1954) has discussed an example of the application of the wave spectra method to wave forecasting and shows that there is an excellent agreement between the forecast and observed data using the PNJ method. The use of this method for preparing wave charts for shipping has been discussed by James (1957), who states that the prognostic charts have been found rather accurate. 85% of the forecast heights were within $\pm 1\cdot22$ m of observed heights, many of which were over $7\cdot6$ m.

One difficulty in attempting to assess the relative accuracy of the different methods is the lack of detailed measurements of complete wave spectra in the oceans. Neumann and Pierson (1957) have made a detailed comparison of four different families of curves with one measured spectrum. The first is J. Darbyshire's (1952) recordings off Cornwall; the second Neumann's (1953; 1954); the third is a modification of Darbyshire's work based on wave recordings made in the open ocean, and lastly Roll and Fischer's modification of Neumann's original curves are used. All use surface winds, except Darbyshire who uses the gradient wind and whose equations were corrected by using 2/3 of the gradient wind as an estimate of the surface wind.

In all the spectra the fully developed sea depends only on the wind strength. The Neumann and Darbyshire spectra grow from high to low frequency with increasing fetch and fixed wind speed. The differences between the spectra are quite considerable, particularly with high winds and long fetches. The area under the Darbyshire spectrum and Roll and Fischer's varies as U^4, but the Neumann spectrum varies as U^5. The variation of wave energy at the high-frequency end of the spectrum varies such that $E_f = 1/f^5$ for Roll and Fischer, $E_f = 1/f^6$ for Neumann and $E_f = 1/f^7$ for Darbyshire.

The stereo wave observations project (S.W.O.P.) attempted to measure a wave spectrum at sea using a wave pole developed by the Woods Hole Oceanographic Institute. One problem was the elimination of swell and waves from other directions. The spectrum measured was developed by an 18·7 knot wind measured 5·5 m above the ground, with a duration of at least 10 hours. The spectrum calculated from the observations has been compared with three different theoretical spectra. Compared with Darbyshire's spectrum the peak of the calculated spectrum is too far to the left, giving a maximum height at too long a period. The Roll and Fischer curves come nearer, but now the peak of the calculated curve for the 18·7 knot wind is too far to the right, implying too short a period for the maximum height, which is also a little too low. Of the three spectra the Neumann one fits best, giving the correct period for the maximum height wave.

The significant height of the waves can be given in the three equations approximately as follows: Darbyshire:

$$\bar{H}_{1/3} = 6·18 \times 10^{-5}U_g{}^2 \quad or \quad 1·39 \times 10^{-4}U^2$$

where U is the surface wind and $U = 2/3 \times U_g$, the gradient wind. Roll and Fischer:

$$\bar{H}_{1/3} = 2·667 \times 10^{-4}U^2,$$

which is also SMB's value. Neumann:

$$\bar{H}_{1/3} = 7·065 \times 10^{-6}U^{2·5},$$

with $\bar{H}_{1/3}$ in cm and the wind in cm/sec. These equations only apply to fully developed seas, which are rarely obtained for the higher wind velocities, hence it is difficult to check the curves for high winds. It appears that the Darbyshire results are too low and that the $U^{2·5}$ law gives more reliable results in this one instance. The calculated wave spectrum, however, is open to various interpretations from the measurements on which it is based.

Bretschneider (1957) has considered the various powers of the wind speed that have been proposed to govern the height of the waves. He concludes that the square of the wind speed is the correct value, rather than the 2·5 power, and that at high wind speeds (above 35 knots) the Neumann method is liable to error.

The average period also appears to fit the observed data most closely from Neumann's equation. Darbyshire's periods are too long for low wind speeds, implying that the orbital velocity is greater than the wind velocity at low speeds. The wave steepness value, for Roll and Fischer's equation, which gives a constant steepness for all wind speeds, appear to be much too high: these are 0·175 for the highest 1/10 waves and 0·14 for the highest 1/3. Darbyshire's results, on the other hand, appear to give rather too low steepness values for low wind speeds, according to Neumann and Pierson. They consider too that the Roll and Fischer results lead to waves with impossible statistical properties.

Darbyshire (1957b) gives an example of his own use of the PNJ equations to determine wave dimensions generated by winds averaging 40 knots on 8–10 October 1954 at 59° N, 19° 20′ W. Darbyshire's prediction in this instance, although rather lower than the recorded values at some times, is much closer than the PNJ value, which is very much too high. Other examples given also show that Darbyshire's results are closer to the measured heights and periods.

Roll (1957) has shown that 1232 measurements of waves in the North Sea are much closer to the computed values of Darbyshire than the PNJ values, which are too high by 50% or more, especially for longer fetches and durations. The waves were, however, generated over a shallow bottom, and Neumann and Pierson (1957) have criticized the method of presentation.

D. E. Cartwright and J. Darbyshire (1957) have drawn attention to the importance of the air–sea temperature difference in the generation of waves, and R. G. Fleagle (1956) has shown that an 11° decrease of air temperature relative to the sea temperature causes a doubling of the wave height for the same wind speed. This factor may account for some of the scatter between the recorded and computed values.

Darbyshire considers that a fetch of 100 nautical miles is all that is needed to generate a full sea for a wide range of wind speeds. Neumann, on the other hand, requires increasing fetches and durations for increasing wind speeds. According to his curves a 50 knot wind requires 1420 nautical miles and 69 hours duration to produce a fully developed sea. The extreme rarity of such conditions makes it difficult to test the upper part of the scale. Records of a severe storm in the north Pacific gave observed wave heights of 14·6 m, which were generated by winds of 45 to 55 knots, blowing for 33 hours over a fetch of 500 nautical miles. Forecasts by Neumann (1953) and Bretschneider (1952) both agreed with this value, but Darbyshire's result gave a height of only 11 m. According to Neumann, it appears that Darbyshire's results are liable to be too low for high winds and long durations. Darbyshire (1957), however, pointed out that the value of 14·6 m could be 20 to 30% in error. A reduction of this order would bring the value into agreement with instrumental observations under similar conditions in the Atlantic Ocean. At low velocities Bretschneider's curves give too high waves, probably owing to dead sea in some of the data used.

Observations show that on Lake Superior, where the fetch is of the order of 100 to 250 nautical miles, waves much greater than 6·1 m are not produced, while in the open Atlantic over long fetches 18·3 m waves are generated. F. Ursell (1956) has pointed out that Cox and Munk's (1954) work on sun glitter of the sea surface is consistent with Neumann's spectrum, but not with Darbyshire's.

The difficulty of testing the various wave forecasting techniques considered is illustrated by L. Moskowitz (1964). He selected sets of wave spectra that were comparable in terms of wind speed for winds of 20, 25, 30, 35 and 40 knots, and tested them statistically to ascertain whether they were likely to have come from the same population. The results showed that some variability in the waves and weather conditions had not been removed, and that spectra chosen for the same wind speed, but without allowing for other criteria, were nowhere near coming from the same population. In Moskowitz's mean spectra the area under the curve is proportional to the fourth power of the wind speed, and so the wave height is proportional to the square of the wind speed. Darbyshire's predicted heights fit the measured waves better after allowing for a recalibration of the wave recording device, on which the results were based. His results then agree reasonably with those of the PNJ and the SMB methods.

Until wave spectra can be measured easily and accurately at sea, it will be impossible to assess or to improve substantially the reliability of the various wave forecasting methods. They do, however, provide a useful means of estimating probable wave dimensions.

Summary

The properties of ideal waves in deep water have been analysed mathematically by Airy and Stokes. They are sinusoidal in form, the particles moving in open circles that are rapidly reduced in diameter with depth. Mass transport causes a slow water movement in the direction of wave travel. The wave velocity in deep water depends on the wave length, these two properties being related also to the period. Wave energy is half kinetic and half potential, the wave train moving at half the speed of the waves within it.

Waves in the generating area, where they are being actively formed, are called sea. As they move out beyond the generating area they become longer crested and more regular, and are called swell. A number of devices have been developed to record wave dimensions in deep water, of which the N.I.O. wave buoy is an important example, as it can record a two-dimensional wave spectrum.

A number of theories concerning the generation of wind waves have been put forward. The size of the waves depends on the strength and duration of the generating wind and the fetch across which it is blowing. The two most recent theories, developed by O. M. Phillips and J. W. Miles, provide a mechanism for wave development and growth. Phillips's theory is based on random velocity fluctuations of the stresses, both normal and tangential, induced by unstable eddies carried along in the air stream. Miles's theory is based on the instability of the interface between the air flow and the water. Miles's mechanism takes over as the waves continue to grow, while Phillips's theory can account for their initiation and early growth.

As waves move out of the generating area they are propagated over the ocean at a speed equal to half the wave velocity. They can be traced for thousands of miles across the ocean, and as they travel the separate wave periods are sorted out and the sea becomes swell. The decay of the waves results in a loss of height, but an increase in crest length.

Microseisms result from the interference of two wave trains of equal length moving in opposite directions. This situation can arise where waves are reflected from a steep coast or where winds are blowing in opposite directions on either side of a small, intense storm. The period of the microseisms is half that of the waves that cause them.

Three main methods of waves forecasting have been proposed, the Sverdrup–Munk–Bretschneider method, the Pierson–Neumann–James method and Darbyshire's method. The first is based on empirical relationships and includes curves for estimating wave attenuation as well as wave generation. The second is based on the wave spectrum and is partly theoretical and partly empirical. Darbyshire's method is based on studies in a variety of fetches and also allows for attenuation. The difficulty of measuring an accurate spectrum in the ocean has meant that the relative accuracy of the different methods has yet to be fully resolved.

References

AIRY, G. B. 1845: On tide and waves. *Encycl. Metropolitana* **5,** 241–396.

BARBER, N. F. and URSELL, F. 1948: The generation and propagation of ocean waves and swell, 1.: wave periods and velocities. *Phil. Trans. Roy. Soc.* A **240,** 527–60.

BEACH EROSION BOARD 1933: *Interim report.* Washington D.C.

BONNEFILLE, R., CORMAULT, P. and VLEMBOIS, J. 1967: Progrès des méthodes de mésure de la Houle naturelle au laboratoire national d'hydraulique. Chapter 9 in *Proc. 10th Conf. Coast. Eng.*, Tokyo, 115–26.

BOTT, M. H. T. 1971: *The interior of the Earth.* Arnold, London. (316 pp.)

BRETSCHNEIDER, C. L. 1952: The generation and decay of wind waves in deep water. *Trans. Am. Geophys. Un.* **33**(3), 381–9.

BRETSCHNEIDER, C. L. 1957: Review of Pearson, Neumann and James, 1955. *Trans. Am. Geophys. Un.* **38**(2), 264–6.

BRETSCHNEIDER, C. L. 1965: The generation of waves by wind. State of the art. *Nat. Eng. Sci. Co. Off. Nav. Res.* SN **134–6.** (96 pp.)

BURLING, R. W. 1959: The spectrum of waves at short fetches. *Deutsch. Hydrog. Zeits.* **12,** 45–64, 96–117.

CARTWRIGHT, D. E. 1967: Modern studies of wind generated waves. *Contemp. Phys.* **8,** 171–83.

CARTWRIGHT, D. E. and DARBYSHIRE, J. 1957: Discussion of chapter 7 in Neumann, G. and Pierson, W. J. (Editors), A comparison of various theoretical spectra. *Proc. Sym. on the behaviour of ships in a seaway*, Wageningen, 16–24.

COASTAL ENGINEERING RESEARCH CENTER 1966: *Shore protection, planning and design*. C.E.R.C. Tech. Rep. 4, 3rd Edition. (401 pp.)

CORNISH, V. 1934: *Ocean waves and kindred geophysical phenomena*. Cambridge University Press.

COTÉ, L. J. *et al.* 1960: The directional spectrum of a wind generated sea as determined from data obtained by S.W.O.P. *Meteor Pap.* **2**(6), New York. (88 pp.)

DARBYSHIRE, J. 1952: The generation of waves by wind. *Proc. Roy. Soc.* A **215**, 299–328.

DARBYSHIRE, J. 1955a: An investigation of storm waves in the north Atlantic Ocean. *Proc. Roy. Soc.* A. **230**, 560–9.

DARBYSHIRE, J. 1955b: Wave statistics in the north Atlantic Ocean and on the coast of Cornwall. *The Marine Observer* **25**(168), 114–18.

DARBYSHIRE, J. 1956: The distribution of wave heights. A statistical method based on observations. *Dock and Harbour Auth.* **37**, 31–4.

DARBYSHIRE, J. 1957a: Attenuation of swell in the north Atlantic Ocean. *Quart. J. Roy. Met. Soc.* **83**, 351–9.

DARBYSHIRE, J. 1957b: A note on the comparison of proposed wave spectrum formulae. *Deutsch. Hydrog. Zeits.* **10**(5), 184–90.

DARBYSHIRE, J. 1963: The one-dimensional wave spectrum in the Atlantic Ocean and coastal waters. *Ocean wave spectra*, Rep. of Conf., Englewood Cliffs: Prentice-Hall, 27–31.

DARBYSHIRE, M. and DRAPER, L. 1963: Forecasting wind-generated sea waves. *Eng.* **195**, 482–4.

DEACON, G. E. R. 1949: Waves and swell. *Quart. J. Roy. Met. Soc.* **75**(425), 227–38.

DEARDUFF, R. F. 1955: A comparison of the deep water forecasts by the Pierson–Neumann, the Darbyshire and the Sverdrup–Munk–Bretschneider methods with recorded waves for Point Arguello, California for 26–29 Oct., 1950. *Bull. B.E.B.* **9**(1), 5–13.

DONN, W. L. 1949: Studies of waves and swell in the western North Atlantic. *Trans. Am. Geophys. Un.* **31**(4), 507–16.

DRAPER, L. 1967: The analysis and presentation of wave data—a plea for uniformity. *Proc. 10th Conf. Coast. Eng.*, Tokyo, 1966, **I**, 1–11.

DRAPER, L. and FRICKER, H. S. 1965: Waves off Land's End. *J. Inst. Navig.* **18**(2), 180–7.

DRAPER, L. and SQUIRE, E. M. 1967: Waves at Ocean Weather Ship Station 'India' (59° N, 19° W). *Trans. Roy. Inst. Nav. Arch.* **109**, 85–93.

DRAPER, L. and WHITAKER, M. A. B. 1965: Waves at Ocean Weather Ship Station 'Juliet' (52° 30′ N, 20° 00′ W). *Deutsch. Hydrog. Zeits.* **18**(1), 25–30.

ECKART, C. 1953: The generation of wind waves over a water surface. *J. Applied Phys.* **24**, 1485–94.

FLEAGLE, R. G. 1956: Note on the effect of air–sea temperature difference on wave generation. *Trans. Am. Geophys. Un.* **37**(3), 275–7.

GAILLARD, D. D. 1904; *Wave action in relation to engineering structures*. Corps of Eng., U.S. Army Prof. Pa. **31**, Washington, D.C.

GERSTNER, F. 1802: Theorie der Wellen. *Abh. Konigl. Bohm. Ges. Wiss.* 412–45.

HINDE, B. J. and GAUNT, D. I. 1967: Microseisms. *Contemp. Phys.* **8**, 267–83.

JAMES, R. W. 1954: Wave forecasts based on the energy spectra method. *Trans. Am. Geophys. Un.* **35**(1), 153–60.

JAMES, R. W. 1957: Application of wave forecasts to marine navigation. *U.S. Hydrog. Off. Sp. Pub.* (78 pp.)

JASPER, N. H. 1955: Chapter 34 in Proc. 1st Conf. on 'Ships and waves'. *Counc. for Wave Res. and Soc. of Naval Arch. and Mar. Eng.*

JEFFREYS, H. 1925: On the formation of water waves by wind. *Proc. Roy. Soc.* A **107**, 189–206.

KINSMAN, B. 1960: Surface waves at short fetches and low wind speeds—a field study, volumes 1, 2 and 3. *Chesapeake Bay Inst., Tech. Rept.* **19**, Ref. 60–1. (581 pp.)

KINSMAN, B. 1965: *Wind waves, their generation and propagation on the ocean surface.* Englewood Cliffs: Prentice-Hall.

LEONIBUS, P. S. DE 1963: Power spectra of surface wave heights from recordings made from a submerged hovering submarine. *Ocean wave spectra.*, Rep. of Conf., Englewood Cliffs: Prentice-Hall, 243–50.

LEVI-CIVITA, T. 1925: Détermination rigoureuse des ondes d'ampleur finie. *Math. Ann.* **93**, 264–314.

LIGHTHILL, M. J. 1962: Physical interpretation of the mathematical theory of wave generation by wind. *J. Fluid Mech.* **14**, 385–98.

LONGUET-HIGGINS, M. S. 1952: On the statistical distribution of the heights of sea waves. *J. Mar. Res.* **11**, 245–6.

LONGUET-HIGGINS, M. S. 1962: The direction spectrum of ocean waves, and processes of wave generation. *Proc. Roy. Soc.* A **265**, 286–315.

LONGUET-HIGGINS, M. S., CARTWRIGHT, D. E. and SMITH, N. D. 1963: Observations of the directional spectrum of sea waves using the motions of a floating buoy. *Ocean wave spectra*, Rep. of Conf., Englewood Cliffs: Prentice-Hall, 111–31.

MARKS, W. and TUCKERMAN, R. G. 1961: A telemetering accelerometer wave buoy. *Ocean wave spectra*, Rep. of Conf., Englewood Cliffs: Prentice-Hall, 281–4.

MILES, J. W. 1965: A note on the interaction between surface waves and wind profiles. *J. Fluid Mech.* **22**(4), 823–7.

MILES, J. W. 1967: On the generation of surface waves by shear flows. Part V. *J. Fluid Mech.* **30**(1), 163–75.

MITCHIM, C. F. 1940: Oscillatory waves in deep water. *Mil. Eng.* **32**, 107–9.

MOSKOWITZ, L. 1964: Estimates of the power spectrums for fully developed sea for wind speeds of 20 to 40 knots. *J. Geophys. Res.* **69**(24), 5161–79.

MUNK, W. H. 1957: Comments on Bretschneider, C. L., 1957. *Trans. Am. Geophys. Un.* **38**.

MUNK, W. H., MILLER, G. R., SNODGRASS, F. E. and BARBER, N. F. 1963: Directional recording of swell from distant storms. *Phil. Trans. Roy. Soc.* A **255**, 505–84.

NEUMANN, G. 1953: An ocean wave spectra and a new method of forecasting wind generated sea. *B.E.B. Tech. Memo.* **43**.

NEUMANN, G. and JAMES, J. W. 1955: North Atlantic coast wave statistics hindcast by the spectrum method. *B.E.B. Tech. Memo.* **57**.

NEUMANN, G. and PIERSON, W. J. 1957: A detailed comparison of theoretical wave spectra and wave forecasting methods. *Deutsch. Hydrog. Zeits.* **10**(3), 73–92; **10**(4), 134–46.

NEUMANN, G. and PIERSON, W. J. 1966: *Principles of physical oceanography.* Englewood Cliffs: Prentice-Hall.

PHILLIPS, O. M. 1957: On the generation of waves by turbulent wind. *J. Fluid Mech.* **2**(5), 417–45.

PHILLIPS, O. M. 1966: *The dynamics of the upper ocean.* Cambridge University Press.

PIERSON, W. J., Editor, 1962: The directional spectrum of wind-generated sea as determined from data obtained by the Stereo Wave Observation Project. *College of Engineering, NYU, Met. Paper* **2**(6).

PIERSON, W. J., NEUMANN, G. and JAMES, R. W. 1955: Practical methods for observing and forecasting ocean waves by means of wave spectra and statistics. *Hydrog. Off. Pub.* **603,** Hydrog. Off. U.S. Navy.

RANKINE, W. J. H. 1863: On the exact form of waves near the surface of deep water. *Phil. Trans. Roy. Soc.* A, **153,** 127–138.

ROLL, H. U. 1957: Some results of comparison between observed and computed heights of wind waves. Chapter 24 in *Proc. Symp. on the behaviour of ships in a seaway*, Wageningen, 418–26.

ROLL, H. U. and FISCHER, G. 1956: Eine kritische Bemerkung zum Neumann Spektrum des Seeganges. *Deutsch. Hydrog. Zeits.* **9**(1), 9–14.

ROSSBY, C. G. and MONTGOMERY, R. B. 1935: The layer of frictional influence in wind and ocean currents. *Papers Phys. Ocean. Met.* **3**(3), Mass Inst. Tech. and Woods Hole Oceanog. Inst. (101 pp.)

RUSSELL, R. C. H. and MACMILLAN, D. H. 1952: *Waves and Tides.* London: Hutchinson.

SAVILLE, T. 1954: North Atlantic wave statistics hindcast by Bretschneider revised Sverdrup–Munk method. *B.E.B. Tech. Memo.* **55.**

SHEMDIN, D. H. and HSU, E. Y. 1967: Direct measurements of aerodynamic pressure above a simple progressive gravity wave. *J. Fluid Mech.* **30**(2), 403–16.

SILVESTER, R. 1955: Practical application of Darbyshire's method of hindcasting ocean waves. *Australian J. Appl. Sci.* **6**(3), 261–6.

SNODGRASS, F. E., GROVES, G. W., HASSELMAN, K. F., MILLER, G. R., MUNK, W. H. and POWERS, W. H. 1966: Propagation of ocean swell across the Pacific. *Phil. Trans. Roy. Soc.* A **259,** 431–97.

SNYDER, R. L. and COX, C. S. 1966: A field study of the wind generation of ocean waves. *J. Mar. Res.* **24,** 141–78.

STANTON, T. E., MARSHALL, D. and HOUGHTON, R. 1932: The growth of waves on water due to the action of the wind. *Proc. Roy. Soc.* A **137,** 283–93.

STOKES, G. G. 1847: On the theory of oscillatory waves. *Trans. Camb. Phil. Soc.* **8,** 441.

STRUIK, D. J. 1926: Détermination rigoureuse des ondes irrotationelles périodiques dans un canal à profondeur finie. *Math. Ann.* **95,** 595–634.

SVERDRUP, H. U. and MUNK, W. H. 1947: Wind, sea and swell—theory of relationships in forecasting. *Hydrog. Off. Pub.* **601,** Hydrog. Off. U.S. Navy. (47 pp.)

TUCKER, M. J. 1952: A wave-recorder for use in ships. *Nature* **170,** 657–9.

TUCKER, M. J. 1963: Recent measurements and analysis techniques developed at the National Institute of Oceanography. *Ocean wave spectra*, Rep. of Conf., Englewood Cliffs: Prentice-Hall, 219–26.

URSELL, F. 1956: Wave generation by wind. Chapter 6 in Batchelor, G. K. and Davies, R. M. (Editors), *Surveys in mechanics*, Cambridge University Press.

WALDEN, H. 1956: Vorschlag zur Anderung der Neumannschen Konstaaten c bei der Bereschnung der Wellenhohe aus der Windstarke. *Deutsch. Hydrog. Zeits.* **9**(1), 14–17.

WALDEN, H. 1963: Comparison of one directional wave spectra recorded in the German Bight with various 'theoretical' spectra. *Ocean Wave Spectra*, Rep. of Conf., Englewood Cliffs: Prentice-Hall, 67–80.

WIEGEL, R. L. and KIMBERLEY, H. L. 1950: Southern swell observed at Oceanside, California. *Trans. Am. Geophys. Un.* **31**(5), 717–22.

4 Waves in shallow water

1 **Ideal waves in shallow water :** a) Wave velocity and length; b) Wave height; c) Wave steepness; d) Wave form; e) Wave energy; f) Orbital velocity; g) Type of breakers; h) Breaking on structures; i) Wave refraction; j) Wave diffraction.

2 **Wave measurement and wave spectra**

3 **Wave records in shallow water**

4 **Wave forecasting in shallow water**

5 **Water movement and mass transport in shallow water :** a) Mass transport; b) Water velocity in shallow water and breakers.

6 **Longshore wave-induced currents :** a) Theory; b) Model experiments; c) Field observations.

7 **Long waves in shallow water :** a) Surf beat; b) Tsunami; c) Storm surges.

Summary

It is essential to know how waves are generated in deep water and transmitted across the ocean, but even more important as far as the beach and coastal studies are concerned is a knowledge of wave behaviour and characteristics in shallow water and at the coastline. In this chapter the changes that ideal waves undergo as they enter shallow water will be summarized first, after which observations of waves in shallow water, their recording, generation and forecasting will be considered. Some aspects of these matters have already been touched upon, but in this chapter the waves will be traced right up to their break-point and final dissolution as swash on the beach. A particularly important aspect of waves in shallow water, as far as coastal studies are concerned, is the longshore movement of water to which waves can give rise. This aspect is, therefore, considered from three points of view—theoretical, scale-model results and field observations. Long waves of varying types are locally and occasionally of great significance, and these are discussed in the final section.

1 Ideal waves in shallow water

The rejuvenation of swell as it approaches the coast is due to changes the waves undergo as they enter shallow water. Nearly all the characteristics of a wave change as it begins to feel the bottom. Only the period remains constant.

a Wave velocity and length

The velocity of an ideal wave ceases to depend entirely on the wave length when it enters shallow water: the equation

$$C^2 = \frac{gL}{2\pi} \tanh \frac{2\pi d}{L}$$

shows that it is now affected by depth and gradually decreases as the water grows shallower. When the depth of the water is less than 0.05d/L, tanh $2\pi d/L$ becomes almost $2\pi d/L$. The equation now becomes $C^2 = gd$. In very shallow water, therefore, the wave velocity depends

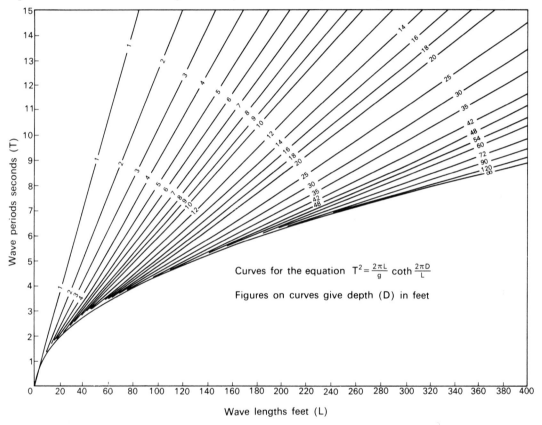

Curves for the equation $T^2 = \frac{2\pi L}{g} \coth \frac{2\pi D}{L}$

Figures on curves give depth (D) in feet

Wave periods seconds (T)

Wave lengths feet (L)

Figure 4-1 The relationship between water depth, wave period and wave length.

only on the depth of water, and solitary waves may occur. As the wave velocity decreases so the wave length decreases in proportion. The relationship between wave length, water depth and wave period is given in the curves shown in figure 4-1. The length can be read off from the measured period for any required water depth.

b Wave height

The increase of wave height with decreasing depth depends on Stokes's (1847) theory of wave motion in shallow water and can be verified by observation. There are, however, factors which modify the theoretical increase in wave height as the waves enter shallow water. One cause of a

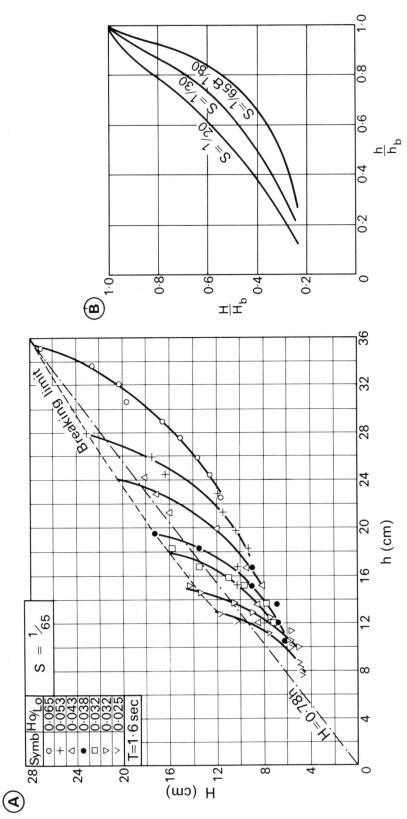

Figure 4-2 A: Transformation of wave heights inside the surf zone on a 1 : 65 bottom slope. H is the wave height and h is the water depth.
B: Effect of the bottom slope on the wave attenuation inside the surf zone on different slopes. The subscript b refers to breaking conditions.
(A, B after Horikawa and Kuo, 1967.)

decrease of wave height is bottom friction. The problem has been considered theoretically by J. A. Putnam and J. W. Johnson (1949) and by J. A. Putnam (1949). They point out that the development of ripples is largely responsible for the loss of energy, which is reflected in a reduction of wave height. This factor is more important than the roughness of the sand. The effect is only really significant, however, when the bottom is shallow and its slope very flat, as for example along parts of the coast of the Gulf of Mexico. The reduction of wave height is much greater for a gradient of 1 in 300 than it is for one of 1 in 10.

The changes in wave height from bottom friction do not become apparent for the first 60% of the distance from the point where d/L_0 is 0·5 to the break-point. In Putnam and Johnson's analysis the friction factor was taken as 0·01 and considered to be constant, which may not be justified. The vertical velocity of water flow was ignored, but this is probably allowable in view of its low value, compared with the horizontal velocities. Bottom friction was found to cause the waves to break in shallower water because of the reduction in wave height. For a bottom slope of 1 in 300 the maximum reduction for a 1·52 m wave in deep water with a period of 12 seconds was 21% of its frictionless value, and for a six second wave of the same height it was 22%. Thus where the bottom slope was 1 in 10, for a 12 second wave of the same height, the maximum reduction in height would be less than 1%.

The effect of percolation is even less marked and would only be significant on a flat slope of shingle, which is unlikely to occur in nature. The term is used to describe currents set up by waves within the bed material. The currents, however, are rapidly attenuated by friction. The maximum effect on a beach of 1 in 300 slope and with a permeability of 100 Darcys is to reduce the wave height by 7·3% for a 1·52 m wave of 12 seconds period or 8·7% for a six second wave. C. L. Bretschneider and R. O. Reid (1954) have developed graphs for computing the values from the equations given by Putnam and Johnson.

K. Horikawa and Chin-Tong Kuo (1967) have made experimental studies of wave shoaling on flat and sloping bottoms. Their results for the former agree well with theory, but the agreement is not so close for the latter. The bottom slope was 1 in 20 and 1 in 30 in one set of experiments and 1 in 65 and 1 in 80 in another. The results for a slope of 1 in 65 are shown in figure 4-2,

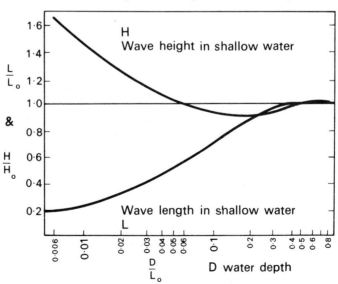

Figure 4-3 The change of wave length and wave height in relation to the ratio of depth to wave length. (*After Russell and Macmillan, 1952.*)

which also gives the dimensionless results for the other gradients. The slope can be seen to have a considerable influence on wave transformation in shallow water.

When the waves enter shallow water, wave height does not vary with such regularity as the length and velocity. According to H. B. Bigelow and W. T. Edmonson (1947), when the ratio d/L falls below 0·5, there is a slight decrease in wave height, which amounts to less than 0·9 H/H_0. The original height is regained when d/L is 0·06, and thereafter there is a rapid increase in height until the break-point is reached, as shown in figure 4-3. The increase is greater for longer waves than for shorter ones of the same height. Thus a very flat wave may double its deep-water height before it breaks, while a very steep wave will only increase a little.

c Wave steepness

The changes in wave length and height cause a change in wave steepness. The increase is small at first, because although the waves are becoming shorter their height is not yet increasing. In depths less than d/L 0·06, however, the increase is very rapid, because the wave length is decreasing and the height is increasing. The steepness increase is rarely sufficient to cause the waves to reach the limiting steepness value of 0·14.

d Wave form

With the change in steepness there is also a change in the wave form. The crest of the wave becomes narrower and sharper while the trough becomes longer and flatter. This change in the wave form is most marked in a long, low swell, in which the smooth sinusoidal crests change to become sharp and conspicuous.

e Wave energy

While the wave length is decreasing and the wave height is increasing the wave energy may remain more or less constant, although some energy is lost by contact with the bottom, leading to the height reduction already noted above. The energy, which is uniform along the wave crest in deep water, does not necessarily remain so when the wave enters shallow water. The convergence and divergence of energy in waves in shallow water are the result of wave refraction (see section 2-3(b) above). It plays an important part in explaining the concentration of wave attack along parts of the coast and dissipation elsewhere (see section 4-1(i) below).

f Orbital velocity

According to classical wave theory the orbital paths of the water particles within the wave are also modified as the waves enter shallow water. They change from being open circles to become open ellipses, with the long axis horizontal. The orbital speed of movement no longer remains constant, but changes with the wave form. Under the sharp crest of the wave there is a short but rapid landward acceleration, while under the long, flat trough there is a much slower, but more prolonged, seaward movement of water.

The movement along the bottom is particularly significant in shallow water as this exerts a very strong influence on the movement of material on the sea bed. The water moves to and fro along the bed approximately horizontally, accelerating landward under the crest and flowing slower seaward under the trough. The increase of wave height with the constant wave period leads to an increase in the orbital velocity of the particles when the wave gets into shallow water. The elliptical orbit is larger than the deep-water circular one, and this also causes an increase in the orbital velocity.

g Type of breakers

The increase of the orbital velocity is a significant factor in the breaking of the waves in shallow water. A wave will break when the increasing velocity of the water at the wave crest exceeds the decreasing velocity of the wave form. The water then overtakes the wave form, and the wave falls over and breaks.

Another factor affecting the breaking of waves is the decrease in volume of water within the wave form. As the particle orbits increase in size, the water in the wave is reduced by the decrease in wave length. There is thus insufficient water remaining to complete the orbit, causing the front of the wave to become unsupported. The crest therefore collapses into the trough and the wave breaks. Breaking will occur when the depth of water is about 4/3 of the wave height at break-point. A flat wave may break in water that is twice as deep as its deep-water height, owing to the increase in its height from deep water to the break-point.

There are two types of breakers, depending largely on the beach gradient and the wave steepness. These are plunging and spilling breakers. The former, in which the crest of the waves falls into the trough enclosing a pocket of air, normally occurs when a fairly low wave approaches a steep beach. This type of breaker is, therefore, common on steep shingle beaches. The form of the wave is lost in the process of breaking.

A spilling breaker, on the other hand, advances at the correct speed for the depth with a foaming crest. The wave does not loose its identity, but gradually decreases in height until it becomes swash on the beach. Such waves are often fairly steep in deep water and advance over a gently sloping, usually sandy beach. The waves produce several rows of breakers advancing shoreward simultaneously, and they are called surf waves. In all plunging breakers some part of the front face of the wave must be vertical as they break; this is not necessarily the case in spilling breakers. The two types of breakers can grade into each other.

h Breaking on structures

Whenever a wave approaches a beach it almost always breaks. This does not necessarily happen when a wave approaches a vertical cliff or sea-wall extending into relatively deep water. In this case the wave may be reflected without breaking, and an equal and opposite wave then travels seawards from the structure. It is rare, however, for the structure to be truly vertical and smooth, with a sufficient depth of water below it, to allow a perfect reflection; furthermore the waves must approach parallel to the shore.

Where a vertical barrier does descend into deep water, the reflected wave interacts with the primary wave to form a standing wave or deep-water clapotis, as shown in figure 4-4A. The wave crests do not advance under these conditions, but the wave troughs and crests rise and fall as shown in the diagram, with nodes occurring every half wave length. If the incoming wave is not parallel to the structure they will be reflected at an angle equal to their angle of incidence. A diagonal crest pattern will result. Such a pattern is only rarely seen well developed in nature, but can be generated in a model tank.

A more likely result when waves approach a sea-wall or cliff is the formation of a shallow-water clapotis, which occurs when the depth of water is not sufficient for a perfect reflection (figure 4-4B). The reflected wave is not now perfectly formed, owing to the loss of energy of the advancing wave over the relatively shallow bottom. The retreating wave, of smaller amplitude, can be seen passing through the advancing wave. In both deep and shallow water clapotis the pressures exerted on the cliff or wall are approximately equal to the hydrostatic pressure of the water.

When the water is still shallower the returning wave will not be formed, as the energy of the advancing wave will be destroyed by breaking. The wave breaking against the wall subjects it to the force of the moving particles, which will be approximately equal to the wave velocity at that point, but shock pressures will not result (figure 4-4C).

When, however, the water is sufficiently shallow to allow the breaking wave to trap a pocket of air between the wall and the water as it breaks, then shock pressures are likely to be set up

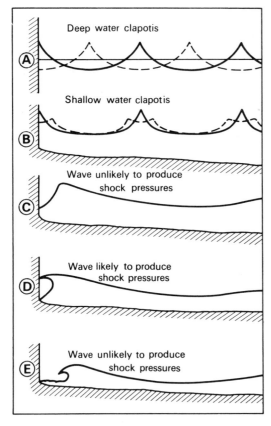

Figure 4-4 The effect of waves on vertical structures in relation to the depth of water. (*After Russell and Macmillan, 1952.*)

leading to damage of the structure or erosion of the cliff. High pressures are set up by the compression of the air as the wave breaks (figure 4-4D). This process is considered further in chapter 17-2.

If the water is so shallow that the wave breaks before it reaches the base of the wall, no shock pressures will be experienced and the wave form will be lost (figure 4-4E).

i Wave refraction

Refraction starts as soon as the wave begins to feel the bottom. It results from the change of wave length and velocity as the wave enters shallow water, in consequence of which the wave crest turns to approach more nearly parallel to the shore. The part of the wave in deeper water moves more rapidly than the part in shallower water, causing the crest to swing round parallel to the bottom contours. As the crests bend so the distribution of energy along them ceases to be uniform. The orthogonals indicate the amount of concentration or dispersion of energy. The energy concentrates on the headlands and is dissipated in the bays if the waves approach the coast at right-angles and the bottom contours are parallel to the coast as shown in figure 4-5. (The method of construction of wave-refraction diagrams has been described in section 2-3(b)(i).)

Some of the effects of wave refraction are worthy of comment. Fan-type refraction diagrams (such as figure 2-8) are useful in demonstrating from which direction wave energy may approach a sheltered site. They are constructed by drawing wave rays from the beach out into deeper water. The amount of energy increase and decrease can also be shown. Where the bottom relief is very steep (1/10), however, the results may not be accurate. Transference of energy along the wave crests, where they bend abruptly, may also cause some inaccuracy in the energy distribution shown by the orthogonals.

Wave refraction is intimately linked with the bottom relief and this can account for abnormal wave energy concentration, which will occur over a submarine ridge for instance. Over a submarine valley, on the other hand, wave energy will be spread out. This occurs, for example, near

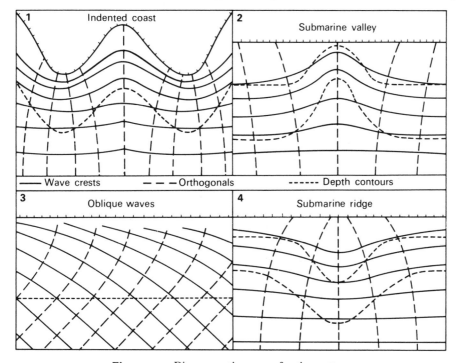

Figure 4-5 Diagrammatic wave refraction patterns.

La Jolla where a submarine canyon approaches the beach. Local shelter, used by fishermen, is caused by this process, whatever the weather.

The pattern of wave refraction is complicated by the fact that waves usually arrive in a spectrum, each element of which is refracted differently. If two waves of slightly different frequency are travelling in the same direction in deep water they will form a long-crested pattern. When they are refracted the pattern tends to become short-crested. Particularly complex patterns of refraction occur when long waves approach over an irregular bottom relief. Wave rays commonly cross in this situation, causing a caustic, where theoretically the wave energy becomes infinite. The interpretation of the effects of wave refraction is made difficult by this occurrence.

A method of dealing with complex refraction phenomena is discussed by J. R. Hardy (1964) in connection with studies at Blakeney Point in Norfolk. He constructed wave-refraction diagrams for swell waves coming south down the North Sea and found that nearly all the wave rays crossed in a very complex manner owing to the shoals and channels offshore. He calculated the distance apart of adjacent deep-water orthogonals when they arrived at the coast, and determined the incoming energy on this basis. The increments of energy at any stretch of coast were then added to give an indication of the total incoming energy at that point. The results are tentative owing to the complexity of offshore relief and the uncertainty of the physical results of crossing orthogonals. The areas of concentration of the constructive swells did, however, correspond to the area of greatest accretion on the beach for three wave directions and periods. Nevertheless conclusions drawn from studies of this type must be tentative until more accurate refraction diagrams can be constructed, which will be difficult owing to the complexity of bottom relief.

j   Wave diffraction

Wave diffraction takes place as energy is transferred along a wave crest in the lee of a breakwater or other obstruction. The transference of energy along the wave crest means that waves can affect the water in the lee of the structure, although their height is much reduced. The reduction in height can be calculated from theory, and depends on the nature of the barrier. The wave length and depth at the end of the barrier must be known. Diagrams have been prepared by the C.E.R.C. (1966) for waves approaching from different angles to the barrier. Wave heights are given in terms of the ratio to the incident wave height, and curves are drawn for equal value of K', the ratio of incident wave height to diffracted wave height. The diffraction through gaps of different widths relative to the wave length is also calculated theoretically and illustrated graphically. The amount of diffraction increases as the angle between wave crests and the barrier increases, resulting in rapidly decreasing wave heights for large angles.

I. E. Mobarek and R. L. Wiegel (1967) have studied a two-dimensional method of analysing wave diffraction behind breakwaters, based on the two-dimensional wave spectra. A laboratory study was used to test the theoretical results. The two-dimensional spectrum was treated as though the waves came from five directions at angles of 30° apart, and the calculations were repeated for each frequency band. The energy for each direction and frequency was found for selected sites in the lee of the breakwater, and the individual results summed to give the diffraction value at that site.

The results showed that the total amount of energy reaching the area in the lee of the breakwater by diffraction was the same for the laboratory tests as in the calculations. The peak energy was about the same, but it occurred at a lower frequency for the measured spectra than the theoretical ones. The evidence supports the assumption of linearity in the theory of diffraction.

2 Wave measurement and wave spectra

Perhaps the best method of recording waves in relatively shallow water is to use the shipborne wave recorder, which can conveniently be installed in lightships that are continuously on station, thus providing a long-term record.

Another instrument, developed by Dutch research laboratories, is the Waverider buoy. It is an accelerometer buoy, the records of which are transmitted by high-frequency radio for distances of up to 20 km. The data are punched onto tape at the receiving station and a pen record of continuous wave height is also given.

For wave observations close to the shore some type of pressure wave gauge, connected to the shore by cable, is probably most useful. Some of the disadvantages of these instruments, when they are placed more than 0·8 km offshore, resulting in long cable connections, have been overcome by the development of a pressure transducer fixed below the wave trough level. Such instruments do not give reliable results in areas of strong currents as they tend to become inclined at an angle.

A simpler mechanism is the flexible rubber bag held below the surface with the pressure recording device on shore and connected to the instrument by air line. The pressure changes are recorded by pen on a revolving drum. The instrument must not be more than 91 m from the shore recorder. Inverted echo-sounders sited on the sea bed can also be used, but they only operate effectively where the waves are long and local storms are rare, because during storm conditions the boundary between the sea and the air is ill defined.

Measurement of wave direction is not so easy, but can be achieved by an array of three or more wave recorders, which must be fixed about a wave length apart. Interpretation is complicated by the refraction of the waves. There are four instruments capable of measuring wave direction:

1   The T.C.B. wave gauge developed in California and capable of measuring waves of two to 25 seconds period and up to 7·6 m high in depths up to 15·2 m, adaptable to 30·5 m.

2   The C.E.R.C. ultrasonic wave direction recorder, which is mounted on a structure, such as a pier. Experiments with the instrument show it to be promising in giving information of wave direction.

3   The Veldi wave velocity meter, which is being developed at Delft Hydraulics Laboratory. This is only suitable for waves of periods greater than ten seconds. It measures water speed and direction of movement.

4   The electro-magnetic flowmeter, which is being developed at N.I.O. and Liverpool University. This measures the motion of water particles beneath the surface to give information concerning direction of waves. The instrument is fixed to a structure and its depth adjusted to give the required range of frequencies. Horizontal velocities in two directions are measured and the mean direction of wave approach and height can be obtained, the former by the ratio V/U and the latter by $(U^2 + V^2)^{1/2}$. Where a broad spectrum rather than a narrow beam is required the wave pressure fluctuations must also be measured, preferably with a digital system to ease computer analysis. Either a smoothed directional spectrum or the mean directions of the waves in each frequency band can be obtained (L. Draper, 1967a).

H. Walden (1963) has recorded a shallow-water wave spectrum from the German Bight and compared it with theoretical spectra. The spectrum was observed from the Mellum Plate lighthouse by means of a wave pole 85 m from the lighthouse in 10 to 15 m water. Water levels were recorded by cinematograph camera on the pole and by electrical methods, the former providing the means for calibrating the gauge. This provided a good wave record, which was used to test an accelerometer, floating about 15 m from the pole.

Fully developed seas, coming from the west-northwest to northeast, can be recorded at this site. One example, developed by a 9·5 to 10 knot wind, shows little agreement with theoretical wave spectra. The recorded spectral peak is at higher frequencies than the theoretical, whereas at the low-frequency end of the spectrum the recorded spectrum gives much lower values than the theoretical ones, which have a peak at the low end of the spectrum. This peak is probably over-emphasized in the theoretical spectra. The recorded spectrum also had a very much lower total energy than the theoretical ones, although it had the same general shape for a 15 to 16 knot wind. This result could be partly due to the narrowness of fetch, although its length was adequate for a fully developed sea. Much still remains to be done in perfecting the analysis of wave records to provide spectra and in relating these to theoretical spectra in shallow water.

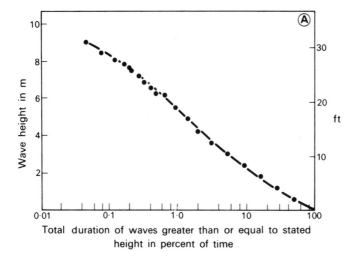

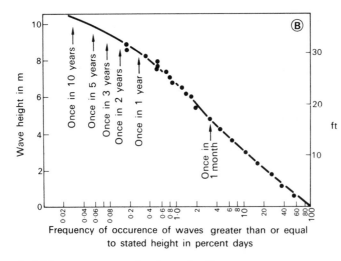

Figure 4-6 A: Wave rose to show percentage frequency of waves of different height coming from various directions off New York Harbour Entrance.

Figure 4-6 B: Frequency of occurrence of waves above a given height.

3 Wave records in shallow water

Wave records are now available for waves in the Irish Sea (M. Darbyshire, 1958) and the North Sea (M. Darbyshire, 1960). These observations were made with wave recorders fitted to light-ships. They show that waves in the shallow enclosed seas are generally much shorter in period and lower in height than those generated in the open ocean. The effect of depth on wave generation has already been noted, and some wave records at coastal sites were mentioned in chapter 3.

T. Saville (1954) has analysed the probable pattern of wave attack for four stations on the east coast of the U.S.A. in the percentage time that waves of different height come from different directions. His results are based on Bretschneider's curves for deep-water wave generation and have been modified by the use of refraction equations to obtain the shallow-water wave pattern. The refraction diagrams were complicated by the Hudson Canyon, which caused the orthogonals to cross in a complex pattern. To check the accuracy of the data wave recorder, observations were

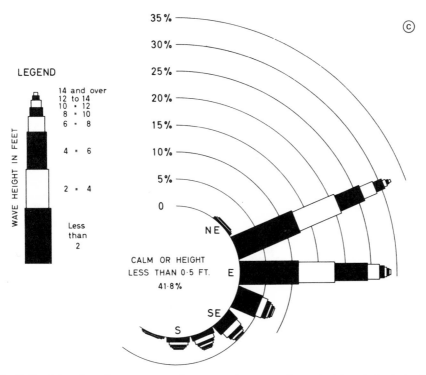

Figure 4-6 C: Total duration of waves greater than or equal to a stated wave height. (*A, B, C after Saville, 1954.*)

made in a depth of 6·1 m for the period from April 1948 until October 1949. The computed and observed waves agreed well for heights up to about 1·52 m but for higher waves the disagreement increased considerably. This was thought to be due to the method used for refraction analysis, which tended to over-emphasize the convergence of waves coming from due east, one of the assumed directions. Waves coming from only 5° to either side would be considerably less refracted. The danger of generalizing the direction of attack to 16 points of the compass is illustrated. A great improvement between the observed and computed data was obtained by splitting all the waves in each segment arbitrarily into three groups and assigning each part its appropriate refraction value.

T. Saville (1954) has calculated the total number of occasions on which waves of a certain height and period group will come from each direction in the form of diagrams, one of which is shown in figure 4-6. They are based on statistical analysis, which gives the expected frequency of specified wave heights. Thus at one station near Cape Cod 6·1 m waves may be expected on 2% of the days; 3·05 m waves will probably occur on 16% of the days; but a 11·0 m wave will only be expected once every three years.

A useful summary of the available wave records at coastal sites in the U.S.A. has been given by J. M. Darling and D. G. Dumm (1967). The instruments are of the surface and submerged types and the records are analysed to give significant wave height and period for a seven minute run each four hours. A spectrum is analysed for a 20 minute run each day, but the duration will increase as the analysing methods improve. Fourteen stations are available on the Atlantic coast, four on the Gulf of Mexico coast and five on the Pacific coast. In addition there are 27 visual observing stations at coastguard stations. They record details of the surf characteristics, which are

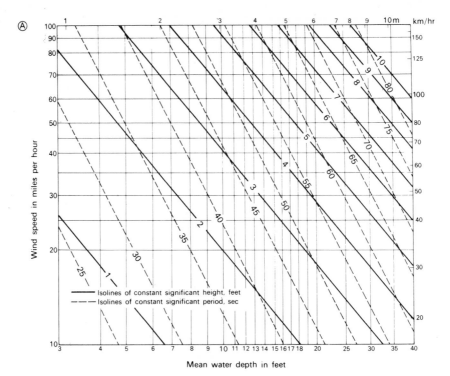

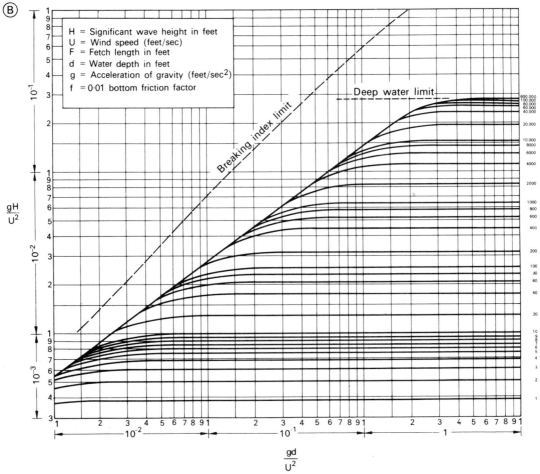

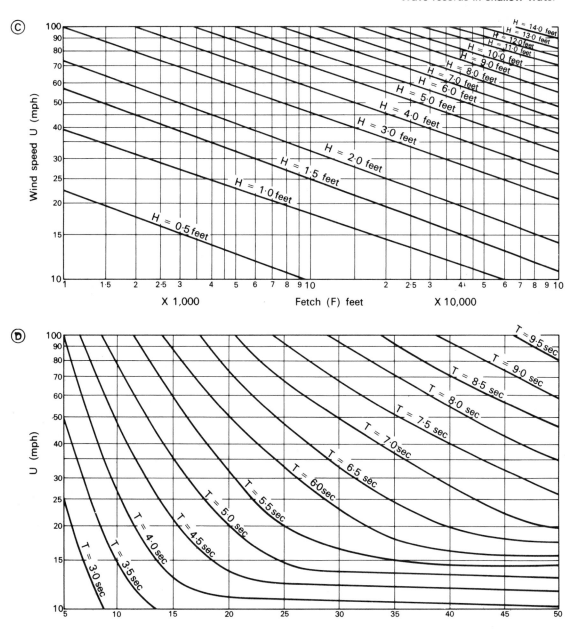

Figure 4-7 **A:** Wave forecasting relationships for shallow water of constant depth. **B:** Generation of wind waves over a bottom of constant depth for unlimited wind duration : presented as dimensionless parameters. **C:** Forecasting curves for shallow-water waves in a constant depth of 50 feet (15·2 m). **D:** Forecasting curves for significant wave periods for constant water depth. (*A, B, C, D after Bretschneider, in Coastal Engineering Research Center, 1966.*)

important for beach studies. These data are given in the form of number of observations and percentages of heights for each breaker period band, and also in terms of direction of approach for both breaker heights and wave periods.

L. Draper (1967) has recorded waves at Skondi in Ghana from June to October 1958, covering the rough time of the year. The significant wave height was found to exceed 1 m for 70% of the time, but only exceeded 1·22 m for 20% of the time. The most common situation was a significant height of just over 1 m and period of 10 to 11 seconds. Waves rarely exceeded 3 m. The waves had a low steepness value, characteristic of the swell environment.

4 Wave forecasting in shallow water

The generation of waves in shallow water is less efficient than in deep water, as shown by C. L. Bretschneider (1965). This is partly due to the dissipation of wave energy by bottom friction, but to provide an estimate of waves generated in shallow water, this factor must be combined with the deep-water forecasting curves. The best agreement between wave data and the numerical calculations was found when the friction factor was $f = 0·01$. A new set of curves can be derived in this way for waves generated over a specified water depth with unlimited fetch and wind duration. Limitations of fetch and wind duration can be allowed for. The curves in figure 4-7 take the effects of friction and permeability of the sea bottom into account. The accuracy of the curves will be improved as more data on the friction factor and more records for the conditions specified for the curves become available. Allowance must be made for the change of wave speed and length in shallow water. Changes in wave height only become considerable for the longer fetches and higher wind speeds (above 80 km/hour) for depths between 1·52 m and 15·2 m. The curves provide good agreement between wave spectra for Atlantic City, New Jersey and the shallow-water hindcast wave spectrum, which contains much less energy than the deep-water hindcast spectrum.

In considering the problems of forecasting waves near the break-point, B. J. Mehauté and R. C. Y. Koh (1966) suggest that the most convenient method is based on the principle of conservation of energy flux between wave orthogonals. This method provides a good approximation for very gentle slopes. Partial reflections occur where there are abrupt changes in depth, which complicate the analysis. Bottom friction must also be considered as it is not negligible. There may be transference of energy across orthogonals where the relief is complex, owing to variations of wave height along the wave crests. Recent development in wave theory now allows higher-order approximations to be applied to the problem.

Calculations of breaking-wave characteristics are based on several different breaking criteria by Mehauté and Koh. The first was proposed by R. Miche in 1944 for waves on a horizontal bottom, the second is based on experiments with a horizontal bottom, and the third takes a sloping bottom into account. The calculations allow for the waves to arrive at an angle and assume conservation of energy flux. Third- and fifth-order approximations have been calculated.

The results of the calculations are given in graphs in which α_0 and α_b are plotted on the x and y axes and values of d_b/L_b and $2\pi H_0/gT^2$ or H_0/L_0 are given. Some of these graphs are shown in figure 4-8. The graphs may be used in conjunction with suitable tables to determine values of α_b, d_b, L_b and H_b, when values of T, H_0, α_0 and the beach slope are known. α refers to the angle of wave approach (the angle between the wave crest and the shore). If the first-, third- and fifth-orders of approximation are compared, the results show in general that the higher the order of approximation, the longer and higher the theoretical waves will be at their break-point and the

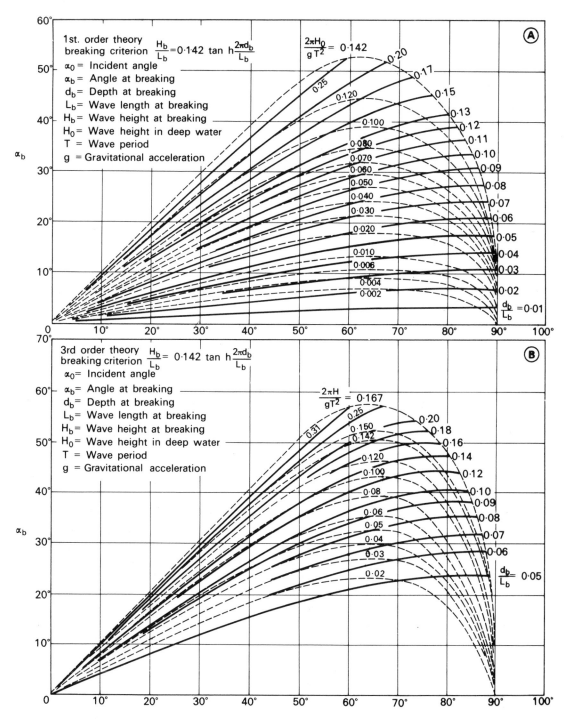

Figure 4-8 Breaking wave characteristics as a function of incident wave characteristics. First (**A**) and third (**B**) order theory are shown. (*A, B after Mehauté and Koh, 1966.*)

greater the breaking depth will be. Nonlinear effects on breaking characteristics are not negligible because wave length, which appears in Snell's law, is strongly affected. The highest-order approximation is not necessarily the best, as for example in two-dimensional wave shoaling. Experiments using varying wave steepnesses show that the effect of beach slope is more important with low wave steepness.

The relationship for angle of approach and deep-water wave steepness approximates to

$$\alpha_b/\alpha_0 = 0.25 + 5.5 H_0/L_0 \quad \text{for } 0 < \alpha_0 < 50°$$

for the linear theory and the Miche breaking criterion. The effect of slope is seen in the modified relationships

$$\alpha_b/\alpha_0 = 0.23 + 5.2 H_0/L_0 \quad \text{for } 20° < \alpha_0 < 40°$$

on a 1 in 10 slope, and

$$\alpha_b/\alpha_0 = 0.06 + 7.5 H_0/L_0 \quad \text{for } 20° < \alpha_0 < 40°$$

on a 1 in 20 slope. The Miche criterion becomes better as the slope decreases, as expected. The nonlinear effects are more important for larger initial wave steepness.

These results are significant for littoral drift currents. The maximum angle of the breaking wave occurs when the deep-water wave angle is 45°, whatever the deep-water wave steepness. This angle will also produce the maximum longshore current.

5 Water movement and mass transport in shallow water

a Mass transport

When the movement of material by waves is considered the character of the mass transport in shallow water is very important, as it affects the movement of material. The theoretical side of this problem has been discussed by M. S. Longuet-Higgins (1953), while experimental data on this topic have been discussed by R. A. Bagnold (1947) and R. C. H. Russell and J. D. C. Osorio (1958). In water where d/L is $\frac{1}{2}\pi$, according to the classical wave theory of G. G. Stokes (1847), there is a steady increase of landward velocity from nil at the bottom to a maximum at the surface. In shallow water this theoretical pattern has not been observed: Bagnold, for example, found in a model tank experiment that the reverse flow in fact occurred, and that there was a strong forward movement on the bottom, with a slower seaward drift in the upper part of the tank. The dividing line between the landward and seaward flow varied between 0.2 and 0.35 d (depth), while the backward movement was about 1/5 of the landward thrust along the bottom. A. F. H. Caligny (1878) also found both forward movement on the bottom and a surface movement in the direction of wave propagation.

Experiments carried out by the Author in the wave tank at Cambridge showed the same pattern of water movement as found by Caligny. The experiments were made with dye, which was dropped into the water at a depth of 12 cm forming a thin streak. Its movement after the passage of 10 waves was recorded. In nearly all runs the same pattern was observed. The bottom water moved rapidly forward, the central water moved seaward a smaller distance, and the surface water moved landwards. This pattern is shown in figure 4-9. The amount of seaward movement in the central layers appeared to depend on the deep-water wave height, increasing with increasing wave height in a constant depth, although there was a considerable scatter of the data.

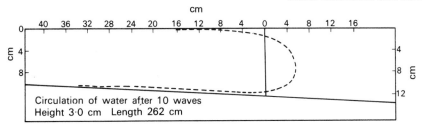

Figure 4-9 Water movement in a model tank to show forward thrust on the bottom and surface with seaward flow in the centre.

At a depth of 40 cm with a short wave of 77 cm length, which would therefore be in deep water, it was found that there was no landward movement on the bottom. The landward movement increased rapidly, however, as the depth decreased (figure 4-10). In the deep water there was still a landward movement on the surface. The observations agreed with the theoretical concept of the classical wave theory for deep water.

The forward thrust on the bottom was found to be dependent on the character of the bottom. It only occurred when the bottom was of smooth sand. As soon as the bed became rough with ripples the forward thrust was no longer observed. The presence of ripples greatly increased the turbulence of the water and prevented the forward movement of the dye. The same result was

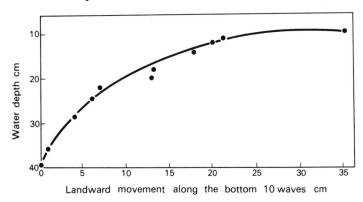

Figure 4-10 Graph relating landward movement of water on the bottom to water depth.

also recorded by Bagnold (1947). He noted that when the dyed tongue of water approached close to the break-point the tongue moved vertically upwards and became dispersed by turbulence. Near the surface the dyed water started to drift away from the beach. Dye dropped into the water in front of the break-point became dispersed in front of it, but did not move seaward of the break-point. This double circulation system agrees with observations in nature.

One point concerning the laboratory results of mass transport studies is worthy of note. Bagnold (1963) suggests that when the width of the experimental beach is such that narrow channel constraints no longer apply, the wave drift shows signs of instability. This state occurs when the channel width exceeds a certain multiple of the water depth. The mass transport becomes greater on one side of the channel than the other. In still wider channels and on the open beach the wave currents may break up into circulations in a plane parallel with the bed. Under these conditions a random scattering of sediment would tend to be superimposed on a smaller landward drift. This movement could account for the circulatory motion of the swash on a sand beach.

The theory developed by Longuet-Higgins (1953) accounts for the forward velocity on the bottom by considering the boundary effects and the viscosity of the water. This leads to markedly different results from those derived from the classical theory. The velocities observed by Bagnold agree well with the value predicted by Longuet-Higgins's theory, which is further confirmed by experimental work by Russell and Osorio (1958).

M. S. Longuet-Higgins and R. W. Stewart (1962) have analysed certain situations from the point of view of their effect on mass transport and variations in mean sea level. Their first analysis deals with wave groups in uniform water depth. The second-order currents are found to be proportional to the square of the local wave amplitude when, firstly, the lengths of the groups of waves are large compared with the mean depth, and secondly, when the groups are all of equal length. In these conditions the surface is depressed under the group of high waves and the mass transport will be negative. This is because the radiative stress under the high groups of waves tends to expel water from the area.

In the second analysis the waves are considered to be of steady amplitude, but the water of varying depth. The waves must change in amplitude to maintain the energy flux in a horizontal direction. This produces a negative tilt in the mean surface level as the depth diminishes. Where the wave height is limited by breaking the tilt becomes positive. The results agree with Fairchild's observations. The magnitude of the changes in level are similar to those caused by wind stress on the surface.

b   Water velocity in shallow water and breakers

The mass transport discussed in the last section indicates the net drift direction of the water at different depths. The actual velocities of the water at different points are also important in the movement of material. D. L. Inman and N. Nasu (1956) found that the particle velocities agreed fairly closely with the theoretical values for the solitary wave theory, which applies to waves in very shallow water. In this theory each solitary wave is said to be independent of its neighbours and consists only of a crest. The velocity is dependent on the depth of water below the trough, d, and the wave height, H, and is given by $C = \sqrt{g(H + d)}$. Each crest is separated from its neighbour by flat water in which the particles are at rest. The water particles under the wave crest move in the direction of wave propagation. The theoretical maximum bottom velocity is shown in figure 4-11, which relates the bottom velocity to the depth for various wave heights. According to the theory the particles are virtually at rest at a horizontal distance of 10 d from the wave crest. As the wave crest approaches, the particles move up and forward; as the crest passes they slow down and move downwards to a new position of rest. It is probable that a slow uniform return velocity is superimposed on the landward velocity. The return flow would slightly reduce the landward velocity under the wave crest and produce a seaward velocity under the trough.

In order to test the theoretical velocities Inman and Nasu (1956) measured orbital velocities from the Scripps Institute pier and made instrumental and visual observations of the wave characteristics (see figure 4-11). The orbital velocities were measured with a current meter set at 0·82 feet (25 cm) above the bottom, which consisted of well-sorted sand of median diameter 0·18 mm, with a gradient of 1 in 35. The meter was designed to record both vertical and horizontal velocities at the point selected. It was placed just seaward of the breaker zone, in water varying in depth from 1·52 to 4·6 m.

Many sources of error have to be considered. The horizontality of the meter and its direction relative to the wave approach are important and particularly affect the relatively low vertical velocities. Another difficulty is the acceleration of the currents between the trough and crest, and to overcome this difficulty Inman and Nasu considered only the maximum trough and crest

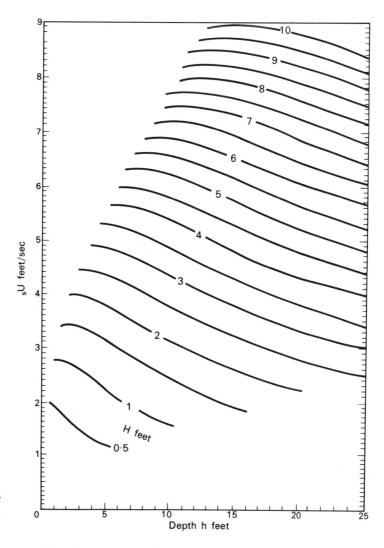

Figure 4-11 Relation between bottom velocity and depth of water for various wave heights. (*After Inman and Nasu, 1956.*)

velocities. A wave meter was mounted on the same tripod as the current meter and was calibrated by reference to visual observations on a graduated staff placed near the orbital velocity meter tripod.

Each wave had to be treated individually in relating the observed to the theoretical group velocity. For each series of waves the wave profile, obtained from the pressure gauge, and the orbital velocities were plotted together, as shown in figure 4-12. The graphs relating the orbital velocity to the wave profile show that the velocity is greatest not at the highest point, but where the wave form is changing most rapidly. Where the waves become asymmetrical near the break-point, the orbital velocities are also asymmetrical. The flow was always onshore under the wave crest, where velocities were nearly always greater than the seaward velocity under the wave trough.

The results have been compared with the theoretical velocities obtained from the solitary wave theory and from the Airy–Stokes shallow-water progressive wave theory by plotting the observed orbital velocities against the wave height for different depths. The curves of the theoretical values were added for comparison. Because the period affects the orbital velocity in the Stokes's theory the theoretical curves were drawn for three different periods. The relation between the observed and theoretical velocities show a considerable scatter on all the graphs, but particularly for the lower wave heights. The scatter may be due in part to the decreasing sensitivity of the meter at low velocities and the consequently greater possible error of observation. In general the observed points agree more closely with the solitary wave theory, especially for waves of period over six seconds, because the shorter-period waves tended to be associated with lower orbital velocities. The agreement is best for waves with relatively simple profiles. The increase in particle velocity

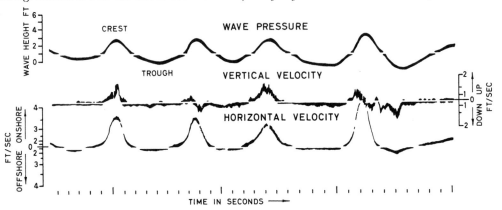

Figure 4-12 Profile of a wave off Scripps Pier with related orbital velocities in horizontal and vertical directions. (*After Inman and Nasu, 1956.*)

was almost linear with increasing wave height. Speeds of between 1·83 to 2·13 m/sec are recorded for waves of 1·52 m height in depths of 2·14 to 2·44 m.

The study of orbital velocity just described was carried out just seaward of the break-point. Owing to the difficulty of observations it has not been possible to obtain reliable full-scale data for the breaker area. Observations in a model tank have been made by H. W. Iverson (1952). Here the aim was to establish relationships between the breaker characteristics, the wave dimensions and the beach slope. The model tank had a smooth bottom slope varying in angle from 1 in 10 to 1 in 50. The breakers were studied by introducing recognizable particles of the same specific gravity as the water and by filming the wave. The results gave the particle velocities and the change in form of the breaking wave. The generated waves were not true deep-water waves, but their deep-water steepness could be calculated. Figure 4-13 shows the relationship between the wave steepness, and the breaker index—the ratio of breaker height to deep-water height, H_b/H_0—for two different versions of the deep-water wave height, one being derived from the laboratory data and the other from the theoretical relation between deep-water and breaker-wave height. Both graphs, however, show the effect of beach slope on the breaker index—on the whole the steeper the slope the greater the index, the latter being about 40% higher on a 1 in 10 slope than one of 1 in 50. Slope also affected the form of the breaker: as the slope became steeper the breaker was steeper in front and flatter behind and had a greater tendency to plunge.

The velocities, determined from the photographs, included backwash and crest velocities. The former were obtained by averaging all velocities in the region of the minimum depth. With high backwash velocities there was a tendency to produce plunging breakers. With high steepness values the breakers tended to spill, but with very low values they tended to surge, particularly

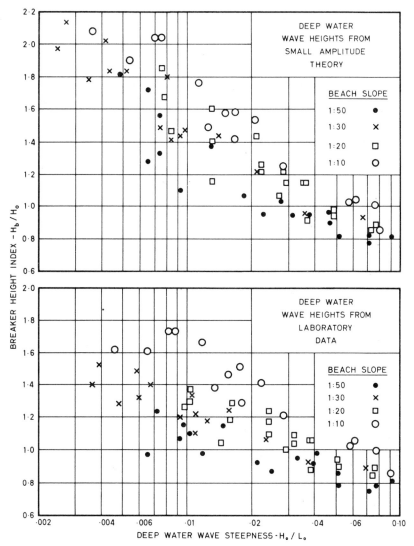

Figure 4-13 Relationship between breaker height and deep water wave height and wave steepness and beach slope in model experiments. (*After Iverson, 1952.*)

on the steeper slopes. The pattern of velocity actually measured in a breaking wave is shown in figure 4-14. The form of the breaker is shown: as the two extreme beach slopes are represented, this can be evaluated, the steeper slope of the wave being associated with the steeper beach. Values for different wave steepnesses are shown. The velocity is given in the form $\dfrac{\text{velocity}}{\text{g crest elevation}}$. As would be expected the maximum velocity is found near the crest of the wave.

Wave velocities reach their maximum values in the turbulent zone of breaking, but the velocity may also be appreciable at considerable depths under storm-generated waves. M. L. Hadley (1964) has considered the velocity of wave-induced bottom currents in the Celtic Sea. According to the generating curves prepared by Darbyshire, the waves analysed were those generated by a

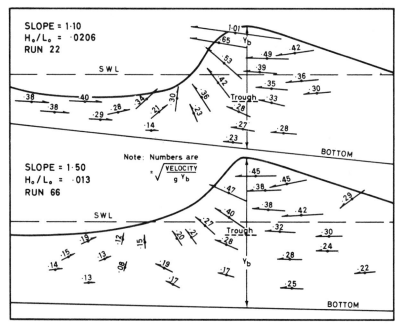

Figure 4-14 Direction and speed of movement in a breaking wave on flat and steep slopes. (*After Iverson, 1952.*)

force 10 gale. The estimate of the wave energy may be 20% in error. Other possible errors in the functions relating the mean square bottom velocity, $\sqrt{\bar{v}_b{}^2}$, to v_{50}, may give a value 10% too large at 10 fathoms and 6% at 20 fathoms. Other errors are probably less than 2%. The values in terms of v_{50}, the velocity for the largest wave in a set of 50, for different depth are given in table 4-1. The relationship between v_{50} and v_b is given by $v_{50} = 3 \cdot 2 \sqrt{\bar{v}_b{}^2}$. The increase for v_{100} is

Table 4-1 Depths and bottom velocities of wave-induced currents

Depth		v_{50}		Depth		v_{50}	
fathoms	m	knots	cm/sec	fathoms	m	knots	cm/sec
10	18·3	8·7	450	60	109·6	2·0	103
20	36·6	5·5	284	70	128·0	1·6	82
30	54·8	4·0	206	80	146·4	1·4	72
40	73·2	3·2	165	90	164·6	1·2	62
50	91·5	2·3	118	100	183·0	1·0	51

7%, for v_{500} 20% and for $v_{50,000}$ 50%. These wave-induced currents are oscillatory, but could assist tidal currents to move material. Storms capable of generating these velocities are rare, only occurring for about one or two weeks in the year, but the results do indicate that waves cause currents throughout the continental shelf under extreme conditions.

L. Draper (1967c) has given further information on this matter. He shows that the most severe conditions occur on the edge of the continental shelf in depths of 90 to 120 m where the wave energy has not been reduced by contact with the bed, a process which takes more energy out of

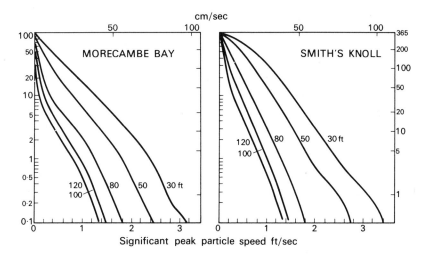

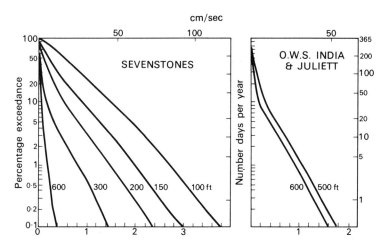

Figure 4-15 Comparison of wave peak particle speeds at different depths and in different positions. The percentage exceedance of specified peak particle speeds is shown. (*After Draper, 1967c.*)

the waves than the wind puts into them in shallower water. The results are presented in terms of the relationship between the peak particle speeds plotted against the percentage exceedance time for Morecambe Bay, Smith's Knoll, Sevenstones and the O.W.S. stations *India* and *Juliet* in the open Atlantic. Some of the results are shown in figure 4-15.

6 Longshore wave-induced currents

a Theory

One of the more important aspects of wave action in shallow water is the generation of longshore currents, because these play an important part in the longshore movement of material, which is fundamental to the formation of many coastal features.

Longshore currents can be generated by winds blowing along the coast at an angle. Water movements of this type are also related to the generation of storm surges on open coasts. The generation of longshore currents is based on the assumption that net transport shoreward is insignificant compared to longshore transport and becomes zero under steady state conditions. C. L. Bretschneider (1966) considers four cases according to the angle between the wind direction and the coast. In the first the wind is blowing onshore at an angle less than 90° with the coast to the right. In the second the wind is blowing offshore with the coast to the right. In the third the wind is blowing offshore with the coast to the left. In the fourth the wind is blowing onshore with the coast to the left. The current induced by the wind is divided into two components, one parallel to the coast and the other perpendicular to it. In all cases the flow parallel to the coast increases from zero at the bottom to a maximum in the direction of the wind at the surface. The perpendicular element is directed towards the coast with the onshore component of the wind

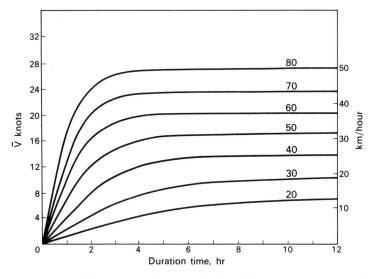

Figure 4-16 Generation of longshore wind currents for 18·3 m (60 feet) water depth. The lines refer to the wind speed in knots parallel to the coast. (*After Bretschneider, 1966.*)

at the top of the water column, and the offshore in the lower, deeper portion, reducing to zero at the bottom. The reverse pattern applies to offshore winds.

The first case will generate the highest water levels in the northern hemisphere owing to the Coriolis effect. The velocity of the longshore current for different wind speeds and durations for a depth of 18·3 m is shown in figure 4-16. For a wind of 60 knots, the current increases as the depth increases for duration times in excess of six hours, but decreases with depth for durations less than two and a half hours. The steady state condition is set up in a few hours, but it takes several days to decay. This applies to both current velocity and the level of the sea, suggesting that the bottom friction factor is greater during generation than during decay. The current velocities are 25 to 50% greater for winds blowing at an angle to the coast than for winds blowing perpendicular to the coast. The bottom friction during generation of the currents lies between 0·006 and 0·01.

J. A. Putnam, W. H. Munk and M. A. Traylor (1949) have considered the generation of longshore currents induced by waves from two different points of view, firstly, the energy approach and, secondly, the momentum approach. If a specific volume of water landwards of the breakpoint of the waves is considered, as shown in figure 4-17, the total energy entering this volume over a width of beach, dx, equals CE cos α dx, where C is the wave velocity, E the mean energy

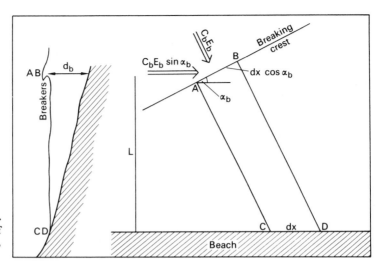

Figure 4-17 Diagram to illustrate the theoretical analysis of longshore currents. (*After Putnam, Munk and Traylor, 1949.*)

per unit surface area of the breaking waves, and α the angle between the wave crests at the break-point and the shore. Only a small part of this energy is actually used to generate longshore currents. Much of it is lost in the breaking of the wave and in other ways. Energy is also lost by frictional resistance of the bottom. The frictional force per unit width of beach is given by $k\varrho v^2 l^1 \, dx$, and the rate at which energy is lost in the volume ABCDE equals $k\varrho v^3 l^1 \, dx$, where k is a friction parameter V is the velocity of the longshore current and l^1 is the distance along the sea bed to the break-point. l^1 can be taken as l, and $d_b/l = \beta$, where β is the beach slope. If a steady state is assumed the energy entering the area must equal the loss by friction so that

$$s_t CE \cos \alpha \sin \alpha \, dx = \frac{k\varrho V^3 \, dx \, d_b}{\beta}$$

Equations derived from the solitary wave theory can be used to give V in terms of the wave height, period, angle of approach and beach slope as follows:

$$V = K\left[\left(\frac{\beta H_b^2}{T}\right) \sin 2\alpha\right]^{1/3}$$

where K^3 is $0.871g(S_t/k)$; S_t is the sand surface texture, and k is a function of the hydraulic roughness of the beach. The equations apply to a steady state current in an area where there is no interruption of the current from obstructions on the beach. Observations have shown that the steady state is achieved remarkably quickly. Five minutes is sufficient for the current to reach a steady state after a train of waves starts to break on the beach. The current will reach its full value only 200 m from an obstruction such as a breakwater.

The momentum approach considers the momentum given to a volume of water put into motion in the direction of wave propagation when the wave breaks. A component of this movement is directed alongshore and this provides the energy of the longshore current. In figure 4-17, the cross-sectional area of the breaking wave crest is Q; C and L are its velocity and length respectively; α its angle to the shore, and ϱ the density of the water. The average momentum per unit surface area is $\rho QC/L$. The component of momentum flux parallel to the shore equals

$$C \sin \alpha (\rho QC/L) \cos \alpha \, dx.$$

The velocity of the current, V, can be given by

$$V = \frac{a}{2}\left[\sqrt{1 + 4C \sin\left(\frac{\alpha}{a}\right)} - 1\right]$$

When the balance of the frictional drag along the bottom is considered

$$C = (2 \cdot 88 g H_b)^{1/2}$$

and

$$a = \frac{2 \cdot 61 \beta H \cos \alpha}{kT}$$

k is given by

$$k = \frac{(2 \cdot 61 \beta H \cos \alpha)(C \sin \alpha - V)}{TV^2}$$

V may now be found in the same terms as before. The same limitations apply however, and the results are only true for a straight beach of uniform bottom slope. k was found by the substitution of observed data in the equation above, for the different types of beach tested. The values of k, K and S_t are given in table 4-2. S_t is the sand surface texture, which was found to be comparable for natural and laboratory sand, although k was very different in each case.

Table 4-2   Values of k, K and S_t

Beach	k	K	S_t	
Field	0·0078	8·2	0·15	
Laboratory 1	0·0397	5·12	0·19	Natural sand cement bonded
Laboratory 2	0·0070	11·02	0·33	Sheet metal, smooth concrete
Laboratory 3	0·385	....	....	¼ inch pea-gravel

The theoretical approach to the study of longshore currents aims to predict their velocity. Most of the methods are semi-empirical being based in part on the results of laboratory and field studies. D. L. Inman and R. A. Bagnold (1963) show that the relations provided by Putnam, Munk and Traylor (1949) give values of k—the drag coefficient or friction parameter—that varied in the field by a factor 10^4. The variations shown in these results may be due to the presence of rip currents, which were poorly developed in the laboratory conditions, but which were important in the field. A steady state is also less liable to be set up in the field, where much energy is consumed to create accelerations, owing to the pulsating nature of the currents.

Inman and Bagnold (1963) introduce a theoretical approach, taking continuity into consideration. They give a relationship

$$\bar{U}_1 = \frac{q l_1}{d_b{}^2} \tan \beta \sin \alpha \cos \alpha$$

where $\bar{U}_1$ is the mean longshore current velocity; q is the gross incoming wave discharge in unit time per unit length of wave crest entering the surf zone at angle α; l_1 is the separation between rip currents; β is the beach slope, and d_b is the depth at the break-point. The power needed to accelerate the surf to the velocity $\bar{U}_1$ and to overcome bed drag and internal resistance to flow comes from the longshore component of the flux of wave momentum. At a distance l_1 from a previous rip the acceleration would cease and the longshore discharge break outwards to form a

116

new rip current. The longshore current must next be evaluated in terms of the wave characteristics, and the relationship

$$V = 4\sqrt{\frac{\gamma l_1}{3T}} \tan \beta \sin \alpha \cos \alpha$$

is given, where γ is H/d, T the wave period, H the wave height and d the water depth.

C. J. Galvin (1967) points out that 12 different equations have been proposed to give longshore current velocities. These equations divide into three classes. The first based mainly on the conservation of energy of momentum, includes Putnam *et al.*'s (1949) and P. S. Eagleson's (1965). The second set, based on the conservation of mass, includes that of Inman and Bagnold (1963) just discussed, and the third, obtained by empirical correlation of data, includes those of Brebner and Kamphuis (1963) and Harrison and Krumbein (1964).

Galvin points out an objection to the conservation of momentum equations, by showing that the longshore component of the breaker velocity, which is assumed to drive the current, must exceed the current velocity, with which it is equated in the theory. In fact the longshore current velocity must have a component in addition to the longshore component of breaker velocity.

P. S. Eagleson (1965) has developed a model for longshore current velocity in which V, the longshore current velocity, is the only unknown. His equations are:

$$\frac{V^2(x)}{A} = 1 - \left[1 - \frac{V^2(O)}{A}\right]e^{-Bx}$$

$$A = \frac{3}{8}\frac{gH_b^2 n_b}{d_b f}\beta \sin \alpha_b \cos 2\alpha_b$$

$$B = \frac{2}{5}\left(\frac{f}{\beta d_b \sin \alpha_b}\right)$$

where β is beach slope, α is angle of wave crest to shore, and f is a constant. The predictions made with this model do not, however, agree with available data, in that the steady state is not always approached faster for lower values of α_b as theory demands.

P. Bruun's equation, based on the conservation of mass gives the relationship

$$V = f\left[H_b^{3/2}\beta\left(\frac{\sin 2\alpha_b}{T}\right)\right]^{1/2}$$

where f is a constant equal to 0·25 in the laboratory and 0·13 in the field. This theory is based on the presence of rip currents, in the same way as Inman and Bagnold's. The equations are difficult to test since some of the values required are not available. It appears, however, that Bruun's results would be too high but that Inman and Bagnold's would be reasonable. Another equation in this category given by Galvin and Eagleson (1965) is

$$V = Kg\beta T \sin 2\alpha_b$$

where $K = (1 + B - \sigma)/2a^2$. K can range between 0·6 and 1·1 according to the choice of B and a, and can be considered to be unity, thus simplifying the relationship.

W. Harrison (1968) has suggested an empirical relationship for longshore current velocity, based on 98 observations of velocity, $\bar{V}$, beach slope, $\bar{\beta}$, breaker height, $\bar{H}_b$, wave period, $\bar{T}_b$, wave angle, $\bar{\alpha}_b$, wave crest length and trough depth made on an Atlantic coast beach of the U.S.A. There was an offshore (submarine) bar parallel to the shoreline for two-thirds of the study. The analysis is based on linear multiple regression. The results differed significantly from those of W. Harrison *et al.* (1965), which were based on deep-water data, the more recent values being for mean breaker characteristics. The variables give the following values for R^2, the coefficient of determination: $\bar{\alpha}_b$ 0·46; $\bar{\alpha}_b$ and $\bar{T}_b$ 0·53; $\bar{\alpha}_b$, $\bar{T}_b$ and $\bar{H}_{bs}$ 0·55; $\bar{\alpha}_b$, $\bar{T}_b$, $\bar{H}_{bs}$ and $\bar{\beta}$ 0·57. These results show that angle of approach is the most important variable, followed by the wave period and the wave height. The predictive equation is given as:

$$V = -0\cdot170455 + 0\cdot037376\bar{\alpha}_b + 0\cdot031801\bar{T}_b + 0\cdot241176\bar{H}_{bs} + 0\cdot030923\bar{\beta}$$

The plot of the points is shown in figure 4-18. The equation is similar to that given by C. J. Sonu *et al.* (1967) apart from the effect of wave period, which has a different sign. In view of the unreliability of theoretical prediction equations, the empirical approach by multiple linear regression provides a useful alternative, as it is based on field observations. It can, however, apply strictly only to the conditions occurring in the area investigated.

One of the difficulties in the theoretical evaluation of longshore currents is the need to make many assumptions concerning the variables, hence simplifying reality very drastically. Descriptions of breaker types are also difficult to quantify. Variation in the nearshore relief is important, while rip currents, ignored in some theories and incorporated into others, further complicate the problem: they are themselves in part dependent on the longshore currents. The theories based on momentum flux appear unreliable owing to the small amount of total flux that goes into the longshore current. The approximations necessary in the mass flux theories are extreme and detract from them. Perhaps the best method at present is to develop suitable empirical relations but these can only be as good as the data on which they are based. Good experimental and field data are essential to an improvement in the accuracy of longshore current prediction.

b   Model experiments

T. Saville (1950) has conducted some experiments into the movement of sand along the shore in a model tank 20 m by 37 m. Part of the work was devoted to a study of longshore currents, the observed velocities of which were compared to the theoretical velocity as determined by the theory of Putnam, Munk and Traylor. The waves approached at an angle of 10° in deep water, breaking on a beach with an initial gradient of 1 in 10. The velocity of the longshore current was obtained by timing the movement of dye over a 3·05 m length parallel to the beach. It ranged between 2 and nearly 12·2 cm/sec, and showed an increase of strength as the waves became steeper. This can be explained partly by the refraction of the longer, less steep waves, which approached the beach at a smaller angle. The current was reduced by an increase of wave length, but increased as the wave height increased. The highest waves were also the steepest, which accounts for the positive correlation of both these variables with the longshore current velocity.

In order to compare the observed and predicted current, the friction factor, k, must be known. This was determined from the observed velocities and found to be k = 0·0135. The graph showing the relationship between the theoretical momentum approach and the observed velocities indicates a good agreement between the two values. They are mostly within 10% of each other until the steepness value becomes very low.

The maximum current velocity was always along the break-point bar in the tank. There was a very rapid reduction in speed seaward of the bar, while landward of it the current also slackened, but less rapidly, the velocity remaining fairly uniform over a considerable distance.

C. J. Galvin and P. S. Eagleson (1965) have reported model experimental studies of the characteristics of breaking waves and the longshore currents to which they give rise, for 34 combinations of wave height, period and breaker angle, in waves breaking on a smooth concrete beach with a

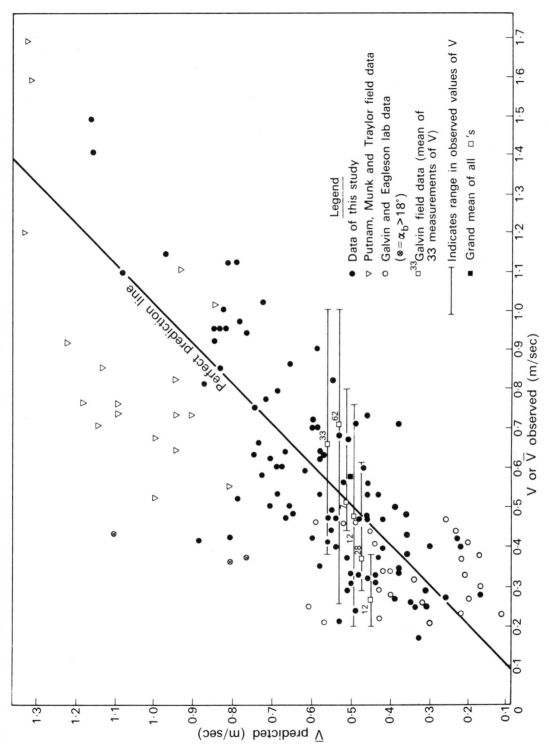

Figure 4·18 The relationship between observed and predicted longshore current velocity. (*After Harrison, 1966.*)

slope of 1 in 10 (0·104) and a 6 m test section. The results showed that most of the water in the surf zone remains there and that the longshore current increases downstream form an obstacle. The energy that maintained the longshore current was less than 1/10 of the energy brought into the shoaling zone by the waves. The variables observed in the wave tank included wave height, speed, and form, breaker position, angle and runup limit, change in mean water level due to the waves, and the longshore current velocity, which was measured by miniature current meters and floats. Tests were made to establish repeatability of the observations and the operator variance factor. The longshore currents were measured in both vertical and longitudinal distribution, giving bottom, mid-depth and surface values. The test area was bounded by training walls.

At the upstream end of the beach water was rapidly drawn into the longshore current, the longshore component increasing with distance from the training wall, while the net onshore water motion decreased with distance from it. No strong net offshore movements occurred except at times near the downstream training wall. The surface velocity showed the most consistent shoreward trend.

The conclusions from this study suggest that most of the water injected into the surf zone when a wave breaks has been drawn from the surf zone, and therefore already has a longshore velocity, V_b, when it becomes part of the breaker. The velocity of the longshore current increases first at an accelerating rate downstream from an obstacle, and then at a decelerating rate, approaching a constant velocity at a large distance from the obstacle. The theoretical momentum flux approach appears to give the best results. The mean velocity of the uniform longshore current, using field and laboratory data, is given approximately by

$$V = g\beta T \sin 2\alpha_b$$

c Field observations

A survey of coastal and longshore currents obtained on an open coast is reported by F. P. Shepard and D. L. Inman (1950). The area studied was around the Scripps Institute in southern California. The coast is fairly straight, but the southern beaches are partly protected from the south by La Jolla Point. The offshore relief is very complex. Two submarine canyons come close to the shore. Between them the continental shelf slopes gently seawards at 1·3°. The bottom relief has a marked effect on the refraction of the longer waves, a process which helps to generate longshore currents.

The methods used to measure the circulation of water near the shore were fairly simple. Measurements outside the breakers were made with triplanes, or current-crosses, attached by line to small surface floats. The triplane thus showed the direction of drift below the surface at any required depth. The surface currents were measured by drift bottles. The positions of the triplanes and bottles were determined by horizontal sextant angles to fixed positions from a boat. The triplanes could not be followed into shallow water as they grounded, and in the surf zone currents were observed by dye on the surface, while bottom currents were obtained by means of a weighted ball. On some occasions numbered floats were released beyond the breaker zone, followed into the surf and recovered from the beach. These observations were made on calm days. Wave characteristics were recorded visually and instrumentally at the same time as the current observations.

Various different types of currents were distinguished on the part of the Californian coast that was studied. The deep-water coastal currents, which dominate the longshore movement outside the breaker zone, are fairly uniform in velocity and depend on the wind-driven oceanic circulation or tidal streams. The extent to which they affect the shallow water is variable, being greatest on a steep beach with weak wave action. The nearshore currents are related largely to the wave action and are the most important from the point of view of beach processes. Currents are caused, firstly, by the mass transport velocity acting shoreward and secondly, in the case of longshore currents, by the oblique approach of the waves owing to wave refraction and to variations in water level along the coast, that result from uneven shoreward transport of water by mass movement. A third factor is the possible division of the seaward flow between uniform return flow and the irregular flow in rip currents. The former is due to the seaward movement in intermediate depths.

The general pattern of circulation was found to vary with different types of waves. The wave period, height and the direction of deep-water approach were the most important variables. For the longer waves the direction of approach was not so important because these waves were greatly refracted. As a result zones of convergence and divergence were strongly developed, and these in turn induced rapid longshore currents, flowing away from the zones of convergence. Currents formed in this way may flow against the direction of wave approach, and here they turned seaward as rip currents some distance away from the convergence. Weaker currents flowed out from the heads of the submarine canyons.

The maps in figure 4-19 indicate the nature of the circulation under different wave conditions. Shorter waves approaching the coast normally did not suffer much refraction, and hence the zones of convergence were not so marked and rip currents were smaller and more numerous. When short waves approached at a considerable angle to the coast the longshore currents were almost continuous in the direction of wave approach and reached velocities of 1 knot or more. The longer waves produced a few, much larger zones of convergence with associated fast rip currents.

The direction of the currents was the same from the surface to the bottom in 73% of the observations. Most of the remainder showed a diagonal offshore movement at the bottom and an alongshore movement at the surface. Only 1% showed surface onshore and bottom offshore movements. The observations were, however, made under calm conditions.

An analysis of rip currents and their associated longshore feeder currents has been made by P. McKenzie (1958) from observations on the sandy beaches of New South Wales, Australia. He concluded from many observations that in heavy seas a few strong rips are produced. These may be fed by longshore currents up to 0·8 km long and from a few centimeters to about 2 m deep. The currents and the rips themselves cut channels along the beach and through any sand bars which may be lying parallel to the shore. He found that each pattern of wave approach tended to produce a characteristic pattern of longshore currents and rips. Smaller waves produced smaller, but more numerous, rip currents.

A comprehensive series of field observations was carried out over a period of 26 days in 1966 on Virginia beach, including measurements of longshore current velocity. The other variables measured were depth to the water table in the foreshore, altitude of the foreshore surface, tide height, angle between breakers and the coast, height of breakers, period of breakers, rainfall, radiant energy balance over the water, water and air temperatures, wind speed and direction, positions of the top of the uprush, position on the inshore margin of the breaker zone, height and period of the significant waves 240 m offshore. Water and sand samples were also analysed. Most variables were measured every four hours, but some were measured every 6·25 hours to coincide with high and low tide. The results of these comprehensive measurements are set out in W. Harrison *et al.* (1968). They are used in the analysis by W. Harrison (1968), to which reference has been made on pp. 117, 118.

C. J. Sonu *et al.* (1967) have studied the relationship between longshore currents and nearshore relief along the Outer Banks of North Carolina. A multiple regression analysis showed that the angle of wave incidence was the most influential variable for both linear and nonlinear regressions. The analytical methods result in a random scatter of some field observations, while others show

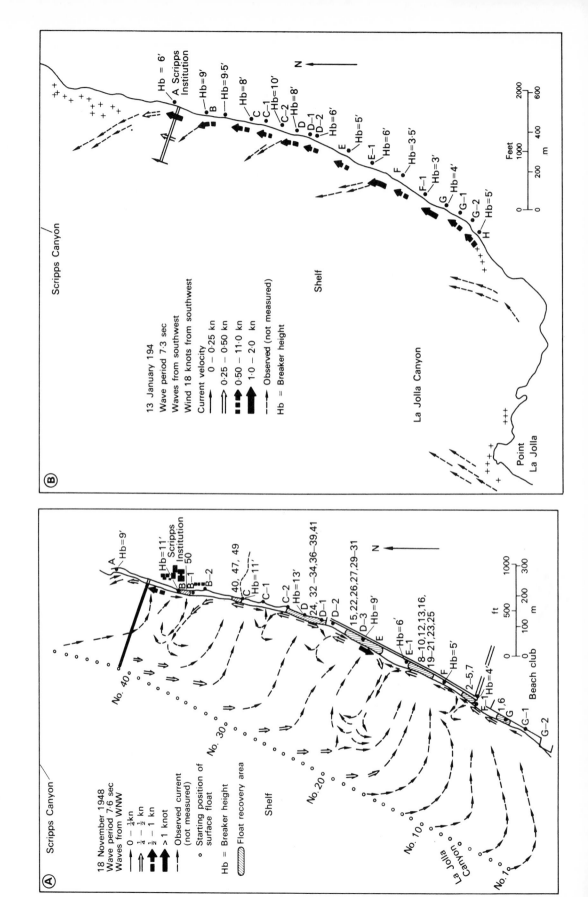

A

Scripps Canyon

18 November 1948
Wave period 7·6 sec
Waves from WNW

Current velocity
0 – ¼ kn
¼ – ½ kn
½ – 1 kn
> 1 knot

○ Starting position of
surface float

Observed current
(not measured)

Hb = Breaker height

Float recovery area

Scripps Institution

Hb=9'   A
Hb=11'
50   B   B–1
B–2
40, 47, 49
Hb=11'   C
C–1
C–2   Hb=13'   D
24, 32 –34,36–39,41   D–1
D–2
15, 22,26,27,29–31   D–3
19 –21,23,25   Hb=9'   E
8–10,12,13,16,   E–1
Hb=6'
2–5,7   Hb=4'   F
F–1
1, 6   G
G–1
Beach club   G–2

No. 40
No. 30
No. 20
No. 10
No. 1
La Jolla
Canyon
Shelf

N

ft
0   500   1000
0   100 200 300
m

B

Scripps Canyon

Hb = 6'   A   Scripps Institution
Hb = 9'   B
Hb=9·5'
Hb = 8'   C
C–1   Hb=10'
C–2   Hb = 8'   D
D–1
D–2   Hb=6'
Hb = 5'   E
E–1   Hb = 6'
F
Hb = 3·5'
Hb = 3'
Hb=4'   G
G–1
H   G–2   Hb = 5'

N

13 January 194
Wave period 7·3 sec
Waves from southwest
Wind 18 knots from southwest

Current velocity
0 – 0·25 kn
0·25 – 0·50 kn
0·50 – 11·0 kn
1·0 – 2·0 kn
Observed (not measured)
Hb = Breaker height

Shelf

La Jolla Canyon

Point
La Jolla

Feet
0   1000   2000
0   200   400   600
m

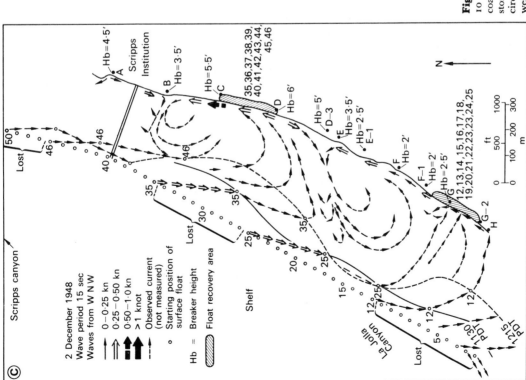

Figure 4-19 **A:** Typical nearshore circulation pattern resulting from waves less than 10 second period approaching normal to the Scripps beach and a southerly flowing coastal current; **B:** Typical nearshore circulation pattern resulting from short period storm waves approaching the Scripps beach from the southwest; **C:** Typical nearshore circulation pattern resulting from long waves of 15 second period coming from west-northwest. (*A, B, C after Shepard and Inman, 1950.*)

systematic deviations. The latter include the observations of Galvin and Eagleson (1965), and of Brebner and Kamphuis (1963). The variability in time of the current pattern was small compared with the spatial variability. The temporal variability was greatest on the submarine bar, in both speed and direction, this being caused in part by the nearshore relief. The current field was generated by the breakers plunging over the bar, and the mass transfer resulted from spilling breakers and the swash. The hydrostatic potential was dissipated by the rip currents.

7 Long waves in shallow water

a Surf beat

The discovery of waves very much longer than normal waves is of interest because, although they are much lower than normal waves, they may influence the velocities of the water particles under wave action, and furthermore, owing to their great length, they are effective in much deeper water than normal waves. One type of long wave has been termed 'surf beat'. W. H. Munk (1949) has recorded the presence of surf beat with a period of about two minutes and heights about 1/11 of the normal waves. The surf beat is related to groups of high waves, which raise the water level temporarily at the shore. It represents about 1% of the wave energy returned seawards from the shore. Where the normal waves in deep water were 1·37 m and 8 second period, the surf beat had a height of 15 cm, and at the break-point of the normal waves, it rose to 1·83 m. The respective horizontal orbital velocities in deep water and at the break-point were 18·9 cm/sec and 1·8 m/sec. In a depth of 6·1 m the surf beat was 14·3 cm high and had a horizontal orbital velocity of 9·15 cm/sec, compared with 0·76 m/sec for the normal wave. In depths in excess of 61 m the horizontal orbital velocity associated with the surf beat exceeded that of the normal wave although both were small—1·58 cm/sec for the normal wave and 2·44 cm/sec for the surf beat.

Similar surf beats of 1 to 5 minute period were recorded by M. J. Tucker (1950) on the coast of Cornwall. Their heights correlated closely with that of the normal waves. A high group of ordinary waves was followed by a group of long waves after about 4 to 5 minutes, the time it would take the waves to travel to the shore and back to the recorder 915 m offshore. It was therefore suggested that the surf beat was formed by groups of high waves breaking on the beach. The surf beat reached heights of 12·7 cm for ordinary waves of 1·83 m, a ratio of 1/12. There is a linear correlation between the two. The surf beat was thus said to result from an increase of mass transport landwards in the breaker zone which causes an acceleration both on and offshore. The depression between the two resulting elevations has been observed in the record and is followed by the reflection of the shoreward elevation from the beach.

M. S. Longuet-Higgins and R. W. Stewart (1962) explain both the linear relationship shown by Tucker between the height of the surf beat and the group of high waves, and the fact that the long wave was a depression and not an elevation. The group of high waves generates a depression of mean sea level beneath it owing to the increased radiation stress at this point, thus accounting for Tucker's observation. The long wave generated by the stresses may be reflected to cause the surf beat, which is a free wave. Loss of energy by breaking before reflection may account for the relationship being more nearly linear than proportional to the square of the wave height.

Surf-beat waves have been recorded by J. Darbyshire (1957) at Tema, Ghana. Their period was between one and ten minutes with most activity in the two to four minute range. Their amplitude approximated to 1/20 of the normal waves, their maximum height being 12·7 cm. They were formed partly by the acceleration of water towards the shore and partly by deformation of the wave form.

D. E. Cartwright (1967) has shown that in surf beat the primary waves are destroyed on the beach, whereas the free waves that result from the modification of the secondary waves are released into the ocean. They can echo back and forth for days. These waves account for the energy in the spectrum below 30 c/ks. They can also cause range action in some harbours that resonate with this particular period or frequency. Tertiary waves may also cause surf beat owing to the narrow wave frequency band. These surf beats have periods of two to three minutes and length of a few km and result from differences of close pairs of primary waves, which produce the secondary surf-beat waves. The surf beat is a forced wave, but it can become modified into a free wave close to the shore.

J. K. Adams and V. T. Buchwald (1969) draw attention to spectral waves with a frequency of nine days in summer and five in winter, the variations in level correlating highly with pressure. These waves are generated by the longshore component of geostrophic wind on a sloping shelf; the process does not operate on a flat shelf. Waves of this type, with an amplitude of several cm, travel north along the coast of eastern Australia at 350 cm/sec, north along the west coast of the U.S.A. at 250 cm/sec, and south along the west coast of Australia at 300 to 600 cm/sec. Long waves with periods of a few minutes to several hours have also been reported on the wide shelves of Argentine. The shelf waves are a form of seiche activity. A critical intensity can cause sea level fluctuations of up to a meter or more in height. They are probably due to meteorological causes, as they frequently occur when sharp pressure fronts come from central Patagonia (D. L. Inman et al., 1962).

S. Unoki and I. Ichiro (1967) suggest that indentations along the coast or variations in water depth of the sea floor can form oscillations. When the natural period of oscillation is close to that of the incoming waves a forced standing oscillation develops, causing second-order variations in sea level. If the wave height varies slowly with time, the mean surface fluctuates with a period similar to that of the envelope of the sea waves. The fluctuations will return offshore as a surf beat when they are released by the breaking of the original sea waves. The surf-beat waves may correlate positively or negatively with the envelope of sea waves, depending on the relief of the basin and the period of the incoming waves. A similar long wave could be generated in front of a breakwater or a steep beach.

b Tsunami

Another type of long wave is the tsunami. These are generated by an earthquake that disturbs the sea floor, and may travel great distances across the ocean. The main difference between tsunami and wind-generated waves is the great length of the former compared with the latter. Tsunami waves have lengths up to 160 km. They therefore behave as shallow-water waves in that their velocity is dependent only upon the water depth. In the deep ocean they can travel at speeds up to 800 km/hour according to the relationship $C = \sqrt{gd}$. Because their movement is dependent upon the water depth, tsunami waves are liable to refraction, but owing to their great length they lose energy slowly and can, for example, travel right across the Pacific Ocean, in which structural instability makes them relatively common.

As the tsunami waves approach shallow water their length diminishes rapidly and their height increases. This accounts for the great damage they do where their energy is concentrated by refraction. They may be only 0·6 m high in deep water, but this height may increase to 6 m before they break on the shore.

The tsunami created by an earthquake off Chile in 1960 travelled at between 670 and 745 km/hour across the Pacific to reach Guam in 20 hours at a distance of 15,100 km (A. H. W. Robinson, 1960). Even as far away as Hokkaido and Honshu the tsunami caused waves 9·15 m high, and one of 3·35 m was recorded at Lyttleton, New Zealand. This occasion did not affect the Hawaiian Islands so badly as that of 1946, although they are considerably nearer the epicentre than Japan. This was probably due to the refraction pattern, as the 1946 tsunami waves were generated off Alaska in the Aleutian trench. This rare type of long wave can cause immense damage if it breaks along a low coast, because of the greatly raised water level that results.

One of the most recent and severe series of tsunami waves was initiated by the strong earthquake that occurred in Alaska in 1964, a detailed account of which has been prepared by B. W. Wilson and A. Tørum (1968). The earthquake took place on 27 March 1964, and had an intensity of 8·5 on the Richter scale—an intensity expected to occur once in 30 years in this area. Extensive earth movement took place on the continental shelf off Prince William Sound in 61·1° N. The main tsunami waves travelled all over the Pacific and subsidiary ones were caused by submarine slumping of deltaic sediments. Seismic sea waves were generated as far away as the Gulf of Mexico as a result of ground vibration. Damage was, however, reduced by the coincidence of the main tsunami with low tide on the open coast of Alaska.

The tsunami waves generated by this earthquake had an inferred period of about 1·8 to 2·5 hours on the coast of Kodiak and Alaska, the first wave being a negative trough caused by subsidence. The first waves were over-ridden by free waves of 1·3 and 1·8 hours periods, followed by the free shelf oscillation, which had a period of 5 hours. The waves that spread right across the Pacific were fairly pure in form, having a period of 1·8 hours. They were recorded on tide gauges all round the Pacific. In some areas higher-frequency waves were formed on shelves, as at Hilo Bay in Hawaii where fifth harmonic waves with a period of 21·5 minutes and third harmonic waves with a period of 36 minutes, were experienced. These periods appear to approximate to the free oscillation period of the shelf in this area. A similar response to the third harmonic occurred at San Francisco. Other areas where resonance allowed exceptionally high waves to occur were along the indented Canadian coast, such as at Port Alberni, where the wave height was increased by a factor of 10 between the mouth and the head of the bay. The waves reached Lyttleton in New Zealand in remarkably pure form. The height of the waves in the west and central Pacific suggests a height decay law of $H = r^{-2/3}$. A relationship between the main period, 1·8 hours in this case, and the intensity of the earthquake, M, has been suggested in the form $\log_{10} T = (5/8)M - 3·31$.

Large intensity earthquakes thus always yield long-period tsunami. Wilson and Tørum's (1968) study has brought out the importance of resonance in the height of the tsunami waves at different points along the coast. The resonance depends on the relative depth and the square of the shelf slope. The probable initial height of the tsunami waves on the Alaskan shelf was between 9·15 and 18·3 m. It had a continuous front of about 650 km. There were five waves in the first beat. Refraction may have given rise to caustic effects due to interference with refracted waves.

c Storm surges

Storm surges are another manifestation of wave action in shallow water. They are induced by abnormal weather conditions that set up long waves which can cause exceptionally high water levels for short periods. In tidal seas they are manifested as exceptionally high tides, since the period of the surge often approximates to that of the tide, travelling at a similar velocity in the same direction. This is particularly true of the North Sea, where high surges develop in certain conditions. Hurricanes can also cause storm-tides on the east coast of the U.S.A.

Surges can be described as sea-surface disturbances with periods ranging from 1 to 100 hours, falling between tsunami and astronomical tides of lower frequency (P. Groen and G. W. Groves, 1962). One of the difficulties in studying surges is that of separating them from the astronomical tide, because the change in water level, due to the surge itself, affects the movement of the tidal wave in a rather complex way. It is not accurate, therefore, merely to deduct the predicted astronomical tide from the recorded change of level to determine the surge wave form. These effects are particularly important in shallow seas.

The period of some surges is determined mainly by the variation of the atmospheric factor involved, such as wind stress or pressure differences, and of others by the properties of the water body where they occur, in which case the atmospheric conditions act only to initiate the surge. The first situation applies either if the atmospheric process oscillates within a very narrow spectrum, or if changes are slow compared with the reaction time of the water body, so that the water body is nearly always in quasi-equilibrium with the atmosphere. The second situation will occur when the atmospheric process shows a random variation in time with a broad spectrum, or has a short time-scale period compared with the natural period of oscillation of the water body. In fact these two extremes rarely occur, and most surges are generated by intermediate conditions. Sometimes the meteorological period is nearly the same as the natural period of oscillation of the water body, so that a state of resonance is set up.

Surges which occur in partly enclosed seas and affect the whole sea area simultaneously and the running-wave type of surge may be considered as internal surges. The running-wave type travels over a sea area that is large compared with the area of the generating disturbance in the atmosphere. The surges in the North Sea belong to the first of the classes, while those generated by tropical cyclones or hurricanes belong to the second and occur on open coasts.

The surges resulting from tropical hurricanes are probably the most intense. They occur especially where wide, shallow shelves are liable to hurricane activity. These are the conditions along the Gulf of Mexico and the Atlantic coast of the U.S.A. The typical hurricane surge in this area consists of three stages, the forerunner, the hurricane surge and the resurgences. The forerunner begins several hours before the storm arrives and is a slow change of level over a wide area, as shown by the correspondence between several neighbouring areas. The forerunner occurs as a rise of water level if the longshore movement of the surge is upcoast (i.e. to the right along the coast facing away from the sea towards the land). If the longshore movement is downcoast then there is a fall in water level. The hurricane surge is a sharp rise in level that occurs when the hurricane centre passes near the point of observation. This phase lasts from two and a half to five hours and water levels can attain heights of 3 to 4 m above normal. Adjacent areas do not now show similar changes, indicating that only the strongest winds in the centre of the hurricane are now responsible. The peak water level occurs to the right of the hurricane track in the northern hemisphere. The resurgences occur after the passage of the hurricane. They may be higher than the main surge if they occur at the time of high water of the astronomical tide. The resurgences are free waves that are probably generated in the wake of the hurricane, and so are somewhat similar to a ship's wake. Their period is that of a free edge wave, having a velocity equal to that of the speed of movement of the hurricane. Some of them may be due to the development of an onshore–offshore standing wave on the shelf.

On an irregular coast of bays and estuaries the forecasting of hurricane surges is complicated by the configuration of the coast, as indicated by the work of B. W. Wilson (1960), who has studied the prediction of hurricane storm surges in New York Bay. The normal empirical or semi-empirical methods do not operate successfully in this area because of the local environment and the omission of inertial effects.

The method Wilson adopted was to correlate observed storm-surge data with meteorological parameters of the hurricanes that induced them. The hydrodynamical equations were used, taking into account wind stress and pressure. The Coriolis factor and edge-wave effects were allowed for. The final correlation and prediction equations involved eight terms. The two hurricanes of 1938 and 1944 and two other storms of 1950 and 1953 were analysed. Data concerning the character of a design-hurricane were evaluated for six different storm wind speeds from 20 to 50 knots. The highest surge height was found to occur with the 35 knot design-storm and this reached a height of 2·7 m. The results confirmed the empirical correlation between height of surge and the central pressure of the hurricane. Predicted storm-surge wave heights were given for a number of stations in New York Bay. The maximum surge height is shown to be likely to reach 4·67 m at Sandy Hook or Port Hamilton, exclusive of the astronomical tide. A method of surge prediction on the open coast is given by C.E.R.C. (1966), and takes into account wind stress—acting both perpendicular and parallel to the bottom contours—and the atmospheric pressure.

Expected hurricane-surge frequency has been calculated by B. R. Bodine (1969) on the basis of actual hurricane occurrence in conjunction with mathematical methods of prediction. 19 hurricane surges that occurred during the period 1900 to 1965 were used in the analysis. The term beta hurricane referred to the hurricane that has a central pressure index of a once in 100

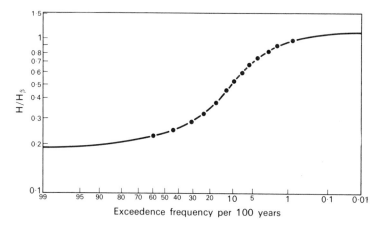

Figure 4-20 Generalized surge frequency for Texas hurricanes. (*After Bodine, 1966.*)

H/H_β

Exceedence frequency per 100 years

years occurrence probability. The surge elevation on the open coast of Texas, in the Gulf of Mexico, was predicted and adjustments were made for other locations. Three components were considered—hurricane winds, other high winds and astronomical forces.

The probability of a surge of height H is compared with the H_β surge height, and expressed in years recurrence interval. Figure 4-20 shows the expected recurrence interval in terms of exceedance frequency per 100 years and includes surges due to the three components mentioned above. The surges above $H/H_\beta = 0·6$ are generated only by hurricanes. The relationships apply to the Gulf coast of Texas only, although the method of analysis could be applied to other areas where there are sufficient data. Further data are also required to improve the predictions for the Gulf coast of Texas, which is particularly liable to this type of sea level disturbance.

T. Ijima and F. L. W. Tang (1967) have devised a computer method of calculating waves generated in shallow water by typhoons. The results apply well to the coasts of Japan. Growth and decay are taken into account and refraction, in enclosed shallow seas of limited fetch, is allowed for.

The North Sea is particularly susceptible to storm surges owing to its shape. It is a shallow, more or less rectangular basin, which opens northwards to the Atlantic Ocean, from which direction the normal tidal energy comes. The small outlet through the Straits of Dover to the south is significant. In some respects the behaviour of the surges resembles the normal tide. Abnormal rises of sea level are especially dangerous on part of the coasts of the North Sea since for considerable stretches they are low-lying, and require artificial protection in the form of sea-walls and banks. These structures often protect areas that are below the high-tide level. A breach in the defences, therefore, has very serious consequences for the coastal hinterland. The great damage and loss of life caused in parts of eastern England and Holland during the 1953 surge illustrates the danger. This type of surge occurs when suitable meteorological conditions prevail.

Eight major surges occurred between 1900 and 1953, and a very severe one in 1897. These included both internal and external types. R. H. Corkan (1950), in his analysis of the 1949 surge, has calculated the amount of disturbance of sea level for all places in the North Sea coasts, for which data are available, by eliminating the normal tidal curve from the records of sea-level changes. The time of the maximum disturbance, as shown by this analysis, occurred within one hour of the time of high water at nearly all stations on the east coast of the British Isles. At the time of the surge the tide was nearly neap, so that in some places the surge only raised the level to that of a normal spring tide. The greatest rise of sea level was about 1·7 m at King's Lynn. Its situation in the Wash may account for this abnormality. The disturbance travelled around the North Sea in an anti-clockwise direction with the normal tide, the amplitude of the maximum disturbance decreasing in the same way as the normal tide.

A weather situation similar in some respects to that of 1949, caused the surge of 1953. A deep depression passed eastwards to the north of Scotland, causing strong southwest winds to veer suddenly to the north. Figure 4-21 shows the character and course of the depression. Wind and pressure affect water level in a number of ways. Firstly, the pressure acts as an inverted barometer: a very low pressure will cause a rise of sea level at the rate of 30 cm for a fall in pressure of 34 millibars. Secondly, the friction of the wind blowing over the sea sets up gradients, and thirdly, water flows in and out from neighbouring water bodies. The third factor caused a change in mean sea level in the North Sea from −15·2 cm to +21·3 cm in one day. Water flowing into the North Sea from the north, owing to the rotation of the earth, comes in largely on the western side of the sea, relatively little change occurring on the coast of Denmark and Norway.

The storm surge of 1953 caused very much greater elevations in sea level and was more disastrous in its effect on the coast than the 1949 surge. It occurred during the period of spring tide, when the predicted levels were high. Had the surge, however, occurred a fortnight later, when one of the highest tides of the year was predicted, the maximum water levels would have been at least 60 cm higher in some areas. The predicted height of sea level was increased by 2·75 to 3·35 m in some places in the southern North Sea, often occurring near high tide.

J. R. Rossiter (1954) used all available data from tide gauges around the North Sea and in the eastern English Channel in his analysis of the surge. The height of the surge was calculated by deducting the normal tide and the effect of barometric pressure so that the effects of the wind could be studied. The surge was caused by a small secondary depression, which developed on a trailing cold front and deepened rapidly as it passed to the north of Scotland and turned southeast to travel across the centre of the North Sea and into northwest Germany. The depression reached a minimum pressure of 966 millibars in its passage across the northern North Sea. When the centre of the depression passed into the North Sea very strong northerly winds developed in its rear, owing to the build up of a strong ridge of high pressure behind it. The geostrophic wind reached a speed of 280 km/hour and in itself caused much damage in Scotland.

The variation of sea level during the passage of the storm and the period of the surge have been calculated for the whole of the North Sea. Most of the extra water came into the North Sea between

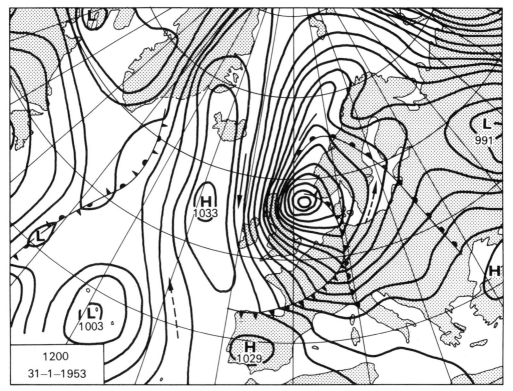

Pressure at centre of North Sea depression 967 mb

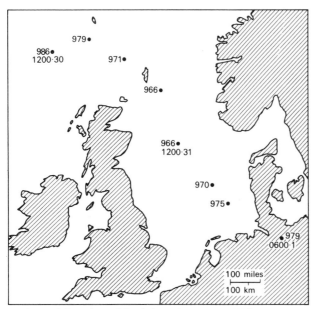

• Centre of depression at 6 hourly intervals pressure in MBS

Figure 4-21 Synoptic chart for the north Atlantic (*above*); Track of depression centre in the North Sea from 30 Jan. to 1 Feb. 1953 (*below*).

Scotland and Norway. The reason for the influx of water was the action of the gale force north winds. It has been estimated that 42.5×10^{10} m³ (15×10^{12} cubic feet) of water entered the North Sea between 2100 hours on 31 January and noon on 1 February. The increase in level averaged over the whole of the North Sea was more than 61 cm during this period, as illustrated in figure 4-22.

The records of tide levels for Dover, Newhaven and Dieppe show that the surge was partially transmitted through the Straits of Dover. Owing to the rotation of the earth the water was deflected to the right, giving higher elevation on the English coast than in France. Thus at Dover the surge was over 1·83 m and at Newhaven 1·22 m, but in Dieppe it was only a little over 0·915 m. The rise in level at Newhaven took place in spite of a very strong offshore northerly wind, which would usually cause a fall in level. The total volume of water escaping from the North Sea through the Straits of Dover has been estimated to be 31.1×10^9 m³ (1.7×10^{11} cubic feet), enough to cause a fall in level in the southern North Sea between Orfordness and Brouwershavn of 27·4 cm approximately. The Straits of Dover acted as a safety valve to a certain degree, although only about 1/100 of the excess water escaped this way.

To account for the nature of the surge along the coast, it is necessary to take into account both

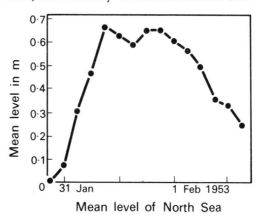

Figure 4-22 Height of the North Sea above the mean level during 31 Jan. and 1 Feb. 1953. (*After Rossiter, 1954.*)

the changes in level in the North Sea and the progress of the external surge southwards down the coast of the British Isles. The arrival of this maximum disturbance can be traced along the coast and differentiated from changes due to the level of the North Sea in different areas. By 1200 on 31 January the north winds were becoming established over the northwestern North Sea and sea level was rising, owing to the traction effect of these winds. By 1500 the general level had risen by 30·5 cm and the maximum disturbance had reached Aberdeen. At 1800 the maximum wind forces were experienced, and the water level had risen by 1·22 m in the latitude of Northumberland. The approach of the main surge, which had now reached the Firth of Forth, was tending to cause an anti-clockwise rotation of the co-disturbance lines. By 2100 the surge peak reached Yorkshire and the major disturbance lay between Norfolk and Holland, where the height of the surge was about 2·44 m. The mean level of the North Sea had now reached its maximum, above the undisturbed level, of 6·7 m. By 0001 on 1 February the surge peak had passed the coastline between the Humber and Thames and was approaching the south coast of Holland, with maximum heights of nearly 2·44 m in the Thames and between 2·74 and 3·05 m in the Scheldt. The peak of the surge was at Chatham and Ostend at 0001. To the south of a line joining these places it occurred later, at 0100 at Dover and 0500 at Newhaven and Dieppe. By 0300 the winds were starting to moderate and the surge was passing northwards up the coast of Holland, reaching

131

Ijmuiden at 0400, the Friesian Islands at about 0600 and Nordeney at 0700. At 1000 the surge reached Esbjerg, by 1200 the coast of north Denmark, and by 2200 the extreme southern tip of Norway. The effect of the shallowing of the sea compensated for the effect of friction in maintaining the height of the surge as it progressed anti-clockwise round the North Sea.

The time of the maximum disturbance was within about 2 hours of predicted high tide at many places along the east coast of Britain. Had the high water of the tide and surge coincided exactly, the actual level would have been considerably higher. Along the Lincolnshire coast the height of the water level would have been about 1·22 m higher at its maximum if the high waters of astronomical tide and surge had coincided a fortnight later, when the predicted tide was higher. At Gibraltar Point in south Lincolnshire the water reached a height of 2·4 m above the predicted tide level. The swash of the waves, which were estimated to be 6 m high in the North Sea, would reach a height greatly in excess of this figure. Some indication of the worst possible conditions that could be expected to occur can be obtained from these figures, and it is important to know these in relation to the height to which coastal defences in areas such as Lincolnshire should be built.

N. S. Heaps (1969) has analysed three subsequent surges in the North Sea. He prepared a computer program to establish sea-level disturbances due to surge generation in the North Sea. Three models were used for each surge. One considered the Straits of Dover closed, the second included them in the model and the third also included the deeper-water area northwest of the continental shelf between Scotland and Norway. Water depths were averaged for rectangular units of 37 km of longtitude and 25·8 km of latitude at the northern boundary and 37·2 km at the southern. The time steps for the iterative procedure were 0·1 hours.

The first surge tested occurred on 13–15 September 1956. It was an external surge generated by a depression that passed to the north of Scotland with strong west-to-northwest winds in its rear. Conditions were fairly calm in the North Sea. The computed sea level agreed closely with the observed for the most part. The external surge was generated mainly on the shelf—as indicated by the small difference between models 1 and 3—and passed as a free wave south down the east coast of Britain between 0600 and 1800. It then lost its progressive character and produced a general rise of level, which rotated anti-clockwise around the southern North Sea, decreasing in amplitude as it moved. The water was piled up to the north of the North Sea by strong south-to-southwest winds off northwest Scotland. This excess water was then released southwards and forced to travel along the east coast of Britain by the influence of the Coriolis parameter.

The second surge, which occurred on 24–26 February 1958, was an internal one. It was created by a depression passing east along the English Channel and southern North Sea, with strong northeast winds on its northern flank. The surge was generated in the southern North Sea between Holland and Lincolnshire and the Straits of Dover. A negative surge occurred at Esbjerg of 1·37 m and at Cuxhaven of 1·07 m. Flow through the Straits of Dover significantly lowered the level at Southend by nearly 1·5 m, as indicated by the comparison of models 1 and 2. Model 2 gave a current flowing out of the North Sea at 55 cm/sec at its maximum. Actual measured values varied between 46 cm/sec and 82 cm/sec.

The third surge investigated occurred on 15–17 February 1962, when it caused serious damage in Hamburg. A depression passed eastwards to the north of Scotland, with strong west-to-northwest winds at its rear, producing a major North Sea surge. The rise in sea level at Southend and Esbjerg was nearly 2·14 m, but at Cuxhaven it was over 3·36 m. Part of the surge effect was external, and the low pressure was also responsible for a sea-level rise of 30 cm at Esbjerg and 49 cm at Bergen, but elevations were smaller elsewhere.

The models show well the progressive wave character of the external surge, owing to weak reflection from the southern end of the North Sea. This type of computer model offers much scope for similar studies, and refinements could be added.

Summary

Nearly all the properties of ideal waves change as they enter shallow water. The waves decrease in velocity and length, and after a slight initial decrease, increase in height. Their form becomes more asymmetrical and their orbits change from open circles to open ellipses. The speed of the water particles increases as the speed of the wave form decreases, and in time the water overtakes the form and the wave breaks. Breakers are either plunging or spilling in type depending on the beach slope and wave steepness. Waves breaking on structures are reflected if there is deep water in front of the structure, but if they break onto the structure shock pressures may be set up when a pocket of air is enclosed. Refraction, due to the decrease of wave velocity in shallow water, is an important process and leads to the unequal incidence of wave energy along the coast. Energy is high in zones of convergence of orthogonals and low in zones of divergence. The offshore relief is an important factor in determining the refraction of waves.

Many new types of instruments are being developed to measure the height and direction of waves in shallow water. Wave records are available for shallow water lightship sites and coastal stations. Wave forecasting in shallow water can be achieved by means of curves especially designed to establish the size of waves generated in shallow water. The effects of refraction must also be considered. Most of the curves are based on empirical methods.

The open ellipses of shallow water particles leads to mass transport. In shallow water there is a forward thrust of water on the bottom, with seaward movement in mid-depths and a shoreward movement on the surface. This pattern may be modified to give a circulatory movement with a horizontal base. The landward transfer of water is sometimes compensated for by the development of seaward-flowing rip currents. The velocity of water particles both in breaking waves and in deeper water has been measured or calculated.

One of the most important aspects of shallow-water wave action is the development of wave-induced longshore currents. Many theoretical and empirical relationships exist to forecast the velocity of the longshore currents. The angle of wave approach is one of the most important variables on which the velocity depends. Movement is most rapid along the crest of a submarine bar, if one exists, or if not, where the waves are steep, in the breaker zone. If the waves are flat the velocity is greatest in the swash zone. The theoretical results have been tested by laboratory studies of longshore currents and by field observations. Rip currents play an important part in the generation of longshore currents and these in turn depend to a considerable extent on the refraction of the waves when these are long. When the waves are short the direction of approach is more important.

Surf-beat waves have periods of about one to ten minutes, and are caused by the reflection of excess water due to a group of high waves from the coast. Tsunami waves have lengths up to 160 km and are generated by earthquakes. They can travel right across the Pacific without losing much energy, their speed depending on the depth of water. Surges are generated by abnormal weather conditions, and have periods ranging from one to 100 hours. Hurricanes generate surges on the east coast of the U.S.A., and the North Sea is also liable to surge activity.

References

ADAMS, J. K. and BUCHWALD, V. T. 1969: The generation of Continental shelf waves. *J. Fluid Mech.* **35**(4), 815–26.

BAGNOLD, R. A. 1947: Sand movement by waves: some small-scale experiments with sand of very low density. *J. Inst. Civ. Eng.* Paper **5554**, 447–69.

BAGNOLD, R. A. 1963: Beach and nearshore processes. In Hill, M. N. (Editor), *The sea* **III**, Part I, *Mechanics of marine sedimentation*, New York: Wiley, 507–28.

BARBER, N. F. and TUCKER, M. J. 1962: Wind waves. Chapter 19 in Hill, M. N. (Editor), *The sea* **I**, New York: Wiley, 664–69.

BIGELOW, H. B. and EDMONSON, W. T. 1947: Wind waves at sea, breakers and surf. *Hydrog. Off. Pub.* **602.** Hydrog Off. U.S. Navy.

BODINE, B. R. 1969: Hurricane surge frequency estimated for the Gulf coast of Texas. *C.E.R.C. Tech. Memo.* **26.** (32 pp.).

BREBNER, A. and KAMPHUIS, J. W. 1963: Model tests on relationships between deep-water wave characteristics and longshore currents. *Queens Univ. Civ. Eng. Res. Rep.* **3**, 1–25.

BRETSCHNEIDER, C. L. 1965: The generation of waves by wind: state of the art. *Nat. Eng. Sci. Co.,* Off. Naval Res., SN **134–6.** (96 pp.)

BRETSCHNEIDER, C. L. 1966: On tides and longshore currents over the continental shelf due to winds blowing at an angle to the coast. *Nat. Eng. Sci. Co.,* Off. Naval Res., SN **134–13.** (45 pp.)

BRETSCHNEIDER, C. L. and REID, R. O. 1954: Modification of wave height due to bottom friction, percolation and wave refraction. *B.E.B. Tech. Memo.* **45.**

BRUUN, P. 1963: Longshore currents and longshore troughs. *J. Geophys. Res.* **68**, 1065–78.

CALIGNY, A. F. H. 1878: *C.R. Acad. Sci.* **87**, 10, Paris.

CARTWRIGHT, D. E. 1967: Modern studies of wind generated ocean waves. *Contemp. Phys.* **8**, 171–88.

COASTAL ENGINEERING RESEARCH CENTER 1966: Shore protection, planning and design. *Tech. Rep.* **4**, 3rd Edition, 50–114.

CORKAN, R. H. 1950: The levels in the North Sea associated with the storm disturbance of 8 Jan., 1949. *Phil. Trans. Roy. Soc.* A **242**, 493–525.

DARBYSHIRE, J. 1957: Sea conditions at Tema Harbour. *Dock and Harbour Auth.* **38**, 277–8.

DARBYSHIRE, J. 1962: Microseisms. Chapter 20 in Hill, M. N. (Editor), *The sea* **I**, New York: Wiley, 700–19.

DARBYSHIRE, M. 1958: Waves in the Irish Sea. *Dock and Harbour Auth.* **39**, 245–8.

DARBYSHIRE, M. 1960: Waves in the North Sea. *Dock and Harbour Auth.* **41**, 225–8.

DARLING, J. M. and DUMM, D. G. 1967: The wave record program at C.E.R.C. *C.E.R.C. Misc. Pap.* **1–67.** (30 pp.)

DRAPER, L. 1963: Derivation of a 'design wave' from instrumental records of sea waves. *Proc. Inst. Civ. Eng.* **26**, 291–304.

DRAPER, L. 1967a: Instruments for measurement of wave height and direction in and around harbours. *Proc. Inst. Civ. Eng.* **37**, 213–19.

DRAPER, L. 1967b: The analysis and presentation of wave data, a plea for uniformity. *Proc. 10th Conf. Coast. Eng.* Tokyo, 1–11.

DRAPER, L. 1967c: Wave activity at the sea bed around northwestern Europe. *Mar. Geol.* **5**, 133–40.

DRAPER, L. 1967d: Waves at Sekondi, Ghana. Chapter 1 in *Proc. 10th Conf. Coast. Eng.*, 12–17.

DRAPER, L. and DOBSON, P. J. 1965: Rip currents on a Cornish beach. *Nature* **206**(4990), 1249.

EAGLESON, P. S. 1965: The theoretical study of longshore currents on a plane beach. *M.I.T., Hydrodynamics Lab. Tech. Rep.* **82**, 1–31.

GALVIN, C. J. 1967: Longshore current velocity: a review of theory and data. *Rev. of Geophys.* **5**(3), 287–304.

GALVIN, C. J. and EAGLESON, P. S. 1965: Experimental study of longshore currents on a plane beach. *C.E.R.C. Tech. Memo.* **10**. (80 pp.)

GROEN, P. and GROVES, G. W. 1962: Surges. Chapter 17 in Hill, M. N. (Editor), *The sea* **I**, New York: Wiley, 611–46.

HADLEY, M. L. 1964: Wave induced bottom currents in the Celtic Sea. *Mar. Geol.* **2**, 164–7.

HARDY, J. R. 1964: The movement of beach material and wave action near Blakeney Point, Norfolk. *Trans. Inst. Brit. Geogr.* **34**, 53–69.

HARRISON, W. 1968: Empirical equations for longshore current velocity. *J. Geophys. Res.* **73**, 6929–36.

HARRISON, W. and KRUMBEIN, W. C. 1964: Interaction of the beach–ocean–atmosphere system at Virginia Beach, Virginia. *C.E.R.C. Tech. Memo.* **7**. (102 pp.)

HARRISON, W., PORE, N. A. and TUCK, D. R. 1965: Predictor equations for beach processes and responses. *J. Geophys. Res.* **70**, 6103–9.

HARRISON, W., RAYFIELD, E. W., BOON, J. D. III, REYNOLDS, G., GRANT, J. B. and TYLER, D. 1968: A time series from the beach environment. *E.S.S.A. Res. Lab. Tech. Memo.* A **OL-1**. (85 pp.)

HEAPS, N. S. 1969: A two-directional numerical sea model. *Phil. Trans. Roy. Soc.* A **265**(1160), 93–138.

HORIKAWA, K. and CHIN-TONG KUO 1967: A study of wave transformation inside the surf zone. Chapter 15 in *Proc. 10th Conf. Coast. Eng.*, Tokyo, 217–33.

IJIMA, T. and TANG, F. L. W. 1967: Numerical calculations of wind waves in shallow water. Chapter 4 in *Proc. 10th Conf. Coast. Eng.*, Tokyo, 38–49.

INMAN, D. L. and BAGNOLD, R. A. 1963: Littoral processes. In Hill, M. N. (Editor), *The sea* **III**, New York: Wiley, 529–53.

INMAN, D. L., MUNK, W. H. and BELAY, M. 1962: Spectra of low frequency waves along the Argentine Shelf. *Deep Sea Res.* **8**, 155–64.

INMAN, D. L. and NASU, N. 1956: Orbital velocity associated with wave action near the breaker zone. *B.E.B. Tech. Memo.* **79**.

IVERSON, H. W. 1952: Laboratory study of breakers. *Nat. Bur. of Stand. Circ.* **521**, 9–32.

LONGUET-HIGGINS, M. S. 1953: Mass transport in water waves. *Phil. Trans. Roy. Soc.* A **245**, 535–81.

LONGUET-HIGGINS, M. S. and STEWART, R. W. 1962: Radiation stress and mass transport in gravity waves, with applications to 'surf beats'. *J. Fluid Mech.* **13**, 481–504.

MACMILLAN, D. H. 1966: *Tides*. London: C. R. Books.

MCKENZIE, P. 1958: Rip current systems. *J. Geol.* **66**(2), 103–13.

MEHAUTÉ, B. J. and KOH, R. C. Y. 1966: On the breaking of waves arriving at an angle to the shore. *Nat. Eng. Sci. Co., Off. Naval Res.*, S **134-10**. (80 pp.)

MICHE, R. 1944: Movements ondulatoires de la Mer. *Ann. Ponts. Chaussées* **114**, 25–78.

MOBAREK, I. E. and WIEGEL, R. L. 1967: Diffraction of wind generated water waves. Chapter 13 in *Proc. 10th Conf. Coast. Eng.* **I**, 185–206, Tokyo.

MUNK, W. H. 1949: Surf beats. *Trans. Am Geophys. Un.* **30**, 849–54.

MUNK, W. H. 1962: Long ocean waves. Chapter 18 in Hill, M. N. (Editor), *The sea* **I**, New York: Wiley, 647–63.

PUTNAM, J. A. 1949: Loss of energy due to percolation in a permeable sea bottom. *Trans. Am. Geophys. Un.* **30**(3), 349–56.

PUTNAM, J. A. and JOHNSON, J. W. 1949: The dissipation of wave energy by bottom friction. *Trans. Am. Geophys. Un.* **30**(1), 67–74.

PUTNAM, J. A., MUNK, W. H. and TRAYLOR, M. A. 1949: The prediction of longshore currents. *Trans. Am. Geophys. Un.* **30**(3), 337–45.

ROBINSON, A. H. W. 1953: The storm surge of 31 Jan.–1 Feb., 1953. *Geog.* **38,** 134–41.

ROBINSON, A. H. W. 1961: The Pacific Tsunami of May 22, 1960. *Geog.* **46,** 18–24.

ROSSITER, J. R. 1954: The North Sea storm surge of 31 Jan. and 1 Feb., 1953. *Phil. Trans. Roy. Soc.* A **246,** 371–99.

RUSSELL, R. C. H. and MACMILLAN, D. H. 1952: *Waves and Tides.*

RUSSELL, R. C. H. and OSORIO, J. D. C. 1958: An experimental investigation of drift profiles in a closed channel. *Proc. 6th Conf. Coast. Eng.*, Council of Wave Res. Univ. of California, 171–83.

SAVILLE, T. 1950: Model study of sand transport along an infinitely long straight beach. *Trans. Am. Geophys. Un.* **31**(4), 555–65.

SAVILLE, T. 1954: North Atlantic wave statistics hindcast by Bretschneider, revised Sverdrup–Munk method. *B.E.B. Tech. Memo.* **55.**

SHEPARD, F. P. and INMAN, D. L. 1950: Nearshore circulation related to bottom topography and wave refraction. *Trans. Am. Geophys. Un.* **31**(2), 196–212.

SONU, C. J. and MCCLOY, J. M. and MCARTHUR, D. S. 1967: Longshore currents and nearshore topography. Chapter 32 in *Proc. 10th Conf. Coast. Eng.*, Tokyo, 524–49.

STOKER, J. J. 1957: *Water waves.* New York: Inter. Sci. Pub.

TUCKER, M. J. 1950: Surf beats: sea waves of 1 to 5 minute period. *Proc. Roy. Soc.* A **202,** 565–73.

UNOKI, S. and ISHIRO, I. 1967: A possibility of generation of surf beats. Chapter 14 in *Proc. 10th Conf. Coast. Eng.*, Tokyo, 207–16.

WALDEN, H. 1963: Comparison of one-dimensional wave spectra recorded in the German Bight with various 'theoretical spectra'. *Ocean wave spectra.* Englewood Cliffs: Prentice-Hall, 67–80.

WILLIAMS, L. C. 1969: C.E.R.C. wave gages. *C.E.R.C. Tech. Memo.* **30.** (117 pp.)

WILSON, B. W. 1960: The prediction of hurricane storm-tides in New York bay. *B.E.B. Tech. Memo.* **120.** (107 pp.)

WILSON, B. W. and TØRUM, A. 1968: The tsunami of the Alaskan earthquake, 1964: Engineering evaluation. *C.E.R.C. Tech. Memo.* **25.** (401 pp.)

5 The tide

In contrast to the variable and unpredictable nature of waves, the rise and fall of the tide is normally both regular and predictable, but like the waves it exerts a considerable influence on many beach processes. In this chapter the significance of the tide to beach problems is considered and a short account is given of the main factors on which its type and range depend. Some of the features developed by tidal streams in shallow water are also discussed.

The tide affects beach processes in two ways—firstly, through the rise and fall of the water level, and secondly, through tidal streams which this causes. On a tideless coast the area of beach coming under any particular part of the wave action is small and is limited by the size of the waves. As long as the waves remain constant the position of the break-point and the extent of the swash will remain constant. Where, however, the tidal range is considerable, the break-point of the waves is never fixed in position for long periods, and the effect of the swash can be exerted over a wide stretch of beach. These differences have an important bearing on the formation of certain types of beach profile and on the cutting of abrasion platforms.

At one time many coastal features were explained by reference to tidal streams, but these are now thought to be of less significance than wave action on many coasts. On others, however, they are very important, and some examples will be cited later in the chapter. The fact that tidal streams are reversing reduces their capacity to move beach material for long distances. The flood stream usually flows in one direction while the ebb flows in the opposite direction, often with nearly the same velocity. The slight residual net flow can, however, be significant. The two opposing streams will also probably be acting at different levels on the beach, and thus material on the upper beach may be carried in one direction by the flood stream at high water, while at low water the lower beach will be under the influence of streams in the reverse direction.

On the open coast tidal streams are rarely of sufficient velocity to enable them to pick up material from the sea bed, but even if they are weak they can move material that has first been thrown into suspension by the waves. In river mouths and estuaries, on the other hand, the currents may attain sufficient velocity to enable them to carry considerable quantities of coarse material. At the southern extremity of Orfordness in Suffolk, for example, the tidal streams reach 4·10 to 4·64 m/sec (8 to 9 knots) at their maxima.

1 Tide-producing forces

The tide-producing forces are caused by the gravitational attraction of the sun and moon on the earth and are, therefore, closely related to the movement of these bodies. These movements are complex as the orbits of neither the earth nor the moon are circular. Also the earth's orbit, or ecliptic, lies at an angle of $23\frac{1}{2}°$ to the equator, while the moon's orbit lies at an angle of $5·9°$ to the ecliptic. The values of the tidal forces at any one place thus vary with the changing declination of the sun and moon. The tidal forces are susceptible to harmonic analysis, a method by which the complex curves can be simplified. Owing to the sun's greater distance away the tractive forces due to it are only 0·46 those of the moon. The cube of the distances more than balances the one power of the masses of the sun and moon, as both quantities enter into the equation giving the tractive tidal generating forces of the bodies. This equation is

$$T = \tfrac{3}{2}g\frac{M}{E}\frac{e^3}{r^3}\sin 2C$$

where T is the tractive force; g is gravity; M and E are the masses of the moon and earth respectively; e is the earth's radius; r is the moon's distance from the earth, and C the angular distance of the point measured at the centre of the earth from the line of centres. It is the tractive force exerted by the moon and sun that is important in generating the tide, and not the direct attractive force. The latter force only acts perpendicularly to the earth's surface, while the tractive force acts horizontally along the surface and can therefore set the water in motion. The tractive force has a maximum value of 0·000,000,084g, when the moon is at its mean distance.

When the moon is above the equator (zero declination) the tractive forces are symmetrical, producing two maxima and two minima during the lunar day (24·8 solar hours) and the actual value of the force varies with the latitude. This is the semi-diurnal tide-producing force. If the declination of the moon is not zero, the forces no longer remain symmetrical. Their value can most easily be appreciated by considering figure 5-1, which is for a lunar declination of 15° N. From a stereographic projection the direction and value of the tractive force at latitude 30° N, for example, can be found for every hour. This gives the complex curve shown in figure 5-1B. The curve can be simplified by splitting it up into its northerly and easterly components, as shown in figure 5-1C. These curves are still asymmetrical. The process can be carried further by splitting the curves into their symmetrical components. Figure 5-1D shows the northerly component. The two resulting curves differ in that one has two maxima and the other only one. The tide-producing force has been split into its semi-diurnal and diurnal components. The diurnal component is a function of the declination of the moon. It is nil when the declination is zero and a maximum when the moon's declination is greatest. The semi-diurnal force on the other hand will be reduced at times of high declination. The forces due to the sun will be similar but smaller, and their period solar time, not lunar.

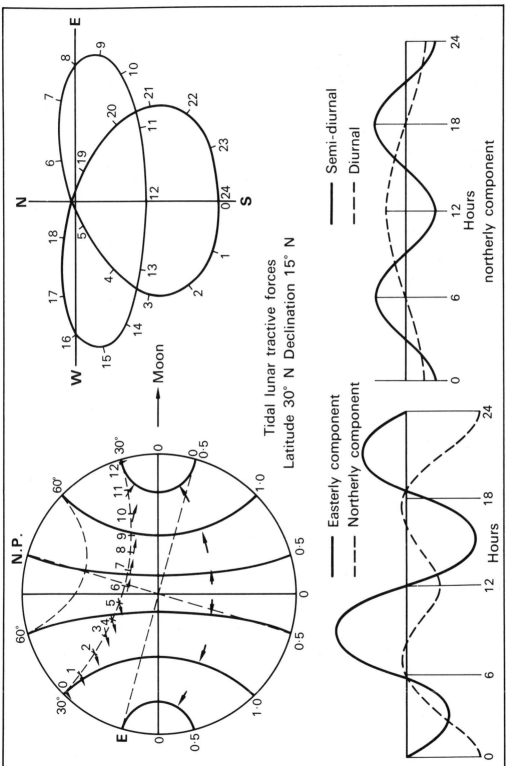

Figure 5-1 Lunar tractive forces for a lunar declination of 15° N at latitude 30° N. (*After Doodson and Warburg, 1941.*)

2 Types of wave motion in tides

In order to appreciate the reaction of the oceans to the tractive forces, the types of wave motion and the effect of the rotation of the earth on them must be mentioned. One type of wave motion is the progressive wave. Its main characteristics are that the maximum flow occurs at the crest of the wave in the direction of propagation, and at the trough in the opposite direction. Its velocity, c, is given by $\sqrt{gd}$, where d is the depth of water. Like the long waves considered in the last chapter, the velocity depends only on the depth of water.

A progressive wave advancing against a vertical barrier will be reflected from it to form the second type of wave, the standing oscillation or stationary wave. When a perfect reflection takes place an equal wave moves in the opposite direction to the primary one. It reacts with it in such a way that at the maximum and minimum elevations there will now be no streams, which reach their maximum velocity when the surface is flat (figure 5-2A).

This type of wave may also be formed in an enclosed basin by the oscillation of the water within it. In a standing wave of this type the water will oscillate about a nodal line. When the water reaches its maximum slope the streams will be nil, but when the surface is flat, they will reach their maximum velocity. The period of oscillation, T, of such a basin is given by

$$\frac{2L}{\sqrt{gd}}$$

where L is the length of the basin and d is its depth. The period of the stationary wave is equal to that of a progressive wave, the length of which is twice that of the basin. The natural period of oscillation of any water body will, therefore, depend largely on its length and depth. This relationship is important as the tides in the ocean are mainly of the standing oscillation type.

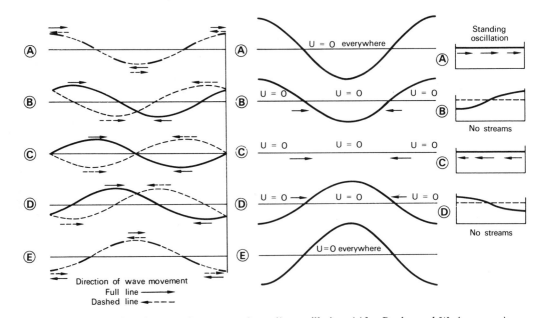

Figure 5-2 Reflected progressive wave and standing oscillation. (*After Doodson and Warburg, 1941.*)

3 Effects of the rotation of the earth

The tides cannot, however, be closely related to the simple standing oscillation, as another modifying factor must be taken into account. This is the rotation of the earth or the Coriolis parameter, which has the effect of deflecting moving water to the right of its path in the northern hemisphere and to the left in the southern. The force causes transverse currents to build up or transverse gradients to develop, the water on the right being higher in the northern hemisphere and vice versa in the southern. The adjustment may take place either by transverse streams or by transverse gradients, or by a combination of both.

The application of the Coriolis parameter to a standing oscillation may be considered. In a rectangular basin, as shown in figure 5-3, there will, in the absence of rotation, be high water

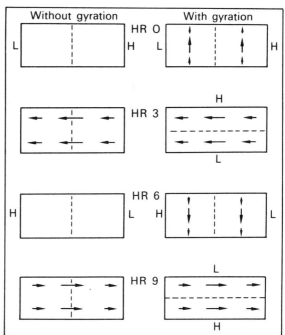

Figure 5-3 Standing oscillation modified by gyration. (*After Doodson and Warburg, 1941.*)

at one end and low water at the other with no streams at hour 0. At hour 3 the surface will be flat, but a stream will be flowing west across the nodal line. Hour 6 is the reverse of 0 and hour 9 of hour 3, completing the cycle. The rotation of the earth adds the subsidiary elevations and streams shown in the figure. When the streams are flowing west at hour 3, a gradient will build up giving high water at the north of the basin. At hour 9, when the stream is flowing east, the secondary elevation will be at the southern end of the basin. In between subsidiary streams will be directed southwards at hour 6 and north at hour 0.

The two sets of movement combined are called an amphidromic system because the tide now moves round a nodal point. High water progresses round the basin in an anti-clockwise direction in the northern hemisphere. The currents also move anti-clockwise round the basin. At high water the current moves in the same direction as the wave crest, while at low water it moves in the opposite direction. This is a characteristic of a progressive wave. The type of motion is now that of a progressive wave moving round a point, anti-clockwise in the northern

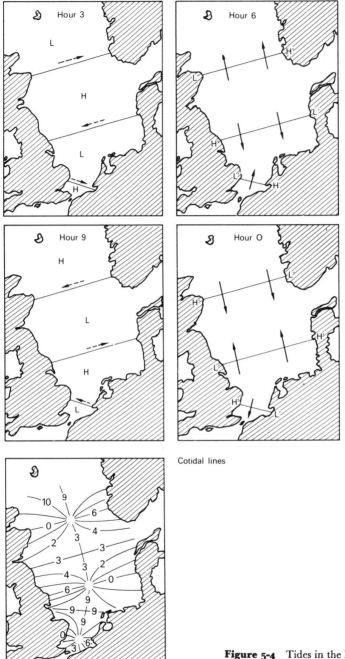

Cotidal lines

Figure 5-4 Tides in the North Sea. The figures in the lower map refer to times of high water. (*After Doodson and Warburg, 1941.*)

hemisphere and clockwise in the southern. The range of the tide will be greatest at the coast and least in the centre near the amphidromic point, where it is nil.

4 Oceanic tides

To a greater or lesser degree the tides in the oceans and adjacent seas are based on the operation of a series of amphidromic systems. The response of the different water bodies to the tide-producing forces depends to a large extent on the principle of resonance. Any body of water has a natural period of oscillation, dependent upon its dimensions. If this natural period of oscillation approximates to the period of one of the tide-producing forces, the body will react to that period, and a state of resonance will be set up. At the end of the last century Harris was one of the first to emphasize the importance of resonance. He drew a co-tidal chart of the oceans divided into oscillating areas, but because he ignored the rotation of the earth his map did not reflect reality. The co-tidal chart constructed by Sterneck in 1920 shows a pattern of amphidromic systems in the Atlantic Ocean.

Most of the coasts of the Atlantic Ocean have tides which are predominantly semi-diurnal in type, and the diurnal inequality of the tide is therefore small. This is because the Atlantic Ocean is of dimensions which respond most readily to the period of the semi-diurnal tide-producing forces. On many Pacific coasts, for example in British Columbia and California, there is a marked diurnal inequality of the tide, one high water being much higher than the other. This is due to the fact that the Pacific Ocean is large enough to react to the diurnal as well as the semi-diurnal tide-producing forces, and there is hence a variation of the tide as the moon progresses through its cycle of declination, the inequality being greatest at times of high declination, when the diurnal factor is also greatest. In parts of Borneo and elsewhere in the southeastern Pacific the diurnal lunar component is dominant for most of the tidal cycle. In other parts of the Pacific Ocean the tides follow the sun, for example in Tahiti, which is near the amphidromic point of the lunar oscillating system, but far away from that of the solar amphidromic system.

5 Tides around the British Isles

The same principles of resonance can be applied to gulfs and seas as to the main ocean basins. The Bay of Fundy, with its very high tidal range, has a natural period of oscillation of between 11·6 and 13 hours, which corresponds closely to the tidal semi-diurnal period. The North Sea also demonstrates resonance. Its dimensions are such that it responds to the tidal movement in the Atlantic to produce three amphidromic points (figure 5-4). The position of the points as shown on Admiralty Chart 301 (5058) (figure 5-5) demonstrate the effect of friction. In the shallow North Sea, friction has the effect of moving the amphidromic points eastwards away from the source of tidal energy, which comes in from the north and moves anti-clockwise round the basin.

The tidal chart of the English Channel shows a further stage in this process. Here the amphidromic point has moved inland and become degenerate. The result is a greatly decreased tidal range on the coast in the neighbourhood of the Isle of Wight, in comparison with the range on the French coast, where it is very large in the region around St Malo. This is also probably due to friction influencing the position of the amphidromic point, which, if there had been no friction, should have been in the centre of the channel, with the tide moving anti-clockwise

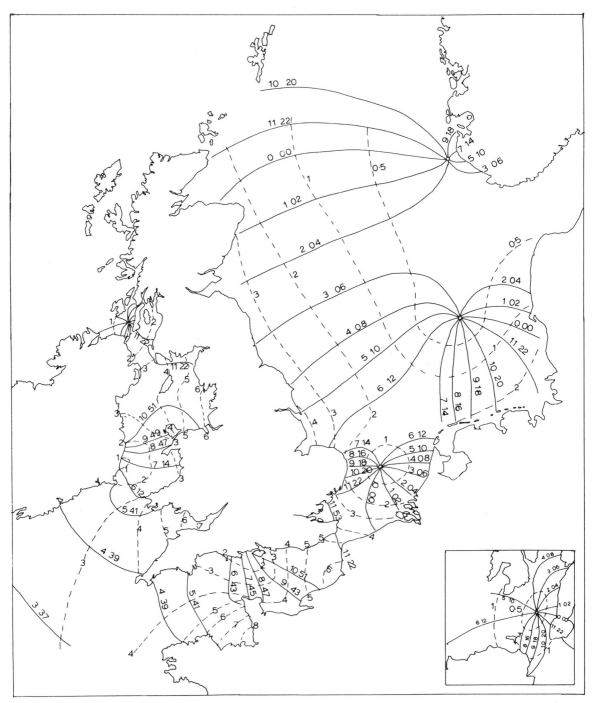

Figure 5-5 Co-tidal and range lines for the North Sea tides. (*Based on Admiralty Chart 5058.*)

round it, eastwards along the French coast and westwards along the English coast. The same feature is also found in the southern Irish Sea, where there is a degenerate amphidromic point off Ireland, south of Dublin.

6 Shallow-water effects

The presence of an area of low tidal range off the south coast of England is one of the factors which helps to explain the interesting double tidal phenomena that occur around the Solent. This feature is probably due to the shallow-water effect. The deformation a progressive wave undergoes as it enters shallow water is shown in figure 5-6A. The smooth sine wave form is

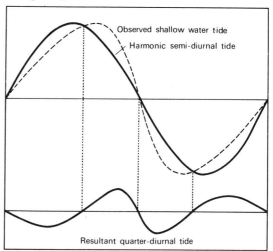

Figure 5-6 Shallow water tidal modification of a progressive wave. (*After Doodson and Warburg, 1941.*)

modified because the crest of the wave is in deeper water: as the speed depends on the depth of water this causes an acceleration of the wave crest, and a retardation of the trough. The form of the wave becomes asymmetrical, with a steep front and a gentle back slope.

The asymmetrical curve can be split into its component parts in the same way, as shown in section 5-1. The two components consist of a large sine curve and a smaller asymmetrical curve which has two maxima to one of the main curve. The small amplitude curve is called a quarter-diurnal tide as it has two crests. It can itself be split into its component sixth-, eighth- and higher-order tidal curves, by the same technique of harmonic analysis. The curves have a phase lag of about 90° so that they can never combine to give a double high or low water.

When a standing oscillation enters shallow water the deformation appears to be such that when the tidal curve is analysed harmonically the phase lag is often about 0° or 180° as shown in figures 5-7A and B. This means that the maxima or minima semi-diurnal tides coincide with the maximum or minimum of the quarter-diurnal tide. Thus with a phase relationship of 0° the two curves combine to give a double low water, if the amplitudes are suitable, while if the phase relationship is 180° a double high or low tide should result.

The simplest occurrence of double high or low tide is when the amplitude of the quarter-diurnal tide is more than one quarter of the semi-diurnal tide, or the sixth-diurnal tide is more than one ninth of the semi-diurnal tide. This is most likely to occur with respect to the quarter-diurnal tide near the node of the semi-diurnal tide. Figure 5-7C shows that it is also likely to be near the maximum of the quarter-diurnal tide if they occur in a closed channel as shown.

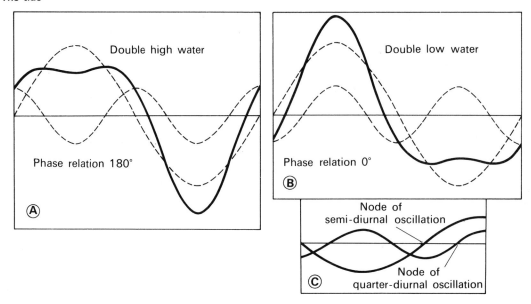

Figure 5-7 Shallow water tides. **A:** Double high water; **B:** Double low water; **C:** Relation of ½ and ¼ diurnal nodes. (*A, B, C after Doodson and Warburg, 1941.*)

These conditions are well fulfilled in the Solent area, which is near the node of the degenerate amphidromic system in the English Channel. Freshwater, Isle of Wight, illustrates the formation of a double low water by the simplest means. The phase relation is $+176°$; the semi-diurnal tide has an amplitude of 2·02; the quarter-diurnal tide has an amplitude of 0·53, giving $4 \times 0·53 = 2·12$. The conditions at Portland are favourable for the formation of a double high water, with a phase relation of $-002°$. The amplitude relationship is not quite suitable, because four times the quarter-diurnal tide is not quite equal to the semi-diurnal tide. However, the sixth and higher species fulfil the necessary conditions to produce a double high water.

7 Tidal streams

a Theory

So far little has been said about the pattern of tidal streams on the open coast. Their reversing nature in the immediate vicinity of the beach has been mentioned, but a little further offshore the tidal streams are often rotatory in character. A combination of the streams for different hours in figure 5-3 is shown in figure 5-8 for an ideal amphidromic system. Everywhere the pattern is one of anti-clockwise rotatory streams in the northern hemisphere. They become more asymmetrical towards the edge of the basin.

Another type of rotatory tidal stream pattern may be set up by the effect of the rotation of the earth on a progressive wave in a fairly narrow channel, where the compensation is achieved by the development of transverse streams rather than by the setting up of subsidiary gradients. The streams in this instance will rotate clockwise in the northern hemisphere.

Much of the material on which this section and the preceding ones are based is from the *Admiralty manual of tides* (1941) by A. T. Doodson and H. D. Warburg, which provides one of the best accounts of modern tidal theory and observation.

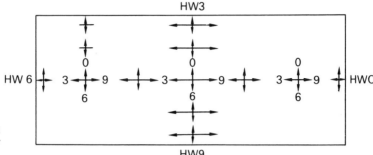

Figure 5-8 Tidal streams in an ideal amphidromic system. (*After Doodson and Warburg, 1941.*)

b Observations

The theoretical pattern of tidal streams is in general found to occur in reality, but actual measurements of tidal streams are of great value because small differences between the local streams and the theoretical pattern can be significant. The net residual of tidal flow is of particular importance as it determines the direction of sediment transport under tidal action. At any one station an hourly record of tidal streams can be used to draw a vector diagram, as shown in figure 5-9. The vector between the first and last points gives the residual of the streams over a complete tidal cycle. The residual indicates the net movement of water and sediment carried in suspension. Bed load may only be moved at the higher velocities and hence may have a different residual movement. The examples show a rectilinear pattern of tidal flow close inshore off the Lincolnshire coast. Further offshore the pattern is more rotatory in character.

Methods of observing tidal streams have been briefly mentioned in chapter 2. Now some of the results of these techniques of measurement will be considered. The jelly bottle gives values of the current at one point at one time, but observations can be made hourly over a complete tidal cycle, thus enabling the calculation of residuals. The other method, which has been extensively used during the last decade, is the Woodhead sea-bed drifter. This method supplies information on the long-term residual tidal stream pattern, and hence indicates the movement of the water near the bottom due to all the currents that are operating. The tidal streams have usually been found to be dominant in the areas where most observations have been carried out around the British coasts. The method can supply useful information concerning the sources of beach material in the recovery areas.

(i) Jelly bottle results: The jelly bottle can be used in depths up to 60 fathoms (110 m) and it can be adapted for deeper currents. It records currents from ¼ to 6 knots (0·46 to 11 km/hour). It was used to check the dispersion of radio-active tracer on Caistor Shoal, a bank near Great Yarmouth. The tracer, which was in water 7 m deep according to the chart, moved south about 0·6 to 1·6 km under the influence of the flood tidal stream. It was not influenced by onshore wave currents. Current meter readings over a complete tidal cycle gave 2·1 knots (3·86 km/hour) for the flood south-going current and 0·8 knots (1·47 km/hour) for the ebb, north-flowing stream. These measurements were made 1 m above the bottom on a tide of 2·44 m range at Lowestoft.

Another set of measurements was made by J. N. Carruthers (1962) in the same position by means of the jelly bottle closer to the bottom. The tidal range was 2·2 m when the observations were made and the greatest south-going flood stream recorded was 2·75 knots (5 km/hour), while the north-going ebb stream reached 2·35 knots (4·3 km/hour). Both results show a

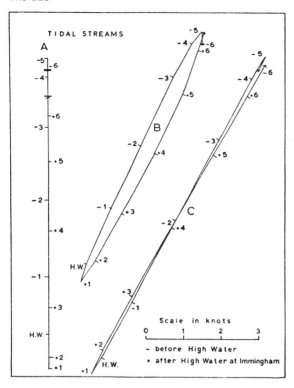

Figure 5-9 Tidal stream vectors for the three positions shown in figure 5-13A.

southerly residual, but the bottom currents are shown to be considerably stronger than those only a few feet above the bed.

The importance of the much stronger velocities on the bottom is that if the bed is loose and mobile it will change configuration with changing stream direction. The presence of sand waves of asymmetrical form is thought to reflect the dominant direction of tidal residual flow, but where the bottom velocities are high the form of the waves may reverse with the reversal of the tidal streams. This aspect of the study of tidal streams will be considered in more detail in the next section.

Observation of tidal streams in deeper water have shown that the water movement can move sediment in considerable depth, where the tidal range is large. The La Chapelle bank 160 km in a direction of 240° from Ushant in the Bay of Biscay has been studied by J. N. Carruthers (1963). This bank has a shallowest depth of 151 m and lies near the edge of the continental shelf, with rapidly deepening water to the southwest, where the gradient is 1 in 9. There are reports of shoals or rocks appearing above sea level in the area, but these reports probably confused marked turbulence above the bank with outcrops of rock.

Echo-soundings over the bank have revealed sand waves on the bank surface, suggesting strong currents. One explanation, advanced by D. E. Cartwright (1959), suggests that the sand waves are the result of stationary internal waves, generated by the disturbance of tidal streams coming onto the shelf when a strong thermocline (separating the warm surface waters in summer from the colder bottom water) is present, and these internal waves have since been identified by thermistor observations.

The tidal range in the area is 3 m. Direct current measurements 12·2 m below the surface revealed a maximum velocity of 1·8 knots (3·3 km/hour) towards N 17° E and 2·1 knots

(3·86 km/hour) towards S 17° W, which is normal to the trend of the sand waves. The maximum speed is directed towards the deep ocean. Currents close to the bottom were measured in 1962 at 47° 40′ N, 7° 14′ W in 155 m at 25 cm above the bottom by the jelly bottle method at hourly intervals for 17 hours. The tide was half way between mean level and neap tide. The maximum stream was 0·55 knots (1·0 km/hour) at 190° with a reciprocal direction 6 hours later of 0·42 knots (0·72 km/hour). At no time was the current weaker than 0·25 knots (0·46 km/hour). The maximum streams were normal to the sand wave crests. These observations show that sand can be moved at very considerable depths by tidal streams, where the range is considerable.

(ii) Sea-bed drifters: Drifter studies differ from those already discussed in that the trajectories of the water are followed, rather than the flow past a fixed point. The drifters are released at one point and move with the water at a predetermined depth. The individual drifters have serial numbered cards attached, offering the finder a small reward if the card is returned with the time and place of recovery entered on it. The method has the advantage of cheapness and independence of weather conditions.

On the other hand, however, it has the major disadvantage that only the starting and end points are known. Only a mean speed can be established, which must be a minimum, especially for drifters recovered from the coast. These are, however, the most useful for beach studies. Some drifters are recovered by fishing boats, particularly in the North Sea. Another disadvantage is that the drifter does not move with the water particle, which may well change level due to turbulent flow, while the drifters maintain one level. Either surface or sea-floor drifters may be used, the former being liable to be influenced by the wind. The latter are not necessarily representative of the true residual flow, owing to their being affected differently by varying current velocities.

A series of drifter studies have been carried out by J. G. Harvey (1967) in the Irish Sea. The surface drifters appeared to be influenced mainly by the wind. Drifters released in the North Channel moved, under some conditions, south into the Irish Sea. Winds between west and north caused the drifters to move to the coast of Ireland, whereas southwest winds drove the drifters to the northeastern part of the sea.

In a study of the dispersion of sea-bed drifters from the Menai Straits in 1962–3, the drifters were dropped at hourly intervals in 12 equal batches to ascertain movement at different states of the tidal cycle. The recoveries showed a southwesterly movement followed by a northwesterly one along the west coast of Anglesey. After a longer time interval recoveries extended further, reaching South Wales and Blackpool after 255 and 202 days respectively. Drifters released in the North Channel were distributed in all directions from Galloway in the southeast, Portrush in Northern Ireland in the west, Ayr in the northeast and Tiree in the north. Drifters in the Solway Firth moved with the tides, but only penetrated into the inner estuary at spring tide at the equinoxes. A comparison of surface and bottom drifters indicated that the patterns do not coincide. On the bottom there is a general easterly movement onto the beaches east of a line from the Mull of Galloway, the Isle of Man to Anglesey. The recovery rate for surface drifters was about 50% (J. G. Harvey, 1967).

The Irish Sea study, which covered a large part of the northern part of the sea, may be compared with studies made by A. H. W. Robinson (1964; 1968) in the North Sea, at the mouth of the Humber in estuarine conditions. The Humber has a complex relief resulting from tidal processes, with interdigitating channels between elongated banks. The origin and character of these features will be discussed in the next section. Tidal streams in the channels are quite rapid, attaining 5 knots (9·2 km/hour) near Spurn Point. Three drifter experiments were made by releasing drifters simultaneously at one or more points in the estuary. One factor that must be considered in beach recoveries is the beach's attraction for people, who are relied on to find and return the drifter cards.

In one experiment 240 drifters were released 4·8 km east of Spurn Point at the seaward end of the main Humber ebb channel near the Outer Binks shoal at low water. The pattern of recovery is shown in figure 5-10. The total recovery was 121 or just over 50%, most of which

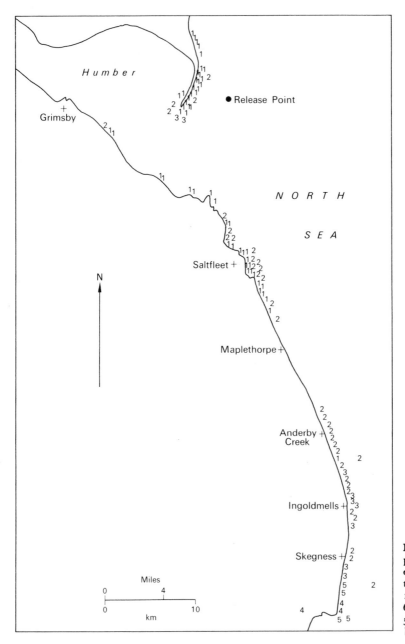

Figure 5-10 The recovery pattern of drifters from the 1961 experiment. The figures refer to recovery intervals as follows: 1, 0–30 days; 2, 31–60 days; 3, 61–90 days; 4, 91–120 days; and 5, over 121 days. (*After A. H. W. Robinson, 1964.*)

were returned within a period of 6 months after release. During the first 3 months 33% of the returns were from Spurn spit and 7% from the southern bank of the Humber between Donna Nook and Cleethorpes, the remainder coming from the Lincolnshire coast south of Donna Nook.

There were two barren areas within the general area of recovery. One was within the Humber near Tetney, and the other was near Mablethorpe. The absence in the latter area probably helps to account for the long-continued erosion and low beaches in this vicinity, as it suggests that the offshore circulation is such that sediment cannot readily reach this part of the coast. The Tetney area has a large channel which precludes easy access to the beach, and this accounts for the low recoveries. This factor cannot explain the absence of recoveries around Mablethorpe, where the beach is narrow and well frequented.

The wind direction during the period of the experiment was mainly southwesterly and on the whole was opposite to that of drifter movement, suggesting that waves were not responsible for the movement of the drifters. Most of the waves would have been generated by the local winds. This assumption would be reasonable in this locality, which is relatively sheltered from long swells coming from the north.

In 1962 drifters were released within the Humber and many of these were recovered from Spurn Point, the others mainly from the south bank of the Humber opposite Hull and near Grimsby. It seems likely that the drifters oscillate up and down the tidal channels in the estuary, moving in the residual direction of the tidal streams. The drifters located on the Lincolnshire coast, on the other hand, appear to move with the main flood stream residual on the main North Sea tidal amphidromic system. The tidal residual seems a more likely means of movement than beach drifting, as experiments showed that once stranded on the beach the drifters did not move subsequently. Had they moved by beach drifting they would have reached the area around Mablethorpe. The bottom material can clearly cross the Humber in both directions via the tidal channels, as shown in figure 5-10.

The main importance of this type of observational data is the emphasis it throws onto the processes operating in the offshore zone, chiefly by means of the action of tidal streams. The offshore zone is a vital part of the beach environment in the Humber estuary and elsewhere. Processes operating in it determine to a considerable extent the development of the beach and foreshore. This is true of much of the coast of Britain, of other areas where tidal streams are vigorous and rectilinear, and where there is an abundance of loose sediment close offshore. The tidal streams give rise to a distinct offshore morphology, which will be considered in the next section.

8 Forms generated by tidal processes

a Sand waves

Forms created by tidal streams include both large features, and small ones superimposed on the larger ones. The smaller features, which are widespread in their occurrence, are the sand waves already mentioned (section 5-7-b (i)) in the discussion of the La Chapelle bank.

The patch of sand waves on the La Chapelle bank is about 19 km long, ending abruptly at the edge of the continental shelf. The sand waves extend laterally for 8 km. Their crests have an average height of 7·6 m, reaching a maximum of 12·2 m. The mean wave length is 854 m, but there is considerable variation. The waves are orientated at about 110°, parallel to the edge of the shelf and normal to the tidal streams. They are composed mainly of sand with some shell gravel. Their asymmetry is such that a westward transport of sediment is suggested, as their

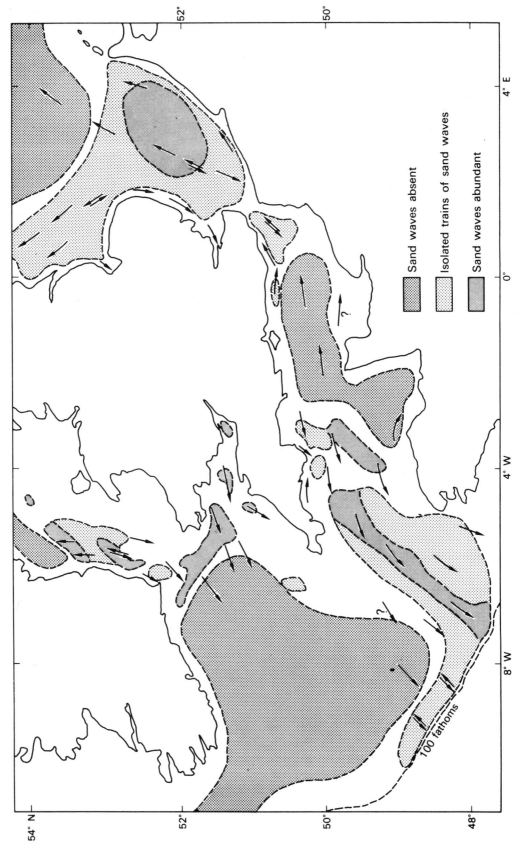

Figure 5-11 Distribution of sand waves and presumed direction of sand transport around southern Britain. (*After Stride, 1963.*)

Sand waves absent

Isolated trains of sand waves

Sand waves abundant

100 fathoms

steeper face is to the west. This is confirmed by the current measurements already mentioned (section 5-7-b (ii)).

An extensive part of the seas around southern Britain and Ireland has been explored by A. H. Stride (1963) in his study of the effects of tidal streams on the sea floor in shallow water. Sand waves can be readily identified on echo-sounder traces, and their asymmetry gives a useful indication of the residual direction of sediment transport. Stride has found sand waves up to 18·3 m high and 915 m long. The waves off the coast of East Anglia are often 4·6 m high and 137 m long, with the largest waves near the edge of the continental shelf. The waves are most regular in size where there is most sediment.

The straightness of the wave crests also varies, tending to be straight in the northern Irish Sea and the Bristol Channel, but more sinuous in the southern Celtic Sea and the western English Channel. The straighter crests seem to occur where the tidal streams are rectilinear and reach diametrically opposed peak velocities. The sinuous crests occur where the streams are similar in strength over a wider angular range.

The distribution and direction of sediment movement is indicated in figure 5-11. The sand waves occur in those areas where the surface tidal streams are in excess of 1·84 km/hour (1 knot),

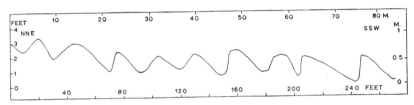

Figure 5-12 Profile surveyed across a series of sand waves on the Inner Dog's Head Bank, off the south Lincolnshire coast.

and where sand is abundant. They are found in a belt 96 km wide off the east coast of England and the west coast of Germany, over much of the Irish Sea, the Bristol Channel, the English Channel and the Celtic Sea where sand is plentiful. Most of the sand waves are asymmetrical, and even a difference of 5 cm/sec (0·1 knots) in the ebb and flood stream peak velocities is sufficient to cause asymmetry and net sediment transport. The general pattern of movement is indicated on figure 5–11 and shows an important movement northwards, estimated at 40 million m³/year in a 64 km wide belt, up the coast of the Netherlands, with a movement south in a 16 km wide belt off East Anglia. The movement is to the north off Lincolnshire and Yorkshire. The pattern in the English Channel is more complex. The movement off the Netherlands coast has been confirmed by radio-active tracers: here the general pattern of movement is parallel to the coast, particularly in the North Sea. Some sediment probably is moved into the Wash by tidal streams. The pattern of movement inferred from the sand waves applies to a belt a little distance from the shore. The pattern close inshore is more complex, but sand waves still occur in the immediate vicinity of the shore.

A survey of sand waves on the Inner Dog's Head Bank, off the south Lincolnshire coast, shown in figure 5-12, indicates a very asymmetrical pattern (C. A. M. King, 1964). The waves had a mean height of 36·5 cm and a mean wave length of 8·4 m, their trend being normal to the main tidal streams. Their asymmetry indicates that they were formed by the ebb tidal stream, which flows at 2 knots (3·65 km/hour) in a direction of 205° at spring tide. It is possible that the asymmetry changes with the reversal of the streams in this area of strong rectilinear streams, because the sand waves are quite small and occur on banks that dry out at low spring

153

tide. Their orientation indicates that they are formed by the tidal streams and not by the waves, even though they are exposed to wave action as the tide falls and they emerge above water level. These waves were surveyed at low tide when they had emerged.

In the English Channel there appears to be a more circulatory pattern of movement in the bays off the south coast of England. At the eastern end of the channel the waves are symmetrical, suggesting that they may be stationary. In the western part of the channel the main direction of transport is to the west, changing to southwest as the shelf edge is approached.

A detailed study of the sand waves on Warts Bank, southwest of the Isle of Man, by N. S. Jones et al. (1965) showed that the waves travelled at an average rate of 5 to 10 cm/day, one crest covering 74 cm on a single flood tide. The ridge is elongated roughly east to west. The waves on the northern side moved southwest while those on the south side moved northeast, on the evidence of their asymmetry. One side of the bank is thus affected by the flood tide and the other by the ebb. The streams over the bank reach a maximum of just over 1 knot (1·84 km/hour). The waves occur in depths between 10 and 40 m below lowest water.

R. L. Cloet (1954a) has described waves on the northern part of Brake Bank in the southern North Sea. They varied from 46 cm to 2·15 m in height and 30·5 to 137 m in length, and lay perpendicular to the elongation of the bank; their steeper slope faced north. The sand waves increased in size up the channel where currents reached a maximum velocity of 3·2 knots.

J. H. J. Terwindt (1971) has observed sand waves in the southern bight of the North Sea. Repeated detailed surveys of the 3 to 15 m high sand waves did not reveal systematic movement. The waves were asymmetrical; those immediately north of the Hinder Banks had steep southern slopes, while those still further north had the opposite asymmetry. The wave crests were eroded by waves during heavy storms and built up again during ensuing calmer conditions, changes in height reaching a maximum of 2 m. Large current ripples, 0·2 to 2·0 m high, covered many of the sand waves, tending to increase in height towards the crest of the sand waves where tidal streams were stronger. The asymmetry of the mega-ripples suggested movement from both sides to the sand wave crests. The sand waves were thus built up by tidal streams.

Another set of sand waves surveyed off the Yorkshire coast (R. V. Dingle, 1965) support the view that the tidal streams converge off Flamborough Head. The records were obtained by Continuous Reflection Profiler. The sand waves were of two types, one variable and one uniform in wave length. The former type were characteristic of areas of thicker sediment. The latter type occurred nearer the coast, where the tidal streams were more rectilinear. The sand waves did not occur in depths greater than 55 m (30 fathoms), because the stream velocities were too low at this depth.

A very uniform set of small sand waves has been recorded in St Andrew Bay, Florida (G. G. Salsman et al., 1966). The movement of the waves has been observed for two years. They are orientated normal to the tidal streams, are composed of fine sand, and are 30 to 60 cm high and 13 to 20 m long. The ridges are advancing into a muddy area, and covered 11·44 m in 849 days. The sand waves, which are in a tidal channel behind an offshore barrier, move more rapidly when the tidal streams are strongest. The streams reach 40 cm/sec when the lunar declination is at a maximum during the flood tide. This tidal stream is dominant, flowing northeast, in the direction of wave migration. There is also a longer-term acceleration in the migration over the whole period, due to long-term tide effects.

b Sand ribbons

In some areas instead of sand waves there are ribbons of sand on the bottom, but these also can be used to assess the direction of sediment transport by tidal streams. Acoustic sounding has shown that ribbons of sand occur over a large part of the area off southern Britain where the sea floor consists of patches of sand, sand and gravel and stones or shells. The general trend of the sand ribbons is parallel to the coast, elongated along the English Channel, the Bristol Channel and the Irish Sea. The pattern also parallels the direction of the strongest tidal streams. The ribbons vary from place to place, becoming more diffuse at the edge where the tidal streams are less than 1 knot (1·84 km/hour) on the sea surface. They are sharply defined when the streams exceed this value, and when the streams exceed 2 knots (3·65 km/hour) their length to breadth ratio increases. They are often only a few cm thick, but may be up to 2·4 km long and a maximum of 100 m wide in the Bristol Channel.

c Ebb and flood channels and tidal banks

One of the factors on which longer-term beach changes depend in some areas is the slow migration of offshore banks. The significance of offshore changes in relation to the coast was first recognized by Van Veen (1936; 1950), who studied the effect of tidal streams on the form and movement of offshore sand-banks. R. L. Cloet (1954a and b), A. H. W. Robinson (1956) and Robinson and Cloet (1953) have applied these ideas to parts of the coast of southeast England.

The form and pattern of the banks and channels are related to the position and strength of the ebb and flood tidal streams and their respective sediment carrying capacities. The ebb and flood channels formed by this process develop an interdigitating pattern, often with almost parallel channels. They develop best where the tidal flow is rectilinear. The streams associated with the flood and ebb tide tend to follow different paths to avoid each other, each of which scours according to its capacity, while accumulation takes place to form elongated or parabolic banks between the tidal channels. The flood stream continues to flow in the flood channel after the tide has begun to fall, while the ebb channel is used by the ebb stream after the tide has started to rise. There is thus a net transport of material in the direction of the ebb tidal stream in the ebb channel and the same is true of the flood channel. The channels and banks often interdigitate in a complex pattern, with divergences and curved branches at times. These patterns allow the streams to avoid those of the opposite tidal state. They are related to the shape of the whole estuary or coastline (A. H. W. Robinson, 1960).

The channels and banks form only in areas where much loose sediment is available offshore. They are widespread in the southern North Sea and Irish Sea, because in both areas a large amount of loose sediment was left as a result of fluvioglacial deposition. Much of this material has been re-sorted and formed into banks by the tidal streams.

A good example of these features is found in the Goodwin Sand area off Kent in the southern North Sea. The area has been surveyed frequently because of its danger to navigation. Detailed evidence is, therefore, available of the form and movement of the Goodwin sand-bank (Cloet, 1954a). This large sand-bank has been more or less in its present position for a considerable time, and is maintained in it by the interplay of the ebb and flood tidal streams. It has, however, gradually been moving since detailed surveys were started in 1844. The feature as a whole is more or less elliptical in shape, with the major axis trending a little east of north. It is about 13 to 14 km long above 11 m depth. To the northwest it is separated by the Gull stream from Brake Bank, which lies less than 3·2 km off the Kentish coast between Deal and Ramsgate in Sandwich Bay. The Goodwin bank is cut at its southwestern end by the flood channel in Trinity Bay. Another flood channel follows the coast between Deal and Brake Bank, both being directed north. The intervening ebb channels, directed south, flow down the Gull and round the east side of the bank. The bank reaches its greatest width where the two opposed streams are least able to counteract each other. The whole of the Goodwin Sand is tending to rotate anti-clockwise, its northern end moving west and its southern end east, and it is widening slightly. Brake Bank, meanwhile, has been moving slowly shorewards.

Since the beginning of this century a deep cut has developed in the northeast part of the bank, forming Kellett Gut, first surveyed in 1926. It is 23·8 m deep and cuts across the widest part of the bank. Its formation may represent an attempt of the ebb and flood tidal streams to balance one another, or it may represent a stage in the formation of a new Brake Bank. The North Goodwin bank is becoming further separated from the South and the present Brake Bank is moving towards the shore, onto which it may be welded. It appears that as the sediment content of a bank increases so it tends to move towards the shore.

Evidence has been put forward by Robinson and Cloet (1953) to suggest that the process of shoreward migration of offshore banks has already taken place to form the Stonar shingle bank, which lies inland of the present shingle and sand mass of Brake Bank. The Stonar Bank, extending south from Ebbsfleet, now lies inland of a sand and shingle spit extending north from near Deal. The outer bank has grown northwards by longshore movement of material along the coast from the south. The Stonar Bank is an extensive feature nearly 4 km long, 553 m across and extending down to a depth of 12·2 m below Ordnance Datum and up to a height of 4·9 m above O.D. It is formed of rounded flint shingle.

The offshore Brake Bank lies 2·4 km from the coast and is 305 to 1220 m wide and 6·4 km long, much of it being in less than 3·65 m of water. It has a steep slope of 1 in 40 facing landwards into the Ramsgate channel, which separates it from the shore. Its seaward slope is much flatter at 1 in 500. It is similar in form and composition to the Stonar Bank. It has been suggested that the latter feature represents an earlier offshore bank that has slowly been driven landwards either by the tidal streams, which cause an anti-clockwise rotation such as that taking place in the Goodwin area, or by wave action. The Brake Bank is now moving onshore, probably as a result of wave action, moving shingle to its steep landward face. This may also represent the process by which the Stonar Bank formed. A similar process may supply the material to the beach in other areas. Some of the shingle of Orfordness may be derived from offshore. Extensive beds of shingle have been located 8 km offshore in this area (A. H. W. Robinson and R. L. Cloet, 1953).

Offshore banks are particularly well formed in many estuaries, and along the east coast of England. This pattern of offshore relief is especially well developed off the southern Lincolnshire coast. The area has already been mentioned (in section 5-7b (ii)) in connection with the retrieval of Woodhead sea-bed drifters released off Spurn Point and carried southwards with the residual of the tidal streams. The offshore banks and their associated tidal channels are extensively developed in the Wash and off Gibraltar Point, but they die out further north. Figure 5-13A shows the pattern of the banks and suggested type of channel in this area, while 5-13B shows a set of profiles surveyed across the banks (C. A. M. King, 1964).

The tidal streams of the south Lincolnshire coast are almost entirely rectilinear, being exactly so off Skegness at point A, where there is a southerly residual of 1·47 km/hour (0·8 knots), indicating a flood tide dominance at this point. Closer inshore a tidal channel develops and it also has a flood residual. The flood stream reaches 7·35 km/hour (4 knots) in this channel. The channel runs up onto the lower foreshore near profile 3. It seems likely that much material travels along this channel onto the beach at this point, as it is in this vicinity that particularly rapid beach accretion has taken place during the last two decades, a fact indicated by the rapid rise of the sweep zones in this area. The accretion here is discussed further in section 16-3. The main flood channel also swings close to the lower foreshore near the outlet of the River Steeping. The vigour of the stream in this channel is indicated by the very coarse nature of the sediment

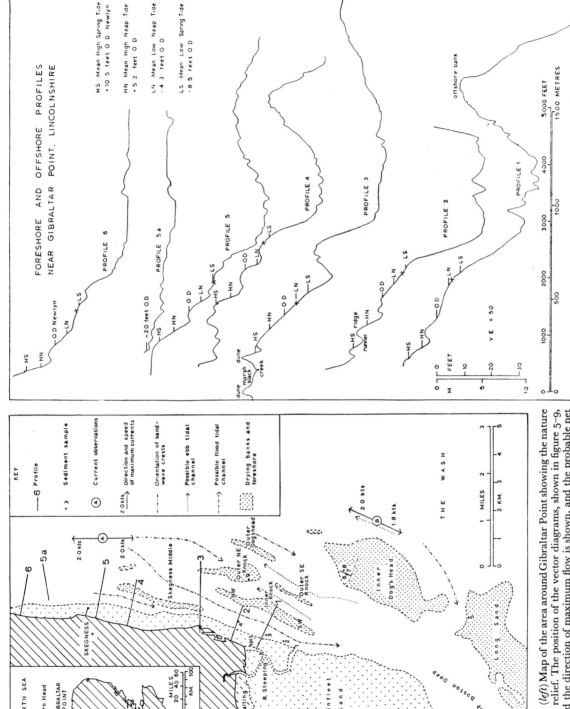

Figure 5-13 (*left*) Map of the area around Gibraltar Point showing the nature of the offshore relief. The position of the vector diagrams, shown in figure 5–9, are shown, and the direction of maximum flow is shown, and the probable net direction of tidal flow in some of the channels is indicated; (*right*) Foreshore and offshore surveys along the lines indicated on the left-hand figure.

on the floor of the channel, which gets coarser southwards in the direction of flow of the flood stream. Another flood channel runs along the seaward side of the Outer Dogshead and Outer southeast Knock Banks, while ebb channels are developed on either side of the Outer Knock Banks, carrying sediment to the north. The pattern of sand waves on the Inner Dog's Head Bank supports this interpretation.

It seems likely that the pattern of the tidal channels and intervening banks controls the movement of sediment in this area, and determines where it can most easily reach the foreshore, to build up the ridges that characterize this stretch of coast. The coast has been growing out eastwards for some centuries, but the zones of maximum accretion have varied through time. The variations are probably connected with the slow movement of the offshore banks, which can be traced on successive charts of the area. These indicate that during the last hundred years the Skegness Middle Bank and associated flood channel between it and the shore have been developing and moving south. This movement has probably allowed the major zone of accretion to form at this point, just south of the town of Skegness. The pattern of the Knock and Dog's Head Banks has also become more complex with new channels developing. These have probably increased the importance of the ebb channels, which now form a circulation by which material moving in from both directions can come ashore in the area (A. H. W. Robinson, 1964).

The drifter experiments support the morphological interpretation of the channels and banks, and the two forms of evidence together provide useful information concerning the trajectories of material and water under the influence of tidal streams off the Lincolnshire coast. The tidal morphology helps to account for the large number of recoveries of drifters from the southern Lincolnshire coast. The pattern of tidal channels indicates that much of the sediment moving into the Wash stays there, because the flood tidal channels are dominant and these allow southerly movement of material.

The banks themselves are often very steep and massive. Those off Gibraltar Point consist of fine, well-sorted sand. Five samples varied between a mean of $2 \cdot 10$ and $2 \cdot 42$ ϕ units, the sorting coefficients being $0 \cdot 30$ and $0 \cdot 59$, using Inman's measures. This fine uniform sand contrasts strongly with the coarse, poorly sorted material in the channels, in which the mean size was $-0 \cdot 90$ to $-1 \cdot 29\phi$, and the sorting $1 \cdot 19$ to $1 \cdot 64$. On the lower foreshore the sediment was fine mud and the slope was very gentle.

Another example of the importance of the tidal morphology in coastal analysis is given by J. R. Hardy (1966). There is a small zone of accretion forming the protruberance of Winterton Ness on the Norfolk coast, and separating two areas of erosion to north and south. The ness has migrated southwards since the beginning of this century. Surveys made in 1884, 1905 and 1956 show that neighbouring areas underwent erosion or deposition in a complex pattern. Changes in the offshore zone have been taking place also. There are well-developed offshore banks and tidal channels in this zone. A north-trending bank has developed on the sea bed since 1945. This bank trends away from the coast immediately adjacent to the growing ness. It seems likely that a flood channel has developed between the ness and the new bank. This channel would allow sediment to come ashore in the vicinity of the ness, while an ebb channel probably carries material offshore on the eastern side of the north–south bank. The bank now rises to less than $1 \cdot 83$ m depth below chart datum. In this instance the change on the foreshore seems to have occurred before the formation of the bank. It is, however, possible that the tidal streams were at least partially responsible for the changes both on the foreshore and in the offshore zone.

A. H. W. Robinson (1966) has shown that Winterton Ness is the northernmost of a series of similar nesses along the coast of East Anglia (figure 10·13). The other nesses are, from north to south, Caistor Ness, Lowestoft Ness, Benacre Ness and Thorpe Ness. The same pattern of tidal stream channels and banks is repeated in nearly all of these nesses. There is a flood channel carrying material southwards onto the northern flank of the ness, while an ebb channel carries material northwards on the southern flank. The growth and movement of the individual nesses can be traced and related to the development of offshore banks, which are the result of the tidal streams. Benacre Ness has moved furthest north, a direction contrary to the normal beach drifting direction on this coast. A well-developed flood–ebb channel system is established off the coast at this point. A study of the changing offshore relief shows that between 1824 and 1965 an ebb channel became established off the position then occupied by Benacre Ness. Successive charts after 1865 show the gradual northerly shift of the ebb channel, and this shift has been followed by the northward migration of the ness. The dominance of the ebb stream immediately off the ness has been demonstrated by observations. The change in position of the channels has led to the formation and migration of the Barnard Shoal where the flows become opposed to one another. Since 1824 the ness has moved rather more than 2 km to the north.

The coast illustrates particularly clearly the importance of the offshore zone, in which tidal streams are the dominant process in explaining changes that are taking place on the foreshore. It is an area of fairly vigorous tidal streams which attain 3·4 knots (6·25 km/hour) 6·4 km off-shore and 2·3 knots (4·2 km/hour) close inshore in Yarmouth Roads. There is also a plentiful supply of sand in the offshore zone.

Similar features also occur on the south coast of England and one example has been discussed by A. H. W. Robinson (1961). He shows that in Start Bay beach material cannot be replenished from offshore as ebb and flood tidal channels cause movement of material parallel to the shore. There is an offshore component near Hallsands, owing to a northeast trending minor flood channel. The main offshore feature in this area is the north-northeast trending Skerries Bank, a stable feature that shows relatively little change over a period of 100 years between 1853 and 1951, when surveys were made. The bank is covered in sand waves with amplitudes varying from 30 cm to 5·2 m. They are aligned perpendicular to the main ebb stream that flows parallel to the elongation of the bank across it from the north-northeast. The offshore relief is not conducive to foreshore replenishment here and erosion results along the coast. The present supply of beach material is probably not being augmented and is relict in character.

A sand-bank formed by tidal action is described by J. Dungan-Smith (1969) in Vineyard Sound off Martha's Vineyard near Cape Cod. The bank, called Middle Ground, is orientated west-southwest to east-northeast and is about 5 km long and $\frac{1}{2}$ km wide. It is wholly formed of sand and carries sand waves on its crest. The sand waves are 2 m high and are reformed every half tide cycle. An anti-clockwise circulation takes place around the bank, owing to the dominance of the northeast-flowing flood stream on the southern side of the bank, and the southwest-flowing ebb stream on the northern side. The average maximum shear velocity of the tidal stream is 4·5 m/sec. The bank owes its origin to the tidal streams, though its position is determined by a remnant of morainic material. Some of the banks in the area are basically morainic —only thinly veneered with sand—although they have been shaped by the tidal streams.

These examples illustrate how important the offshore zone can be in a consideration of the supply of material to the foreshore. For this reason it is necessary to take into account the offshore relief and the processes that fashion it, particularly when tidal processes are active and strong tidal streams may carry much sediment in directions very different from that supplied by the waves alone. The morphology of the offshore zone provides valuable information concerning the tidal processes, and these processes cannot be ignored in many areas where the tidal range is large and the streams are strong.

Another way in which tidal processes are important on the beach is in the causing of a cyclic variation in the water level and hence in the level at which waves are operating. This cyclic element will be considered briefly in the next section.

9 Tidal cycles on the foreshore

One interesting cyclic change concerned with tidal processes has a biological consequence. On some of the beaches of California, at Long Beach and to a certain extent at La Jolla, there is a regular change in sand elevation with the tidal cycle of spring and neap tide. W. F. Thompson and J. B. Thompson (1919) and E. C. Lafond (1939) show that a few days after neap tide the beach a few feet below mean tide level reaches its minimum elevation, while the beach a short distance above the mean tide level reaches its maximum elevation. The reverse changes occur after the spring tide. The cut now occurs at the higher level and the fill below mean tide level. These changes in the elevation of the sand on the beach are used by a species of fish, *Leuresthes tenuis* or Grunion, to protect their eggs after spawning. They lay their eggs two or three days after spring tide above mean tide level. The eggs are then buried by sand during the neap tide period when deposition occurs at this level. When the next spring tides occur the sand is again removed and the eggs are ready to hatch, having been protected by sand meanwhile. The spawning of the grunion takes place during the period from March to August when the sand movements resulting from tidal action are most regular. During other times of the year the changes in sand level due to variation in wave size are much greater than those due to tidal action, and they therefore mask the latter changes. The changes in level are related to the different levels at which the waves act during different parts of the tidal cycle. In most areas the waves are too variable for such changes to be observed, and it was thus not possible, for example, to detect changes of this type due to the tidal cycle on a beach in County Durham where weekly surveys were carried out for more than a year.

A very consistent wave pattern combined with a regular tidal cycle produces cyclic changes on the beach at Estrella on the northwestern coast of the Gulf of California (D. L. Inman and J. Filloux, 1960). A sea breeze blows onshore during the hotter time of the day and this combines with a tidal cycle in which the highest of the fortnightly spring tides also occurs in the early afternoon. Thus the waves are at their maximum intensity at the time of the highest water level once a fortnight and this results in a fortnightly beach cycle. The maximum tidal range is 7 m at spring tide, and there is a marked diurnal inequality in the tidal range. The beach profile is steep, ending in a broad low tide terrace, which is a characteristic profile for a beach with small waves and a large tidal range. The waves reach a normal maximum of about 0·61 m significant height and a period of three to four seconds, owing to the limited fetch. The beach face has a gradient of 1 in 7, rising 7·6 m above the low-tide terrace, which is 1370 m wide ending in an outer bar at 3·05 m below mean sea level. This bar is formed by the waves at lower, low water.

A berm is formed at the top of the beach at higher, high water. The level of the berm follows the level of the higher, high water as the tide rises, but the combination of the time of the highest tide with the largest waves causes cutting of the beach. Rebuilding takes place during the succeeding days as the tide level falls until the cycle is complete. Heavy minerals are concentrated in the beach face at each high tide, and these concentrations record the variations in tide height through the fortnightly cycle.

Detailed effects of rising and falling water level on the movement of sand on the foreshore have been studied by A. N. Strahler (1964) and M. L. Schwartz (1967). The former made half-hourly observations of the foreshore near Sandy Hook, New Jersey, during the summer period when the general beach level was stable. A rhythmic pattern of deposition and scour took place over the tidal cycle. As the tide rose there was deposition near the inner limit of the swash, followed by scour in the swash-backwash zone. A wedge-like step of deposition moved up the beach. The scour gave way to deposition of coarser, poorly sorted material at a lower level. The maximum deposition occurred at the step, where well-sorted pebbles and gravel occurred, in the breaker zone. In many of the cycles the layer of sand involved was 6 cm thick at mid-tide level. The fall in tide level reversed the changes, bringing the profile back to its original form.

M. L. Schwartz (1967) used tracers in his study of tidal changes on the foreshore on pocket beaches on the Atlantic coast of Nova Scotia. He found that during the flood tide a small portion of the sediment eroded in the lower backwash scour zone was deposited just seaward of the upper swash limit. This material consisted of the finer fraction. Most of the eroded material was carried to the breaker zone, where the coarser material accumulated in building the step under the breaker zone, while some finer grains went further seaward. There were minor differences during ebb-tide sedimentation. The lower backwash scour zone was translated seaward and the sediment eroded from there was deposited seaward of the upper swash limit, thus rebuilding the profile in a previously scoured zone. The step was built up of coarse grains in the same way. When the breaker zone had returned to its original low-tide position, little sediment had moved out beyond the breaker zone to the shoaling wave zone.

E. G. Otvos (1965) has made a somewhat similar study of changes on a beach over a single tidal cycle. Depths of erosion at different phases of the tide on Long Island Sound beaches were recorded by using columns of coloured sand. The stations in the breaker zone during the tidal cycle developed a dual lamination, with coarse grains underlying finer ones. The laminae were several mm thick under many conditions. Occasionally other patterns developed, such as a single fine-grained or coarse-grained lamina.

J. R. Duncan (1965) has also studied the effects of changing water level during the tidal cycle in the swash-backwash zone on a sand beach. The observations were made on Manhattan beach on the Californian coast. The beach level was measured on rods driven into the beach to a predetermined depth, leaving 46 cm exposed. Half-hourly measurements were made over the tidal cycle, where the range was 1·8 m. At high tide the water level in the beach is low and this results in the deposition of a lense of sediment in the swash zone nearer the backshore, with scouring on the surf side of the zone. When the water table in the upper beach is relatively high at low water, erosion takes place in the upper zone due to intensified backwash, with deposition in the lower zone near the surf boundary. The varying water level causes the fluctuations of the zones of sedimentation with the tide. This results in changes of gradient, the slope being steeper at high tide and gentler at low tide. The change is reflected in laminae at varying angles in the foreshore deposits.

These detailed observations show how the variation in water level over the tidal cycle affects the movement of sand as the swash-backwash zone migrates across the beach. The changes only become consistent when the wave action is uniform. For this reason longer-term cyclic changes due to tidal phases are not common. In most areas the variability of the waves more than counteracts the regularity of tidal fluctuations in water level. The examples cited mostly apply to areas with only a low to moderate tidal range. Where the tidal range is large specific beach profile types can form. These will be considered, together with profiles characteristic of tideless seas, in chapter 12.

Summary

The tides are produced by the gravitational attraction of the earth, moon and sun. The tractive forces can be split into their component semi-diurnal and diurnal lunar and solar constituents. The response of the oceans to these forces is based on the amphidromic system, which is a standing oscillation modified by the rotation of the earth to produce a progressive wave moving round a central nodal point. Each water body has a natural period of oscillation. When this natural period is the same as that of one of tidal forces then a state of resonance is set up and a large tidal response results. The tide around the British Isles is also based on a series of amphidromic systems. Some of these have become degenerate owing to the effects of friction. This has the effect of moving the amphidromic point towards the shore. There is a degenerate amphidromic system near the Isle of Wight; this is associated with double tidal phenomena that are due to the effect of shallow water on a standing oscillation.

Tidal streams tend to be rectilinear near the coast and rotatory further offshore. The velocity of flow can be measured at one point by means of jelly bottles, while sea-bed drifters can be used to determine the longer-term trajectories of the tidal residuals. These observations give useful information concerning beach sedimentation. Tidal streams generate specific morphological forms. Small-scale features include sand waves, which indicate by their asymmetry the net direction of sediment transport. They occur where sediment is abundant offshore. Sand ribbons also occur where streams and sediment supply are suitable. The larger-scale features are the tidal banks and the interdigitating channels that surround them. The latter are used predominantly either by the flood or the ebb tide, and both these tidal morphological features are common in estuaries and occur along the coast where tidal streams are rectilinear and sediment is abundant. They are common along the east coast of England, and are associated with the growth and movement of nesses of accumulation along the coast of East Anglia and with the zone of accretion in south Lincolnshire. In these areas it is essential to consider the tidal processes offshore in explaining the changes that take place on the foreshore.

On some beaches where wave action is regular, tidal cycles can be observed as the tide rises and falls. On some beaches the cycles are fortnightly, related to spring and neap tide. On others systematic changes occur over one tidal cycle. These changes are related to the water content of the beach, which is lower as the tide rises than as it falls. Deposition tends to take place at the top of the beach at high tide and erosion as the tide falls. The changes are reversed lower down the beach.

References

CARRUTHERS, J. N. 1962: The easy measurement of bottom currents at modest depths. *Civ. Eng.* **57**(669), 486–8.

CARRUTHERS, J. N. 1963: History, sand waves and nearbed currents of La Chapelle Bank. *Nature* **197**(4871), 942–7.

CARTWRIGHT, D. E. 1959: On submarine sand waves and tidal lee waves. *Proc. Roy. Soc.* A **253,** 218–41.

CARTWRIGHT, D. E. and STRIDE, A. H. 1958: Large sand waves near the edge of the continental shelf. *Nature* **181,** 41.

CLOET, R. L. 1954a: Hydrographic analysis of the Goodwin Sands and the Brake Bank. *Geog. J.* **120,** 203–15.

CLOET, R. L. 1954b: Sand waves in the southern North Sea and in the Persian Gulf. *J. Inst. Navig.* **7,** 272–9.

DINGLE, R. V. 1965: Sand waves in the North Sea mapped by continuous reflection profiling. *Mar. Geol.* **3**(6), 391–400.

DOODSON, A. T. and WARBURG, H. D. 1941: *Admiralty manual of tides.* London: H.M.S.O. Hydrog. Dept. Admiralty.

DUNCAN, J. R. 1965: The effects of water table and tide cycle on swash-backwash sediment distribution and beach profile development. *Mar. Geol.* **2**(3), 186–97.

DUNGAN-SMITH, J. 1969: Geomorphology of a sand ridge. *J. Geol.* **77,** 39–55.

HARDY, J. R. 1966: An ebb–flood channel system and coastal changes near Winterton, Norfolk. *East. Mid. Geogr.* **4**(1), 24–30.

HARVEY, J. G. 1966: Large sand waves in the Irish Sea. *Mar. Geol.* **4**(1), 49–56.

HARVEY, J. G. 1967: Drifter studies in the Irish Sea. *Liverpool essays in geography.* London: Longman, 137–56.

INMAN, D. L. and FILLOUX, J. 1960: Beach cycles related to tide and local wind wave regime. *J. Geol.* **68**(2), 225–31.

JONES, N. S., KAIN, J. M. and STRIDE, A. H. 1965: The movement of sand waves on Warts Bank, Isle of Man. *Mar. Geol.* **3**(5), 329–36.

KING, C. A. M. 1964: The character of the offshore zone and its relationships to the foreshore near Gibraltar Point, Lincolnshire. *East. Mid. Geogr.* **3**(5), 230–43.

LAFOND, E. C. 1939: Sand movement near the beach in relation to tides and waves. *Proc. 6th Pacific Sci. Congr.,* 795–9.

MACMILLAN, D. H. 1966: *Tides.* London: C. R. Books.

OTVOS, E. G. 1965: Sedimentation–erosion cycles of single tidal periods on Long Island Sound beaches. *J. Sed. Petrol.* **35**(3), 604–9.

PHILLIPS, A. W. 1969: Sea-bed water movements in Morecambe Bay. *Dock and Harbour Auth.* **45**(580), 379–82.

ROBINSON, A. H. W. 1956: The submarine morphology of certain port approach channel systems. *J. Inst. Navig.* **9,** 20–46.

ROBINSON, A. H. W. 1960: Ebb–flood channel systems in sandy bays and estuaries. *Geog.* **45,** 183–99.

ROBINSON, A. H. W. 1961: The hydrography of Start Bay and its relationship to beach changes at Hallsands. *Geog. J.* **127**(1), 63–77.

ROBINSON, A. H. W. 1964: Inshore waters, sediment supply and coastal changes of part of Lincolnshire. *East. Mid. Geogr.* **22,** 307–21.

ROBINSON, A. H. W. 1966: Residual currents in relations to shoreline evolution of the East Anglian coast. *Mar. Geol.* **4**(1), 57–84.

ROBINSON, A. H. W. 1968: The use of sea-bed drifters in coastal studies with particular reference to the Humber. *Zeits. für Geomorph.* NF **7,** 1–23.

ROBINSON, A. H. W. and CLOET, R. L. 1953: Coastal evolution of Sandwich Bay. *Proc. Geol. Assoc.* **64,** 69–82.

SALSMAN, G. G., TOLBERT, W. H. and VILLARS, R. G. 1966: Sand-ridge migration in St Andrews Bay, Florida. *Mar. Geol.* **4**(1), 11–20.

SCHWARTZ, M. L. 1967: Littoral zone tidal cycle sedimentation. *J. Sed. Petrol.* **37,** 677–83.

STRAHLER, A. N. 1964: Tidal cycle changes in an equilibrium beach, Sandy Hook, New Jersey. *Tech. Rep. 4 Proj. NR* **388–057,** Off Naval Res. Geog. Br. (51 pp.)

STRIDE, A. H. 1963: Current-swept sea floors near the southern half of Great Britain. *Quart. J. Geol. Soc.* **119,** 175–99.

STRIDE, A. H. and CARTWRIGHT, D. E. 1958: Sand transport at the southern end of the North Sea. *Dock and Harbour Auth.* **38**(447), 323–4.

TERWINDT, J. H. J. 1971: Sand waves in the southern Bight of the North Sea. *Mar. Geol.* **10**(1), 51–67.

THOMPSON, W. F. and THOMPSON, J. B. 1919: The spawning of the grunion. *Calif. State Fish and Game Comm. Fish Bull.* **3.**

VAN VEEN, J. 1936: Onderzockingen in de Hoofden in Verband met de gesteldheid der Nederlandsche Kust. 's-Gravenhage (Ministerie van Waterstaat).

VAN VEEN, J. 1950: Eb en vloedschaar systemen in de Nederlandse getijwatern. *Tijd van Let. Kon. Ned. Aardr. Gen.* **67,** 303.

6   The effect of wind

1   Model experiments with an onshore wind : a) Water circulation; b) Ground perspex experiments; c) Movement of sand under wind and wave action; d) Effect of wind on beach profiles.

2   Observations in nature of beach profiles in relation to wind action

3   Coastal sand dunes : a) Sand size characteristics; b) Sand movement by wind; c) Dune vegetation; d) Dune stabilization; e) Types of coastal dunes : (*i*) *U-dunes and their orientation*; (*ii*) *Transverse and longitudinal dunes*; (*iii*) *Cliff-top dunes*; (*iv*) *Tropical dunes*; f) Examples of coastal dune systems : (*i*) *Holland*; (*ii*) *Parana*.

Summary

The wind, quite apart from its major function of generating waves, plays an important part in the movement of beach material. In this chapter model experiments made to establish the effect of onshore wind on sand movement are described first, and then the full-scale effects of wind action on the beach are considered. The third section is devoted to coastal sand dunes, which are an important aspect of wind action on the coast.

1 Model experiments with an onshore wind

a   Water circulation

It has been shown that under the action of waves in shallow water both the major acceleration of the water particles and the transport of sediment is predominantly in a landward direction outside the break-point. There is thus a general tendency for accretion to take place. In places rip currents can carry sediment seawards through the breaker zone, but such movement does not extend far beyond the breakers.

One factor that can cause a seaward current along the bottom is an onshore wind. This causes a landward movement of the surface water which may be compensated by a seaward current at a lower level. A series of experiments was made in a narrow wave tank to examine the effect of an onshore wind on the water movement and sediment transport on the bottom both inside and outside the break-point. A fan was fixed above the wave generator so that either wind alone or a combination of wind and waves could be tested.

The first series of experiments was designed to study the pattern of water flow under the action of an onshore wind without wave action. The tank was not long enough for the wind of the strength used to generate any measurable waves itself. The water circulation examined, therefore, was the result of the wind only. The circulation was measured by using dye in depths from 8 to 18 cm, with winds varying from 16 to 21 km/hour. The pattern was the same in all depths. A rapid landward flow on the surface, extending downwards to between one third and one quarter of the total depth, at most positions became a seaward drift in the lower part and along the bottom. The maximum current where the wind speed was 21 km/hour (580 cm/sec) was 5·8 cm/sec landwards on the surface with a seaward current of nearly 2 cm/sec near the bottom.

A series of measurements as made of the seaward bottom water velocity by timing the travel of small wax balls about 2 mm in diameter and with a specific gravity of 1·1. The results are shown in figure 6-1, which indicates that on a smooth sand bed of gradient 1 in 15 in depths of water

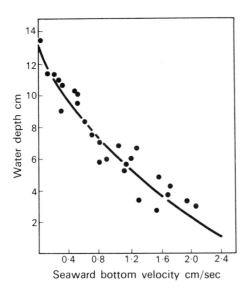

Figure 6-1 Relationship between water depth and seaward bottom velocity with an onshore wind in the wave tank.

ranging from about 3 to over 13 cm there was a decrease of bottom velocity seawards from about 2 cm/sec in a depth of about 3 cm to a very low seaward velocity in depths greater than 12 cm. A landward velocity on the surface was maintained in all depths.

In a narrow tank of the type used there must be a return seaward of the water blown towards the shore. In shallow water this must be accomplished in a relatively narrow zone and hence a faster current is generated. Where the water is deeper the return flow can be spread through a greater depth of water and is not, therefore, so rapid at the bottom where the velocity was measured. The distribution of velocity on the bottom under wind action is just the reverse of that under wave action alone. The movement on the bottom under wave action is always landwards although it increases in velocity towards the shallower water as far as the break-point. The expected seaward return current occurred in the narrow tank, but its velocity was not sufficient to move quartz grains. The weak current can have a very significant effect on the movement of sand on the bottom when it is combined with wave action.

b   Ground perspex experiments

The effect of the wind-generated current on the bottom was tested by using perspex ground to a median diameter of 0·63 mm. This material is very light, having a specific gravity of only 1·18. It is much more mobile than quartz sand and reacted to the low velocity of wind-generated currents. The ground perspex was formed into a beach with a gradient of 1 in 15 and experiments were made by varying the depth of a trap similar to the one used for the experiments described in section 9-2(a). The strength of the wind over the trap was 41·5 km/hour. The results are shown in figure 6-2, in which the water depth is plotted against the seaward transport of ground perspex in gm/minute over the width of the tank. The points plotted are the mean values for the depth specified. There was a very rapid increase in the amount of seaward transport as the water became shallower, due to the increase in velocity with decreasing depth. In depths over 6 cm less than 5 gm/minute moved seawards, but in a depth of 2 cm the amount was nearly 15 gm/minute. The seaward velocity and the amount of ground perspex moved seawards showed a positive linear correlation.

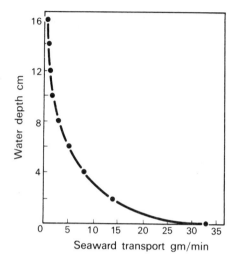

Figure 6-2 Relationship between water depth and seaward transport of perspex sand under an onshore wind in the wave tank.

When the trap was placed in a constant depth of water and the wind velocity varied at this point, there was a very rapid increase of seaward transport as the wind velocity increased and exceeded 35 km/hour. The experiment was made in a depth of 4 cm on a beach gradient of 1 in 15. The relationship is shown in figure 6-3.

c Movement of sand under wind and wave action

The wind-generated currents could not under the conditions of the experiment move the quartz sand grains. The effect of the wind, therefore, had to be studied together with that of the waves,

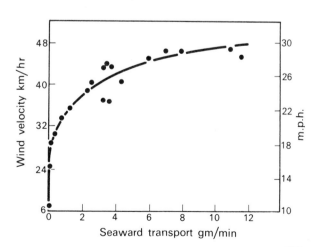

Figure 6-3 Relationship between wind velocity and seaward transport of perspex sand under an onshore wind in the wave tank.

a state which is likely to occur in nature when the wind is usually accompanied by waves. Inside the break-point with constructive waves the direction of current flow is reversed. For steep destructive waves, however, under both wind and wave action the flow is seaward inside the break-point and the two currents will reinforce each other. Outside the break-point the wind and wave currents are opposed under all conditions. Experiments to verify these suggestions were made by trapping sand. The addition of wind-generated currents modified both the gross and net transport of sand on the bottom.

For a flat wave of steepness 0·01, on a beach gradient of 1 in 15, the gross transport without wind increased steadily till the break-point was reached and then fell off sharply. Similar waves combined with a wind of 45 km/hour moved a considerably lower gross volume of sand. The reduction is the result of the partial cancellation of the wind and wave currents, thus reducing the sand movement. The reduction in volume transported occurred in all depths, but was most marked near the break-point.

The net transport of sand is more important, as changes in the beach profile are dependent upon it. The effect of wind-generated currents was examined on waves of two types—the steep destructive waves that move sand seawards inside the break-point and the flat waves that move sand landwards in all depths. Each run was made without wind and then repeated with similar wave conditions and with a wind of 45 km/hour blowing over the trap. In all runs the beach gradient was 1 in 15.

For the runs made with the steep waves (H/L = 0·046) without wind, the curve plotted of sand movement against distance from the break-point shows a landwards movement outside the break-point and seawards inside it. The runs made with a strong onshore wind show that in all depths the seaward movement of sand is much greater in volume, especially inside the break-point where the seaward generated current has been shown to be strong. The effect on the movement outside the break-point is not very great. The results, shown in figure 6-4A, confirm the suppositions concerning the wind effect.

The flat wave used had a steepness of 0·01. The plot of sand transport against proximity to the break-point showed landward transport in all depths under wave action alone. In this experiment the wind effect was more marked. In the deepest water the slight landward movement under calm conditions was reversed and a slight seaward movement took place under the onshore wind. In the shallower water outside the break-point the strong landward movement under calm conditions was considerably reduced under the action of the onshore wind. The position of the maximum landward movement was no longer at the break-point, but about 30 cm seaward of it. Inside the break-point the landward movement under calm conditions was also reversed, becoming a fairly marked seaward movement as shown in figure 6-4B.

The results illustrate the effect of the seaward wind current on the normal landward wave-generated currents. The wind currents reverse the landward current in the shallowest and deepest water. In the former the wind current reaches its greatest strength, where the wave current is rather weaker inside the break-point. In the deepest water the wind-generated current is still appreciable where the rather low wave used had little effect on the bottom. These experiments show that landward movement outside the break-point may be reversed in some conditions, and that the effect of an onshore wind is strong inside the break-point, causing an increased or reversed seaward movement.

d   Effect of wind on beach profiles

A strong onshore wind has a marked effect on the amount of sand moved on the bottom by waves. This must affect the development of beach profiles in the model tank. An experiment was made

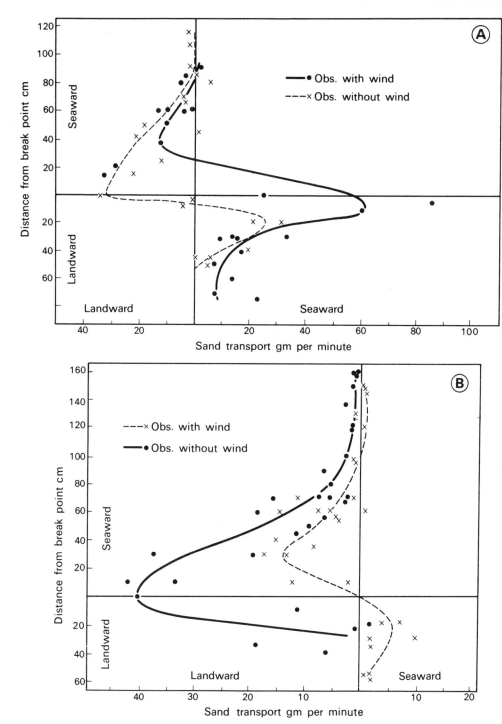

Figure 6-4 **A:** The effect of wind on the transport of sand with a steep wave, H/L 0·046; **B:** The effect of an onshore wind on the transport of sand with a flat wave, H/L 0·010.

to examine this effect, using a flat wave, 4 cm high and 350 cm long, giving a deep-water steepness of 0·0114. The waves would be expected to produce a swash bar. The experiment was carried out on a gradient of 1 in 15. The waves were allowed to shape the beach profile for 1½ hours by which time the profile shown in figure 6-5 had formed. This is typical of a flat wave profile, showing a well-developed swash bar, built 5 cm above the still water level. There is a loss of sand in the

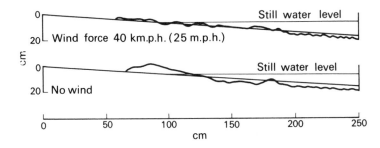

Figure 6-5 To show the effect of an onshore wind on a beach profile built by flat waves.

deeper water owing to the landward transport to build the swash bar. The second profile shows the effect of the same waves accompanied by a strong onshore wind. The waves and wind were allowed to act for the same period, but the profile that was formed was very different: the swash bar was completely lacking and the only deposition of sand was a very small accumulation near the break-point of the waves. The waves were destructive when accompanied by the onshore wind throughout almost all the beach profile, confirming the results of the sand transport experiments.

2 Observations in nature of beach profiles in relation to wind action

If it can be shown that the results of the model experiments on the effect of an onshore wind on sand movement are applicable to natural beaches then the frequency and intensity of onshore winds must be very important in the beach regime. The winds could reverse the effect of waves that would normally cause accretion on the upper part of the beach.

A series of surveys was made on the east coast of England at Marsden Bay, County Durham, to study the effect of the wind on the movement of sand on the beach (C. A. M. King, 1953). The wind is likely to have a double effect on the water movement on a natural beach. It will generate currents near the shore in a similar way to that discussed in the tank experiments but it will also affect the character of the waves themselves. When a strong onshore wind is blowing it will often be accompanied by the steep waves of a locally generated sea, which may be superimposed on and conceal a longer, lower swell. With a strong offshore wind, on the other hand, the height of the advancing waves will be reduced by the head wind and the waves reaching the coast will be flattened, and therefore liable to be constructive. Observations of the steepness of the waves at Marsden Bay confirmed this argument. The mean deep-water wave steepness measured with an offshore wind was 0·0014, with a maximum of 0·0060 for very short waves and a minimum of 0·0002. With an onshore wind the mean steepness was 0·0059, the maximum was 0·010 and the minimum 0·002. Even without the effect of the wind-generated currents near the beach, the waves accompanied by a strong onshore wind tended to be more destructive on the foreshore than waves working with an offshore wind.

The wind-generated current will enhance the effect of the wind on the wave characteristics. On an open beach, however, the seaward flow observed in the narrow wave tank may be concentrated in the form of localized rip currents instead of a general seaward bottom current. In order to investigate the possible connection between wind and beach changes wind roses were prepared for the weekly period between the beach surveys at Marsden Bay. In many cases the wind was predominantly onshore or offshore during the week. The results of the observations with an offshore wind showed that on 13 occasions accretion occurred on the upper foreshore above mean tide level, while erosion only took place on three occasions. With an onshore wind erosion took place 13 times, while accretion only occurred four times. On the lower foreshore below mean tide level the changes were reversed on most occasions.

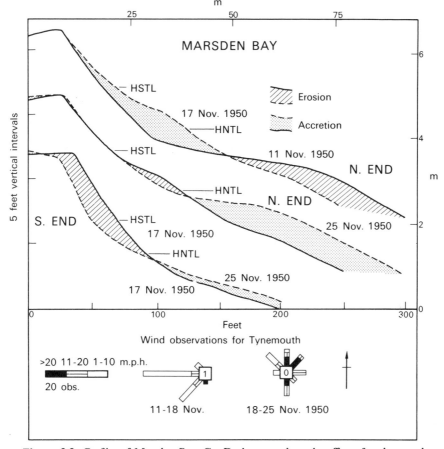

Figure 6-6 Profiles of Marsden Bay, Co. Durham, to show the effect of onshore and offshore winds.

A good example of the effect of an offshore wind is shown in the profiles drawn for 11 and 17 November 1950 (figure 6-6), during the whole of which time between surveys the wind blew offshore from the west, and low, long swells reached the beach. During the period between 17 and 25 November 1950, winds were blowing mainly between south and northeast in an onshore direction. They generated short, high waves and these, combined with the wind, caused considerable erosion on the upper beach, while accretion took place on the lower foreshore. At the south end of the bay 1 m of sand was removed from the berm at the top of the beach and the berm was largely removed. These observations suggest that the results of the model experiments can be applied to natural beaches.

The effect of an offshore wind was observed on a tideless beach in the Mediterranean where a fairly wide expanse of sand was exposed above the water line. The sand was partially protected by a hard salt crust. Measurements showed that a 38 km/hour wind blew 95 gm of sand per 30 cm width of beach into the sea in one minute. This caused accretion in the shallow water.

The wind blows alongshore at times and under these conditions it will tend to set up currents acting along the coast. Waves may be generated, which will be short and will hence approach the shore at a very oblique angle because they will not be greatly refracted. Both the oblique waves and the wind-generated longshore currents will cause considerable movement of material alongshore. F. P. Shepard and D. L. Inman (1950) have pointed out the importance of wind stress in the generation of longshore currents, although they state that it is difficult to separate these currents from those generated by wave action.

3 Coastal sand dunes

One of the most important processes associated with wind action on the coast is the formation of coastal sand dunes. The sand forming the dunes is derived from the foreshore where it is exposed to wind action at low tide, and from the backshore zone, in which the dunes form.

a   Sand size characteristics

A considerable amount of work has been done on the differentiation of beach and dune sands by means of their sedimentological characteristics. The results of mechanical analysis of samples from both environments have been compared. Such studies also throw light on the processes by which wind transports sand. A more detailed consideration of the methods of analysis of sedimentological data will be deferred to chapter 8, but in this section some of the characteristics of dune sand will be mentioned. These characteristics often allow dune sand to be distinguished from beach and other types of sand.

C. C. Mason and R. L. Folk (1958) suggested that the graphic skewness and kurtosis measures may be used to differentiate beach and wind-blown sand. Observations on Mustang Island barrier beach in the western Gulf of Mexico gave the following results:

	Mean size	Sorting	Skewness	Kurtosis in ϕ units
Beach	2·82	0·309	+0·03	1·09
Dunes	2·86	0·273	+0·14	1·07
Flats	2·83	0·286	+0·17	1·20

The mean values do not distinguish between the environments, but the dune sand was significantly better sorted than the other types, while the skewness allowed the beach sand to be distinguished from the other two. The kurtosis distinguished the aeolian flats from the other types.

G. M. Friedman (1961) has shown that by plotting the skewness against the mean for 267 samples derived from dunes, ocean and lake beaches and rivers, it is possible to distinguish between the dune and beach sand in terms of these two characteristics. The dunes tended to have a positive skewness, which implies a tail of finer particles, while the beach sands mostly had a very small or negative skewness, indicating a tail of coarse particles. These results emphasize the more vigorous environment of sedimentation on the beach and the preferential choice of sand grains by the wind. Friedman used moment measures rather than graphic measures in his analysis.

Another study by J. R. Hails (1967) in eastern Australia confirms the importance of skewness in distinguishing between beach and dune sands and barrier island sands. His analysis is based on 1500 samples obtained from various dunes, barriers and fluvial deltaic plains as well as beaches.

The sands in these features, which are of differing ages, are polygenetic, having been reworked during the post-glacial rise of sea leval, when the series of barriers were formed. All the dune samples showed a positive skewness, while only the inner barrier samples did so. Most of the beach samples were negatively skewed (81%). Hails found that it was not possible to distinguish beach and dune sand in terms of its roundness, where the sand was of polygenetic origin.

F. P. Shepard and R. Young (1961), on the other hand, were able to distinguish these two types of sand on the basis of their roundness. They fitted the sand grains, viewed under a microscope, into one of six classes of roundness. The categories were determined by the pivotability of the sand grains: the highest pivotability was that of the most angular grains. The dune samples showed the greater roundness, the roundness being most consistent where the wind blew mainly onshore. The wind can pick up the rounder grains more easily, as the angular ones become readily trapped amongst their neighbours. This criterion is only useful where the sands show a considerable range in roundness, which was not found in the Australian sands analysed by Hails, where all the sands were well rounded.

J. Chappell (1967) argued that skewness is the best moment for differentiating beach and dune sands, provided the skewness is calculated by the moment measure method. He based his conclusions on the analysis of beach and dune sands from the west coast of New Zealand. Analysis showed that the sands were bimodal, containing two logarithmic normal populations 1ϕ unit apart. This may be attributed to the large proportion of heavy minerals in these 'black' sands. The mixed density gives the sands an intrinsic positive skew. The beach sands are, however, negatively skewed. This property allows them to be separated from the dune sands with a fairly high degree of confidence. In older deposits the difference is less marked. The contrast between dune and beach sand is much greater where the prevalent wind blows onshore. The offshore wind blows sand from the dunes onto the foreshore, thus mixing the populations.

The value of textural parameters in differentiating sand and studying depositional processes has been tested by R. J. Moiola and D. Weiser (1968). They used 120 samples of sand from beaches, coastal and inland dunes and rivers. The coastal dunes and beach sands were collected along the panhandle of Florida. They used Folk and Ward's graphic measures. The results indicated that these measures were not efficient in differentiating between coastal dune and beach sand. They were more successful, however, in distinguishing between beach and inland dunes, the latter having sand of smaller mean size and a high positive skewness. Coastal and inland dunes could be fairly effectively distinguished by plotting mean diameter against skewness, and kurtosis against skewness. The inland dunes were finer and for any size more positively skewed. Mean diameter plotted against standard deviation separated coastal dunes from river sands. Their results confirm those of Chappell in suggesting that the graphic measures are not so useful in distinguishing between beach and coastal dune sand, although in the area to which their analysis applies the wind may not have been predominantly onshore in direction.

R. T. Giles and O. H. Pilkey (1965) collected 50 pairs of samples from beaches and dunes along the Atlantic coast of the southern U.S.A. and compared these with samples from rivers in the vicinity. Measurements of median size, sorting, calcium carbonate percentage and heavy and light minerals were determined. Both beach and dune sands appeared to be derived from nearby rivers and also from the sediment on the adjacent shelves. The main differences between the beach and dune sands were the coarser mean size of the beach samples and the better sorting of the dune samples. The average carbonate content was lower in the dunes, but considerable variation occurred in the measures. The sands were mineralogically distinct. The wind picked up the equidimensional minerals as opposed to the elongate ones, which were more concentrated on the beaches.

B. Greenwood (1969) has used discriminant analysis to differentiate between dune and wave-deposited sands from a number of different areas. He compares samples derived from the dunes with those derived from the backshore and foreshore zones. Quarter ϕ sieves were used and moment measures calculated by computer. The samples were obtained from the dunes and beach at Braunton Burrows and other areas in Barnstable Bay, Devon. Both foreshore and dunes are wide and well developed in this area. A total of 112 samples were analysed, including some from St Ives Bay, Christchurch Bay and Padstow Bay. The results of the analysis showed that the multiple discriminant analysis could be used to differentiate the different environments. The most important variables that were used were the skewness, followed in order by the mean size, standard deviation and the kurtosis. The dune sands tended to be smaller in size than the foreshore sands and were better sorted. They tended to be mesokurtic and to have very low skewness values, some of which were positive and some negative. The foreshore sands on the other hand were strongly negatively skewed. The results confirm the findings of other workers.

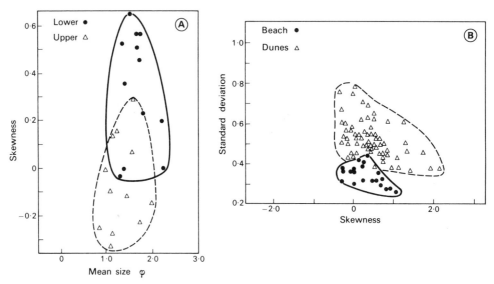

Figure 6-7 Relationship between mean sand size and skewness at two positions on coastal dunes and relationship between standard deviation and skewness of sediment size distribution on the beach and dunes on Plum Island, Massachusetts. (*After Anan, 1969.*)

F. S. Anan (1969) has discussed the matter further with reference to samples from the coast of northeast Massachusetts and New Hampshire, using beach and dune samples. The sampling plan was meticulous. The beach samples were obtained from the beach and were of three types, the details of which are considered in chapter 8. The dune samples were of two types: one group was collected from the upper third of the slip face, and consisted of 3.2 mm thick samples; the others were collected within 30 to 60 cm of the base of the slip face. Both moment measures and Folk and Ward's measures were calculated after dry sieving at $\frac{1}{4}$ ϕ intervals.

The results were presented as scatter plots of various measures plotted against each other, some of which are shown in figure 6-7. The first and second dune samples are best differentiated by plotting skewness and mean size against each other. The upper samples show higher positive skewness on the whole than the lower samples, although there is some overlap. The lower samples show some negative skewness values. The lower samples were slightly coarser than the upper ones. The larger particles rolling down the slip face give the negative skewness to the lower samples, while their loss gives the high positive values to the upper samples. The best type of beach sample can be distinguished from the dune samples by the better sorting of the beach samples. This is contrary to many earlier findings. The result is probably due to the care in sampling the beach, in which only one sedimentological unit was collected. The wide range of grain sizes available helps to account for the poorer sorting in these dunes. Anan's plot of skewness against kurtosis, using moment measures, also provides an effective means of differentiating the sand types, the dune sands having positive skewness values.

The emphasis on proper sampling is important. This brief account of a number of studies of the character of beach and dune sands indicates that they can be separated by moment measures, the skewness being the most diagnostic. The positive skewness characteristic of the dune environment is due to the inclusion of a tail of finer particles, which can readily be carried by the wind, and which, once deposited, require a higher velocity to be eroded. The loss of larger grains by rolling to the base of the dune also renders the higher samples positively skewed. On the beach, on the other hand, the vigorous swash and breaker zones do not allow the deposition of the finer particles, and so a tail of coarser ones gives the negative skewness often found in this environment.

b Sand movement by wind

A number of different types of trap have been devised to measure the movement of sand by wind in the coastal environment. K. Horikawa and H. W. Shen (1960) tested two types of horizontal trap and five vertical traps. A horizontal trap was used to measure surface creep. It was divided into sections perpendicular to the wind direction. The sand moving by creep was assumed to fall into the first section and the sand moving by saltation into the others. Creep was found to account for about 20% of the total transport for all wind speeds. The horizontal trap has the advantage that it does not disturb the wind flow. The vertical trap does suffer from this, but allows the level at which the sand is moving to be recorded. Vanes can be attached to the trap to make it face always into the wind.

P. Y. Belly (1964) measured the sand moving in a laboratory wind tunnel. His results confirmed the rate of transport equation put forward by previous workers. Belly used a variety of sand sizes and sorting. His experiments showed that the threshold velocity for movement was lowered when sand was fed into the tunnel, closely agreeing with Bagnold's values. The value fell from 40 to 30 cm/second. Sand feed did not change the amount of sand in transport at wind velocities in excess of 9·15 m/second, but it did at lower velocities. The poorer sorting of Belly's experimental sand may account for a difference between his results and Bagnold's.

Belly also tested the time required for sand transport to become adjusted to a new wind velocity and found this to be about four minutes or less. A smaller sand of 0·30 mm diameter was then used, and the threshold shear velocity was found to be 16 cm/second, agreeing with Bagnold's value. This sand was better sorted and the amount moved agreed closely with values given by the equations of Bagnold and Karamura.

The effect of moisture in the sand was also tested. This is a feature of importance in coastal dunes and coastal wind transport. The sand and wind were both moistened to prevent the wind drying out the sand. The sand used for the experiment was 0·44 mm. It was found that the moist sand moved less easily than dry sand and the threshold shear velocity was higher. When the moisture was confined to the air the effect was not great for the normal range of humidities experienced. The dampness of the sand was much more effective, and even when the water content was only 2 to 3%, the wind strength needed to initiate movement was greatly increased. The threshold shear velocity for a water content of 0·1% was about 34·5 cm/second, but it increased to 58 cm/second for a moisture content of 3%. The results showed that for fine sand less than 0·20 mm the threshold velocity is best determined empirically. The flying distance of particles was found to be greater than in earlier studies.

Measurements in the field on sand movement by the wind have been made by F. D. Larsen (1969) on Plum Island, Massachusetts. In this area once-stable dunes have been deforested and it is now difficult to stabilize them. This may possibly indicate a desiccation of the climate during the last few thousand years. The orientation and movement of active slip faces in the coastal dune area were measured.

The beach is backed by a foredune ridge 19·5 to 10·7 m high, with blow-out gaps, slip faces and new dunes. Behind this ridge is an interdune area, followed by a discontinuous backdune ridge, which is partially stabilized, rising to over 15 m in places. Behind is an area of small stabilized dunes and a tidal salt-marsh containing some wind-blown sand. The foredunes have a steep east-facing slope and gentle west-facing slope. The east-facing slope is wave-cut, while the west-facing slopes are stabilized by dune grass and other plants. Internally the dunes consist mainly of westward-dipping layers of aeolian sand, but there are also high-angle seaward-dipping cross beds. The interdune area has northwest to southeast lineations, caused by blow-outs resulting from the action of northwest winds. There are some dunes with active slip faces in this area: these are building into the northwest sides of the depressions. The backdune ridge has an active slip face moving into heavily forested land.

Movement of sand was recorded by measuring the changing position of the active slip faces. One moved 15 cm in 31 days. Their slope angle is between 30° and 32°. Estimates of the direction and amount of sand moving by wind were obtained by means of a multidirectional sand trap. The trap had eight 1·27 cm copper tees screened at one end and arranged radially. The opening was fixed 2·28 cm above ground level to allow saltating grains to enter the trap from eight directions. The trap was buried in the interdune area and sand was collected for two weeks in one test. This type of trap is not intended to trap all the sand moving, but to indicate the relative importance of winds from different directions in the movement of sand. The results were correlated with wind measurements. The degree of correlation was highest when the wind velocities were added cumulatively for winds over 9 knots. The plot of the third power of the wind velocity with the amount of sand moved showed little correlation. The moisture of the sand at times caused lack of correlation between the wind and the amount of sand trapped. The method, however, does show a general relationship between the sand moved and the wind velocity. It is not yet possible to ascertain sand transport from wind data alone on the basis of these experiments. The results did show the importance of the north and northwest winds during the period of the experiments.

The deforestation of the Plum Island dunes probably took place in the middle of the seventeenth century. Since this time winds have piled up the sand to form the discontinuous backdune ridge, where sand is moving into a forested area. Buried soils in the interdune area indicate the destruction of the vegetation cover. The dunes were formed not more than 6300 years ago, when Plum Island according to radio-carbon dates formed as a barrier island.

c Dune vegetation

One of the most significant differences between coastal dunes and those of the desert is the presence of vegetation on many of the former and its general lack on the latter. The part played by vegetation is very important in establishing the character of many coastal dunes. It plays a large part in the stabilization of the dune and also promotes its growth, by providing a trap for wind-blown sand.

There is a definite order of colonization by plants of developing dunes. It may differ from place to place but it exerts an important influence on the character of the dunes. The most important dune plants are the grasses which flourish in loose sand. Of these Marram Grass (*Ammophila arenaria*) is the best known. This grass only grows well when it is being continually covered by fresh wind-blown sand. Other grasses common on dunes in the British Isles are *Agropyron junciforme* and *Elymus arenaria*. *Agropyron* can withstand rather more salt spray then *Elymus*, and both are more tolerant of salt than Marram. *Agropyron* is, therefore, often the first colonizer of shingle and sand near the limit of the high spring tide. It helps to trap sand and form an embryo dune. The Marram follows it and grows well as long as sand is being added to the dune, but when the dune becomes stabilized the Marram dies off. Its place is taken by other plants including Sea Buckthorn (*Hippophae rhamnoides*) and Dewberry (*Rubus caesius*) or Elder (*Sambucus nigra*) and many other plants grow as a soil begins to develop.

The southern part of the Lincolnshire coast illustrates the various phases of coastal dune development and vegetation on a shore which is actively building out. The beach is wide and sandy, providing plenty of sand to blow onto the dunes. There are two major dune ridges of different ages. The inner one is about 100 years old and the outer ridge has developed since 1924. Newer dunes are forming in front of the latter at present. Both main dune ridges are shown in figure 6-8, they are both fully stabilized and colonized by mature vegetation.

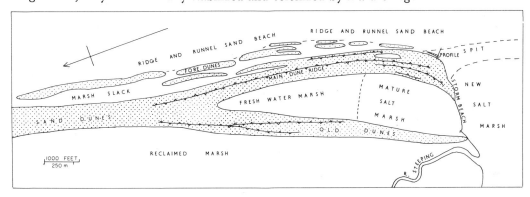

Figure 6-8 Dune pattern at Gibraltar Point, Lincolnshire.

Only on the outer dunes, which are actively growing, are the typical dune plants found. The earliest colonizers on these foredunes are *Cakile maritima* (Sea Rocket) and *Salsola kali* (Prickly Saltwort), which are annuals and which colonize small wind-blown accumulations of sand collected in the lee of some obstacle on the upper beach. On this beach a large amount of flustra collects near high tide level and facilitates the first accumulation of sand. The lowest level at which vegetation will colonize growing sand accumulation is about 3·73 m O.D. (Liverpool), where the mean high spring tide level is 3.32 m O.D. The height range of *Salsola kali* is between 3·73 m and about 4·58 m O.D. At heights above about 4·27 m O.D., *Agropyron junceum* and *Ammophila arenaria* take over and induce further upward dune growth. Under favourable conditions dune growth can be rapid. Figure 6-9 shows that over 1·50 m of sand accumulated over a period of six years on the foredunes at Gibraltar Point over a considerable horizontal distance. At higher level *Elymus areneria* grows in clumps.

All these plants have an important effect in helping to bind together the sand by their complex root system and thus help to protect the dunes from erosion. If the vegetation is weakened for any reason, as by trampling of people walking over the dunes, sand is exposed to the wind and the loose grains blown away. In extreme cases blow-outs may occur. The even line of the dune crest

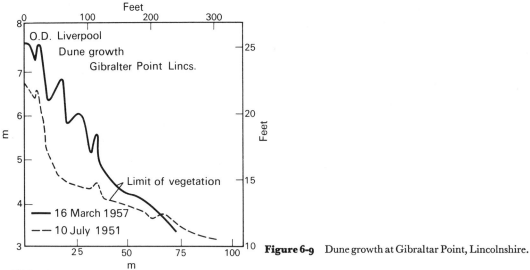

Figure 6-9 Dune growth at Gibraltar Point, Lincolnshire.

will be broken and the form of the dunes altered. Dunes form an important protection to the coast, especially if the hinterland is low-lying, as will be considered in chapter 17.

One of the best areas of natural dune vegetation in England occurs at Braunton Burrows in Devon, where sand reaches the dunes by onshore winds blowing across the sandy estuaries of the Taw and Torridge. The natural vegetation on the dunes was however disturbed by military use during the Second World War. Subsequent attempts to repair the damage have been described by C. Kidson and A. P. Carr (1960).

d   Dune stabilization

The dune system at Braunton Burrows is 6·4 km long, and consists of a foredune system of more or less continuous dunes about 4·6 m high above the beach level, behind which lies a seaward dune ridge about 15·3 m high. Still further east a central and landward ridge rises to over 30 m. In their natural conditions the ridge show instability, as sand is always blowing from the beach and from some parts of the dunes, leaving bare patches of active sand. The pioneer plants, many of which are annuals, grow mainly on the seaward and foredune ridges and these are the most mobile. Other plants, such as moss and shrubs, give greater stability to the landward dunes.

The major problems of maintenance occur when the generally slowly acting natural processes are disturbed by artificial destruction of the vegetation. Early records of the changes in the central part of the dune area show that between 1885 and 1957 the landward dunes had grown in height and migrated 122 m landward. At the same time the seaward dunes had maintained themselves. The reclamation initiated in 1952 had three problems to deal with. These were, firstly, destruction of the foredunes, secondly, blowouts on the seaward dune ridge, and thirdly, instability in the central and landward dunes. As a result of military use the central ridge had been lowered 1·83 m to 2·44 m between 1952 and 1957 over an area of 10 ha. The sand passed through two large blow-outs in the landward ridge, piling up on the landward side of the system and leaving much bare sand exposed. The remedial measures consisted of planting *Ammophila arenaria* extensively. Before the plants could take root some stability was achieved and sand accumulation encouraged by placing brush-wood fences in exposed situations. The fences must have some permeability so that the wind can blow through them, but they must also allow sand to be deposited around them. Planting was carried out first on the seaward main ridge apart from the blow-outs. This work resulted in the rebuilding of the foredunes, and the high-water mark receded 61 m between 1954 and 1958 in a seaward direction. The foredunes grew 2·44 m in height during the period. The growth of the foredunes and the sealing of the blow-outs, however, deprived the inner dunes of some of their nourishment. As a result the middle ridge lost sand where it was still unprotected by vegetation. This ridge was, therefore, replanted between 1955 and 1959. About two to three years are needed before the replanted areas reach stability and to be effective planting must cover the whole bare area. Block planting, which leaves bare strips and patches, is not effective. Nor is it desirable to leave clumps in a replanted area, as the aerodynamics of the wind causes scour around the clumps. Any irregularity that causes hummocks to develop, thus increasing the irregularity, is deleterious. An even slope is much better suited to smooth the aerodynamic flow, and this leads to natural and stable dune formation.

In more recent dune-stabilizing projects, particularly on small areas, preliminary stabilization of the bare sand has been achieved by spraying the sand with a solution that holds the sand in place, preventing loss of sand while the Marram seedlings are taking root. This technique has been applied in the severely depleted dune areas of the Lancashire coast near Southport.

W. W. Woodhouse and R. E. Hanes (1967) have discussed the effects of different plants in dune-stabilizing experiments. They tested four different types of grass on the east coast of the U.S.A., American Beachgrass (*Ammophila breviligulata*), the Sea Oat (*Uniola paniculata*), Dune Panic Grass (*Panicum amarum*) and Saltmeadow Cordgrass (*Spartina patens*). The experiments were carried out on the coast of North Carolina, which is characterized by sandy barrier islands. The outer barriers require preservation because recent erosion has reduced large areas to low, bare sandy flats only 1·22 to 1·52 m above mean sea level.

Experiments included the testing of fertilizers, and providing suitable plants, because *Ammophila arenaria* is not very well suited to the American Atlantic coast. Randomized blocks with at least three replications were used to test the validity of the experiments. The most critical area on this coast, where most of the tests have been carried out, is the zone 152 to 183 m from the high tide mark and only 1·22 to 1·83 m above mean sea level. Where foredunes exist they are 3·66 to 4·27 m above mean sea level.

It was found that only the perennial plants make much contribution to the trapping of sand. Annuals, such as Sea Rocket, are only temporarily effective. The four grasses tested grow naturally in the area and offer the best possibilities for stabilization. The American Beachgrass has been used most extensively and appears most satisfactory. It can grow through rapidly accumulating sand and is easily propagated in a nursery. It is not so successful in hot dry conditions and does better in North than in South Carolina. It is reasonably tolerant of salt spray and will survive occasional salt-water flooding in cool weather. It will also spread rapidly in suitable conditions. Average accumulation in plantings of this grass show a 1·27 m gain between February and November. The Sea Oat grows in warmer climates and is also a good sand catcher, but it grows sparsely naturally and hence produces hummocky ground. It usually grows nearer the surf than the American Beachgrass where they grow together. None of the four grasses mentioned is suitable for areas with heavy traffic, where a turf-forming grass is needed. Bermuda Grass (*Cynodon dactylon*) and Knotgrass (*Paspalum vaginatum*) provide suitable species.

Experiments with fertilizers showed that the response to nitrogen of American Beachgrass was very marked. Fertilization of the sand at Cape Hatteras was carried out by helicopter in the spring of 1963. This method of application prevented damage to the dunes. 2000 acres (810 ha) were fertilized and after three years a full cover had been achieved on 90% of the area, where three years earlier there were only thin degenerating stands. The improved cover has already trapped a considerable amount of sand and led to gains of height. Once a full cover has been achieved the fertilizer will be reduced to a maintenance level. Much of the area planted has been planted mechanically.

B. O. Gage (1970) has described methods of creating and stabilizing dunes on the barrier coast of Texas. Intermittent hurricane damage has destroyed some of the experimental dunes. The sites for the experiments were all low, being 0·76 to 1·37 m above sea level. The tidal range varies between 0·37 and 0·76 m. The sand in the area is fine (between 0·08 and 0·20 mm in diameter) and the prevailing winds blow onshore. An experiment using old car bodies to trap sand showed that these were less effective than wood fencing. Wood slat fencing was found to trap more sand than low-porosity fabric fencing, and the latter more than higher-porosity fabric fencing. Attempts to stabilize low areas by means of vegetation were hindered by high tides, which destroyed most of the plants. Fencing accumulated about 4·05 m³/30 cm of beach. The optimum placing of the second level of fencing when the first becomes buried requires further study. The fencing should be placed some distance away from the lower fence to increase the width of the dune. Porosities of 40 to 60% gave the best results on this coast.

The considerable amount of effort that has been devoted to the study of dune regeneration by planting and fertilizing demonstrates the importance of vegetation in the stability of the dune and in its value as a coastal defence. Vegetation also plays a part in the morphological types of many coastal dunes. The variety of coastal dunes will now be considered.

e Types of coastal dunes

The extent and type of coastal dunes vary widely. H. T. U. Smith (1954) gives a height range from less than 3 m to over 600 m, with a width of less than 30 m to many kilometres. The distribution of coastal dunes is very wide. They occur along much of the Atlantic coast of the U.S.A. and along the Gulf coast, on the Pacific side they occupy one third of the coast of Oregon and considerable stretches of the coasts of Washington and California. In Europe dunes are widespread along the north coast of Germany, the west coasts of Denmark, Holland, Belgium and north France and in the Bay of Biscay. They are more scattered round the coast of Britain and the Mediterranean. Many other coasts also have dunes, such as the desert coast of Peru, parts of Australia and the northern part of the North Island of New Zealand.

Smith (1954) lists the types of coastal dunes as follows:

1   *Foredunes*—mounds up to 3 m high adjacent and parallel to the beach.
2   *U-shaped or parabolic dunes*—arcuate sand ridges which open towards the beach.
3   *Barchans or crescentic dunes*—steep slip-off slope on the lee side away from the beach.
4   *Transverse dune ridges*—these trend parallel or oblique to the shore and are elongated perpendicular to the dominant winds. Their form is asymmetrical with steep lee slope and gentle windward slope.
5   *Longitudinal dunes*—these are elongated parallel to the wind direction and extend oblique or perpendicular to the shore and are symmetrical in form.
6   *Blow-outs*—are hollows or troughs cutting into the dune of the previous types. Large mounds with steep lee slopes occur landward of the larger ones.
7   *Attached dunes*—these depend on some obstacle round which sand accumulates.

(1) and (2) are the most common of these types on many coasts, of which the latter will now be considered.

(i) U-dunes and their orientation: A study of the orientation of dunes in relation to the wind direction has been published by S. Y. Landsberg (1956), to which J. N. Jennings (1957) has suggested

slight modifications. The type of dune considered is probably the most common in the British Isles and Europe and on part of the coast of the U.S.A. The part played by vegetation in the dune formation is important. In its early stages the dune is an oval accumulation, which may have a slip face on the lee side, if it is moving fast. Marram Grass will become established on the front face, but will still be fairly sparse. The vegetation helps to anchor the flanks of the dune, and these tend as a result to drag behind the movement of the centre. This movement is the reverse of that of a desert dune, where the flanks travel fastest, forming the horns typical of a barchan in areas where the wind is unidirectional. Dunes in the early stage are found at Forvie in Scotland and on the Danish coast at Raabjerg Mile near Skagen.

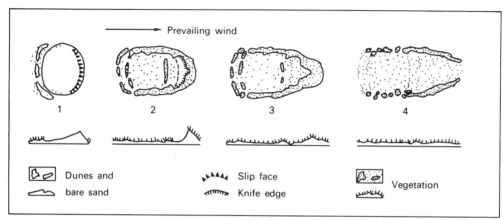

Figure 6-10   U-dune formation. (*After Landsberg, 1956.*)

The stages of evolution are shown in figure 6-10. The mass of the dune diminishes by removal from the centre. During the next phase, in which erosion is dominant, almost the whole surface of the dune becomes vegetated. The U-shape is now clearly seen, opening towards the dominant wind direction. A small zone of bare sand may, however, occur near the forward edge of the dune, facing up-wind with a very steep crest line. In time the dune becomes completely vegetated and gradually elongates its flanks by moving slowly down-wind in the centre. The erosion face is now eliminated.

Sometimes the front face of the dune is broken through completely by the formation of a blow-out near the leading edge, which is least protected from the wind. The dune then consists of its two trailing flanks, while a new one forms in front, giving an *en echelon* pattern to the dune field. The final phase of the U-dune is not found in Britain or Denmark, but occurs in Germany.

In order to relate the direction of the flanks of the U-dune to the wind direction it is necessary to analyse the wind observations. Landsberg used a slightly modified form of the vector diagram method suggested by Bagnold (1951). An earlier method of analysing wind is that used by M. Musset (1923) in which he employed the equation

$$c = \sum_{1}^{10} nj$$

where n is the number of occasions a particular wind was recorded and j is the Beaufort force. A. Schou (1945) modified the equation by using only winds of force 4 or more, and calculating c for each vector of 45°. This equation does not take into account the fact that the sand-moving power of the wind depends on the cube of wind velocity above 16 km/hour, as shown by Bagnold (1941).

The equation Landsberg used took the sand-moving power of the wind into account. The vector terms were given as

$$b = s \sum n_j (v_j - v_t)^3$$

where s is a scaling factor of 10^{-3}, j is the Beaufort force, v_t is $16\cdot0$ km/hour, n is the number of occasions, and v is the wind speed in km/hour. The figures calculated for all vectors can be drawn as a continuous line to give the wind resultant vector (figure 6-11). The second of the two equations gives better results in all examples tested, except for two of the areas studied in Britain and Denmark. In the former, the Culbin Sands of Morayshire, both the methods give a northwest

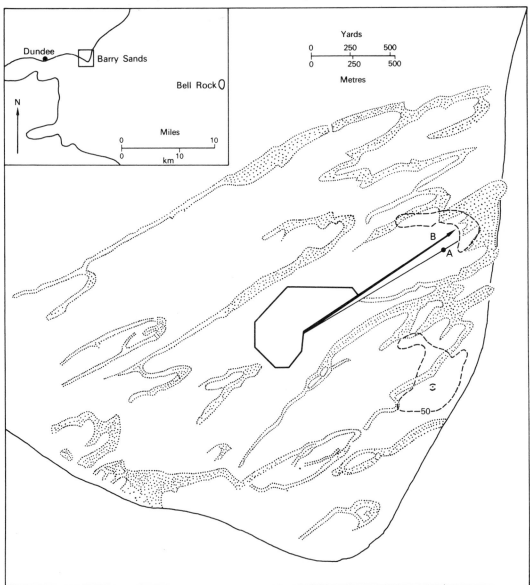

Figure 6-11 The relationship between dune orientation and wind direction. Sands of Barry. (*After Landsberg, 1956.*)

wind, while J. A. Steers (1937) has observed that the prevailing winds in the dune area are southwesterly. The wind values used cannot, therefore, be typical of the dune area.

One of the conclusions of this study is that the wind regime, as defined by the second equation (Bagnold, 1941) is a major factor in determining the orientation of U-dunes, although local variations affect some of the results. J. N. Jennings (1957) has applied the equation to dunes on King Island, Tasmania. He found that, particularly for the dunes on the lee shore, the relationship between wind direction and dune orientation was much closer if the onshore winds only were used for drawing the vector diagrams. The onshore winds have a great advantage as far as dune formation is concerned, because the sand is derived from the beach to which only the onshore winds have access for dune-building processes. Figure 6-12 illustrates the correlation between wind vector and dune orientation on King Island.

Even when erosion is an important process, it can be argued that where the vegetation cover is less complete on the windward side blow-outs are more likely to occur with onshore winds. There is still room for improvement in the method. For example, the wind data are rarely available for the immediate vicinity of the dunes nor for the significant wind that is near the ground. Irregularities of the solid rock relief also affect the dune orientation, as shown in the southeastern part of King Island. The U-dunes, which are amongst the most common type of coastal dune, can in general, however, be related to the direction of the winds responsible for their formation.

(ii) Transverse and longitudinal dunes: W. S. Cooper (1958) has described the coastal dunes of Oregon and Washington, where U-dunes are rare and transverse and oblique dune patterns are found. The oblique type might be placed in the fifth group of Smith's classification, as they have much in common with longitudinal dunes. Cooper also mentions another type, referred to as a 'precipitation ridge'. All these dunes differ from most of those already mentioned in that vegetation is not involved in their formation and growth. This is partly because Marram Grass, which is such an important and common dune plant elsewhere, is not native to this area. It is only since the introduction of this grass that well-stabilized foredunes have developed along this coast. Marram was introduced to San Francisco in 1869 and to Coos Bay, Oregon, in 1910.

The transverse dunes characteristic of much of the dune coast of Oregon and Washington are formed by the summer winds, which blow mainly from the north and northwest. These dunes have long, gentle windward slopes of 3 to 12° and steep slip faces to leeward. There is a tendency for the distance between crests to increase inland over the range 25 to 50 m. The ridges move under the influence of summer winds, and tend to be destroyed by the southwesterly winds of the wet winter season. They form where the ground is fairly level and where the sand supply is adequate. This type of dune is found all over the world where suitable conditions prevail. One of these conditions is the constancy of the wind direction for at least one season of the year, and the direction of this wind will be closely parallel to the lee projections that extend down-wind from the higher parts of the transverse crests. The trend of the main transverse dune ridge is almost perpendicular to the dune-forming wind.

The oblique ridges form only where the sand is plentiful over a wide area which is fully exposed to the seasonal winds, the northwest-to-north summer winds, and the southwest winter winds. The alignment of the dune ridge is dependent on the relative importance of the two winds and lies along the mean direction of summer and winter winds, greater weight being given to the summer winds. The position of this type of ridge is more or less fixed. They are about 200 to 300 m apart, with crests extending for over 1000 m. The summer winds tend to elongate the ridge, while the winter winds, which blow nearly perpendicular to the elongation of the ridge, drive

BC—I

sand onto it and thereby add to its bulk. Cooper suggests that the oblique type of ridge is ultimately stabilized to form a precipitation ridge at the edge of the forest. The feature is an active slip face, which forms in a mass of sand driven towards the forest edge. A large mass of sand is involved in the advancing precipitation ridge, which gradually drives over and destroys the forest in its path.

(iii) Cliff-top dunes: J. N. Jennings (1967) has discussed possible ways in which dunes can occur on cliff tops. There are a number of examples of dunes in this situation in Australia. This type of dune could be formed by sand moving from the landward side of a fairly narrow peninsula, or alternatively during a period of high sea level. Another possibility is that dunes reached the cliff top as climbing dunes, the lower parts of which have subsequently been destroyed by erosion.

Evidence from King Island in Bass Strait shows dunes on top of cliffs 30 to 52 m high. The dunes are of two ages. The older, which are podsolized, are probably Pleistocene in age. The younger ones are Holocene and have only weakly organic soils. Dunes are also growing actively at present behind the extensive sandy beaches. No obvious source is at present available at the cliff foot to account for the older dunes on the cliffs. The U-dune form indicates that these dunes were formed of sand moving from the west, that is from seaward. The highest Pleistocene shoreline in the area was at 36·6 m. The older dunes are younger than this, as they transgress onto the boulder beds marking this high sea level. Evidence of a sea level at 19·8 m shows that the old dunes are genetically associated with a sea at this level. The young dunes are associated with a sea level 3 m above the present. This does not, however, solve the problem of the emplacement of the younger cliff-top dunes. High sea levels do not, therefore, appear to be involved in the formation of the cliff-top dunes. The form of the cliffs indicates that little recession has taken place since the younger cliff-top dunes formed.

The effects of lower sea levels must be considered, as these would expose considerable areas of sand for blowing onto the cliff foot area. There is some evidence for a low sea level stand at −45·8 m. When the sea level is lowered sand can blow inshore. It is well established that climbing dunes can ascend cliffs of considerable height and even a vertical gradient is no barrier. This method of formation of cliff-top dunes is probably the most common. Under special circumstances, however, all the other possibilities cited may explain the presence of cliff-top dunes. These dunes provide a good example of 'convergence' of land forms, when different processes lead to similar end results.

(iv) Tropical dunes: Another problem discussed by J. N. Jennings (1964; 1965), concerns dunes in humid tropical climates. There is a general paucity of coastal dune development in tropical climates and this can probably be accounted for by a number of factors. Even on coasts on which sandy barriers are well developed, and hence much sand is available, there is an almost complete absence of dunes, as on the coasts of Malaya and Johore. On some tropical beaches the sediments appear to be too coarse to allow dune formation, but this is certainly not true everywhere. One possible explanation is the damp climate which prevents the sand drying out.

Areas in which coastal dunes are rare or absent include the coast of Guiana, eastern Brazil, the Ivory coast, the Dahomey coast of Africa, New Guinea, Salvador, Jamaica and tropical Australia where there is no dry season. Dunes do, however, form extensively in Java, where there are large bare dunes, but they are not common in Indonesia as a whole.

P. Birot (1960) has suggested that the density of tropical vegetation may militate against dune formation. E. C. F. Bird (1965) has rejected the effect of dense vegetation. The binding of the

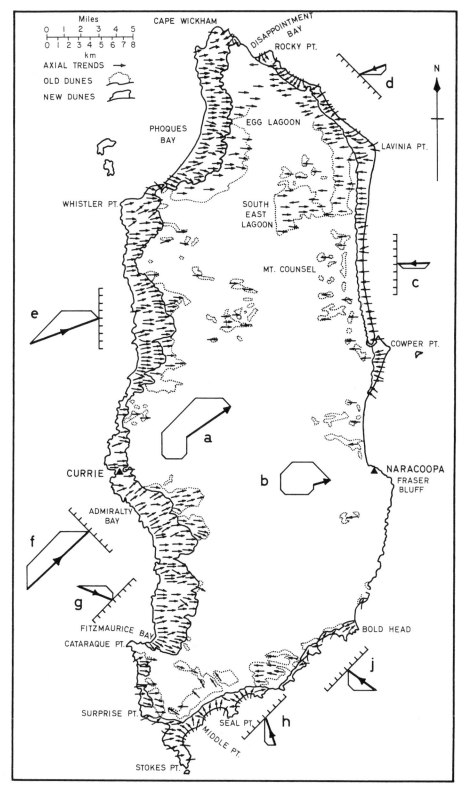

Figure 6-12 The relationship between dune orientation and wind direction. King Island, Tasmania. (*After Jennings, 1957.*)

sand by the formation of a salt crust might be one factor inhibiting dune formation. Such caking has not, however, been observed on many tropical beaches. The effect of moisture in the sand does not necessarily prevent dune formation, as sand can be seen blowing even when it is raining and dunes form in very damp areas in the temperate zone, such as the Hebrides of Scotland.

A more important factor appears to be the considerably lower wind velocity characteristic of the tropics. Jennings considers that there is an order of magnitude difference between the wind data in terms of the cubic function of the velocity that determines sand transport by the wind, for tropical and temperate areas. This factor would operate both in those parts of the tropics that have a dry season as well as the humid tropics. The lower wind velocity in the latter areas would not be sufficient to move moist sand, which could be moved by much stronger winds.

Beach profiles may be another factor that causes fewer dunes in the tropics. The light winds are likely to produce small waves and hence steeper profiles. Many tropical coasts, however, such as parts of Africa, are affected by distant swells, and these create wide sandy beaches with berms. These beaches are often not associated with dune formation. Another factor that may reduce the availability of sand is the type of weathering characteristic of the tropics. The products of weathering are more likely to be silt- or clay-sized in the tropics than sand-sized. Even the rivers are thought to have a fine grade load. Thus a wide variety of different processes may help to account for the paucity of coastal dunes in many tropical areas, particularly the humid tropics.

f Examples of coastal dune systems

(*i*) *Holland:* L. M. J. U. Van Straaten (1961) has described the dunes of the Dutch coast and shown that both bare and stabilized dunes occur. The bare dunes which are small and occur near the beaches are ephemeral and change orientation frequently. The fixed dunes show a variety of patterns. One of these consists of parallel ridges, closely spaced, narrow and continuous: these represent a series of foredunes on a prograding coast. They occur, for example, on southwestern Texel. A second pattern on southwestern Voorne shows one foredune seaward of a series of parallel parabolic and longitudinal dunes about 10 m high. A third pattern consists of higher dunes, up to 20 m or more, with wider ridges and troughs 100 m apart, and still parallel. The fourth pattern occurs between Scheveningen and Wassenaar, where the dune landscape is irregular, with closely spaced high dunes, reaching 25 to 30 m. There are also large dune pans in the area. At Ijmuiden and Zandvoort there are very large parabolic dunes and long, longitudinal dunes: pans 400 m wide occur in this fifth pattern. The final pattern consists of three or four high, continuous transverse dunes up to 56 m high, with parabolic dunes to seaward. These occur between Bergen and Schoorl.

The dunes are of various ages, the oldest being small and decalcified. The largest are post-Roman, as indicated by the finds of Roman pottery beneath them in places. Some of the dunes are young, but the bulk of the high dunes appear to have formed during the Middle Ages. Some of the dunes accumulated after 1610, such as those on the southeast of Rockanje on the island of Voorne. Much sand was probably drifting in the sixteenth to eighteenth centuries, and only since then have efforts at stabilization been successful. The directions shown in the older dunes cannot be related to recent meteorological records, as they are of much older origin. The orientations are also dependent on that of the dunes from which they have developed. Dunes growing out of southeast to northwest trending dunes have a lower azimuth than those originating from southwest to northeast dunes. The elongated dune pans tend to decrease in azimuth as they become wider. The weak and moderate winds have a lower azimuth (N 242° E) than the stronger winds (N 267° E), which are more important in building both the positive and negative features (J. D. de Jong, 1962). The orientation of the dunes suggests that the pattern of winds has changed.

These coastal dunes have an important part to play in coastal defence, and they also provide a valuable supply of fresh water.

(*ii*) *Parana:*   A detailed study of the structures of coastal dunes in Parana, Brazil, has been published by J. J. Bigarella *et al.* (1969). They made sections through the coastal dune ridges both parallel to and perpendicular to the mean wind direction. The structures of dunes of two ages were compared with desert dune structures. Dunes of various types occur between the Amazon and the Rio Grande do Sul in the south. There are transverse dunes, U-shaped dunes, and ridges parallel to the shoreline. The last are smaller and can form by either erosion or accretion; they often occur by coalescence of small tongue-shaped masses of sand banked against the coastal vegetation. The dunes are linear, with an undulating crest line and protuberances at the crests stretching landward. On the coastal plain in the state of Parana there are several parallel dune ridges of this type, which are 5 to 10 m high.

Wave erosion has exposed a section through the ridge showing dune strata overlying beach deposits. Trenches were dug across the dunes in the rainy season (to prevent collapse of the near vertical walls). Winds are from a direction between east and south for most of the time, and are therefore onshore. The trade winds blow northeast during the summer and east-southeast during the winter. Only the southeast winds are strong enough to carry the sand and form the dune structures. They are also associated with drier conditions. Sand sizes are very similar on the beach and in the dunes and sand ridges, the dune sands being better sorted. There are small foredunes only 12 to 14 m across, which have convex layers. Blow-outs reveal a basal cross-bedded structure with average dips of 19·2°. Angles of repose vary between 34 and 39°, indicating deposition under moist conditions. The mean dip direction is N 34° W, which agrees well with the southeast trade wind direction. The inner dune ridges are higher, indicating damper conditions or stronger winds during their formation. They also contain palaeosols and are better vegetated. Trees growing on these dunes have destroyed the structure to a depth of 1 to 2 m below the surface. The convex upwards form of bedding is common in many of the dunes, indicating growth of a stationary feature. This is due to the heavy vegetation cover and winds that are not strong enough to remove earlier deposits. These are some trough fillings, which have concave upwards bedding.

Another common type of structure in the coastal dunes of Parana, Brazil, results from slumping causing deformation of the bedding. Such slumping occurs shortly after deposition and is characteristic of the upper slip face area, especially where the beds are curved. The preservation of the contorted strata results from the inability of the dune to move landward into the vegetated area. The high angle of the foreset beds helps to account for the slumping. Both folding and faulting occur in the contorted strata. The structures form under both wet and dry conditions in the loosely packed sand of the lee side of the dune. They are mostly produced by slumping and avalanching of the slip face. Slumping in a damped layer of sand may cause the layer to become contorted to the level of water penetration. The damp crust breaks up, resulting in faulting and folding of this group of strata. Such movement tends to destroy structures in the underlying dry sand. The windward face of the dunes is more stable, owing to denser packing of the sand on this side.

Summary

Model experiments with an onshore wind in a narrow wave tank showed that the water near the bottom flowed seawards to compensate the water blown shoreward on the surface. The seaward bottom flow was strongest in the shallowest water. Experiments with ground perspex showed that the seaward current was capable of moving the light material seaward, although quartz sand was not moved by the wind currents alone. Wind and waves combined tended to cancel each other so that the gross volume of sand moved was decreased. Under the action of constructive waves with a strong onshore wind the landward movement was reversed in the shallowest and deepest water and reduced near the break-point in water of intermediate depth. The effect of destructive waves was enhanced inside the break-point by the onshore wind. These effects were also noted in the formation of profiles with waves and wind. The normally constructive waves did not build up a swash bar when they were accompanied by an onshore wind.

Observations on Marsden Bay beach in County Durham confirmed that the same effects applied on a natural beach when the wind was blowing onshore, while an offshore wind caused constructive action on the upper foreshore.

Coastal dunes are one of the most conspicuous features due to wind action at the shoreline. Dune sand can be differentiated from beach sand by its sedimentological characteristics. Dune sands are normally better sorted and tend to have a positive skewness, owing to a tail of finer particles. This property is the most diagnostic according to several studies. Vegetation is one of the most important properties that distinguish coastal dunes. Annuals, such as *Salsola kali* and *Cakile maritima*, are often the first colonizers of growing sand accumulation. The sand-loving grasses, including Marram (*Amophila arenaria*) and *Agropyron junciforme*, take over and are able to increase the height of the dune as they thrive in freshly blown sand. These grasses and others are important in the stabilization of dunes, which form a valuable coastal defence.

There are a number of types of coastal dunes, including foredunes, U-dunes or parabolic dunes, barchans or crescentic dunes, transverse dunes, longitudinal dunes, blow-outs and attached dunes. The U-dunes are common and their orientation correlates highly with the resultant of winds over force 4 raised to the power of 3. Transverse and longitudinal dunes develop where dunes vegetation is not so abundant. They are also related to the direction of the dune-building winds. Cliff-top dunes can form by a number of mechanisms, of which changes in sea level may be important. Coastal dunes are rare in the tropics, partly due to the greater moisture and also to the less strong winds. The nature of the products of weathering, which are finer than other areas, may also play a part. The dunes of Holland are complex and varied and have grown over a considerable period, although most of them are young.

References

ANAN, P. S. 1969: Grain-size parameters of the beach and dune sands, northeast Mass. and New Hampshire coasts. In *Coastal environments: northeast Mass. and New Hampshire*, Coastal Res. Group, Dept. of Geol., Univ. of Mass, 266–80.

BAGNOLD, R. A. 1941: *The physics of blown sand and desert dunes*. London: Methuen.

BAGNOLD, R. A. 1951: Sand formations in south Arabia. *Geog. J.* **117**, 77–86.

BARNES, F. A. and KING C. A. M. 1951: A preliminary survey at Gibraltar Point, Lincolnshire. *Bird Obs. and Field Res. St. Gib. Pt. Lincs., Rep.*, 41–59.

BARNES, F. A. and KING C. A. M. 1957: The spit at Gibraltar Point, Lincolnshire. *East Mid. Geogr.* **8**, 22–31.

BELLY, P-Y. 1964: Sand movement by wind. *C.E.R.C. Tech. Memo.* **1**.

BIGARELLA, J. J., BECKER, R. D. and DUARTE, G. M. 1969: Coastal dune structure from Parana (Brazil). *Mar. Geol.* **7**(1), 5–56.

BIRD, E. C. F. 1965: The formation of coastal dunes in the humid tropics: some evidence from north Queensland. *Aust. J. Sci.* **27**(7), 258-9.

BIROT, P. 1960: *Géographie physique génèralé de la zone intertropicale.* Paris: C.D.U.

CHAPPELL, J. 1967: Recognizing fossil strand lines from grain size analysis. *J. Sed. Petrol.* **37,** 57-165.

COOPER, W. S. 1958: Coastal sand dunes of Oregon and Washington. *Geol. Soc. Am., Mem.* **72,**

COOPER, W. S. 1967: Coastal dunes of California. *Geol. Soc. Am., Mem.* **104.** (131 pp.)

DUANE, D. B. 1964: Significance of skewness in recent sediments, West Pamlico Sound, North Carolina. *J. Sed. Petrol.* **34,** 864-74.

FRIEDMAN, G. M. 1961: Distinction between dune, beach and river sands from their textural characteristics. *J. Sed. Petrol.* **31,** 514-29.

GAGE, B. O. 1970: Experimental dunes on the Texas coast. *C.E.R.C. Misc. Pap.* **1-70.** (30 pp.)

GILES, R. T. and PILKEY, O. H. 1965: Atlantic beach and dune sediments of the southern United States. *J. Sed. Petrol.* **35**(4), 900-910.

GREENWOOD, B. 1969: Sedimentary parameters and environmental discrimination: an application of multivariate statistics. *Canad. J. Earth Sci.* **6**(6), 1347-58.

HAILS, J. R. 1967: Significance of statistical parameters for distinguishing sedimentary environments in New South Wales, Australia. *J. Sed. Petrol* **37**(4), 1059-69.

HIDEO MII, 1958: Coastal sand dune evolution of the Hachiro-Gata, Akita prefecture. *Saito Ho-on Kia Mus. Res. Bull.* **27,** 7-22.

HORIKAWA, K. and SHEN, H. W. 1960: Sand movement by wind action—on the characteristics of sand. *B.E.B. Tech. Memo.* **119.** (51 pp.)

JENNINGS, J. N. 1957: On the orientation of parabolic or U-dunes. *Geog. J.* **123,** 474-80.

JENNINGS, J. N. 1964: The question of coastal dunes in tropical humid climates. *Zeits. für Geomorph.* NF **8,** 150*-54*.

JENNINGS, J. N. 1965: Further discussion of factors affecting coastal dune formation in the tropics. *Australian J. Sci.* **28**(4), 166-9.

JENNINGS, J. N. 1967: Cliff-top dunes. *Australian Geog. Stud.* **5**(1), 40-49.

JONG, J. D. DE 1962: The coastal dunes near the Hague. *Med. van d. Geol. Sticht.,* New Series **15,** 21-3.

KIDSON, C. and CARR, A. P. 1960: Dune reclamation at Braunton Burrows, Devon. *Chart. Surv.* (Dec.), 3-8.

KING, C. A. M. 1953. The relationship between wave incidence, wind direction and beach changes at Marsden Bay, Co. Durham. *Trans. Inst. Brit. Geogr.* **19,** 13-23.

LANDSBERG, S. Y. 1956: The orientation of dunes in Britain and Denmark in relation to the wind. *Geog. J.* **122,** 176-89.

LARSEN, F. D. 1969: Eolian sand transport on Plum Island, Mass. In *Coastal environments: northeast Mass. and New Hampshire,* N.E. Mass. and New Hants. Coastal Res. Group, Dept. of Geol., Univ. of Mass., 266-80.

MASON, C. C. and FOLK, R. L. 1958; Differentiation of beach, dune and aeolian flat environments by size analysis, Mustang Island, Texas. *J. Sed. Petrol.* **28,** 211-26.

MOIOLA, R. J. and WEISER, D. 1968: Textural parameters: an evaluation. *J. Sed. Petrol.* **38,** 45-53.

MUSSET, M. 1923: Über Sandwanderung, Dunenbildung und Veranderung an der Hinterpommerischen Küste. *Zeits. für Bauw.*

SCHOU, A. 1945: Det Marine Forland. *Folia Geog. Dan.* **4.**

SHEPARD, F. P. and INMAN, D. L. 1950: Nearshore circulation related to bottom topography and wave refraction. *Trans. Am. Geophys. Un.* **31**(2), 196-212.

SHEPARD, F. P. and YOUNG, R. 1961: Distinguishing between beach and dune sand. *J. Sed. Petrol.* **31,** 196–214.

SMITH, H. T. U. 1954: Coast dunes. *Coastal Geog. Conf., Feb. 1954,* Off. Naval Res., 51–6.

STEERS, J. A. 1937: The Culbin Sands and Burghead Bay. *Geog. J.* **90,** 498–528.

STRAATEN, L. M. J. U. VAN 1961: Directional effects of winds, waves and currents along the Dutch North Sea coast. *Geol. en Mijnbouw.* **40,** 333–46.

WOODHOUSE, W. W. and HANES, R. E. 1967: Dune stabilization with vegetation on the Outer Banks of North Carolina. *C.E.R.C. Tech. Memo.* **22.** (45 pp.)

7 Sea level

1 **Seasonal fluctuations in sea level**

2 **Longer-term variations in sea level:** a) Eustatic effect: (*i*) *Types of eustatic change*; (*ii*) *Eustatic curve for the glacial and post-glacial period*; (*iii*) *Present changes*; b) Isostatic changes in sea level: (*i*) *General effects*; (*ii*) *Uplift and emergence curves*; (*iii*) *Areal aspects*; c) Raised shoreline features.

Summary

Beach processes and coastal development are both affected strongly by variations in sea level. The variations can be short term, either regular or occasional, medium term or long term. The short-term regular variations are the semi-diurnal and diurnal tidal cycles that were considered in chapter 5. The short-term occasional changes are associated with phenomena such as tsunami and surges, which were considered in chapter 4. These are short lived, but because they cause an abnormally high sea level and are difficult to predict, they are often disastrous in their consequences on the coast. The short period oscillations of sea level are of more importance in their effect on the beach processes, while the longer-term changes, to which most of this chapter is devoted, exert a major influence on coastal development. In this chapter a brief account of medium-term sea level fluctuations is given: these are the seasonal changes in level. Then the longer-term irregular variations of sea level during the glacial and post-glacial period are mentioned. This is a very complex topic about which much has been written. It is, therefore, not possible to do more than indicate some of the theories and evidence for changes of sea level during this time.

1 Seasonal fluctuations in sea level

Seasonal changes in sea level have been known to occur for a long time, but data collected recently have clarified the pattern. The variations seem to affect large stretches of coast similarly, and values are the same on both sides of an ocean in the same latitude.

Charts of sea level variations have been prepared by J. G. Pattullo (1963) for March, September, June and December. In March sea level is lower than the mean in the Northern Hemisphere and higher south of the equator. The exceptions in the Northern Hemisphere are in the Arabian Sea and the Gulf of Siam and between 40° and 60° N. The only negative values in the south occur along the south coast of Australia. The largest deviations occur in the Bay of Bengal, where values of −40 cm occur. Values of −19 cm are found off Mexico, Central America and in northeast Siberia. A positive value of +16 cm occurs off northeast Australia. The Arctic Ocean has negative values in March and positive ones in September. In September the values are similar to those of March, but the sign is reversed. The Bay of Bengal is now +54 cm and positive values of +13 and +27 cm are found off west Mexico and northeast Siberia. The main exception to the reversal is a positive value off southeast U.S.A. and Iceland, while south Australia has negative deviations at both seasons. June and December do not have such regular patterns. The central oceans in June tend to show negative deviations. Large positive values occur in the north Indian Ocean, the western third of the Pacific, north and south of the equator and around south Australia. Small positive values occur in the central south Pacific, parts of eastern U.S.A. and in the tropical and subtropical Atlantic. The largest deviations in June are −18 cm in the Gulf of Siam, −13 cm in north Norway, +30 cm in the Bay of Bengal and +14 cm in south Australia. In December the largest positive values of +20 cm occur in the Gulf of Siam, +16 cm along the coast of Norway, negative values of −26 cm occur in the Bay of Bengal and −10 cm in south Australia. In December in the Arctic Ocean all except the coast of north Alaska and northeast Siberia is positive, while in June the negative values occur along the north coast of Greenland, Europe and Asia.

The positive variations are due to a number of factors, which include falls of local atmospheric pressure, increase in heat content of the ocean, decrease in salinity, increase in onshore wind component, increase in longshore current component, annual or semi-annual high astronomic tide, increase in total mass of water in the ocean and decrease in mixing of water. The last two are probably negligible, but the first four could cause variation in the pressure on the sea floor as mass is conserved.

The causes of the seasonal changes may be summarized for different areas. In the subtropics the changes average 10 to 15 cm, and are mainly due to seasonal variations in heat storage in the oceans, induced by seasonal variations in local heating. In the tropics the deviations are largest at the solstices, and seem to be due to variations in heat content. North of 40° N subarctic levels are highest in December, with a range of about 15 cm. The changes are due to variations in atmospheric pressure. Regional effects include the monsoon. Changes off the tropical coasts of Mexico and Australia and off north Europe are due to changes in precipitation, wind and the water mass.

2 Longer-term variations in sea level

Longer-term changes of sea level can be broadly divided into eustatic changes (those that affect the volume of the ocean water or the size of the ocean receptacle) and isostatic changes (those that depend on the movement of the land by warping relative to a static sea level). The two main processes often act together, producing a very complex result.

a Eustatic effect

(i) *Types of eustatic change:* Eustatic changes of sea level over much of Quaternary time have been discussed by R. W. Fairbridge (1961). He discusses the possible types of eustatic change. One of these is tectono-eustatism, which is the result of tectonic changes in the shape of the ocean basins. The tectonic processes can be local, regional or ocean-wide in their extent, although the level of the whole ocean is affected by changes of this type, which alter the capacity of the ocean basins. In general in the later Tertiary earth movement appear to have resulted in foundering of parts of the ocean basins, causing a eustatic fall of sea level during this time.

Another form of eustatic change is sedimento-eustatism. A decrease in the capacity of the ocean basins is caused by infilling with sediment. This process may be responsible for the widespread slow transgressions that characterize some geological epochs, but it is of minor importance at present.

The third major type of eustatism is currently the most important. This is glacio-eustatism, which depends on the growth and decay of ice sheets and glaciers. This process has caused the large recent changes of sea level on a world-wide scale. Minor eustatic changes include the effects of changes in water temperature, but glacio-eustatism is the process that has determined the major changes of sea level on a large scale during the last few million years, and particularly during the last 25,000 years.

By contrast the large-scale effects of isostatic sea level changes are local and large changes are restricted to heavily glaciated areas. They depend on the response of the crust to the addition and removal of load in the form of ice. The eustatic changes that have been established in stable areas will be considered first, as these are world-wide in their effect and are superimposed on the isostatic changes, and so must be allowed for in calculating uplift curves in glaciated areas.

(ii) Eustatic curve for the glacial and post-glacial period: The eustatic curve covering the last 300,000 years, which is the period since the Gunz or Nebraskan glaciation, shows wide fluctuations with high levels during the interglacials and low levels during the glacial periods. Each successive high and low value, however, was lower than the earlier one. Thus the Gunz–Mindel interglacial level was +100 m, the Mindel–Riss was +50 m and the Riss–Würm varied from +20 m to +3 m above the present sea level. The glacial lows were respectively −10 m, −40 m, −70 m and −100 m for the Gunz, Mindel, Riss and Würm glaciations, according to Fairbridge (1961). Each one of these periods was complex, but these values give the probable lowest sea levels during each glaciation. Variations of this amount can account for the presence of large erratics, weighing many tons, on the beaches of Devon and Cornwall beyond the limits of glaciation. These large rocks could have drifted in icebergs onto the shore during the earlier glacial periods when sea level was similar to its present level.

The late Quaternary and post-glacial events are, however, of more direct relevance to many coastal problems and are very important in accounting for many features of the modern coast and beach. The last glacial period, the Würm, Weichsel or Wisconsin, started about 74,000 years ago, and a final major advance occurred about 20,000 years ago, with subsequent minor advances during the general deglaciation. The last important advance took place after the warm Allerød period from 12,000 to 10,800 years ago; this cold phase, in zone III, lasted from 10,800 to 10,300 years ago and was the final occasion in which glaciers grew in Britain to any appreciable size.

Fairbridge has suggested a large number of minor oscillations of sea level during this late and post-glacial period from 13,000 to the present. These fluctuations, he considers, were superimposed on a generally rising level, leading to a rapid transgression between the beginning of the period and 6000 years ago. This period of rapid rise of sea level, called the Flandrian transgression, played an important part in establishing the present form of the coast. Since 6000 years ago, Fairbridge considers that sea level has oscillated about its present level, extending both above and below it by about 3 to 4 m. These minor changes appear to be related to climatic oscillations. He states that every minor glacial advance during the last 5000 years has been accompanied by a lowering of sea level of about 3 to 7 m.

A somewhat different view of sea-level changes during the last 35,000 years has been proposed by F. P. Shepard (1963). His eustatic curve is given in figure 7-1, which shows the rapid rise of sea level between 20,000 years ago and 5000 years ago. Since this date, apart from a few observations in Australia, there is little evidence that sea level has been higher than the present level. The Australian data are open to different interpretations and one may conclude that during the last 5000 years the level has been fairly constant. Shepard's conclusion is based in part on the availability of radio-carbon dates on peat and other organic deposits.

A particularly complete record is available in Holland, where salt marsh peats are more or

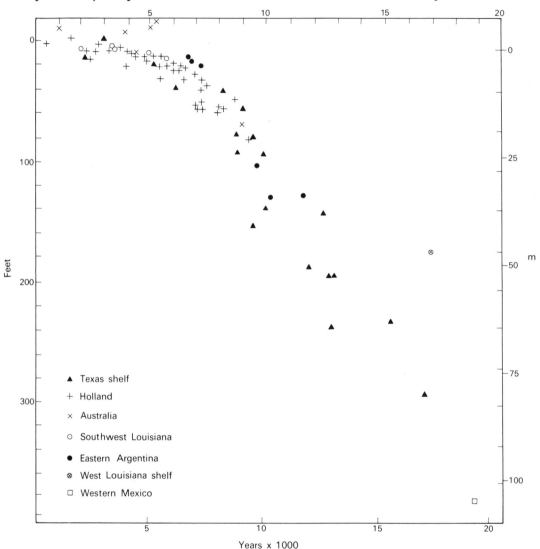

Figure 7-1 The rise of sea level indicated by Carbon 14 dates obtained in relatively stable areas. (*After Shepard, 1963.*)

less continuous over the period. There would have been gaps in the record had the level been higher than the present as suggested by Fairbridge. He considered that sea level was higher than present at 1000, 2200, 2400, 3700, 4900, and 5700 years ago. Workers in the Gulf coast area, on the other hand, consider that sea level has been constant during the last 5000 years, although some evidence that this period is only 3000 years long has been put forward. A difficulty concerning the record from Holland is that subsidence may have occurred and more than compensated for a falling sea level. Subsidence has also to be taken into account when the data for the Mississippi delta area are considered.

The curve back to 18,000 years ago in Holland is fairly well substantiated, but there is more doubt as to the variations in the period between 18,000 and 35,000 years ago. One view suggests stability of sea level during this period, while other evidence points to a lowering of sea level between 18,000 and 25,000 years ago. There is some evidence that sea level was at about its present height between 25,000 and 35,000 years ago. The low sea level centred around 20,000 years ago would represent the last major ice advance that occurred at this time. This was the main Würm maximum. The high sea level preceding this phase would represent an interstadial, probably the Farmdale. Shells from a 3·66 m terrace in Oahu, in the Pacific, have been dated 31,540 and 31,840 B.P. and some from a 1·52 m terrace were dated at 26,640 and 24,140 years B.P.

A detailed study of the changes in sea level in the Netherlands has been made by S. Jelgersma (1961) covering the Holocene period. The chronology is based on radio-carbon dating of the peat in salt marsh deposits. Processes that must be taken into consideration in studies of sea level include the effects of tectonic movements. In the Netherlands such movements are related to the slow downwarp of the southern North Sea basin. This subsidence has been going on for many millions of years. Compaction of the sediment must also be considered. This is effected

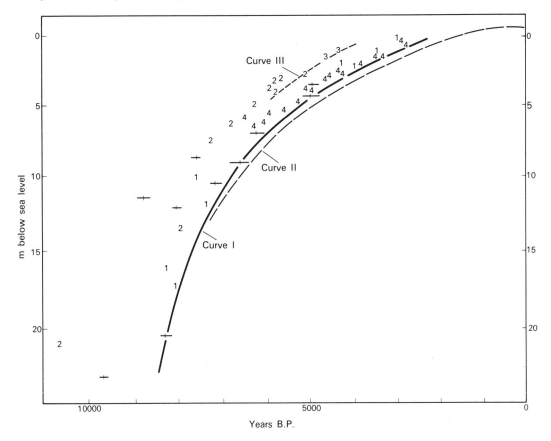

Figure 7-2 Curves of relative changes in sea level in the Netherlands. **1:** Donken (Rhine–Meuse estuary); **2:** Zeeland; **3:** Zeeland (base upper peat); **4:** Friesland and Groningen. (*After Jelgersma, 1961.*)

by increasing load, and changing hydrological conditions. It varies with the type of sediment, being high in clay and peat, and low in sand. The variation in the tidal range must also be taken into account. Jelgersma assumes that the marsh deposits grew to the level of the high tide, but this varies along the coast at any one time, and may vary with time at any one place. The curve of sea level change, shown in figure 7-2, is based on 52 radio-carbon dates ranging from 9300 to 2700 years B.P. The symbols show that the dates for Zeeland lie about 2 m above those obtained in other areas. This difference could be due to higher tidal range or greater subsidence, the former being the more likely. The level during the Roman period was probably 1 m lower than the present. The problem of subsidence during the last 5000 years is difficult to resolve definitely. The conclusion was reached that tectonic subsidence during this period could be between 1 and 12 cm/century. The latter value is thought to be too high and a more realistic value is between 1·5 and 3·4 cm/century. The value of 3 cm/century may be taken as a reasonable rate.

There is a general agreement in all the published eustatic curves that sea level rose very rapidly during the period between 20,000 and 5000 years ago, with either a very rapid deceleration of movement during the last 5000 years or a stable sea level. The gradual extension of the North Sea, spreading up from the south, during this period is shown in figure 7-3. About 9000 years ago the southern North Sea was a narrow gulf extending as far north as East Anglia, with the final separation of Britain from the continent taking place about 8600 years B.P. at a point on the latitude of the Humber. By 8300 the North Sea has extended widely, nearly to its present dimensions.

In a more recent paper Jelgersma (1966) considers that a slowly rising sea level after 5000 years ago is the most likely, thus supporting the earlier curve. The evidence for higher sea levels than the present during this period is derived from observations in New Zealand and Australia. The date from Australia have been reinterpreted by J. R. Hails, who sees no evidence for a higher sea level. All the data referring to higher sea levels come from mountainous areas. It seems likely, therefore, that these areas have been liable to tectonic disturbance. This applies to the Firth of Thames in New Zealand, where a series of beach chenier ridges suggest a slowly falling sea level between 4000 years ago and the present.

Evidence for the slow continued rise of sea level during the last 5000 years has been put forward by D. W. Scholl and M. Stuiver (1967) from observations in south Florida. In this area the sea level was 4·4 m below present 4400 years ago, but during the last thousand years it rose to 1·6 m below present at a fairly rapid rate. Since then it has only risen 1·6 m, which is small but not negligible. Mangrove swamp overlying fresh-water deposits are used to obtain the levels. This area appears to be a tectonically stable one, thus revealing the true eustatic movements. The curve for the Netherlands agrees closely with the Florida values, as shown in figure 7-2, in which the dashed curve indicates the best estimate of mean sea level. Because of continuous fluctuations in climate and the other controls on eustatic sea level, a slowly rising sea level seems more likely than a static one during the last few thousand years. This is also supported by current changes in level.

F. P. Shepard and J. R. Curray (1967) discuss the evidence of higher sea level provided by elevated terraces on oceanic islands. Dates have been obtained for included shells and these range from 7500 to more than 50,000, which do not support post-glacial high sea levels. Dates on shells in these situations are liable to be inaccurate. The coral of which the terraces are formed has been dated at between 100,000 and 160,000 years old, which would belong to one of the earlier warm interglacial periods, probably the Yarmouth. It is possible that the low terraces were built up as flood conglomerates. The evidence is still somewhat conflicting.

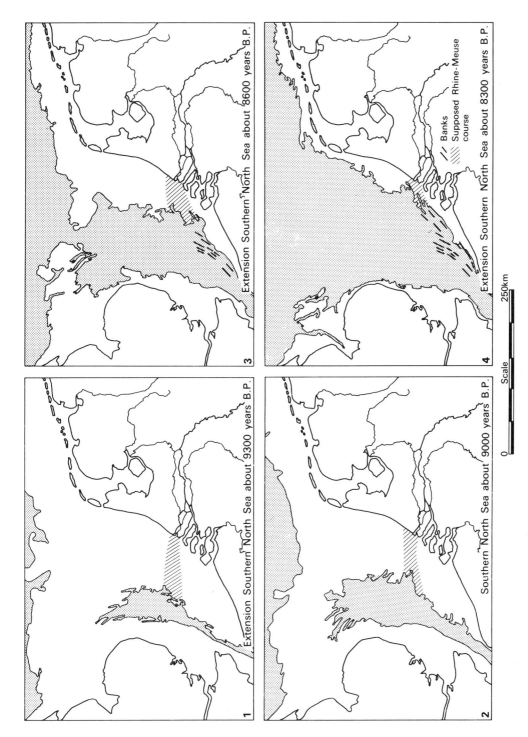

Figure 7-3 Hypothetical maps of the extension of the southern North Sea during the early Holocene. Dates derived from pollen analysis of moorlogs. (*After Jelgersma, 1961.*)

Extension Southern North Sea about 8600 years B.P. 3

Extension Southern North Sea about 8300 years B.P. 4

Extension Southern North Sea about 9300 years B.P. 1

Southern North Sea about 9000 years B.P. 2

Banks

Supposed Rhine-Meuse course

Scale

0   250km

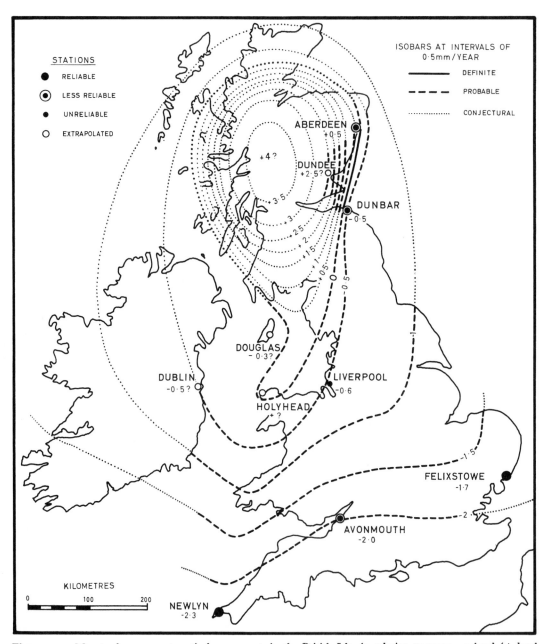

Figure 7-4 Map to show present vertical movements in the British Isles in relation to mean sea level (+ land emerging; − land submerging). (*After Valentin, 1953.*)

A study of a series of beach ridges in Tasmania (J. L. Davies, 1961) gives some information concerning possible sea level changes related to coastal features. At several points on the Tasmanian coast there are series of low ridges, parallel with each other and the coastline, and with a height ranging from a few cm to about 6 m. They represent slow gradual progradation and lie between the sea and the older and slightly higher sea level shoreline, which marks the maximum post-glacial transgression. The ridges must have formed during the last 6000 years. They get older inland, and each consists of a beach berm surmounted by a low dune. They are mostly formed of sand. The series of beach ridge systems has been analysed by linear regression to establish the best fit line that indicates the fall of sea level that took place during the emplacement of the ridges. The results were on the whole consistent, indicating a fall of sea level of 0·61 to 1·22 m in southeast Tasmania and 1·5 to 3 m elsewhere in the island. This evidence, therefore, suggests that sea level has fallen during the last few thousand years.

J. R. Hails (1965), in commenting upon these findings in southeastern Australia, suggests that a series of descending beach ridges, which are often used as evidence of a falling sea level, could be due to a decreasing supply of sediment during the period of progradation. Other possible factors are changes in offshore relief, affecting the refraction pattern, and a variation of littoral currents. Another possibility is that the ridges really do indicate a falling sea level, but that this is the result of minor earth movement and not a eustatic fall of sea level. Hails considers that many of the barrier and lagoon systems of eastern Australia have developed while sea level has been nearly static or rising very slowly during the last 5000 years. His evidence does not support a high sea level during this period.

(*iii*) *Present changes:* The evidence of tide gauges during the last few years suggests that sea level is still rising slowly. The suggested rate is 1 mm/year or 10 cm/century at present. The rise in southern England is estimated at the rate of about 2 mm/year, with a zero line running across the country from Anglesey to Aberdeen, with isostatic rising to the northwest of the line in Scotland. Figure 7-4 shows H. Valentin's (1953) map of current sea level changes in Britain. Many of the lines are, however, conjectural. It is probably true that the northern part of the British Isles is tending to rise, while the southeastern part is certainly sinking relative to the sea.

Good evidence of the continued and steady fall of sea level off the west coast of Scotland is given by S. Ting (1936), who describes a series of shingle beach ridges built up by storm waves on the west coast of Jura. There are 20 ridges, grading down gradually from a height of 8·85 m to near sea level, in which small and large quartzite shingle alternates regularly. Their arrangement and height suggest a gradual lowering of sea level, following the cutting of the '25 ft' beach in the area.

The report on secular changes of sea level published in 1954 records the data available for the last few decades. The only countries which show persistently falling sea levels are Norway, Sweden, Finland, Alaska and Canada north of 46·5° N. These are all areas affected by glacial-isostatic recovery. Everywhere else, with a few exceptions, sea level is rising at varying rates. On the Atlantic coast of America at many places the rise is between 4 and 7 mm/year. Slight rises of sea level of about 1 mm/year are recorded from Poland, Latvia and Germany. In Denmark the average value is 0·5 mm/year, but in Holland and Portugal it is 1·5 mm/year, France 1·4 mm/year, Italy, 1·7 mm/year, western North Africa 0·6 mm/year. Van Veen has calculated a rise of 7 to 16 cm since 1860 in the Netherlands. Table 7-1 gives some recent values of current changes.

The current general rise in ocean level is due to the amelioration of climate that has caused retreat of the glaciers in the northern hemisphere, and elsewhere, during the last 100 years. The

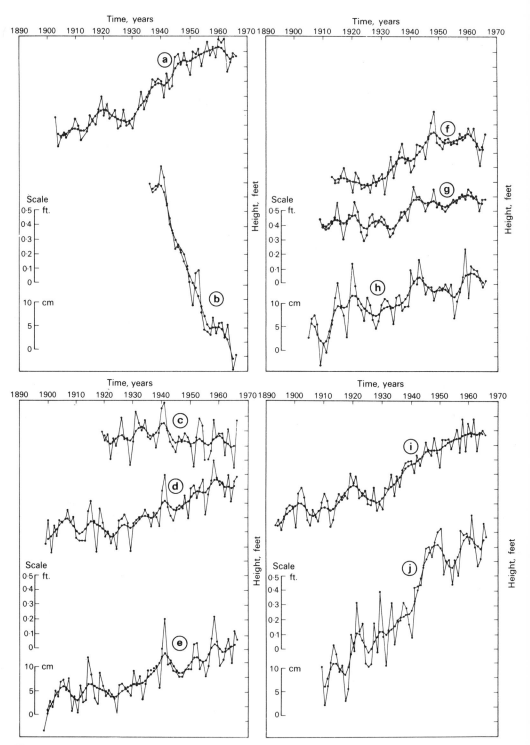

Figure 7-5 Sea level variations around the coasts of the U.S.A. **a:** Baltimore; **b:** Juneau; **c:** Ketchikan; **d:** Seattle; **e:** San Francisco; **f:** Key West, Florida; **g:** Cristobal, Canal Zone; **h:** Honolulu; **i:** New York; **j:** Galveston. (*From 'Shore and Beach', 1968.*)

Table 7-1 Current sea level trends

	Formosa	2·2 mm/year
	Japan	1·0 mm/year

U.S.A.	Trend for 1940–62 (mm/year)	Trend for 1940–66 (mm/year)
Atlantic coast		
Portland, Me.	2·74	1·22
Boston, Mass.	1·83	0·91
Newport, R.I.	3·05	1·83
New York, N.Y.	3·36	2·44
Sandy Hook, N.J.	6·10	4·53
Atlantic City, N.J.	2·74	2·13
Baltimore, Md.	4·27	2·44
Washington, D.C.	3·68	2·44
Portsmouth, Va.	3·96	3·05
Charleston, S.C.	3·36	1·83
Fernandina, Fla.	2·44	1·83
Miami Beach, Fla.	2·13	1·83
Pacific coast		
Yakutat, Alaska	−7·33	−6·10
Juneau, Alaska	−15·25	−13·70
Sitka, Alaska	−3·68	−3·05
Seattle, Wash.	2·13	2·13
Astoria, Oreg.	−0·61	−0·91
Crescent City, Cal.	−2·13	−1·52
San Francisco, Cal.	0·91	1·52
Santa Monica, Cal.	1·52	1·52
Los Angeles, Cal.	−0·61	−0·305
San Diego, Cal.	2·13	1·83
Gulf coast		
Galveston, Tex.	5·19	3·96
Eugene, I., La.	10·05	9·15
Pensacola, Fla.	1·83	0·61
Key West, Fla.	2·13	0·91
Cristobal, C.Z.	0·305	0·061
Honolulu, Hawaii	−0·0305	0·305

Some of the trends are shown in figure 7-5.

retreat has been accelerating during the last few decades. The ocean waters have also warmed slightly, resulting in a small rise of sea level. There are, however, some areas where sea level has not been rising. The most important are those affected by the major Pleistocene ice sheets. These are still experiencing isostatic recovery due to the melting of the ice.

b Isostatic changes in sea level

The changes in sea level are more complex in those areas that have been subjected both to eustatic and isostatic changes resulting from deglaciation. In a study of the purely isostatic effect, the most reasonable results are obtained when correction for the eustatic effect is made by means of the curve published by F. P. Shepard (figure 7-1), and supported by the results of Jelgersma. This curve indicates a rapidly rising sea level until 5000 years ago, followed by a period of very much slower rise to the present.

(i) General effects: Some useful general points have been made by A. L. Bloom (1967) who draws attention to the fact that both ice and water change volume, and therefore affect isostatic depression and later recovery, during the growth and dissipation of ice sheets. The isostatic effects are the result of changes in the hydrological cycle, which is essentially a closed system.

At present 2·9% of the land surface is covered by ice. At the height of the last glacial maximum about 20,000 years ago it was 7·9%, which means that 5% of the land has lost its load of ice since that date. Three fifths of the area is in North America, one fifth in northern Europe and one fifth scattered in high areas. The estimated thickness of the ice was such that the added load would approximate to 140 to 170 bars, assuming a mean ice thickness of 1·6 to 1·9 km. This load has now been removed, but it has been added to the ocean area, which covers 70% of the earth's surface, amounting to an excess load of 10 to 12 bars. The fact that the weight moves from one area to another must mean that compensation at depth must also result in reverse movements, if isostatic balance is to be maintained. There is little evidence of peripheral bulges, which would be required in a simple model of isostatic adjustment ignoring the ocean effect. The rapid rate at which compensation takes place in response to change of load suggests that this takes place in a layer of low viscosity at a depth of a few hundred km.

Another problem is the lack of evidence for coastal deformation resulting from oceanic compensation, if this is sufficient to cause such isostatic response. A pressure of 10 bars is the generally accepted loads that leads to isostatic response. This value is likely to be exceeded if the estimates are right. Observations along the Atlantic coast of the United States show that submergence has not been uniform, as would be expected along a stable coast on which only a eustatic change was taking place apart from changes due to variations in tidal range and other factors. Five sites along the coast have provided good, dated submergence curves. These are Everglades, in Florida, Clinton, Connecticut, Plum Island, Massachusetts, Brigantine, New Jersey and Barnstable, Massachusetts. The Florida site has submerged less than the other four. This fact supports the theory that the Atlantic coast has been downwarped due to added load in proportion to the increase in the depth of water offshore.

The theory is based on the assumption that the deformation extends 50 km from the edge of the load. Deep sea and coastal areas will respond differently to the load. On the coast a fall of sea level of 100 m is followed by a sea floor rise of 30 m, due to isostatic response, causing a rise of sea level along the coast. When sea level rises by 100 m, the sea floor is depressed, causing a relative fall of sea level along the coast. The total change in level could be one third greater than the eustatic change at the coast. The coastal sea level variations result from changes in the capacity of the ocean basin. They are based on the assumption that the coast is stable and does not move, while the ocean floor responds to the change in load. Thus a single oscillation of sea level could result in the formation of elevated coastal features at four levels, if the isostatic response lags behind the eustatic change. These isostatic effects in the extra-glacial coastal areas are small compared to the isostatic effects on coasts influenced by ice sheets, yet they have important results.

(ii) Uplift and emergence curves: Much of the early work on emergence and uplift curves for shorelines influenced by isostatic rebound was carried out in Scandinavia. The accuracy of such curves has been improved since radio-carbon dating has provided a reasonably accurate time scale, and more precise levelling has been carried out to provide better height data. J. T. Andrews (1968a and b, 1970) has provided much evidence with which to evaluate the nature of isostatic uplift curves for Arctic Canada. There are many raised shoreline features in this area and a considerable number of radio-carbon dates are available. Where different heights of former sea

levels can be dated an uplift curve can be constructed. The total amount of uplift is greater than the emergence, because the coast will only emerge if the uplift is greater than the eustatic rise of sea level. Emergence is measured, but this must be adjusted by allowance for the eustatic effect to give the amount of uplift.

One of the difficulties is the different time at which the sea reached its post-glacial maximum at different places. In eastern Arctic Canada deglaciation took place about 10,000 years ago on the outer coast, but occurred later, up to 5000 B.P., in the inner fjords. By 10,000 years ago there was about 30 m of eustatic rise still to take place. The rate of eustatic rise was likely to be slower than the isostatic rise, which is rapid immediately after deglaciation, thus allowing emergence to take place at least initially. The maximum sea level, or marine limit, therefore, mostly occurred soon after or at the time of deglaciation in this area.

A number of errors are liable to occur in establishing uplift curves. These include the error defining and determining the marine limit, errors in measuring dateable samples, errors in carbon 14 dates, errors in correcting for eustatic sea level and errors in relating the samples to sea level. Despite these possible errors consistent results have been obtained.

The general pattern of uplift is given by $U' = C\,e^{-kt}$, where U' is the amount of uplift remaining after t years (t in 1000s of years), C is the amount of recovery remaining when t is zero—that is the total amount of uplift since deglaciation to the present (J. T. Andrews, 1968a and b). U' is zero at the present day. k is a decay constant, varying with time. It is 0·4 for 10,000 years after deglaciation, rising to 0·5 for 4000 years and 0·9 for 2000 years after deglaciation. The amount of uplift, U, that has taken place in time $t_p = C - U'_p$. Sea level at time q in years B.P. is given by $S_q = (C - U_p) - E_q$, where E is the eustatic correction. A straight-line plot on semilogarithmic paper relates uplift remaining (log. scale) to time since deglaciation (linear scale). The lines for different areas are similar, indicating a uniform response in the earth's crust to deglaciation. The similarity allows a simpler equation to be used. This is

$$U = \frac{A(1 - i_t)}{1 - i}$$

where the value of i for Arctic Canada is given as 0·677 and A is the percentage of uplift in the first 1000 years, its value depending on the total time since deglaciation. It is 33% for 10,000 years, 36% for 6000 years and 59% for 2000 years.

The relationship established between percentage uplift and time since deglaciation allows uplift and emergence curves to be constructed. Figure 7-6 is an example of such a curve drawn for the Henry Kater peninsula in eastern Baffin Island (C. A. M. King, 1969a). The relaxation time, given by $T = 1/e$, or the response time, defined by Broecker as 50% of the total recovery, can be obtained from results of this type. The relaxation time varies in different areas. In Arctic Canada it is $2·5 \pm 0·2 \times 10^3$ years, in Scandinavia it is $3·0 \times 10^3$ years and for East Greenland it is $1·7 \times 10^3$ years. These differences could be due to variations in the viscosity of the mantle. The amount of recovery still to take place is calculated at about 100 m for Hudson Bay. The total depression in this area was 270 m and the amount of uplift to the present has been 170 m. A considerable amount of uplift takes place prior to the retreat of the ice front from the area during thinning of the ice. Complete uplift would take 46,000 years, where the relaxation time is $7·6 \times 10^3$ years.

The complete uplift curve is S-shaped and is symmetrical about the date of deglation. It can be broken into three components, indicated by the equation

$$S = U_r + U_p + U_{rr}$$

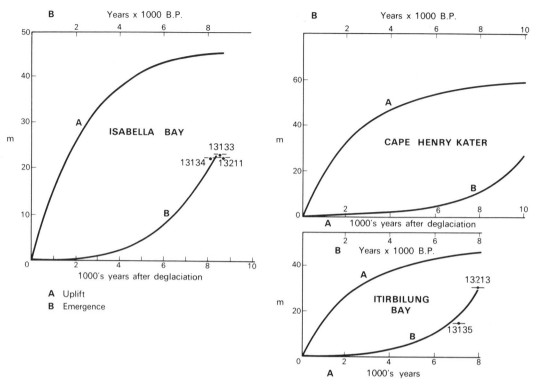

Figure 7-6 Uplift and emergence curves for three sites on Henry Kater peninsula, East Baffin Island.

where S is the amount of isostatic depression, U_r is the uplift that takes place prior to deglaciation as the ice is thinning. Its curve is in the form

$$U_r = -C\,e^{kt}$$

U_p is the uplift between the time of deglaciation and the present; its form is the negative exponential already given, and this also applies to U_{rr}, which is the amount of uplift that still has to take place at present. The whole curve thus consists of an accelerating section followed by a decelerating one, the point of inflection being the time of deglaciation.

(iii) Areal aspects: The uplift and emergence curves apply only to one point. It is also necessary to consider the areal distribution of uplift and emergence. This can be done either by considering changes along a line perpendicular to the lines of equal uplift to which the observations are adjusted—this is called a shoreline relation diagram—or alternatively by using the three-dimensional pattern of emergence determined by trend surface analysis for any one time. The shoreline relation diagram can provide information covering a period of time and has been used to analyse raised shorelines in Scandinavia by J. J. Donner (1966; 1969), by F. M. Synge and N. Stephens (1966) in northwest Britain, and J. T. Andrews (1969) in Arctic Canada. Andrews constructed the shoreline relation diagram from the information provided by uplift curves of the type already mentioned. In this diagram the x axis is the elevation of the reference strandline while the y axis represents the heights of higher strandlines above the reference level, which must be synchronous and accurate to provide a reliable diagram. Canada provides useful

evidence because the uplift started later than in Scandinavia where the eustatic rise had slowed down, thus making transgressions rare. The rate of uplift is also more rapid than in highland Britain or Fennoscandia. The shoreline relation diagram given by Andrews, corrected for eustatic sea level using Shepard's curve, is shown in figure 7-7. The reference level was chosen at 2000 years ago and curves for the preceding years from 3000 to 14,000 years ago are entered on the diagram, assuming a 10,000 year period of uplift for total uplifts of 25 m, 50 m, 75 m and up to 325 m at intervals of 25 m.

The three-dimensional approach to the analysis of coastal uplift is used by J. T. Andrews (1968b) in his analysis of the pattern of uplift in Arctic Canada. There were 67 sites in Arctic Canada where marine limit heights and dates were known. The cubic trend surface explained 74% of the variance in the data for the 67 sites. It showed two centres of maximum uplift, one

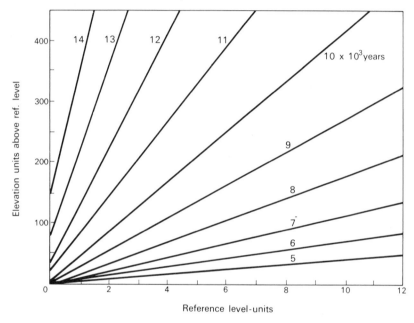

Figure 7-7 The shoreline relation diagram corrected for eustatic sea level changes using Shepard's curve. (*After Andrews, 1969*).

over Queen Maud Gulf and the other over Labrador–Ungava, with a saddle between them over Hudson Bay, and low levels along east Baffin Island. The saddle over Hudson Bay may be due to later deglaciation at this site, as it was the centre of the Foxe Basin ice sheet, which reached a maximum about 9000 B.P. Trend surface analysis of the uplift during the last 6000 years shows a maximum of about 100 m centred in Hudson Bay, the explanation of the quadratic surface being 84%. The position of the trend surface contours is supported by radio-carbon dates and measured elevations. Present rates of uplift in Hudson Bay are about 0·6 m/century and between 0·2 and 0·3 m/century in east Baffin Island, but to counteract this uplift sea level is rising at between 0·1 and 0·35 m/century, so submergence could be taking place where uplift is slowest.

The trend surface method has also been applied to western Scotland by S. B. McCann and R. J. Chorley (1967), who fitted a surface to the main post-glacial beach of highland Britain. The surface slopes down from 13·7 m east of Oban to 6·1 m over northern and western Skye, and 5·5 m in western Mull and near Ullapool. F. M. Synge and N. Stephens (1966) also use this main post-glacial beach as the reference level for their shoreline distance diagram for northeast Ireland and southwest Scotland. They plot the earlier shorelines with reference to this one. The axis of the diagram is assumed to lie perpendicular to the lines of equal uplift. The late glacial shorelines show a much steeper tilt than the post-glacial ones, the gradient gradually flattening with time.

J. B. Sissons et al. (1966) have carried out very detailed work on the sea level changes in southeastern Scotland, showing that the late glacial shorelines are associated with late glacial advances, and that they possess a considerable tilt. Re-advances produced renewed downwarping, followed by a very rapid recovery after the ice retreat.

Similar studies in Scandinavia by J. J. Donner (1969) indicate that in this area the isostatic recovery was dome-shaped, the summit of the dome lying along the eastern part of the Scandinavian mountains. On a profile 1090 km long across Scandinavia from west to east the only irregularity shown is a possible hinge zone in the Gulf of Finland. The lines of current uplift are parallel to the ice margin of the Weichsel and Salpausselka moraines. The maximum rate of present uplift is 9·3 mm/year at the head of the Gulf of Bothnia. The rate falls to zero across central Denmark. The shorelines slope more steeply towards the west than the east, parallel to the contours of the ice sheet.

c Raised shoreline features

The raised shoreline features of the Canadian Arctic are well developed, owing to the continuous fall of sea level over much of the area since deglaciation. As an example of the features associated with a consistently falling sea level the raised beaches of Foley Island and the neighbouring mainland of west Baffin Island will be considered briefly (C. A. M. King, 1969b).

The raised coastal features are more conspicuous than the modern shore forms for several reasons. Firstly, sea level was nearly 100 m higher when the raised features were formed and the offshore slope was very much steeper at this time, allowing more effective wave action at the shore. At present Foxe Basin is extremely shallow and is frozen over most of the year, thus inhibiting effective wave action. The second factor is the availability of beach material to build beach ridges and other forms of accretion. At the time of the marine limit the ice front lay close to the present coastline, and outwash material—forming extensive fluvioglacial deltas—was being deposited into the sea. This material was shaped by the waves into conspicuous beach ridges. Now the ice has retreated inland and is relatively inactive. Only a limited amount of material can reach the coast, much being trapped in lakes so that it cannot reach the sea. The third factor is the climate, which was warmer when sea level was higher, thus shortening the period of ice cover and enhancing the effect of waves in building shore forms.

Most of the conspicuous coastal forms at higher levels are depositional, consisting of ridges of coarse, rounded shingle. The mean size of the stones is around 5 cm, being larger on the crests than in the troughs of the beach ridge sequences. The curvature of the ridges indicates that wave refraction was effective during their formation. The ridge patterns show that long waves could have been generated in Foxe Basin at this stage. Beach ridges have formed in sheltered bays and these must have been built by very refracted waves. Tombolos that linked islands to the mainland were also formed, resulting from the meeting of refracted waves behind the islands. Barrier beaches were built when sea level had fallen slightly from its maximum height: these form elevations along the seaward margins of the deltaic spread and can be identified by their rounder pebbles. The mean roundness of samples of 50 barrier pebbles was 364 compared with 312 for the neighbouring delta stones, using Cailleux's roundness index. The difference is statistically

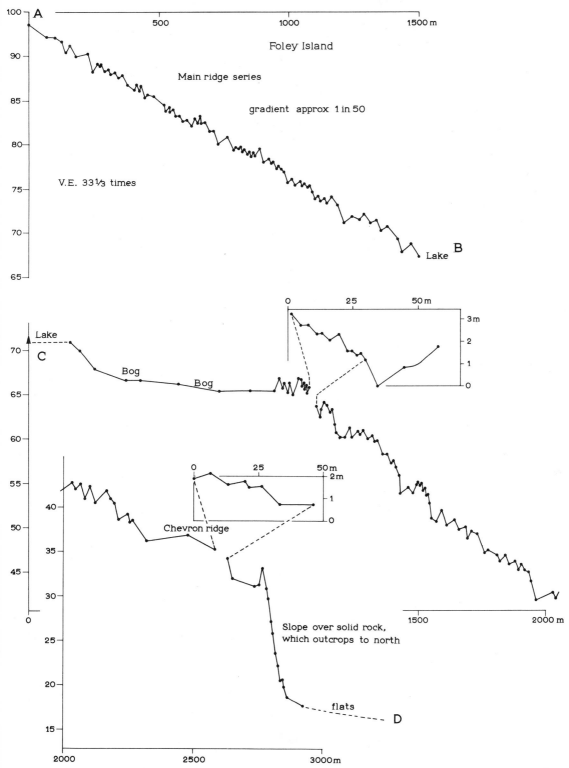

Figure 7-8 Profiles of raised beach ridges on Foley Island, off west Baffin Island.

significant. These raised shore forms are very similar in many respects to those formed in the Åland Islands in the Baltic off Finland, which were also affected by isostatic recovery resulting in a falling sea level (C. A. M. King and R. A. Hirst, 1964).

The most intricate pattern of ridges and the longest suite of beach ridges of those studied occur on Foley Island, a few km off the western coast of Baffin Island. This island is formed of limestone and the ridges are built of small chips of this rock, but many granite–gneiss erratics are included in places. The marine limit covered the top of the island, which reaches a maximum elevation of 94 m. There are two main series of ridges. The upper one extends from 93 m to 68 m above present sea level and was built by the most effective waves approaching across the open waters of Foxe Basin, between 6800 and 5600 years B.P. It consists of a series of 42 ridges. The mean gradient is smooth and is 1 in 50. Thirty years were available for the formation of each ridge, some of which are complex, containing smaller ridges. The ridges were probably built by storm waves, and so represent the action of a storm that has a recurrence interval of about 30 years.

Between 6000 and 5500 years ago there was a hiatus, when sea level stood between 65 and 70 m. Larger and more complex patterns formed at this stage. The ridge sequence then begins again, covering the period from 5500 to 4800 years ago, and forms the lower series with a height range from 65 to 40 m above present sea level. A thinly veneered limestone cliff outcrops between 32 and 20 m above sea level, below which the ground becomes very flat and ridges are rare and isolated. There are 48 ridges in the lower series, but again some are complex. The two sets are shown in figures 7-8 and 7-9. If the time scale is correct ridge building must have been more frequent during the later period, when sea level was falling more slowly.

During the hiatus between 6000 and 5500 years ago a complex fan-shaped pattern of beach ridges developed in a south-facing embayment (figure 7-9). During the period of ridge formation sea level must have been gradually falling and each successive ridge swings round slightly to face in a more southerly direction, changing from north–south to northeast–southwest. This pattern suggests that wave refraction caused a variation in wave approach as the water became shallower. The amplitude of the ridges is between 1 and 1·5 m and they are formed of poorly sorted limestone chips. The whole sequence probably formed during 120 years prior to 5800 B.P. The low gradient in the shallow embayment meant that considerable changes in the pattern of wave refraction could occur during this period as the water level gradually fell. Exposure of low-lying islands to the south and southwest may have affected the available fetch and hence the refractions of the waves, by changing their length.

N. Edelman (1968) has surveyed the raised shorelines on islands off Finland and reports that they occur at all levels and can, therefore, form without stillstands of sea level. He shows that where the mean gradient is steeper there are fewer more widely spaced terraces. The terraces he describes were formed during a continuous regression, as were those on Foley Island. Edelman suggests that the terraces were built by seaward movement of material, as a result waves built a terrace below water level. This process goes on until the depth is so shallow that material can no longer be transported seawards. A new terrace then begins to form as the waves erode into the face of the higher one. At this stage a terrace reaches its maximum width, and its inner part emerges above wave action. This hypothesis would not account for the back slope that is characteristic of many of the ridges on Foley Island. In this area, therefore, it is more likely that the ridges were formed by the waves from material thrown up to the top of the beach by the swash of extra powerful waves.

Some raised beach ridges form distinctive patterns, such as the chevron beach ridges. This type is considered in more detail in chapter 13.

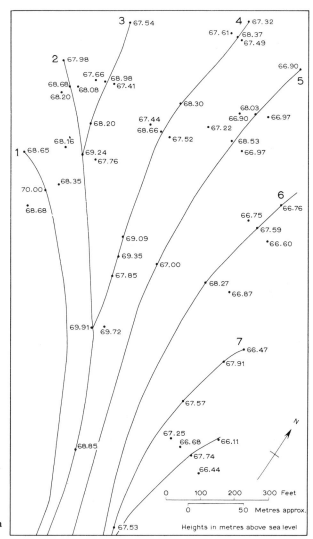

Figure 7-9 Pattern of fan-shaped ridges on Foley Island.

Summary

Seasonal changes of sea level are mostly about 20 cm or less. In March sea level is generally lower in the northern hemisphere and higher in the south, with the reverse pattern in September. Largest deviations occur in the Bay of Bengal, and are −40 cm in March and +54 cm in September. Longer-term changes are due to eustatic and isostatic effects. The most important of the eustatic changes is the glacio-eustatic rise of sea level that was very rapid between 20,000 years and 5000 years B.P. Since 5000 sea level has probably been rising slowly, but has not exceeded its present height in stable areas. Current changes in level are associated with continued glacial retreat so that sea level is rising slowly in stable areas, and more rapidly in areas liable to subsidence. Only in areas affected by isostatic recovery are current changes related to a falling sea level due to uplift of the land. Isostatic changes are mainly due to increase and decrease of ice volumes and associated changes in water volume in the ocean. Uplift in glaciated areas follows an S-shaped curve, with the point of inflection being at the time of deglaciation. Uplift following deglaciation is rapid at first and then slows down. Uplift and emergence curves can be constructed, the former allowing for the eustatic change in level. Three-dimensional patterns can be established by trend surface analysis and shoreline diagrams.

References

ANDREWS, J. T. 1968a: Postglacial rebound in Arctic Canada: similarity and prediction of uplift curves. *Canad. J. Earth Sci.* **5**(39), 39–47.

ANDREWS, J. T. 1968b: Pattern and cause of variability of post glacial uplift and rate of uplift in Arctic Canada. *J. Geol.* **76,** 404–25.

ANDREWS, J. T. 1969: The shoreline relation diagram: physical basis and use for predicting age of relative sea levels (Evidence from Arctic Canada). *Arctic and Alpine Res.* **1**(1) 67–78.

ANDREWS, J. T. 1970: A geomorphological study of post-glacial uplift with particular reference to Arctic Canada. *Inst. Brit. Geog., Sp. Pub.* **2.** (156 pp.)

BLOOM, A. L. 1963: Late Pleistocene fluctuations of sea level and postglacial crustal rebound in Coastal Maine. *Amer. J. Sci.* **261,** 862–79.

BLOOM, A. L. 1967: Pleistocene shorelines: A new test of isostasy. *Bull. Geol. Soc. Am.* **78,** 1477–94.

BLOOM, A. L. and STUIVER, M. 1963: Submergence of the Connecticut coast. *Science* **139**(3552), 332–4.

DAVIES, J. L. 1961: Tasmanian beach ridge systems in relation to sea level change. *Paps. and Proc. Roy. Soc. Tasmania* **95,** 35–40.

DONNER, J. J. 1966: A comparison between the late glacial and postglacial shorelines in Estonia and southwest Finland. *Comm. Phys.-Math. Ed. Soc. Sci. Fennica* **31**(11), 1–14.

DONNER, J. J. 1969: A profile across Fennoscandia of Late Weichselian and Flandrian shorelines. *Comm. Phys.-Math. Ed. Soc. Sci. Fennica* **36**(1), 1–23.

EDELMAN, N. 1968: Raised shore terraces as the result of continuous regression. *Bull. Geol. Soc. Finland* **40,** 11–15.

EMERY, K. O. 1958: Shallow submerged marine terraces of South Carolina. *Bull. Geol. Soc. Am.* **69,** 39–60.

FAIRBRIDGE, R. W. 1961: Eustatic changes in sea level. *Phys. Chem. of the Earth* **IV,** New York: Pergamon, 99–185.

GODWIN, H. 1940: Studies of the post-glacial history of British vegetation. III and IV. *Proc. Roy. Soc.* B **230,** 239.

GODWIN, H. SUGGATE, R. P. and WILLIS, E. H. 1958: Radio-carbon dating of the eustatic rise in ocean level. *Nature* **181,** 1518–19.

HAILS, J. R. 1965: A critical review of sea level changes in eastern Australia since the last glacial. *Australian Geog. Stud.* **3**(2), 65–78.

HARRISON, W. and LYON, C. J. 1963: Sea level and crustal movements along the New England–Acadian shore, 4500–3000 B.P. *J. Geol.* **71**(1), 96–108.

JELGERSMA, S. 1961: *Holocene sea level changes in the Netherlands. Med. Geol. Sticht,* Series C **VI.** (101 pp.)

JELGERSMA, S. 1966: Sea level changes during the last 10,000 years. *Roy. Met. Soc. Sym. on world Climate from 8000 to 0 B.C.*

JOLLY, H. L. P. 1939: Supposed land subsidence in the south of England. *Geog. J.* **93,** 408–13.

KING, C. A. M. 1969a: Glacial geomorphology and chronology of Henry Kater Peninsula, East Baffin Island, N.W.T. *Arctic and Alpine Res.* **1**(3), 195–212.

KING, C. A. M. 1969b: Some Arctic coastal features around Foxe Basin and in east Baffin Island, N.W.T., Canada. *Geogr. Ann.* A **51**(4), 207–18.

KING, C. A. M. and HIRST, R. A. 1964: The boulder-fields of the Åland Islands. *Fennia* **89**(2), 5–41.

MCCANN, S. B. and CHORLEY, R. J. 1967: Trend surface mapping of raised shorelines. *Nature* **215** (5101), 611–12.

PATTULO, J. G. 1963: Seasonal changes in sea level. In Hill, M. N. (Editor), *The sea* **II,** New York: Wiley, 485–96.

SCHOLL, D. W. and STUIVER, M. 1967: Recent submergence of southern Florida: a comparison with adjacent coasts and other eustatic data. *Bull. Geol. Soc. Am.* **78**(4), 437–54.

SHEPARD, F. P. 1963: Thirty-five thousand years of sea level. In *Essays in Marine Geology in honor of K. O. Emery*, Univ. S. Calif. Press, 1–10.

SHEPARD, F. P. and CURRAY, R. J. 1967: Carbon 14 determination of sea level changes in stable areas. In *Progress in oceanography* **IV,** Oxford: Pergamon, 283–91.

Shore and Beach 1948: Sea level variations around the coasts of the U.S.A.

SISSONS, J. B., SMITH, D. E. and CULLINGFORD, R. A. 1966: Late-glacial and postglacial shorelines in southeast Scotland. *Trans. Inst. Brit. Geogr.* **39,** 9–18.

STEPHENS, N. 1968: Late glacial and postglacial shorelines in Ireland and southwest Scotland. **VIII** *Proc. VII INQUA: Means of correlation of Quaternary successions,* 437–56.

SYNGE, F. M. and STEPHENS, N. 1966: Late and post-glacial shorelines and ice limits in Argyll and Northeast Ulster. *Trans. Inst. Brit. Geogr.* **39,** 101–25.

TING, S. 1936: Beach ridges in south-west Jura. *Scot. Geog. Mag.* **52,** 182–7.

UNION GEOD. ET GEOPHYS. INTER. ASSOC. D'OCEANG. PHYS. 1954: Secular variations of sea level. *Pub. Sci.* **13,** 21.

VALENTIN, H. 1953: Present vertical movements of the British Isles. *Geog. J.* **119,** 299–305.

VALENTIN, H. 1954: Gegenwürtige Niveauveranderungen in Nordseeraum. *Petermanns Geog. Mitt.* **246,** 1–118.

Part III

Beaches

8 Beach material

1 **Types of beach material**

2 **Sampling**

3 **Size distribution:** a) Measurement methods; b) Graphic and mathematical moment measures: (*i*) *Central tendency*; (*ii*) *Sorting*; (*iii*) *Skewness and kurtosis*; (*iv*) *Comparison of methods*; c) Size of beach fill.

4 **Shape analysis**

5 **Source of beach material**

6 **Differentiation of beach material**

Summary

Three aspects of beach material are considered in this chapter: firstly, the description and character of the material, secondly the source of the material, and thirdly, methods and results of studies that have been made to differentiate various types of sedimentary material. Three other major aspects of beach material are discussed in this part of the book—the movement of material normal to the shore, in chapter 9; movement of material along the shore, in chapter 10; and sorting of material, both normal to and along the shore, in chapter 11.

1 Types of beach material

The loose material forming the beach may range from clay particles to large blocks of rock. Various classifications have been proposed to define the categories. The British Standard Code of Practice (1947) issued on behalf of the committee by the British Standards Institution gives one of these. Table 8-1 shows the size range in mm of the various groups of this classification. Another classification, known as the Wentworth scale, is based on a geometrical division of the mm scale. This classification can be easily converted into the third one, which uses the same divisions but expresses the values in ϕ units, where ϕ is $-\log_2$ of the mm values. This is the most commonly used scale at present. Both these classifications are given in table 8-2. The ϕ unit classification was proposed by W. C. Krumbein in 1934.

Although there are minor differences in the ranges covered by the different materials in the first and last two classifications, the range covered by sand is almost the same in each. The differences increase at the extremities of the scales. The ϕ unit and Wentworth classifications are rather more detailed, having 15 types of material. W. F. Tanner (1969) has listed the many advantages of the ϕ scale for the description of sediment and shown it to be superior to any of the

Table 8-1 British Standards classification of sediment size

Types		Predominant particle size (mm)	Field identification
Stone	boulder	more than 200	Larger than 8 inches
	cobble	60 —200	Mostly between 3 and 8 inches
	coarse	20 —60	
Gravel	medium	6 —20	Mostly between 7 B.S. Sieve
	fine	2 —6 ⎫	and 3 inches
	coarse	0·6 —2 ⎭	Mostly between 7 and 25 B.S.
Sand	medium	0·2 — 0·6	Mostly between 25 and 72 B.S.
	fine	0·06 — 0·2	Mostly between 72 and 200 B.S.
	coarse	0·02 — 0·06 ⎫	Particles mostly invisible or barely
	medium	0·006— 0·02 ⎭	visible to the naked eye
	fine	0·002— 0·006	Some plasticity and dilatancy
Clay		less than 0·002 ⎫	Smooth to touch, plasticity but no
		more than 30% ⎭	dilatancy

Table 8-2 Wentworth and ϕ unit (Krumbein, 1934) sediment classification

Types	ϕ units	Wentworth (mm)
Boulder	more than −8·0	more than 256
Cobble	−8·0 to −6·0	256 —64
Pebble	−6·0 to −2·0	64 — 4
Granule	−2·0 to −1·0	4 — 2
Very coarse sand	−1·0 to 0	2 — 1
Coarse sand	0·0 to 1·0	1 — 0·5
Medium sand	1·0 to 2·0	0·5 — 0·25
Fine sand	2·0 to 3·0	0·25 — 0·125
Very fine sand	3·0 to 4·0	0·125 — 0·0625
Coarse silt	4·0 to 5·0	0·0625 — 0·0312
Medium silt	5·0 to 6·0	0·0312 — 0·0156
Fine silt	6·0 to 7·0	0·0156 — 0·0078
Very fine silt	7·0 to 8·0	0·0078 — 0·0039
Coarse clay	8·0 to 9·0	0·0039 — 0·00195
Medium clay	9·0 to 10·0	0·00195 — 0·00098

others. One of the main advantages of the ϕ scale is that the cumulative plot of sediment size distribution on arithmetic probability paper gives a straight line if the size distribution is logarithmic normal, which is a characteristic of many beach materials.

Sediments in the different size groups possess important and distinctive properties. The types of material can be divided broadly into two groups. The coarser material, sand and gravel, are non-cohesive especially when they are dry; the finer materials are cohesive. The coarser non-cohesive materials can be distinguished by their capillarity, which is negligible in gravel, but may be appreciable in sand. Although sand is non-cohesive when dry, if it is damp it can stand at any angle up to vertical. This is not possible in gravel.

The finer material—silt and clay—possesses cohesion. The silts can, however, easily be reduced to powder when they are dry. Clays on the other hand shrink on drying, and although they can be broken into lumps when dry, they cannot be powdered and are highly cohesive. The term 'dilatancy' is applied to sediments which, when shaken in a wet state, will exude water. If a pat of silt, for example, is shaken and then pressed, the water retreats into the silt leaving a shiny surface, because of an increase in volume of pore space. In its dilatant state the deposit is hardened and rendered more resistant to shear. This is due to the closer packing of the grains, rendering the material more resistant. At the same time, however, its capacity to hold water increases, because the volume of the pore spaces increases.

Experiments (G. Chapman, 1949) designed to demonstrate the state of dilatancy in beach material showed that, although the physical state was apparently present, it did not affect the resistance of the sand under the conditions of the experiment. The material used consisted of very fine sand, with 1 to 3% silt and clay, 80% of the material passing through a sieve with apertures of 0·12 mm (100 B.S.). These tests did, however, demonstrate thixotropy, which is present in some finer grain beach sediments. This is a state which shows a decrease of viscosity upon agitation, or a decreased resistance to shear when the rate of shear increases. Unlike dilatancy, thixotropy in the sediment results in a reduction in resistance with increased rate of shear. The decrease in viscosity ceases as soon as agitation is discontinued. The semi-quicksand character, which can be induced in some beach materials, is the result of their thixotropic property. This property becomes more effective as the sediment approaches saturation.

2 Sampling

Beaches consist of a very large number of individual particles, mainly sand grains or pebbles. With such a large total population sampling is a necessity. The method of sampling is made more difficult because of the large number of different beach environments and because of the considerable variability of beach sediment within and between these environments. The aim of the sampling plan must be to represent the total populations of the different environments in as statistically correct and representative a way as possible. The samples must, therefore, be selected randomly within each environment, and allowance must be made for the assessment of the variability within each environment. Thus stratified random sampling with several samples from each stratum provides a good sampling plan. Analysis of variance can then be used to test the ratio of the between and the within strata variations of the sediment (see J. C. Doornkamp and C. A. M. King, 1971, 162–8).

The problem of beach material sampling has been studied by W. C. Krumbein and H. A. Slack (1956), who investigated the problem in two different environments. One was the sandy and gravelly shore zone of part of Lake Michigan near Waukegan, Illinois, and the other was the sandy shore at Ocean Beach, Maryland. The sediments of Lake Michigan were very mixed and the environment included sand dunes as well as a beach with berms of mixed sand and a few pebbles. The problem of describing the sediments accurately was complex.

The observations made on the ocean beach included the analysis of underwater sediments. A series of samples was taken above low water along six profiles, of which the outside ones were spaced 490 m apart, while the four profiles in the centre were spaced 30 m apart. Three of the central profiles were extended 610 m seaward to a depth of 9·15 m. The above-water samples were taken in pairs every 15·25 m along the profiles and 16 samples were taken in each end profile. The samples could then be used to consider the variation size in different zones across the beach and variations along the beach.

The analysis of the results showed that there was no significant difference between the means obtained from the four centre profiles, but the upper and lower samples taken on the backshore and foreshore respectively did show significant differences. The mean sand for this particular part of the beach was obtained from all 64 samples. This value could then be compared with different combinations of samples. For all the samples the ϕ median diameter was 1·67, or 0·314 mm, the computed standard error for this value being 0·08, or a relative error of 4·8%. For all four profiles but for only one sample from the backshore and one from the foreshore, the relative error was 6·6%. For all samples from only one profile the relative error was 9·6%. For one sample from one profile the relative error was 19·2%, but for a pair from only one profile the error was 16·8%. When the analysis was extended to the outer profiles along the beach the relative errors calculated were of the same order, but rather larger, reaching a maximum of 24·7% for only one sample.

The underwater samples were taken every 76·3 m from low-tide level along three profiles. A double tube sampler was employed with the samplers fixed 45 cm apart. All except one pair of samples were satisfactory. Each of the pairs was used separately to compute the mean diameter, the values being 0·145 mm and 0·168 mm, but discarding the poor sample, the figures were 0·150 mm and 0·157 mm. The results show how one bad sample can affect the result. The standard error of the results of this sampling plan was less than 10%. It was concluded that the additional effort of collecting double samples was not necessary to keep the error under 10%.

Samples must be taken from the different beach zones in proportion to their width, extending from the backshore to about 10 m depth to obtain a sound value of the mean particle diameter. If one zone is very variable more samples should be taken from it. Samples should also be taken from more than one profile along the beach. If there are five beach zones, and these are each covered by six profiles, providing 30 samples, these 30 should provide an adequate number for analysis. The relative error should not exceed 10% at the 95% confidence level.

3 Size distribution

a Measurement methods

The most important sediments on beaches are sand and shingle, the former being the most common on a world scale. Several methods have been developed to study the size distribution in sands and other sediments. A useful review of parameters developed to describe the distribution of particles size has been prepared by R. L. Folk (1966). He is particularly concerned with grain size statistics. The first step in an analysis of grain size is to obtain a representative sample of the sediment being analysed. Once the sample has been obtained the frequency size distribution must be measured. The larger particles, the cobbles or shingle, can be measured individually and their shape assessed. This matter is considered in section 8-4.

The sand-sized particles can either be dry sieved, which is probably the most common method, or measured by settling tube. Pipette or hydrometer analysis is essential for the finer silt and clay-sized particles. Sieving seems to be the most useful method of analysing sand. Other characteristics of sand grains can be studied by examining them under a microscope. The work of F. P. Shepard and R. Young (1961) illustrating this method has been discussed in chapter 6, when other techniques were also referred to. The sieves used for sand and gravel analysis should be spaced at $\frac{1}{2} \phi$ or $\frac{1}{4} \phi$ units apart. A spacing of 1 ϕ is not sufficient to indicate bimodality and other characteristics of the cumulative frequency curve. Sieving divides the sediment into volume frequency classes suitable for further analysis. As a method it measures a different characteristic of the sediment than that measured by settling tube methods, which measure the hydraulic properties of the sediment. Some authorities would advocate the latter as more meaningful (D. L. Inman, 1952). The settling tube can only use very small samples, and Folk (1966) considers it least accurate, although it is quick.

When the laboratory analysis is completed the results can be plotted on a graph. Probability paper, on which a normal curve is plotted as a straight line, is the best. The results are plotted as a cumulative percentage frequency curve. The normality of the distribution can then readily be assessed. It is also possible to calculate moment measures directly from the laboratory analysis, using the volume frequency results for each $\frac{1}{2}$ or $\frac{1}{4}$ ϕ class. The advantage of drawing the cumulative frequency graph is that it can reveal the nature of the curve. The tails are often particularly important in revealing the depositional environment of the sediment. The nature of mixed curves can also be better appreciated from a graph.

b Graphic and mathematical moment measures

A large number of different measures for describing distribution have been suggested. Four descriptive measures are usually calculated: (1) a measure of central tendency, the first moment

Table 8-3 Mathematical and graphic moment measures for sediment analysis

GRAPHIC MEASURES

Central tendency			Efficiency—McCammon
Trask	Median	$Md = mm_{50}$	64%
Inman	Mean	$M\phi = (\phi_{16} + \phi_{84})/2$	74%
Folk and Ward	Mean	$M_z = (\phi_{16} + \phi_{50} + \phi_{84})/3$	88%
McCammon	Mean	$(\phi_{10} + \phi_{30} + \phi_{50} + \phi_{70} + \phi_{90})/5$	93%
McCammon	Mean	$(\phi_5 + \phi_{15} + \ldots \phi_{85} + \phi_{95})/10$	97%

Standard deviation		
Trask (1932)	$So = \sqrt{Q_1/Q_3}^*$ mm	37%
Otto, Inman (1952)	$(\phi_{84} - \phi_{16})/2$	54%
Folk and Ward (1957)	$(\phi_{84} - \phi_{16})/4 + (\phi_{95} - \phi_5)/6{\cdot}6$	79%
McCammon	$(\phi_{85} + \phi_{95} - \phi_5 - \phi_{15})5{\cdot}4$	79%
McCammon (1963)	$(\phi_{70} + \phi_{80} + \phi_{90} + \phi_{97} - \phi_3 - \phi_{10} - \phi_{20} - \phi_{30})9{\cdot}1$	87%

Skewness

Trask $Sk = Q_1 Q_3^*/Md^2$ mm

Inman $\alpha_\phi = \dfrac{\phi_{16} + \phi_{84} - 2\phi_{50}}{\phi_{84} - \phi_{16}}; \quad \alpha_{2\phi} = \dfrac{\phi_5 + \phi_{95} - 2\phi_{50}}{\phi_{84} - \phi_{16}}$

Folk and Ward $Sk_1 = \dfrac{\phi_{84} - \phi_{16} + 2\phi_{50}}{2(\phi_{84} - \phi_{16})} + \dfrac{\phi_{95} - \phi_5 + 2\phi_{50}}{2(\phi_{95} - \phi_5)}$

Kurtosis

Inman $\beta\phi = \dfrac{(\phi_{95} - \phi_5) - (\phi_{84} - \phi_{16})}{\phi_{84} - \phi_{16}}$

Folk and Ward $K_g = \dfrac{\phi_{95} - \phi_5}{2{\cdot}44(\phi_{75} - \phi_{25})}$

MATHEMATICAL MEASURES

Mean	$m = \Sigma fx/n$	
Standard deviation	$m_2 = \Sigma (x_i - m)^2 f_i,$	$\sigma = \sqrt{m_2}$
Skewness	$m_3 = \Sigma (x_i - m)^3 f_i,$	$\alpha_3 = m_3/\sigma^3$
Kurtosis	$m_4 = \Sigma (x_i - m)^4 f_i,$	$\beta_2 = m_4/\sigma^4$

* Q_1 is the lower quartile; Q_3 is the upper quartile.

219

or mean of the distribution; (2) the sorting or standard deviation of the distribution, the second moment about the mean; (3) the skewness, the third moment, which describes the asymmetry of the distribution: some reference to the importance of skewness as a diagnostic variable has already been made in chapter 6, and further examples will be cited in sections 3(c) and 6 of this chapter; (4) the kurtosis, which defines the peakedness of the curve. A curve that is more peaked than the normal is leptokurtic, while a less peaked one is platykurtic.

A large number of graphical methods for obtaining moment measures have also been developed. These use specific percentiles that are read off the cumulative frequency graph. Some of the more commonly used measures are shown in table 8-3. Folk has pointed out some of the disadvantages of the mathematical moment method. He shows that faulty sieves can less easily

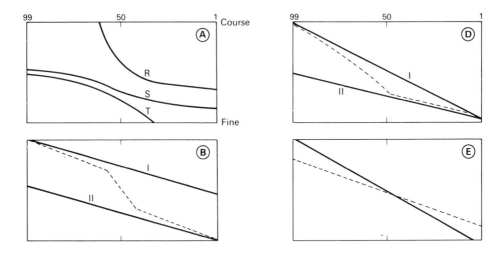

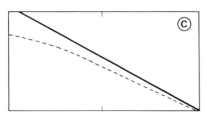

Figure 8-1 Size distribution in different depositional environments. R—curve for deposition in river or strong marine current. S—curve for currents with decreasing capacity downstream. T—stagnant water conditions. These three types are shown in **A. B:** The dashed line shows a mixture of two sediments with different means. **C:** The truncation of a single sediment is shown. **D:** The dashed line shows a mixture of two sediments with different means and variances. **E:** The dashed line shows the double truncation of one sediment. (*After Tanner, 1964.*)

be identified. Open-ended curves—that is sediments having a large percentage of unanalysed fine material—require considerable arbitrary assumptions. The assumption that the material is all of the size of the centre point of the class also leads to erroneous results. Although some workers advocate moment measures, calculated mathematically, others, including G. M. Friedman (1962) and G. V. Middleton (1926), consider that the different methods measure rather different properties. There are advantages and disadvantages in both methods, and unless the differences between the sediments are very slight both will differentiate between different sedimentary environments and give useful information concerning the character of the material.

W. F. Tanner (1964) has shown the effect on cumulative frequency distribution of the possible modification of a normal distribution by different processes. He illustrates several examples, some of which are shown in figure 8-1, and compares them to curves characteristic of different conditions. Some of the modifications are due to mixing, others to truncation of the curve at one or both ends, and also to filtering processes, whereby parts of the distribution are missing. Sediments may show one or more of these characteristics combined.

(*i*) *Central tendency:* R. B. McCammon (1962a) has summarized the relative efficiency of various measures to determine the central tendency. The median is the simplest, but least accurate, with only 64% efficiency. Other degrees of efficiency are given in table 8-3. The mean gives the general size of the material. Most sediments fall into one of three classes, gravel, sand with coarse silt, or clay. Very coarse sand or very fine gravel are rare in beach sediments. Both the source of the material and the processes of deposition affect the size distribution of beach materials. Bimodality or multimodality can be revealed by the higher moments, which is one of the main values of the higher moments.

(*ii*) *Sorting:* Various sorting measures are given in table 8-3, together with McCammon's values for their efficiency. The method of Folk and Ward (1957) has been used a great deal, and Friedman (1962) has shown that it is almost as good as the second moment measure, giving an accurate value of the standard deviation. It takes in a reasonable part of the distribution and is more efficient than Inman's measure of sorting, except in very well-sorted sediments, in which both methods are equally good. Most verbal scales of sorting are based on a geometrical scale. The relationship between mean values and sorting shows that for sands the two values increase together, finer sands being better sorted. The sorting, however, becomes worse for both very coarse sediments and very fine ones in the clay grade. The cause of these relationships is probably due to polymodal sources, resulting from the common occurrence in nature of pebbles, sand and clay, and the relative scarcity of granules and finer silt.

(*iii*) *Skewness and kurtosis:* The measures of skewness and kurtosis give an indication of the non-normality of the sediment. The skewness measures the asymmetry of the curve, or the difference between the median and the mean. Both Inman's and Folk and Ward's measures have values ranging from -1 to $+1$, the negative values indicating a tail of coarser particles and the positive one of finer particles in the ϕ notation. Most natural sediments do not have a skewness value exceeding 0·8.

The kurtosis measures the ratio between the spread in the central part of the distribution and that in the tails. Folk and Ward's graphic kurtosis value is 1·0 for a normal curve, but very platykurtic curves have values as low as 0·6. The latter are often bimodal. Very leptokurtic curves may have values up to 3·0, and contain coarser and finer tails. The relationships between the third and fourth moments can be used to distinguish different environments as will be considered in section 8-6.

(*iv*) *Comparison of methods:* W. D. Sevon (1968) has compared the various moment measures by regression analysis. He analysed 220 samples of sand from beaches, dunes and rivers, using $\frac{1}{2}\phi$ sieves and compared the moment measures derived by the methods of Trask, Inman, Folk and Ward and Friedman. He fitted both first- and second-degree polynomials to the data. Nearly all the regression coefficients were close to unity, indicating a good linear agreement between the results. The constants of the regression equation were also close to zero for the first three moment measures, but increased rapidly for the kurtosis.

These results are reflected in the correlation coefficients, which are very high for the mean and standard deviations, indicating that all the methods give a reasonable value for these measures. The second-degree regression equation provides little improvement in the first two measures. The methods of calculating skewness and kurtosis show little correlation, although the second-degree regression does improve some of the relations. The results show that care must be taken in comparing results using the third and fourth moments when these have been obtained by different methods of analysis.

c Size of beach fill

A practical application of the size distribution analysis of beach sand will be briefly referred to before the consideration of shape analysis in the next section. W. C. Krumbein and W. R. James (1965) discuss the importance of studying the size distribution of sand used for beach replenishment. The material used for beach maintenance must be of suitable size in relation to the natural sand if it is going to remain on the beach. At times fill must be used that is not of the best size, and as a result more material must be put on the beach, because the finer part of the borrow-material will not remain in equilibrium.

The assumptions made in the model are that (a) the native sand is in equilibrium; (b) only the fill material that corresponds to the native sand size distribution will stay; (c) only the size distribution is important; (d) the native and fill materials are log-normally distributed. The critical ratio between the two sand sizes is found from

$$R_{\phi \text{ crit}} = (s_{\phi}b/s_{\phi}n) \exp \left[-(M_{\phi}b - M_{\phi}n)^2/2(s_{\phi}n^2 - s_{\phi}b^2) \right]$$

where M is the mean, s is the standard deviation and s^2 is the variance. The critical ratio, $R_{\phi \text{ crit}}$ refers to the ratio between the frequency of the natural sand to the borrow-sand at the critical ϕ class point. The critical value of ϕ is where this ratio reaches a maximum. The value of $R_{\phi \text{ crit}}$ can be calculated from the equation given and its value will determine whether the borrow-material can be converted into the natural material by selection.

Table 8-4 Comparison of natural sands and borrow-sands

Case	Relation between native sand and borrow-material	Remarks
I	Means are not equal; borrow-sand less well sorted	$R_{\phi \text{ crit}}$ is a maximum and borrow-material can be transformed into natural material
II	Means are not equal; borrow-sand better sorted	$R_{\phi \text{ crit}}$ is a minimum and borrow-sand cannot be transformed into natural material
III	Means are equal; borrow-sand less well sorted	$R_{\phi \text{ crit}}$ is a maximum and occurs at ϕ mean. The borrow-sand can be transformed into the natural sand
IV	Means are not equal; sorting is equal	$R_{\phi \text{ crit}}$ is at an inflection point and borrow-material cannot be transformed into the natural sand

A number of cases can be tabulated, as shown in table 8-4, and the likely effect on the borrow sand can be established. The optimum adjustment is likely to occur where the native sand is better sorted than the fill. The amount of extra fill required will depend on the difference between the means. Such studies are of considerable value in view of the increasing use of artificial nourishment in beach improvement schemes. The value of $R_{\phi \text{ crit}}$ defines the amount of sand required to produce a distribution similar to that of the native sand. For example,

when $M_{\phi n} = 1{\cdot}50$; $M_{\phi b} = 2{\cdot}96$; $s_{\phi n} = 0{\cdot}91$; $s_{\phi b} = 1{\cdot}76$

then R_ϕ crit $\simeq 3{\cdot}0$

4 Shape analysis

The shapes of both sand grains and shingle have been analysed, but more studies have been made using the latter because these do not require microscope analysis. A considerable number of shape parameters and indices have been established. They are based either on the geometry or the functional aspects of the particles.

N. C. Flemming (1965) used the term parameter to describe direct measurements on the pebbles and indices for combinations of the parameters. He distinguished between form indices and functional indices, the latter describing the behavioural characteristics. The form measurements and indices compare the pebble in relation to a reference body. Flemming considers the

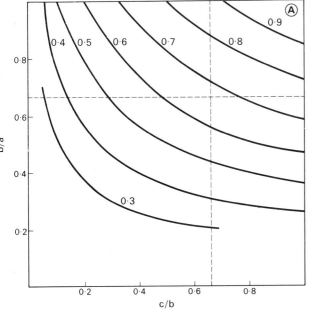

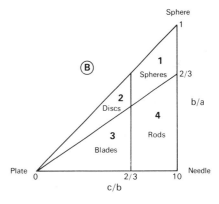

Figure 8-2   A: Sphericity measures using ratio of b/a and c/b axes; **B:** Zingg's shape classes. (*A after Krumbein, 1941.*)

skew ellipse to be a useful reference body: the pebble's shape can be specified by the three major axes—a, b and c—which are assumed to intersect at a point. Then α, β and γ are the distances between the point of intersection and the mid-points of the axes. Each octant of the figure is considered an ellipsoid.

13 measurements can be made on a pebble. These are: a, b and c axes, α, β and γ values, M the mass, ρ, the density, V_t, the true volume, A_t, the true area, C_t, the true circumference, and A'_t, the true circumference at a given cross-section, r, radius of curvature of any corner, n, the number of corners. There are 6 axial ratios. The Zingg system uses the ratios b/a and c/b, giving values ranging between 0 and 1. These are illustrated in figure 8-2. Asymmetry can be given by α/a, β/b and γ/c. The skew ellipse can be defined by four functions. The first is the

223

perimeter index, C_t/C_e. The second is the profile factor, A'_t/A'_e. The third is Wadell's sphericity index, A_t/A_e. The fourth is the volume ratio V_t/V_e, the subscript e referring to the reference ellipse.

A. Cailleux's roundness measure (see chapter 7) refers to the radius of curvature in the principal plane, using the long axis also, to give a roundness index, $R = 2r/a \times 1000$, where r is the minimum radius of curvature in the principal plane. A sphericity measure is given by $\sqrt[3]{ab/c^2}$, or $c/\sqrt{ab}$.

This is a measure called the portance, which governs the settling velocity. Flatness is given by $(a + b)/c$ in Cailleux's system. Some roundness measures are not independent of sphericity, for example Wadell's roundness, c/a, plots as a hyperbola on Zingg's diagram. The radius of the sharpest curvature on an ellipsoid is $c^2/2a$, and this can be related to the radius of the smallest inscribed sphere, which is $c/2$, so the ratio is c/a. Roundness measured in this way correlates with sphericity.

Cailleux's (1945) roundness is important as a measure of the severity of abrasion. Particles undergoing abrasion start with angular corners, and in the early stages of abrasion the roundness indices give a good measure of shape. At later stages the particles change from skew ellipses to regular ellipses. A measure of the skewness of the ellipse is useful, therefore, in the later stages of abrasion. Flemming proposes the mean radius of curvature to that of the reference ellipsoid to measure this index.

C. A. M. King and J. T. Buckley (1968) have tested several shape measures on samples from many different environments, and it was found that Cailleux's roundness index provided the most diagnostic measure. The data were analysed by factor analysis and the mean roundness had the highest factor score on the first factor, together with the flatness ratio. These two measures were shown to be strongly negatively correlated with each other. Raised beach pebbles could be readily distinguished from those in other environments by means of Cailleux's roundness index. Some results will be considered further in the next sections. Each roundness value quoted is the mean of a random sample of 50 stones. Sometimes the standard deviation of the samples provides useful data in addition to the mean roundness.

5 Source of beach material

The material on the beach can come from one or more of four sources:

1   The cliffs behind the beach and the rock platform beneath it
2   from the land via rivers or glaciers, or to a lesser degree by the wind
3   from offshore
4   from alongshore.

The material moving alongshore must itself have been derived originally from one of the first three sources, while much of the material offshore also has a terrigenous origin. Some beach material is of direct organic marine origin, however, including shell sand, foraminiferal and coral sand.

The relative proportion of material from these different sources varies in different areas. A beach backed by cliffs of glacial sand and gravel, for example in Holderness, Norfolk and Suffolk, will derive much material from this source as the cliffs are easily eroded by the sea and mass movement. However, not all material eroded from such cliffs goes to replenish the beaches. On the other hand beaches backed by cliffs of hard rock, as in Cornwall, receive little from this source. The evidence of interglacial features on such coasts indicates that this source is negligible over a considerable period of time. Cliffs cannot provide beach material on those beaches which are so thick and high that they are an effective protection to the cliffs.

The supply of material reaching the beaches from inland will depend on the nature of the hinterland. The type of rock, stage of erosion, vegetation and climate are all relevant factors in determining the amount and calibre of the load which the rivers carry to the sea. Observations reported by the Royal Commission on Coast Erosion (1911) show that at the mouth of the Humber the water is much less charged with sediment in suspension than further up the river. This observation indicates that in this area the finer sediment is derived largely from inland. In areas of inland drainage the wind may be more important in carrying sediment to the sea. In other places material may be brought to the sea by glaciers and fluvioglacial streams, as for example in southeast Iceland.

Heavy mineral analysis of river sediment has been carried out by P. D. Trask (1952) in California to enable him to trace its movement along the coast. The technique of heavy mineral analysis has been used in some areas to trace the source and distribution of marine sediment. A very detailed study of the sediments of the southern North Sea has been made by Baak (1936). He divided the area into different zones, each of which has its own characteristic assemblage of heavy minerals. On the eastern side the H group includes the mixed allochthonous sand of the Dutch group. The A groups are related to fluvioglacial and glacial material from Scandinavia. On the English coast an E group, rich in garnet and augite, is recognized, while the sediment brought down by the Rhine makes up the final North Hinder group. The sand along the coast of north France, Belgium and Holland, from Dielette eastwards, is very similar, owing to the re-sorting by waves of large quantities of glacial detritus brought into the North Sea and washed through the Straits of Dover. This material largely belongs to the H group, with some admixture of the North Hinder group.

Detailed work on the mineralogy of the sands of the coasts of Picardy and the Flemish coast has been done by D. C. Pugh (1953), which also includes work on the English coast in the neighbourhood of Worthing and Folkestone. This work shows that there is a distinctive sand called the Sussex group. The nature of the heavy minerals in marine sediments can also help to establish the source. J. A. Baak's (1936) study in the North Sea has already been mentioned. K. Venkataratnam and M. P. Rao (1960) in studying the sediments along the Visakhapatnam coast of India show that garnet and sillimanite indicate that the sand and finer sediments were derived from the metamorphic rocks that outcrop along the coast in the area.

Material from offshore can reach the beach under the influence of wave action, but the depth from which it can be moved is limited. Work done on the beaches of California by P. D. Trask (1955) shows that this movement can only take place to an appreciable extent in water which is less than 18·3 m deep. Movement in large quantities is probably confined to 9·15 m or less. The exposure of the beach is one of the variables that determines the depth from which material can reach the beach. Where the coast is exposed to long fetches over which long swells can reach the coast, the zone from which sediment can reach the shore is wider, because the long waves move sediment in greater depths than off those coasts where only short waves can reach the shore. This aspect will be considered further in the next chapter, in which movement normal to the shore is discussed.

The nature of the beach material often provides information concerning its source. Some examples from the west coast of Donegal are of interest in this respect (C. A. M. King, 1965). Most of the largest beaches along this indented part of the coast occur near the mouths of river valleys, down which a large volume of glacial outwash is carried. This material, eroded from the quartzites and granites of the area, consists of quartz sand. Each small bay has a different type or size of material: some have coarse pink sand, derived from the granite of the hinterland; some have beaches of large boulders; others consist of fine sand. Away from the estuaries many of the beaches consist of predominantly organic sand. Ballymanus beach has much siliceous material, including sponge spicules and radiolaria, while Dooey beach, a few miles further south, consists mainly of Calcareous Globigerina foraminifera.

The beaches must have been fed from different sources, and only those with direct access to the interior have largely terrigenous sediment. Those that cannot receive much sediment from inland must have obtained their material from offshore by wave action. Long swells can reach this coast, which faces the open Atlantic so that a fairly large area would be available to provide the organic material. This material only forms the dominant element of the beach in those areas where the generally more plentiful quartz sand is in short supply. Coarse material can reach the beach from offshore by attachment to sea weed (K. O. Emery and R. H. Tschudy, 1941).

Organic sand, consisting of Calcareous foraminifera, mainly Globigerina, also forms the beach material further south in Connemara. The small beaches that make the tombolo linking a gabbro island to the mainland consist entirely of this material. The beaches are considerably steeper than those associated with quartz sand, owing to the lower density of the foraminiferal sand (A. Guilcher and C. A. M. King, 1961). The gradients on the organic sands vary between 1 in 16·95 and 1 in 23·4, compared with 1 in 71 to 1 in 89 for quartz sand beaches of similar material size and exposure.

A study of shingle shape has been used by B. J. Bluck (1967) to establish the source and movement of shingle on beaches in south Wales. He used the Zingg classes, shown in figure 8-2, which divide the pebbles into spheres, rods, discs or blades. He also related the shape classes to size groups. The pebbles were found to be concentrated in zones on the beach, each zone being characterized by pebbles of a different shape class. The landward zone consisted of large discs; the next zone showed an imbricate structure of disc pebbles, seaward of this was a fill zone consisting mainly of rod and spherical pebbles, beyond which lay the frame of spherical cobbles. The source of the pebbles was the till which lay at the back of the beach.

Their shape is partly due to post-glacial weathering and partly due to marine abrasion. Both factors split up the softer greywackes into discs. With continued abrasion the larger pebbles have the most mature shape, which is spherical. The zonation on the beach of the different shapes is the result of selective movement of the different shapes by the waves. Discs and blades move in the same way, but they differ in this respect from rods and spheres. Lag deposits can also form where the particles have a shape that prevents them moving past obstructions.

Shape influences tractive movement in three ways. Round particles can roll, whereas discs shuffle along and some shapes cause a type of creep, especially where they have a low standard deviation. Large spherical particles can move over the surface of smaller disc-shaped ones. The discs travel seaward far slower than the rods and spheres, thus leaving the large discs at the top of the beach in the storm ridge, forming a capping to the reservoir of pebbles. The width of the imbricate zone of discs is a measure of the length of time the storm ridge has been breaking down to form the modern beach. Its width increases with time. The pattern of shape distribution on the beach is a function of selective sorting by wave action from mixed source material.

Quartz is by far the most common constituent of sand on most beaches, but some examples of other types of sand have been mentioned. The organic sands tend to be most common on tropical beaches where coral and other organisms can flourish. Beaches in areas of basic rocks often have black, basaltic sand. South Iceland provides one example, while there are black sand beaches in New Zealand, the West Indies and all over the central Pacific inside the Andesite line, which delimits the zone of basic volcanic rocks. The beaches of Hawaii illustrate this type of sediment.

R. Moberly (1968) has described some of the properties of this basaltic sand, and the budget of Hawaiian sands. The reservoir of beach sand was estimated at $3 \cdot 0 \times 10^6$ m³, most of which is found in Oahu and Kauii. The sand is mainly in the medium grade but varies from gravel to sandy mud. The finest grain sizes mostly occur on the more exposed beaches on the windward side. This is the result of more rapid weathering and of finer sediment passing to the coast in drainage basins which have exposed aspects. Marine abrasion and sorting in the more vigorous environment also helps to reduce the size of the sand. The wide reefs of the south coast prevent effective wave action and the beaches have coarse, poorly sorted material. The beaches show a consistently coarser sand in winter than summer by about a $\frac{1}{2}\phi$ class.

All the beaches show a mixture of organic calcareous grains and black silicate grains derived from basalt. Some samples were mainly detrital in origin, but most showed a very large proportion

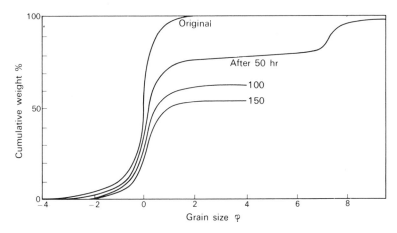

Figure 8-3 Size reduction of basaltic sand during experimental testing. (*After Moberly, 1968.*)

of organic material. The loss of sand from Hawaiian beaches is partly brought about by the abrasion of the particles. Abrasion of quartz sand is so slow as to be negligible in most beach studies, but the sands of the Hawaiian beaches do show measurable abrasion under experimental conditions. This is an important factor in the loss of beach sand in this area. Figure 8-3 illustrates the results of experimental abrasion of sand grains. The amount of silt in the sample increased very rapidly, the sand being reduced to half silt after 150 hours. The coarse grains were abraded slightly faster than the finer ones. Most of the basalt-rich sands lost about 20% of their mass in a 50 hour run. The rate was greatest in the most weathered basalts that accumulated in the most sheltered environments. The unweathered sands of the vigorous northeast coast environment abraded at a much slower rate. The carbonate sands mostly lost about 10% of their mass during 50 hours in the experimental mill. Other losses of sand in Hawaii occur in the building of storm beach ridges, the formation of dunes, extraction by man, cementation to beachrock, but the principal loss is by passage through sand-bottomed channels out to deeper water. These channels were cut during periods of low sea level in the Pleistocene. New sand is always entering the system but at the same time some is permanently lost. On the whole the Hawaiian beach sand volume is in approximate equilibrium, but loss by abrasion is a very important factor on these beaches. It is not one which affects quartz beaches, on which abrasion is 1 to 2 $\times$ 10^3 slower.

6 Differentiation of beach material

Some of the work on the differentiation of environments in terms of their sedimentary characteristics has already been mentioned in chapter 6, in discussing the differentiation of beach and dune sand. Some further examples and other methods of studying the differentiation of beach sediments will be considered in this section.

D. B. Duane (1964) has considered the significance of skewness in recent sediments in western Pamlico Sound, North Carolina. He has shown that skewness is environmentally sensitive. Negative skewness is found in sediments laid down by a fluid flow of moderate or strong intensity, such as on beaches, the littoral zone and tidal inlets. The negative skewness results from the winnowing action of the current that removes the finer particles. Sheltered lagoons, on the other hand, generally show a positive skewness. Duane demonstrated that most of the differences were sufficiently great to be reproducible whichever equations were used, including those of Inman, Shepard and Young, and Folk and Ward's graphic measures. Pamlico Sound is the largest coastal embayment off the eastern U.S.A., being 96 km long and 42 km wide at its maximum behind the barrier beaches that separate it from the open ocean. A total of 136 samples were analysed, falling in the range 0·7 to 6·2 ϕ, of which 84% were finer than 1 ϕ. The range of skewness was from −1·59 to +1·60, 60% being negatively skewed. Only 15% had a skewness value between −0·1 and +0·1. Duane concluded that negative skewness was characteristic of those coastal environments that are undergoing erosion or non-deposition, while positive skewness was found in areas of deposition, such as the sheltered lagoons, where the finer deposits could accumulate. The results calculated by Folk and Ward's equations agreed most closely with the mathematical moment measures, but only Inman's measures differed in sign. The settling tube method of analysis may cause too high a negative skewness value compared with sieve analysis.

A. O. Fuller (1962) studied sands from water of varying depth between 1·83 and 3·66 m. He found that the cumulative frequency curves showed two inflection points at 0·8 and 2·0 ϕ. These points may represent the size at which traction replaces suspension as the sand becomes coarser. The 2·0 ϕ size is often missing from sediments in this shallow-water environment, suggesting that this size moves either onshore or offshore from this depth. This result may be due to the relative ease with which this size of material moves.

J. R. Hails and J. H. Hoyt (1969) have analysed many sediment samples from the coastal plain of lower Georgia. The sediments included a series of six Pleistocene barriers and the present barrier, and the intervening marsh deposits of the lagoons. The lagoon deposits include estuarine and tidal channel deposits, while the barriers include dune, littoral, shallow neritic and offshore deposits. The samples were analysed by $\frac{1}{4}$ ϕ sieving; computer analysis gave mathematical moment measures and graphic measures. The moment-measures programs used interpolated values to improve the estimation of the statistical values. The mathematical moment measures were compared with those derived graphically according to the Trask (1952), Inman (1952) and Folk and Ward (1957) methods. Roundness values were also estimated according to Shepard and Young's (1962) method.

The results showed that the majority of the samples were negatively skewed. The skewness, mean and standard deviation all have diagnostic value in the study. Barrier island deposits were better sorted than the lagoon deposits, although all the samples were larger than $1 \cdot 50 \phi$. The coarsest barrier island samples occurred in the tidal channels and inlets. Of the barrier samples 70% were negatively skewed, while 90% of the present beach sands were negatively skewed. On the other hand about 70% of the dunes showed positive skewness. Some of the positively skewed barrier sands may be the result of diagenesis. Skewness was considered to be a valid measure in differentiating the sediments of different environments, in which it also reflected the energy variations, thus confirming earlier results in this field.

J. E. Klovan (1966) has used the multivariate technique of factor analysis to consider the depositional environment in terms of grain-size distributions. He points out that an empirical approach to the problem is likely to be valuable owing to the relatively poor knowledge of the laws governing movement and deposition of particles. He considers that each sediment can be described by the frequency with which its constituents fall into the ϕ classes. If, for example, the sediment falls into ten ϕ classes, then the amounts in each class represent ten variables that characterize that sediment. The similarity between each class value can be determined by the $\cos \theta$ matrix, in which the vector of each variable is compared with every other. The value is unity when the vectors coincide and zero when they are 90° apart. Factor analysis can be used to determine the relationship between the matrix of $\cos \theta$ vectors. Mutually orthogonal axes reduce the number of variables to a significant number of factors that best account for the variability of the data.

Klovan analysed data from Barataria Bay on the Mississippi delta by this method. Some of the samples come from the coast in a surf environment; some are dominated by current activity within the bay; others occur in a depositional environment. The first factor accounts for 77·22% of the sums of squares, the second for 14·34% and the third for 5·91% totalling 97·46%, in terms of the loading of the samples on the first three factors. Figure 8-4 illustrates that most samples fall near the apices of the diagram, in which the data have been normalized. The samples concentrate at the apices and few fall along the bottom or middle. The samples far from the corners appear to be mixed sediments, while those at the corners are end members reflecting three different modes of deposition—wind-wave action, current action and gravitational settling. Many samples, however, have a mixed origin.

Kovan's method uses the whole of the sediment size structure and is not dependent on calculated moment measures or graphically derived ones. The method is, therefore, more objective, the only subjective element being an assumption of log normality and the choice of ϕ class interval. His results are both geographically and geologically meaningful in terms of the resultant groups of sediment. These groups are expressed by three variables, which are the loadings on the first three factors. Together these loadings account for most of the variability of the data.

All the examples given in this section so far have been concerned with the size distribution of the samples. The differentiation of beach material by shape will be exemplified by brief reference to two different areas.

In Dingle Bay in western Ireland there are three spits extending towards the centre of the bay. The outermost two, Inch and Rossbehy spits, are mainly composed of sand and have been built up by wave action (A. Guilcher and C. A. M. King, 1961). The inner spit at Cromane is different in character, having been modified only in a relatively minor way by wave action. These spits are discussed in more detail in chapter 19, but a study of the stone roundness provides a useful confirmation of this difference in formation.

The mean roundness of the stones on Rossbehy spit is 575, using Cailleux's index, and the mean length is 58 mm. The roundness of three samples from Cromane spit gives the following values: western beach, 425; north end of the spit, 325; and the central mound, 275. There is a

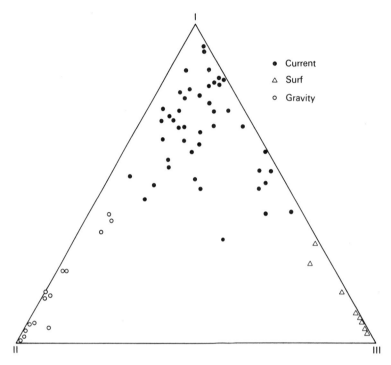

Figure 8-4 Factor loadings from factor analysis of sand size classes. Three environments of sedimentation can be distinguished. (*After Klovan, 1966.*)

very significant difference between the western sides of the two spits, and there is also a considerable difference between the different sections of Cromane spit. The central mound has the lowest value, which is that of the morainic material that forms the mound. The sea has slightly rounded the material at the end of the spit, and has progressed further in this process on the more exposed western side of the spit. The growth of the other spits to seaward, however, has stopped vigorous wave action on this spit, so that its stone roundness is not nearly so great as that on the more exposed spits further seaward.

The other example relates to a series of stone roundness measurements on raised beaches in eastern Baffin Island. Samples were measured on five different beaches, the mean values being as follows:

		Height (m)	Cailleux roundness
1	Eskimo Point terrace	8	207
2	Eskimo Point beach ridge	10	314
3	Cape Henry Kater ridge	2	369
4	Cape Henry Kater marine limit	22	375
5	Cape Henry Kater modern beach	0	591

Analysis of variance shows that these values are significantly different. The modern beach (5) has the roundest pebbles because it is in an exposed situation, facing the open waters of Davis Strait. Sea level is now falling only very slowly, if at all, at this position on the outer coast. There has, therefore, been sufficient time and wave energy to round the beach stones thoroughly. The roundness on the marine limit (4) is similar to that on the low ridges at Cape Henry Kater (3). The similarity can be accounted for by the longer time the low ridges have been influenced by the waves, which compensates for the greater exposure of the marine limit beaches that face the open Davis Strait, with the same aspect as the modern beach.

The smaller roundness index of the marine limit beaches compared with the modern beach is due to the shorter time that sea level remained at the marine limit. The low ridges at Cape Henry Kater (3) have a roundness value considerably greater than that of the beaches and terrace at Eskimo Point. The latter samples were from features in a much more sheltered position, further from the open sea. Thus both longer time and greater exposure have allowed the low ridges at Cape Henry Kater (3) to become rounder than samples (1) and (2) from the more sheltered and higher locality, 19 km further up the fjord.

The significant difference between the two sites at Eskimo Point is due to at least two factors. Firstly, unweathered stones were sampled on the ridge, while some of the terrace stones were weathered, thus increasing their angularity. The nature of the deposit is also relevant. The terrace is flat and stones thrown by the waves onto it can no longer be modified by them. It is possible that the terrace is an erosional feature rather than one built up by wave action. On the steeper slope of the beach ridge, which must have been a depositional form, effective wave action could continue the rounding process for longer. The time factor is not important. However, in samples 1 and 2 both time and exposure must be considered as both are relevant in accounting for the difference in roundness of the beach pebbles in different parts of this area, which has been uplifted isostatically.

Summary

Beach material varies from clay to boulders, although sand is by far the most common material. The ϕ classification is used mostly now to describe the size of sediment, where ϕ is $-\log_2$ mm. In order to study beach sediment a good sampling plan is essential. Random stratified sampling is most suitable, so that all environments within the system are adequately represented. Large particles can be measured individually, but sand must be analysed by sieving or settling tube, the former being the more common. Finer sediments must be analysed by pipette or hydrometer. The results are usually plotted as a cumulative percentage graph on probability paper, and mathematical moment measures can be calculated. The various graphic and mathematical moment measures are summarized in table 8-3. The central tendency gives a mean value of the sediment size; the sorting indicates the spread; the skewness shows the asymmetry of the curve and the kurtosis its peakedness. Combinations of these moment measures have been shown to be diagnostic of environments of sedimentation, the skewness being especially useful. Various shape indices have been proposed. Cailleux's roundness index is most useful for the early stages of abrasion.

Beach material is derived from inland, via rivers or glaciers, the cliffs or platform, or from offshore, when it may be organic in origin, such as coral or shell sand. Most sand is formed of quartz, but in some areas basaltic sand occurs. This is much less resistant and measurable attrition occurs, especially where the basalt is weathered. A useful application of sediment size studies is in projects for beach nourishment where borrow-sand is added to the beach. The relationship between the mean size and sorting of the natural and borrow-sand determines the amount of borrow-sand that will remain on the beach. Table 8-4 displays the relationships between the two sands.

Size characteristics of the sediments can be used to differentiate different environments. The vigorous environments, such as the beach, tidal inlets and nearshore zone, usually show negative skewness, owing to the inability of the fine material to settle. The depositional environments, such as lagoons, on the other hand, usually show a positive skewness, as fine material can settle in the quiet conditions. Shape can also be used to differentiate features formed under different conditions. This type of analysis is usually carried out on larger particles. Both time of formation and exposure must be considered in accounting for differences in stone roundness, which is the best variable to use in such studies.

References

BAAK, J. A. 1936: *Regional petrology of the south North Sea.* Wageningen.

BLUCK, B. J. 1967: Sedimentation of beach gravels: examples from South Wales. *J. Sed. Petrol.* **37**(1), 128–56.

BRITISH STANDARD INSTITUTE 1947: *British Standard code of practice.*

CALDWELL, J. M. 1960: Development and tests of a radioactive sediment density probe. *B.E.B. Tech. Memo.* **121**. (28 pp.)

CHAPMAN, G. 1949: The thixotropy and dilatancy of a marine soil. *J. Mar. Biol. Assoc. U.K.* **28**, 123–40.

CHAPPELL, J. 1967: Recognising fossil strand lines from grain size analysis. *J. Sed. Petrol.* **37**(1), 157–65.

DOORNKAMP, J. C. and KING, C. A. M. 1971: *Numerical analysis in geomorphology.* London: Arnold; New York: St Martin's Press. (384 pp.)

DUANE, D. B. 1964: Significance of shewness in recent sediments, West Pamlico Sound, North Carolina. *J. Sed. Petrol.* **34**(4), 864–74.

EMERY, K. O. and TSCHUDY, R. H. 1941: Transportations of rock by kelp. *Bull. Geol. Soc. Amer.* **52**(6), 855–62.

FLEMMING, N. C. 1965: Form and function of sedimentary particles. *J. Sed. Petrol.* **35**(2), 381–90.

FOLK, R. L. 1962: Of skewness of sands. *J. Sed. Petrol.* **32**, 145–6.

FOLK, R. L. 1966: A review of grain size parameters. *Sedimentology* **6**, 73–93.

FOLK, R. L. and WARD, W. C. 1957: Brazos River bar, a study of the significance of grain size parameters. *J. Sed. Petrol.* **27**, 3–27.

FRIEDMAN, G. M. 1962: On sorting, sorting coefficients and the log, normality of the grain size distribution of sandstones. *J. Geol.* **70**, 737–56.

FRIEDMAN, G. M. 1967: Dynamic processes and statistical parameters compared for size frequency distribution of beach and river sands. *J. Sed. Petrol.* **37**, 327–54.

FULLER, A. O. 1962: Systematic fractionation of sand in shallow marine and beach environment of the South African coast. *J. Sed. Petrol.* **32**, 602–6.

GILES, R. T. and PILKEY, O. H. 1965: Atlantic beach and dune sediments of the southern United States. *J. Sed. Petrol.* **35**, 900–10.

GREENWOOD, B. 1969: Sedimentary parameters and environmental discrimination: an application of multivariate statistics. *Canad. J. Earth Sci.* **6**(6), 1347–58.

GUILCHER, A. and KING, C. A. M. 1961: Spits, tombolos and tidal marshes in Connemara and west Kerry, Ireland. *Proc. Roy. Irish Acad.* **61**B(17), 283–338.

HAILS, J. R. and HOYT, J. H. 1969: The significance and limitations of statistical parameters for distinguishing ancient and modern sedimentary environments of the lower Georgia coastal plain. *J. Sed. Petrol.* **39**(2), 559–80.

HARRISON, W. and ALAMO, R. M. 1964: Dynamic properties of immersed sand at Virginia Beach, Va. *C.E.R.C. Tech. Memo.* **9.** (52 pp.)

INMAN, D. L. 1952: Measures for describing the size distribution of sediments. *J. Sed. Petrol.* **22**(3), 125–45.

KING, C. A. M. 1965: Some observations on the beaches of the west coast of County Donegal. *Irish Geog.* **5**(2), 40–50.

KING, C. A. M. and BUCKLEY, J. T. 1968: The analysis of stone size and shape in Arctic environments. *J. Sed. Petrol.* **38**(1), 200–214.

KLOVAN, J. E. 1966: The use of factor analysis in determining depositional environments of grain size distribution. *J. Sed. Petrol.* **36**(1), 115–25.

KRUMBEIN, W. C. 1941: Measurement and geological significance of slope and roundness in sedimentary particles. *J. Sed. Petrol.* **11,** 64–72.

KRUMBEIN, W. C. and JAMES, W. R. 1965: A log-normal size distribution model for estimating stability of beach fill material. *C.E.R.C. Tech. Memo.* **16.** (17 pp.)

KRUMBEIN, W. C. and SLACK, H. A. 1956: Relative efficiency of beach sampling methods. *B.E.B. Tech. Memo.* **90.**

MCCAMMON, R. B. 1962a: Efficiency of percentile measures for describing the mean size and sorting of sedimentary particles. *J. Geol.* **70,** 453–65.

MCCAMMON, R. B. 1962b: Moment measures and the shape of size frequency distributions. *J. Geol.* **79,** 89–92.

MIDDLETON, G. V. 1962: On sorting, sorting coefficients and the log. normality of the grain size distribution of sandstones—a discussion. *J. Geol.* **70,** 754–6.

MII, HIDEO 1959: Grain size, roundness and shape of the beach pebbles of Kujinshama, Aomori prefecture. *Saito Ho-on Kai Museum Res. Mem.* **28,** 30–39.

MOBERLY, R. 1968: Loss of Hawaiian littoral sand. *J. Sed. Petrol.* **38**(1), 17–34.

PUGH, D. C. 1953: Étude minéralogique des plages Picardes et Flamandes. *Bull. d'Inform. Com. Cent. d'Oceanog. et d'Études des Cotes.* **5**(6), 245–76.

SEVON, W. D. 1968: First and second degree regression correlations of the size analysis statistical parameters of Trask, Inman, Folk and Ward and Friedman. *J. Sed. Petrol.* **38**(1), 238–40.

SHEPARD, F. P. and YOUNG, R. 1961: Distinguishing beach and dune sands. *J. Sed. Petrol.* **31,** 196–214.

TANNER, W. F. 1964: Modification of sediment size distribution. *J. Sed. Petrol.* **34,** 156–64.

TANNER, W. F. 1969: The particle size scale. *J. Sed. Petrol.* **39**(2), 809–12.

TRASK, P. D. 1932: *Origin and environment of source sediments of petroleum.* Gulf Pub. Co. (323 pp.)

TRASK, P. D. 1952: Sources of beach sands at Santa Barbara, California, as indicated by mineral grain studies. *B.E.B. Tech. Memo.* **28.**

TRASK, P. D. 1955: Movement of sand around the southern Californian promontories. *B.E.B. Tech. Memo.* **76.**

VENKATARATNAM, K. and RAO, M. P. 1960: Studies in grain size, coarse fraction and mineral content of marine sediments off Visakhapatnam. *Quart. J. Geol. Min. and Metal. Soc. India* **32**(4), 205–11.

9 Movement of material normal to the shore

1 Theory

2 Model experiments: a) Sand movement outside the break-point: (*i*) *Wave height*; (*ii*) *Wave period*; (*iii*) *Wave steepness*; (*iv*) *Water depth and distance from the break-point*; (*v*) *Beach gradient*; (*vi*) *Character of the bottom*; b) Sand movement inside the break-point.

3 The equilibrium line

4 Surf base and wave base

5 Movement in deeper water outside the break-point

6 Movement landward of the break-point: a) Sand in suspension; b) Tracer studies.

7 Depth of disturbance of sand by waves

8 Artificial beach nourishment

Summary

In this chapter the movement of sediment normal to the shore is considered from the theoretical point of view, and experimental and field observations are discussed. The theory of sediment movement by wave action is more complex than that by other fluid media owing to the reversing nature of the flow in wave action. Model experimental results provide useful data to test the theory. Field observations are also needed to apply the results to natural conditions. These observations are not easy to make owing to the large number of uncontrollable variables, which complicate the problem.

1 Theory

R. A. Bagnold (1963) has shown that the physics of movement of material by waves involves the flow of dispersed grains within a fluid. Certain concepts are required to understand the nature of flow of this type. In hydraulics the friction factor or coefficient, c_d, is the ratio of the fluid shear stress over the flow boundary, τ, to the square of a representative flow velocity, u, so that $c_d = \tau/\rho u^2$, where ρ is the density of the fluid. The friction factor in solid physics is the ratio of the shear stress or force to the normal stress across the plane of contact, or T/P. This ratio is defined as the tangent of the friction angle ϕ.

The term 'concentration' is used to denote the ratio of space occupied by the sand grains to the whole space in which they exist. The sediment is heavier than the fluid, and the normal stress exerted by it is given by

$$[(\rho_s - \rho)/\rho_s]\text{gm} \cos \beta$$

where ρ_s is the sediment density, m is its mass and β is the angle of the bed. The tangential or shear stress is given by

$$[(\rho_s - \rho)/\rho_s]\text{gm} \sin \beta$$

The sediment movement involves shearing of the sediment grains over each other and the bed—a process that necessitates some upwards dispersion of the grains. A normal stress must support the moving grains. In suspension load this is achieved by turbulent eddies. For bed load, however, turbulence is absent or incompetent to support the grains. The collisions between grains set up stresses that tend to make each grain layer repel its neighbours. The repelling stress must be equalized by the force of gravity, or it must take place between two parallel boundaries that the grains cannot penetrate. The dispersive pressure is in equilibrium with the weight of the grains.

The total applied stress consists of the stress transmitted from grain to grain, the solid phase, and the shearing of the fluid—the fluid phase. The solid stress is about 100 times that of the fluid stress. As a first approximation, therefore, the whole resistance to motion may be considered as being due to the shearing of the solid phase. Only when the concentration is as low as 9% does the fluid element begin to dominate.

The dynamic grain stresses, T and P, are proportional to one another. The angle ϕ', which is the ratio T/P, is similar to that of the angle of repose of the grains. At the surface of the bed the tangential stress equilibrium state is given by

$$T_F = \frac{\rho_s - \rho}{\rho_s}\text{gm}_b \cos \beta(\tan \phi - \tan \beta) + \tau_0$$

regardless of the degree of grain dispersion. T_F is the externally applied stress resulting from the fluid flow; m_b is the whole mass of the bed load; and τ_0 is the residual fluid stress and may be neglected when the transport mass is considerable. When the bed-slope angle, β, is small $\tan \beta$ may be ignored; but when β equals ϕ, the bed will move by avalanching without any fluid stress being applied. As T_F increases, τ_0, the residual fluid element, decreases to a negligible value. An increase in T_F must cause erosion of the grains, with the bed load weight increasing as a result.

It is possible to compute the dynamic transport rate in terms of the equation given, where j_b is the mass transport of grains per unit width. This is the mass of grains m_b multiplied by their mean velocity $\bar{U}_b$. It is possible to measure j_b if no load is carried in suspension. The tangential thrust needed to transport the load is given by

$$[(\rho_s - \rho)/\rho_s]\text{gm}_b \cos \beta(\tan \phi - \tan \beta)$$

which can be multiplied by $\bar{U}_b$, to give the fluid power expended in transporting bed load. The dynamic transport rate, i_b, is the quantity

$$[(\rho_s - \rho)/\rho]\text{gj}_b \cos \beta$$

The fluid power expended is then $i_b (\tan \phi - \tan \beta)$. This fluid energy is converted into heat by intergranular friction.

The available fluid power, ω, must exceed

$$i_b(\tan \phi - \tan \beta)$$

where i_b is given as

$$i_b = \omega \frac{\varepsilon_b}{\tan \phi - \tan \beta}$$

in which ε_b is an efficiency factor, and must be less than unity. For waves of height, H, travelling over a constant depth

$$\omega = \tfrac{1}{4}\rho g H \frac{dH}{dx} Cn$$

where C is the wave phase velocity, and n is that proportion of it moving forward with the wave phase velocity C. The power ω is also measurable in terms of T_F and u_*, the drag velocity. The flow velocity u' at an effective distance above the bed is $c_r u_*$, c_r being a numerical coefficient that must be determined experimentally. Wave power can now be defined as

$$\omega = c_r T_F^{3/2}/\sqrt{\rho} = c_r \rho u_*^3$$

From this equation Bagnold could calculate i_b for laboratory wave tanks.

When the grains are smaller than 1 mm diameter, movement causes spontaneous rippling, but larger grains do not develop ripples. The initial disturbance of sediment by waves is defined by the critical shear stress, τ_t, when the shear stress overcomes gravity and friction. The natural threshold criterion, θ_t, is the ratio of the critical shear stress, τ_t. to the immersed grain weight, $(\rho_s - \rho)gD$, where D is the grain diameter. θ_t varies between 0·04 and 0·06 for flat beds, which do not become spontaneously rippled. It increases to 0·25 as the grains become smaller, owing to the drag exerted by ripples where these have been formed by a previous flow. Thus

$$\theta_t = \tau_t/(\rho_s - \rho)gD$$

In alternating wave flow the threshold grain velocity on an unrippled bed is determined both by the orbital velocity and the end-of-stroke acceleration, which is related to wave amplitude. The value of θ_t varies for a smooth and rippled bed. The relationship $\tau_t = gd \tan \beta$, allows τ_t to be measured in a flume. Information on conditions of rippled beds is still scanty and there is no reliable information for conditions in the sea.

Once movement has been initiated the individual grains are likely to move more slowly than the mean mass transport velocity $\bar{U}_b$. The grain velocity $\bar{U}_G$ is given by

$$\bar{U}_G = \bar{U}_b(2bD/\eta)$$

where b is the number of sand layers moving, which is about 2, and η is the ripple height. As the ripples move forward, the grains appear to advance over the ripple crest and to retreat at the level of the ripple trough. The mass transport velocity is related to the orbital velocity close to the bed by the equation

$$\bar{u} = \tfrac{5}{4}u_0^2/C$$

where $\bar{u}$ is the predicted drift velocity or mass transport velocity; u_0 is the orbital velocity just above the boundary layer; and C is the wave phase velocity. The equation applies when d/L is small. The equation for $\bar{u}$ can be stated as

$$\bar{u} = \tfrac{5}{4}(H/2d)^2C,$$

according to Longuet-Higgins's theory. The theory no longer strictly applies when the boundary layer contains dispersed sediment, although the forward thrust on the bottom that it predicts has been observed, as was noted in chapter 4. Experiments showed that the transport rate increased with increasing wave length. Bagnold (1963) suggests the equation

$$i = k''\omega H/2d,$$

where i is the wave drift transport; k'' is probably a function of wave length; ω is the available power attributable to bed drag; H is the wave height and d the water depth.

These relationships require testing and verification by specially prepared laboratory experiments and field tests, some of which have been carried out and are mentioned later.

2 Model experiments

Experiments to study the direction and amount of sand moved at varying depths under different wave conditions were carried out in the wave tank in Cambridge University. The material used had a median diameter of 0·41 mm. The experiments were carried out with a trap, which has already been described. It enabled the net amount and direction of sand movement normal to the beach to be determined. The experiments tested the effect of several variables, both outside and inside the break-point.

a Sand movement outside the break-point

In 98% of the observations the net movement was in a landward direction. The few exceptions involved very small amounts and were obtained with very steep waves. The result can be explained by the orbital movement on the bottom discussed in chapter 4. The landward transport continued, however, when the bottom was rippled; in this state the landward thrust, observed with a smooth bottom, no longer continued. The following variables determine the volume of sand moving—wave height, wave period or length, water depth or proximity to the break-point, beach gradient and bottom character, whether it be rippled or smooth. As only one sand size was used the effect of this variable was not determined.

(*i*) *Wave height:* The wave height is an important variable in determining the amount of material moved landwards, as shown in figure 9-1. For any given wave period at a specific distance from the break-point the amount of sand transported increases very rapidly with increasing wave height.

(*ii*) *Wave period:* As the period lengthens for any given wave height so the volume of sand moved increases (figure 9-1). The greater volume of transport with lengthening wave period is more rapid as the waves become higher, due to increasing wave energy. A long wave may be expected to move more sand in the same depth owing to the smaller value of d/L, which is one of the parameters determining the horizontal amplitude of movement on the bottom. Thus for a short wave (L = 100 cm) in a depth of 20 cm, d/L will be 0·2; but for a wave 300 cm long, d/L will be 0·067. This will produce a theoretical amplitude of oscillation of 0·6 H for the short wave and 2·3 H for the long one.

(*iii*) *Wave steepness:* Wave steepness does not affect sand movement nearly so much as the wave dimensions. A short, high wave can move as much as a longer, lower one.

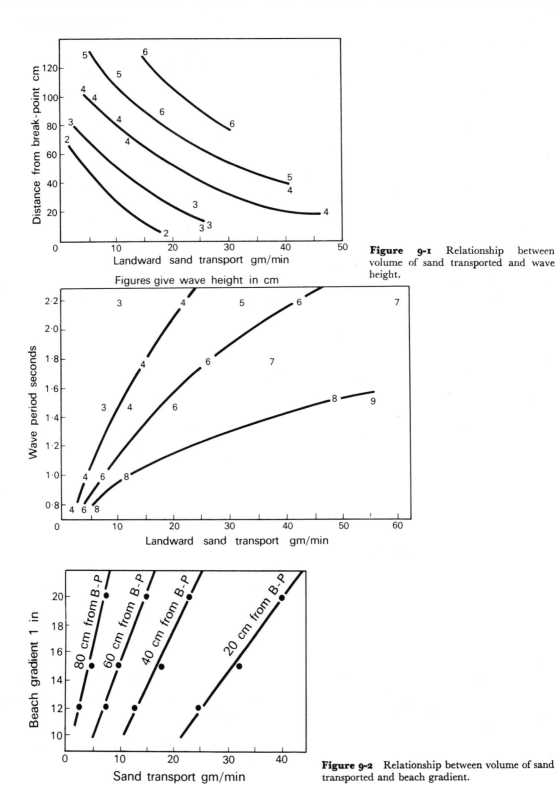

Figure 9-1 Relationship between volume of sand transported and wave height.

Figures give wave height in cm

Figure 9-2 Relationship between volume of sand transported and beach gradient.

(*iv*) *Water depth and distance from the break-point:* The volume transported is considerably greater as the water becomes shallower, reaching a maximum just seaward of the break-point. The same relationships that explain the increase of transport with increasing wave period apply also in this instance. The d/L ratio is decreased as the break-point is approached. The depth at which no movement takes place is a function of the wave height and length. For the larger waves, the limit at which movement ceased was not reached in the wave tank. For the lower waves the limit of movement appeared to be reached when d/L exceeded a value between 0·015 and 0·02.

(*v*) *Beach gradient:* Greater transport of sand took place on flatter beach gradients. The gradients used were 1 in 12, 1 in 15 and 1 in 20. Figure 9-2 shows the effect of changing gradient at different distances from the break-point for one wave height and length.

(*vi*) *Character of the bottom:* The experiments already discussed were made with an initially smooth sand bed, but before the end of the usual five minute run the bed had nearly always become rippled. Another series of experiments was made to determine the effect of the character of the bed on the volume of transport. The bed was smoothed at the beginning of the run and as soon as ripples started to form the waves were stopped. One wave length and height were used and the gradient was kept at 1 in 15.

Figure 9-3 shows that for any given distance from the break-point the sand transport on a

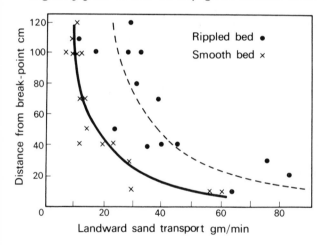

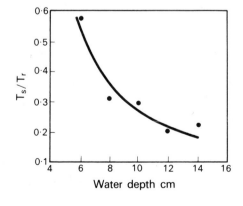

Figure 9-3 Relationship between volume of sand transported and character of the bed.

smooth bed was considerably less than on a rippled bed. The scatter of points for the rippled surface is partly accounted for by the varying number of ripple crests that passed over the trap during the run. The effect of rippling is much more marked in deep water, where the ratio T_s/T_r is about 0·2, T_s being transport on a smooth bed and T_r that on a rippled bed. In shallow water the ratio increases to over 0·5. When the bottom is rippled sand movement begins in deeper water than on a smooth bed. This result is partly due to the greater turbulence in the lower layers when rippling develops: much more sand is put into suspension. There is little sand in suspension when the bottom is smooth, and transport is achieved by the rolling of sand grains along the bottom.

The narrowness of the wave flume used for the experiments constrained the direction of the sediment transport due to wave drift. In a wider tank or on a natural beach it is likely that the wave drift would break up into circulations, according to Bagnold (1963). This would result in random scattering of sediment superimposed on a small landward drift. The circulatory motion of the swash could also be related to a similar lateral instability.

b   Sand movement inside the break-point

As stated above, sand outside the break-point nearly always moved landwards in the experiments described. Inside the break-point, however, the movement was not so regular. Different variables are important in this zone. Landward of the break-point in the tank the action of the swash and backwash moved the material. The waves in the tank were not at first working on an equilibrium profile, but on a uniform gradient, which was 1 in 12 for most of the experiments. This gradient is flatter than the equilibrium gradient. This fact probably influenced the direction of movement in the very shallow water.

Inside the break-point the effect of wave height and period is less easy to demonstrate, because the sand is not moving in a constant direction. The wave steepness determined the direction of movement, as shown in figure 9-4. Landward transport is shown to the left of the axis, while seaward transport increases to the right of it. There is an abrupt change in the pattern of movement at the break-point. Each graph is drawn for one specific wave length and three wave heights, giving three steepness values on each graph. The waves of different steepness will break in varying depths of water dependent upon their height.

The position of maximum transport, with few exceptions, was found to be just seaward of the break-point, where material moved landwards. The steepest waves, with a steepness of more than 0·04, moved relatively little sand outside the break-point, probably because they were very short. Inside the break-point they moved a very large volume of sand seaward, the amount decreasing with decreasing depth. Seaward movement inside the break-point took place for all waves above a critical steepness. Below this steepness value sand was moved landwards in all depths, although the amounts were less than those moved just outside the break-point. The critical steepness under the conditions of the experiments was about 0·012.

These results agree with the well-known fact that steep waves are destructive on a beach, while flat waves tend to build it up. The model experiments thus appear to apply to natural beaches. The same critical steepness will not apply under all conditions. The size of the beach material is one of the variables that determines the value of the critical steepness. In other experiments the critical steepness varied between 0·03 and 0·025. T. Scott (1954) found that a destructive effect was obtained with a steepness value of 0·019, which lies nearer to the value found in the experiments under discussion.

The results of the experiments may be explained by the velocities of the swash and backwash respectively. The swash acts with a high velocity for a short period and the backwash with a lower velocity for a longer period. Assuming a constant wave length, the volume of water descending the beach increases as the wave height increases. The period remains constant so that the amount lost by percolation remains constant. The increased volume will cause increased velocities in both swash and backwash. These will be raised above the critical velocity for sediment transport in both directions of flow as the wave steepness increases. When the velocity of the backwash is raised above the critical velocity the sand will be moved seawards owing to the longer duration of the backwash current. The greater turbulence associated with higher waves will also help to put sand into suspension, so that it can be more easily moved. The return

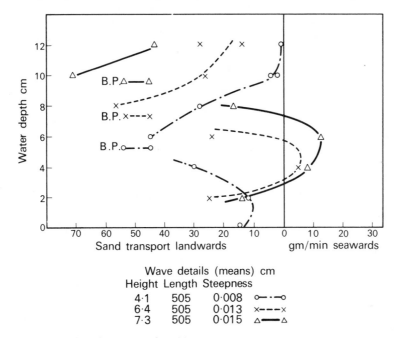

Wave details (means) cm

Height	Length	Steepness	
4·1	505	0·008	o——·—o
6·4	505	0·013	x———x
7·3	505	0·015	△——△

Figure 9-4 Direction of transport of sand in relation to wave steepness inside the break-point.

flow relating to the mass transport velocity will be relatively great for the higher waves. It will be most strongly felt in the shallow water inside the break-point.

Experiments were made on a much flatter gradient of 1 in 40. On this gradient the waves broke in a series of rather feeble breakers, the nearest likeness to surf waves that could be achieved. The steep waves were still destructive inside the break-point, and the flat ones were constructive throughout the tank. The gradient, therefore, did not alter the direction of movement, although the volume of sand moved was affected. In the deeper water outside the break-point more sand was moved on the flatter gradient, but inside the break-point the reverse was true. This result may be explained by the much greater horizontal distance over which the wave energy was dissipated inside the break-point on the very flat gradient compared with the steeper slope.

3 The equilibrium line

The amount of transport of material on the bottom under natural conditions is difficult to measure. Both experimental studies and theoretical consideration, however, suggest that movement of material under normal wave conditions takes place in an onshore direction seaward of the break-point. As long ago as 1887 P. Cornaglia put forward a theory in which he suggested that a neutral line existed, landward of which the bottom material moved landward, while outside it the material travelled seaward. He supposed that the depth of the neutral line depended upon the character of the waves, the slope of the bottom and the size and density of the bottom particles. The depth reached a maximum of 10 m for the exposed beaches of the Mediterranean. P. D. Timmermans (1935), who also discussed the neutral line, suggested that its depth was $2\frac{1}{2}$ times the wave height. This relationship does not, however, take into consideration the particle size, and this is relevant.

A. T. Ippen and P. S. Eagleson (1955) have shown that the transport of sediment on the bottom under wave action is mainly a function of the hydrodynamic drag and the weight of the particle. Their observations suggest that there is a zero-transport null point landward of which transport of sediment is onshore, and seaward of which transport is offshore. The seaward movement at depth is never rapid, because in this zone the velocities of the water particles under wave action are only sufficient to move the grains by rolling. A short distance seaward of the null point friction causes all movement to cease.

The existence of the null point is also suggested by the change in direction of ripple movement. The direction of movement of the ripples does not necessarily, however, determine the direction of net sand movement on the bottom. At times the ripples can move landwards, while the net transport is in a seaward direction.

Ippen and Eagleson's experimental results on a model beach slope of 1 in 15 and using a range of steepness between 0·01 and 0·08, suggest the relationships governing the position of the null point to be $(H/d)^2$, L/H, $C/W = 11·6$, where H is the wave height, L is the length, C is

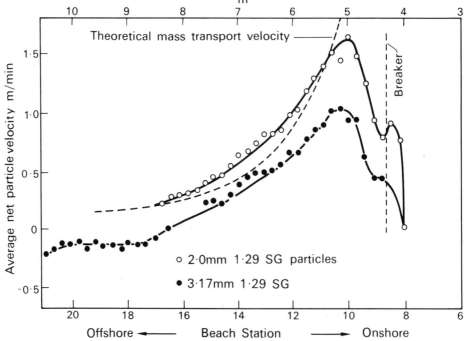

Figure 9-5 Particle velocity related to distance offshore towards null point in the model tank. L = 2·72 m; H = 5·67 cm; T = 1·428 sec; H/L = 0·0209; beach gradient 1 in 15; beach coated with quartz sand 0·787 mm diameter.

the wave velocity, d the local depth of water and w the terminal velocity of fall of the particles in fresh water. The wave characteristics refer to those at the point in question. The constant applies only to a slope of 1 in 15 and probably varies with slope. Figure 9-5 illustrates their results.

The neutral line would be closer inshore for coarse sediment on a natural beach. There would be a sorting of the sediment, as a result of the differential velocities. This will be considered in more detail in chapter 11; in this section the depth of the so-called neutral line is considered as it will determine the maximum depth to which waves cause movement of material on the bottom. In general it appears that the offshore motion on a natural beach will be very much less in volume and importance than the onshore movement, and can be ignored for most purposes.

V. P. Zenkovich (1967) has examined the neutral line concept in some detail. He considers first the case where the wave acceleration is the same in the landward and seaward directions. Under such conditions particles will move landward when their critical velocity is exceeded by the landward wave motion adjusted for the slope of the bed. When the water is moving seaward, their critical velocity will be exceeded for a longer period, owing to the slope of the bed being down in their direction of movement. Material will thus move offshore by the amount of the difference made by the slope to the landward and seaward transport. Where the bottom is horizontal there will be no net sediment movement.

When the water accelerations are not symmetrical the situation is more complex, and the response of the particles will depend on their size. When the particles exceed a certain size they will move landward under the greater acceleration of the wave crest. There will, therefore, be an equilibrium or neutral line for each size of material, the position of the line being governed by three factors:

1   The steeper the gradient, the nearer the neutral line will be to the shore and the shallower the depth, for any given size of material.
2   The neutral line will be further offshore at a greater depth as the waves become larger, and their asymmetry develops sooner.
3   The larger the particles the further offshore will be the neutral line.

The operation of the forces that determine the position of the neutral line are such that particles of one size may have a net movement in the opposite direction from particles of another size. Complications occur when some of the particles are small enough to be carried in suspension during part of the wave cycle, which occurs when the wave velocities are high.

The movement of particles associated with the equilibrium line will cause both sorting of material and modification of the bottom profile. These two aspects of sediment movement will be considered in chapters 11 and 12 respectively. The equilibrium line is important in that it determines the depth at which sediment begins to move, which has been called the 'wave base' or 'surf base'. Only sediment in water shallower than this can be moved by the waves and is available to feed the beaches from offshore. Some of the observations concerning the depth of the surf base will be considered in the next section.

4 Surf base and wave base

The waves first feel the bottom when the depth is equal to half the wave length. It is not until the depth is much shallower, however, that any appreciable amount of sand is transported and changes of the bottom contours resulting from wave action can take place. It is difficult to obtain precise data on this point, and evidence is often conflicting, due to the many variables that can affect the depth of movement.

The existence of strong tidal or other currents in deeper water may be effective in some areas, which would not be disturbed by waves at the depth in question. Another difficulty is to obtain precise measurements of the amount of movement taking place in deep water. The accuracy of most types of hydrographic survey is not great enough to record small changes of elevation resulting from bottom movement in deep water.

Some of the most precise data concerning the movement of material in fairly deep water on the bottom is reported by D. L. Inman and G. A. Rusnak (1956), who carried out observations to a depth of 21·3 m on the shelf off La Jolla, California. The accuracy of the observations was such that the standard error in the determination of the sand level was ±15·2 mm. The changes in level recorded at depths of 21·3 m were of the same order of magnitude as the irregularities of the bottom, so that it was difficult to determine their exact value. On the whole the magnitude of recorded changes decreased with increasing depth and was small in depths greater than 9·15 m. The changes of sand level over the period of observation was about 45·8 mm at a depth of 21·3 m, 48·8 mm at a depth of 15·85 m, 88·4 mm at a depth of 9·15 m, and at 5·5 m it was 19·9 cm. For all except the shallowest depths the surveys covered a period of 40 or more months.

There was a steady decrease of sand size—which was very fine on the whole—with increasing depths. At 5·5 m the median diameter was 0·15 mm; at 9·15 m it was 0·12 mm; at 15·85 and 21·3 m it was 0·11 mm. The maximum changes in level are shown in figure 9-6. The amount of change at 5·5 m was probably rather greater in total amount than indicated, at times exeeding 0·61 m.

The depths at which the bottom movement becomes small were found to be similar to Trask's (1955) values which have just been discussed. Trask was concerned with the transport of material round the rocky peninsulas of part of the Californian coast, which he studied by detailed analysis of the sediment in different depths. He was able to show that material does move around the headlands of Point Arguello and Conception. The movement cannot take place on the beach itself as the headlands descend into relatively deep water and only small and isolated beaches occur at intervals along the coast.

Some information concerning the state of the sea bed was observed off the California coast by divers. The depth at which ripples were first developed was about 15·25 m and there was evidence of slight water movement at a depth of 18·3 m. Below this depth to a maximum of 39·7 m the sea bottom was covered by a fine powdery deposit, like brown 'rust', and the water was quite quiet. At a depth of about 13·7 m the passing waves were observed to disturb the sand grains. The median diameter of the sand at this depth was 0·149 mm. On another profile ripples were first encountered at a depth of 17·7 m. In this area movement of the bottom sediment was limited to quiet deposition in depths greater than 18·3 m.

Trask divides the sea bed into three zones above a depth of 18·3 m. Beyond this depth is a passive zone of little or no movement. Between 18·3 and 9·15 m is a zone of intermediate character, in which sand is moved at intervals. An active zone extends between 9·15 m and the surf zone. The third zone is the surf and beach zone.

Later observations by D. L. Inman (1957) have shown that in depths of 21·3 m the 'rust' reported by Trask is not a permanent feature of the sea bed. According to Inman's observations a quiescent state, in which 'rust' can form and burrowing animals can destroy the ripple pattern, is found in about 30% of the observations. This state of the sea bed can develop in a few hours after the orbital velocity falls below that necessary for the formation of ripples. The period of quiescence at 15·85 m was 12%, while at 9·15 m it was zero. Ripples were also measured at

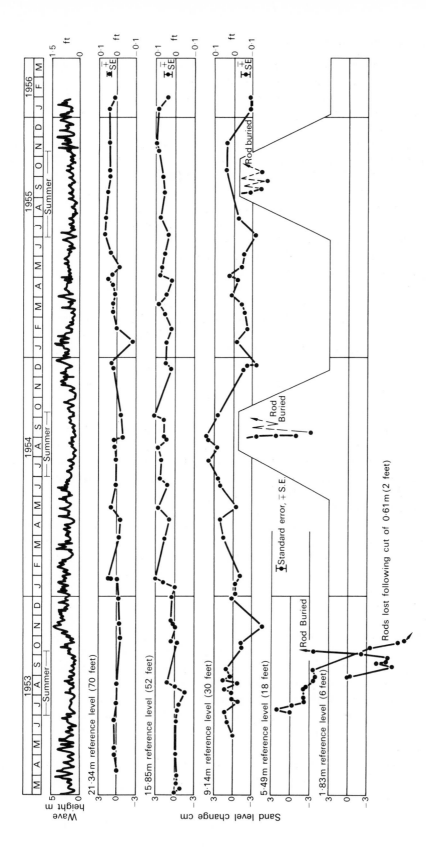

Figure 9-6 Changes in sand level at various depths off the Californian coast (positive axes refer to fill, negative to cut). (*After Inman and Rusnak, 1956.*)

depths of 33·6 m and observed at a depth of 51·9 m. During periods of strong wave activity the waves can cause some movement of material at very considerable depths, although such movement is not likely to cause much change in sand level. F. P. Shepard and D. L. Inman (1951) do show that changes in level at a depth of 30·5 m off the Scripps pier occasionally amount to as much as 30 to 60 cm.

On the other hand the dumping of beach fill in a depth of about 12·2 m showed that movement in this depth was very slow (R. L. Harris, 1955). The dumped material did not move landwards to replenish the beach at Long Branch, New Jersey. To nourish the beach 460,000 m³ of sand were dumped in water 0·8 km offshore, where the water depth was 11·6 m at mean low water. Surveys of the offshore area and dumping ground were made before, during and after the dumping operations, and wave observations were made. Only 3·4% of the waves were able to move the stock-pile of sand. The minimum size of waves capable of moving the stock-pile was 1·22 m high with a period of 6 seconds. After four years the stock-pile, which had originally formed a ridge 2·14 m high, 228 m wide and 1130 m long, had been flattened out, but was still substantially intact.

It was concluded that this method of beach nourishment had little influence on the processes operating along the shore, where the annual loss of sand was 119,000 m³ after the dumping, only slightly less than the pre-dumping figure of 135,000 m³. These results show that substantial movement of sand is a very slow process in a depth of 12·2 m, although the larger waves were able to effect slow changes. During the four year period from July 1948 to October 1952 there was a slight decrease in the median diameter of the sand in the stock-pile area. The material when dumped had a median diameter of 0·34 mm where the original sand size was 0·39 mm. The size had decreased to 0·32 mm in 1952.

Experiments reported by S. Inose and N. Shiraishi (1956) were made with radio-active sand at Tomakomai, Hokkaido, in Japan. They show that sand of median diameter of 0·13 mm started to move at a depth of 6 m, when the wave height exceeds 1·77 m. Knaps (in Zenkovich, 1967) showed that changes in the sandy profile off the Baltic coast ceased at depths equal to three times the average storm wave height according to Zenkovich (1967).

The observations that have already been discussed apply mainly to sand. Shingle can move only in depths considerably less than those in which sand is moved. Observations of the movement of radio-active pebbles have been carried out on the east coast of England at Orfordness, Suffolk, by C. Kidson, A. P. Carr and D. B. Smith (1958). These showed that for the duration of the observations over a period of about six weeks, pebbles in a depth of 9·15 m of water were not moved by the waves. Similar experiments off Scolt Head Island in Norfolk, showed that pebbles were moved in a depth of 5·5 to 7·3 m by moderate waves of about 0·91 m height at the break-point.

Where the tidal currents are very strong the movement of shingle may occur at considerably greater depths. A tidal stream of 230 cm/sec (4·5 knots) running between Hurst Castle spit and the Isle of Wight in a depth of 57 m was able to scour shingle. In the absence of tidal streams the depth of movement of shingle is probably only about 2 m below the lowest tide level. R. A. Bagnold (1940), using the results of model experiments with the equivalent of shingle, found that the depth at which movement ceases is equal to the height of the waves. This height determines the position of the edge of the shelf, shown in figure 9-7, regardless of the size of the shingle in the offshore zone.

The extent of wave activity on the sea bed around the northwest of Europe has been discussed by L. Draper (1967). The area where wave activity is greatest on the bed is around the western approaches, which are directly exposed to the long Atlantic swell and storm waves. Particle speeds were calculated using the Darbyshire wave spectrum. The differences between theory and experimental results ranged between 1 and 2% at the maximum depths, increasing to about 15% at shallow depths. The significant wave height was used to calculate the water particle speeds, which are given in terms of significant peak speeds. These are the fastest speeds attained for any given wave size and may be of short duration. The results are given as the percentage time that any given particle speed will be exceeded in different depths.

Near Sevenstones, off the southwest Cornish coast, for example, at a depth of 61 m a significant peak particle speed of 46 cm/sec will be expected to be exceeded for 1% of the time, or about 3 to 4 days a year. Draper concluded that surface waves can cause a particle speed of 43 cm/sec

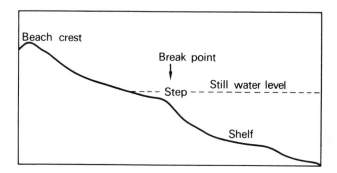

Figure 9-7 Diagram of model shingle beach.

at a depth of 152 m on the edge of the continental shelf, a state that should persist for one day each year. The longer waves cause a much greater disturbance than shorter waves. The disturbance at 183 m on the edge of the exposed shelf will be as great as that at 30.5 m in the northeastern Irish Sea. The results apply to the movement of water particles. It is also essential to estimate the movement of sediment on the sea bed.

The term surf base may be used to delimit the zone of substantial movement. This is restricted to the shallow water where depths do not exceed about 12.2 m. The term wave base, on the other hand, can be applied to the slow and small changes that occur in deeper water and which do not involve the movement of substantial amounts of material over considerable distances. They cause more stirring of the sediments than consistent movement of material. The problems of surf base and wave base are referred to again in chapter 21.

5 Movement in deeper water outside the break-point

A study involving experimental and theoretical data by G. Kalkanis (1964) provides equations to estimate the bed load carried by wave action. The waves considered were long relative to their height. The problem was considered in two parts, firstly, the description of the flow field in the boundary layer, and secondly, the dynamic effect of this field on the solid particles that form the bed. A combination allowed the prediction of the motion of the particles and hence of the bed load.

The variables that affect the sediment transport on the bed are the wave amplitude, H, the wave length, L, the angular velocity, ω, the water depth, d, the water temperature, T°, which together give the kinematic velocity, ν, the grain diameter, D, and the density of the material, ρ_s which was assumed to be uniform. The flow in the boundary layer was assumed to be unstable and this must be tested first. The flow field in the boundary layer could then be found and the value of ψ calculated by the equation

$$|\psi| = \frac{\rho_s - \rho_t}{\rho_t} \cdot \frac{gD}{|\bar{u}|^2}$$

where $\bar{u}$ is the velocity measured at $0 \cdot 35D$ from the theoretical bed. A curve allowed ψ to be used to find the value of Φ, the oscillatory bed load, by means of the equation

$$\Phi = \frac{q_B}{v_s} \sqrt{\frac{\rho_t}{g(\rho_s - \rho_t)}} D^{-3/2}$$

The rate of sediment transport was predicted by means of the relationship

$$Q_B = c_0 \int_0^{2D} U(y) \, dy$$

where c_0 is the concentration found by

$$c_0 = 0 \cdot 618 \frac{q_B}{2D(\bar{u}_B)}$$

$U(y)$ could be found by equating it with $\bar{U}$ in the equation

$$\bar{U} = \frac{a^2 \omega k}{2 \sinh^2 kd} \left\{ 5 - 8 \, e^{-\beta y} \cos \beta y + 3 \, e^{-2\beta y} \right\}$$

This method allowed a quantitative value of the bed transport to be calculated, but its accuracy depended on the validity of the assumptions that were made. The most important of these was that the wave height was small so that the equations could be linearized. The second was that the depth was fairly large and uniform.

The method applies only where sediment is carried on the bed in the bed layer, i.e. outside the break-point, where material in suspension is of little importance. The velocity of the boundary layer used in the curves was derived from experimental values in the wave tank, but these probably apply fairly well to natural conditions. The depth at which ψ was calculated may not be accurate for oscillatory flow: the curve relating ψ to ϕ depends on the accuracy of the data used to produce it. More accurate field data are required to confirm the validity and accuracy of the method. The determination of the sediment transport was based on the average discharge of fluid in oscillatory flow under wave action, which is only an approximation. Field measurements are again required to test the accuracy of the equations.

The experimental work carried out by D. L. Inman and T. K. Chamberlain (D. L. Inman and R. A. Bagnold, in Hill, 1963) provides one of the few field observations made to test the theoretical methods of assessing sediment movement outside the break-point. A sample of 1 kg irradiated sand was deposited in a water depth of 3 m outside the surf zone 300 m from the shore and its scatter over 24 hours was observed. At the time the wave velocity was 540 cm/sec, the value of the mean wave drift, $\bar{u}$, as predicted was $2 \cdot 7$ cm/sec along the bed: the mean rate of sediment drift, $\bar{U}_b$, would be about $\frac{1}{3}$ of this, or about 1 cm/sec. The mean sediment size was $0 \cdot 0125$ cm and the ripple height $1 \cdot 5$ cm. Taking the number of moving grain layers, b, as 2, the value of $\bar{U}_G$, the average migration speed of individual grains, should be $0 \cdot 25$ cm/sec. The greatest observed migration distance in $7\frac{1}{2}$ hours was 30 m shoreward, giving an average speed of $\bar{U}_G$ of $0 \cdot 1$ cm/sec. The recorded rate was, however, increased by some sand moving in suspension. The depth to which the marked grains were found was equal to the ripple height as predicted by the theory.

Field-work by R. W. Sternberg (1967) in Puget Sound, Washington, has shown that natural conditions are similar to those found in laboratory experiments. The threshold grain velocities agreed with theoretical values, where the movement was by tidal currents, which reached a maximum velocity of 75 cm/sec. The sediment only moved during one two hour period, covering the three-day programme.

The critical drag velocity that initiated sediment movement was found to be 2·2 cm/sec. The mean velocity 1 m from the bed, associated with this value, was 38·8 cm/sec. The generalized friction coefficient was 0·07. These values agreed with laboratory results. Subsequent field observations to test erosion velocity curves also agreed with laboratory results for grain sizes between 0·3 and 1·10 mm.

Observations of sand movement outside the breaker zone have been made by J. C. Ingle (1966) by means of fluorescent tracers. Marked sand must be released mechanically in water depths greater than 46 m. False-bottomed oil drums have been used off California. The recording of the movement of the tracer can be achieved by sampling with grease-coated sampling leads in depths up to 91·5 m. In deeper water grabs must be used or automatic fluorescent counters. In shallow water divers can press grease-coated cards onto the bottom to obtain samples. The interpretation of the results requires adequate observations of waves and currents. Measurements immediately seaward of the breakers indicated that the theoretical and experimental landward movement of sediment did in fact take place. In one test at a point 22·8 m seaward of the breaker zone, on the beach north of Santa Monica, fluorescent sand was released in a depth of 3·36 m. The breaker height was 0·76 m. Most of the marked sand moved diagonally landwards parallel to the wave orthogonals. The low concentration at the release point 40 minutes after release showed that dispersion was rapid. None of the grains released seaward of the breakers was found inside the breaker zone, although a few did penetrate from inside the breakers to the seaward side. The breaker zone does appear to form a boundary that coarse grains at least find difficult to cross.

In another test 7·7 kg of fluorescent red sand within a median diameter of 0·18 mm was deposited in 3·66 m of water 84 m seaward of the breaker zone. The sand dispersed over a wide field, but the predominant direction was landwards. Calculation indicated that the average tracer grain velocity $\bar{U}_G$ was about 0·60 cm/sec. Bagnold's equation to estimate the velocity of shoreward wave drift, $\bar{u} = \frac{5}{4}(H/2d)^2 C_s$ where C_s is the wave velocity, gave a value for $\bar{u}$ of about 1·74 cm/sec. $\bar{u}$ is about 3 times the velocity of sediment drift U_b, and thus the predicted sediment drift is 0·57 cm/sec. This velocity may be compared to the value of 0·1 cm/sec considered by Inman and Bagnold.

The greater value found by Ingle is probably due to the action of longshore currents during his test. The presence of these was the main difference in conditions between his and Inman and Bagnold's tests. Other tests made by Ingle in deeper water showed that sand movement is often complex. In 9·15 m of water off San Diego, sand moved predominantly onshore–offshore parallel to the wave orthogonals. The maximum average grain velocity of 0·304 cm/sec agreed fairly well with estimates using Bagnold's equation. The formation of ripples, however, which were ubiquitous where the experiments were made, complicates the travel patterns.

The loss of sand down submarine canyons can be tested by use of fluorescent tracers but results so far are not extensive. They do confirm that this is a source of loss of beach sand, especially where the canyon head is close to the shore. The Dume Canyon appears to be too far offshore to take much sand from the shelf.

A. W. Johnson and P. S. Eagleson (1966) have calculated the volume of sediment moving landwards under wave action off the coast of California, where the average slope was 0·014. The median diameter of the sand was 0·30 mm, the average wave height was 46 cm and the wave period was 13 seconds. $\bar{U}_s$ reaches a maximum when the backwash begins to operate. It refers to the mean instantaneous sediment velocity and is zero where $D = D_i$, which is the incipient motion sediment size. The mean value of d/L_0 between the points where $\bar{U}_s$ is zero and its maximum, was 0·034. This value was taken to be related to the average transport rate. Volumetrically this is given as $q_s = A\bar{U}_s t$, where A is the cross-sectional area per unit of beach and t is the decimal percentage of time that this wave operates. $q_s = 3\cdot4 \times 10^3$ At tons/square feet/year. The submerged unit weight of transported solids is assumed to be 100 pounds/cubic foot. If the sediment only moves to the depth of one particles, then $A = nD$ square feet/foot, in which n is the porosity. If n is taken as 0·1 and t as 0·3, which are reasonable estimates, then $q_s = 0\cdot1$ tons/foot/year (310 kg/m/year), q_s is 528 tons/mile/year (335,000 kg/km/year) and for the 245 miles (392 km) of the coast the transport would be 130,000 tons (132×10^6 kg)/year. This amount is 17% of the bed material supplied by the largest river on this stretch of coast. q_s is calculated by

$$\bar{U}_s = Kf_1(d/L_0) - J \sin \alpha$$

$$K = 0\cdot92\pi^2(H_0/L_0)^2 D/L_0(\beta D)^{8/7} \text{ foot/sec}$$

$$J = 6.94 \times 10^{-2} \frac{DTg}{\nu}\left(\frac{S_s - 1}{S_t}\right) \text{ feet/sec}$$

$$f_1(d/L_0) = \frac{\coth h^2 kd}{\sinh^2 kd - k_0 d}$$

$$\beta = (\pi/\nu T)^{1/2}$$

6 Movement landward of the break-point

Landward of the break-point the conditions become more complex and much sand is carried in suspension. Attempts to measure the amount of sand moving in this way have provided some quantitative data. Fluorescent sand tests have also been carried out in the surf zone, and in the swash–backwash zone.

a   Sand in suspension

The amount of material in suspension on a sand beach is at a maximum at and inside the break-point. This material can be carried in the direction of the littoral currents, even if they are of low velocity. Quantitative data from observations made at Long Branch, New Jersey, were published in the Interim Report of the Beach Erosion Board (1933) and are shown in figure 9-8. Only near the break-point was the proportion of sand moved in suspension as much as 5%, amounting to about 17,000 parts per million by weight. At a point only 7·6 m seaward of the break-point the quantity of sand in suspension had fallen to only 4000 parts per million, while it was less than 1000 parts per million 84 m further seaward. At the break-point the sand in suspension extends evenly from the bottom to the surface. In the swash zone the sand grains are fairly evenly spaced throughout the whole water depth, but in the backwash the movement is confined to a layer close to the bottom. Seaward of the break-point the level to which sand

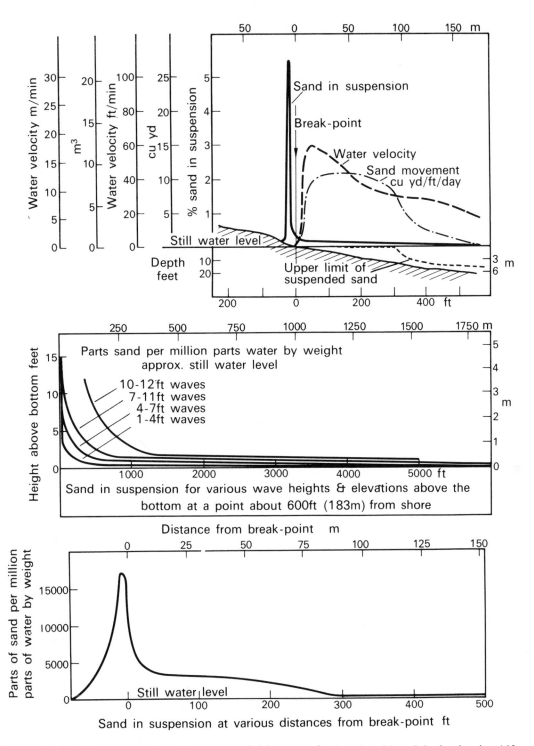

Figure 9-8 Sand in suspension in relation to wave height, water depth and position of the break-point. (*After Beach Erosion Board, 1933.*)

in suspension rises depends partly on the height of the waves. At a point 183 m from the shore, there is very little sand above 3 m from the bottom except for waves over 3 m high. For all waves, sand in excess of 2000 parts per million is not found above about 0·6 m from the bottom.

A field sampler devised to measure the amount of sediment in suspension has been described by G. M. Watts (1953a). This is an instrument of the pump type working by suction. A nozzle is held vertically downwards, at right-angles to the horizontal flow. The sampler is calibrated in a laboratory tank where known volumes and sand concentrations can be obtained at specified velocities of flow. Watts tested various widths and velocities of flow in the nozzle and found that the instrument was much more accurate when the nozzle velocity was greater than the flow velocity in the tank. If the nozzle velocity was twice the maximum orbital velocity of the wave motion, and the nozzle width was 1·27 cm, the results were correct to within 15% even without a correction factor.

Field tests were carried out on the pier at Mission Bay, California. Runs were made for 5 minutes and 290 observations taken, of which 238 were inside the breakers and 52 outside. The observations provided 170 acceptable figures inside and 22 outside the breakers. Clogging

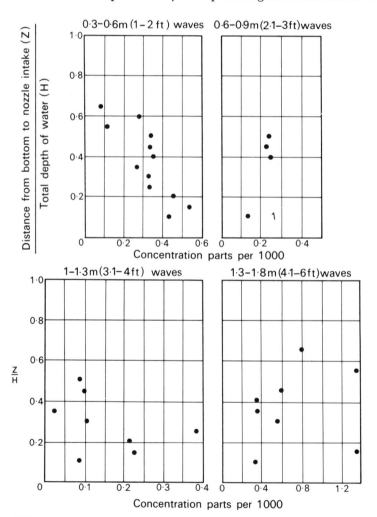

Figure 9-9 Sand in suspension in relation to wave height and water depth. (*After Watts, 1953a.*)

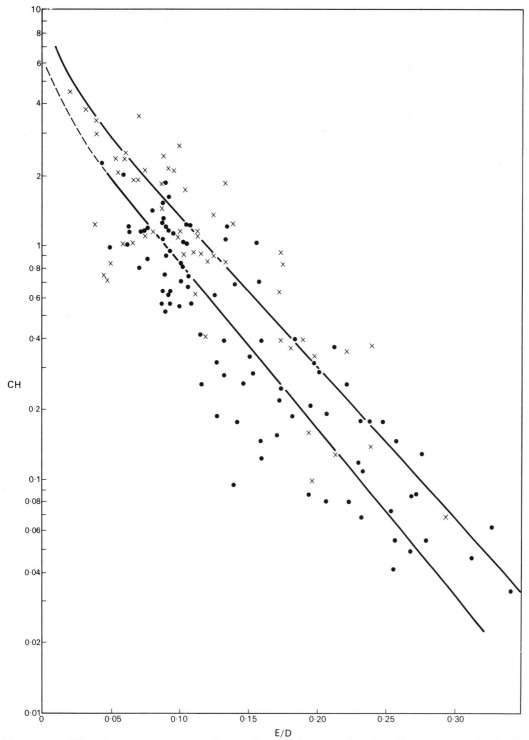

Figure 9-10 Effect of water temperature on the quantity of sand in suspension: C—sediment concentration (ppt by weight); H—wave height in feet; E—elevation of intake nozzle above sand ripple crest (feet); D—water depth (feet). The upper curve is for cold water at 53°F (12°C), and the lower for warm water at 80°F (27°C).

of the nozzle by seaweed reduced the nozzle velocity below the allowable minimum in some of the runs.

The results show some scatter but the mean of several values is probably fairly accurate. The results are plotted for different wave heights at several levels from the bottom and in varying depths of water. One example gives a mean value of 241 parts per million with a maximum of 482 parts per million and a minimum of 155 where the depth of water was 1·86 to 2·44 m and the waves were 0·64 to 0·915 m high at 0·6 to 0·915 m above the bottom. The greatest volume of material in suspension was found in depths of 1·22 to 2·44 m just inside the break-point. The results of these measurements are shown in figure 9-9. The median diameter of the sand in suspension was 0·14 mm. On the foreshore it was 0·22 mm, grading down to 0·10 mm at a depth of 15·2 m. The median diameter was 0·15 mm at depths between 0 and 6·1 m.

J. C. Fairchild (1959) has reported on suspension-sediment sampling in laboratory conditions with waves from 10 cm to 1·83 m in height. The tests with the small waves were intended to study the effect of temperature on the amount of sand in suspension. The results are shown in figure 9-10. Two temperatures were tested 12°C and 27°C (53 and 80°F). A consistently larger volume of material was in suspension at the lower temperature. The difference was 50 to 75% more in the colder water, and was greater at higher elevations above the bottom. When the large waves were tested more sand was found to be in suspension when the period was shorter, but this may be partly due to the higher waves associated with the shorter periods. It was difficult to establish a relationship between wave height and sand in suspension. The tests were difficult to make owing to the great variability of sand concentration in the turbulent area near the break-point of the waves. The variability may exceed a factor of 1000 in these conditions.

b   Tracer studies

Movement of sediment inside the break-point has been shown, by the model experiments discussed in section 9-2(b), to be more complex than that outside, partly because of the greater turbulence and the greater amount of sand in suspension. Detailed studies with fluorescent tracers have thrown some light on the way in which sand moves inside the break-point normal to the shore.

J. C. Ingle (1966) has made detailed observations on the short-term dispersal of sand in the surf zone along the coast of California. He found that under surf conditions there was a tendency for a significant proportion of the marked sand to move offshore to the break-point. The sand grains moved along paths nearly parallel to the breaker line, at right-angles to the wave orthogonals, until they reached the breakers.

Three major forces cause sediment movement inside the break-point. Firstly, the force of the breaking wave moves particles onshore or offshore. Secondly, longshore currents move the particles along the shore. Thirdly, the beach slope increase causes an increase in the effectiveness of gravity. The diagonal movement of the sediment is a resultant of the action of these three forces. When the longshore component is weak the tracers moved directly towards the break-point. One problem raised by the consistent movement of tracers towards the breaker zone is to account for the periodic build up of the level of the foreshore. The destructive offshore movement of sediment normally takes place much more rapidly and less selectively than the slower, longer-lasting onshore movement. Ingle considers that the predominance of offshore movement of marked sediment may be the result of selective sorting of the particles by size. This would occur if the tracer grains were not in equilibrium with the surrounding grains after injection on the beach. Some tests with different-sized particles were made to test this idea, and it was found to be generally true.

The tracer tests also showed the effectiveness of rip currents in moving sediment seawards in concentrated zones towards and through the breaker zone, and that the rips were intermittent or pulsating in their operation. The coarser sand of the foreshore zone landwards of the breakers could travel by this means to the zone seaward of the breakers. The seaward movement of the sediment landward of the breakers may have been assisted by the wind, which was blowing onshore on all except three occasions covering 31 observations. A weak positive correlation was found to exist between average tracer grain velocity and maximum depletion rate, and the onshore wind velocity.

7 Depth of disturbance of sand by waves

Experiments were made on several sandy beaches round the coasts of England and Wales to determine the depth to which waves disturb the sand in different positions on the beach and in various sand sizes (C. A. M. King, 1951). The experiments were made with dye sand. A small quantity of sand was taken from the beach and dyed purple to contrast strongly with the natural sand colour. The dyed sand was placed in a vertical column in the beach at low tide and the surface of the sand carefully smoothed. The site of the dyed sand was marked by fixing two thin pegs about 6 mm diameter and 0·61 m long on either side of the dyed sand and far enough away not to influence its movement. The pegs also enabled the change in sand level to be measured. After the tide had risen and fallen the position of the dyed sand was located and then under-mined from below. The undisturbed column of purple sand was followed up until it came to an abrupt end at the point where the dyed sand had been dispersed by wave action. The depth of disturbance was given by the distance from the top of the dyed sand to the surface and was measured to the nearest millimetre. Whenever possible the observations were only made when the change in sand level was very small. It was impossible to know whether accretion or erosion of sand took place before or after the maximum disturbance.

At high water some of the samples were in a depth of up to 6·1 m of water, some were near the break-point, and others were only in the zone of the swash and backwash of the waves. It is impossible by this method to measure the amount of disturbance in water deeper than that in which the maximum disturbance takes place. The observations to determine the depth of the maximum disturbance were made at Rhossili, South Wales. The beach is wide and sandy and has a large tidal range of 7·9 m at spring tide. The sand is fine, with a median diameter of 0·23 mm.

The results indicate that the depth of disturbance was as great in the shallow water under the swash and backwash, as it was under the break-point and in deeper water, since all the results were similar. The gradient of this beach is flat, being about 1 in 80, so that the waves formed spilling breakers and a wide surf zone was normally present. On a wide sand beach the depth of disturbance is greatest at or slightly landward of the break-point in the surf zone. This is the area where the wave energy on the bottom reaches its maximum value and turbulence is greatest.

The depth of disturbance was plotted against the breaker height. Figure 9-11 shows an approximate linear relationship between these variables. The small values shown apply to three of the four beaches on which observations were made, those at Rhossili, Blackpool in Lancashire and Whitbeck in Cumberland. A similar relationship held for the fourth beach at Druridge in Northumberland, but the amount of disturbance on this beach was greater for a given wave height. The coefficient of correlation for the first three beaches was $r = 0·9548$ and

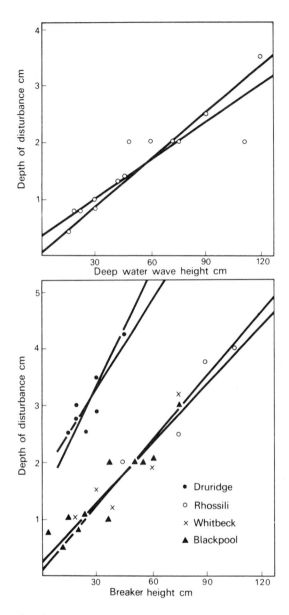

Figure 9-11 Graphs to show the relationship between wave height and depth of disturbance of sand.

for the Druridge observations, which are fewer in number, r = 0·859. Both values are highly significant, and show that the depth of disturbance of the sand is a function of the wave height.

As might be expected there is also a fairly close correlation between wave energy and depth of disturbance. The relationship is shown in figure 9-12. The observations at Druridge again produce a greater depth of disturbance than those of the other three beaches for the same wave energy. The correlation of disturbance depth with wave length was not close, indicating the greater significance of wave height, which is important in determining the wave energy.

The differences between the first three beaches and the Druridge beach can be explained by the median diameters of the four sands. These are 0·22 mm at Blackpool, 0·23 mm at Rhossili and 0·29 mm at Whitbeck, but Druridge sand had a median diameter of 0·40 mm. The first three are finer than the last. The depth of disturbance increased as the material became coarser. This agrees with observations that coarse beaches are more mobile than fine ones. The mobility is particularly great in the zone landward of the break-point, which is also the zone of maximum disturbance depth. On a coarser beach, which is steeper, the zone of wave energy dissipation is narrower, and hence turbulence on the bottom is greater.

If the results obtained are extrapolated for higher waves it seems unlikely that even very high waves of about 6·1 m would disturb the sand to depths greater than about 20 cm. It is unlikely, however, that such large waves would not affect the level of the beach. The experiments show that only a relatively thin cover of sand is enough to protect a wave-cut platform beneath the beach from erosion by the waves, unless the sand is removed entirely by destructive waves.

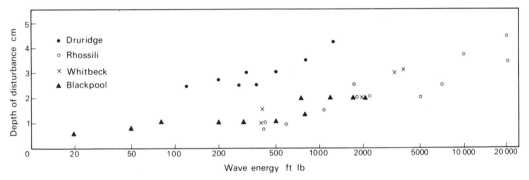

Figure 9-12   Graph to show the relationship between wave energy and the depth of disturbance of sand.

On a thick sand beach it is unlikely that all the sand would be removed except on very rare occasions. Erosion of the wave-cut platforms can only occur, therefore, with any reasonable speed where they are not protected by beaches.

A test of disturbance depth on a coarse sand beach was carried out by W. E. Yasso (1962) at Sandy Hook, New Jersey. Marked sand was placed in a cylindrical hole to a depth of 15 cm near low tide and also near high-tide levels. The waves acting during the experiment had a maximum breaker height of 61 cm, a period of 6·75 seconds and a deep-water approach of 30°. The break-point moved across the lower site during high water. After the tide had fallen 2·9 cm of the original marked gravel remained, covered by 15·4 cm of sand. At the upper site 9·15 cm of marked sand was covered by 7 cm of coarse unmarked sand and 7 cm of fine unmarked sand. The median diameter at the lower site was 0·463 mm. At this site 12·34 cm of disturbance occurred with a wave height of 61 cm, which is about twice the results found on British beaches, though the upper site showed a very similar disturbance depth.

8 Artificial beach nourishment

Beach nourishment by means of artificially placed beach material is becoming a more common method of maintaining and improving beaches in areas where erosion is likely to cause deterioration of the natural beach. The search for a suitable borrow-material has led to a study of the behaviour of beach fill of different size distribution to the natural beach sand. Some comments on this topic have already been made in the last chapter in dealing with sand-size distribution. The effect of wave action on material dumped offshore has also been mentioned in this chapter, in connection with the depth to which waves can move appreciable volumes of material. In this section some examples of the behaviour of beach fill will be mentioned on both Great Lakes beaches and those of the Atlantic coast of the U.S.A.

One area that has suffered from prolonged erosion is the beach of Presque Isle Peninsula in Lake Erie (D. W. Berg, 1965). The net rate of loss was estimated at 19,100 m³/year. To make good this loss 525,000 m³ of fill was placed on the beach in late 1960 and early 1961. A higher proportion than expected of the fill was lost from the beach, and this was thought to be due to the grain size distribution of the fill. The optimum size was 1.73ϕ, but 2.32ϕ material was used as this was readily available. The finer fractions of the fill were removed by the waves, thus gradually restoring the original size. The finer material was deposited in the offshore zone, the rate of removal being especially rapid soon after the deposition of the fill.

Since the first fill was put on the beach erosion has continued, and in 1965 1.27×10^4 m³ of coarser sand was put on the beach. This fill was even coarser than the natural beach sand. After the coarser sand was placed on the beach the whole area gained sediment and the area above water level was extended. The rate of erosion was thus reduced after the placing of the coarse fill.

The response of this beach to the fill operations showed that beaches of coarse sediment are more stable than finer ones in a given set of circumstances, require less frequent filling, and may have decreasing rates of erosion. Fill should be fairly well sorted, covering the whole range of grain size of the natural material. The rate of erosion on Presque Isle beach is directly related to the lake level. The mean grain size is reduced offshore and an offshore transport of sediment occurs in the area. It is probably representative of other parts of Great Lakes, so that the experience gained in this area can be applied elsewhere (D. W. Berg and D. B. Duane, 1968).

The behaviour of beach fill at Virginia Beach, Virginia, has been discussed by G. M. Watts (1959). The natural beach material was 0.30 to 0.40 mm in size, decreasing to 0.12 mm at a depth of 6.1 m. A total of 1,032,000 m³ of fill were placed on the beach between 1952 and 1953 to restore the beach. Thereafter smaller volumes were placed to maintain the beach. Before the fill was placed the beach lost 177,000 m³/year between 1946 and 1952. The massive stabilizing programme undertaken in 1952–3 appears to have been successful, as during the period 1952 to 1958 1,192,000 m³ were placed on the beach of which 1,149,000 m³ still remained. This stability was maintained with an annual replacement of 32,000 m³. Groynes would not help to stabilize this beach as the net alongshore transfer is probably small. Most of the sand was lost in offshore transport. The study of respective costs showed that the cheapest means of stabilizing this beach was by means of artificial nourishment.

Another successful example of beach nourishment was that carried out at Prospect Beach in 1957 (W. H. Vesper, 1961). Previous to this date the beach had a steep slope of coarse shingle and boulders, with rock outcrops. The original fill material had a median diameter of 1.22ϕ. Surveys showed that between 1957 and 1960 29,000 m³ of material was carried away from between high and low water. The eroded material was carried northwards as well as seawards of the low-water line, but was not lost altogether from the area. Only about 9% of the fill was lost from the foreshore, and the beach width above high-water level increased from 13.7 m to 53.4 m as a result of the fill, and was still 46 m in 1960. It is estimated that the average annual loss from the foreshore is about 9950 m³. The size distribution remained more or less constant throughout the three years, indicating that the sand used was suitable for the wave conditions of this area. The borrow area was situated offshore 305 m to 458 m from the high-water mark in depths of 1.53 to 7.63 m below low-water level. 334,000 m³ were dredged from this area and surveys showed that 19,100 m³ accumulated in the borrow-pit between 1957 and 1960. The results show that the sand fraction in the vicinity of the borrow-pit was not transported any significant distance during the period, and that sand put on the beach did not reach the borrow-pit. The area lies in the shelter of Long Island so that wave intensity is not great and wave action does not seriously disturb the bed in shallow water.

Two similar beach nourishment schemes have been carried out at other places on the coast of Connecticut in the shelter of Long Island (W. H. Vesper, 1965; 1967). At Seaside Park, Bridgeport, between 1957 and 1962, 9170 m³ and 45,300 m³ respectively were lost from above high water and on the foreshore. The offshore zone gained 48,200 m³. The net result was a loss of 1280 m³/year. The borrow area was sited offshore at an initial depth of 1·52 m below low water and about 366 to 488 m offshore. A total of 488,000 m³ were dredged from this area in 1957, which regained 11,200 m³ after dredging. The changes on the beach since the fill was deposited indicate an offshore movement of sand, but only 1% of the total fill has been lost from the project area. Very similar results were obtained in the other area, Sherwood Island State Park, Westport, which was treated in a similar manner. Both areas showed a movement out of the foreshore zone into the shallow offshore zone. Little sand movement, however, takes places at depths more than 1·53 m below low water in the sheltered situations.

Summary

Movement normal to the shore depends upon the nature of the fluid stress on sand grains under wave action. The sediment movement involves shearing of the sediment grains over each other and the bed. Equations are given to relate the stress applied to the grains to the nature of the load, the slope and the wave characteristics. Model experiments on the movement of material seaward of the break-point show that this movement in a narrow tank is nearly always landwards. The volume transported increases as the waves become higher, as their period lengthens, as their energy increases and as the beach becomes flatter and rippled. Inside the break-point the direction of transport depends on the steepness of the waves. Under the conditions of the experiment the critical steepness was 0·012; with steeper waves, movement was seaward, and with flatter waves, it was landwards on gradients between 1 in 12 and 1 in 40. The equilibrium line concept suggests that there is a line landward of which sediment moves towards the shore and seaward of which the movement is very slowly offshore. The offshore movement is often negligible. The theoretical and experimental results support this suggestion. The position of the neutral line depends on the sediment size, being closer to the shore for larger material. Surf base is defined as the maximum depth to which large movements of material can take place under the influence of waves near their break-point. Observations have shown that this depth is about 10 to 12 m under most conditions. Sediment can, however, be moved slightly and ripples form in water considerably deeper than this. The term 'wave base' can be applied to the depths at which these minor movements cease. Records show that some movement can take place in depths as great as 50 m, but substantial changes are very slow even in depths of 10 m, as indicated by the slight disturbance of material dumped in this depth of water over four years. Shingle can be moved by waves at only shallow depths as indicated by experiments with tracers, some movement occurring in 6 m, but none at 9 m. The water particles can move at depths as great as 183 m on the edge of the continental shelf off western Europe. Surface waves can cause a particle speed of 43 cm/sec at a depth of 152 m, but movement in this depth is only expected one day a year on average. Experiments have been carried out to record the mean rate of sediment drift, using tracers, in order to test theoretical calculations. The recorded rate was rather more than the theoretical rate owing to some sand moving in suspension. Other observations with marked sand showed a general shoreward movement outside the break-point with a general seaward movement to the break-point landwards of it. The latter result may have been affected by the marked grains having been out of adjustment with their environment. Measurements of sand in suspension show that high concentrations only occur very close to the break-point. Water temperature makes a considerable difference, amounts in suspension being 50 to 75% higher for 53°F (12°C) compared with 80°F (27°C). The depth of disturbance of sand on the foreshore was recorded with dyed sand and found to be closely related to wave height: for each 30 cm of wave height the depth of disturbance was about 1 cm on fine sand beaches. Disturbance was greatest at and inside the breaker zone, and increased as the material became coarser. Examples of beach replenishment by artificial fill show that this is successful where the fill is coarser than the natural sand, and also where the area is fairly sheltered. Fill can be obtained from offshore borrow-pits in these conditions.

References

BAGNOLD, R. A. 1940: Beach formation by waves: some model experiments in a wave tank. *J. Inst. Civ. Eng.* **15**, 27–52.

BAGNOLD, R. A. 1946: Motion of waves in shallow water. *Proc. Roy. Soc.* A **187**, 1–15.

BAGNOLD, R. A. 1963: Mechanism of marine sedimentation. Chapter 21, part I in Hill, M. N. (Editor), *The sea* **III**, New York: Wiley, 507–28.

BEACH EROSION BOARD 1933: *Interim Report*. U.S. Army, Corps of Engineers.

BERG, D. W. 1965: Factors affecting beach nourishment requirements at Presque Isle Peninsula, Erie, Penn. *Gt. Lakes Div. Univ. of Michigan Pub.* **13**, 214–21.

BERG, D. W. and DUANE, D. B. 1968: Effect of particle size and distribution on stability of artificially filled beach, Presque Isle Peninsula, Penn. *Proc. 11th Conf. Gt. Lakes Res.* 161–78.

BOON, J. D. 1969: Quantitative analysis of beach sand movement, Virginia Beach, Virginia. *Sedimentology* **13** (1/2), 85–104.

CORNAGLIA, P. 1887: *Sul regime della spiagge e sulla regulazione dei porti*. Turin.

DRAPER, L. 1967: Wave activity at the sea bed around northwestern Europe. *Mar. Geol.* **5**, 133–40.

DUNCAN, J. R. 1964: The effects of water table and tide cycle on swash–backwash sediment distribution and beach profile development. *Mar. Geol.* **2**(3), 186–97.

EAGLESON, P. S. and VAN DE WATERING, W. P. M. 1964: A thermistor probe for measuring particle orbital speed in water waves. *C.E.R.C. Tech. Memo.* **3.** (50 pp.)

EMERY, K. O. 1968: Relict sediments on continental shelves of the world. *Bull. Am. Assoc. Petrol. Geol.* **52**, 445–64.

FAIRCHILD, J. C. 1959: Suspended sediment sampling in laboratory wave action. *B.E.B. Tech. Memo.* **115.** (25 pp.)

HADLEY, L. M. 1964: Wave-induced bottom currents in the Celtic sea. *Mar. Geol.* **2**, 164–7.

HARRIS, R. L. 1955: Restudy of test shore nourishment by offshore deposition of sand, Long Branch, New Jersey. *B.E.B. Tech. Memo.* **62.**

HARRISON, W. and ALAMO, R. M. 1964: Dynamic properties of immersed sand at Virginia Beach, Virginia. *C.E.R.C. Tech. Memo.* **9.** (52 pp.)

INGLE, J. C. 1966: The movement of beach sand. *Developments in Sedimentology* **5.** (221 pp.)

INMAN, D. L. 1957: Wave generated ripples in nearshore sands. *B.E.B. Tech. Memo.* **100.**

INMAN, D. L. and BAGNOLD, R. A. 1963: Littoral processes. Chapter 21, part II in Hill, M. N. (Editor), *The sea* **III,** New York: Wiley, 529–53.

INMAN, D. L. and RUSNAK, G. A. 1956: Changes in sand level on the beach and shelf at La Jolla, California. *B.E.B. Tech. Memo.* **82.**

INOSE, S. and SHIRAISHI, N. 1956: The measurement of littoral drift by radio isotopes. *Dock and Harbour Auth.* **36,** 284–8.

IPPEN, A. T. and EAGLESON, P. S. 1955: A study of sediment sorting by waves shoaling on a plane beach. *B.E.B. Tech. Memo.* **63.**

JOHNSON, A. W. and EAGLESON, P. S. 1966: Coastal processes. Chapter 9 in Ippen, A. T. (Editor), *Estuary and coastline hydrodynamics, Eng. Soc. Mono.* New York: McGraw-Hill, 404–92.

KALKANIS, G. 1964: Transportation of bed material due to wave action. *C.E.R.C. Tech. Memo.* **2.** (38 pp.)

KIDSON, C., CARR, A. P. and SMITH, D. B. 1958: Further experiments using radio-active methods to detect movement of shingle over the sea-bed and alongshore. *Geog. J.* **124**(2), 210–18.

KING, C. A. M. 1951: Depth of disturbance of sand on beaches by waves. *J. Sed. Petrol.* **21,** 131–140.

MANOHAR, M. 1955: Mechanics of bottom sediment movement due to wave action. *B.E.B. Tech. Memo.* **75.**

MONROE, F. F. 1969: Oolitic aragonite and quartz sand: laboratory comparison under wave action. *C.E.R.C. Misc. Pap.* **1–69.** (29 pp.)

MOORE, D. G. and CURRAY, J. R. 1964: Wave base, marine profile of equilibrium and wave-built terraces: discussion. *Bull. Geol. Soc. Am.* **75,** 1267–74.

RUSSELL, R. H. C. and MACMILLAN, D. H. 1952: *Waves and tides.* London: Hutchinson.

SCHWARTZ, M. L. 1966: Fluorescent tracer: transport in distance and depth in beach sands. *Science* **151**(3711), 701–2.

SCOTT, T. 1954: Sand movement by waves. *Inst. Eng. Res.* Wave Res. Lab., Univ. of California.

SHEPARD, F. P. and INMAN, D. L. 1951: Sand movement on the shallow inter-canyon shelf at La Jolla, California. *B.E.B. Tech. Memo.* **26.**

STEERS, J. A. and SMITH, D. B. 1956: Direction of movement of pebbles on the sea-floor by radio-active methods. *Geog. J.* **122,** 343–5.

STERNBERG, R. W. 1967: Measurements of sediment movement and ripple migration in a shallow marine environment. *Mar. Geol.* **5**(3), 195–205.

STRIDE, A. H. 1963: Current swept sea floors near the southern half of Great Britain. *Quart. J. Geol. Soc.* **119,** 175–99.

SWIFT, D. J. P. 1970: Quaternary shelves and the return to grade. *Mar. Geol.* **8**(1), 5–30.

TIMMERMANS, P. D. 1935: Proeven over den invloed van golven op een strand. *Leidsche Geol. Med.* **6,** 231–386.

TRASK, P. D. 1955: Movement around southern Californian promontories. *B.E.B. Tech. Memo.* **76.**

VESPER, W. H. 1961: Behaviour of beach fill and borrow area at Prospect Beach, West Haven, Connecticut. *B.E.B. Tech. Memo.* **127.** (29 pp.)

VESPER, W. H. 1965: Behaviour of beach fill and borrow area at Seaside Park, Bridgeport, Connecticut, *C.E.R.C. Tech. Memo.* **11.** (24 pp.)

VESPER, W. H. 1967: Behaviour of beach fill and borrow area at Sherwood Island State Park, Westport, Connecticut. *C.E.R.C. Tech. Memo.* **20.** (25 pp.)

WATTS, G. M. 1953a: Development and field tests of a sampler for suspended sediment in wave action. *B.E.B. Tech. Memo.* **34.**

WATTS, G. M. 1953b: A study of sand movement at south Lake Worth Inlet, Florida. *B.E.B. Tech. Memo.* **42.**

WATTS, G. M. 1956: Behaviour of beach fill at Ocean City, New Jersey. *B.E.B. Tech. Memo.* **77.**

WATTS, G. M. 1959: Behaviour of beach fill at Virginia Beach, Virginia. *B.E.B. Tech. Memo.* **113.**

YASSO, W. E. 1962: Fluorescent coatings on coarse sediments: an integral system. Off. Naval Res. Proj. NR 388–057, *Tech. Rep.* **1.** (48 pp.)

ZEIGLER, J. M. 1964: Some modern approaches to beach studies. In Barnes, H. (Editor), *Oceanagr. and Mar. Biol. Ann. Rev.* **2,** 11–30. London: Allen & Unwin.

ZEIGLER, J. M., TUTTLE, S. D., GIESE, G. S. and TASHA, H. L. 1964: Residence time of sand composing beaches and bars of Outer Cape Cod. *Proc. 9th Conf. Coast. Eng.* **26,** 403–16.

ZENKOVICH, V. P. 1946: On the study of shore dynamics. *Trudy. Inst. Okeanolog.* **1,** 99–112.

ZENKOVICH, V. P. 1967: *Processes of coastal development.* (Edited by J. A. Steers) Edinburgh: Oliver and Boyd, 92–191.

10 Longshore movement of material

The movement of material alongshore is one of the most important processes at work on the coast. It is responsible for the development of a large number of shore features, such as the various types of spit that are considered in chapter 19. It is also an important cause of many instances of coastal erosion. Theoretical aspects of longshore transport will be considered first, then model experiments and then field observations. The third method of investigation has been greatly extended by means of experiments with tracers. Finally, some general assessments of the pattern of longshore transport and beach sediment budgets for different stretches of coast are given.

1 Theory

The theory of longshore currents has already been dealt with in section 4-6(a). The movement of sediment by these currents is considered by D. L. Inman and R. A. Bagnold (1963), who give a model for longshore transport of sand. The total immersed weight of sediment transported per unit time past a section of beach is given by the equation

$$I_1 = \frac{\rho_s - \rho_f}{\rho_s} g J = K \frac{ECn}{u_0} \frac{\cos \alpha}{\tan \phi} \bar{u}_1$$

where I_1 is the dynamic transport rate; ρ_f is the fluid density; ρ_s is the sand density; J is the sediment discharge in mass per unit time; K is a proportionality factor; E is the mean energy per unit surface area of a wave approaching a long straight beach at an angle α; ECn is the rate of transport of energy available for dissipation; C is the wave phase velocity; Cn is the velocity at which energy is propagated forward; u_0 is the mean friction velocity; $\tan \phi$ is the intergranular friction coefficient, and $\bar{u}_1$ is the longshore current velocity.

The value for I_1 can be given also in the simplified form

$$I_1 = \frac{8}{\sqrt{(3\gamma)}} \frac{\tan \beta}{\tan \phi} K (l_1/CT) \, P_1 \cos \alpha$$

where the terms γ, β and ϕ depend respectively on the type of breaking wave, the slope of the beach and the physical properties of the sand, and P_1 is the longshore component of wave power ($P_1 = P \sin \alpha \cos \alpha$). The first part of the expression varies from 0·1 to 1 on a sandy beach. The last part of the expression is proportional to the total longshore component of power available. The value reaches a maximum when the breaker angle, α, is 35°. K is the ratio of work done in transporting sand to the total power available, and is, therefore, an efficiency factor. The value of K for laboratory data is 3%, but for field data with $l_1 = 400$, K is 17%, l_1 being the average separation between rips. K will be zero with velocities below the threshold of sand movement, and reaches a maximum when sand is moving everywhere.

Longshore movement of material takes place primarily in two zones on the beach. Beach drifting takes place along the swash–backwash zone, particularly in coarse material, such as shingle, when waves break at the foot of the swash slope. On a sand beach the bulk of the longshore movement frequently takes place in the breaker zone. Both laboratory and field evidence for this movement will be presented.

V. P. Zenkovich (1967) calculates the horizontal displacement in beach drifting for various angles of wave approach, using the equation

$$\frac{h + m}{l} = \frac{1 + \sin \alpha}{\cos \alpha}$$

where h is the perpendicular distance, m is the slant distance moved by the swash up the beach, and l is the horizontal displacement, α being the angle of wave approach. The smaller the pebble the larger the path it traverses and hence the greater the value of l. Increasing beach slope reduces the size of the parabola traversed by a pebble. Waves of medium size are more effective because they are less refracted.

The empirical study of K. Vollbrecht (1966) attempts to derive the intensity of longshore drift from wind records. He used wind data to forecast the waves, by means of the Sverdrup–Munk–Bretschneider forecasting curves described in chapters 3 and 4. In a consideration of longshore drift only the wave intensity and direction of approach are required. Vollbrecht states that the amount of material moving alongshore is considerably greater than that moving normal to the beach.

One important factor is the component of wave energy moving parallel to the shore and causing littoral drift, designated E_t.

$$E_t = E_0 \sin \alpha_0 \cos \alpha_0 (L^*/L_0)$$

where L^* is the wave length at the shore, α is the wave crest angle, and the subscript $_0$ refers to deep-water values. The value of E_t reaches a maximum with α of 45°, being zero at angles of 90 and 0 degrees. Owing to wave energy spread the curve becomes somewhat distorted. Alongshore energy is provided even by slightly offshore winds, the maximum efficiency occurring at 47°. The efficiency pattern is shown in figure 10-1. The values shown can be used to establish the variation of efficiency along a shoreline that changes direction relative to waves coming from a standard direction. Diagrams of this type, as shown in figure 10-2, can be used to indicate possible areas of erosion and accretion.

Vollbrecht (1966) has calculated the pattern of energy relevant to longshore sand transport

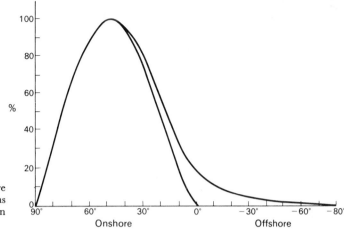

Figure 10-1 Percentage of longshore transport volume for different directions of wave approach relative to the shore in the south Baltic. (*After Vollbrecht, 1966.*)

along parts of the Baltic coast. The method used in this study only applies to relatively enclosed seas, such as the Baltic, because no allowance is made for swells that travel from distant generating sources. The wind data, used to determine the direction of wave approach and wave energy, were obtained from the lightship *Kiel*, and showed a predominance of southwest and east winds.

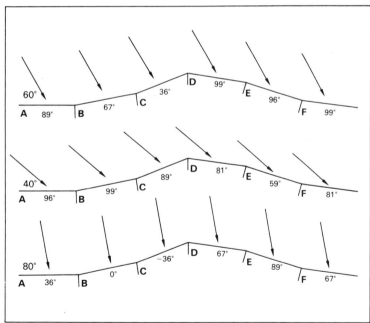

Figure 10-2 Effect of direction of wave approach relative to shoreline orientation on volume of longshore transport on the shore in the south Baltic. (*After Vollbrecht, 1966.*)

The wind records gave a value for E*, and the longshore component of energy was derived from this value (figure 10-1). The pattern of alongshore energy could then be summed consecutively for each point on the coast. Vertical or steep sections on the cumulative graph indicate periods of strong longshore transport, while horizontal sections indicate periods of little longshore

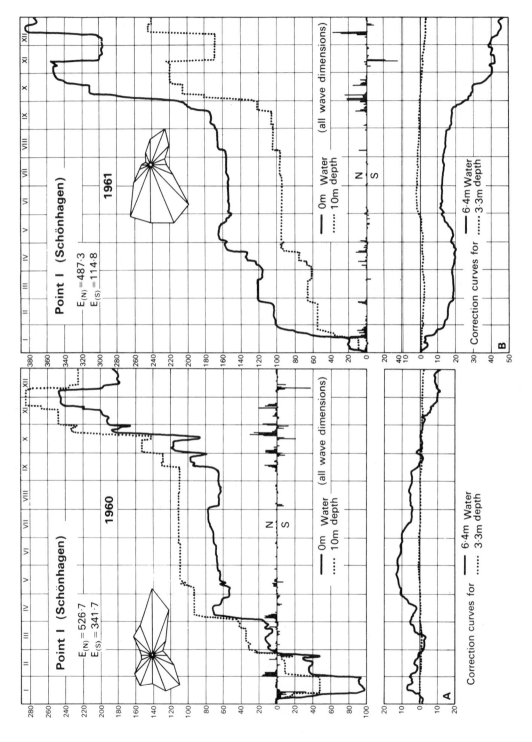

Figure 10-3 Pattern of energy responsible for longshore material transport at Schönhagen, 1960 and 1961. (*After Vollbrecht, 1966.*)

movement. The net movement over a given period of time can be readily obtained from the graph, an example of which is shown in figure 10-3, referring to Schönhagen, which lies on a north–south coastline. This method provides a convenient means of comparing successive years. The heavy line on the graph (figure 10-3) shows the calculations for all winds and waves. Values for deeper water (in which the weaker waves were omitted) and corrections for intervening depths are also given. The latter are small and the pattern is essentially similar under all conditions. A northerly drift of material, which is confirmed by field evidence, is indicated.

Other stations for which Vollbrecht made calculations were situated on an east–west stretch of coast. In this situation the fetch was much greater to the east than to the west. The influence of fetch on longshore movement could thus be studied. The most westerly of the stations on this stretch of coast showed the strongest western component of drift, caused by the longer fetch of the waves generated by the east winds. There was little movement to the east. The most easterly station showed a stronger easterly movement, which almost cancelled the westerly movement.

It is possible to build up an energy budget at any point between two stations for which drift information is available. A value is considered positive if the up-drift point has the higher value, and negative if it has the lower. It is now necessary to develop a means whereby the balance of drift energy can be transformed into volumes of material moving alongshore in different depths. The relationship between drift energy and amount of material carried along the shore is probably not linear. The stronger winds exert more influence on the pattern of drift energy than the weaker ones. This type of analysis should provide useful information concerning the likely direction and amount of longshore movement of sediment, and can readily be derived from wind observations. It would be of value to establish similar methods for coasts exposed to swell waves.

2 Model studies

Model studies of sand transport along a straight beach with differing angles of wave approach have been made by T. Saville (1950). He used the wide wave tank, 20·5 m by 37·2 m in plan and 0·61 m deep, which has already been described in chapter 2. A beach was constructed at one end 1·83 m wide. The initial slope was 1 in 10 and the sand size was 0·30 mm. A trap was fixed at the downwave end with a pump to ensure that the sand transport was not upset by currents at the end of the tank. An infinitely long beach was thus simulated. Traps were fixed at various levels in the centre of the tank to measure bed-load transport. Sand was introduced at the up-wave end at the same rate as it moved out at the down-wave end.

It was found that once stability had been reached, after a period of about 2 to 3 hours, the amount of sand transported remained relatively constant. The traps were divided into four parts so that the transport in different zones on the profile could be measured. The transport of beach material took place in two main zones: one was the zig-zag transport on the beach foreshore in the form of beach drifting; the other was the transport in suspension in the breaker zone over the submarine bar. The type of transport varied with the wave characteristics. With steep waves about 60% of the material was carried in suspension, while for low, flat waves only a small percentage was carried in suspension. The different zones in which transport took place are shown in figure 10-4. 10-4(A) shows that transport under steep waves took place mainly on the submarine bar, while 10-4(B) shows that with flat waves transport was mainly by beach drifting in the swash zone. The critical steepness causing a change in transport occurred at 0·03.

The observations in the wave tank showed that there is an optimum wave steepness between 0·02 and 0·025 at which transport reaches a maximum. There is a very rapid decrease for smaller

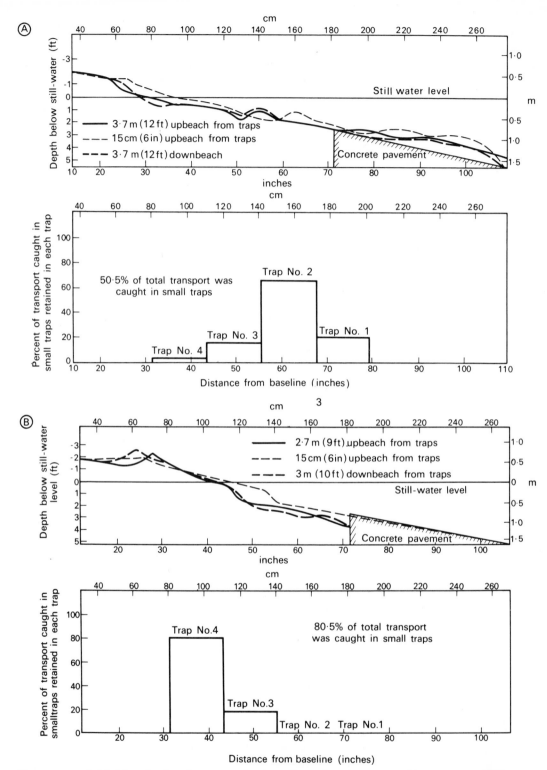

Figure 10-4 **A:** Model study of sand transport, beach profiles and total transport with steep waves, H/L 0·0597; **B.** Model study of sand transport, beach profiles and total transport with flat waves, H/L 0·0151. (*A, B after Saville, 1950.*)

steepness ratios. The peak value was three times that taking place with very steep waves. The wave energy also had a marked effect on the amount of sand transported. The results apply to an equilibrium beach, which is unlikely to occur often in nature. The relationship between model and prototype is uncertain. In the model the strength of the alongshore current alone was not great enough to move the sand grains, although it often is rapid enough to do so in nature.

Saville's tests were extended by E. A. Shay and J. W. Johnson (1953) to examine a greater range of wave approach directions. All Saville's results were obtained with waves that approached the beach at 10°. The later observations extended the range to angles up to 50°. The maximum alongshore movement of material was found to occur when the waves approached at an angle of about 30° to the coast. The rate at which the transport takes place was also found to slow down with time, if the waves causing it are in process of adjusting the beach profile to a new equilibrium slope.

Experiments have been carried out by the Hydraulics Research Board (1956) to examine the longshore movement on a model of a particular stretch of coast at Dunwich in Suffolk. One aim was to assess the effect of different types of groynes on the sand movement. The model profile, which was on a horizontal scale of 1 in 30 and a vertical scale of 1 in 20, was moulded to represent the beach at Dunwich, and the waves and tidal range were adjusted by trial and error until the profile remained in equilibrium. The direction of wave approach was fixed at 30° north of normal and the wave size, according to the scale, would have been 0·61 m in deep water, increasing to 0·915 m at the break-point. The amount of longshore movement was measured by collecting the sand in trays, each covering the equivalent of 18·3 m width of beach in the prototype or 0·61 m in the model. The total transport was the equivalent of 347,500 m³/year in the prototype on an open beach with no groynes, over the width of the three upper trays, or 54·9 m. The movement was found to be greatest around the high-tide position. About half this amount moved in the zone immediately above the low-tide level. The tidal range is 1·83 m in nature. The amount moved below low-water level was very small.

It was shown that groynes 54·9 m long normal to the shore and 0·915 m above the beach level, greatly reduced the volume of longshore transport of sand. The groynes, which were spaced 110 m apart, reduced the transport to the equivalent of 91,700 m³/year. The experiment gave useful information concerning the probable maximum amount of longshore movement which might be expected at Dunwich. Because the optimum wave direction was used and only one wave size was tested the experiments could not, however, give the true value of longshore movement along this stretch of coast.

Experiments on sand transport by waves and currents were carried out by D. L. Inman and A. J. Bowen (1963) at the Hydraulics Research Station at Wallingford. The sand was moved first by waves alone and then by waves and currents over a horizontal sand bed in water 50 cm deep. The wave height was 15 cm and the periods 1·4 and 2·0 seconds. Currents of 2, 4 and 6 cm/sec were tested. Sand was trapped at both the up-wave and down-wave ends of the tank. The sand diameter was 0·22 mm.

The total amount of sand caught in both traps was largest with the longer wave period, while the largest amount of net transport occurred with the shorter wave period. The 2 cm/sec current doubled the amount of sand moved for both wave periods, but there was a slight decrease of transport with the higher current velocities. The conclusion was reached that about 1/10 of the wave power was used to transport sediment. The value of the efficiency coefficient k was 0·29 for the first run and 0·12 for the second. The value of k was reduced as the current became greater than 2 cm/sec, and for the 4 cm/sec current its value was negative and the sand transport was also slightly reversed in direction. These results were unexpected and show that more work remains to be done on the action of waves and currents combined, in studying longshore transport.

A model study of the behaviour of groynes under different wave conditions has been made by P. H. Kemp (1962). The tank he used was 4·58 m by 2·74 m, and waves, tides and currents could be simulated. Littoral drift material was fed into the model on a conveyor belt and caught in a trap at the down-wave end. Changes in beach volume were obtained by photographing cords laid along the beach contours. The material used was pumice sand of median diameter of 0·9 mm, designed to simulate a natural shingle beach. The pumice sand moved 14 times the rate of quartz sand of the same size.

Preliminary experiments showed that the storm or bar type profile occurred with waves above a certain height. These waves caused surf conditions, in which the swash of one wave reached its limit at the same time as the next broke. The summer or step type profile occurred with waves below a critical height, which produced surge conditions. The surf conditions are likely to give rise to rip currents. The littoral currents increased linearly and rapidly with increasing wave height, while the increase in transport was even more rapid. The littoral current velocity also increased in proportion to the sine of the angle between the wave crest and the shore. The combined action of mass transport and wind-induced currents will tend to cause shingle to remain in the active zone close to the shore. The reorientation of the shore, as a result of groynes, will modify the littoral currents.

The groyne experiments were made under conditions of constructive wave action, with a spell of destructive waves causing denudation and bar formation acting in the middle of the run. Three types of groynes were tested—low groynes, long high groynes and short high groynes—in three different groyne alignments—normal to the shore, 30° in an up-drift direction and 20° in a down-drift direction. The results are set out in table 10-1, which shows the percentage of material caught in the down-drift trap, compared with that moving on the beach without groynes. The orientation of the groynes had a marked effect on the efficiency, particularly with the low groynes and the long high groynes. Orientation did not, however, change the efficiency of the short high groynes. All groynes produced some reduction of the littoral drift, particularly on the up-drift side. The low groynes normal to the shore produced the best conditions for progradation after the storm. During storm conditions the littoral drift was higher, the bulk of the material moving alongshore being that eroded from the upper beach. The transport rate was reduced with time, because the erosion slowed down. The figures for change of shoreline orientation are given after those for percentage littoral transport in table 10-1. They show the extent to which the groynes caused the shoreline to change angle under different conditions. Such shoreline reorientation can reduce littoral drift.

Experiments have been made in a much larger wave tank by R. P. Savage (1959). The tank was 91·5 m by 45·7 m and 0·915 m deep. The experimental beach had a gradient of 1 in 20, and sand traps caught the material moving alongshore at different levels on the beach. A test was made first with no groynes and then four tests were run, using different groyning systems and positions on the beach. The results can best be seen in figures 10-5A and B, which show the cumulative amount of sand caught under each condition and the position on the beach where the sand was trapped. The low short groynes reduced the rate of drift by 12%, the high short groynes by 25%, and the long high groynes by 60%. It was found that the velocity of the littoral current varied inversely with the wave period. Three periods of 34, 40 and 46 waves per minute were used in the experiment. The wave crests were aligned at 30° to the beach in the tests and the wave heights were 6·1, 7·6 and 9·2 cm respectively. This series of tests in a very large wave tank shows clearly the effectiveness of long high groynes in slowing down longshore drift.

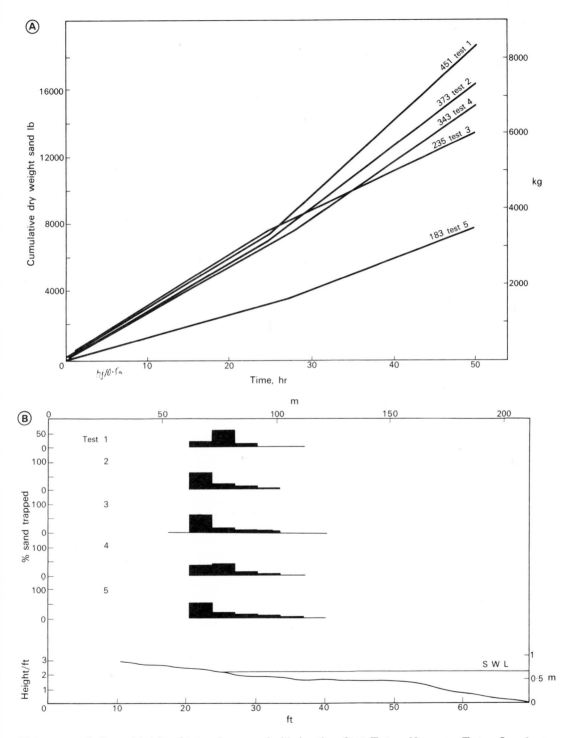

Figure 10-5 A: Dry weight of sand trapped compared with duration of test. Test 1—No groyne. Test 2—Low short groyne at station 30. Test 3—High short groyne at station 30. Test 4—High short groyne at station 45. Test 5—High long groyne at station 45; **B:** Percentage of total sand in east test trapped in the individual traps, showing the relative position of the traps on the 150 hour profile. (*B after Fairchild, 1966.*)

Table 10-1 Effect of groynes on longshore transport

1 *Wave height 1·2 cm, wave period 0·544 second: Two tides, one preceding and one following a storm tide*

GROYNE TYPE	30° UP-DRIFT		0°		20° DOWN-DRIFT	
	%		%		%	
Low	48	15	61	18	95	21
High long	35	6	42	9	48	13
High short	58	6	63	9	56	18

2 *Wave height 3·0 cm, wave period 0·422 second: one tide*

GROYNE TYPE	30° UP-DRIFT		0°		20° DOWN-DRIFT	
	%		%		%	
Low	57	11	57	18	70	20
High long	59	9	65	20	68	33
High short	86	8	86	20	88	33

3 *Average computed for the total cycle of three tides*

GROYNE TYPE	30° UP-DRIFT		0°		20° DOWN-DRIFT	
	%		%		%	
Low	51	17	60	10	87	16
High long	43	8	50	10	55	21
High short	67	3	71	10	67	21

Note: All groynes produced some reduction of the littoral drift.
Values give transport as percentage of transport without groynes for three alignments.
The second figure gives the change in alignment of the coastline between groynes as a result of longshore movement in degrees.

3 Observations and calculations of longshore transport in nature

a Sand beaches

(*i*) *Surveys in relation to coastal structure, artificial and natural:* It is not easy to measure directly the total transport of sand along a shore. Estimates have been made, however, of the longshore transport in different areas and under different wave conditions. Such studies can be made most readily where the natural movement of sand alongshore has been interrupted by some barrier, such as a breakwater. By repeated surveys it is possible to estimate the volume of material accumulating on the up-drift side of the barrier and that lost by erosion on the down-drift side. In some instances more accurate volumetric figures are available where sand has either been dredged from the up-drift side or dumped on the down-drift side. Studies of this type are easier to make where there is a dominant direction of drift along the coast.

Estimates of the amount of longshore transport have been made for various parts of the coasts of the U.S.A., including California, Florida and New Jersey. Data on the longshore drift of sand has been collected over a considerable period at Santa Barbara in California (J. W. Johnson, 1953). In 1929 a breakwater was constructed to form a harbour at Santa Barbara, as shown in figure 10-6. The structure intercepted the west to east longshore movement of sand. Silting of the harbour was also caused by the breakwater and the up-drift beaches accreted. Erosion occurred for a distance of at least 16 km down-drift along the coast after only a few years. A system of harbour dredging and feeding of the down-drift beaches was initiated in 1935 to overcome this problem.

Surveys of the harbour have enabled annual accretion to be calculated since 1932. The average amount of annual transport for the period 1932–1951 was 214, 360 m³/year. Since 1950 more precise figures are available, based on more frequent surveys. They can be correlated with wave recordings, which were not available for the earlier period. The wave recorders were fixed in 9·15 m of water off the breakwater at Santa Barbara and 16 km to the west in 12·2 m of water. Wind observations were also available but no recording of the direction of approach of the waves was made. It is known, however, that except for a very few days each year the waves cause an easterly drift of sand. The period of detailed observations extended from April 1950 to the end of February 1951, an average period as far as sand transport here is concerned. The median diameter of the sand moving into the harbour was about 0·2 mm.

Results of the more detailed surveys revealed several occasions when the daily rate of transport was higher than the average daily rate. These periods were in general those with greater wave power, where wave power is expressed as $E\,2T$, E being the wave energy and T the wave period. On one occasion the transport was much greater than usual, which was probably due to a more oblique wave approach, as the wave power was not above average. In all observations the wave steepness was low, never exceeding 0·017. By analogy with model experiments transport should have been taking place in the shallower water, and therefore nearly all of the drift alongshore should have been trapped in the harbour. Very frequent surveys were found necessary to establish precise relationships between waves and transport. A value for the direction of wave approach was also found to be essential.

R. P. Savage (1957) has discussed the sand by-passing project at Port Hueneme, California. This plan was put into operation in an attempt to alleviate severe beach erosion. The area is 104 km northwest of Los Angeles (figure 10-10). The harbour consists of an entrance protected by jetties, extending to a depth of 9·15 m in a natural salient of the coast. A submarine canyon extends right into the mouth of the harbour, which was built during 1938 to 1940. Before the construction of the harbour the beaches north of it had accreted since observations were first made in 1855, while the coast south of the harbour had been remarkably stable during the same period. Since the building of the harbour the down-drift or southern beaches have eroded rapidly and sea-walls have been built. The predominant direction of wave approach is from the north-west, particularly during the summer. The waves tend to be rather lower in summer than in winter, when a greater proportion come from other directions. The deep-water waves are modified in direction and height by refraction. The presence of offshore islands protects the area from northwesterly waves and refraction reduces their height so that they rarely exceed 1·22 m. The mean tidal range is 1·13 m, with a diurnal range of 1·65 m mean higher high water to mean lower low water, the extreme range being 3·2 m.

It appears that most of the material moving along the coast in the neighbourhood of Port Hueneme comes from inland via the Santa Clara River. Estimates of the amount of material added to the up-drift beaches north of the jetties suggest that about 306,000 m³/year of sand are

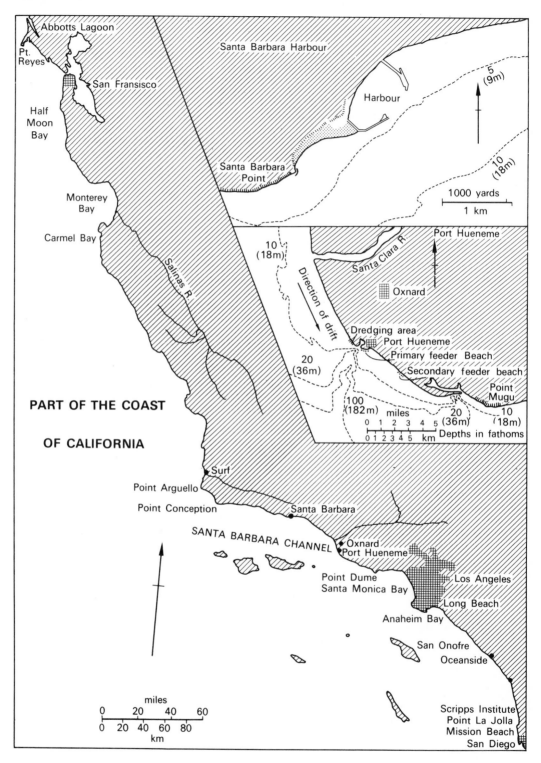

Figure 10-6 Map of California to show places mentioned. Inset of Santa Barbara and Port Hueneme.

deposited in this area, while about 915,000 m³/year are moved along the coast from the down-drift area. This amount has been lost from the down-drift beaches since the construction of the harbour works. The total transport along this coast is about 915,000 m³/year, of which ⅓ remains on the up-drift beaches and ⅔ is lost into the Hueneme Canyon. Some material, probably only a small amount, may be lost by wind erosion. Later surveys and computation between 1948 and 1952 suggest a total rate of annual transport of about 840,000 m³.

In an attempt to stabilize the down-drift beaches extensive dredging operations from the up-drift area were started in September 1953. By June 1954 1,552,000 m³ had been moved to the down-drift beaches. Surveys were carried out during this period and subsequently. It was estimated that from June 1954 to June 1955 only 620,000 m³ reached the dredging area, considerably less than the previous estimate of 915,000 m³/year. Some of the material was probably lost down the canyon. On the down-drift beaches immediately adjacent to the harbour, 1,070,000 m³ was lost from the beach during the year June 1954 to June 1955, while 4·8 to 6·4 km further down-drift from the harbour 317,000 m³ was lost. This figure is probably too small for the average movement in this area. Later surveys showed an acceleration in the longshore transport.

Another estimate of longshore movement of sand in California was made by J. M. Caldwell (1956) in the area near Anaheim Bay (figure 10-6). Jetties had been constructed in this area during 1944. They served as a trap for longshore transport of sand and hence provided suitable conditions for the correlation of the amount of longshore movement with wave data. The building of the jetties interrupted the normal sand movement to such an extent that the down-drift area to the south of the structures had to be artificially replenished. The transport of this beach fill was measured in seven surveys between March 1948 and August 1949. The wave data correlated with the amount of transport included estimates of wave energy from synoptic charts, analysis of wave records from gauges of two types and photographic data.

The results of the different techniques indicated that the hindcast data provided reasonably accurate values from which the alongshore component of wave energy could be calculated. The total energy in foot-pounds transmitted alongshore is given by the equation

$$E = 41 T H_s^2 n (\tanh 2\pi d_s / L_s) t \sin \alpha \cos \alpha$$

where

$$n = \frac{1}{2}\left(1 + \frac{4\pi d_s / L_s}{\sinh 4\pi d_s / L_s}\right)$$

T is the wave period; H_s is the wave height; d_s is the depth and L_s the wave length in this depth; α is the angle of the wave crest with the beach at the point of analysis; and t is the time in seconds over which the energy, E, is transmitted.

The alongshore wave energy was averaged for the six periods between the surveys. In four of the periods the net direction of alongshore energy was directed to the south and on only one occasion was the direction of drift contrary to the computed alongshore wave energy, which was very small. In figure 10-7 the amount of transport alongshore in cubic yards/day has been correlated with the wave energy. This figure also includes data of a similar type derived from observations made in Florida (G. M. Watts, 1963). The two sets of data show a similar correlation, suggesting that the method of analysis has a wider application. The relationship between the variables can be expressed as $Q_i = 210 E_i^{0·8}$, where Q_i is the intensity of alongshore sand movement in cubic yards/day and E_i is the intensity of alongshore energy in millions of foot-pounds per foot of beach per day (1 foot-pound = 0·1383 kg/m).

The size of sand on the beach in California near Anaheim Bay varied between 0·30 and 0·48 mm.

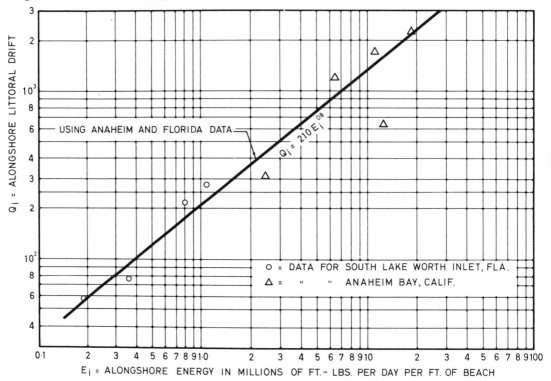

Figure 10-7 Volume of sand transported alongshore in California and Florida. (*After Caldwell, 1956.*)

At the time of the first survey the material was finer to the south and was the original beach material, while the sand fill to the north was coarser. At the end of the period the northern area had a median diameter of 0·36 mm and the southern one of 0·39 mm. The change was due to the transfer of the fill south by longshore movement.

The movement of sand along the coast of South Lake Worth inlet in Florida has already been mentioned (G. M. Watts, 1963). The drift in this area is to the south and it has been estimated that about 152,500 m³/year move alongshore. There is a fairly strong selective action in the size of the sand moving south. Only the coarser particles are moved southwards, though all the sand is fairly coarse as the median diameters range from 0·33 to 0·84 mm.

Further north along the Atlantic coast of the U.S.A. measurements of longshore movement, reported by G. M. Watts (1956), have been made on the beaches in front of Ocean City, New Jersey (figure 10-8). This area is now suffering erosion owing to changes in configuration of the channels through the Great Egg Inlet immediately northeast of the beach under consideration. The deepening of the channel through the inlet has reduced the amount of sand travelling along-shore to the Ocean City beaches from the northeast, which is the dominant direction of movement on this stretch of coast. During the period 1842 to 1949 the Ocean City beach advanced seaward and towards the northeast into Great Egg Inlet. A little further north along the coast at Atlantic City the amount of sand moved southwest has been estimated to be about 305,500 m³/year. This amount must reach the Great Egg Inlet each year. The shifting of the channels in the inlet has meant that about 38,100 m³/year has been lost from the Ocean City beaches between 1930 and 1950. In order to make good this loss it was decided to put beach fill on the foreshore. 1,947,000 m³ of sand were placed on the beach between May and July 1952. The sand was very fine with a median diameter of about 0·16 mm. This is finer than the natural sand, which was about 0·23 mm at mid-tide level. It was found that quite a large proportion of the finer part of the fill was taken offshore to a depth of about 3·66 m. Later it moved alongshore to replenish neighbouring beaches.

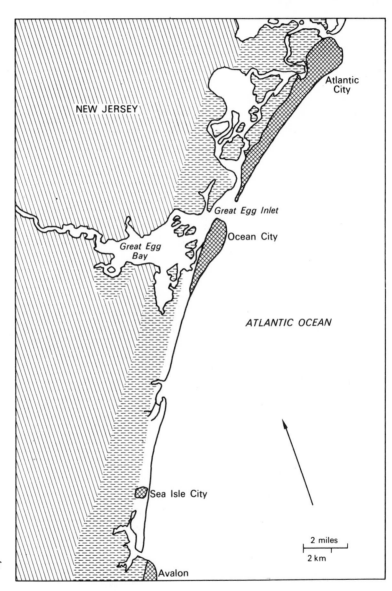

Figure 10-8 Map of part of the coast of New Jersey.

The loss in the Ocean City beach area may be partly due to its position, which is further seaward than the adjoining beaches, making it more liable to erosion.

Longshore movement took place in general in the shallower water along the beach or in the surf zone to a depth of about 6·1 to 9·15 m. It is often suggested that rocky headlands on the coast prevent the movement of material along the shore. This is true as far as the beach and foreshore are concerned and probably often applies also to the surf zone. J. A. Baak (1936) has put forward convincing evidence in support of this view. He used heavy mineral analysis of the sands of the west coast of Brittany and Normandy to establish that each bay in this area of varied geology had its own particular type of heavy mineral assemblage. The material is local in character and sand from this part of the French coast does not pass through the Straits of Dover.

Further evidence on this point is given by V. P. Zenkovich (1946), who stated that the shingle in a small bay on the south coast of the Crimean Peninsula in the Black Sea was of local origin. No shingle can move into or out of the bay along the shore round the rocky headlands enclosing it. Each bay contains only material of local origin.

P. D. Trask (1955) worked on the problem of transport around the rocky headlands along the Californian coast north of Los Angeles. He suggested that the uniform offshore slope and uniform size and sorting of the sediments, particularly between 9·15 and 18·3 m depth, is strong evidence that sand migrates along the coast between Surf and Point Conception: at these depths sand can move around the headlands, which prevent movement of material along the foreshore and in the surf zone.

(ii) Tracer experiments: Radio-active isotopes are being increasingly used for studying the movement of sand on beaches. An experiment in this field made in Sweden has been reported by J. Davidsson (1958). The beach was situated on the west side of the Island of Maklpäpen and was of quartz sand with a diameter between 0·20 and 0·60 mm, mainly in the finer part of the range. Active northerly longshore movement takes place along the coast, owing to the predominance of west to southwest winds.

The radio-active sand was placed on the sea bed in an area less than $\frac{1}{2}$ m square. Its movement was traced mainly in the swash zone by using a scintillation counter, which was moved along a square grid across the beach. During the experiments the direction and size of the waves were measured or calculated. Longshore movement was studied on a small recurved spit where the activated sand was laid in a line 2 m long from the upper limit of the swash to the break-point of the waves. After half an hour the radio-active sand was found in two lines, one at the limit of the swash and the other immediately inland of the break-point. The sand extended alongshore for 11 and 8 m respectively. The sand did not move into depths greater than 25 cm, at which depth a terrace was formed by the breaking waves. The sand moved in a down-drift direction. After $1\frac{1}{2}$ hours the sand had moved further down-drift, but there was also a slight movement in the reverse direction, where the sand had first been deposited. After three hours, the final stage recorded, most of the activated sand had reached the tip of the spit about 21 m away from the starting point.

Extensive coastal observations, including measurements of longshore transport of sand, have been planned for the Netherlands coast (J. J. Arlman *et al.*, 1957), in connection with the proposal to dam the estuaries of the Scheldt. Radio-active tracers will be used to establish the longshore movement using techniques devised and tested in a model flume.

Experiments involving the use of radio-active sand in greater depths have been carried out off Sandbanks, Dorset, by the Hydraulics Research Board (1956). The sand was activated with the isotope scandium–46, which has a half-life of 85 days. The material had a mean diameter of 0·18 mm, where the beach sand was 0·22 mm. Observations showed that the tidal streams in the area did not exceed 30 cm/sec, which was too low to move the sand. The activated sand was deposited at a point 855 m offshore in a depth of 5·79 m. It was dropped from a height of 2·44 m above the sea bed, causing a considerable scatter of the finer particles, which may have spread 168 m during the first hour after injection. The subsequent movement of the activated sand was traced over a period of four months by means of Geiger counters. The activated sand moved very little during the first six weeks after its injection when the weather was relatively calm. During November, however, a period of south easterly gales produced waves which moved the sand to the north and northeast, causing a general scattering of the original patch. It was concluded that only storm waves could move the material in this depth of water. The experiments also showed that radio-active sand could be traced for at least four months.

S. Sato and N. Tanaka (1967) describe an example of sand drift affected by the construction of Port Kashima, which faces the Pacific Ocean in Japan. The coast is characterized by submarine bars, lying 100 to 150 m offshore under normal conditions, but 100 to 400 m under storm conditions. The tidal range is 1·4 m. Sand drift was measured for two years before the construction of the harbour was started in 1963. The predominant wave direction was from northwest to north-northwest, nearly normal to the shore. The median wave period was 8·7 seconds and median significant height was 0·93 m. Sand movement was measured by radio-active and fluorescent tracers. In the surf zone the direction of movement coincided with the longshore component of wave action or with rip currents. Offshore the same applied, except that for low waves the tidal streams were dominant. The net alongshore transport was trapped by the breakwaters when they were completed and amounted to $64 \times 10^4 \, \text{m}^3/\text{year}$ to the south and $60 \times 10^4 \, \text{m}^3/\text{year}$ to the north. The difference between the two is estimated as less than $10^5 \, \text{m}^3/\text{year}$ allowing for errors, the direction varying from year to year. The stability of this coast is consistent with these results.

The development and increasingly extensive use of fluorescent materials for tracing the longshore movement of material has provided many useful studies. The technique of tracing fluorescent sand on the beach is described by F. F. Wright (1962) when it was still in the developmental stage. It has the advantage of low cost, rapid application, ready identification and complete safety, compared with the use of radio-active materials. Wright used anthracene in his study on a beach on the west side of Sandy Hook, New Jersey. The dispersion of the sediment was measured after dark with an ultra-violet lamp. Anthracene is brilliantly fluorescent and insoluble in water. It can be applied directly to the sand grains and will survive 24 hours of constant agitation or 3 to 4 weeks on a beach. Marked grains can be identified in a dilution of 1 in 500,000. The use of this method has the advantage that sand from the beach being studied can be used. Tracer studies do not give direct values of volumetric longshore transport, but they do provide an indication of direction and distance of sand transport under specific conditions.

W. E. Yasso (1964) records a very rapid rate of movement of marked sand on the sand beaches of Sandy Hook, New Jersey. After only two swashes the marked sand had moved 5·5 m along the beach and 1·52 m down it, giving a rate of movement of 17·1 m/minute. These beaches are open to the Atlantic waves.

An extensive study of sand movement by means of fluorescent tracers has been carried out on various Californian beaches by J. C. Ingle (1966). Some of his work has been mentioned in the last chapter. He dyed 45 kg of sand from each of five test beaches, using green and red fluorescent dyes. The dyeing process does not affect the hydraulic qualities of the sand. One problem arises through change of particle size on the beaches between the collection of sand for dyeing and its return to the beach for tracing. Tests could be repeated at monthly intervals without contamination from previous dyed sand in these high-energy environments.

When the release point was within the surf zone (where most of the experiments were made), the dyed sand was deposited on the bottom at the release point from a plastic bag, in which it was mixed with wetting agent. Several samples of different colours were released simultaneously. The sampling was carried out on a grid pattern by pressing greased 7·6 cm by 7·6 cm sampling cards into the bed. The sand adhering to the card, which was numbered, was later examined under ultra-violet light in the laboratory and the marked grains were counted. Samples were collected at specific intervals after release, beginning with a 5 minute interval and usually continuing for 2 to 3 hours. At the same time observations were made on the beach profile, the currents, the wave approach direction, height and period and the wind. Maps showing lines of equal corrected tracer concentration were drawn for the different sampling periods following the release time.

The general pattern of tracer dispersion shows a scatter of grains in all directions, usually with one direction predominant. Ingle also attempted to express the results in volumetric terms. He discusses R. C. H. Russell's (1960) concentration method, which applies strictly to shingle beaches and where there is repeated injection at the same point. This general three-dimensional diffusion equation is based on a statistical prediction of the tracer diffusion. The mean square displacement of a number of tracer grains can be calculated for each test.

Ingle arrived at an estimate of longshore drift from his tests by a relatively simple method, based on a number of assumptions: firstly that the isopleths of concentration of tracer correctly represented the pattern of dispersion and concentration; secondly that only a small percentage of grains was lost by burial; and thirdly that at least 90% of the sand drift took place between the breaker zone and the edge of the sea. The first two assumptions are probably valid, because the greased card sample recovers the whole of the mobile layer.

The depletion rate was established by measuring the area within the isopleth concentration curves for each dispersal map. The number of tracer grains within each sample grid at each elapsed time was calculated and depletion curves were then constructed for each test. Each curve was found to have an abrupt inflection point. The time taken for half the grains to move out of the sample grid was computed from the average distance of grain travel and the average rate of tracer flux below the inflection point. From these values the average velocity of sand grains travelling in the surf zone could be calculated for each test. The grain velocities ranged between 1·1 m and 6·9 m/minute, which is about $\frac{1}{6}$ of the average velocity of the longshore currents. This illustrates the inefficient nature of the surf system.

The average grain velocity increased with increasing kinetic wave energy, with relative wave energy as determined by breaker height, and with the velocity of the longshore currents, although in all cases the scatter of points was considerable. The best correlation was between alongshore component of wave energy or wave power and average grain velocity. This relationship is shown in figure 10-9, in which Y = 5·60 + 1·28 X, where Y is the mean tracer grain velocity and X is the alongshore energy.

$$E_i = 0 \cdot 0625 w H_b^2 (L_b/T) \sin 2\phi$$

(r = 0·73). The alongshore energy takes into account the breaker height and angle of wave incidence. There was also an increase in grain velocity with the cross-sectional area of the water overlying the foreshore–inshore zone.

The depth of the mobile layer or active layer was then calculated by means of known volumes of longshore transport derived from earlier studies, and by the average grain velocity and the average distance between the shore and the break-point. The results were plotted against average grain size and the resulting straight line allows the depth of the mobile layer to be calculated for beaches without previous information of sand transport. The depth of the mobile layer was 0·51 mm with a sand size of 0·17 mm, and about 2·54 mm for a sand size of 0·24 mm.

The drift rates were found to vary greatly owing to variations in surf conditions. The frequency of the drift rates was bimodal, and heavily skewed to the low values, showing that the greatest

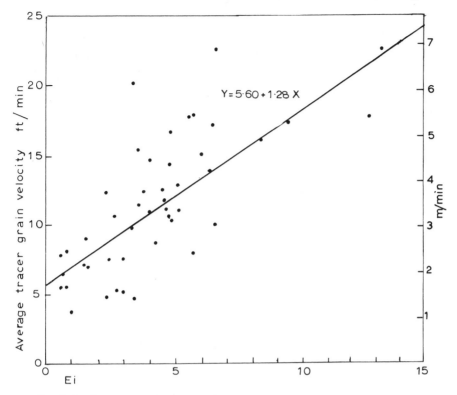

Figure 10-9 Correlation between a value representing the intensity of net longshore energy and average tracer-grain velocity: $r = 0.73$; $E_i = 0.0625 wH_b^2 (L_b/T) \sin 2\phi$. (*After Ingle, 1966.*)

volume of sand was carried alongshore under low-energy conditions. Only a fairly small proportion of the total annual load was carried under storm conditions. The mean rate of transport was 305 m³/day, the maximum and minimum rates were 1430 m³ and 56·5 m³/day. The rates in general increased with increasing breaker angle and the greatest rates occurred with deep-water wave steepness between 0·003 to 0·0045. The relationship between alongshore energy and drift in relation to material size is shown in figure 10-10: more energy is needed to sustain the same drift as the particle size falls below 0·18 mm; a lower energy is needed to move grains between 0·20 and 0·28 mm, but a higher value to move grains over 1·00 mm. In general the longshore movement of sediment was closely associated with the intensity of the longshore current.

In nearly all tests in which tracer was released in the surf zone, some of the marked grains moved into the swash zone, indicating a shoreward component of movement in most conditions. Where submarine bars were present on the profile the major longshore movement took place on the outer bar where the wave first broke and only secondary movement took place on the inner bar, on which re-formed waves were breaking. Grains just seaward of the inner breaker zone remained in strong concentration for longer than elsewhere. An orbital motion rather than onshore–offshore movement is likely in this area. The tracer grains showed the influence of rip currents on sediment movement very clearly. Movement took place also along runnels that fed into rip channels.

D. L. Inman, P. D. Komar and A. J. Bowen (1969) have made observations on three beaches in California in order to relate the longshore transport of sand to the nature of the waves. Wave sensors were used to measure the direction and flux of wave energy in and near the surf zone.

The longshore component of wave power was calculated, using the equation $E = \frac{1}{8}\rho g H^2_{rms}$, where ρg is the weight of a unit volume of water and H^2_{rms} is the root mean square wave height. $P = EG$, where P is the wave power, E is the wave energy and G is the group wave velocity. The longshore component of P is given by $P_1 = P \sin \alpha \cos \alpha$, where α is the angle between the breaking wave and the shore. The rate of sand transport was obtained from tracer studies. The

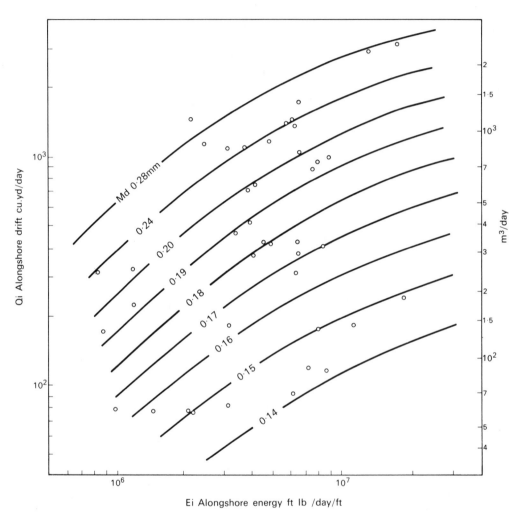

Figure 10-10 Relationship between longshore component of wave energy, rate of longshore sand transport and average median grain diameter across the foreshore–inshore slope as computed or measured from 45 tests using fluorescent sand. (*After Ingle, 1966.*)

value of the longshore transport rate, L_1, is given by $L_1 = (\rho_s - \rho)ga_iS$, where a_i is a correction for pore space and S is the volume transport per unit time. The best fit curve for six sets of data under differing wave conditions was given by $L_1 = KP_1$, with a value for K of about 0·7. The study, therefore, shows that the rate of sand transport is directly proportional to the longshore component of wave power, and is independent of sand size between 180 and 600 microns. It is thought that bed load transport in the surf zone is the most important process.

In order to arrive at valid relationships between transport rates and wave dimensions both variables must be accurately measured. W. A. Price (1969) has shown that some of the interpretations of tracer experiments may give misleading results. The normal centroid method of estimating transport volumes from tracer experiments is only correct when the dispersion is constant in the area under study. This is not true of a beach environment when movement occurs both normal to the shore and parallel to it. Price gives a mathematical model that shows for a simplified situation that dispersion increases towards the break-point of the waves. The result is an apparent movement of tracer towards the break-point, as found by Ingle (1966) in his tracer studies. This movement is probably not a real effect and requires correction to obtain the true longshore volume of transport.

Another method of overcoming the difficulty of measurement of longshore sand movement is to use a bedload trap, such as that described by E. B. Thornton (1969). The traps he used were fixed to a pier at Fernandina Beach in Florida. The beach is barred and the observations were carried out between the crests of the two bars. The results showed that the volume of sand transport varied with time when observations were averaged for 20 minute periods over a total duration of four hours. The transport was found to be greater as the depth decreased. The kinetic energy of the waves increased in the onshore direction, while their potential energy decreased. The increase of kinetic energy could account for the greater shear stress on the bottom and hence the increase of transport shorewards, and in the shallower water on the bar crests. The results with the bed load traps suggested that between 10% and 40% of the total littoral transport was as bed load, when the results were compared with those derived by use of the C.E.R.C. equation.

The use of fluorescent tracers in beach material movement studies was pioneered by workers in the U.S.S.R. V. P. Zenkovich (1962) describes their use for studying movement in the near-shore zone. The fluorescent tracers have been used for different types of study. In weak wave conditions detailed studies of an area of 100 m² were made to relate movement to wave and beach conditions. The results were often difficult to interpret owing to the complexity of water movements. The experiments were extended to examine conditions in storms by means of a cable built out to sea. Sand movement could be traced over a distance of 1·5 km, but only to a depth of 3 m at first. Since 1960 experiments have extended out to depths of 7 m. Even larger-scale experiments, using a ton of tracer, have allowed longshore movement to be traced over distances of 40 km.

The results showed that conditions were simplest when a strong longshore current was flowing along the coast so that the tracers moved parallel to the shore. Different colours were used for different grain sizes and it was shown that the larger grains moved faster. Different colours were also used for the same sand size placed at different distances from the shore. The sand on the submarine bar moved faster alongshore than sand further inland. The larger-scale experiments showed that marked sand could pass round rocky headlands on the north coast of the Taman Peninsula. The sand on the beaches west of the headland was replenished from offshore. Other observations showed that marked sand travelled about 10 km alongshore in three months on the shore of the Black Sea.

G. A. Orlova (1964) has reported on a series of experiments with fluorescent material on the coasts of the Isthmus of Anapa, in the Black Sea. The beach profile in all the localities studied had submarine bars. Mixed sizes of sand, coloured according to size, were placed on either side of and at the crest of the bar and in the trough landward of it. Samples were taken at distances of 5 to 35 m from the injection points at between 5 and 60 seconds after injection. Wave heights varied between 25 and 100 cm, length from 7 to 24 m and water depths from 1·5 to 2 m. Three fluorescent colours were used for the sand. It was found that the fine sand, 0·1 to 0·25 mm, moved alongshore at 0·64 of the mean speed of the longshore current, while the coarser sand, 1·0 to 3·0 mm, moved at between 0·3 and 0·5 of the longshore current speed. The differences for transverse movement were greater, being 0·687 for the finer sand and 0·06 for the coarser.

The volume of longshore transport was established by means of the constant concentration method devised by R. C. H. Russell (1960; et al., 1963). A constant amount of indicator sand is introduced at uniform intervals at the same point over a prolonged period of time. The concentration is recorded at both sides of the injection point until a constant value is obtained. The method was devised for shingle. With sand there is the problem of an unknown loss of material offshore. An experiment was carried out in simplified conditions of low swell of 20 to 40 cm height and 13 to 15 m length, reaching the coast at 12°. Marked sand was introduced every 10 minutes outside the break-point and at the foot of the beach slope. Samples were collected along lines 10 and 20 m from the injection line every hour with a special sampler that obtained undisturbed cores 15 cm long, a depth that provided a record of deposition for the break-point samples. The amount of sand moved alongshore under the conditions of the experiment was calculated to be 1293 m³ and 1145 m³ in 8 hours by two different methods, one using the speed of sand movement and the depth of disturbance, and the other based on the concentration of tracer in the sample. The two results agree well and give confidence in the methods of assessing the volume of longshore drift from tracer experiments.

The rate of movement of different-sized material alongshore was tested by means of fluorescent tracers by W. E. Yasso (1964) on Sandy Hook. The marked sand was placed in the mid-swash zone two hours before high tide. The waves at the time of the experiment were 0·73 m maximum height and 5·3 seconds period, and they came at an angle of 5° to the coast. A sampling line was established 30·5 m down-drift of the injection point. Samples were obtained from a strip 3·05 m upslope of the limit of the backwash to a depth of 3 cm. The smallest size class (0·701 to 0·589 mm) started to arrive at the sampling line 38·9 minutes after injection, travelling at a mean rate of 0·79 m/minute. The next size class (0·701 to 0·840 mm) started to arrive after 50 minutes, travelling at 0·61 m/minute mean velocity. The maximum number of particles in these two size classes were present at 62·3 minutes after injection. Only two particles of the two larger sizes were found in the samples (1·397 to 1·168 mm and 1·168 to 0·991 mm).

The experiment was designed to measure the rate of beach drifting, which is given by

$$V_a = \frac{L_s \tan \theta_s}{T_s}$$

where V_a is the theoretical alongshore transport velocity; L_s is the mean swash length; θ_s is the angle of the swash to the shoreline; T_s is the period of the swash. L_s was about 6·1 m; θ was less than 5° measured from the normal to the shore, T_s was 8 seconds. Substitution gives

$$V_a = \frac{20(0·01746)}{0·133} = 0·79 \text{ m/minute}$$

which corresponds with the measured value. It is suggested that the equation be multiplied by a factor, C_p, a dimensionless transport constant depending on the slope and density of the particles. This factor could be adjusted to the peak arrival period or the mean arrival period. Further tests are needed to determine the value of C_p and its usefulness in tracer studies of longshore transport.

Field tests have been carried out to test an elaborate method of tracing sand movement in the surf and offshore zones (D. B. Duane, 1970). The sand was marked with radioactive xenon-133 and gold-198–199, with half-lives of five days and three days respectively. Injection was carried out almost simultaneously along a line normal to the coast by use of water-soluble envelopes of tagged sand. Tracing was done by means of a ball-like detector towed behind a boat capable of operating in heavy surf. The vehicle was amphibious for ease of operation on the foreshore as well as in the surf and offshore zones. Computer programs enabled the results to be recorded both visually and on punched paper tape. Wave and wind characteristics were recorded and beach gradients were obtained twice a day during the experiments.

The sand marked with xenon was placed in a line 180 m long from +6 feet (+1·83 m) from mean lower low water to −6 feet (−1·83 m). The tagged sand moved only slightly downcoast, although it is possible that the movement was sufficiently random and spread out to escape detection. Some burial of the marked sand also probably took place, as indicated by coring experiments. The gold-marked sand was placed in a line 130 m long, extending from −1·22 to −3·35 m below lower low water. It was found that the gold-tagged sand yielded better results that the xenon, as it was much more sensitive. The movement was predominantly alongshore, apart from some offshore movement associated with particularly high waves. The pattern of dispersal showed a complex movement predominantly down-drift along the coast, with considerable variations in the rate of movement in different zones. Movement was particularly rapid in the zone immediately landward of the breaker margin, and sediment on the beachface moved slower than that in the inshore zone, but faster than that in the offshore zone, seaward of the breaker zone. Some burial of tagged sand occurred in the inshore zone, but relatively little in the offshore zone.

(iii) *Heavy mineral analysis:* A different type of tracer technique has been used by A. M. Kamel (1962) for tracing the longshore movement of material along the coast of California. The naturally radio-active thorium in the sand was used to detect the direction of littoral drift between Russian River and Point San Pedro. The method is quick compared with mineral analysis. Samples were collected from the surface and in depth along the stretch of coast being studied. Heavy minerals were separated in bromoform and a particular size fraction was tested for natural radio-activity. Naturally radio-active materials were added to the beach at several points along the coast where rivers bring thorium to the sea.

The direction of drift was measured by three methods. In the first the concentration of thorium in parts per million in the heavy minerals of a limited size fraction of the sand samples was analysed. In the second the percentage of heavy minerals in the same sand size fraction was determined: drift was assumed to be in the direction in which both thorium and heavy minerals decreased alongshore. The third method was based on wave refraction patterns, which give a good indication of the drift direction. The first two methods both suggest a southward drift along the coast south of Russian River. Movement along Point Reyes beach is variable according to the wave refraction pattern. The dominant waves approach normal to the shore and drift only occurs when waves come from other directions. In Drakes Bay both thorium decrease and wave refraction indicate eastward movement.

This same stretch of coast has been studied by J. A. Cherry (1966), who used the coast to study the longshore movement of sand because it is in equilibrium. The distribution of heavy minerals along the coast was studied around Point Reyes. Figure 10-11 shows the distribution of six different heavy mineral zones along the coast. The heavy minerals can be divided into distinct provinces, apart from small mixed areas within the active zone, in which material is constantly undergoing movement. The active zone descends out to a depth of about 27·4 m.

The material in the first province is derived from the cliffs at Point Reyes. The second province is in an area of no cliff erosion and material cannot be moving into this zone because if it were

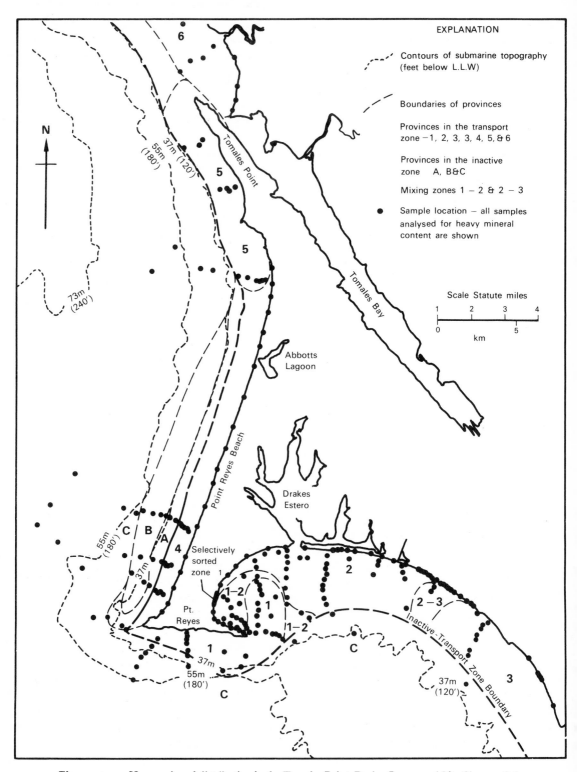

Figure 10-11 Heavy mineral distribution in the Tomales Point–Drakes Bay area. (*After Cherry, 1965.*)

the distinctive heavy mineral suite would not remain. The waves that reach this stretch of coast in Drakes Bay are very refracted. The material of the third province, lying to the southeast of the second, does not appear to come from the southeast. The material could be supplied by cliff erosion and landslides. Province five to the north of Point Reyes beach could also be supplied by local cliff erosion, but not province four, which covers Point Reyes beach to the south of province five.

The heavy mineral analysis of these beach sands suggests that they are in equilibrium, a conclusion that is supported by studies of the beach changes. The cliff recession in zones one and five is not noticeable, but over geological periods it is probably significant. A negligible amount of sand moves southeast round Point Reyes from province four to province one. Transport from provinces five to four must also be negligible. The processes operating at present are not able to account for the distribution of heavy minerals in provinces two and four. The sands on these beaches are probably relict from an earlier cycle. The present beaches are in a state of equilibrium, with no new sand added and no net longshore transport of sand away, owing to their orientation normal to the dominant waves.

Support for the heavy mineral analysis was obtained by means of predicted longshore currents and mass transport.

$$U_{max} = \frac{\pi H}{T} \cdot \frac{1}{\sinh 2\pi d/L}$$

where U_{max} is the horizontal velocity near the bed.

$$U_b = \frac{1 \cdot 25 T}{L} \cdot (U_{max})^2$$

where U_b is the mass transport velocity. These values were calculated from predicted waves to confirm the heavy mineral analysis: the predicted current velocities correlated with grain size distribution and heavy mineral distribution, which are in equilibrium with each other.

(iv) *Estimates of sand budget:* A. J. Bowen and D. L. Inman (1966) have studied the sand budget on the beaches of southern California between Pismo Beach and Santa Barbara. Longshore transport was estimated in two ways, by dilution of heavy minerals and by the longshore component of wave power. The dilution of heavy minerals suggests that little sand moves around Point Buchon, but 214,000 m³/year move alongshore at Santa Barbara. Some of this moves around Point Arguello and Point Conception. A study of the augite content of the sand shows 15% at Surf, 10% at Point Conception and 3 to 4% at Santa Barbara. These percentages indicate a continuous dilution along the coast as no augite reaches the coast south of Surf and little sand is lost offshore or in dune building in this stretch. The sand transport at any point south of Surf, multiplied by the percentage of augite in the sand, should give a constant product, which is the transport rate of the augite. The results give a transport rate of 49,700 m³/year at Surf, 76,450 m³/year at Gato, based on 214,000 m³/year at Santa Barbara (P. D. Trask, 1952; 1955).

These results agree well with the longshore component of wave power method. The longshore component of wave power calculated from the equation

$$P_e = E_0 C_0 n_0 b_0/b_b \sin \alpha_b \cos \alpha_b$$

where subscripts 0 and b refer to deep water and break-point respectively; E_0 is the energy per unit surface area; C_0 is the wave phase velocity; $C_0 n_0$ is the group velocity; and b_0 is the separation between wave rays in deep water and b_b at the break-point. The ratio gives the reduction

287

in wave energy due to refraction. The sin and cos convert the power to the longshore component. The angles are positive when transport is to the south. The power is converted into transport volume by

$$S = 1 \cdot 13 \times 10^{-4} P_e$$

The results of these calculations give a net transport of 40,500 m³/year at Surf, and 764,500 m³/year at Gato, which agree very well with the estimates by the first method. At Surf, where the coast runs nearly north–south, the up-drift and down-drift amounts are nearly equal. At Gato, where the coast runs west–east, the easterly movement is far larger than the westerly one, giving more reliable net results.

Compared with the large volume of material moving alongshore, the onshore–offshore movement is very small, being negligible for depths up to 9·15 m. Sand is lost from the beaches by wind transport, which forms extensive dunes. A total of 176,700 m³/year is lost between Pismo Beach pier and Bear Valley. The computation is based on the rate of dune advance, which is estimated as 0·15 cm/day for a mean dune height of 9·15 m, giving 0·014 m³/m (0·15 ft³/ft) of coast/day. 95% of the sand moves inland, with only 5% moving offshore.

The total annual contributions of the rivers to the sand supply is estimated at 244,200 m³/year. The volume reaching the coast has been considerably reduced since a series of major dams was built in the river valleys, and the figures refer to the present discharge since the dams were built. The cliffs supply relatively little material to the beaches. Cliff retreat is estimated at not more than 15 cm/year and the amount of material supplied 49,700 m³/year. Offshore loss is mainly down the submarine canyons, but none occurs in the area studied, so that loss from this cause is small.

The budget of losses and gains on this stretch of coast is shown in figure 10-12, which divides the coast into five cells. The estimates provide the measured volume of sand passing Santa Barbara at the eastern end of the section. The general trend of longshore movement is to the south in the study area at a rate of about 45,850 m³/year, occurring mainly in depths less than 18·3 m. The loss of a large amount of river sand may be made up by a change of alignment, which reduces longshore transport. A slight decrease in storminess may also have occurred. Seasonal trends differ from the long-term average in that transport northwards frequently takes place in winter, but in the spring and the transition period transport is strongly to the south.

J. C. Fairchild (1966) has compared various methods of estimating longshore transport along the east coast of the U.S.A. between Cape Cod and Chesapeake Bay over a distance of 800 km. Wave data were provided by hindcasting and they were related to littoral drift, measured at a few sites along the coast from maintenance dredging records. Estimates of longshore transport along the south coast of Long Island vary from 344,000 m³/year to 367,000 m³/year, the higher estimate being used. At Sandy Hook 376,500 m³/year move northwards. Wave energy was calculated for three stations from wave height, period and direction measurements, and interpolated for stations in between. Deep-water wave characteristics were thus obtained for any point along the coast. Refraction and inshore energy were then calculated, using wave periods of 9, 13 and 17 seconds. Isolines of equal energy for different directions of wave approach were computed for the three main stations, then the alongshore component of wave energy was calculated.

The results show that there is a nodal zone of littoral transport near Barnegat Inlet where the mean rate of transport approaches zero. Material seems to move away to both north and south, a finding confirmed by the continuous erosion of this area. The alongshore wave energy reaches a minimum here. The plot of alongshore energy against littoral transport suggests that a family

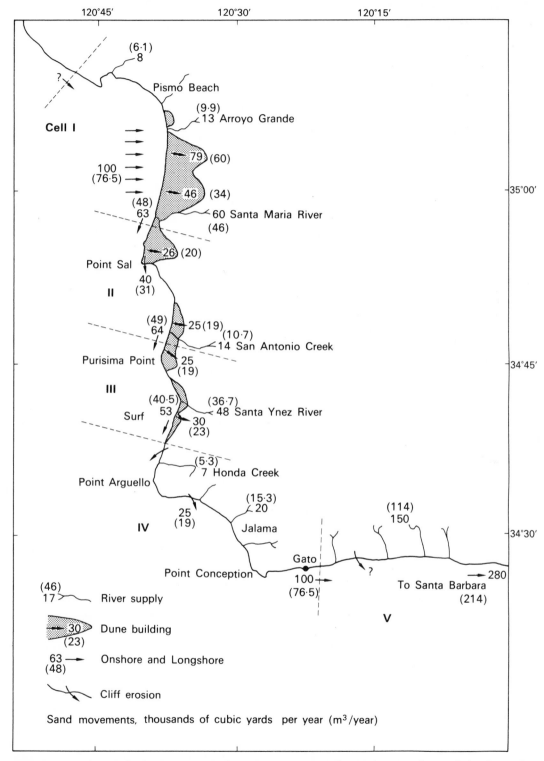

Figure 10-12 Schematic diagram of the budget of littora sands around Point Arguello and Point Conception. (*After Bowen and Inman, 1966.*)

of curves may be needed to define the relationship as different constants apply to different areas: $Q = 213E_a{}^{1\cdot1}$ fits the Atlantic coast data for the upper limits and $Q = 55E_a{}^{1\cdot9}$ fits the lower limits (Q is the transport volume and E_a is the alongshore wave energy). These values provide considerably lower volumes of drift than other estimates, such as from Caldwell's $Q = 210E_a{}^{0\cdot8}$ or laboratory test data.

b Shingle beaches—tracer experiments

In some respects the study of longshore movement on shingle beaches is simpler than that on sand beaches. The shingle is mostly confined to the top of the beach and rarely extends far offshore, so that transference of material into deep water is so small as to be negligible in many instances. The individual pebbles can be marked and traced, and experiments undertaken without the necessity of using radio-active or fluorescent markers.

The study of C. Kidson and A. P. Carr (1961) exemplifies a simple method of observing shingle movement. They used $\frac{1}{4}$, $\frac{1}{2}$ and whole bricks to conform to the natural shingle size in Bridgwater Bay, Somerset. The rates of recovery were large because the beach is sheltered and movement is limited in distance and the shingle did not move offshore. Little movement took place at the lower end of the line along which marked shingle was placed. Here recoveries of up to 100% were possible, although after 7 to 8 months some of the markers were buried by material combed down from the top of the beach in storms. The bricks were marked with galvanized tags and this method was successful. It was concluded that longshore movement in this sheltered locality, far up the Bristol Channel, was very slow: after 6 years the furthest travelled marker had only moved 2280 m. The fastest rate was at Hinkley Point, with a maximum of 24·4 m/month, and an average movement over 6 years of less than 15·25 m/month. The coast is unusual in the slow movement of material alongshore, and the narrow zone in which the material moves. Only the markers near high-water level moved measurably. The different-sized markers moved at different rates and sometimes even in different directions. The larger material was found to move faster than the small. This method of study would not be possible where the rate of movement was greater.

A series of tracer observations were made on Spurn Head, Yorkshire, by A. W. Phillips (1963) using painted pebbles. For each experiment 1000 pebbles were painted with hard enamel paint of bright turquoise, baking at 150°C made the paint resistant to wave action. Spurn Head is a narrow sand and shingle spit and the tracer pebbles were injected 400 m from its tip. Different-sized pebbles were placed in equal proportions in a line down the beach from high to low water. The beach was entirely shingle over the stretch studied. After four days all the pebbles had moved southwest towards the tip of the spit. Those less than 5 cm had moved 32·3 m; pebbles 5 to 10 cm had moved 31·7 m; and pebbles larger than 10 cm had moved 29·2 m. Waves were small during the experiment with a height of 30 cm. The southward movement was assisted by the set of the flood tidal stream in this direction. The results of this and other experiments show that movement is complex under both wave and tidal action. The method of marking pebbles was, however, successful, and marked pebbles were found up to seven months with little sign of wear.

In the Spurn Head experiments the smaller pebbles moved slightly faster than the larger, which is contrary to the Bridgwater Bay results. Other experiments made by I. P. Jolliffe (1964) were carried out with fluorescent tracer to study the relative rate of movement of different-sized pebbles on a beach at Deal and near Winchelsea in southeast England. Pebbles painted with marine paint were used as well as artificial fluorescent pebbles. The latter were made of angular chips of concrete mixed with fluorescent material. The concrete particles used were both abraded and rough.

The experiment at Deal was carried out on a 274 to 366 m stretch of coast between groynes.

There was a clear-cut sand–shingle boundary on the beach. The marked shingle was placed 3·05 m seaward of the high-water line. The waves were small during the experiment and caused a slight northerly drift. After four and a half days the larger pebbles (5–7·5 cm) had moved 17·1 m; the pebbles 2·5 to 3·8 cm had moved 13·7 m; the unbraded concrete stones 3·8 to 9 cm had moved 14·9 m; and unbraded 2·5 to 3·8 cm stones had moved 9·75 m. In both sets the smaller particles had moved less far.

The Winchelsea experiment continued rather longer and used pebbles varying from 1·25 to 10 cm diameter. The markers were again placed on the upper beach where they were influenced by the waves for two hours either side of high tide. The natural shingle varied from 1·25 to 15 cm in diameter. The marked pebbles were placed half way across the shingle between high-water mark and the sand boundary. After 32 tides the 5–7·5 cm shingle had moved nearly 152 m, having travelled furthest. The mean rate of movement for the different sizes is as follows:

7·5 –10 cm	8·25 m/day
5 –7·5 cm	9·15 m/day
2·5 –5 cm	7·90 m/day
1·9 –2·5 cm	7·30 m/day
1·25–1·9 cm	6·40 m/day
0·95–1·25 cm	4·30 m/day

The general conclusion from this study is that the differences between abraded and unabraded pebbles is small after four and a half days, as the concrete rapidly became rounded. Before this the unabraded stones moved faster. The fluorescent concrete stones moved faster than natural ones of the same size. The larger stones travelled further than the small ones up to a size of 5–7·5 cm. As the waves became larger so the differential movement between different sizes of stones became greater.

The results tend to support the view that the larger stones travel towards the zones of greater energy, where large pebbles already occur. This is true, for example, of Lulworth Cove and Worbarrow Bay, where great differences of energy occur around the bay.

Under the auspices of the Coastal Physiography section of the N.E.R.C. in conjunction with the Atomic Research Station at Harwell, experiments were carried out on the Suffolk coast (C. Kidson, A. P. Carr and D. B. Smith, 1958). At a point 640 m offshore and 2·4 km north of the distal end of Orfordness shingle spit 600 radio-active pebbles were placed in water where the depth was 5·8 to 8·5 m according to the tide level. A further set of 2000 radio-active pebbles were placed 11 m seaward of low-water level, 366 m north of the tip of the spit in mid-January 1957. The pebbles had been taken from the beach and a radio-active coating applied to them at Harwell before they were deposited on the sea bed. The isotope barium-140–lanthanum-140, with a half-life of 12 days, was used. This enabled the pebbles to be traced for about six weeks.

Their movement was measured as often as weather conditions allowed. The positions of the pebbles were traced underwater by Geiger counters mounted on a sledge, which was towed behind a launch. The instrument will locate pebbles over a band 1 to 1·22 m wide. Accurate positioning is needed to map the pebbles, and a large number of sweeps was required to be sure of locating them all. Once located the point was fixed by horizontal sextant angles to known positions on shore. A scintillation counter was used on the foreshore: this could locate a single pebble 4·6 m away horizontally and at a depth of 15 to 23 cm beneath the surface of the beach.

During the period of observation, which lasted about six weeks, the pebbles in deep water did not move at all. Those in the shallower water spread out up to more than 1·6 km north of their original position. The mean distance the 93 pebbles, which were located in the first four weeks of observation, had moved was 550 m to the north. During this period southerly winds prevailed and the wave heights never exceeded 61 cm. In the fifth week of the experiment northerly winds occurred and these caused a very rapid southerly movement of the shingle, which is the dominant direction of movement.

When northerly winds blew for two or three days some of the pebbles moved south to the distal end of the spit, and up its inland side for a distance of about 460 m. Others moved across the mouth of the river Orr to Shingle Street on the southern shore, as well as onto the shingle bank, which dries out at low tide at the mouth of the river. River mouths, therefore, provide little obstacle to the longshore transport of shingle, even though tidal currents of 7 to 8 knots occur at ebb and flood of spring tides at the mouth of the river.

Experiments also showed that the movement of the shingle is closely related to the direction of approach of the waves. In the relatively enclosed North Sea the waves are closely connected with the wind direction. When wind direction is opposed to the dominant direction, the beach material will move slowly in the opposite direction of the dominant one. When the waves come from the dominant direction, the movement is reversed and longshore transport is much more vigorous.

4 Patterns of longshore transport

Some examples of longshore transport over considerable stretches of coast have been given, as well as an example of the sediment budget along a stretch of the Californian coast. The pattern of residual sediment movement by tidal currents has been considered in chapter 5. The longshore movement considered in this chapter is the result of oblique incidence of wave energy.

The pattern of transport of beach material along the east coast of England has been discussed by C. Kidson (1961) (figure 10-13). There are several areas of serious erosion along this coast. Holderness in particular, the east coasts of Suffolk and Norfolk, and parts of east Lincolnshire have all suffered either continuous or temporary erosion. Erosion also occurs south of Harwich along the Essex coast. On other stretches of the coast accumulation has been and is rapid, for example in north and south Lincolnshire, and along the north coast of Norfolk. Large spreads of shingle occur between Aldeburgh in Suffolk and Harwich in Essex. Along the generally eroding coasts of east Norfolk and Suffolk there are localized areas of accretion, forming the nesses referred to in chapter 5, in connection with tidal streams.

Early views on the direction of longshore movement along the east coast suggested that movement was in general southwards (J. A. Steers, 1927). A dominant westward drift was postulated on the north Norfolk coast, on account of the form of Blakeney Point and Scolt Head Island, which have grown westwards. The idea of a drift parting near Cromer was considered reasonable in view of the change of coastal orientation at this point. However, the cliffs of the Weybourne–Sheringham area cannot supply the whole of the material deposited along the coast to the west.

Both the source of supply of beach material and the direction of longshore drift are relevant to the problem of large-scale accretion along this coast. It is unlikely that large quantities of sand and shingle can reach Norfolk from the north. Tidal streams are more likely to bring sand from the south to the shoals off the Norfolk coast. There is no evidence that material from offshore reaches the north Norfolk coast. Longshore movement must, therefore, be considered as a source of supply. Even if shingle can be shown to move westwards on this coast, there is no reason why sand should not move in the reverse direction. Even shingle at times moves eastwards along this coast as indicated by the build-up against the groynes. Experiments with radio-active tracers have shown that little shingle reaches the beaches from offshore. Kidson concludes that little sand and no shingle come from offshore onto the north Norfolk beaches directly from the sea bed. Material can move alongshore both above and below low water and it normally moves in both directions at different times. The movement, as shown by tracer studies, is governed by the wind direction, which to a large extent determines the wave approach on the east coast of England.

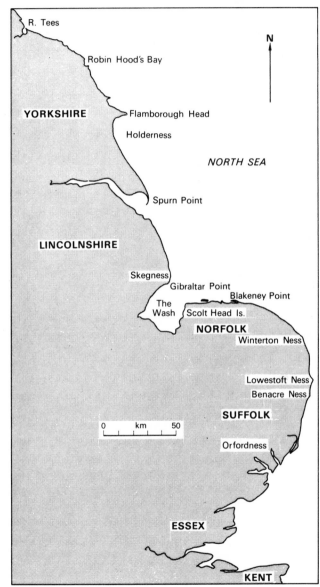

Figure 10-13 Map of the east coast of England.

Much of the material on the coast of north Norfolk may come from the east coast of Norfolk and Suffolk. The material would move north with a southerly component in the wind, and west along the north Norfolk coast when the wind was easterly, a situation common especially in the spring. Owing to the longer fetch, the easterly waves would be more efficient than the westerly waves along this coast: the situation is somewhat similar to that already considered on the Baltic coast. It is concluded that most of the material is derived from the eroding coast to the east and south, with little coming from offshore or the north. Much of the material is probably fossil, in that it reached the area under different conditions, being reworked glacial sediment. The drift parting is, therefore, not a valid concept.

On a much larger scale R. Silvester (1962) has attempted to outline the direction of sediment movement around the coastlines of the world. He uses as evidence the shape of bays between fixed headlands. His argument is based on the results of model experiments, in which waves from an oblique direction eroded a straight sedimentary coastline until a stable shape was formed between fixed headlands. The equilibrium shape is a half heart with the curved portion up-drift and the tangent section down-drift. The asymmetry of the form indicates the direction of coastal drift in the bay. The half heart shape was found to exist on many maps, for example in southwest Africa, the west coast of America and the east coast of Malaya. In all these areas the swells come from one main direction and it is the influence of these constructive waves that determines the coastal pattern.

About 250 Admiralty charts covering most of the world's coastline were examined and maps drawn on the basis of the form of the bays. The maps do not indicate the rate or amount of sediment transport, but only the direction material would move if it were available. The direction indicates net movement and does not preclude reversals of drift. Only general movement can be shown on the scale used and more complicated patterns occur where the coastal outline is intricate. The half heart shape bay is a stable form in which the amount of longshore movement is reduced to a minimum. The form of the coast is thus shown to be a response to the direction of longshore transport. The longshore movement is also responsible for erosion and accretion. These relationships will be considered in more detail in later chapters.

Summary

The amount of longshore transport is shown by theory to depend on the longshore component of wave power, which depends on the angle of wave approach. An assessment of longshore transport can be established from wind records, related to waves generated by them in enclosed seas. Model studies show that with steep waves movement alongshore takes place mainly under the breakers, and with flat waves it takes place in the swash zone, the maximum movement is found to occur with a wave approach angle of 30°. The effect of groynes can be tested in models, and they are shown greatly to reduce longshore transport. Observations of longshore transport in nature can be made by recording accretion and erosion where artificial breakwaters have been built that interrupt the longshore movement of material. Tracer experiments have been used increasingly to measure short-term movements of material alongshore. These movements may be related to the wave conditions during the experiment. Volume of transport can also be calculated. Studies can be carried out on both sand and shingle beaches. The latter studies in particular show that different-sized material moves at different speeds. The form of the coast can be used as evidence to assess the net direction of longshore transport of material.

References

ARLMAN, J. J. SANTEMA, P. and SVASEK, J. N. 1957: Movement of bottom sediment in coastal waters by currents and waves: measurements with the help of radio-active tracers in the Netherlands. *Prog. Rep. Deltadienst Rijkwaterstaat.* (56 pp.)

BAAK, J. A. 1936: *Regional petrology of the south North Sea.* Wageningen.

BOON, J. D. III 1968: Trend surface analysis of sand tracer distributions on a carbonate beach, Bimini, B.W.I. *J. Geol.* **76**(1), 71–87.

BOWEN, A. J. and INMAN, D. L. 1966: Budget of littoral sands in the vicinity of Point Arguello, California. *C.E.R.C. Tech. Memo.* **19.** (41 pp.)

BRAUKHOLL, K. and GRIESSEIER, H. 1967: Sandtransportuntersuchungen mit lumineszenten Sandes im Küstengebiet der Halbinsel Zingst. *Acta Hydrog.* **11**(3), 137–69.

CALDWELL, J. M. 1956: Wave action and sand movement near Anaheim Bay, California. *B.E.B. Tech. Memo.* **68.**

CALDWELL, J. M. 1966: Coastal processes and beach erosion. *Boston Soc. Civ. Eng.* **53**(2), 142–57.

CHERRY, J. A. 1965: Sand movement along a portion of the north Californian coast. *C.E.R.C. Tech. Memo.* **14.** (125 pp.)

CHERRY, J. A. 1966: Sand movement along equilibrium beaches north of San Francisco. *J. Sed. Petrol.* **36**(2), 341–57.

COASTAL ENGINEERING RESEARCH CENTER 1966: Shore planning and design. Section 2.3 in *Tech. Rep.* **4,** 3rd edition, 154–80.

DAVIDSSON, J. 1958: Investigations of sand movement using radio-active sand. *Lund studies in Geog., Ser. A, Phys. Geog.* **12,** Lund: Gleerup, 107–26.

DUANE, D. B. 1970: Tracing sand movement in the littoral zone: progress in the radioisotopic sand tracer (RIST) study, July 1968–February 1969. *C.E.R.C. Misc. Paper* **4–70.** (46 pp.)

FAIRCHILD, J. C. 1966: Correlation of littoral transport with wave energy along shores of New York and New Jersey. *C.E.R.C. Tech. Memo.* **18.** (35 pp.)

FOREST, G. 1957: Observations du chariage littoral au moyen d'éléments radio-actifs. *J. de la Marine.* No. Sp. *Nouveautés techniques maritimes.*

GORSLINE, D. S. 1966: Dynamic characteristics of west Florida Gulf coast. *Mar. Geol.* **4,** 187–206.

GRIESSEIER, H. and VOIGT, G. 1965: Lumineszenter Sand und sein Nachweis in Bodenproben. *Acta Hydrog.* **9**(3), 151–68.

HOURS, R. NESTEROFF, W. D. and ROMANOVSKY, V. 1955: Méthode d'étude de l'évolution des plages par traceurs radio-actifs. *Trav. Centr. Rech. d'Études Oceanog.* 1–11.

HYDRAULICS RESEARCH BOARD 1956: *Annual Report.* D.S.I.R., 33–6.

INGLE, J. C. 1966: The movement of beach sand. *Devel. Sediment.* **5,** Amsterdam: Elsevier. (221 pp.)

INMAN, D. L. and BAGNOLD, R. A. 1963: Littoral processes. In Hill, M. N. (Editor) *The sea* **III,** New York: Wiley, 529–53.

INMAN, D. L. and BOWEN, A. J. 1963: Flume experiments on sand transport by waves and currents. Chapter 11 in *Proc. 8th Conf. Coast. Eng.,* 137–50.

INMAN, D. L., KOMAR, P. D. and BOWEN, A. J. 1969: Longshore transport of sand. Chapter 18 in *Coastal engineering* **1,** Proc. *11th Conf. Coastal Eng.,* London, 1968, Am. Soc. Civ. Eng., 298–309.

JOHNSON, J. W. 1953: Sand transport by littoral currents. *Proc. 5th Hydraulic. Conf.,* 89–109.

JOLLIFFE, I. P. 1964: An experiment designed to compare the relative rates of movement of different sizes of beach pebbles. *Proc. Geol. Assoc.* **75,** 67–86.

KAMEL, A. M. 1962: Littoral studies near San Francisco using tracer techniques. *B.E.B. Tech. Memo.* **131.** (86 pp.)

KEMP, P. H. 1962: A model study of the behaviour of beaches and groynes. *J. Inst. Civ. Eng.* **22,** 191–217.

KIDSON, C. 1961: Movement of beach materials on the east coast of England. *East Mid. Geogr.* **16,** 3–16.

KIDSON, C. and CARR, A. P. 1961: Beach drift experiments at Bridgwater Bay, Somerset. *Proc. Bristol Nat. Soc.* **30**(2), 163–80.

KIDSON, C. and CARR, A. P. 1962: Marking beach material for tracing experiments. *J. Hydraulic Div. Proc. Am. Soc. Civ. Eng.* **3189,** HY 4, 43–60.

KIDSON, C., CARR, A. P. and SMITH, D. B. 1958: Further experiments using radio-active methods to detect movement of shingle over the sea-bed and alongshore. *Geog. J.* **124**(2), 210–18.

NEIHEISEL, J. 1965: Source and distribution of sediments at Brunswick Harbor and vicinity, Georgia. *C.E.R.C. Tech. Memo.* **12.** (49 pp.)

ORLOVA, G. A. 1964: Nouvelles recherches sur la dispersion des sables en mer à l'aide des luminophores. *Cah. Oceanogr.* **16**(10), 875–91.

PHILLIPS, A. W. 1963: Tracer experiments at Spurn Head, Yorkshire, England. *Shore and Beach* **31**(2), 30–35.

PRICE, W. A. 1969: Variable dispersion and its effects on the movements of tracers on beaches. Chapter 21 in *Coastal engineering* **1,**, *Proc. 11th Conf. Coast. Eng.*, London, 1968, Am. Soc. Civ. Eng., 329–34.

RUSSELL, R. C. H. 1960: Use of fluorescent tracers for the measurement of littoral drift. *Proc. 7th Conf. Coast. Eng.*, 418–44.

RUSSELL, R. C. H., NEWMAN, D. E. and TOMLINSON, K. W. 1963: Sediment discharges measured by continuous injection of tracers from a point. *Int. Assoc. Hydrog. Res. 10th Cong., London* **1,** 69–76.

SATO, S. and TANAKA, N. 1967. Field investigation of sand drift at Kashina facing the Pacific Ocean. Chapter 35 in *Proc. 10th Conf. Coast. Eng.*, 595–614.

SAVAGE, R. P. 1957: Sand bypassing at Port Hueneme, California. *B.E.B. Tech. Memo.* **92.**

SAVAGE, R. P. 1959: Laboratory study of the effect of groins on the rate of littoral transport: equipment development and initial tests. *B.E.B. Tech. Memo.* **114.** (55 pp.)

SAVILLE, T. 1950: Model study of sand transport along an infinitely long, straight beach. *Trans. Am. Geophys. Un.* **31**(4), 555–65.

SHAY, E. A. and JOHNSON, J. W. 1953: Model studies on the movement of sand transported along a straight beach. *Inst. Eng. Res. Univ. of Calif.* Issue **7,** Series **14.** (Unpub.)

SILVESTER, R. 1962: Sediment movement around the coastlines of the world. *Conf. on Civ. Problems Inst. Civ. Eng.* Paper **14.** (16 pp.)

STEERS, J. A. 1927: The East Anglian coast. *Geog. J.* **69,** 24–48.

THORNTON, E. B. 1969: A field investigation of sand transport in the surf zone. Chapter 22 in *Coastal engineering* **1,** *Proc. 11th Conf. Coast. Eng.*, London, 1968, Am. Soc. Civ. Eng., 335–51.

TRASK, P. D. 1952: Sources of beach sands at Santa Barbara, California, as indicated by mineral grain studies. *B.E.B. Tech. Memo.* **28.**

TRASK, P. D. 1955: Movement of sand around southern Californian promontories. *B.E.B. Tech. Memo.* **76.**

VOLLBRECHT, K. 1966: The relationship between wind records, energy of longshore drift, and energy balance off the coast of a restricted water body, as applied to the Baltic. *Mar. Geol.* **4**(2), 119–48.

WATTS, G. M. 1953: A study of sand movement at south Lake Worth Inlet, Florida. *B.E.B. Tech. Memo.* **42.**

WATTS, G. M. 1956: Behaviour of beach fill at Ocean City, New Jersey. *B.E.B. Tech. Memo.* **77.**

WATTS, G. M. 1959: Behaviour of beach fill at Virginia Beach, Virginia. *B.E.B. Tech. Memo.* **113.** (26 pp.)

WRIGHT, F. F. 1962: The development and application of a fluorescent marking technique for tracing sand movement on beaches. *Off. Naval Res. Geog. Br. Tech. Rep.* **2,** Proj. NR 388–057. (19 pp.)

YASSO, W. E. 1964: Use of fluorescent tracers to determine foreshore sediment transport Sandy Hook, New Jersey. *Off. Naval Res. Geog. Br. Tech. Rep.* **6,** Proj. NR 388–057. (18 pp.)

ZENKOVICH, V. P. 1946: On the study of shore dynamics. *Trudy. Inst. Okeanologie* **1,** 99–112.

ZENKOVICH, V. P. 1962: Applications of luminescent substances for sand drift investigation in the nearshore zones of the sea. *Die Ingenieur* **13,** 81–9.

ZENKOVICH, V. P. 1967: *Processes of coastal development.* Steers, J. A. (Editor), Edinburgh: Oliver and Boyd.

11   The sorting of beach material

Some aspects of differential transport of different-sized particles in both onshore–offshore movement normal to the coast, and in longshore movement, have already been noted in chapters 9 and 10, respectively. In this chapter the sorting of material both normal and parallel to the shore is considered according to size and other characteristics. Theory, model experiments and field observations are discussed.

1 Sorting normal to the shore

a   Theory

Movement of sediment particles under wave action is affected by the unequal accelerations that occur in the landward and seaward directions, as already pointed out in chapter 8 in connection with the equilibrium line. The difference between the shoreward and seaward acceleration has the effect theoretically of sorting the sand in particle sizes, parallel to the shore.

If the beach were composed of uniformly graded sand so that the mean and median diameters coincided, A. T. Ippen and P. S. Eagleson (1955) suggest that this uniformity would be disturbed by the waves. They suggest that in deep water some of the finer particles will move offshore and some will move onshore, the latter travelling all the way to the break-point. As the water becomes shallower, larger and larger particles will be capable of movement and will move onshore, so that a greater proportion of coarser particles should be found as the water becomes shallower. The general direction of transport outside the break-point is towards the shore. It might be expected, therefore, from theory that at this point the sand should have the poorest sorting, because sand of all sizes will tend to accumulate at this point. This has in fact been verified.

P. S. Eagleson, B. Glenne and J. A. Dracup (1961) have extended the theoretical approach to sediment sorting normal to the shore. They distinguish between incipient motion at which a certain size particle is just capable of motion, D_i being used to designate its size. There is also an equilibrium point at which the particle oscillates without moving seaward or shoreward: the particle in this condition has a size D_e. The sizes can be found by solving equations for D_i and D_e as follows. The original size distribution is assumed to be as shown in figure 11-1. The beach material size changes after several hours' wave action according to whether D_e/D_i is less than or greater than 1.

$$D_i = 258 \cdot 7 \frac{(\nu)^{1/2} H_0}{T^{3/2} g} [s_f/(s_s - s_f)] \frac{f_2(d/L_0)}{\sin \alpha + \tan \phi} (1 - K)$$

$$D_e = \left[6 \cdot 81 \frac{H_0^2 N \nu (1 - K^2)}{gTL_0} [s_f/(s_s - s_f)] \frac{f_1(d/L_0)}{\sin \alpha} \right]^{7/6} (\pi/\nu T)^{2/3}$$

where ϕ is angle of particle repose in radians, K is the reflection coefficient, ν is the kinematic viscosity, α is the beach slope, H_0 and L_0 are wave height and length in deep water, N is a constant, and f is a function.

At an offshore position the size distribution becomes bimodal if the ratio D_e/D_i is less than 1. The smaller-size mode is that of the particles in equilibrium. Particles yet smaller than this mode will move towards the breakers, while larger particles will move offshore. The larger-size mode occurs at the point where the fluid forces can no longer move the larger sizes.

If the ratio D_e/D_i is greater than 1 the tail of fine particles is cut off. A negative skewness in ϕ units results, because the particles larger than the incipient size will not be moved. The smaller

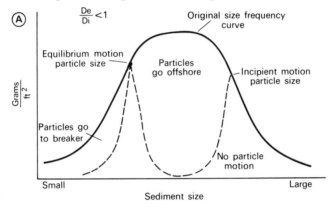

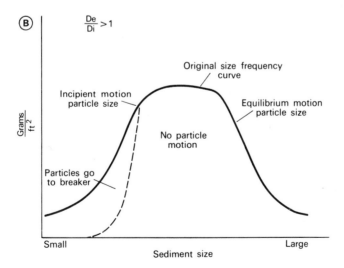

Figure 11-1 **A:** Theoretical sorting for incipient size smaller than the equilibrium size at a given beach position; **B:** Theoretical sorting for incipient size larger than the equilibrium size at a given beach position. (*A, B after Eagleson; Glenne and Dracup, 1961.*)

particles meanwhile will move towards the break-point. The size of both incipient and equilibrium particles becomes progressively larger from the toe of the beach towards the break-point. This means that sand beaches should become progressively coarser towards the break-point.

Sorting should also vary with depth, and should become progressively better in an onshore direction. The theoretical pattern is likely to be modified because of the weakness of the theoretical offshore motion. Observed values are even less than the predicted ones.

b   Model experiments

P. S. Eagleson *et al.* (1961) spread 50 gm of rounded silica sand over each square foot (0·093 m²) of experimental tank floor. Long waves were used that could move the sand in fairly deep water, and the waves were run for 139 hours. Sorting occurred most rapidly at the beginning of the run. Sand on either side of the breaker over a distance of 3·05 m was swept to the breaker zone and to the swash limit, leaving a clear bottom in between and offshore. The fine material moved to the swash limit and the coarse to the break-point. Very fine material was taken in suspension into deep water offshore.

The results of one of the runs agreed very well with theory. Two distinct peaks occurred at 0·15 mm and 0·59 mm. The sizes between 0·297 and 0·15 mm were probably in oscillating equilibrium in the offshore zone. Sizes between 1·19 and 0·59 mm were in the incipient size range for $D_e/D_i < 1$. The greatest differences occurred with the larger sizes. These decreased in frequency as the breakers were approached. This result can only be explained if $D_e/D_i < 1$, and if D_i is larger than the maximum size in the sample. In this case the larger sizes should move offshore. They were not, however, recorded in this position. Some other factor, not included in the theory, must account for this result. This factor is probably related to the influence of the breakers. There was, however, a slight increase in mean sediment size near the toe of the beach, agreeing with the theory. An increase of 30% was recorded in one run. The decrease of the mean size nearer the breaker is probably the result of sand being put into suspension near the breaker, where the large particles accumulate. They are removed in this way from the zones adjacent to the breaker. The degree of sorting of the samples became progressively better in the onshore direction.

T. Scott (1954) experimented with sand that was originally well sorted. Wave action caused differential movement of the grains, thus changing the median diameter in different parts of the tank. The coarser grains moved towards the water line, while the finer ones moved offshore. Superimposed on this sorting, the coarse grains collected on the crests of the break-point bars, while the finer grains collected in the troughs. The variation in grain size is shown in figure 11-2.

These changes could be related to the variation in orbital velocity, which was relatively great in the shallower water and over the bar crests, where the waves tended to break. The sorting of the grains of sand was influenced by the formation of ripples on the bottom. There is a correlation between the size of the sand and the horizontal amplitude of the orbital water movement.

The sorting of the larger particles between 0·5 and 0·9 cm in a wave tank has been described by R. A. Bagnold (1940). He found that on the shelf from the point where movement first started to the foot of the step, the particles became smaller in size. They reached a minimum at the base of the steep slope leading up to the step. The largest particles were found on the steep slip face below the step. The step itself, as far as half way up to the beach crest, was composed of particles of mean size. Towards the top of the upper beach the size again increased, the maximum-sized particles being found at the beach crest. Any finer particles among the shingle were removed to deeper water. The selective grading appeared to be confined mainly to the surface layer of pebbles, except at the top of the beach crest. There is a strong similarity between the grading in the tank and on natural shingle beaches.

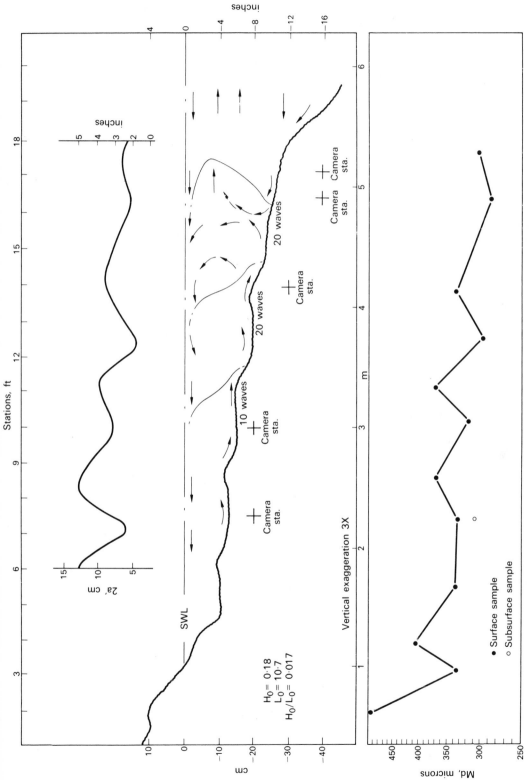

Figure 11-2 Horizontal amplitude of orbital water motion (2a'), water drift and variation of median diameter along the final profile. *(After Scott, 1954.)*

c Field observations

It is well known that on a beach of mixed sand and shingle the shingle is usually found at the top of the beach. This pattern agrees with the experimental data just described. It can be explained by the fact that shingle is only in suspension actually at the break-point and, therefore, progresses by rolling on the bottom. It is influenced by the differential velocity and moves landwards under the greater acceleration at the wave crests. The sorting of sand both on the foreshore and in the

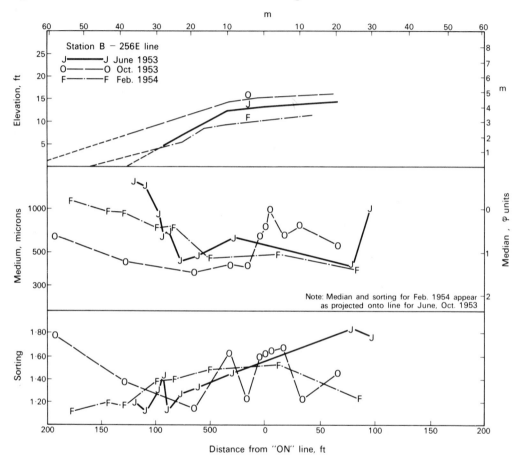

Figure 11-3 Beach slope and elevation, median diameter of sand and its sorting, for Abbotts Lagoon. (*After Trask and Johnson, 1955.*)

offshore zone is much more difficult to study, as it is only apparent after careful sampling and analysis.

Many sandy beaches, particularly if the sand is fine, do not show any marked variation of sand size with the seasons or with changing wave conditions. Some coarser sand beaches are, however, very variable both from place to place and from time to time. It is generally true that the particle size is larger where the wave energy is greater. This relationship applies both in space and time.

Detailed work on the variation of sand size with the seasons has been carried out by P. D. Trask and C. A. Johnson (1955) and P. D. Trask (1956) on the beach at Point Reyes, California (see figures 11-3 and 10-6). This is a variable beach facing the open ocean about 56 km northwest of San Francisco. Its variability makes it suitable for a study of this type. The range of grain size lies between a median diameter of 0·35 mm and 4·0 mm, although most of the samples lie between 0·56 mm and 0·77 mm (0·84 ϕ and 0·38 ϕ). The median diameter varies with the seasons. It is 0·77 mm (0·38 ϕ) in February, which is the maximum size, 0·710 mm (0·50 ϕ) in March, 0·62 mm (0·68 ϕ) in June, 0·67 mm (0·58 ϕ) in May, 0·65 mm (0·62 ϕ) in August, 0·56 mm (0·84 ϕ) in October, which is the smallest size, and 0·62 mm (0·68 ϕ) in December. These figures are for the period October 1955 to August 1956. They show that the finest sediments are found during the early autumn after the lower wave energy during the summer season. The coarsest sand is found on the beach during February, when the waves have the most energy.

In a consideration of the variation of sand size on the profile at any one time it was found that the finer sand is on the upper foreshore, with coarser sand on the lower foreshore, and on the crest of the berm. The lower foreshore receives more energy than the upper foreshore, which is at the limit of wave action. The coarse sand on the berm crest is probably due to the rapid percolation of the swash here, so that the backwash cannot carry the coarse particles down the slope. The winnowing effect of the wind on the berm crest may also play a part. This particular beach showed poorer sorting than most beaches.

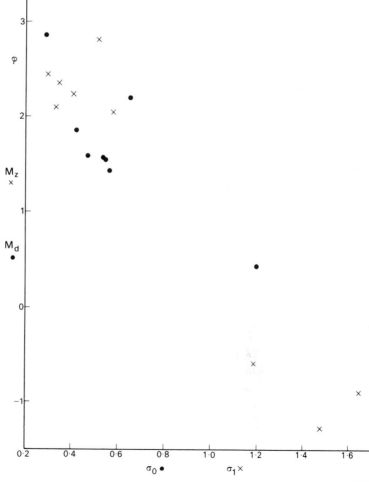

Figure 11-4 Relationship between sediment mean size and sorting for samples from western Irish beaches (dots) and from Gibraltar Point, Lincolnshire (crosses).

In general there appears to be a rather crude correlation between sorting and sand size, the finer the sand the better the sorting. The best-sorted sands tend to have median diameters of 0·15 to 0·20 mm. As the material becomes finer than this, however, its sorting deteriorates. It is significant that the best-sorted sand size is also that moved at the lowest velocities. An example of the correlation of size and sorting is shown in figure 11-4, on which mean and sorting of sand from a set of samples from Gibraltar Point, Lincolnshire, and some west Irish beaches are shown.

The variation of sediment size in deeper water has been studied by D. L. Inman (1953) and P. D. Trask (1955) in various localities along the coast of California. The latter has taken 175 bottom samples from depths of 24·4 m and less in the area around Point Arguello, Conception and Dume (see figure 10-6). The samples taken in the offshore zone showed that the median diameter decreased consistently with depth. For all profiles the sand between 0 and 12·2 m had a

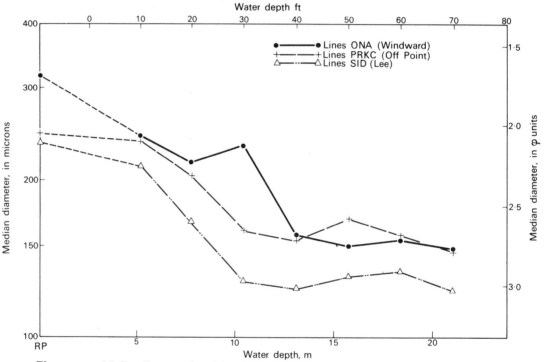

Figure 11-5 Median diameter of sand in relation to water depth and exposure. (*After Trask, 1955.*)

median diameter average of 0·165 mm (2·60 ϕ). Between 12·2 and 24·4 m the diameter varied between 0·145 and 0·150 mm (2·80 and 2·74 ϕ). The seaward decrease of grain size was at the rate of 0·02 to 0·05 mm per 3 m depth increase between 3 m and 9·15 m. Between 9·15 m and 18·3 m the sand size was nearly constant, while in greater depths it decreased in size at the rate of 0·005 to 0·015 mm for every 3 m increase in depth.

The effect of the wave energy on the sand size on the foreshore is also shown by the decrease in median diameter from 0·311 mm (1·70 ϕ) on the windward beaches to 0·273 mm (1·89 ϕ) off the Points and 0·239 mm (2·07 ϕ) in their lee, where the wave energy was reduced by refraction. The values for the three different exposures in the 6·1 to 12·2 m depths were 0·179 mm (2·48 ϕ) windward beaches, 0·173 mm (2·53 ϕ) off the Points and 0·139 mm (2·85 ϕ) in their lee. For the 12·2 to 24·4 m depths the figures were 0·149 mm (2·75 ϕ), 0·154 mm (2·70 ϕ) and 0·130 mm (2·95 ϕ) respectively. These values are shown in figure 11-5.

A detailed study of the variation of the beach and offshore sediments at La Jolla has been reported by D. L. Inman (1953), who found that the sediments are aligned in zones parallel to the shore, each zone having distinctive properties. A beach zone, surf and shelf zone and slope zone were differentiated. Inman found an area of coarser sediment and heavy mineral concentration at the edge of the shelf in depths of 18·3 to 27·4 m. This may be related to tidal scour at the major break of slope, or perhaps to the convergence of long-period waves or surf beat. It may also represent relict sediment belonging to a low glacial sea level (D. J. P. Swift, 1970).

Inman gives the following types: (1) beach and foreshore, with diameter of 0·165 mm (2·60 ϕ), best sorted; (2a) surf zone, coarse and poorly sorted, size 0·203 mm (2·30 ϕ), which grades into (2b)—surf zone and shelf to 30·5 m, size 0·105 mm (3·25 ϕ), well sorted, very fine sand with less than 3% silt, (3) slope, size 0·072 mm (3·80 ϕ); this zone shows an increasing amount of silt.

Experiments carried out by diving in the Black Sea are reported by V. P. Zenkovich (1946). These illustrate the effect of waves in sorting material that is out of equilibrium with the rest of the bottom sediment. A mixture of dyed sand of equal quantities of the following grain sizes was placed between marked stones at a depth of 6 m. Sizes were 7–5 mm, 5–2·5 mm, 2·5–1·0 mm, 1·0–0·5 mm, 0·5–0·25 mm, 0·25–0·1 mm and less than 0·1 mm. The waves during the experiment were 80 to 120 cm high and their period was five seconds. Samples were taken every 11 minutes after the placing of the material on the bottom at distances of 1 m and 3 m on either side of the original strip. The results showed that some of the larger grains moved shorewards while the finer ones (0·5–0·25 mm) tended to move offshore. The grains of size 1·0–0·5 mm appeared to be more or less in equilibrium. They were close to the size of the natural sand, which had a median diameter of 0·6 mm. Zenkovich also (1967) quotes observations by Leont'ev who studied changes in sand size off the shallow beaches of the north Caspian Sea. Some of the beaches showed a marked increase in material size between 1000 and 2000 m offshore; on some size decreased progressively offshore, while on others it increased steadily offshore in size.

W. T. Fox *et al.* (1966) have analysed the variation in the first four moment measures of samples of sand along a profile normal to the shore at South Haven, Michigan. The profile covers the backshore zone, the berm, foreshore, break-point, nearshore zone, a submarine bar and the offshore zone. There is a close parallelism of the four moment measures. The mean is fine in the backshore zone and on the berm. It rises sharply to give coarse material under the break-point. It then falls to the same fine size, with only a very small increase offshore, until the submarine bar is reached. The material again becomes coarser on the bar. The finest sizes occur in the offshore zone. The sorting is almost exactly similar, with the poorest sorting at the break-point and on the submarine bar. The skewness is negative throughout the profile, with the exception of the plunge-point samples. The highest negative skewness values were found between the break-point and the submarine bar, on which the skewness becomes rather smaller, but remains negative. The highest kurtosis values are also in the area between the break-point and the bar. The values are small, approximating to normal, on the foreshore, berm and submarine bar.

During his observations with fluorescent tracers, J. C. Ingle (1966) made useful observations on the sorting of material off the Californian coast. The presence of irregularities on the profiles complicates the sorting pattern. His observations were mainly made inside the surf zone, where ripples are absent and high-velocity flow is characteristic. Sheet flow probably only affects a layer a few grains thick, except immediately under the plunging breakers and in the swash surf boundary zone. The upper layers of water move shoreward in the surf zone, but there is a seaward return flow in the bottom layers. There is a general tendency for the larger grains to move towards the zones of greatest energy, which is the breaker zone. The swash surf transition zone is another area of high energy. In the swash zone gravity plays an important part in sorting grains on a coarse beach. Coarse lag deposits form at the foot of the swash slope. Even on shingle beaches there is a tendency for pebbles to move to the break-point.

Where rip currents are common, bands of coarser particles are likely to occur on sand beaches. These bands perpendicular to the shore will also be less well sorted. Complications occur on tidal beaches through migration of the swash and breaker zones with the tide. Variations in wave dimensions will also mean that the ideal theoretical sorting will rarely have a chance to be fully developed in nature.

An experiment was made with different sized tracers on Trancas Beach. Grains over 0·50 mm were dyed green and those less than 0·50 mm were dyed red. The mixed sand was released half way between the breaker zone and the swash zone. Eight samples were collected every four minutes for 34 minutes, beginning two minutes after injection. Both fine and coarse grains moved away from the release point in all directions. Longshore current velocity was less than 30 cm/sec, so that onshore–offshore movement predominated. The finer grains on average moved away from the release point more than twice as fast as the coarser grains. The larger ones moved first offshore and alongshore but after 16 minutes the movement was mainly onshore. The finer grains moved in both directions. After 4 minutes the coarser grains had moved mainly offshore and the finer mainly onshore. The offshore movement of the coarse grains was probably caused by their approach to the high-energy breaker zone. Once in motion their greater momentum allowed them to move faster. Their movement was probably aided by the seaward return flow and gravity.

Another test was made by Ingle (1966) on the same beach with sand coarser than 0·25 mm dyed one colour and finer than this another. The median diameter of the coarse sand was 0·351 mm and of the finer 0·168 mm. The mixed dyed sand was released at six points on the beach under fairly heavy surf conditions. Maximum breaker heights exceeded 2·24 m, and the longshore current velocity was 46 cm/sec. The median diameter of the sand on the foreshore–inshore zone was 0·219 mm, the size increasing to 0·340 mm just landward of the break-point. After 20 minutes grains of the finer size dispersed rapidly in all directions, but mainly alongshore. Coarser grains moved rather more slowly and mainly diagonally offshore. After 45 minutes the finer grains appeared to be oscillating in the surf zone and moving mainly alongshore, while the coarser grains moved mainly onshore–offshore. The strong surf had more or less completely dispersed the marked sand after 105 minutes.

A further experiment using bi-coloured sand was made under 1·16 m high waves of 11 second period, with a mean longshore current of 30 cm/sec. Grains finer than 0·25 mm moved primarily alongshore, while the coarser grains moved on diagonal offshore vectors to the breaker zone. The sizes present on the beach at the time of the experiment showed finer grains on the foreshore-inshore slope and coarser ones at the break-point. Each of the marked grain sizes moved towards the zones in which that size was in equilibrium. The results, therefore, suggest that the absolute grain size does influence its direction of movement, each size seeking the zone in which it is in equilibrium. This would account for offshore movement in many tests.

2 Sorting of material parallel to the shore

The sorting of sediment normal to the shore appears to be related to the type of water movement and to the distribution of energy. It has already been suggested that variation in energy is partly responsible for variations in size parallel to the shore so that now specific examples of this effect will be described.

One very good example of lateral sorting of sand is described by W. N. Bascom (1951) in Half Moon Bay in California. This bay is protected at its northern end from the prevailing northwesterly swell, while the southern end of the bay is fully exposed to the waves. The differences of exposure are reflected in a continuous decrease in particle size from the exposed southern end

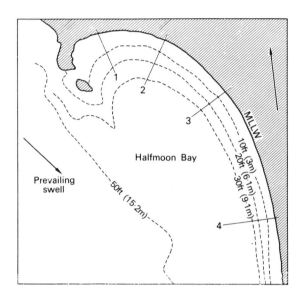

Figure 11-6 Half Moon Bay, California, showing position of samples. (*After Bascom, 1951.*)

to the sheltered northern end of the bay. Four samples from the positions shown in figure 11-6 were taken at mid-tide level on the beach. They had the following diameters from south to north along the bay respectively, 0·65 mm (0·63 ϕ), 0·39 mm (1·37 ϕ), 0·20 mm (2·31 ϕ), and 0·17 mm (2·56 ϕ). The finer sand accumulates in the area where refraction reduces the wave energy to a minimum.

A very striking example of the lateral sorting of shingle is found on Chesil Beach in Dorset. This beach extends from Bridport in the west to Portland in the east and is 28·8 km long. For the eastern 19·2 km of its length it is separated from the coast by the Fleet, as shown in figure 11-7.

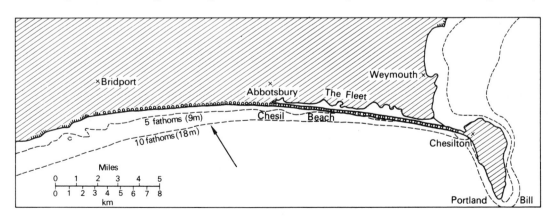

Figure 11-7 Map of Chesil Beach.

The beach becomes wider and higher towards the east. At Abbotsbury, where it leaves the land, it is 155 m wide and about 7 m above high water, while at Portland it is 183 m wide and nearly 13·1 m high. Throughout its length the beach is made of shingle which varies in size from pea-sized at Bridport in the west to large shingle about 6 cm in diameter at Portland. At Abbotsbury the stones are about 1·25 cm in diameter.

Various views concerning the development of this beach have been put forward (J. Coode, 1853; J. Prestwich, 1875; V. Cornish, 1898). These need not be considered in detail. As yet there is no really satisfactory theory to account for the very even grading of the shingle. It is generally agreed that the main force causing the sorting of the pebbles is the waves. Chesil Beach is aligned however to face approximately the direction of approach of the dominant waves according to W. V. Lewis (1938). These come from the southwest and because they reach the beach more or less at right-angles, they do not cause significant lateral movement of material. A. Guilcher (1954) suggests that there are slight variations between the direction normal to the shore, that of the dominant wind vector and the maximum fetch. He gives the direction of maximum fetch as $224\frac{1}{2}°$. The direction of simplification of the beach, which is the resultant of these two factors, giving greater weight to the wind force, is $217\frac{1}{2}°$. The beach is not, however, quite straight and faces more to the south of southwest at the northwest end.

In general the beach is perpendicular to the approach of the dominant waves. The next longest waves come from the west of southwest. These waves would produce an easterly drift of material and would probably reach the eastern end of the beach with more energy than the western end. They would, therefore, tend to drift the larger pebbles towards the east. The smaller waves, generated in the English Channel, would come from a direction to the south of southwest and would be capable of moving the smaller shingle westwards. Lewis has suggested that these different waves are responsible for the sorting.

The relative heights of the beach at Abbotsbury and Portland indicate that waves are able to throw larger shingle to higher elevation at the east end, than the waves that can attack the central and western part of the beach. This suggests that the energy of the waves at the eastern end is much greater than that of the waves at the western end. It has already been shown that the largest particles tend to accumulate in the zones of greatest energy. There is no reason why this argument should not also apply to Chesil Beach. Deeper water occurs off the southeast end of the beach, which would help to concentrate the wave energy here as shown in figure 11-7.

Observations on Chesil Beach made by L. Richardson (1902) have suggested that pebbles larger than the average at any particular part of the beach move rapidly southeast under normal conditions, until they reach an area where the pebbles are of a similar size. A correlation of the distance along the beach with the size of the pebbles, derived partly from the values given by D. J. M. Neate (1967), gives a very high coefficient of correlation. The regression equation is $Y = 2·934 + 0·098 X$, for $n = 9$, and $r = 0·9929$. X is the distance from West Bay, Bridport, in km, and Y is the size of stones in ϕ units, using the positive rather than the negative, owing to the larger size of the material. The results are shown in figure 11-8B.

There is also a significant correlation for the relationship between the distance offshore to the 18·3 m (10 fathom) depth contour and the size of the pebbles. The regression equation is $Y = 5·6145 - 1·845 X$, $r = -0·9526$ for $n = 8$. Y is the pebble size and X is the offshore slope. The gradient is expressed as a cotangent of the slope and the value is thus large for a gentle slope and small for a steep one. The negative correlation shows that the size of the material is largest where the offshore slope is steepest, as indicated in figure 11-8A.

The gradient is related to the wave energy and size of shingle on Chesil Beach, so there appears to be a positive relationship here between wave energy and size of shingle. The same explanation

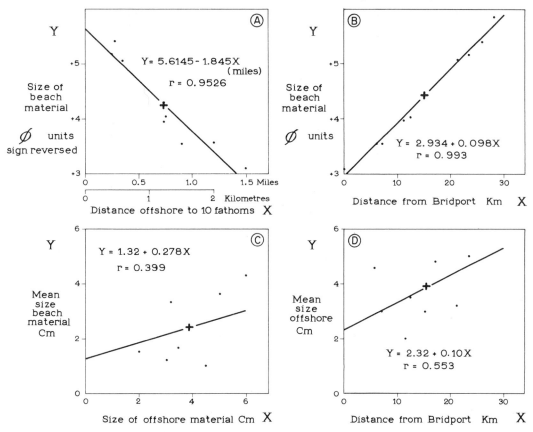

Figure 11-8 Graphs to show relationship between material size along Chesil Beach and other variables.

may be applicable to the grading of Chesil Beach as that applied to Half Moon Bay in California. Sorting can only take place so perfectly on a beach which is virtually a closed system. This applies to Chesil Beach, which is probably receiving little new material, and which has become adjusted to lie at an equilibrium orientation in relation to the wave regime that affects it.

Further data on the variations of pebble size on Chesil Beach have been collected by A. P. Carr (1969). Some points are significant in explaining the marked sorting along the beach. The eastern end of the beach is subject to the largest waves with maximum fetch, and wave height and direction of approach vary progressively along the beach. There are no coast defence works along the beach to restrict longshore movement. Little new material can reach the beach under present conditions and coarse material does not reach the beach from offshore as shown by the under-water investigations of D. J. M. Neate (1967). The pebbles consist of 98·5% flint and chert above the low-water mark. Of the remainder 90% are quartzite.

The beach was sampled by A. P. Carr at half-mile intervals at the eastern end, where the rate of change of size is greater, and at one-mile intervals at the western end. Samples were taken on the beach crest, and at high-water and low-water mark between three and 11 sites being sampled at each of the 17 points along the beach. A total of 89,000 pebbles were measured in 1965. Thereafter monthly samples were taken until July 1966. A series of boreholes was also sunk through the beach. Each sample normally consisted of 500 pebbles. The long and short axes and

309

the weight were recorded. Only the long axis was recorded in the later samples, because there was a close correlation between the long axis, the short axis and the cube root of the weight.

All the high-water samples were unimodal, but they had a tendency to a negative skewness. They were well sorted on the whole. Some of the low-water samples were bimodal. A few of those on the backslope seem to belong to a different population, and are not associated with present conditions. They do not appear to have been washed over the beach crest during storms. Immediately landward of the main crest the sorting is less good owing to the occasional throwing of larger pebbles over the crest during storms, and the little opportunity for sorting in this position. The size of the stones on the ridge crest was smaller in 14 out of 23 sites than the high-tide samples, but at no site were the smallest stones on the beach crest. On the whole the variation down the beach was small.

A. P. Carr's measurements show a rapid decrease in size from east to west at the eastern end, but with a steady decrease continuing all the way to the western end of the beach at high-water level. The correlation between the size of the underwater pebbles, as given by Neate, and the distance along the beach is not high. There is little evidence of an underwater size increase in the opposite direction to the high-water level pebbles, as was suggested by J. Coode (1853). A. P. Carr's sampling shows some slight irregularities along the beach, due to removal of pebbles at some points and addition of weaker pebbles near the western end. He suggests that some of the irregularities are due to wave refraction under storm conditions.

The pattern of pebble-size variation has been very constant over a period of more then 50 years. A comparison of the pebble sizes recorded by V. Cornish in 1897 with those of Carr in 1965 shows remarkable agreement. This indicates that alignment is not affected by infilling with pebbles of a different size. If the alignment of the beach were changing, alterations of pebble size would be expected.

The variations in the size of low-water samples indicate that the processes causing the high-water level sorting are not operating at low-tide level. Finer material is more often found at low-water level, except when destructive waves have combed down the coarser material from higher up the beach. Bimodal samples were often recorded during the monthly sampling at low-water level for this reason. The variation of the high-water samples month by month showed that changes are the result of different wave conditions. The boreholes showed that finer material underlies the coarse at the beach crest at a level corresponding to the high-water mark. This material resembles the finer material at present at low-water level. Most boreholes showed pebbles as well as sand at depth, but the pebbles tended to be more angular and to contain a larger proportion of limestone. The greater roundness of the modern beach pebbles is most likely due to progressive rounding by attrition.

The remarkable grading of Chesil Beach is thus to a large extent due to the relict nature of its material and to its alignment, which prevents vigorous longshore movement. The variation of wave energy along its length is also significant.

Blakeney Point is a shingle feature on the north coast of Norfolk, which makes an interesting contrast to Chesil Beach. The sorting of pebbles on this spit has been studied by J. R. Hardy (1964). Observations showed that shingle on the beach moved in both directions according to the direction of the wind and wave approach. The shingle on this beach is also a fossil mass, which is not being added to substantially under present conditions. It increases in size from west to east. The mean size at the western end was 1·5 cm, while at the eastern end at Sheringham it was 4 cm. The range in size is thus fairly small, and suggests that there is no permanent longshore movement of shingle along this stretch of coast, although the eastern movement may predominate slightly over the western. The eastern end is rather more exposed to the largest waves coming from the north or northeast, and the energy reaching this end of the spit would be rather higher. It is also possible that if the larger pebbles moved faster than the smaller, then these would be expected to reach the eastern end as this is the predominant direction of movement in a nearly balanced system.

Sorting is much less in evidence on Orfordness in Suffolk. This spit is subject to very rapid longshore movement of shingle under suitable conditions. The movement along it was discussed in chapter 10.

Summary

Theoretically sorting normal to the shore should result from the asymmetry of flow velocities under waves in shallow water. The movement depends on the size of the particle. An incipient motion particle size can be distinguished from a particle size that is in equilibrium according to the depth of water. Sorting should vary with depth, becoming better as the water becomes shallower. Sand beaches should become progressively coarser towards the break-point. Model experiments on the whole confirmed the theoretical findings, but in some respects the results differed. On some natural beaches there was a seasonal variation in sand size, the material being coarser after the stormier conditions of the winter months and finest after the calmer summer conditions. Field observations also showed a decrease of material size with increasing depth off-shore. Material was coarser in the zones where energy was greatest, particularly at the break-point. Observations with tracers showed that finer grains of sand moved faster than the larger grains. Sand grains tended to move towards those of the same size into an equilibrium position.

It seems that good sorting parallel to the shore can only occur where longshore movement is restricted and the amount of material on the beach is static. The material can then move to that part of the beach where it is in equilibrium with the prevailing conditions. This will apply both to sorting normal to and parallel to the shore. The most marked sorting occurs where the variation in wave energy is greatest in both directions of sorting. Thus it seems the most important element that accounts for the sorting of the beach material is the energy of the waves. The coarser material is associated with the zones of highest energy. The energy is related to variations in the character of wave motion in transverse sorting. The longshore distribution of energy in the swash–surf zone is responsible for longshore sorting of material.

Chesil Beach in Dorset displays the most perfect sorting on any shingle beach in Britain. The material becomes coarser towards the southeast end of the 29 km long beach. The beach is aligned to face the direction of approach of the dominant storm waves from the southwest. There is a positive correlation between the steepness offshore (indicating greater wave energy on the beach) and the size of material. Blakeney Point in Norfolk shows somewhat similar but less well-developed sorting, the eastern end having the larger material. This is also the more exposed part of the spit.

References

BAGNOLD, R. A. 1940: Beach formation by waves: some model experiments in a wave tank. *J. Inst. Civ. Eng.* **15,** 27–52.

BASCOM, W. N. 1951: The relationship between sand size and beach face slope. *Trans. Am. Geophys. Un.* **32**(6), 868–74.

BRUNN, P. 1962: Tracing of material movement on sea shores. *Shore and Beach.* **30,** 10–15.

CARR, A. P. 1969: Size grading along a pebble beach: Chesil Beach, England. *J. Sed. Petrol.* **39**(1), 297–311.

CARR, A. P. and BLACKLEY, M. W. L. 1969: Geological composition of the pebbles of Chesil Beach, Dorset. *Dorset Nat. Hist. and Arch. Soc.* **90,** 133–40.

CARR, A. P., GLEASON, R. and KING, A. 1970: Significance of pebble size and shape in sorting by waves. *Sediment. Geol.* **4,** 89–101.

COODE, J. 1853: Description of the Chesil Bank, with remarks upon its origin, the causes which have contributed to its formation, and upon the movement of shingle generally. *Minutes Proc. Inst. Civ. Eng.* **12,** 520–57.

CORNISH, V. 1898: On the grading of the Chesil Beach shingle. *Proc. Dorset Nat. Hist. and Antiq. Field Club* **19,** 113–21.

EAGLESON, P. S., GLENNE, B. and DRACUP, J. A. 1961: Equilibrium characteristics of sand beaches in the offshore zone. *B.E.B. Tech. Memo.* **126.** (66 pp.)

FOX, W. T., LADD, J. W. and MARTIN, M. K. 1966: A profile of the four moment measures perpendicular to a shoreline, South Haven, Michigan. *J. Sed. Petrol.* **36**(4), 1126–30.

GUILCHER, A. 1954: *Morphologie littorale et sous-marine.* Paris. Translated by Sparks, M. N. and Kneeze, R. H. W. as *Coastal and submarine morphology,* London: Methuen.

HARDY, J. R. 1964: The movement of beach material and wave action near Blakeney Point, Norfolk. *Trans. Inst. Brit. Geogr.* **34,** 53–69.

INGLE, J. C. 1966: The movement of beach sand. *Devel. Sediment.* **5,** Amsterdam: Elsevier, 86–100.

INMAN, D. L. 1953: Areal and seasonal variation in beaches and nearshore sediments at La Jolla, California. *B.E.B. Tech. Memo.* **39.**

IPPEN, A. T. and EAGLESON, P. S. 1955: A study of sediment sorting by waves shoaling on a plane beach. *B.E.B. Tech. Memo.* **63.**

JOLLIFFE, I. P. 1964: Experiment designed to compare the relative rates of movement of different sizes of beach pebbles. *Proc. Geol. Assoc.* **75,** 67–86.

LEWIS, W. V. 1938: Evolution of shoreline curves. *Proc. Geol. Assoc.* **49,** 107–27.

MILLER, R. L. and ZEIGLER, J. M. 1964: A study of sediment distribution in the zone of shoaling waves over complicated bottom topography. In Miller, R. L. (Editor), *Papers in marine Geology: Shepard commemorative volume,* New York: Macmillan, 133–53.

NEATE, D. J. M. 1967: Underwater pebble grading of Chesil Bank. *Proc. Geol. Assoc.* **78,** 419–426.

PRESTWICH, J. 1875: On the origin of the Chesil Bank, and on the relation of the existing beaches to past geological changes independent of the present coast action. *Minutes Proc. Inst. Civ. Eng.* **40,** 61–114.

RICHARDSON, N. M. 1902: An experiment on the movements of a load of brickbats deposited on the Chesil Beach. *Proc. Dorset Nat. Hist. and Antiq. Field Club* **23,** 123–33.

SCHIFFMAN, A. 1965: Energy measurements in the swash-surf zone. *Limnol Oceanog.* **10,** 255–260.

SCOTT, T. 1954: Sand movement by waves. *Inst. Eng. Res.* Univ. of California: Wave Research Lab.

SWIFT, D. J. P. 1970: Quaternary shelves and return to grade. *Mar. Geol.* **8**(1), 5–30.

TRASK, P. D. 1955: Movement of sand around southern Californian promontories. *B.E.B. Tech. Memo.* **76.**

TRASK, P. D. 1956: Change in configuration of Point Reyes beach, California, 1955 to 1956. *B.E.B. Tech. Memo.* **91.**

TRASK, P. D. and JOHNSON, C. A. 1955: Sand variations at Point Reyes, California. *B.E.B. Tech. Memo.* **65.**

ZENKOVICH, V. P. 1946: On the study of shore dynamics. *Trudy. Inst. Okeanologie* **1,** 99–112.

ZENKOVICH, V. P. 1967: *Processes of coastal development.* Steers, J. A. (Editor), Edinburgh: Oliver and Boyd, 101–11.

12   Beach profiles

Summary

In the first part of this chapter the results of experiments in a model wave tank on the nature of beach profiles, and the factors influencing their form, are considered. In the second section natural beach gradients and in the third section beach profiles are discussed. The types of profiles and their variability through time are considered.

1 Experimental results—beach profiles

The effect of different waves and other variables on the laboratory beach profiles will be considered first. Then the two main types of profile will be described and the factors on which they depend assessed.

a   The effect of the material

In some of his experiments R. A. Bagnold (1940) used material that would be the equivalent of shingle in nature, according to his ratio R = H/d, where H is the wave height and d is the diameter of the particle. The profiles he obtained agreed closely with the known features of shingle beaches. His model beach profile showed a step at the break-point of the waves. This feature is common in nature, and a shelf often occurs below the step. The size of the material he used varied between 7 and 0·5 mm. The model shingle beaches were built with the coarser particles.

A wave tank in which the effect of different sizes of sand could be studied has been described by G. M. Watts (1955), G. M. Watts and R. F. Dearduff (1954), and R. L. Rector (1954). The tank used was 25·9 m long and 4·3 m wide, being divided longitudinally into four equal parts each 1·03 m wide. Different-sized sand was placed in each section, the median diameters for the first three sections being 0·22 mm, 0·46 mm, and 3·44 mm. The fourth section contained a mixture of the two coarser sands, with a median diameter of 1·22 mm. It was found that the finest sand was the most mobile, and most sensitive to different wave conditions. This is the reverse of what would be expected for the shallower depths in nature, but may well apply to the deeper water outside the break-point, where some of the changes recorded in the wave tank were taking place. Coarser beaches in nature are more mobile than fine beaches landwards of the break-point. This is due to the steeper gradient associated with coarser beaches. In the tank the initial gradient of 1 in 20 was the same for all sands.

R. L. Rector found that, for any specific wave dimension and steepness, there was a greater tendency for the beach material to move shoreward as the grain size of the material increases. It was also found by Watts that the finer sand of 0·46 and 0·22 mm produced more conspicuous bars than the coarser sand. This finding agrees with observations in nature. Watts, however, considered that at least some of the bars may have been due to reflection of waves from the beach at the top of the tank. It appears that reaction in the tank is broadly similar to that of natural beaches of similar material.

b Effect of wave characteristics and tide

Many model experiments on the formation of beach profiles have shown that the most important wave characteristic in determining the type of profile is the wave steepness. With steep waves a so-called 'storm' profile is formed, while flat waves produce a 'summer' profile. The experiments discussed in section 9-2 on the transport of material inside and outside the break-point, helps to explain this fundamental difference. Steep waves transport sand seaward inside the break-point, and landward outside it. This pattern must result in an accumulation of sand at the break-point, forming the break-point bar, which is one of the distinguishing features of the storm profile. With flatter waves it has been shown that material is moved landwards in all depths. There must, therefore, be an accumulation at the limit of wave action. The accretion associated with summer profiles can be explained in this way.

The value of the critical wave steepness which determines which profile will form, varies somewhat in different experiments. Rector and Watts both state that waves flatter than 0·016 will produce the summer profile. The experiments described in section 9-2 showed that the critical steepness was about 0·012. It is likely that these variations depend partly on the size of the material. The higher values were found with the coarser material.

Watts examined the effect of slight variations in the wave period in the formation of the beach profile. The variations were of 10% and 30% covering periods of ten minutes to one hour in a total test time of 40 hours. The results showed that the 10% change had little effect on the profiles, which differed little from the standard test with uniform period. The 10% variation in period did show some reduction in the formation of bars, while the 30% change nearly eliminated them. Changes in wave period of 25% caused a 62% change in the wave steepness. This change was probably responsible for variations in the formation of the bars.

Watt also made a series of tests to show the effect of variation in water level in simulating the effect of a tide. The tidal range used was 15 cm and 7.5 cm. The former was the same as the wave height 4·6 m from the generator. Both steep and flat waves were used. The greater tidal range was found to increase the amount of material moving, but decreased the size of the bars.

c Break-point bars—storm profiles

Two main types of profile develop in sand depending on the steepness of the waves. Steep waves produce a storm profile, characterized by a bar at the break-point of the waves. Because this feature depends on the position of the break-point, it is called a 'break-point' bar. Experiments have been made to examine their character in the tank illustrated in figure 2-3. The bars form at the break-point of steep waves, where the sand moving landward outside the break-point meets the sand moving seaward inside the break-point (figure 12-1).

The crest of the bar never grows above the water level, but the bar reaches a specific equilibrium size. The initial formation of the bar is easily explained, but it is less easy to explain why it does

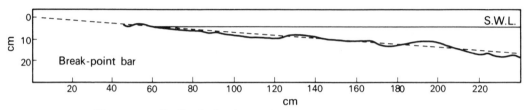

Figure 12-1   Profile of a break-point bar formed in the model wave tank.

not continue to grow above a certain height. The effect of the bar on the action of the waves is probably responsible. When the bar reaches its maximum height it deforms the waves breaking on it, so that they tend to reform landwards of the bar. They can now apparently move the sand landwards inside the original break-point. The surplus sand is moved landwards onto the beach across the bar trough. In one experiment the bar reached maturity after about 30 minutes, but the water continued to deepen outside it after this time. Deposition was meanwhile taking place landward of the break-point on the foreshore despite the continued high value of wave steepness in deep water. The bar moved inland, owing to the increase in the water depth outside it, which caused a landward shift of the break-point.

(*i*) *Wave height:*   The position and height of the break-point bar depends on the position of the break-point, which is closely related to the height of the waves (see section 4-1(g)). The depth in which the wave breaks is a function mainly of the wave height. The higher waves will produce a larger bar in deeper water.

There is also a very close relation between the position of the bar on the profile, primarily determined by the wave height, and the height of the bar crest above the original profile. Figures 12-2 and 12-3 illustrate the relationship. There is a constant ratio of 1 in 2 between the height of the bar crest above the original profile and the depth of water over the bar. Figure 12-3 also shows that this ratio is independent of the beach gradient, which varied from 1 in 10 to 1 in 20. If the form of the original profile and the position of the bar is known, it is possible to establish the depth of water over the bar crest from this relationship. The depth of water over the bar crest is also clearly related to the wave height, because this determines the position of the bar crest on the profile. If the wave height at break-point is known, it is possible to deduce the depth of water over the bar crest. If this can be shown to apply to natural beaches the relationship can be of considerable value in some circumstances, such as the landing of boats on barred beaches where there is a danger of grounding.

(*ii*) *Wave length:*   The wave length does not itself appear to be an important variable in the formation of a break-point bar. It is important, however, in relation to the wave height as this determines the wave steepness.

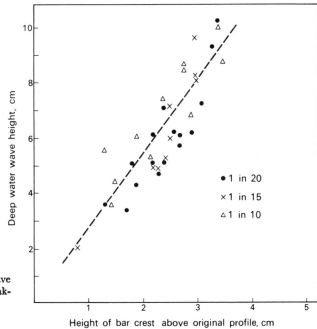

Figure 12-2 The relationship between wave height and the height of the crest of the break-point bar above the original profile.

Height of bar crest above original profile, cm

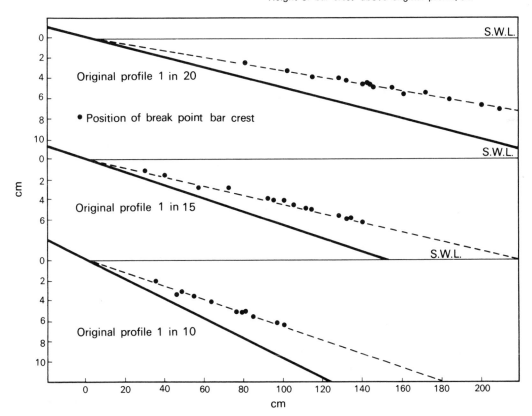

Figure 12-3 To show the ratio of the depth of water over the bar crest in relation to the height of the crest above the original profile.

(*iii*) *Wave steepness:* The fundamental importance of the wave steepness has already been discussed. It determines whether a break-point bar will form or not, and affects the ratio of the trough depth to crest height of the bar—the steeper the wave the greater the depth of the trough landward of the bar in relation to the height of the crest from the original profile. The ratio of trough depth to crest height varies from 1·4 for a steepness of 0·0265 to 0·4 for a steepness of 0·013 on an original gradient of 1 in 15. The ratio is unity for a steepness of 0·022.

(*iv*) *Beach gradient:* The position and height of the fully formed break-point bar is independent of the beach gradient. This variable is important, however, in relation to the wave steepness. It determines, for one sand size, the critical steepness at which the bar will form as shown in figure 12-4. As the gradient becomes steeper, so the critical steepness of waves which will form a

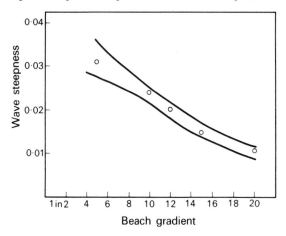

Figure 12-4 Relationship between beach gradient, wave steepness and break-point bar formation. The upper line gives the approximate steepness at which the break-point bar is fully formed. The lower line indicates the steepness at which the break-point bar first forms.

break-point bar increases. For a gradient of 1 in 5 the steepness must exceed 0·034, but for a gradient of 1 in 20 the steepness need exceed only 0·0115. The latter is a fairly flat wave which will not form a fully developed bar trough. The variation in critical steepness, given by different workers, may be partly explained by this factor.

(*v*) *Change in wave size:* Because the break-point bar is dependent on the wave height, a change in its dimensions will affect the position and character of the bar. A large wave will form a bar in deep water. If the wave size is suddenly reduced, without decreasing the steepness below the critical value for the conditions obtaining, a second smaller bar will be formed landward of the first, at the break-point of the smaller waves. The smaller waves are unable to cause any very great change in the larger bar to seaward. This now comes under the action of unbroken waves, where the movement of material is landward, so there is a very slow landward shift of the large bar crest. If the larger waves now attack the beach again, the smaller bar will be rapidly destroyed, and the sand moved seaward onto the larger bar (see figure 12-5).

A slow change in wave height will cause a bodily migration of the bar in the direction of the change of wave height. An increasing wave height will move the bar seawards, as the waves break in deeper water, while a decreasing wave height will move the bar landwards.

(*vi*) *Change in water level:* The effect of a change in water level is similar to that of varying wave size because it also alters the position of the break-point, if the wave height remains constant. With a continually changing water level, as on a tidal beach, a break-point bar will never have

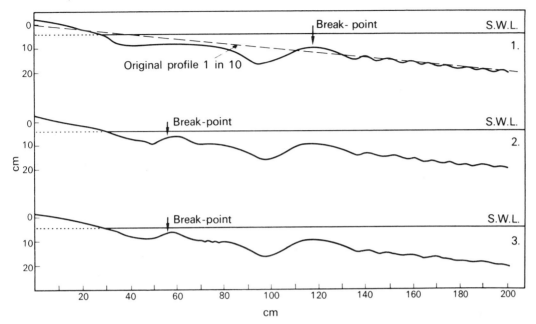

Figure 12-5 Profiles to show the formation of two break-point bars: **1:** Wave height 9 cm, length 240 cm, run 10 minutes; **2:** wave height 3·7 cm, length 88 cm, run 10 minutes; **3:** same waves as **2,** run 10 minutes.

time to form fully. A bar formed at low-water level will not be disturbed if there is a rapid rise of level. The change will be similar to a reduction in wave height. If the change is slow enough the bar will move forward with the break-point.

If the water level starts to fall after a mature bar formed it is completely destroyed by the time

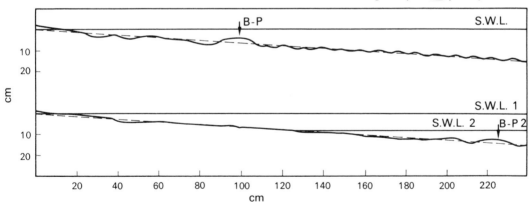

Figure 12-6 The effect of a falling water level on a break-point bar.

the water level falls below the original position of the bar. The area where the waves were pre-viously breaking now comes under the action of the swash and backwash, and their action destroys the bar. The results of experiments showed that a break-point bar cannot remain above the water level with a falling tide (see figure 12-6).

It can be concluded that the break-point bar in the tank is dependent on the stability of the break-point for its formation and can only form where the wave steepness is above the critical value for the conditions. The application of these results to full-scale beaches is considered in section 12-3(b).

d Swash bars—summer profiles

The flat waves which produce a summer profile in the wave tank will form a bar if conditions are suitable. This feature is in every respect different from the break-point bar already discussed. It is called a 'swash' bar, as it is formed in front of the break-point, by the action of the swash and backwash. It has been shown that flat waves move sand towards the land in all depths both outside and inside the break-point (C. A. M. King and W. W. Williams, 1949). The sand must accumulate at the top of the beach where it forms the swash bar. A bar of this type, unlike the break-point bar, can be raised above the still-water level and up to the limit of the swash. A profile of a typical swash bar is shown in figure 12-7. This was built on a beach having an original gradient of 1 in 20 by waves 3·7 cm high and 512 cm long, giving a steepness ratio of 0·007. The sand had a median diameter of 0·41 mm. After a period of ten minutes sand had begun to accumulate landwards of the break-point. A slip slope facing landwards had formed after 11 minutes at the angle of rest of sand in water. It formed where the advancing sand was pushed over the growing accumulation of material. The position of the slip face was 20 cm seaward of

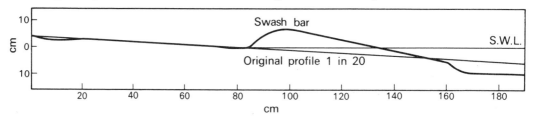

Figure 12-7 A typical swash bar formed in a model wave tank.

the original water line. Once the slip face had formed the growth of the bar was rapid. After 37 minutes it had grown above the still-water level, nearly to the limit of the swash. The continued deposition of material by the swash on the bar crest led to the elevation of the crest above the normal limit of the swash. The bar was now permanently above the level of wave action and extended across the tank. After a period of 45 minutes, when the profile was drawn, the bar crest was above the swash throughout its width. Landwards of the bar a deep lagoon formed, in which the still-water level was appreciably above that in the main part of the tank, as long as the waves were running.

The bar crest in this particular example was 7 cm above the still-water level, while the wave forming it was only 3·6 cm high in deep water. The landward slope of the bar was steep, at the angle of rest of sand in water. The seaward gradient varied with the size of the wave that formed the bar, and will be discussed in sections 12-2(b) and (c). The position of the break-point is indicated by the abrupt change of gradient at the foot of the swash slope. Outside this point 5 cm of sand had been moved landwards, the amount decreasing offshore.

(i) Wave steepness: Again wave steepness is fundamental to the formation of a swash bar. It must be lower than the critical value for the conditions. The wave steepness also influences the amount of accretion. The ratio of crest height above the original profile to deep-water wave height increases as the wave steepness decreases. A flatter wave is thus considerably more constructive, in proportion to its height, than a steeper wave. In this experiment the original gradient was 1 in 15 and the runs were continued until stability was reached.

(*ii*) *Wave height:* The height of the wave exerts an important influence on the height of the mature swash bar as it determines the limit of the swash on the beach. Figure 12-8 illustrates the relationship between the deep-water wave height and the height of the crest of the swash bar above the still-water level. It shows that the two amounts increase together at an almost linear rate for any one wave-steepness value on a beach gradient of 1 in 10. The greater energy of the larger waves enabled their swash to extend further up the beach, thereby building a higher swash bar.

(*iii*) *Wave length:* The variation of wave length causes a change in the gradient of the swash slope, a relationship that will be examined in section 12-2.

(*iv*) *Beach gradient:* A swash bar will only form if the original gradient of the beach is less than the gradient built up by the swash of the waves in their constructive action. However flat the

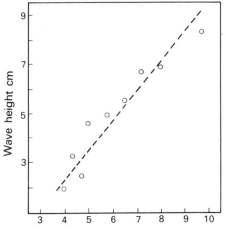

Figure 12-8 The relationship between wave height and the height of the swash bar above still water level.

waves, they could not build up a swash bar on a gradient of 1 in 2. If the original gradient is very flat, on the other hand, the swash bar is built to a considerably greater height above the original profile, for any given wave height and steepness, than on a steeper profile. The swash bar is also formed further seaward and a wider lagoon results, the lowest point of which is further below the still-water level than it is on a steeper original gradient. The bar forms a much more conspicuous feature as the original gradient becomes flatter.

(*v*) *Change in wave type:* A change in the size of the waves that does not alter their steepness ratio will not produce a very marked effect on the bar. If the waves are decreased in size the bar will remain little altered. If they are increased in size the bar will be raised in height because of the greater vertical reach of the swash of the more powerful waves.

If the waves are changed to steeper ones, which are destructive on the swash slope, the bar will undergo erosion. This change of wave type was examined experimentally, the results being shown in figure 12-9. A swash bar was formed by waves of steepness 0·006 on an original gradient of 1 in 20. These waves were 3·2 cm high and had a period of 1·8 seconds. They built a swash bar to a height of 6 cm above the still-water level after 5 hours 15 minutes. The waves were then reduced in length, to increase their steepness, and were allowed to attack the mature bar for 1 hour. Their destructive action is shown by a considerable reduction in the volume of the swash bar.

Beach profiles

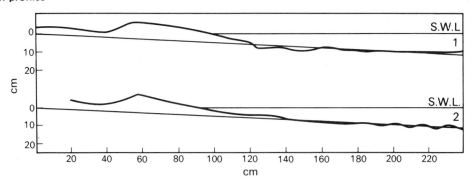

Figure 12-9   The effect of steep waves on a swash bar. **1:** Wave height 3·2 cm, length 504 cm, run 5 hours 15 minutes; **2:** Profile after one hour of wave action by short steep waves.

Owing to their shorter length, however, they were not able to wash over the bar, the position of which remained unchanged.

(vi) Change in water level: The effect of changing water level on the swash bar was also investigated in the wave tank. The effects of both rising and falling water levels were examined. A bar was first formed with a very low water level. The waves were then stopped and the level raised 13 cm. At the new level waves of a similar deep-water height formed a bar at the top of the beach in 40 minutes. During this time the former bar, now deep under the water, was not disturbed by the waves as its crest was covered by 8 cm of water. The water level was then slowly lowered 6 cm to an intermediate position and a third bar formed. During the fall in level the uppermost bar was not disturbed by the falling water level. Waves at the intermediate level, however, affected the lowest bar, as the depth of water over its crest was only 2 cm. The first bar was ·elongated and pushed forward, but it did not lose its height or identity. The experiments showed that swash bars may exist at or above the water level and also below the water level. In this latter position their form is likely to be modified, as they are affected by different processes.

   It has thus been shown that two very different types of bars can be formed in the wave tank and that they require opposite wave characteristics. The break-point bar can never extend above the still-water level. The essential feature of the swash bar is the fact that it is built above the still-water level at the limit of wave action. One type of bar does not develop into the other. They are not merely two stages in one process, but two different features.

e   Time to reach equilibrium in a model tank

The rate at which equilibrium profiles are formed in a wave tank is of interest in assessing the effect of different waves acting on beaches in nature for relatively short periods of time. From the experiments that have been described it can be seen that the general character of the profile becomes apparent after the waves have been acting on it for only a short period of time. After only 30 minutes a well-formed swash bar could develop. A considerably shorter period of time was required for the growth of a break-point bar to its maximum height above the original profile. These profiles had not reached a state of static equilibrium, however. Slow changes continued throughout most of the profile.

   T. Scott (1954) has recorded the progressive changes in a beach profile over a period of 450 minutes. Figure 12-10 shows a graph of the rate of change of the profile in terms of volume of sand moved per unit time. Although no precise volumes could be given, the graph does show the relative rate at which the profile changes with time. The total net change is shown as curve 1, the other curves show various parts of the profile. The foreshore and inshore areas are shown on curve 2, the area around the break-point bar is shown on curve 3, and 4 and 5 cover the middle and far offshore zones respectively. The rate of change is most rapid in the breaker zone, while the break-point bar is forming. When the profile of the bar is mature, greater changes take place in the nearshore zone inside the break-point. The curve for total movement, where the time is plotted on a logarithmic scale, shows that the rate of profile change decreases steadily with time.

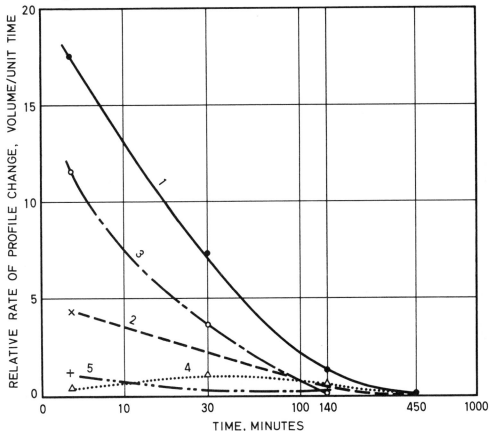

Figure 12-10 The rate of change of beach profiles with time. (*After Scott, 1954.*)

The rate is logarithmic for about the first 50 minutes. Thereafter the change is at a slower rate and becomes very small after 140 minutes, practically ceasing after 450 minutes or $7\frac{1}{2}$ hours.

The changes were brought about by changing the waves to a higher steepness value. The steepness was 0·041 and the waves were modifying a profile previously built by waves of steepness 0·017. The flatter waves had acted on the beach for 44 hours, when slow changes in the profile were still in progress. The changes suggest that late in the formation of a profile the rate of change does not reach zero, but instead begins to increase again. This may be due to standing waves in the experimental wave channel.

Even in the controlled conditions of uniform waves in a model tank complete equilibrium is rarely completely reached. It is, therefore, much less likely that equilibrium is ever reached in nature. Natural waves are more complex, and additional variables, such as the tides and winds and irregular coastal configuration, increase the number of variables. Perfectly formed bars of the types described are unlikely to be found in natural conditions. Nevertheless, it is possible to equate the bars described with natural features (see sections 9-3(b) and (c)).

2 Beach gradient

The gradient of a beach in the swash zone depends mainly on three variables. These are the size of the beach material, the length and steepness of the waves. These three variables affect both natural and model beaches.

a   Size of material

Shingle and coarse sand beaches are much steeper than those of fine sand. Steep beaches allow wave energy to be absorbed over a relatively narrow zone, and they are, therefore, more mobile. Before the effect of material size on natural beach gradient is considered, the results of model experiments will be mentioned.

R. A. Bagnold (1940) has recorded the gradients of beaches formed of three different sizes of material. He refers to the angle that a line joining the beach crest to the top of the steps makes with the horizontal. He states that the beach angle depends only on the size of the grains composing the beach, and was independent of wave height. The gradient was 22° for a size of 0·7 mm, 19·5° for 0·3 mm and 14° for a finer material of 0·05 mm. Experiments carried out by R. D. Meyers (1933) also show that the coarser of two sands formed the steeper beach slope. The sands had diameters of 0·368 mm and 0·472 mm. They showed a consistent difference of gradient on a logarithmic scale. The different sands did, however, produce quite a variety of gradients under different wave conditions. Meyers measured the tangent of the angle of slope at the water line.

The Beach Erosion Board in their Interim Report of 1933 show that there is an increase of gradient with increasing material size on beaches along the coast of New Jersey. The relationship was linear, ranging from a gradient of tan 0·15 for a median diameter of 0·50 mm to a tangent of about 0·06 for a median diameter of 0·20 mm. W. N. Bascom (1951) has given further evidence of this relationship from observations on the coast of California. He takes the gradient of the beach at mid-tide level. The range of diameters found on the beaches he measured are given in the following list:

Gradient	Median diameter in mm
1 : 90	0·17
1 : 82	0·19
1 : 70	0·22
1 : 65	0·235
1 : 50	0·235
1 : 38	0·30
1 : 13	0·35
1 : 7	0·42
1 : 5	0·85

This relationship is shown in figure 12-11, in which the minimum probable slope for any size of material is given. Half Moon Bay shows very clearly the relationship between foreshore slope and sand size. In the sheltered part of the bay the size is finer and the gradient correspondingly less. Four points in the bay are shown in the figure to illustrate this correlation.

The gradient of shingle beaches is considerably steeper than that of sand beaches. Slopes of between 1 : 2 and 1 : 3 have been recorded on Chesil Beach near Abbotsbury. This is about the maximum beach gradient that waves can build up, and the beach is not always so steep.

The cause of the decrease of slope with decreasing grain size is the variation of the percolation rate through the beach material. Coarse shingle is very permeable and a large proportion of the advancing swash sinks into the beach, and the backwash is reduced correspondingly in volume.

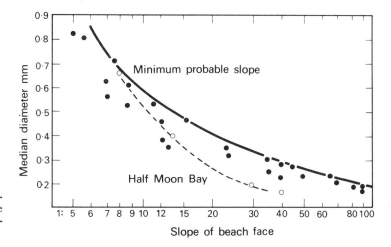

Figure 12-11 Relationship between beach slope and sand size from observations made in California. (*After Bascom, 1951.*)

On a fine sand beach only a relatively small volume of swash is lost by percolation, owing to the much-reduced permeability. The volumes and force of the swash and backwash are more nearly equal in this instance. The force of gravity, which is proportional to the slope, tends to equalize the force of the swash and backwash. When the two are very different, as they are on a shingle beach, the slope must be steep to render gravity more effective. On a fine sand beach the two opposing forces of swash and backwash are more equal. Gravity need not be so powerful and a flatter slope is formed.

b Wave length

The effect of wave length on the gradient of the swash slope has been studied both in model experiments and in nature. In order to eliminate the other variables the same sand was used throughout the model experiments and the waves were of constant steepness. Two series of runs were made. In the first the original gradient was 1 : 15 so that the waves, which had a steepness of 0·011, were constructive and built a swash bar. In the second series the original gradient was 1 : 2, which was steeper than the gradient formed by these waves. In one set, therefore, the beach was built up and in the second it was combed down. The results of the experiments are shown in figure 12-12. The relationship between wave length and gradient is linear, and for any one wave length similar gradients were produced whether the beach was built up or combed down.

Figure 12-13 combines the experimental data with full-scale observations made in the tideless Mediterranean Sea on the south French coast. The model sand had a median diameter of 0·41 mm and the Mediterranean beach sand one of 0.30 mm. The results show that there is a continuous linear relationship of the logarithmic scale between beach gradient and wave length covering the range of both model and full-scale observations.

Further observations were made at Marsden Bay, County Durham (C. A. M. King, 1953).

325

Beach profiles

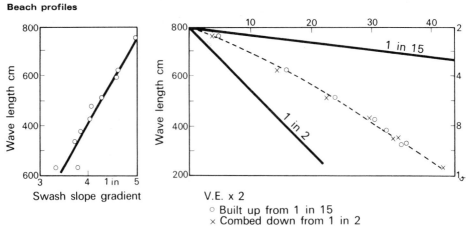

○ Built up from 1 in 15
× Combed down from 1 in 2

Figure 12-12   Relationship between beach slope and wave length in model experiments.

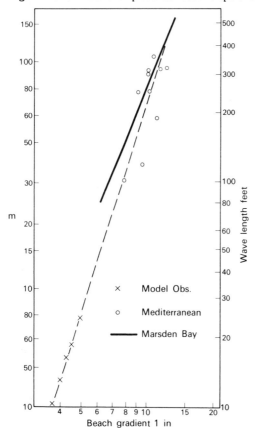

Figure 12-13   Relationship between beach gradient and wave length on natural and model beaches.

The results are shown in figure 12-14, in which beach gradient is plotted against wave period, which is directly related to wave length. There is a significant correlation of 0.56 between the variables. The sand in this bay had a median diameter of 0.37 mm at the north end and 0.35 mm at the south end. The scatter of points is due to the impossibility of controlling the other variables during observations. The other variable that is important in this instance is the wave steepness, as the sand size remained more or less constant. The wave steepness can be controlled

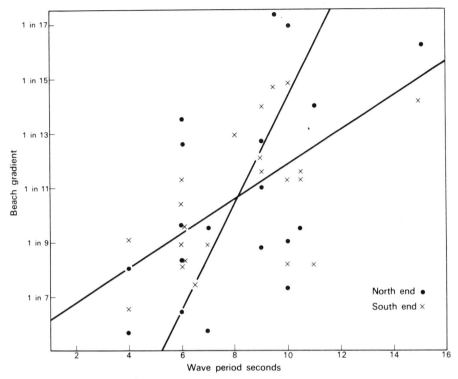

Figure 12-14 Relationship between beach gradient and wave period in Marsden Bay, Co. Durham.

by the statistical means of partial correlation, and this considerably improves the correlation between wave length and beach gradient.

The flatter gradient produced by longer waves cannot be explained by variations in the rate of percolation as the material size remains constant. If it is assumed, however, that a larger volume of backwash leads to a flatter gradient, then it can be argued that a larger wave will produce more swash and if the percolation remains constant, then the proportion of backwash will increase. The increasing proportion of backwash is responsible for the flatter gradient with the longer waves.

c   Wave steepness

A series of model experiments has been made by R. L. Rector (1954) on the equilibrium profiles of model beaches. In these he has shown that the slope of different parts of the beach depends on the material size. For any one size, however, it is related to the wave steepness. He gives the following equations to relate the wave steepness to the beach gradient. He defines the foreshore slope as extending from the crest of the break-point bar for steep waves or from the foot of the swash slope for flat waves. The equation he gives is

$$y_t/x_t = 0 \cdot 07 (H_0/L_0)^{-0 \cdot 42}$$

The foreshore slope above still water level has the equation

$$y_s/x_s = 0 \cdot 30 (H_0/L_0)^{-0 \cdot 30}$$

The values are derived from dimensionless log. log. plots of the data. The equations show that as the wave steepness increases so the gradient of the beach decreases. The median diameter of the sand was 0·22 mm.

The experimental work of R. D. Meyers (1933) shows the same relationship. He finds a straight-line correlation between the wave steepness and the tangent of the beach gradient at the water line. The tangent varied from 0·21 for a wave steepness of 0·008 to a value of 0·111 for a wave steepness of 0·080. The median diameter of the sand was 0·368 mm.

Experiments were carried out in a model tank in which the sand size and wave length were kept constant, but the wave steepness was varied. The sand size was 0·41 mm and the original gradient was 1 : 15. The range of gradients built up varied between 1 : 3·7 and 1 : 7·5. Figure 12-15 shows the relationship between the tangent of the angle of slope and the wave steepness to be linear. The line agrees fairly well with that of Meyers.

The relationship between beach gradient and wave steepness has been observed also on natural

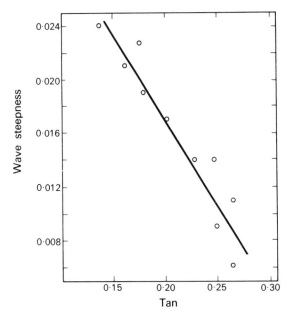

Figure 12-15 Relationship between wave steepness and the tangent of the angle of beach slope in the model wave tank.

beaches of both sand and shingle. The swash slope of Chesil Beach in Dorset has been observed to have a gradient of 1 : 4 or steeper under normal conditions of fairly flat waves in calm weather. As the result of a storm, during which steep storm waves attacked the beach, the gradient was flattened to 1 : 9, by removal of shingle.

The surveys made on the sand beach at Marsden Bay also illustrate this relationship. The profiles in figure 12-16 show one instance when the gradient was steepened by the action of flat constructive waves. Other profiles illustrate the flattening of the slope by the action of steep storm waves. A cliff of sand was cut by the destructive waves, but below this the gradient was considerably flattened by the swash and backwash. F. P. Shepard (1950) has published profiles at the beach at Cape Cod that also illustrate the effect of steep storm waves on the gradient of the beach. These are reproduced in figure 12-17. The steep waves, by moving sand seawards from the upper beach, reduced the mean gradient above sea level.

Similar reasoning explains the cause of the variation of beach gradient with wave steepness. For all three variables the proportion of the swash volume to that of the backwash will change as

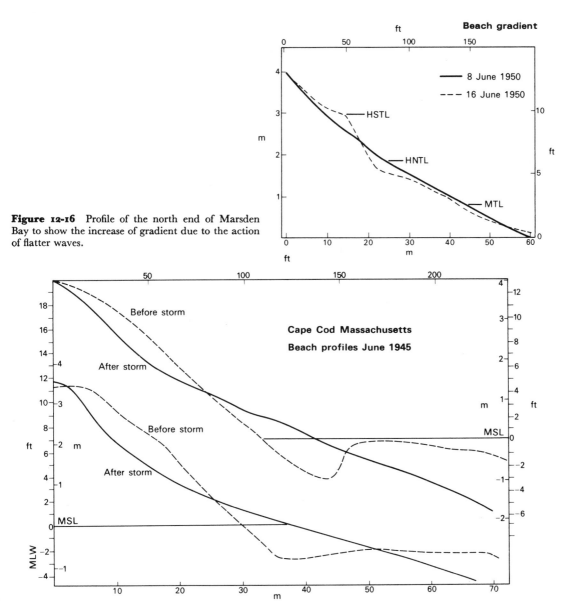

Figure 12-16 Profile of the north end of Marsden Bay to show the increase of gradient due to the action of flatter waves.

Figure 12-17 Profiles of the beach near Cape Cod to show the decrease of gradient resulting from the action of storm waves. The removal of the ridge near low water level by storm waves is also shown. (*After Shepard, 1950.*)

the variables alter. If the steepness is varied by changing the wave height, as was done in the model results illustrated in figure 12-15, the wave length will remain constant. The period of the swash and backwash will, therefore, be the same in each run. The volume of the swash will, however, increase with increasing wave steepness. If the percolation volume is constant, the proportion of backwash will increase. This leads to a flatter gradient.

d The equilibrium gradient

Beach gradient has been shown to vary with at least three different variables, the sand size, the wave length and steepness. An analysis to assess the relative importance of these and other variables has been made. The results were obtained from observations on 27 beaches in widely varying conditions. The variables tested were foreshore gradient, material size in ϕ units, sand sorting, the tidal range and a measure of exposure. The fetch distance adjusted for the orientation relative to the dominant waves was used as a measure of energy reaching the beach in terms of its exposure. The data were analysed by simple, partial and multiple correlation. The simple correlation matrix and the significant results of the partial and multiple correlations are shown in

Table 12-1   Correlation between beach gradient and other variables

(a) SIMPLE CORRELATION COEFFICIENT MATRIX

	Slope	Size	Sorting	Tide	Energy
Slope	1	*0·840*	−0·148	0·301	0·313
Size		1	−0·311	0·178	*0·489*
Sorting			1	0·023	−0·397
Tide				1	0·056
Energy					1

Correlations significant at 99 % confidence level are italicized

(b) PARTIAL CORRELATIONS (variable in brackets is the controlled one)

Significant at 99 %		Significant at 95 %	
Slope and size (sorting)	+0·845	Size and energy (slope)	+0·438
Slope and size (tide)	+0·838	Size and energy (sorting)	+0·419
Slope and size (energy)	+0·829	Sorting and energy (tide)	+0·399
Size and energy (tide)	+0·487		

(c) MULTIPLE CORRELATIONS (the first variable is correlated with the last two, all correlations are positive)

Significant at 99 %		Significant at 95 %	
Size—slope and energy	0·873	*Energy*—slope and sorting	0·473
Size—slope and sorting	0·861	*Slope*—tide and energy	0·423
Slope—size and tide	0·854	*Sorting*—size and energy	0·419
Slope—size and sorting	0·848	*Energy*—sorting and tide	0·402
Slope—size and energy	0·847	*Sorting*—tide and energy	0·400
Size—slope and tide	0·844	*Sorting*—slope and energy	0·398
Energy—size and sorting	0·553		
Energy—slope and size	0·520		
Size—tide and energy	0·512		
Size—sorting and energy	0·505		
Energy—size and tide	0·490		

table 12-1. The highest simple correlation is with sand size, while there is also a correlation significant at 99% between energy and size, but there is no significant correlation between beach gradient and tide, sand sorting or energy. The analysis confirms that material size is the most important variable affecting beach slope. This relationship is shown also by trend surface analysis using sand size and the energy values as the independent variables in relation to the beach gradient in the form of the logarithm of the cotangent of the beach slope. The linear surface accounts for 71·82% of the variability of the beach slope, the equation is

$$Z = +407·71 + 4·20U − 0·71V,$$

where U is the sand size in ϕ units, and V is the logarithm of energy and Z is the beach slope. The pattern of the cubic surface is shown in figure 12-18. It brings out the importance of sand size in controlling beach slope. The minimum gradient is associated with the finest material and the maximum value of wave energy or fetch. These are fine-sand beaches exposed to long swells in exposed situations. The greater wave length in these areas helps to reduce the beach gradient. At the opposite extreme are the steepest beaches where the size is greatest and the energy lowest. The beaches are in sheltered positions where waves will be short and hence the equilibrium gradient steeper.

The equilibrium gradient of any beach in nature is not a static slope, but one which will be continually tending to adjust itself to the changing variables on which it depends. On any one beach the material is usually more or less constant in size, although even this variable changes greatly from time to time on some beaches. Even on those beaches where it is constant, however, the equilibrium gradient is a dynamic one. The fact that wave length is important in determining the equilibrium gradient of a natural beach is significant in explaining the different types of beach profiles. The average wave length depends partly on the exposure of the beach. Where the beach is exposed to the open ocean, the average waves reaching it will be much longer than those reaching a relatively enclosed sea beach. Thus the dynamic equilibrium of the different beaches will fluctuate around a different mean point according to the mean material size and the beach exposure.

In his study of the coast of Jutland, P. Bruun (1954) showed that the beach profiles along this coast have tended to steepen during the period since erosion started. Recession was initiated by the artificial cutting of a channel through a barrier. The mean gradient of the beach to a considerable depth was measured. His results are not, therefore, directly, comparable with those already considered, which refer mainly to the swash slope gradient. Bruun used the 'stc' or 'steepness characteristic', which is found by dividing a specified depth by the distance of this specified depth from the shoreline, to record the increase in gradient. The stc has increased since the barrier was first breached. Its greatest value is given by stc $\times$ 10^3 = 13·5.

Bruun considers that there are three types of profiles. The first is overnourished, the second is sufficiently nourished and the third is undernourished. In the first type the profile is irregular, with shoals and bars, while the last two have a smooth equilibrium form. The importance of this distinction will be discussed in the next section dealing with the formation of different types of bars and ridges on the beach profile.

Laboratory studies of equilibrium beach profiles have been carried out by P. S. Eagleson, B. Glenne and J. A. Dracup (1961). The original beach profiles had a constant slope and the sands were well sorted. The study aimed to predict profiles in connection with their work on incipient motion and established sediment motion. These sediment motion characteristics were used to define predicted profiles for sand beaches. The profiles defined by means of the incipient motion criterion were far too steep. Only the established motion criterion was, therefore, used.

The slope for the established motion criterion is given by

$$\sin \alpha = K/Jf_1(d/L_0)$$

where K is proportional to the effective mass transport velocity for d/L_0; J is a coefficient associated with the wave and sand parameters; d is the depth, and L_0 the deep-water wave length. Four tests were carried out with varying wave steepnesses. The steep theoretical slopes suggest that the mass transport velocities are not so large as those predicted, a result that may be due to bed rippling, which reduces mass transport velocity. The profile depends on the relative positions of the incipient motion point and the equilibrium point; if the former lies offshore of the

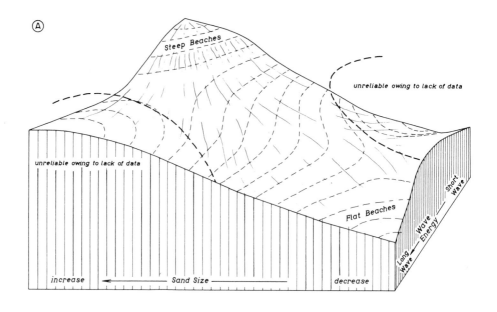

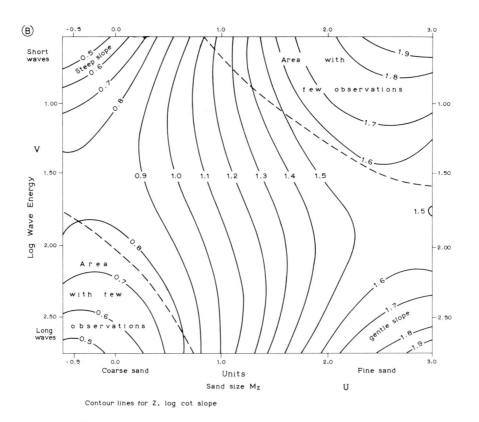

Figure 12-18 A and B: Trend surface analysis of the relationship between sand size, wave energy and exposure as the independent variables, and beach gradient as the dependent variable.

latter, the offshore area builds up. If the reverse applies, a flatter profile results from erosion. In the first three tests the incipient point was offshore of the equilibrium, indicating a building beach. In the fourth the reverse was true, resulting in an eroding profile. The results also agreed with the direction of movement suggested by previous work on wave steepness (see section 12-2(c)), except for the first test in which the profile was eroded rather than built up.

Some useful general conclusions emerged from the study. According to theory, the final gradient should be independent of the initial one, but the experimental results showed that this was not so. The theory does not predict the profile in the breaker zone. It was found that profiles for all four tests were very similar in the breaker zone. Eagleson *et al.* conclude, therefore, that the profile in the breaker zone is independent of the wave size and steepness, as well as the initial slope, over the range of variables tested.

The final foreshore profile was very similar for all tests, although the beach was slightly steeper for the lower wave steepnesses. The mean slope angle was 12°. The breaker exerts the main control over the profile in its vicinity, overshadowing other processes. The second important factor is the amount of material available for movement by the waves. This depends on the initial slope. When the breaker zone profile was stabilized, the offshore zone reached equilibrium only very slowly. Only local sediment was moved in the offshore zone, and none reached it from the breaker zone. The experiments ran for up to 222 hours, allowing plenty of time for equilibrium to be achieved at least in the breaker zone.

V. P. Zenkovich (1967) has discussed the theoretical formation of the equilibrium profile of a beach of uniform material. Sediment moves offshore seaward of the neutral line and onshore landward of it. This results in steepening of the profile both landward and seaward of the neutral line, with portions of flatter profile seaward of the steepened parts. These changes will cause two neutral zones that will spread from the upper and lower parts of the profile towards the initial neutral line. When these two zones merge the equilibrium profile will have become established. The equilibrium profile is steeper than the original uniform gradient near the water line, but flattens in a zone of erosion to a point seaward of the initial neutral line. Accretion at the offshore limit of movement continues the flattened profile beyond the zone of erosion. The form thus becomes parabolic. In producing these changes in the profile the waves are themselves modified by feedback relationships. These theoretical considerations only apply to ideal conditions of uniform material size and constant waves. In reality conditions will not be constant for long enough for the ideal profile to be formed. Nevertheless the profile will be affected by the type of sediment movement considered in relation to the wave-generated water velocities.

In considering the profiles of shingle beaches, Zenkovich (1967) states that the steepest part is at the water line, the slope flattening upwards where the beach forms a ridge. Where the shingle is banked against a cliff the profile is generally smooth. Sometimes shingle beaches with a backslope have a concave unit. This often occurs at the heads of bays. On a straight or slightly convex stretch of coast a convex unit is more common.

By contrast Zenkovich shows that sand beaches are flat and low, often having ridges that are unstable and rarely more than one meter high. Around mean water level the sand profile is generally concave, beyond which the slope steepens before flattening again as it extends out to deep water. A miniature shelf is formed when there is slight erosion, or the beach is being modified by smaller waves. Sand from offshore cannot move up the steep front slope of the shelf. Material on the flat upper part of the shelf is in equilibrium, merely moving to and fro.

The discussion so far has been mainly concerned with laboratory beach profiles, and the theoretical equilibrium profiles as well as some general remarks concerning the essential differences of shingle and sand beach profiles. The most striking difference is one of gradient, the shingle beaches being very much steeper than sand beaches, for reasons already discussed. Sand beaches, as well as being generally flatter, also have a much greater variety of profile. The different types of sand beach profile will be considered next, before the variability of any one beach profile is examined.

3 Beach profiles in nature

a   Smooth profiles

Beaches with a smooth profile may have a wide range of gradients depending on the three variables considered. Most smooth beaches do not have a straight profile, but one which approaches a parabola in form. The example shown in figure 12-19 illustrates this. The parabolic beach profile is partly due to the variation of material size perpendicular to the coast on a normal sandy beach. The coarser material tends to collect at the top of the beach, and as a result the slope is steeper here. The form of the profile allows the waves to break closer inshore at high tide, therefore, their energy at high water would be increased per unit width of beach. It has been shown that the coarse materials will tend to accumulate at the points of maximum wave energy. Thus once this shape of beach profile has been formed considerations of wave energy show that

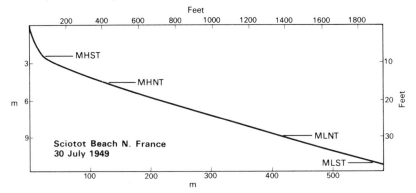

Figure 12-19   Profiles of smooth beaches, Sciotot, north France.

it will be likely to be maintained. It will be initiated by the landward movement under constructive waves, and the building up of the equilibrium swash slope gradient.

Another point that facilitates the development of a parabolic profile on a tidal beach is the relative time during which the different parts of the beach profile come under the influence of the swash and backwash of the waves. The upper part of the beach will come only under the influence of the swash and backwash. Further down the proportion of time of swash action will be reduced. The wave will, therefore, have less time to build up the steeper part of the profile, which is the swash slope.

Smooth beach slopes can have a very great variety of gradient. They range from gradient steeper than 1 : 2, which have been recorded on Chesil shingle beach, to a gradient of 1 : 90, recorded by W. N. Bascom (1951) on a very fine sand beach of median diameter 0·17 mm in Grenville Bay, California.

Smooth foreshore profiles are likely to occur where the tidal range is large and the exposure great. They are also more common where there is not a superabundance of beach material. Below low-water level the smooth profile continues offshore in many exposed areas. However, in some areas irregularities occur under water, forming bars parallel to the coast. They are more common in areas of restricted fetch and tidal range. These bars are considered in the next section.

b Submarine bars

The characteristic profile of a beach in a relatively enclosed tideless sea has a series of submarine bars. They are common for example in the Mediterranean, where work on them was intensified during the Second World War on account of landing operations undertaken in this area. Before considering the method of formation of these bars their characteristics and distribution will be described.

(*i*) *Character:* The term 'submarine bar' is used to describe these features because it indicates an essential fact of their character. They are never exposed above the water level and are most perfectly developed in tideless seas. The term 'longshore' bar, used by F. P. Shepard (1950), draws attention to the fact that they mostly lie parallel to the shore.

Submarine bars were mentioned by L. Elie de Beaumont (1845) together with other types of beach bars. Several German authors including G. Hagen (1863), F. P. W. Lehmann (1884), P. Olsson-Seffer (1910), G. Braun (1911), H. Poppen (1912), T. Otto (1911-12) and W. Hartnack (1926) all discuss the submarine bars of the Baltic and the coasts of Jutland. The bars of the Great Lakes of America have also been studied by I. C. Russell (1885), G. K. Gilbert (1890), and in more detail by O. F. Evans (1940), while more recent work has been done by G. H. Keulegan (1945, 1948) and F. P. Shepard (1950). Work in the Mediterranean was carried out by P. Cornaglia (1887), and during the 1939-45 war by W. W. Williams (1947) and subsequently by C. A. M. King and W. W. Williams (1949).

Most of these observers find that two or three parallel bars occur. Evans, for example, records three bars in Lake Michigan, covered at their crests by 1·22, 2·44 and 3·66 m of water. Poppen and Otto both show three bars on their surveyed profiles of the Baltic beaches. Surveys made in the Mediterranean in three successive years (1948, 1949 and 1950) on the south coast of France also show three bars. The profiles are shown in figure 12-20. The position of the bars varies from year to year. Profiles on the North African shore of the Mediterranean show only two bars, but a third may lie beyond the limit of the profile. There was 0·61 mm of water over the inner bar crest, while the outer one had between 1·93 and 2·44 m. The outer bar showed considerable movement over a relatively short period of six days.

Profiles of submarine bars, surveyed by F. P. Shepard (1950), on the coast of California show that the bars here are much less regular than those of tideless seas. In fact during the summer months they are frequently absent. In this region the tidal range reaches a maximum of about 2·44 m at spring tides, but is only 0·61 to 0·915 m at neap tides. Shepard notes that the bars tend to be higher during the periods of small tidal range at neap tides.

Some of the earlier authors suggest that the bars are the forerunners of barriers, notably Braun (1911) and Hartnack (1926). The latter considers that the submarine bars are transitory forms. Otto's (1912) observations revealed some of the important characteristics of the bars. He noted that there was no systematic landward movement of the bars, making it unlikely that they would become barriers above sea level. He also noted the importance of storm waves in altering the character and position of the bars, destroying some and building others. By associating the breakers with the bar crests, he led the way to the explanation of their formation.

(*ii*) *Distribution:* The description of the bars shows that they are best developed in areas where the tidal range is very small, for instance in the Mediterranean, the Baltic, parts of the North

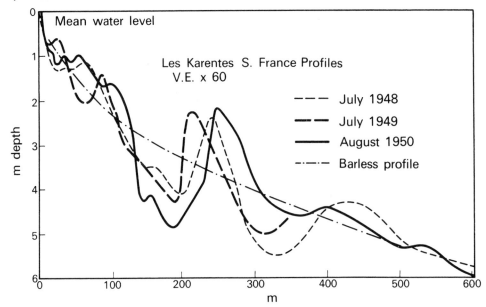

Figure 12-20   Profile of submarine bars, Les Karentes, south France.

Sea near the amphidromic point off Denmark, the Great Lakes of America and the Gulf of Mexico. Where the tidal range is larger, for example along the coast of California and the east coast of the U.S.A., the bars are not so well developed, nor are they always permanent features of the beach profile.

Their formation and disappearance is related to the different types of waves that affect the coast during the two seasons. Waves reaching the coast during the summer months, when the bars are often absent from the west coast, are long, low, constructive swells. In winter, when the bars are best developed, storm waves are more common. The distribution of the well-developed submarine bars is, therefore, partly dependent on the available fetch of the beach, which is related to the beach exposure.

(iii) Formation and movement: The formation of submarine bars on natural beaches may be compared with the formation of break-point bars in the wave tank. The break-point bars in the wave tank were formed at the break-point of steep waves. The relationship between the break-point and the position of the submarine bars of the Baltic has been pointed out by Otto (1912). This relationship was further stressed and amplified by Evans (1940) in his work on the bars of Lake Michigan. The conclusion is reached that the break-point bar in the model tank is the model equivalent of the natural submarine bar. The extent of the similarity will be considered.

In the wave tank a close correlation was found between the position of the break-point bar and the height of the wave forming it. The relationship between the wave height and the depth of water over the bar crest, which is partly a function of its position on the profile, has also been noted in some observations on submarine bars. It is shown by Evans (1940) and Keulegan (1945) as well as in the Mediterranean observations. Shepard discusses the same relationship. In California the bars tend to have deeper crests where the wave heights are larger. The scatter of data is probably due to the difficulty of measuring the particular waves that were responsible for the formation of the bar when the observations are not continuous.

The observations in the model tank showed that there was a constant ratio of 2 to 1 between the depth of water over the bar crest and the height of the crest above the original profile. If this relationship could be demonstrated to apply also to natural beaches it would be of value. The depth of water over a bar could then be established from its distance offshore and the gradient of the smoothed profile or 'barless' beach profile. This latter profile is formed by smoothing out the bars and is the natural equivalent of the original profile of the model experiments. It is shown in figure 12-20 that in general the same relationship between the bar crest height above the barless profile and the depth of water over the crest holds for natural beaches. The bar in the deepest water is an exception. This bar is probably not fully formed, owing to the extreme rarity of waves large enough to break on it.

It has been shown that there are usually two or three bars on any profile, but the number varies with changing wave conditions. The tank experiments also showed that two break-point bars could be formed on one profile if the small steep waves followed large steep ones. The same mechanism can account for the presence of several bars on the natural profile. The outermost bar is formed by the largest storm waves, which are large enough to break in this depth of water. The smaller bars, in shallower water, are formed by the intermediate-sized storm waves. The inner bar is formed by the short, steep waves that affect the beach much more often. They are generated by the sea breezes that often blow onshore during summer afternoons. Otto (1912) has pointed out that the largest storm waves break on the outer bar. Shepard's observations in California confirm that the steep, storm waves form the bars on this coast. The storm waves, in forming the outermost bar, destroy the inner bars, but these are rebuilt quickly when the waves return to more normal dimensions.

Zenkovich (1967) described profile changes in enclosed seas. During storms on sandy beaches the profile becomes very gentle and the wave energy is spread over a wide breaker zone. Submarine ridges form as the storm dies down and they move towards the shore to form terraces. The beach profile becomes steeper as a result. These changes have been recorded frequently from the suspended cable way at Anapa on the Black Sea, from which observations can be made during and immediately after storms.

Many observations have shown that the smaller inner bar is much more mobile than the outer bar (W. W. Williams and C. A. M. King, 1951). This is because the inner bar can come under the influence of the break-point of the waves much more often than the outer bars, which are only affected by the rare severe storms. That these outer bars are not affected by the smaller waves of normal weather was demonstrated in the periodic surveys carried out during a month in summer on the Mediterranean coast of France. Even the inner bar, which had about 0·915 m of water over its crest, was undisturbed by the waves. They were small during the period of observations and did not break on the bar during this set of surveys.

Other surveys carried out when the waves were breaking on the inner bar established that it moved in a similar way to the break-point bars in the wave tank (Williams and King, 1951). A slight increase in height caused a seaward shift of the bar crest, while a reduction in wave height caused the inner bar to move landwards. The profiles in figure 12-21 show the movement of the bar. The change in wave height affects the position of the break-point of the waves and hence the position of the bar crest. A greater change of this type was recorded by Williams on the African coast of the Mediterranean at Sidi Ferruch. As a result of a period of high waves, the bar moved seawards 35 m in 2 days. The crest of this bar was at a depth of 2·15 m and was originally 168 m offshore.

It was shown that the break-point bar was destroyed by a falling water level in the model experiments. This will help to account for the occurrence of well-developed submarine bars in

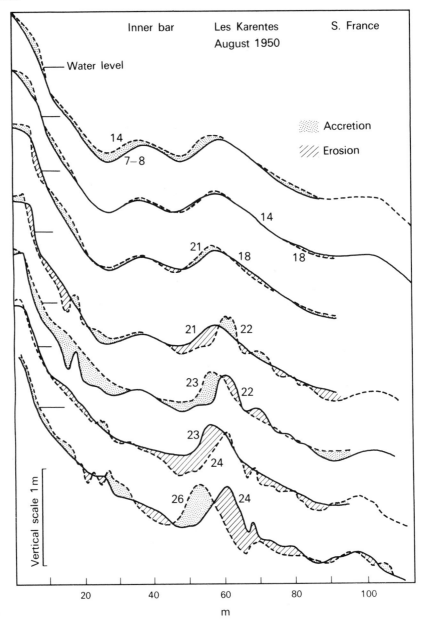

Figure 12-21 Movement of the inner submarine bar at Les Karentes in the Mediterranean Sea.

tideless seas. These depend on the constancy of the break-point of the waves for their formation. In a tideless sea this may be constant, but in a tidal sea the position must vary throughout the tidal cycle and bars formed at high tide would be exposed at low tide. The only position on a tidal beach where a submarine bar is likely to form is where the waves normally break at low tide. A bar in this position will be under the influence of the unbroken waves in deeper water when the tide is high.

The chief characteristics of the waves forming the break-point bars in the model tank was their destructive nature and high steepness value. The relationship of the natural bars with storm conditions, particularly the formation of the bars in deeper water, shows that they are also the result primarily of destructive storm waves. Submarine bars, therefore, result from the action of the steeper waves and form at their break-point. The flat, constructive waves, typical of the Californian coast in summer, have been shown to smooth out the submarine bars. Bascom (1953) has pointed out that there are two major types of beach profile dependent on the wave steepness. Submarine bars are characteristic of the storm wave profile, while flatter, summer waves form a berm above the water level.

(*iv*) *Crescentic submarine bars:*   Submarine bars normally lie parallel to the coast and are continuous from considerable distances. The bars, however, sometimes form a crescentic pattern in plan, with the points of the crescents facing towards the land. There may be two sets of crescentic bars, the inner ones having a shorter distance between the points of the crescents than the outer ones. No really satisfactory explanation of this type of submarine bar has yet been proposed.

C. J. Sonu and R. J. Russell (1967) have drawn attention to the great variability in the beach profile over short distances along the coast off the Outer Banks of North Carolina. Submarine bars and troughs are present, but their position fluctuates. Along one profile there will be a well-developed bar, while a few metres further along there will be no bar. The air photograph of the site shows that the bar pattern is crescentic, which would account for the pattern. The crescentic bars migrate along the coast, thus resulting in rapid profile changes at any one point. A movement of 15 to 24 m in 24 hours has been recorded by Egorov, and 1 km annually by Bruun. The crescentic form appears to develop where longshore currents are present.

Changes on the profiles could be divided into two types. Firstly, changes take place within each envelope, and secondly changes take place between envelopes. The first type occurred with normal wave approach and the second with oblique wave approach, indicating movement of the pattern alongshore. As the wave power increased the changes within the envelope increased and the profile became deeper. Changes between envelopes were not affected by variation of wave power, but by direction of approach. The profile deepened with a southerly approach and shallowed with a northerly one. In the normal wave approach the amount of material moved is given by $Q = 2 \cdot 1 H^{1/2}$, with H in m. Alongshore movement was several times greater than the transverse movement in volume. This pattern of large sand waves or crescentic bars is not uncommon on the Outer Banks.

Where crescentic submarine bars occur in bays along an indented coast it is possible that they are due to the interaction of two sets of waves approaching from different directions. Each set would tend to form a series of bars parallel to their crests. The interaction of the two sets might account for the crescentic pattern as illustrated in figure 12-22. Aerial photographs have shown that the pattern of submarine bars tends to move rapidly in position. Longshore movement of the crescentic bars may cause such changes, which would be much more apparent than similar movement of a straight bar.

c   Ridge and runnel profiles—parallel to the shore

On some tidal sand beaches the profile is made irregular by ridges lying parallel to the shore. They have been referred to by various authors under different names. V. Cornish (1898) and R. K. Gresswell (1937) have used the terms 'fulls' or 'balls' for the ridges and 'swale' or 'low' for the intervening depressions. They will be called ridges and runnels. The beach at Blackpool, where many surveys have been made, provides a good example of a ridged tidal beach. The

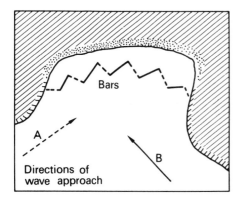

Figure 12-22 Diagram to illustrate a possible method of formation of crescentic submarine bars.

surveys on this beach were started during the 1939–45 war, as the beach is similar to the Normandy beaches on which landings were being planned. These observations were necessary as no detailed theory concerning the formation and movement of the ridges was then available. The ridges, which are covered at high tide, were a danger to landing craft, which might ground on the ridges while deeper water lay in the runnel to landward.

(*i*) *Characteristics:* The beach at Blackpool is composed of fine sand of median diameter 0·22 mm. The tidal range is considerable, being 7·64 m at spring tide. The width of the beach at low spring tide is 1220 m, giving an overall gradient on the foreshore of 1 : 150. The slope of the seaward faces of the ridges is, however, considerably steeper. It ranges from 1 : 32 near the top of the foreshore to about 1 : 60 near low-water level. The ridges tend to increase in size towards low-tide level, causing a conspicuous increase in the depth of the runnels. The one near neap-tide level is often 1·22 m deep. The runnels form outlets for the falling tide, which drains along them, cutting channels across the ridges at their lowest point.

A series of profiles were taken daily at Blackpool beach from March to August 1943, and thereafter weekly observations were made from December 1943 to October 1944, and at less regular intervals subsequently. The profiles, analysed by the author, showed that the positions of the ridges tended to remain more or less constant, as shown in figure 12-23. The most persistent positions of the ridges were at 21·4 m and about 305 m, 550 m, 854 m and 1035 m from the high spring tide level at the top of the beach. The corresponding heights of the ridges were 1·98 m O.D. (Newlyn), −0·915 m, −2·14 m and −3·66 to −3·97 m. The ridge at −0·915 m was least persistent. The mean heights compare closely with the mean tide levels, which are M.H.S.T. 3·74 m, M.H.N.T. 1·77 m, M.L.N.T. −1·86 m and M.L.S.T. −3·88 m. There is a correlation between the most persistent ridges and the positions at which the tide will stand for the longest period during the tidal cycle.

The ridges do not move systematically towards the shore, but they maintain their positions for long periods on this beach. This is because the ridges lie parallel to the coast, which is aligned perpendicular to the direction from which the dominant ridge-building waves come across the Irish Sea at this point. The ridges do, however, change position slightly from time to time, but more often one ridge dies out and another forms elsewhere. The 550 m ridge died out during the second period of observation and a new one formed further up the beach. The ridges tend to be removed during period of storm waves and onshore winds. Calm weather conditions, and particularly the swells following a storm, cause the ridges to build up. R. K. Gresswell (1937) also notes

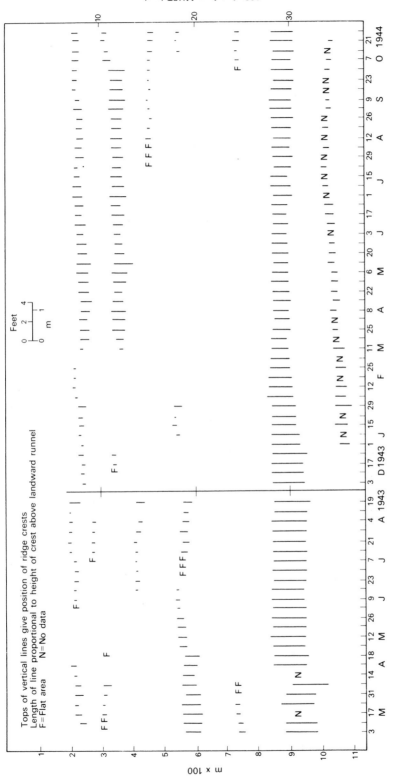

Figure 12-23 Diagram to show the position and movement of the sand ridges on the beach at Blackpool.

the effect of storms in reducing the height of the ridges and moving material seawards. The profiles shown in figure 12-24 illustrate the process.

The character of the beach surface is relevant to a consideration of the method of formation of the ridges. Nearly all the foreshore surface was rippled with the exception of the seaward faces of the ridges, which were composed of very firm, smooth sand. The ridge crests on the other hand were often of soft sand, which had not been firmly packed by wave action.

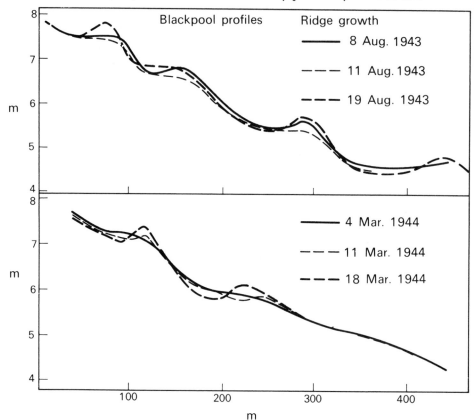

Figure 12-24 Profiles of Blackpool beach to show the growth and removal of ridges during March 1944 and August 1943.

(*ii*) *Comparison with model beach profiles:* A swash bar in the model wave tank is formed by constructive waves in front of their break-point. It is not, therefore, disturbed by a falling water level, and can exist above the water level. Ridges are exposed at low water on a tidal beach in a similar way. The two features have a similar form. Both have a steep landward slope, and the seaward slope is steep compared with the overall beach gradient. The smooth seaward face of the ridge is affected by the swash and backwash of the waves of the falling tide. This process is responsible for its smooth character and its gradient. The flattening of the seaward face during storms has been observed. This shows that the equilibrium gradient of the swash slope responds to the wave steepness as already discussed. The ridge, therefore, has the characteristics of a model swash bar, rather than those of a break-point bar.

Ridges are smoothed by steep destructive waves, but are built up by constructive waves, in the same way as swash bars in the wave tank. The main formative process in both features is the constructive action of the waves in building up the swash slope. On some ridge and runnel beaches a bar may exist below the low-water level. This bar must have the characteristics of a submarine bar.

(*iii*) *Distribution:* Ridge and runnel beaches have a fairly wide distribution. They are found where the tidal range is considerable, for example along parts of the Irish Sea and North Sea, parts of the Firth of Clyde. In the North Sea they occur in Druridge Bay in Northumberland, and along parts of the coast of Lincolnshire and of East Anglia. On the continental coast they occur from north Holland to Cherbourg. They are very well developed near Le Touquet in France and occur all along the Normandy coast. They extend along the east side of the Cherbourg Peninsula, but they are not found on the beaches on the west side of the peninsula. Nor do they occur on the foreshore of the southwest peninsula of England or in South Wales. The ridges and runnels on the coast between Dieppe and Ostend are briefly described by D. C. Pugh (1953). The runnels along some of these beaches penetrate to the clay and peat foundation of the beach. In all these areas the tidal range is considerable, reaching very high values in parts of the Irish Sea and in certain localities in North France.

The main point about this distribution is that the ridges are found on coasts not exposed to the open ocean. They cannot, therefore, be influenced by the very long swells characteristic of really exposed coasts. This distribution is illustrated by their presence on the east coast of the Cherbourg peninsula and their absence on the exposed west coast.

The importance of the exposure on the development of ridges is related to the equilibrium gradient which the waves will attempt to establish on the beach. Long waves produce flatter gradients than short waves, thus a beach that is exposed to long swells will have a flatter equilibrium gradient than one that is only worked on by waves generated in the restricted fetch of a small sea, such as the Irish or North Seas.

Not all beaches in the relatively restricted Irish or North Seas have ridged profiles. There must be an additional factor, therefore, which will also facilitate formation of ridges on the beach. The ridges develop where the overall gradient of the foreshore is much flatter than the gradient of the swash slope of the seaward side of the ridge. A surfeit of sand on the foreshore, which gives a flat overall gradient, appears to be necessary for ridge formation. This is one of the factors that accounts for the distribution of ridge and runnel beaches. In many places the extra beach material is glacial and fluvioglacial sand, deposited in the areas that now form the shallow waters of the offshore zone as a result of the post-glacial sea level rise. The work of J. Van Veen (1936) in the southern North Sea has shown that there is a superabundance of material in this area. The sand forming the ridge and runnel profiles in the northern part of the Irish Sea is also probably mainly derived from glacial deposits, which are sandy in this area. The deposits were laid down by the Irish Sea ice sheet.

Where there is not a surplus of sand on the foreshore the waves can maintain their equilibrium gradient throughout the beach. This will be achieved more easily in areas where the exposure allows very long waves to reach the beach, because, as has already been shown, long waves will produce a flatter beach gradient (section 12-2(b)).

Ridges and runnels on a sandy beach are the result of an attempt by the waves to produce an equilibrium swash slope gradient, suitable to their dimensions, on a beach the overall gradient of which is flatter than the equilibrium gradient. Even where the sand supply is not excessive, if the overall gradient of the foundation of the beach is flat, the sand available will be built into ridges. D. C. Pugh (1953) pointed out that the overall gradient of some of the north French beaches is very flat. At Walde just north of Calais, for example, the upper beach has a slope of

1 : 400 and is soft and muddy. On the lower part of the foreshore sand ridges and runnels have formed. The supply of sand is reduced here and the clay foundation of the flat beach is exposed in the runnels. The beach is suffering erosion at the present time. Pugh stated that there is relatively little sand on the bottom of the Channel in the vicinity of Calais, as it has moved back into the southern North Sea.

(*iv*) *Formation:*   Where waves are adjusting the gradient of the swash slope to suit their dimensions the process will continue most effectively where the waves are at specific levels for the longest period on a tidal beach. These levels will be the position of the mean low spring and neap tides, and the corresponding high-tide levels. The ridges may be expected to be most permanent and best developed at these positions, where the ridges are parallel to the shore. This has been shown to be true at Blackpool.

Another example is illustrated in the profile of the beach at Druridge Bay, shown in figure 12-25. The ridges are at positions in which the swash zone would lie at low neap and low spring tides respectively. On this beach the sand is much coarser than at Blackpool, having a median diameter of 0·40 mm on the two lower ridges. It is even coarser on the berm where the median

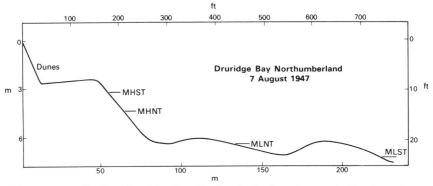

Figure 12-25   Profile of Druridge Bay, Northumberland, to show sand ridge formation.

diameter is 0·84 mm. The tidal range is 4·27 m at spring tide, so there is only room for two ridges to form. The coarse nature of the sand necessitates the formation of ridges because the equilibrium gradient is steep in this size of sand. Figure 12-17 illustrates an example from the east coast of U.S.A., where the level of the ridge is associated with the mean lower low-water level. The figure also gives a good example of the elimination of a ridge by destructive waves.

The initial profile may be assumed to be smooth before the ridges start to form on the foreshore. At low water the waves will expend their energy over a wide zone, owing to the flat gradient. If they are constructive they will deposit some of the sand they carry at the limit of the swash. This deposition will increase the gradient of this area, rendering the wave energy more effective, by concentrating it. The energy can now be used in building up the equilibrium gradient in the swash zone. The growing ridge will first be apparent as a flat area with a steeper seaward slope. This form was often observed in a study of the daily profiles of Blackpool beach. A new ridge was nearly always preceded by the development of a flat area. The flat area will reduce the efficiency of the water drainage from the beach as the tide falls. As soon as a slight runnel has formed, the water draining from the beach as the tide ebbs will cause erosion and deepening of the runnel. These stages in growth are illustrated in figure 12-24, taken from an example on Blackpool beach. A ridge is formed in this way at low-tide level. As the tide rises it quietly fills the runnel behind the ridge, eliminating the action of the swash from the runnels. This accounts for their rippled character. The continued rise of the tide allows the waves to break inland of the low-tide ridge. A new ridge will form where the swash again becomes effective. If this is the mid-tide zone the tide will be rising fast and the ridge will not have time to develop so fully as the low- and high-tide ones. Near the level of high neap and high-spring tide the process can again take place more effectively.

The smaller size of the upper ridges can be explained by the parabolic or concave shape of the overall beach gradient on Blackpool beach. The steeper overall gradient in the upper part requires a smaller ridge to produce the necessary steepening to achieve the equilibrium gradient. The difference between the overall and equilibrium gradients is less at the top of the beach than it is in the lower part. A larger ridge must be formed to produce the required steepening of slope on the lower foreshore. The increase in gradient of the seaward faces of the ridges towards high-water level is the result of the coarser sand accumulating near the top of the beach.

d   Ridge and runnel profiles—ridges at an angle to the shore

On some beaches the ridges are not parallel to the shore. This depends on the direction of approach of the ridge-building waves. Where the waves approach with their crests at an angle to the shore the ridges have a tendency to turn to face the direction from which the waves come. This is true of the orientation of the ridges on the south Lincolnshire coast (F. A. Barnes and C. A. M. King, 1951). R. K. Gresswell (1953) has also drawn attention to this pattern of ridges on the coast between Liverpool and Southport in Lancashire. The ridges here tend to lie at right-angles to the direction from which the dominant waves come. At Ainsdale, where the coast trends at 32° from north, the ridges diverge from the coast northwards. At Formby Point the ridges lie parallel to the coast. South of the Point, they diverge southwards from the coast, which trends south-east at this point. The dominant waves come from a little north of west.

On the north–south coast of Lincolnshire the ridges trend away from the coast southwards, because the dominant waves come from the direction of maximum fetch to the north. The ridges are well developed on the southern part of the coast, which is in an area of active accretion, with a flat overall beach gradient. South of Skegness the ridges sometimes reach considerable heights above the landward runnels. A beach profile surveyed in November 1957, at the southern side of Skegness, showed a ridge 1·68 m high, sloping very steeply to the runnel. The ridge had increased to 2·13 m by 1960. Very thick soft mud frequently collects in the deep runnels; the seaward slopes of the ridge on the other hand are firm, smooth sand, indicating the part played by the swash in shaping them.

Surveys of the beach profiles in Lincolnshire have been repeated many times since 1951. These surveys show that the ridges on each profile move gradually landwards. This movement is very steady and continuous. It is illustrated in figure 12-26, which shows the landward movement of the swash slope of the ridges in front of the spit at Gibraltar Point. The movement is most easily explained by the migration of the whole ridge southwards. If the ridges move in this direction, it will appear that they are moving inland on any one profile because they diverge from the coast southwards. Further reference to these ridges is made in section 16-3.

e   Variability of beach profiles

The variability of beach profiles can be studied by repeated observations of the profile over time spans of varying duration. The interpretation of the variations can be attempted in terms of the controlling process variables, if these are measured at the same time as the profiles are recorded. The movement of beach material normal to the coast is mainly responsible for the very considerable changes which occur from time to time on the foreshore and in the offshore zone.

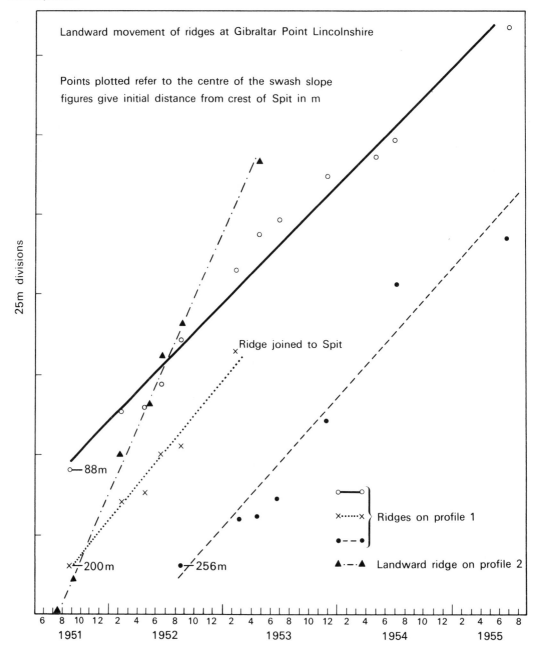

Landward movement of ridges at Gibraltar Point Lincolnshire

Points plotted refer to the centre of the swash slope
figures give initial distance from crest of Spit in m

25m divisions

Ridge joined to Spit

○—88m

×—200m   •—256m

Ridges on profile 1

Landward ridge on profile 2

6 8 10 12 2 4 6 8 10 12 2 4 6 8 10 12 2 4 6 8 10 12 2 4 6 8
1951   1952   1953   1954   1955

Figure 12-26 Landward movement of the ridges at Gibraltar Point, Lincolnshire, from 1951 to 1955.

Such changes are seasonal in some areas, but more erratic in others. The areas undergoing a seasonal variation of beach profile are mainly those which have a regular seasonal change in climatic conditions, which affect wave action on the beach.

The extent of the periodic fluctuation of the beach is partly dependent on the variability of the waves. Perhaps the most important factor, however, is the nature of the beach material. The coarser the material the greater will be the changes on the beach. Changes in level of up to a metre in one week have been recorded at Marsden Bay, County Durham, where the median diameter of the sand was about 0·36 mm. On the much finer sand beach of Rhossili Bay, South Wales, where the sand median diameter was 0·23 mm, the change in sand level over a period of a week was limited to 2 to 5 cm. On shingle beaches the changes are even larger than on coarse sand beaches. On Chesil Beach near Abbotsbury a change in level of 1·5 m was recorded over a period of only two hours. The shingle has a median diameter of 11·4 mm. A similar relationship between the rapidity of beach changes and the size of beach material has also been noted by F. P. Shepard on Californian beaches (1950).

The steep gradient of coarse beaches causes the greater mobility and variability. On such beaches waves break close inshore and their energy is dissipated over a narrow beach zone. The backwash also has greater power on a steeper beach.

(i) *Short-term variability:* W. Harrison (1969) has provided empirical equations that relate changes in the beach profile to the process variables. The beach changes are defined by the net change in the quantity of sand on the foreshore, ΔQ_f, the advance or retreat of the shoreline at mean high-water level, Δs, and the mean slope of the foreshore, $\bar{m}$. 14 process variables were measured:

1	b	breaker distance or run-up
2	d	distance between outcrop of water table on the foreshore and inshore margin of the breakers
3	$\bar{D}$	grain diameter at mid-foreshore
4	h	hydraulic head
5	$\bar{H}_b$	breaker height
6	H_{bs}	height of significant breaking waves
7	t_w	sea water temperature
8	$\bar{T}_b$	mean period of breaking waves
9	u	unsaturated beach surface between outcrop of water table on foreshore and swash reach
10	$\bar{z}$	mean trough-to-bottom distance in front of breaking wave
11	$\bar{\alpha}_b$	mean acute angle between shoreline and breaking wave
12	$\pm\eta$	rate of rise and fall of still-water level at tide gauge
13	ρ_l	density of sea water
14	ρ_s	density of solids on mid-foreshore

The data were analysed by linear multiple regression to provide prediction equations. The analysis showed the importance of the interaction of the swash and groundwater characteristics. Because of the interaction between the variables involved, the physical system is difficult to interpret in terms of the individual variables. Empirical equations, therefore, provide a good method of prediction. The equations presented, however, only apply to the type of beach analysed and the conditions during the measurements. The variables used are best given in meaningful dimensionless form.

The observations on which the analysis was based were carried out at low tide over a period of 26 days at Virginia Beach, Virginia, which is exposed to the Atlantic waves. During the period there were wide ranges of most of the measured variables. The foreshore was generally plane, only developing cusps at one observation. No rainfall affected the water table on the foreshore. A time lag was allowed for in relating the process variables to the response ones. The best lag was selected by using the process variables at sequential three hourly intervals before low water, when the response variables were measured.

The predictor equation for the five most significant variables was found to be

$$\Delta Q_f = 5{\cdot}803 - 113{\cdot}151(\bar{H}_b/gT_b^2)_{0{\cdot}0}^{1/2} - 52{\cdot}111(h/b)_{3{\cdot}0} - 7{\cdot}269(\bar{\alpha}_b)_{6{\cdot}0}$$
$$+ 2{\cdot}724(\bar{D}/\bar{z})_{6{\cdot}0} - 35{\cdot}067(\bar{m})_{12{\cdot}0}$$

The subscripts outside the brackets refer to the time lag before low water. These five variables explain 55% of the variability of the sand volume on the foreshore. The physical meaning of the equation may be summarized by stating that the breaker steepness at the end of the tidal cycle, which is low water, correlated negatively with sand volume. Thus as the breaker steepness increases, erosion occurs. When the tide is high the correlation becomes positive, but is not so strong. This is due to deposition at the top of the swash in the unsaturated upper foreshore at high water. Deposition is greater as the value of h/b decreases. This means that there is an increase in the size of the swash. This result is again due to deposition in the relatively unsaturated upper foreshore as the larger swash extends further up the beach. The negative correlation with $\bar{\alpha}_b$ means that as the breakers become more nearly parallel to the shore, the quantity of swash water increases and the swash moves further up the beach. More deposition results from the swash reaching the unsaturated sand, an effect that is most pronounced at high water. The positive correlation with sand size indicates that as the swash reaches the coarser sand percolation is greater, causing greater deposition. The final correlation indicates the dependence of the volume of sand moved on the beach slope. Where the initial slope is gentle deposition may be expected and vice versa. This is an attempt by the waves to reach equilibrium. The accuracy of the predictions is indicated in figure 12-27A.

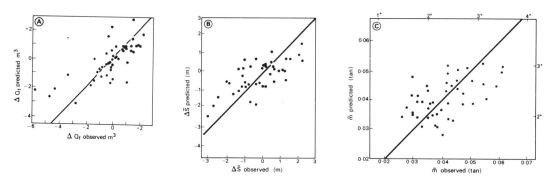

Figure 12-27 A: Predicted versus observed values for change in the quantity of foreshore sand from one low water stand to the next; **B:** Predicted versus observed values for advance or retreat of the shoreline from one low water stand to the next; **C:** Predicted versus observed values for slope of foreshore as measured at the end of the low-tide interval. (*A, B, C after Harrison, 1969.*)

The advance and retreat of the mean high-water line is best predicted by the equation

$$\Delta s = 2{\cdot}312 - 0{\cdot}909(\bar{D}/\bar{z})_{0{\cdot}0} - 61{\cdot}037(\bar{H}_b/g\bar{T}_b^2)_{3{\cdot}0}^{1/2} - 5{\cdot}708(\bar{\alpha}_b)_{6{\cdot}0}$$
$$+ 4{\cdot}682(\bar{\alpha}_b)_{0{\cdot}0} - 22{\cdot}190(h/b)_{3{\cdot}0} + 1{\cdot}874(\bar{D}/\bar{z})_{6{\cdot}0}$$

The most important process variable is related to the size of the material at the time of low water. This is caused by the interaction between groundwater seepage where the sand is unsaturated, the swash velocity, and their ability to carry grains of different sizes. Coarse grains will tend to move downslope, causing a negative value of s, which retreats inland. Smaller grains will tend to remain on the slope as the groundwater flow will be slower. This same variable has a positive correlation at high water, but the effect is not nearly so important. There is a strong negative correlation between b, the runup distance, and $\bar{D}/\bar{z}$, suggesting that the relationship between $\bar{D}/\bar{z}$ and the b value is important. The larger the former is the smaller the latter will be. The relationship may mean that for a given slope and grain size $\bar{D}/\bar{z}$, the swash depth increases with the runup distance. The accuracy of the predictor equation is shown in figure 12-27B.

The predictor equation for the beach slope is

$$\bar{m} = 0.345 + 0.351(h/b)_{9.0} - 0.374(\bar{H}_b/g\bar{T}_b^2)^{1/2}_{3.0}$$
$$+ 0.238(h/b)_{0.0} + 0.032(\bar{\alpha}_b)_{9.0} - 0.011(\bar{D}/\bar{z})_{0.0} + 0.018(\bar{D}/\bar{z})_{3.0} - 0.217(h/b)_{3.0}$$

The strongest variable is h/b, which is the ratio of hydraulic head to runup distance, and this applies at all states of the tide. The slope is thus dependent upon the groundwater conditions in the beach. When the slope is steep the swash runup is small. The correlation becomes negative at falling half tide, due to sand being eroded from the swash slope and carried to the breaker zone, when h is large relative to b. The hydraulic head is larger on the falling tide than the rising one. The relationship of slope with $\bar{D}/\bar{z}$ indicates that, at the half tides, the foreshore slope is related to the grain diameter. The correlation is now positive, while it is negative at high and low water. The large swash length at high water for a given grain size will lead to the build-up of the foreshore and a steeper slope. The swash length will also be great at the final low water. The breaker steepness is also important in determining the foreshore slope. As breaker steepness increases at falling half tide, there is net erosion of material. The water line retreats, and the foreshore slope becomes flatter. A measure of the breaker power has also been shown to correlate strongly with the mean foreshore slope. Substitution of this variable for breaker form did not materially alter the predictor equation. The accuracy of the equation given is shown in figure 12-27C. The analysis as a whole indicates the importance of taking the beach groundwater conditions into account in explaining the response of the foreshore to the processes operating upon it over a short period.

The variability of beach profiles is very well exemplified by the work of J. M. Zeigler and S. D. Tuttle (1961) on four beaches on the inner and Atlantic shores of Cape Cod. They made daily measurements of a series of beach profiles. The foreshore is very changeable, varying between a width of 15.2 m and 45.8 m horizontally and over a vertical distance of 2.44 and 3.05 m. The total measurement period was five years and profiles were surveyed at varying intervals. The inner beaches had a small fetch; the outer ones had longer fetches which were unlimited in some directions. One profile, at Race Point, was situated at the tip of the spit near the end of an offshore bar. The waves were highest on the most exposed profile at Highland. Spring tidal range varies between about 2.75 m and 3.05 m. The area is stormy, resulting in variable wave conditions. The beach profiles were measured by recording the elevation of the top of pipes above the sand surface. Owing to the inadequacy of wave data it was not possible to relate the beach changes directly to the wave conditions.

The results for the whole period of observations showed that changes over a period of two tides were mostly under 7.5 cm but sometimes increased to 15 cm. On one occasion a cut of 2.44 m occurred in ten days. The total envelope of change was greatest on the most exposed beaches and at mid- and low-water levels. The offshore zone in this area is complicated by bars and a series of giant ripples, forming transverse bars between the main bar and the foreshore. The transverse bars move along the coast. The region is thus complex and highly dynamic. Further observations are needed to sort out the effect of the many variables. More accurate wave data especially are needed. The observations do, however, indicate the likely extent of beach profile fluctuation in such an active environment.

Field observations on Del Monte beach, California, by W. C. Thompson and J. C. Harlett (1969) were made on the intertidal part of the beach over a period of 60 days by making daily observations of beach level on fixed poles. On every occasion a change of at least 6 cm was recorded somewhere on the beach, even when the waves were only 15 cm high. Erosion took place more rapidly than accretion, the extremes being 61 cm and 44 cm respectively over a 24·8 hour period. Cutting often occurred on the upper beach and filling on the lower beach and vice versa. The beach cut when the wave steepness increased, and high beach levels were only associated with very low wave steepnesses. Wave power operated in the same way as wave steepness, with cutting associated with greater wave power. Lowest beach levels were associated with the steepest and largest waves and vice versa. The rate at which equilibrium was reached was rapid at first and fell off quickly, 78% of the change occurring in the first interval of time of one day, and 91% in the second and 97% in the third. The time intervals became shorter as the distance between actual and equilibrium beach level increased, at the mid-point of the daily swash zone.

The ridge and runnel profiles on the south Lincolnshire coast have already been mentioned as an example of ridges that lie at an angle to the shore. They, therefore, appear to move inland on any one profile. A detailed study of the movement of the ridges on a profile near Gibraltar Point was based on measurements made on a series of pegs at intervals of two to three days (C. A. M. King, 1968). Most of the changes can be related to the movement of the ridges and the development of runnels across the beach. The southward extension of a ridge across the profile resulted in the burial of one peg and marked accretion on others. Erosion, caused by deepening of a runnel landward of the ridge, amounted to 73·6 cm. The record of detailed measurements covers 15 months and, apart from runnel development, the maximum change of level was one of accretion of 68·5 cm near the bottom of the profile. The results are shown in figure 12-28. The beach showed marked short-term stability. Successive changes on any peg only very occasionally exceeded 5 cm, and for most of the time they were only 2·5 cm or less. Only 22 out of 582 observations recorded changes greater than 5 cm from March to September. The total was 77 out of 1319 observations over the whole period of observations.

There were fewer major changes in level during the summer. This was due to the lower incidence of strong winds and large waves during this period. Most of the large changes were due to runnel formation. These results confirm the stability of fine-grained sand beaches with wide, flat profiles in the relatively sheltered conditions of the south Lincolnshire coast. The coast is a low-energy one because the dominant winds blow offshore, and offshore banks protect the lower part of the foreshore. They also reduce wave action even at high tide. On beaches of this type the profile changes slowly and systematically by the gradual movement of beach ridges southwards along the coast. The movement of the ridges has already been shown to be steady. On a coast of this type, therefore, occasional surveys provide useful information of the longer-term development of the beach profiles and the amount of sand on the beach. The latter aspect is considered in chapter 16 and the former in the last section of this chapter.

Further pipe measurements are reported from the east coast of the U.S.A. by H. D. Urban and C. J. Galvin (1969). Pipes were placed at 15·2 cm intervals from the dunes to the low-tide terrace along two profiles on each of five Atlantic coast beaches. Two were situated on Long Island and the others at Long Beach Island, Atlantic City and Ludlam Island, New Jersey. Wave observations were also obtained and weekly profiles were observed during January to March 1968. The pipe readings were checked against normal surveys and were mostly found to be reliable and accurate. The maximum change in one week was erosion of 1·74 m and accretion of 1·43 m. The three month maximum values were 0·915 m erosion and 1·10 m accretion. The

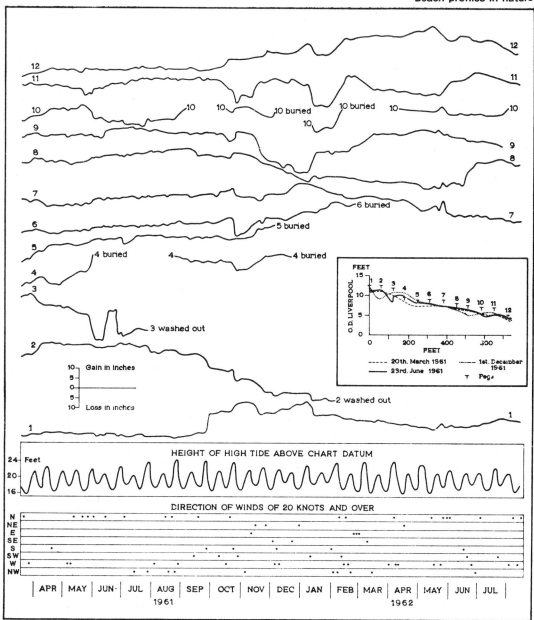

Figure 12-28 Details of beach changes, winds over 20 knots and tidal data for the period 20 March 1961 to 20 August 1962.

Long Island beaches tended to show more variations than the New Jersey ones. There was little evidence of positive correlation of sand levels on different beaches. The waves generally low along the coast, reaching a mode of 0·915 m and a maximum of 2·13 m, with greater values on Long Island. There was a positive correlation between sand level change and mean wave height. The greater changes in level appeared to occur on or above the beach face rather than below it. The profiles are flatter and the sand finer on the more southerly profiles in New Jersey.

(*ii*) *Seasonal and cyclic changes:* A series of profiles surveyed across the foreshore and the open Atlantic side of Sandy Hook during the summers of 1959, 1960 and 1961 indicate the nature of the seasonal beach changes in this area (A. N. Strahler, 1966). The northern profile at Kingmill is less exposed than the southern one, at Spermaceti Cove. The Kingmill station is stable, the shore having moved little more than 100 m between 1836 and 1953. A submarine bar lies off the foreshore 73 m seaward of the foot of the beach face. Waves break on the bar at low tide, the tidal range being 1·22 to 1·52 m. At Spermaceti station the beach has moved about 274 m between 1836 and 1953 and there is no submarine bar. This beach has a higher berm and longer, higher beach face than the other, owing to greater exposure.

The foreshore zone in this area consists of a high winter berm, a lower summer berm and a very regular shore-face slope. The winter berm is at 2·44 to 2·74 m above mean sea level, and the summer one is about 1·83 m. The gradient of the beach face is 10 to 12% and is formed in the swash–backwash zone, covering 2·44 to 2·74 m vertically. Coarse sand and gravel accumulate at the foot of the slope, where a step 15 cm high occurs. The sand becomes finer up the beach face, ranging from 6·0 mm to 0·35 mm between the step at the base and the berm at the top. During the summer season the beach face builds steadily seawards during June and July, but thereafter it is maintained at a very constant position and slope. It is during this season that the tidal cycles considered in section 5-9 occur most regularly. During the winter season the sand that accumulated during the early summer is eroded and the winter berm is reactivated. While the summer growth was taking place the submarine bar at Spermaceti station was removed, and the shore face extended into deeper water by 0·61 to 0·915 m. The amount of progradation, which was similar on four profiles in this vicinity, was 12·2 m to 15·25 m in the four weeks between 29 June and 27 July. The profile then remained similar until 7 September, indicating a stable equilibrium profile, adjusted to the uniform summer wave conditions.

The seasonal changes on the five Atlantic beaches studied by Urban and Galvin have been discussed by J. M. Darling (1964). His observations cover the period from 1962, when a severe storm did considerable damage, to 1964. Beaches in Connecticut, sheltered from Atlantic waves, were also included. These beaches were fairly flat, with sand, gravel and shingle. The Atlantic City beach accreted between January 1963 and August 1963, when 86% of the waves were below 1·22 m, and only 14% above. Between August 1963 and January 1964 erosion occurred. During this period 28% of the waves exceeded 1·22 m, and tides were relatively high. Between 28 October 1963 and 14 November 1963, a hurricane caused considerable erosion. The +0·915 m contour retreated 11·6 m and the +1·83 contour 14·9 m, a loss of 10·5 cubic yards/linear foot (26·3 m³/m). A marked seasonal change in beach level is indicated by these profiles. Erosion occurs during autumn and winter, and accretion during spring and summer, the latter season being generally a stable one. This trend also occurred on the other beaches studied.

Observations from the beaches of west Florida, given by D. S. Gorsline (1966), provide observations from a different wave environment. 15 beach stations were observed at monthly intervals, and both beach profiles and wave and sediment data were obtained. This is a low- to medium-energy environment: maximum waves are 100 cm high, longshore currents are generally high at 30 to 150 cm/sec. The magnitude of profile changes is approximately a direct function of wave height up to a height of about 30 cm, but thereafter wave height does not appear to affect the rate of sand level variation. Profiles extended to a depth of about 1·5 m beyond the low breakers.

The maximum sand elevation changes on the profiles in relation to the breaker heights are shown in figure 12-29. Maximum annual sand level changes were 1·5 m. These do not appear to relate to the wave heights, but rather to the beach exposure. Maximum cutting appears to occur

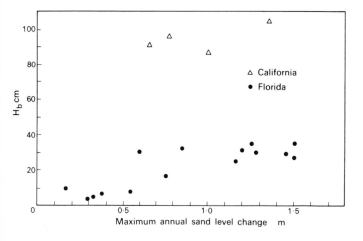

Figure 12-29 Changes in beach level for 1962 at California (open triangles) and Florida (dots). (*After Gorsline, 1966.*)

during the summer and early autumn, when southerly waves are dominant. These have the greatest fetch and hence energy. Some beaches show a cyclic summer fill and winter cut, but others show no systematic pattern. Those in sheltered localities showed little change at all. The beaches in this area on the whole appear to be in near equilibrium.

The foreshore and offshore zone along the Scripps Institute pier in California shows a marked seasonal variation in level (F. P. Shepard, 1950). Figure 12-30 shows the beach profiles for spring and autumn. There is a marked fill on the upper part of the profile over the summer season with a cut in deeper water. This change indicates that the source of material being deposited on the upper beach is at least partly derived from the offshore zone, by transport normal to the shore. During the winter season the reverse change is recorded, with loss of material from the top of the profile and deposition below. These changes can be related to the wave characteristics. Storm waves are common in the winter season and they form a storm-wave profile with a submarine bar. The flatter swells of the summer season remove the submarine bar and build up the foreshore.

Other high-energy beaches in California have been studied by J. C. Ingle (1966). They also showed seasonal changes as demonstrated by Shepard. Ingle studied the beaches at Goleta, Trancas, Santa Monica and La Jolla and they all showed accretion during the summer, when long, low waves arrived from the southern hemisphere. Erosion took place during the winter and spring, when local storms generate high waves. Huntingdon beach was anomalous, owing to its shelter from the violent winter and spring northwest waves. It is exposed to the occasionally damaging waves from the south and west. The breaker height seemed to be the most reliable index to the amount of cut of fill on the profile.

(*iii*) *Long-term variability:* An example of severe and continuous loss of material from the beach profile has been recorded by Prasada Rao and C. Mahadevan (1958). The cause of the change was the construction of an artificial breakwater in 1933 on the central east coast of India. The beach to the north of the breakwater lost large quantities of sand, according to surveys made between 1934 and 1953. Over a mile (1·6 km) stretch of coast about 37,800 m³ of sand was lost. The beach profile retreated a maximum of 117 m and lost its berm, becoming flatter in gradient.

Annual surveys of the profiles at eight stations show a fluctuating decline in beach elevation, the average cut at five stations was 3·96 m, and 2·44 m at the remainder, at positions closest to the breakwater. 300 m further north the average cut varied between 1·22 and 3·96 m. The beaches seem to have reached equilibrium conditions during the 1950s. The beach profiles show a

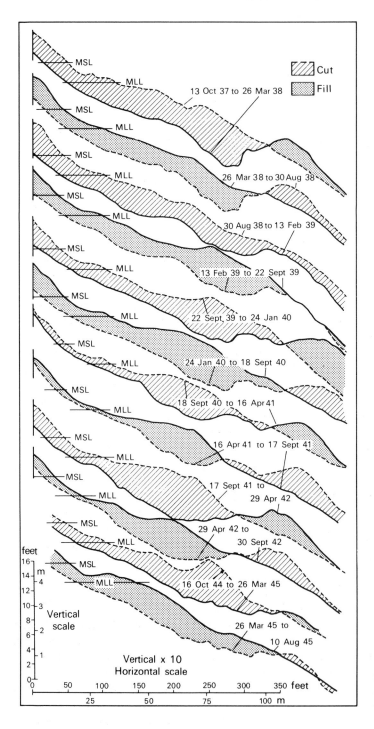

Cut
Fill

13 Oct 37 to 26 Mar 38

26 Mar 38 to 30 Aug 38

30 Aug 38 to 13 Feb 39

13 Feb 39 to 22 Sept 39

22 Sept 39 to 24 Jan 40

24 Jan 40 to 18 Sept 40

18 Sept 40 to 16 Apr 41

16 Apr 41 to 17 Sept 41

17 Sept 41 to
29 Apr 42

29 Apr 42 to
30 Sept 42

16 Oct 44 to 26 Mar 45

26 Mar 45 to
10 Aug 45

MSL
MLL

feet
16
14
12
10
8
6
4
2
0

m
4
3
2
1
0

Vertical
scale

Vertical x 10
Horizontal scale

0   50   100   150   200   250   300   350 feet

25   50   75   100 m

Figure 12-30 Seasonal changes on Scripps Pier profile. (*After Shepard, 1950.*)

354

considerable narrowing of the beach, due to the loss of the berm, although the foreshore slope is flatter.

T. Edelman (1967) has described the records that have been kept for many years of selected profiles along the Dutch coast. In a new series of data, the number and length of the profiles have been increased. The measurements give useful data of the effects of various structures on the coast. They also indicate long-term coastal trends. Some of the results are shown in figure 12-31. The coast of Holland between the Hoek of Holland and Den Helder has changed most near the coastal structures that have been installed along this stretch of coast.

A long-term study of the beach profiles over a stretch of the Lincolnshire coast between Gibraltar Point and Mablethorpe has been carried out between 1951 and 1963 (C. A. M. King and F. A. Barnes, 1964). The southern part of the Lincolnshire coast is one of accretion, on which wide beach profiles have high ridges. North of Skegness the beach becomes narrower and smoother and the coast is liable to erosion unless it is protected by sea walls and groynes. Details of the historical development and the erosion on this coast are considered in chapters 18 and 17 respectively. In this section some examples of the variations in the beach profiles over the period 1953 to 1959 are discussed.

Figure 12-32 shows sweep zones for two separate periods. The sweep zones cover the envelope of beach changes. This method indicates the longer-term changes in the beach profiles because the individual sweep zones cover the variability of the beach profile during the period they represent. The five profiles shown in the figure cover the coast between Mablethorpe in the north, profile 22, and Ingoldmells in the south, profile 13.

Profile 22 shows very little change over the two periods. There is a slight gain on the upper beach, due to the effectiveness of the groynes built during the first period. They have raised the sand to a slightly higher level on the upper foreshore. This beach is at the southern limit of the northern area of accretion on the coast.

Profile 20 exemplifies the zone that is most liable to erosion. During the 1953 storm surge the sand was completely stripped off this beach, exposing the clay foundation of the beach. The second sweep zone shows that the groynes built after the storm have been effective in stabilizing the upper beach. The narrowness of the sweep zone is due to the stability of this generally smooth beach, now that the groynes have raised the level of the upper foreshore. The mean thickness of the sand is now about 1 m.

Profile 17, at Anderby Creek, showed a fall in the sweep zone during the period of observation. The sweep zone has also narrowed due to reduction of ridge size. The loss of sand from this beach may be related to the success of the groynes further north. These may have trapped a considerable proportion of the sand moving south alongshore.

Profile 13 at Ingoldmells Point shows little change during the period. This beach is steeper than the others as it consists of coarser material. The change at Profile 10, a little further south, is one of a narrowing sweep zone. This is due to the reduction of ridge size following the early period when high ridges moved up the beach as sand was returned from offshore after the 1953 storm. The beach is now in a state of reasonable dynamic equilibrium.

The set of sweep zones north of Skegness contrast with those south of the town, which are shown in figure 12-33. The southern profiles represent the zone of accretion. This is indicated by the continued raising of the sweep zones for the successive periods. The accretion is most marked at profile 4, near the southern edge of Skegness, and is least at the spit at Gibraltar Point, profile 1. The set of detailed observations discussed in section 12-3 e (i) refer to a situation near profile 2. This profile has shown a slow but continuous period of growth and the sweep zone has gradually widened. The increase in the width of the sweep zone is the result of the increase in the height of

Beach profiles

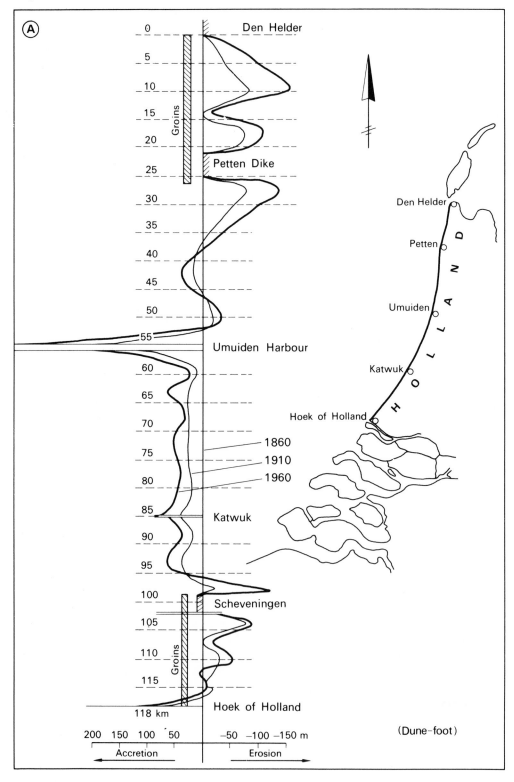

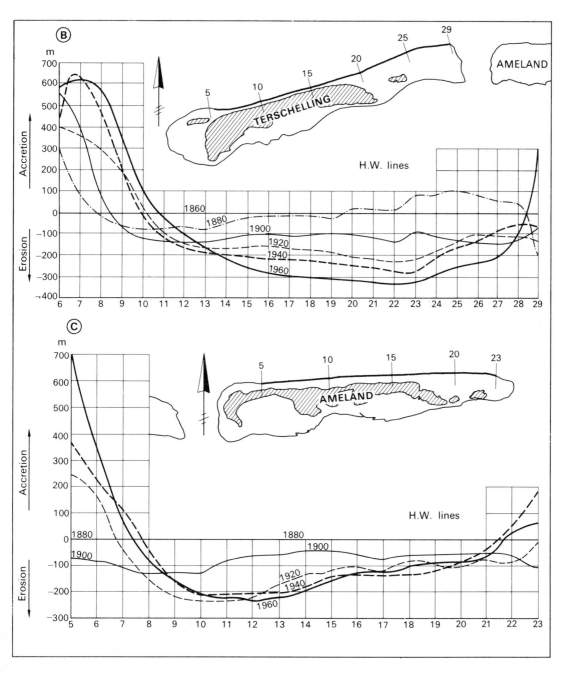

Figure 12-31 **A** (*opposite*): Changes along the coastline of part of Holland between Den Helder and Hoek of Holland. Changes on the coasts of the islands of Terschelling (**B**) and Ameland (**C**). (*A, B, C after Edelman, 1967.*)

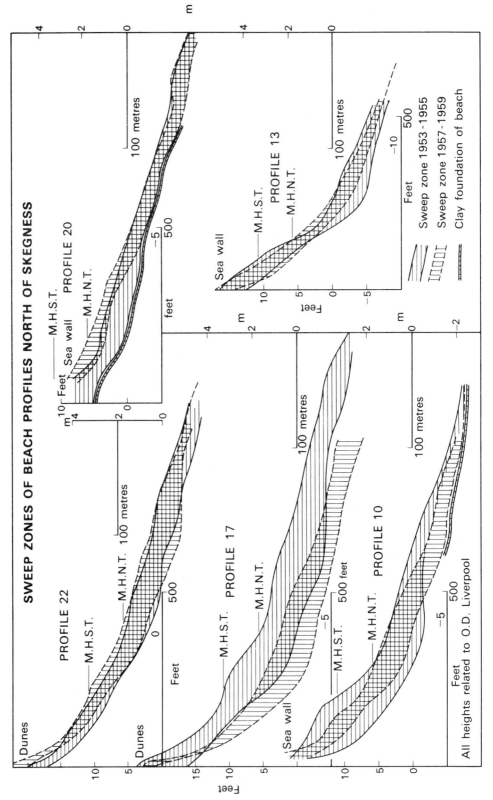

Figure 12-32 Sweep zones of beach profiles north of Skegness on the Lincolnshire coast for the periods 1953 to 1955 and 1957 to 1959.

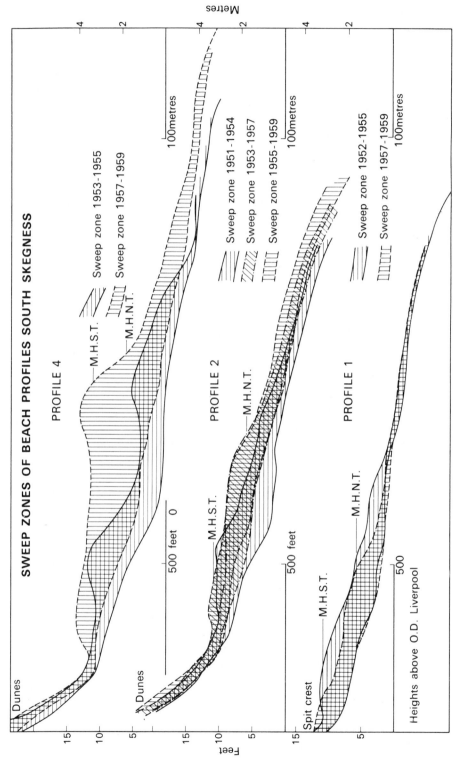

Figure 12·33 Sweep zones of beach profiles south of Skegness on the Lincolnshire coast for the period between 1951 and 1959.

the ridges on the beach. Details of the relationship between accretion and ridge height are considered in chapter 16.

The volume of material on the beach is reflected in the form of the beach profiles along this coast. They tend to be smooth north of Skegness, where sand is not so plentiful, but ridges increase in height as the amount of sand available on the foreshore increases south of Skegness. The profiles provide a useful basis for this type of analysis. They can be used to establish the state of the beach in terms of nourishment and stability. Profile analysis is, therefore, a valuable method of study of beach dynamics as well as beach morphology.

Summary

Beach profiles in a model wave tank fall into two distinct types. With steep waves a break-point bar will form at the break-point of the waves. The position of the bar depends on the height of the waves and the slope of the beach as these variables determine where the waves will break. An increase in wave height will cause the bar to move offshore and vice versa. If a small wave acts after a large, steep wave then two bars can form. A break-point bar is destroyed by a falling water level and it cannot exist above the water level. The bar crest builds to above the original profile to a height half the water depth over the bar crest on all gradients tested.

A flat wave will produce a swash bar at the limit of wave action. This bar can be built up above the still-water level by the constructive action of the swash. It is not disturbed by a falling water level and can exist above water. The bar separates the lagoon that forms landward of it from the sea.

The beach gradient on the swash slope both on natural beaches and in model tanks is shown to depend primarily on the size of the beach material, but also on the wave length and wave steepness. The coarser the material, the shorter and flatter the waves, the steeper the beach swash slope will be. The reason for these relationships is the amount of swash that percolates through the beach. This is large in coarse material with a high permeability, it is also large relative to the backwash in steep and long waves. Waves will attempt to build their equilibrium slope according to the value of these three variables. Because these variables are continually changing, particularly the wave dimensions, the equilibrium gradient of a beach is also liable to change. It is a dynamic equilibrium and not a static one.

Beaches in nature can have smooth profiles, the gradients of which depend on the nature of the beach material. Most smooth beaches are parabolic in form, steepening towards high-tide level where the coarser material accumulates. Beaches in relatively enclosed seas with a small tidal range or no tide often have submarine bars, which normally lie parallel to the coast. These bars are the full-scale equivalent of break-point bars in the model tank. They are characteristic of the storm beach profile and are formed at the break-point of steep, storm waves. Many barred beaches have two or three parallel bars, the outermost being formed by the largest storm waves and the inner one by the smaller steep waves generated often by onshore breezes. The bars may also have a crescentic form, with the points of the crescents facing inland. These bars move along the coast, causing rapid changes in any one beach profile. Submarine bars also form on exposed coasts during the stormy season and may occur below low-tide level on some tidal beaches. On beaches with a large tidal range, a fairly restricted fetch, and a large volume of available sediment, ridges and runnels may develop. These ridges are exposed at low water on the foreshore and are the full-scale equivalent of the swash bar in the wave tank. They are formed by constructive waves and tend to be flattened by storm waves. They represent an attempt by the waves to build their equilibrium gradient on a beach that is flatter than the equilibrium gradient. The gradient is steeper in areas of small fetch where wave lengths will be small, while the large sediment supply ensures a flat overall gradient and hence the necessity for ridge formation.

Short-term variability of the beach profile is related to the groundwater conditions in the beach foreshore and the breaker steepness. Many beaches show a seasonal change in profile, with the beach reaching its maximum build-up on the upper foreshore during calm conditions in summer, while in winter the foreshore is eroded and a submarine bar forms below low water. Longer-term changes also occur where the beach is undergoing more continuous erosion or accretion, which is sometimes induced by artificial beach structures, such as breakwaters, or occasional severe storms.

References

BAGNOLD, R. A. 1940: Beach formation by waves; some model experiments in a wave tank. *J. Inst. Civ. Eng.* **15,** 27–52.

BARNES, F. A. and KING, C. A. M. 1951: A preliminary survey at Gibraltar Point, Lincolnshire. *Bird Obs. and Field Res. St. Gib. Pt. Lincs. Rep.*, 41–59.

BASCOM, W. N. 1951: The relationship between sand size and beach face slope. *Trans. Am. Geophys. Un.* **32**(6), 866–74.

BASCOM, W. N. 1953: Characteristics of natural beaches. Chapter 10 in *Proc. 4th Conf. Coast. Eng.*, 163–80.

BEACH EROSION BOARD 1933: *Interim Report.* U.S. Army, Corps of Engineers.

BEACH EROSION BOARD 1947: A comparative study of waves on model beaches of different scale. *Bull.* **1–2,** 8.

BRAUN, G. 1911: Entwickelungsgeschichtliche Studien an Europaischen Flachlandsküste und irhe Dünen. *Inst. Meereskunde Geog. Inst.* **15,** 1–174.

BRUNN, P. 1954: Coast erosion and the development of beach profiles. *B.E.B. Tech. Memo.* **44.**

CORNAGLIA, P. 1887: *On beaches.* (Translated from Italian.)

CORNISH, V. 1898: On sea beaches and sand banks. *Geog. J.* **11,** 628–51.

DARLING, J. M. 1964: Seasonal changes in beaches of the North Atlantic coast of the United States. *Proc. 9th Conf. Coast. Eng.*, 236–48.

EAGLESON, P. S., GLENNE, B. and DRACUP, J. A. 1961: Equilibrium characteristics of sand beaches in the offshore zone. *B.E.B. Tech. Memo.* **126.** (66 pp.)

EDELMAN, T. 1967: Systematic measurements along the Dutch coast. Chapter 30 in *Proc. 10th Conf. Coast. Eng.*, 489–501.

ELIE, DE BEAUMONT, L. 1845: *Leçons de geologie pratique.* 7me Leçon—Levées de sables et galets. Paris.

EVANS, O. F. 1940: The low and ball of the east shore of Lake Michigan. *J. Geol.* **48,** 476–511.

GILBERT, G. K. 1890: Lake Bonneville. *Monogr. U.S. Geol. Surv.*

GORSLINE, G. S. 1966: Dynamic characteristics of west Florida Gulf coast beaches. *Mar. Geol.* **4**(3), 187–206.

GRESSWELL, R. K. 1937: The geomorphology of the south-west Lancashire coastline. *Geog. J.* **90,** 335–48.

GRESSWELL, R. K. 1953: *Sandy shores of south Lancashire.* University of Liverpool: Studies in Geography.

HAGEN, G. 1863: *Handbuch der Wasserbaukunst.* 3 Teil—Das Meer, Berlin.

HARRISON, W. 1969: Empirical equations for foreshore changes over a tidal cycle. *Mar. Geol.* **7**(6), 529–51.

HARTNACK, W. 1926: *Die Küste Hinterpommerns und besonderer Berücksichtigung der Morphologie.* Stolpmunde.

INGLE, J. C. 1966: The movement of beach sand. *Devel. in Sediment.* **5,** Amsterdam: Elsevier. (221 pp.)

KADIB, A-L. 1963: Beach profiles as affected by vertical walls. *B.E.B. Tech. Memo.* **134.**

KEULEGAN, G. H. 1945: Depths of offshore bars. *B.E.B. Tech. Memo.* **8.**

KEULEGAN, G. H. 1948: An experimental study of submarine sand bars. *B.E.B. Tech. Rep.* **3.**

KING, C. A. M. 1953: The relationship between wave incidence, wind direction and beach changes at Marsden Bay, Co. Durham. *Trans. Inst. Brit. Geogr.* **19,** 13–23.

KING, C. A. M. 1968: Beach measurements at Gibraltar Point, Lincolnshire. *East Mid. Geogr.* **4**(5), 295–300.

KING, C. A. M. and BARNES, F. A. 1964: Changes in the configuration of the inter-tidal beach zone of part of the Lincolnshire coast since 1951. *Zeits. für Geomorph.* NF **8,** 105*–126*.

KING, C. A. M. and WILLIAMS, W. W. 1949: The formation and movement of sand bars by wave action. *Geog. J.* **113,** 70–85.

LEHMANN, F. P. W. 1884: Das Küstengebiet Hinterpommerns. *Zeits. Gesell. Erdkunde zu Berlin* **19,** 391.

MEYERS, R. D. 1933: A model of wave action on beaches. Univ. of California: Unpub. M.Sc. Thesis.

OLSON-SEFFER, P. 1910: Genesis and development of sand formations on marine coasts. *Augustana Lib. Pub.* **7.**

OTTO, T. 1911–12: Der Darss und Zingst. *Jahrbuch. Geog. Gesell. Greifswald* **13,** 235–485.

POPPEN, H. 1912: Die Sandbänke an der Küster der Deutschen Bucht. *Ann. für Hydrog.* **6,** Berlin, 393–403.

PRASADA RAO, R. and MAHADEVAN, C. 1958: Evolution of Viskhapatnam beach. *Andhra Univ. Mem. in Oceanog.,* Series 62, Vol. **II,** 33–47.

PUGH, D. C. 1953: Études mineralogique des plages Picardes et Flamandes. *Bull d'Inf. Com. Cent. d'Oceanog. et d'Etudes des Côtes* **5**(6), 245–76.

RECTOR, R. L. 1954: Laboratory study of the equilibrium profiles of beaches. *B.E.B. Tech. Memo.* **41.**

RUSSELL, I. C. 1885: Geological history of Lake Lahontan. *U.S. Geol. Surv. Mono.* **11,** 92–3.

SCOTT, T. 1954: *Sand movement by waves.* Inst. Eng. Res., Univ. of California: Wave Research Lab.

SHEPARD, F. P. 1950: Longshore bars and longshore troughs. *B.E.B. Tech. Memo.* **15.**

SONU, C. J. and RUSSELL, R. J. 1967: Topographic changes in the surf zone profile. Chapter 31 in *Proc. 10th Conf. Coast. Eng.,* 502–24.

STRAHLER, A. N. 1966: Tidal cycle of changes on an equilibrium beach. *J. Geol.* **74,** 247–68.

THOMPSON, W. C. and HARLETT, J. C. 1969: The effect of waves on the profile of a natural beach. Chapter 23 in *Coastal engineering* **1,** *Proc. 11th Conf. Coast. Eng.,* London, 1968, Am. Soc. Civ. Eng., 352–72.

TIMMERMANS, P. D. 1935: Proeven over den invloed van golven op een strand. *Leidsche Geol. Med.* **6,** 231–386.

URBAN, H. D. and GALVIN, C. J. 1969: Pipe profile data and wave observations from the C.E.R.C. beach evaluation program, Jan.–Mar. 1969. *C.E.R.C. Misc. Pap.* **3–69.** (21 pp.)

VAN VEEN, J. 1936: *Onderzockingen in de Hoofden.* Ministerie van Waterstaat, 's Gravenhage.

WATTS, G. M. 1955: Laboratory study on the effect of varying wave periods on beach profiles. *B.E.B. Tech. Memo.* **53.**

WATTS, G. M. and DEARDUFF, R. F. 1954: Laboratory study of the effect of tidal action on wave formed beach profiles. *B.E.B. Tech. Memo.* **52.**

WILLIAMS, W. W. 1947: The determination of the gradient of enemy held beaches. *Geog. J.* **109,** 76–93.

WILLIAMS, W. W. and KING, C. A. M. 1951: Observations faites sur la plage des Karentes en Août, 1950. *Bull. Inform. du Com. Cent. d'Oceanog. et d'Études des Côtes,* **2**e Pt: *Notes tech.,* 363–8.

ZEIGLER, J. M. and TUTTLE, S. D. 1961: Beach changes based on daily measurements of four Cape Cod beaches. *J. Geol.* **69,** 583–99.

ZENKOVICH, V. P. 1967: *Processes of coastal development.* (Steers, J. A., Editor), Edinburgh: Oliver and Boyd.

13 The beach in plan

Summary

The plan form of beaches is considered in this chapter. The nature of the beach profile was shown to be dependent in part on the nature of the beach material, as well as on the dynamic processes operating upon the beach. The plan form of the beach is also in part dependent on the nature of the beach material. The most permanent features of shingle beaches are built up by waves of a different type than those that form the major sandy features. The different materials determine which type of wave is dominant in the different types. Storm waves will be dominant in shingle beaches and swell waves on sand beaches as a rule.

In this chapter two main aspects of the plan form of beaches are considered, the first of these being the orientation of the beach with reference to the processes operating upon it. Various theoretical methods of approach are commented upon, and then specific examples mentioned of beaches of different types of material and in different settings. The setting of the beach includes its length between fixed headlands, and the general pattern and exposure of the coastline: the pattern may be intricate or crenulate in outline, or it may be relatively straight; it may be fully exposed to the large ocean waves, or it may be in inland sheltered waters and therefore only affected by locally generated waves. Changing sea level at times results in interesting coastal patterns, particularly when sea level is falling.

The second major aspect to be considered is the geometrical form of the beach, and the influence of the beach on the changing form of the coast is also discussed. Some beaches straighten the coastline along which they develop, while others make the coastline more irregular. Examples of these two types of changes in the plan form of the beach in terms of the coast as a whole are cited.

1 Beach orientation

a Theoretical views

A number of theoretical views on the processes that are important in determining the orientation of a beach have been put forward.

(*i*) *W. V. Lewis:* W. V. Lewis (1931; 1938) discussed the tendency for beaches to turn in a direction perpendicular to the approach of the dominant waves. Lewis elaborated the earlier work of H. T. de la Beche (1833) and J. T. Harrison (1948). Lewis considered that any feature of marine deposition will tend to align itself normal to the direction of approach of the dominant waves, which he assumed to be the largest storm waves. If the storm waves approach at an oblique angle they will cause longshore movement in the opposite direction. The coast will, therefore, tend to swing round to a position normal to their direction of approach. Lewis (1938) took as an example of this process the orientation of the forelands in north Cardigan Bay. He pointed out that these structures are orientated to face the direction of maximum fetch, from which the largest waves come across the Irish Sea from the Atlantic Ocean. He concluded that the prevalent waves, which may be oblique to the shore, will bring the material to the beach, but the dominant waves will build it into a beach ridge orientated normal to their direction of approach.

(*ii*) *A. Schou:* A rather different method of establishing the alignment of a coast has been proposed by A. Schou (1945). He considered that the direction of coastal simplification depends on both the direction of maximum fetch and the resultant of winds from all directions, R. This value, the 'direction-resultant of wind work' is calculated by plotting a vector diagram of all winds of Beaufort force 4 and over. Where the fetch maximum direction coincides with the direction of R, or the fetch is equal in all directions, the coast will become orientated perpendicular to the direction of R. If R is in a different direction to the maximum fetch, the coast should become aligned between the two directions.

The examples cited in support of this theory are on the coast of Denmark, where the fetch is limited in many positions and directions. The wind, therefore, is likely to have a greater effect on the size of the waves than in other areas, where long swells, generated far from the area, form an important proportion of the waves. The direction of maximum fetch from which the swells and storm waves can approach is then more likely to play the dominant role in determining the alignment of the coast.

Both Lewis and Schou emphasize the effect of storm waves that are generated by local winds. The wind direction, therefore, plays an important part in determining the orientation of the beach. Their results will apply essentially to shingle structures that are built up by storm waves. Nearly all Lewis's examples are in fact formed of shingle. Schou developed his wind resultant relationship for the intricate and fairly sheltered beaches around Denmark, where, particularly in east Jutland, and on the islands, the fetch is variable but limited in length. The dominant waves are likely to be those generated by the local winds as far-travelled swells cannot reach these beaches.

(*iii*) *J. L. Davies:* The orientation of sand beaches, on which long swells are the dominant waves, has been studied by J. L. Davies (1959; 1960). He has shown how the wave crests approach the shore closely parallel to the orientation of the beach on many of the exposed beaches of southern Australia and Tasmania. The beach fits the waves, but it is not necessarily straight, even if the waves approach from a consistent direction in deep water. The amount of refraction the long swells undergo as they pass through the shallow water plays an important part in determining the orientation of the beach. One of the most important variables on which the beach orientation depends in this situation is thus the offshore relief. This plays a dominant part in determining the amount and character of the wave refraction. The dominant waves off the Australian coast have a period of 14 seconds. Hence their deep-water length is about 305 m and they begin to feel the bottom and to be affected by refraction in a depth of 150 m. In areas of this type the offshore relief to a considerable depth must affect the beach orientation.

Davies advances three major arguments in support of his view. Firstly, he shows that the waves anticipate the beach before they reach it, as they become adjusted to the underwater contours. Secondly, the swell fits the sandy beach, but not the adjoining rocky parts of the shore. This is due to the more easily adjusted beach fitting the waves, while the rocky coast, which cannot readily be changed in orientation, does not necessarily fit the waves. The beach fits the waves rather than the reverse. Thirdly, he argues that swell is of particular importance in building sandy beaches. This point recognizes the fact that long constructive swells build up the berms, which are so common on sandy beaches with an exposure to long swells. Storm waves are destructive on this type of beach and, therefore, it is much more likely that the beach orientation will be determined by the swell.

This hypothesis of beach orientation explains the curvature of beaches, and curved beaches are much more common than straight ones on sandy coasts. The refracted waves develop smoothly curving crests in response to the changes in depth offshore. Davies regards the greater curvature of bay-head beaches than mid-bay beaches as being due to the greater refraction at the head of the bay. The relationship between the length and width ratio of an inlet, and the curvature of the beach within it, can also be explained by this process. Before complete adjustment to the refracted swell is achieved by the beach alignment, the beach curve is likely to be sharper than the refracted wave crest. In a bay this will mean that waves will tend to drift material towards the centre of the bay. This reduces the curvature of the beach and makes it fit the curvature of the wave crest. When the fit has been perfected, longshore movement will be reduced to a minimum because the wave crest everywhere approaches normal to the beach.

b   Field examples

(*i*) *Long swell environment:* Davies (1960) has described a number of examples of beaches in southern Australia that support his view of beach orientation. He has drawn a refraction diagram for a 14 second swell approaching Frederick Henry Bay from the southwest, as shown in figure 13-1. Within the bay is the Seven Mile beach, which is a mid-bay barrier. It forms a sandy beach, about 8 km long, facing east of south in the centre. The gentle curvature exactly fits the wave crests, as reconstructed in the wave refraction diagram. Other beaches within the bay face in a variety of directions between east, southwest and west-northwest. All of them fit the wave crests closely. Thus long waves from one direction in deep water can cause sand beach orientations to develop in a wide range of direction. Beaches on the coasts of central and western Victoria, and in southwest western Australia, appear to be related to swells coming from the southwest. Refraction diagrams for Bass Strait show a similar good fit between the beach orientations and the refracted 14 second swells coming from southwest.

Another effect of wave refraction on the beach in plan has been pointed out by W. Bascom (1954). In places berms built up by constructive waves can dam temporary streams, which eventually break out across the lowest point of the berm. The new stream outlet is thus controlled by the form of the berm, which in turn is controlled by wave refraction. The berm will be lowest where wave refraction is greatest, the orthogonals are most widely spaced, the wave energy is least and, therefore, the wave height is lowest. Thus stream outlets that are free to migrate in a bay will usually occur in the most sheltered part. This may be in the lee of an islet or at the head of a submarine valley that comes close inshore. An example of this is Mugu Canyon in California, where the Mugu lagoon empties into the sea opposite the canyon head. This is the zone where the refraction coefficient reaches a minimum and wave energy is lowest.

An intricate coastline that illustrates well the relationship between beach orientation and the dominant swell waves is that of the west coast of Ireland. There are long deep bays in the south,

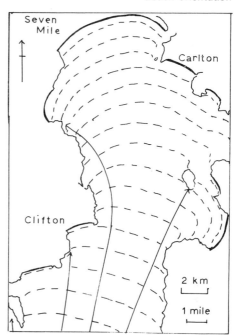

Figure 13-1 Wave refraction diagram to show fit of beach outlines to wave crests in Frederick Henry Bay, south Australia. The waves have a period of 14 seconds and every tenth wave crest is shown. (*After Davies, 1960.*)

and further north the coast is crenulate. An analysis of the relationship between the orientation of the beach, the orientation of the 10 fathom (18·3 m) depth contour and the offshore gradient has been attempted. The distance between the beach and the 10 fathom contour was converted into a tangent, to indicate the offshore gradient. The exposure of the beach was also included. This variable was expressed as the number of degrees between the beach orientation and the direction from which the longest swells and most effective waves would be expected to come. This direction was taken to be from the southwest.

The position of the beaches and their mean orientation are shown in figure 13-2. The mean vector of the beach orientations is 289° with a dispersion of 54°. The offshore contours have an orientation of 292° and a dispersion of 49·5°. It can be shown that the two sets of data are closely related, belonging to the same population with a high degree of confidence. The results support the views of Davies, and suggest that the beach orientation is determined by the offshore relief through refraction of the waves.

A highly significant positive relationship was shown to exist between, on the one hand, the difference between the beach and the 10 fathom depth line orientations, and on the other, the differences between the orientation and the direction of approach of the dominant swells from 225°. This relationship means that as the difference in orientation between the beach and the direction of maximum wave effectiveness increases, so the beach turns at a greater angle to the offshore contour at 10 fathoms. The wave refraction is, therefore, shown to be more effective in those situations where the differences are greatest. The analysis was applied to 14 sets of observations.

A smaller group, consisting of eight beaches, showed a similar relationship, apart from a much larger difference between the orientation at the shoreline and the 10 fanthom line. The mean angle for the first set was 12·6° and for the second set it was 39·2°. There is a significant difference between the mean offshore gradient of the two groups. The first set has a mean offshore gradient of 1 : 173, while for the second set the value was 1 : 360. The essential difference

367

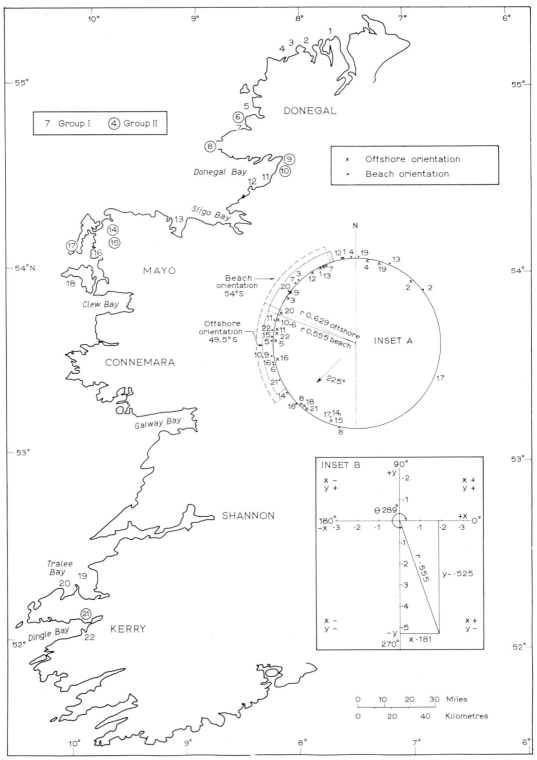

Figure 13-2 Map of western Ireland to show pattern of beach and offshore orientation in inset diagram. The location of the beaches is shown. (*After Doornkamp and King, 1971.*)

between the two sets is the greater shelter of the second set. This factor is related to the lower gradient, which in turn accounts for the greater wave refraction in the shallower water. Hence the larger difference between the 10 fathom line and the shoreline orientation is accounted for.

The analysis as a whole indicates that the orientation of the wide sandy beaches is closely related to the offshore relief, and the effect that this has on the long waves approaching from the open Atlantic ocean from a southwesterly direction. Wave refraction, therefore, provides the link between the offshore relief and the orientation of sandy beaches.

The intricate coast of Donegal illustrates the great variety of beach orientation that can result from the operation of these processes. The pattern of tombolos illustrates some of the processes determining orientation. Two distinct types of tombolo exist in Gweebarra Bay (C. A. M. King, 1965). The first type becomes orientated to face the direction from which the dominant long

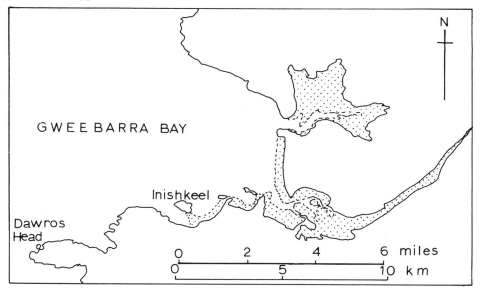

Figure 13-3 Map of Gweebarra Bay, Donegal.

swell waves come. These face the southwest where wave refraction does not alter the deep-water approach direction. Figure 13-3 illustrates the first type at Burnbeg and Termon, which are islands linked to the mainland by a sand and shingle beach ridge tombolo. The second type forms in the shelter of an island, round which the refracted waves meet from both sides, forming beaches orientated nearly at right-angles to the direction of approach of the swell waves. The developing tombolo behind the island of Inishkeel on the south side of Gweebarra Bay illustrates an early stage of this type of feature.

The depth of water determines the extent of refraction. This in turn determines which type of tombolo will form. The first type will form where the water is shallow and sediment is plentiful, so that it can be built up into a beach facing the direction of wave approach. The second type forms where the water is deeper or sediment not so abundant. With an adequate supply of sediment the second type could in time develop into the first, which represents a more mature form.

(ii) Short wave environment: The features considered above are built by long swells, which are considerably refracted and which are not related to the local wind regime. There are, however,

other features that exemplify the processes that Lewis, Schou and Guilcher consider important in determining orientation. These processes are most relevant to shingle beaches, because the most permanent features on these beaches are the ridges built by storm waves. These waves are often generated by local winds. In relatively sheltered waters they are short and, therefore, little refracted. They tend to build features as a result that face in the direction from which the storm waves approach.

Good examples of this type of feature occur around the coasts of southern Britain. One of the best known of these features is Chesil Beach, which has already been considered in section 11-2 from the point of view of the sorting of the shingle along it. The good sorting indicates that relatively little longshore movement takes place. It is reasonable to assume, therefore, that the orientation is adjusted to the dominant waves. The central part of the beach faces almost exactly the direction of simplification as worked out according to Schou's direction resultant of wind work. It thus provides a good example of the application of this theory of beach orientation to a shingle structure.

Hurst Castle spit, situated further east along the English Channel coast, also illustrates the operation of this process. This spit leaves the east–west trending coast and turns to face southwest. It then curves slowly round to run east–west once more. The main spit has many recurves that join it at an acute angle. The recurves face northeast and increase in number and length near the distal end of the main spit. Where the main spit leaves the coast it is orientated to face the direction from which the dominant waves approach. These waves are the Atlantic storm waves, coming across the direction of greatest fetch from the southwest. They build the storm ridge that forms the main line of the spit. The bend of large radius of curvature, which occurs along the main line of the spit, is due to the refraction of these waves as the water deepens towards the distal end of the spit.

The recurve ridges lie at an angle of 150° to the main line of the spit near its proximal end. They are formed by storm waves approaching from the northeast. There is a considerable stretch of open water along the Solent in this direction, in which steep, short waves can be generated. The sharp point at the end of the main ridge is due to the proximity of the Isle of Wight to the southeast, preventing effective ridge-building waves from coming from this direction. The form of the spit is shown in figure 13-4. It is also considered in chapter 2, in which it is used as the model for the development of a simulation computer program.

(*iii*) *Chevron pattern:* A complex pattern of beach ridges is found in some Arctic areas. One form is the chevron pattern, which is well exemplified in south Baffin Island near Nettilling Lake, on Southampton Island in Foxe Basin, and on Mansel Island in the same area. These features consist of long straight beach ridges, aligned perpendicular to the shore, to which are attached short barbs. The barbs vary in their angle of attachment. Sometimes they link to form ridges joining the main ridge nearly at right-angles. When they are short, the barbs are often arcuate. Some of the patterns are shown in figure 13-5, which is drawn from air photographs.

The origin of the chevron patterns is rather doubtful. They do require the following conditions:

1   A suitably low gradient, but the slope must not be too flat so that the wave action is ineffective.
2   There must be loose sediment, usually fine shingle, to form the ridges and barbs.
3   The land must be rising relative to sea level, so that the features gradually emerge from the sea and the main ridge becomes elongated in the process.

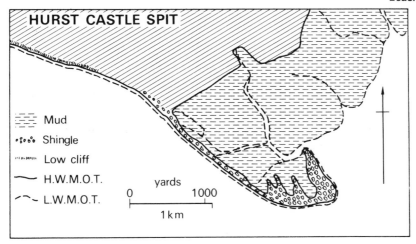

Figure 13-4 Map of Hurst Castle spit, Hampshire.

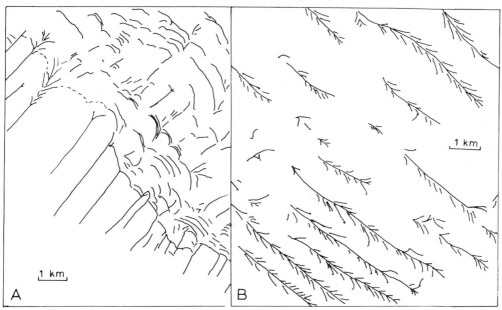

Figure 13-5 Maps to show pattern of chevron ridges, drawn from air photographs. **A:** Mansel Island in Foxe Basin; **B:** Near Nettilling Lake, Great Plain of the Koukdjuak, Baffin Island.

4 Wave action must not be too strong in a direction oblique to the shore. This would destroy the main ridge orientation and prevent the normal symmetry of the barbs. Once the main ridge has emerged, any waves approaching the position of barb formation must approach parallel to the main ridge (C. A. M. King, 1969).

It is difficult to envisage a submarine process that could form the main ridge normal to the coast in these areas of low energy. However, F. Tanner (1967) has drawn attention to features forming perpendicular to the coast. He calls them transverse bars. These bars are characteristic of low to moderate wave energy coasts. Accumulations of sand concentrate advancing wave energy

371

by refraction, so that material is carried landwards along the axes of the accumulations to form the long ridges. The area between the bars is protected, and water moves seawards in this zone, if the bars are not too long. The same mechanism could form the elongated part of the chevron ridges, which would emerge as the sea level falls and thus increase progressively in length. The barbs could be formed by larger than usual constructive waves, the angle of the barb relative to the main ridge being determined by the degree of wave refraction. The angle would be more acute where the central ridge is wide, causing a variation in depth between the main ridges. The barb forms a curve concave to the sea, as its distal end swings out at a wider angle. The spacing between the long ridges varied in the examples studied from about $\frac{1}{2}$ to 1 km.

This particular pattern of beach orientation requires special conditions, such as occur in Arctic areas, in which sea level is falling. Other patterns of beach features typical of this environment were described in chapter 7, including Foley Island. Wave refraction was considered important in the formation of these features.

2 Geometrical beach forms

a Circular arc

Attempts have been made to fit specific geometrical forms to the beach outline in plan. R. McClean (1967) has described the form of 86 beaches on the east coast of New Zealand in terms of their radius of curvature relative to a circular arc. The theoretical radius of curvature of each beach was obtained by measuring the chord length, C, from the end points of the beach, determined from maps or air photographs. At the mid-point of the chord a perpendicular, P, was measured to the shore. The ratio of C to P gives a convenient index of curvature, C/P. The radius of curvature was then found by

$$R = \frac{C^2 + 4P^2}{8P}$$

Beach orientation was also measured by determining the angle between the line P and north.

Of the beaches 45 had values of R less than 1·6 km, 13 had values between 1·8 km and 3·2 km, 12 had values between 3·4 and 8 km and 7 had values between 8·15 and 14·4 km. Nine beaches had radii of curvature greater than 14·4 m. The actual outline of the beaches fitted the circular form very closely regardless of the size of the beach. It was concluded that most of the beaches reach an arc of equilibrium. The closest fit was Waikouaiti beach, which has an angular width of 95°. The deviations from the circular arc occur mainly in the centre or at the ends of the beaches. The curvature often increases towards the ends of the beaches, particularly where the beach is situated just north of a prominent headland that causes much refraction of the southerly swell. The central part of the beach often has too low a curvature: the reason for this is probably the considerable amount of longshore movement that prevents the establishment of the arc of equilibrium owing to the one-way movement of material. In most instances the curvature is concave seawards, but there are two cases where the curvature is convex seawards, the reason being the deltaic nature of these areas.

The majority of beaches face between southeast and east-southeast, which is the direction from which the dominant swells come. Those beaches on the straightest and most exposed parts of the coast approximate most closely to this orientation. The most indented parts of the coast, such as around the Otago and Banks Peninsulas, show the greatest divergence in orientation. The beaches in these areas are those where wave refraction of the southeast swell is greatest.

The plan shape and the orientation can be used to consider the equilibrium character of the beaches. The beach must be supported at both ends to be in equilibrium. It must have a circular curvature. The angle subtended by the radii from the ends of the beach should be 14·3° (0·25 radians). It must be orientated consistent with the prevailing wave conditions, and it must have an equilibrium gradient. Most of the beaches studied by McClean fulfil the first qualification, and many approach the circular form, although some deviate from it. The beaches do, however, show a great variation in subtended angle, ranging from 20° to 110°. The mean for 22 beaches was 64°. The prescribed angle of 14·3° is equivalent to a C/P index of 15, which very few of the New Zealand beaches possess. Most of the beaches are, however, adjusted in orientation. The beaches measured in this study ranged from fine sand to boulders, and from less than 1·6 km to more than 128 km in length, yet they showed a considerable uniformity in plan shape, approximately to the circular form.

b Logarithmic spiral

A detailed study by W. E. Yasso (1964a and b) of the form of the spit-bar shoreline at Horseshoe Cove, Sandy Hook, in New Jersey is concerned with the geometrical form of wave-built sandy features. The spit-bar is attached to the land at its proximal end, but is in deep water at its distal end. It decreases in elevation towards the distal end and has a curvature convex to the sea. The analysis presented by Yasso is based on detailed profile surveying, both transverse and longitudinal, as well as plane-table mapping.

Sandy Hook is a barrier spit 10 km long, lying at the northern tip of the New Jersey Atlantic coastal plain. It connects with a barrier bar that joins the mainland 5·6 km south of Monmouth beach. The tidal range is 1·7 m at spring tide. The feature can be subdivided into an upper-foreshore spit-bar, with a crest near the high-water swash limit, and a lower-foreshore spit-bar with a crest below high water. A tidal lagoon lies landwards of the upper-foreshore spit-bar, while a steep depositional slope lies in front of the lower-foreshore feature. The lower feature moves landwards under the swash of the rising tide but maintains its geometrical form as it moves.

The spit-bars undergo an annual cycle of formation. In winter, waves are large and steep, coming from the northwest, and sediment is transported south. In summer the waves are small and low, coming from the south. These waves push the newly deposited sand into a succession of landward migrating lower-foreshore spit-bars, which merge to form a new upper-foreshore spit-bar by the end of the summer. They also have a long-spiral form, indicating lack of change in form with migration up the beach. The beach is a good one for this type of analysis as the environment is simplified by the exclusion of Atlantic waves from the inner side of Sandy Hook. The convex curvature of the features is caused by wave refraction. The migration of the lower spit-bar during a single tide reached a maximum of 61 cm landwards. Once the spit-bar has become stabilized on the upper foreshore it becomes a broadly convex ridge of low relief. The lowering is due to deflation.

The form of the spit-bars, both in plan and transverse profile, seems to represent an equilibrium form that is maintained even under extreme conditions of tidal range and attack by large waves, such as those generated by hurricanes. The observed changes of the feature can be explained by a simplified model of shore development in which pure translation of the entire shoreline to the southeast takes place in annual increments. The form that fits this beach is the logarithmic spiral, defined by $r = e^{\theta \cot \alpha}$. In this equation r is the length of a radius vector from the long-spiral centre at angle θ and α is the angle between a radius vector and the tangent to the curve at that point. α is constant for the given log-spiral, and varies from about 60° to about 90°. The goodness of fit of the spit-bar plan curvature was assessed by linear regression analysis. The best fit log-spiral curve was fitted by computer, some examples being shown in figure 13-6. The linear regression analysis shows the extremely good fit of this curve. Nearly all the points fall almost exactly on the straight line.

The value of curves of this type in describing the form of spits can be increased if the curve can be successfully extrapolated along a greater stretch of coast than that for which measurements are available. The results of tests of such extrapolation showed that, although it was successful for a certain distance, it could not be carried too far. Other factors tended to modify the curvature, such as the presence of old spit-bars.

W. E. Yasso (1964b) has applied the spiral logarithmic form to headland bays as well as spit

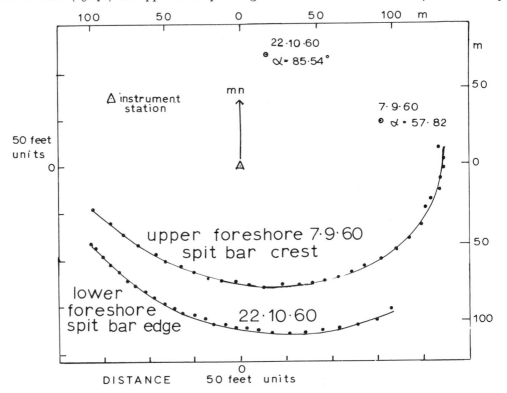

Figure 13-6 Diagram to show fit of logarithmic spiral curve to spit bars on Sandy Hook. (*After Yasso, 1964.*)

outlines. He defines a headland bay beach as one lying in the lee of a headland that is subjected to a predominant direction of wave attack. Beaches in such situations have a seaward-concave plan due to erosion caused by refraction, diffraction and reflection of waves into the shadow zone behind the headland. The radius of curvature of the beach increases with distance from the headland. The log-spiral form, therefore, appeared suitable for testing the goodness of fit.

The log-spiral curve was fitted to four beaches, Spiral beach on Sandy Hook, New Jersey, Halfmoon Bay beach in California, Drakes beach and Limantour spit beach, both north of San Francisco in California. The form of the beach is dependent in these situations on some interruption of the flow of material along the coast. It is also dependent upon dissipation of wave energy by turbulence and reflection, as well as by redistribution of energy by refraction and diffraction. Diffraction has been less studied than refraction, but it could well be the means by which sediment is carried towards the headland, and might be an important factor in the creation of the concave-seaward curve in plan.

The beaches tested differ in their wave regimes. At Sandy Hook 50% of the waves come from the east in deep water, 38% from the southeast and 12% from the northeast, with an average breaker period of seven seconds and waves up to 1·22 m in height are common. On the west coast 85·5% of the waves come from northwest, 8% from the west and their average period is 15 seconds, with the greatest percentage of significant heights falling in the range 0·61 m to 1·83 m.

Spiral Beach lies on the outer or Atlantic side of Sandy Hook and it fits very closely the log-spiral form with an α value of 61·49°. The centre of the log-spiral lies close to the landward end of a groyne that determines the curvature of this small section of the beach. The mean square error in length of radius vector of the best-fitting log-spiral was only 25 cm. The distance over which the curve fitted was a little over 305 m.

The fit of Half Moon Bay is also very close, the mean square error in length of radius vector being only 56 m for each of the 57 data points. The length of beach fitted in this area is about 4·8 km, the fit being least good in the south, which is the open part of the bay, where refraction and diffraction would be least effective. The α value for this beach was 41·26°, with the centre lying near the position of the headland. Drakes beach also fits well with an error in the same terms of 4·9 m. The value was 71·6 m for the adjacent Limantour beach. The α values were 85·64° and 82·20° respectively.

There is little correspondence between the spiral angle α and the shape of the shoreline. This lack of correspondence may be due to different wave conditions at each location. The close fit that has been established, particularly in the small-scale example on Sandy Hook, suggests that such a relationship may be useful in predicting changes in the plan of beaches in the lee of headlands. This would apply when the plan does not yet conform to the log-spiral, if indeed this is the equilibrium form to which beaches in these sites are tending. The form of the spiral is likely to change in time, as the beach increases in length or as the headland is eroded. There should be a sequential change in the spiral angle α as the development proceeds. If the headland is completely eliminated the beach may become straight.

c Half-heart

The half-heart shape is similar to the log-spiral in form, and has been studied in wave tank tests carried out by R. Silvester (1960; 1962). These tests have already been mentioned in chapter 10 in connection with longshore movement of material. They are of interest in this chapter because they indicate a possible equilibrium plan form of model beaches, similar to that suggested by Yasso. Silvester's tests were designed to determine the equilibrium shape of beaches formed by swell from a constant direction. Waves approached the model coast at 45° and broke on an originally straight beach, which was subdivided into bays by concrete sections resembling headlands. No sand was fed in up-drift of the two bays. They were 6·1 m wide in the model tank, and the waves, scaled up, were about 10 seconds period and 1·52 m high. Surveys were made at intervals of several hours of the water line and underwater contours, until stability had been approximately reached.

It was concluded that the form of the beach at the water line was nearly a half-heart shape. The sharply curved portion lay upwave and the tangent portion downwave in each bay unit. The tangent portion on the down-drift side should be aligned nearly perpendicular to the deep-water wave approach direction. The waves reaching this portion would, therefore, be little refracted, while those in the lee of the headland would be both refracted and diffracted around the upwave headland.

The actual form of the bay down-drift of the second headland depends in part on the sand passing to it from the up-drift bay, which itself received no sediment in the experiment. Some of the material eroded from the up-drift bay reached the down-drift one, which still showed modifications after 84 hours in one test.

The model results were tested by reference to part of the coast of South Africa, where there is a predominant direction of wave approach and a suitable configuration. The swell comes from the southwest and the bays have a half-heart form, with the tangential section facing to the southwest at their eastern end. Little sediment can reach this part of the coast around Cape Agulhas and hence it is liable to erosion. This is one of the criteria that determine whether the half-heart form will develop.

Silvester (1960) shows how the tendency of the beach to develop this equilibrium form can be used to stabilize stretches of the coast. The longshore movement of material could be halted by building headlands, about which stable half-heart-shaped bays could form. The headlands could initially be in the form of breakwaters close to the shore, behind which tombolos would develop. The breakwaters could then be extended obliquely offshore until the equilibrium form for the beach had been attained. The headlands should be some miles apart. The final stable form would result in some erosion and some accretion. The breakwaters would be progressively extended offshore and the net longshore movement of sediment halted.

d Circle or ellipse

V. P. Zenkovich (1959) has described the stages by which cuspate spits can develop within lagoons. These features may in time develop in such a way that the lagoon becomes split into circular or elliptical lakes. Lagoons of this form exist in the Chukotsky Peninsula. When winds generate waves that move down the length of a lagoon, there will be a point along the shore where the sediment load moving alongshore becomes constant. If the sediment load is obstructed in any way deposition will ensue and a spit will grow out from the land at an angle of about 45°. The growing spit will form a wave shadow and the process will be repeated along the lagoon shore if it is long enough. Smaller waves from the opposite direction will cause material to be added to the spit, giving it a cuspate form.

The spits once formed will tend to shift along the shore of the lagoon in the direction of the dominant waves. The orientation of the cuspate spits will vary along the length of the lagoon according to the available fetch. They will be symmetrical in the centre, but increasingly asymmetrical towards the ends of the lagoon, where the fetch in two opposite directions is very unequal. Half-heart-shaped bays will develop between the spits, which will slowly migrate towards the ends of the lagoon from the centre. The central ones will be stable. In time the spits become larger and interfere with the generation of waves. If the same process is operating on both shores of the lagoon, it may become segmented into separate elongated elliptical parts. In time when the features have reached stability the spits from either side of the lagoon may meet in the centre, and elongated lakes now result. Waves can now be generated of almost equal length from any direction so that the lakes gradually become more nearly circular. Features of this form appear to be more common in high latitudes, and where lagoons do not become filled with mud and salt marsh vegetation.

e Straight coasts

So far the geometrical forms considered are curved. They are related to coasts in which head-lands are an essential element of the coastal outline. There are, however, long stretches of beach that are essentially straight. Examples of long straight beaches have been discussed by R. J. Russell (1958). They occur in the Gulf of Mexico, where they stretch over distances exceeding 1000 km along the coasts of Texas and Louisiana. They also occur east of the Mississippi delta along the coasts of Alabama and Florida. These beaches are mostly along the seaward face of offshore barriers. They lie seaward of an intricate lagoon shore over much of their length. These long straight beaches are formed in an area of subsidence.

Similar long straight beaches, also on the seaward side of barrier islands, are characteristic of the Atlantic coast of the U.S.A. extending from New York to Florida. Some of these straight beaches are mainland ones. Others, as in the vicinity of Cape Hatteras, lie more than 60 km

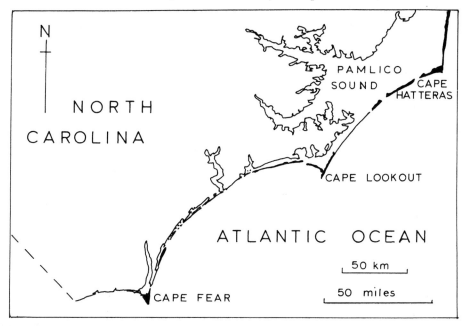

Figure 13-7 Map of North Carolina coast.

offshore. There are, however, prominent capes along the coast at Cape Fear, Cape Lookout and Cape Hatteras in North Carolina. Near Cape Hatteras there is a broad shoal area, and 40 km north of the Cape the Outer Banks change trend. Russell suggests that the change in trend is related to the presence of erosion-resistant material offshore. This material causes tom-bolo formation, and prevents the landward migration of the beaches. The resistant material is probably heavy clay, which is the foundation of some of the offshore barrier islands.

These long straight beaches formed rapidly in about 6000 years, but they have been and are still undergoing modification. Some move landwards and others seawards. When looked at on a small-scale map they do show some curvature of the log-spiral type. Their curvature increases markedly near the major capes along this coast, although over much of their length they are very nearly straight for distances of tens of miles.

The detailed changes of some of the outer capes have been studied by M. T. El-Ashry and H. R. Wanless (1968). The capes, which are shown in figure 13-7, are particularly susceptible to modification by hurricane-generated waves and other major storms. Aerial photographs were used to determine the changes created by these extreme events. The dates of the air photograph surveys are 1945, 1953, 1958, 1959, 1961 and 1962. Charts going back to 1852 have also been consulted, as well as more recent topographic maps.

Three capes were studied. Two of these, Capes Fear and Hatteras, have retreated on the evidence of both maps and photographs. The third, Cape Lookout, advanced seaward, but also showed periods of retreat on the photographic evidence. The spits at the end of the Capes are modified by wave activity in major storms. The normal smooth outline is restored by the smaller waves of calm conditions. During hurricanes material is washed over from the seaward sides of the beaches into the bays. At other times material moves southwards, which is the net direction of drift along this coast, but some is lost permanently into deeper water off the Capes. Waves sometimes breach the low parts of the barrier beaches forming fans in the bays. At other times high water in the lagoons causes break-throughs in the opposite direction. Inlets through the barrier islands migrate southwards.

On the whole the ocean side of the beaches is retreating. The changes in the orientation of the beaches tend to correlate with the direction of prevailing gale force winds during the months preceding photography. The offshore shoals that extend up to 16 km from the capes represents material that is permanently lost from the beaches. Beach material reaches the shoals during storms of major intensity. The oscillating movement of the capes shows that the beach form is on the whole adjusted to the prevailing conditions. The equilibrium form is one of smoothly flowing curves, which have long straight portions in the down-drift sections. The curvature is greater near the fulcrum points of the capes. These are the fixed points along the coast that determine its geometrical form.

Summary

W. V. Lewis put forward the view that beach features have a tendency to turn to a direction at right-angles to the direction from which the dominant waves approach. This view was slightly modified by A. Schou, who considered that the resultant of strong winds also influenced the orientation of beach features in conjunction with the direction of maximum fetch, from which the dominant waves would be expected to come. These views apply mainly to shingle beaches, on which the dominant waves are the steep storm waves. These waves are generated often by strong winds blowing close to the coast and they build up the most permanent features, the storm beach ridges, on shingle beaches. J. L. Davies has shown that on sandy structures the dominant waves are the long, constructive swells. These waves build up the berms that determine the orientation of sand beaches. The orientation of the beaches is determined by the direction of approach of the refracted swells. Thus the offshore relief and the direction and length of the long swells determines the orientation of sandy beaches. Examples of the operation of the orientation process are found in south Australia and Tasmania, where the dominant waves have a period of 14 seconds. The west coast of Ireland, which is intricate in outline, also illustrates these controls on the orientation of sandy beaches. A wide variety of orientations can result from marked wave refraction.

Chesil Beach and Hurst Castle spit on the south coast of England exemplify the orientation of shingle structure normal to the approach of dominant storm waves. The latter feature is shaped by waves from two distinct directions, the major set forming the main ridge and the smaller the lateral recurves. In areas that are rising relative to sea level chevron beach ridges may form.

These are long beach ridges transverse to the shore to which are attached straight or arcuate barbs.

Geometrical forms have been recognized in the outline of beaches. A study of New Zealand beaches has revealed the close approximation of many of the bays to the arc of a circle. The beaches in the bays are also adjusted to the direction of approach of the refracted swell. Other small sections of beach and bays between breakwaters or headlands have been shown by Yasso to approximate very closely to a log-spiral form. This form is also affected by the refraction and diffraction of waves in the lee of headlands or breakwaters. Silvester has also shown that a similar form of bay is the stable shape of bays liable to erosion and affected by wave with an oblique approach. These forms can be used to assess future changes in the coast outline and to assist in stabilizing the beach where it is liable to erosion. Zenkovich has shown that elongated lagoons may be divided up into elliptical or circular lakes by the growth of spits along the lagoon shores. Other beaches have very long straight stretches.

References

ANTONINI, G. A. 1962: Development of the Horseshoe cove shoreline, Sandy Hook, New Jersey. *Tech. Rep.* **3,** Off. Naval Res. Geog. Br., Proj. NR 388–057. (11 pp.)

BASCOM, W. 1954: The control of stream outlets by wave refraction. *J. Geol.* **62**(6), 600–605.

DAVIES, J. L. 1959: Wave refraction and the evolution of shoreline curves. *Geog. Stud.* **5**(2), 1–14.

DAVIES, J. L. 1960: Beach alignment in South Australia. *Australian Geogr.* **8**(1), 42–4.

DE LA BECHE, H. T. 1834: *A geological manual.* London: Researches in theoretical geology.

DOORNKAMP, J. C. and KING, C. A. M. 1971: *Numerical analysis in geomorphology.* London: Arnold; New York: St Martin's Press. (384 pp.)

EL-ASHRY, M. T. and WANLESS, H. R. 1968: Photo interpretation of shoreline changes between Capes Hatteras and Fear (North Carolina). *Mar. Geol.* **6**(5), 347–79.

GUILCHER, A. 1958: *Coastal and submarine morphology.* London: Methuen.

HARRISON, J. T. 1848: Observations on causes tending to alter the outline of the English coast. *Min. Proc. Inst. Civ. Eng.* **8,** 344.

KING, C. A. M. 1965: Some observations on the beaches on the west coast of County Donegal. *Irish Geogr.* **5**(2), 40–50.

KING, C. A. M. 1969: Some Arctic coastal features around Foxe Basin and in E. Baffin Island, N.W.T. Canada. *Geogr. Ann.* A **51**(4), 207–18.

LEWIS, W. V. 1931: Effect of wave incidence on the configuration of a shingle beach. *Geog. J.* **78,** 131–48.

LEWIS, W. V. 1938: The evolution of shoreline curves. *Proc. Geol. Assoc.* **49,** 107–27.

MCCLEAN, R. 1967: Plan shape and orientation of beaches along the east coast, South Island, New Zealand. *N.Z. Geogr.* **23,** 16–22.

RUSSELL, R. J. 1958: Long straight beaches. *Eclog. Geol. Helvetica* **51**(3), 591–8.

SCHOU, A. 1945: Det Marine forland. *Folia Geog. Danica* **4,** 1–236.

SILVESTER, R. 1960: Stabilisation of sedimentary coastlines. *Nature* **188**(4749), 467–9.

SILVESTER, R. 1962: Sand movement around the coastlines of the world. *Inst. Civ. Eng. Conf. on Civ. Eng. Problems Overseas.* Paper **14.** (16 pp.)

TANNER, F. 1967: Finger bars on an ideal low-wave, low-tide beach, Santa Caterina Island, Brazil. *Abs. Vol. 1967 Ann Meeting, New Orleans, Geol. Soc. Am.,* 219.

YASSO, W. E. 1964a: Geometry and development of spit-bar shorelines at Horseshoe Cove, Sandy Hook, New Jersey. *Tech. Rep.* **5,** Off. Naval Res., Geog. Br. NR 388–057.

YASSO, W. E. 1964b: Plan geometry of headland bay beaches. *Tech. Rep.* **7,** Off. Naval Res., Geog. Br., NR 388–057.

ZENKOVICH, V. P. 1959: On the genesis of cuspate spits along lagoon shores. *J. Geol.* **67**(3), 269–77.

14 Minor beach forms

1 **Ripples :** a) Model studies; b) Ripples in nature.

2 **Beach cusps**

3 **Transverse bars**

4 **Tropical beach features :** a) Beach rock; b) Coral reef shoreline features.

5 **Polar beach features**

Summary

In this chapter a number of minor beach forms and features are discussed. Some of these are of widespread occurrence, others are limited to beaches in particular climatic zones. Ripples are the smallest features. They are considered first, as their study is useful in assessing the nature of oscillatory flow and they are widespread on certain zones of most sandy beaches. Beach cusps are larger, but their occurrence is limited to the foreshore, and particularly to high-tide level, on a few sandy and shingly beaches. Still larger, but much less common, are transverse bars, characteristic of some low- to moderate-energy shores. Some of the features found only on tropical coasts are mentioned next: beach rock is one of these and has given rise to a considerable amount of discussion. Corals are also restricted to warmer seas. Finally some of the minor forms that are characteristic of beaches in cold and polar environments will be considered. In the latter areas features associated with the presence of shore ice are particularly significant.

1 Ripples

The study of ripple formation under the oscillatory flow characteristic of wave motion has been carried out both in laboratories and in the field. Some of the results of laboratory studies will be considered first and then these will be related to the field observations. Ripples are characteristic of the area of oscillatory flow seaward of the break-point of the waves. They are only exposed on natural beaches in those areas where they are not destroyed by the breakers and swash of the falling tide. They are, therefore, found in runnels on ridge and runnel beaches and those parts of the foreshore where the gradient is so low that the power of the swash and backwash is not sufficient to destroy them. Because they are due to oscillatory flow under wave action they can be generated by means of an oscillating section of sand bed.

a Model studies
Some mention of the effect of ripple formation on the amount of sand moving outside the break-point in a model tank has already been made. In this section the mode of formation and dimensions of ripples will be considered in more detail. Observations have been made both in ordinary

wave tanks and by oscillating a curved cradle through still water. One very detailed study was made by M. Manohar (1955), using both theoretical and experimental data. His results apply mainly to waves in fairly deep water of about 7·3 m. He discusses in detail the nature of the boundary layer, and concludes that ripples only form when the flow in this layer is turbulent. His analysis applies where the water velocity landward and seaward is nearly the same, so his results are not directly applicable to the formation of ripples near the break-point.

The experiments made by R. A. Bagnold (1946) were also carried out by oscillating a cradle through still water with a simple harmonic motion. A series of angular velocities was used for a number of different semi-amplitudes, R, from 25·0 to 0·5 cm. The range of velocities used covered the speed at which sand first started to be disturbed to a velocity at which the whole sand bed started to move off the cradle. A second series of experiments was made to measure the ripple drag. The motion of the water was studied by using a camera fixed to the cradle and moving with the ripples. The photographs revealed the presence of small eddies and large vortices. Bagnold has described two different types of ripples, which are formed by different forces, but which are superficially similar in appearance. The similarity arises because both depend on the maximum angle at which sand is stable, which is about 30°.

When sand movement first starts the sand grains first move by rolling. The distance at first is short, as only the maximum acceleration raises the speed enough to move the sand. The grains in time form into a pattern of transverse crests only a few grains high. They oscillate to and fro with the passing waves. These small crests eventually grow into a stable pattern, the spacing of which depends on the sheltering effect exerted by one ridge extending to the next. The height of the ridge, which determines the width of the flow-shadow, also affects the repetition distance. The form of the rolling grain ripples depends on the size of the sand. In the larger grains it may become part of a nearly circular arc in profile, while in finer material flat troughs exist. There is no movement in the troughs of the ripples of this type and no vortices are set up. This type of ripple will not form if the initial bed has inequalities of greater amplitude than about 20 grain diameters. The speeds at which it will form vary from the critical speed which first initiates movement to about twice that speed.

If the speed is increased to more than twice the critical speed, the stable system of rolling grain ripples suddenly breaks down and vortex ripples will be developed. The steep lee face first increases beyond a stable height at one point. A vortex forms, creating a new type of ripple, which rapidly extends from this initial position in both directions. Any irregularity on the bed is sufficient to initiate the formation of a vortex and the breakdown of the stable system, and on an irregular bed the velocity need not be so high to initiate vortex type ripples. The effect of the vortex is to move sand grains from the foot of the ripple to its crest, thus controlling its size. With a long stroke the height of the ripple tended to decrease. With a very long stroke, and high velocity, the length to height ratio becomes such that no vortex can develop, due to the high mid-stroke speed. Hence the vortex type of ripple cannot form. With very short strokes, on the other hand, the crests of the ripples are sharply pointed.

The length of the ripples was found to be independent of the speed of oscillation for a variety of sizes and densities of grains. Coal, steel and quartz were used, with diameters varying from 0·25 to 0·09 mm. The variation in size of the grains did, however, affect the length of the ripples. The effect of variation in the stroke of the cradle was not shown in a variation in pitch of the ripple, except for the two largest grain sizes. In these materials the ripples suddenly became shorter as the R/p ratio reached unity, but remained at the same ratio as R increased. The natural length of the ripple appears to be independent of the density of the grain and to vary nearly as the square-root of its diameter. The degree of sorting of the sand also had little effect on the length of the ripple. The experiments were made with sand of much more mixed character than most natural beach sands.

The length to height ratio of the ripples remained at about 4·5 to 5·0 for the shorter amplitude of oscillation. The ratio increased to nearly 8·0 as the value of R increased to a maximum of 32 cm. A modification of the vortex ripple pattern occurred when R was reduced to about $\frac{1}{6}$ of the length of the ripple or p/6. This pattern resembled a brick wall, in that regular transverse bridges were formed between two crests and offset as in brick walling. The pattern has also been observed in nature in deep water, with a short oscillation on a sandy bed. This provides confirmation that the model ripples behaved as their full-scale counterparts (Bagnold, 1946).

Experiments were made in a wave tank by T. Scott (1954) in which he studied the formation of ripples created by the uneven accelerations of water in wave motion on a sloping beach. His experiments apply more nearly to the natural conditions of a sand beach near the break-point than those already discussed which were made in uniform depth with harmonic oscillation. Scott was able to study the movement of the ripples in relation to the direction of the shoreline, to evaluate the effect of differential acceleration under the wave crest and trough, and to relate the dimensions of the ripples to the wave characteristics. He found that the ripples moved towards the land on the upper part of the profile, but moved seawards in deeper water. The position of the change in direction varied slightly from time to time, but was mostly between 2·44 and 3·36 m from the water line in about 30 cm of water. The velocity of movement increased away from the point of change of direction. The landward movement of ripples in the shallow water was caused by more sand being pushed over the crest of the ripples than was carried seaward in suspension by the vortex, which developed as the wave trough passes. This type of movement resulted in the development of an asymmetrical form in which the landward slope was steeper. The form and type of movement appeared to be exactly reversed in the deeper water where the ripples were moving seaward. In intermediate depths the ripples were more symmetrical, implying a more balanced movement. The landward movement of ripples in shallow water was more rapid when the waves were higher.

In order to relate the movement of the ripples to the acceleration of the water ciné photographs were used to measure the orbital velocity of the particles. The accelerations were very much higher in a landward direction in relatively shallow water, while in deeper water the accelerations became more equal and in one case, near the position of change of ripple movement direction, the seaward acceleration was greater. The length of the ripples agreed closely with the amplitude of oscillation of the water horizontally, agreeing with Bagnold's results, when R/p is less than unity.

An analytical model of ripple development in unidirectional flow has been given by J. P. Kennedy (1963), in which he relates wave length and velocity of movement of the ripples to flow characteristics. He also indicates the conditions necessary for different configurations of the bed, such as ripples, anti-dunes and a flat bed. He does not, however, deal with the oscillatory flow characteristic of wave-generated ripples.

A recent analytical and experimental study by M. R. Carstens et al. (1969) has extended the knowledge of ripple formation under oscillatory water motion. In this type of motion fill and cut alternate both periodically and spatially. With smaller velocities this alternation gives rise to the rippled or duned bed. The upstream face of the ripple is an area of scour, as flow accelerates towards the crest. A vortex forms at the crest, while sand grains carried over the crest are deposited on the downstream face. The separated flow joins the surface in the ripple trough, where the particles are at rest. With reversal of flow, areas of cut and fill are also reversed. This complex system is not yet amenable to exact mathematical formulation. The profile of the moving bed is assumed to be a moving sinusoid of varying amplitude and constant wave length. The upstream side of the ripple is taken to extend along the upper boundary of the separation layer in the water beyond the crest. The water motion is assumed to be harmonic, and the ripples small relative to the wave length. With these assumptions, the fluid velocities can be derived. They are then substituted into empirical equations for sediment transport. From these steps, mathematical functions for the velocity of the bed form, and the ratio of ripple amplitude to wave length are derived. The resulting equations are not very satisfactory, but they do point to a possible analytical solution. The velocity distribution along the face of the ripple is given by

$$u/U_m = 2{\cdot}4x/\lambda \cos 2\pi t/T$$

where u is the velocity distribution, U_m is the maximum velocity at the crest, t is time, T is period, and λ is the ripple length. The evolution of the rippled bed can either be induced or spontaneous. Spontaneous ripple formation occurs if the water motion amplitude, a, is greater than a specific value. Ripples then appear by scouring all over the bed. Just before the ripples appear some of the sand grains move to and fro over the bed.

The experiments on which these observations were based were carried out in a large U-tube, in which water could be oscillated horizontally over a sand bed at the bottom of the tube. The test section was 3·05 m long, 30·5 cm high and 1·22 m wide. The period of oscillation was 3·6 seconds, and the amplitude could be varied. This method is more satisfactory for ripple studies, as it is difficult to obtain adequate velocities for ripple formation by generating waves in a long wave tank.

Spontaneous formation continues with bands of grains moving in phase with the water velocity. The moving bands become the ripple crests and the stationary ones the troughs. As ripple amplitude increases the crest motion tends to decrease and vortices begin to develop. The ripples are irregular at this stage as some must be removed to form the final stable pattern. Ripple formation may be induced by a disturbance on the bed. They begin at the disturbance and spread outwards from it. Incipient motion begins when the following criterion is satisfied:

$$\frac{u_c{}^2}{(s-1)gD_g} = \left(\frac{\tan\phi\cos\alpha + \sin\alpha}{1 + \tan\phi}\right)\left(\frac{8{\cdot}2}{C_D{}^1}\right)$$

$C_D{}^1$ is the coefficient of drag, α is the angle of inclination of the bed from horizontal, ϕ is the angle of repose, D_g is the grain diameter and u_c is the critical velocity. Figure 14-1 illustrates the incipient ripple formation velocity requirements.

Once formed the ripples move at a velocity, c, and this value appears to decrease as the ripple system develops. In fact the ripples only appeared to move when $a_c < a < a_s$, where a_c is the water motion amplitude for incipient motion and a_s is the amplitude at which ripples form spontaneously all over the bed. When amplitudes are low the ripple geometry is two-dimensional. The ripple amplitude increases until a/D_g is 775. Ripples are three-dimensional in the range between 775 and 1700, while above 1700 they disappear and the bed becomes flat. When the ripples are two-dimensional their wave lengths are 5 to 6·5 times their amplitude. When the ripples are three-dimensional their amplitude decreases linearly with the water motion amplitude to a zero value, but the wave length is nearly independent of the value of a.

The added dissipation of energy over a rippled bed was compared with that over a smooth bed. The drag coefficients were used to give the difference. These coefficients seemed to be unusually large compared with flow in one direction. This was found to be due to the almost uniform velocity above the bed in oscillatory flow, so that the choice of reference level for the determination of mean velocity was important. The dissipation of energy is due to the develop-

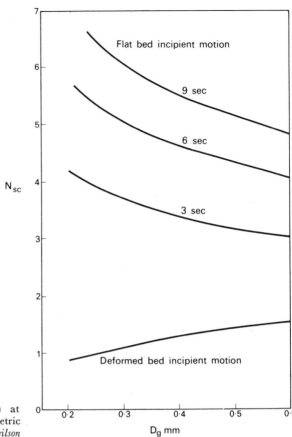

Figure 14-1 Critical sediment number (N_{sc}) at incipient motion for oscillatory flow. D_g is the geometric mean diameter of bed material. (*After Carstens, Neilson and Altinbilek, 1969.*)

ment of vortices, which are generated twice in each cycle of oscillation. Two methods were used to estimate the loss of energy. Considerably more energy was dissipated over the rippled bed, in many runs amounting to more than twice as much as with a smooth bed.

b Ripples in nature

Before true ripples are considered, the rhomboid type of beach marks noted by E. G. Otvos will be mentioned (1964a). These marks form a closed network of shallow grooves on the intertidal beach surface. They are different from rhomboid ripple marks (which are tongues of sand formed in a uniform current), and are formed by the backwash returning down the foreshore. Otvos abandoned the view that they were formed by two sets of grooves made by the swash and backwash respectively. One reason for abandoning this view was that the grooves were often not parallel to the directions of the swash and backwash currents. He considered that the rhomboid rill marks were due to deflection and channelling caused by uniformly distributed irregularities on the otherwise smooth, even sand surface that is swept by the rear part of the backwash. The marks are normally made by relatively small waves, but there is no consistent trend between breaker size and dimensions of the angles between the grooves.

Observations, reported by D. L. Inman (1957), on the formation of ripples under oscillatory waves in nature, have been made by swimmers off the coast of California. These observations were made to depths of 51·8 m. Ripples were always present on sandy floors where the significant orbital velocity was somewhere between 10 and 91·5 cm/sec. The length of the ripples varied between 4·2 cm and 1·22 m. The observations included the length, height, symmetry and form of the ripple. The results showed that the ripples were of two types. Some had flat troughs between the crests, which were called solitary ripples. Others had rounded troughs and were named trochoidal ripples. Whenever possible the wave dimensions were measured at the same time as ripples were observed.

The size of the ripples was found to be related to the sand size. The larger ripples were formed of coarser sand and the smaller of finer sand. The depth of water and exposure also affected the ripple size. Ripples in deeper water and off exposed coasts tended to be larger than those in shallower water and in more sheltered areas. Ripples in bays and lakes were the smallest. This relationship is due to variations in the amplitude of the orbital oscillation of the waves forming them. The trochoidal ripples were found in deeper water and more sheltered sites. They are formed by the development of vortices. The flat-bottomed, solitary ripples were found where the bottom velocities and orbital amplitudes were greater. They occurred in shallower water and on finer sand, where the material is carried in sub-suspension in a layer a few centimetres thick. Where there was a large supply of sand, the coarser grains were found on the ripple crest and the finest and densest grains in the troughs. The finer sand was found at the crest where the supply was limited in areas of rocky bottom. The character of sand at the crest largely determined the dimensions of the ripples.

Observations of ripples on the bottom of the Black Sea off the coast of the Crimea have been made by V. P. Zenkovich (1946). At a depth of 14 m he observed ripples from 90 to 110 cm long and 7 to 10 cm high. They must originally have been 15 cm high, before fine material was deposited in their troughs. The crests of the ripples in a depth of 13 m contained pebbles up to 6 cm in length. An analysis of the material from the crest showed that it had a median diameter of 17 mm, and that in the trough of 3·5 mm. In a depth of 18 m the crest diameter was 3·0 mm and the trough 0·17 mm.

The results of the full-scale observations mostly agree with those of model experiments. There are, however, some differences. The length of model ripples is not as great as that of natural ripples for the same sand size. The longest ripples on natural beaches were found in deeper water, where the velocities were slower. Manohar found that the longest model ripples were formed where the velocity was approaching the upper limiting value, while in nature the ripple length was reduced at higher speeds.

W. F. Tanner (1965) had drawn attention to the occurrence, in the swash zone, of high-index symmetrical ripples. He had observed them on the beaches of the southeast U.S.A. They occur parallel with the step and have lengths of 20 to 50 cm, and indices of 30 to 100. They appear to be shear ridges in an incipient stage before an eddy forms. They are formed by the alternation of the swash and backwash flow.

2 Beach cusps

Beach cusps modify the normal regular sorting of material parallel to the shore. They are formed by the swash and backwash of the waves, and are found near the high-water level on a tidal beach, and in the swash zone of tideless seas and lakes. According to O. F. Evans (1938) they occur in all types of beach material from fine sand to gravel. They are normally best developed in areas where the beach material contains a mixture of sand and shingle or in pure shingle beaches. They occur, for example, on Chesil Beach near Portland, where the shingle is coarse with a diameter of 2·5 to 5 cm.

A laboratory study of beach cusps has been carried out by N. C. Flemming (1964). Nine experiments were carried out with 5 cm high waves acting on a model beach for up to 48 hours. In eight runs beach cusps formed. In only one, however, were the cusps stable. They formed after two hours and thereafter remained constant. In the other runs the cusps varied. The beach material was sorted in such a way that the large particles were concentrated on the upper surface at the top and bottom of the beach. Near the water line the modal size increased vertically downwards. No significant difference in the size sorting was observed in the bays and promontories. The most spherical grains collected at the foot of the beach, and the flatter ones at the back of the bays. The high permeability at the cusp points increased the stability of the system, while the least permeable particles collected in the bays.

The method of formation and conditions necessary for the development of cusps are still open to doubt. D. W. Johnson (1919) discussed most of the earlier theories of beach cusps and reached the conclusion that they are formed by selective erosion of the swash working on irregular initial depressions. The size of the cusps is related to the size of the waves. Johnson considered that the spacing of the cusps was roughly doubled as the wave height doubled. Both he and P. D. Timmermans (1935) thought that cusps formed most readily when the waves were approaching perpendicular to the shore. O. F. Evans (1938) on the other hand, found that cusps could form under the action of both normal and oblique waves.

O. F. Evans (1938) has classified beach cusps into a number of categories, some of which are dependent on features on the beach. The true cusps are, however, independent of fixed objects. From observations on Lake Michigan and other lakes, Evans came to the conclusion that the cusps were formed by erosion of a previously built beach ridge. Small breaches in the ridge led to the rapid development of cusps along the shore by deepening the breaks. The cuspate form is due to the parabolic paths of the water particles in the swash. The resulting cusps are spaced roughly equidistant. Variation of 40%, however, in cusp spacing was the minimum observed, and spacing often varied by over 100%.

P. H. Kuenen (1948) has re-examined the problem of the beach cusps and stressed the relative regularity of the features. Sorting of beach material is also typical of cusps on many beaches. The coarser material is carried to the back and horns of the cusp, while the finer sediment occupies the floor of the depression between the horns. Kuenen emphasized the importance of deposition, as well as erosion of material, in the formation of the cusps. The horns are built up of material washed from the bays. The sideways component of the swash helps to concentrate the backwash along the edges of the horns.

The lateral movement of the swash has also been commented upon by R. A. Bagnold (1940) in explaining the variation of gradient on a model beach. Bagnold compared the model beach with bays, spaced 12 m apart, on the beach near Mersa Matruh on the coast of Egypt. He noted that the swash piles up against the horns, and is divided into two streams, which swing round the head of the bays and unite to flow back, as backwash, down the centre of the bay. The bay is lowered by the vigorous backwash. This scheme is rather different from that of Kuenen, but both show the importance of the lateral movement of water in the formation of the cusp. The breaching of a beach ridge is not necessary to explain the initiation of cusps. They frequently occur where no such ridge is present, particularly on tidal beaches.

One of the few studies of beach cusps that combine a measure of the cusps with that of the waves forming them is reported by M. S. Longuet-Higgins and D. W. Parkin (1962). They measured waves and cusps at Seaford and on Chesil Beach. Some model experiments were also made. In the experiments a regular series of cusps formed. Seaward of each cusp a small accumulation of material collected, while erosion formed a gully at the seaward ends of the intercusp promontories. The profile across the cusps was thus reversed at a lower level. The cusps observed near Seaford occurred at both high- and low-tide level on a steep shingle beach. The cusp spacing was not related to the wave length in a simple manner. From observations made on Chesil Beach a relationship was found between the length of the swash and the spacing of the cusps. There was, however, no correlation between the wave period and the cusp spacing, although there was a weak positive correlation between the cusp spacing and the wave height. Longuet-Higgins and Parkin concluded that cusp spacing is primarily a function of swash length. The cusps appeared to form most readily when there was a vertical stratification of material, with coarse shingle on the surface and a mixed impermeable layer below. This layer increases the power of the backwash relative to the swash, allowing the former to erode the bays. The thicker layer of shingle on the promontories allows more swash percolation and less backwash erosion, thus contributing to the cusp permanence. Cusps are destroyed by waves that are too large for them.

Cusps do not form only in shingle beaches. Observations of cusps in Donegal (C. A. M. King, 1965) showed that they also form on sandy beaches. The best set occurred on Trahane beach where 36 cusps covered 533 m of beach. They had a mean spacing of 14·8 m and a standard deviation of 1·52 m, indicating considerable regularity. The mean height of the crest above the trough was 19·8 cm. The sand of the crest was coarser than that in the troughs, the respective mean diameters being 1·53 and 1·85 ϕ. This difference of sand size would help to maintain the cusps by allowing greater percolation through the sand on the horns or crests, than in the troughs or bays. Waves could only reach the beach normal to the shore. The waves forming the cusps had a period of 9·5 seconds and were low. Remnants of larger cusps occurred higher up the beach. These had presumably been formed by more vigorous waves.

In Glen Bay, a narrow beach contained larger cusps. A mean length of 31·4 m was measured with an amplitude between bay and promontory of 0·7 m. The larger size is probably related to the coarser sand of this bay. The mean sizes of the sand of the cusp horn and bay were 1·43 and 1·58 ϕ respectively. These cusps were not affected by a change of wave period. This supports the results of Longuet-Higgins and Parkin. Similar sized cusps on another beach increased in length towards the centre of the bay, where exposure to the waves was greater. The mean sizes were 25·9 m and 29·9 m. There was a tendency for a positive correlation between the size of the cusps, the size of the sand and the size of the waves forming the cusps, all variables increasing together. There were not, however, enough values to make a significant correlation.

H. Mii (1958) has described a considerable number of cusps along the coast of Japan. Some interesting relationships emerge from his measurements. The formation of cusps was affected by the beach slope, but their size was more closely related to the waves that formed them. Favourable conditions for cusp formation included waves approaching normal to the coast, although this was not necessary. Cusps only formed where there was a destructive element in the wave action. They formed, and were obliterated very quickly, at the line where water drains out of the beach, which was normally in the swash–backwash zone. Small depressions formed at this level and these developed into the cusps. Once they formed the erosive action of the waves became concentrated. The depressions were enlarged horizontally and vertically until a limit was set by the size of the waves and the beach material. Nine different forms of cusps were distinguished according to their position relative to breaks of slope of the beach profile.

E. G. Otvos (1964b) has described cusps at Westbrook, Connecticut, where coarse and fine sediment both occur on the beach. Conditions necessary for cusp formation include adequate amounts of transportable material, and sufficient breaker energy for the accumulation of the coarse material to form the ridges. The balance between swash energy and availability of material must be maintained until the cusp is formed. The shingly cusps form much more rapidly than fine sandy cusps, which form as a result of the combination of erosion and deposition. If the supply of coarse material is maintained as the tide recedes, and the waves maintain their size, the cusp promontories can be elongated down the beach to form long transverse ridges on the foreshore. These become oblique if there is rapid longshore drift of material. The spacing of cusps on the Westbrook beaches was 160 to 500 cm. Wave direction does not appear to have an important control on cusp development. Fine-grained sand cusps were less common than coarse-grain cusps with shingle, and they tended to have wider spacing.

Cusps have been observed on beaches in a wide range of environments by R. J. Russell and W. G. McIntire (1965b). Their observations are concentrated on tropical and southern hemisphere beaches, covering 84 examples of beach cusps. A plot of the spacing of cusps showed a bimodal distribution with a large mode at 13·7 m and a smaller one at 47·3 m. They observed that cusp regularity increases with time. Well-developed cusps occupy a considerable area and are associated with a conspicuous berm at the level of the higher points along the cusp tops. They appear on the seaward face of an advancing berm and grow seawards as they develop. The contrast between cusp and bay material gradually decreases and they lose their sharpness. The spacing depends on the nature of the waves. They originate during the transition from winter to summer beach conditions, and tend to disappear when conditions become more destructive. As the cusps form, a circularity develops in the movement of the swash, with water swinging into the bays where two streams meet, causing turbulence and rapid flow down the bay. This backwash prevents the advance of the next swash in this zone, forcing it up the promontories. Here the turbulence decreases upwards, leading to deposition of the larger particles, while the increasing turbulence in the lower parts of the bays allows entrainment and removal of material. The coarse material characteristic of the cusp horns probably comes from the step zone, where sediments are normally coarser.

A cellular pattern of flow is essential for the initiation of cusps and this may be related to processes that lead to rip current development. Irregularities in the step zone may be the initial cause of cellular flow, and hence cusp initiation. A chi-square and analysis of variance test suggested that, with 99% confidence, there is a relation between cusp spacing and the degree of exposure.

A regular set of cusps was described by G. A. Worrall (1969) on the coast of West Africa. The cusps formed in coarse to medium sand, with some fine gravel but no shingle. They were large, having a length of 30 to 45 m and a height between 0·7 and 1·3 m. Their constancy may be due to the regularity of wave action on the coast. The waves approached obliquely and set up a cellular motion similar to that described by Russell and McIntire (1965), who agree that some regular variation in flow pattern offshore is required to initiate cusp formation.

3 Transverse bars

W. F. Tanner (1967; 1965) has drawn attention to larger features on the beach. They are the transverse bars that develop below low water on some low- to moderate-energy shorelines. The sand accumulations form bars transverse to the coast. They have been mentioned in chapter 13 in connection with the chevron pattern of beach ridges, found on some Arctic coasts that are undergoing uplift. The features form where accumulations of sand in the offshore zone concentrate wave energy by refraction. This results in the landward movement of material. The accumulation is thus elongated into a bar transverse to the shoreline.

Between the growing bars the beach is relatively protected and as long as they are not too long sediment moves seawards in the troughs. When the bars increase in length beyond a critical size, the movement of water develops into two distinct cells, and their formation becomes more complex. The bars can be seen on some aerial photographs of areas where there is an abundance of loose sediment and relatively shallow water in the offshore zone, with only limited wave action. The bars tend to occur near estuaries and other areas where the sediment supply is considerable and the water circulation is complex.

In a more detailed study of transverse bars, A. W. Niederoda and W. F. Tanner (1970) have made both field and laboratory observations on the conditions under which these features form. They are normally restricted to areas of abundant sand supply, wide gently sloping foreshores and beaches and low-average breaker heights. The field observations were carried out on the coast of Florida at St James Island in the Gulf of Mexico. The average breaker height is 6 cm on this low-energy coast and the transverse bars extend to a depth of 1·5 m at a distance that varies between 335 and 1000 m from the shore. The bars are spaced at 107 to 640 m and vary between 64 and 218 m in length. Their maximum relief is about 24 cm and they do not migrate. At low tide the bars cause significant wave refraction and wave crests develop a V-shaped form, with the bar crest under the apex. The wave crests form a crossing pattern over the bar. Current measurements showed that the water is moving shorewards over the bar crest, sometimes at 80 cm/sec, slowing down and splitting into two streams near the shore. The current then returns seaward between the bars in a more diffuse form and at a lower velocity than the more concentrated landward flow over the bar crest. Dyed sand also demonstrated the capacity of the current to move sediment landwards along the bar crest, at a maximum grain velocity of 7 cm/sec.

Wave tank experiments confirmed that a circulatory scheme could be induced by two sets of interfering waves. In a second set of experiments a single wave was generated over a bottom modelled in the form of transverse bars. The same circulatory water pattern was formed, with landward movement along the bar crest. The refraction pattern created by transverse bars was also studied by means of a computer program, which demonstrated the pattern of crossing orthogonals that had been observed in Florida. Energy is greater where the orthogonals cross, thus helping to account for the greater wave current velocity at these positions. In some depths the orthogonals focus at points along the bar crest, thus accounting for variations in height along the bar crests.

The bars are important in that they provide a mechanism whereby sand can be transported landwards from offshore. The circulatory current system is set up as a result of the concentration of energy along the bar crest by refraction. This means that more water approaches the shore along the bar crest and this results in the slower, wider seaward movement between the bars. The current scheme becomes more complex as the bars increase in length and bottom friction becomes an important factor. The shallower water over the bar crest causes more energy to be lost in this zone than in the deeper water between the bars. The velocity over the crest will become less than that over the trough nearer the shore where the bars are long. Thus a reverse circulation will be set up over the shoreward portion of the system. The initial formation of the bars will be facilitated where the bottom is shallow. In these conditions a small variation in depth will cause marked wave refraction. Once wave refraction has been initiated then the bars can develop, and they will be maintained by the refraction pattern and the currents to which it gives rise. Each bar only affects a certain extent of beach, so that in time a fairly regular system is likely to develop. Where bars are initially too close they will tend to merge, where they are widely spaced new ones can form between them. The perpetuation of the system of transverse bars requires a delicate balance to be maintained between the forms and the transporting capacity of the wave-generated currents. These currents are not associated with rip currents, which in fact have an opposite pattern with a concentrated seaward flow balancing a diffuse landward flow. The permanence of the bars depends on the maintenance of the equilibrium conditions under which they form.

4 Tropical beach features

a Beach rock

One of the features characteristic of tropical coasts that has given rise to much speculation is the formation of beach rock. A. Guilcher (1961) has shown that this lithified beach material exists mainly in the regions in which corals flourish. The cement that lithifies beach rock is calcareous in type. High temperatures assist the cementation process. Needles of aragonite or calcite form in the voids between the sand grains, causing an increase in the coherence of the material. Consolidation takes place in the intertidal zone. Beach rock is very occasional in its occurrence, appearing on some beaches but not on others, and also varying in position with time on any one beach. The beach rock often forms small outcrops that are discontinuous both laterally and transverse to the beach, several distinct layers of beach rock forming at different levels on the beach. About 95% of true beach rock is found in the warm waters of tropical seas, although beach rock has been observed in the eastern Mediterranean, Hawaii, Morocco, Portugal and the Loire estuary. The latter areas are almost temperate, but the consolidation in these areas is probably different from that of true tropical beach rock.

Detailed observations have been carried out by R. J. Russell (1962), Russell and W. G. McIntire (1965a) and Russell (1967) on the occurrence and formation of beach rock. The cemented beach material outcrops at about mean sea level in areas where the tidal range is small, or at high neap tide where the range is larger. The material that is cemented can be organic or mineral in origin. It can vary in size from salt marsh mud to a coarse conglomerate, as occurs in south Jamaica. The material is only cemented to form beach rock on retreating, eroding beaches. It forms very quickly in the order of decades in suitable localities. The thickness of the beach rock depends on the degree to which the water table fluctuates. Several bands, up to 9·15 m wide, may outcrop on one beach. The cement is calcareous and beach rock is resistant once it has formed, and changes in the configuration of the coast may be caused by it. Frequently algal growths cover it, but detailed studies showed that the cementation is not algal in origin. An examination of the water table position showed that beach rock forms at the water table, and extends inland for at least 488 m on Mauritius.

In some areas the origin of the calcium carbonate that forms the cement poses a problem. In others limestone hinterlands could provide a source, but such a source is not essential. The sea contains a higher calcium carbonate content than streams in many areas. This is not, however, the normal source of the cement. The calcium carbonate usually comes from the groundwater or from the beach sand. The beaches on volcanic islands usually consist of calcareous fragments, and these provide the calcium carbonate. Grains of beach material above the water table are smooth and abraded and have no depositional coating. Grains below the water table are pitted, having lost material by solution, and are leached, especially where the water has a relatively low salinity. It is within the zone of water table fluctuation that lime coating occurs. The waters are heavily charged with calcium carbonate. The lime forms layers on the grains thereby decreasing the size of the voids. As these are eliminated, the beach rock is indurated to form a mass of concrete. The final fill is sometimes iron-stained and finer in texture. Beach rock has been observed to form in only 2 to 3 seasons at Cluny, Basse Terre. The first stage occurs in fairly stagnant conditions of sluggish groundwater flow, the second in more vigorous conditions. The form of the water table determines the form of the beach rock, and steps may form. Incipient beach rock was found in the Five Islands district of Antigua.

Prograding beaches do not allow time for incipient beach rock to be exposed to complete the cementation process. Areas of high energy also do not allow incipient beach rock time to cement. It forms best, therefore, on retreating beaches in areas of moderate energy. The bands of beach rock dip more gently seaward than the sand laminae. Troughs between them represent periods of more violent wave action, when cementation could not occur. Younger bands appear to dip below older ones, although they do not in fact do so. They are separated from them by a trough of water, and they do not overlap. Retreat of the beach causes a lowering of the water table, which emerges at sea level where the tidal range is low, or at high neap tide level where the range is higher. Retreat of 0·8 km may cause several feet of lowering of the water table. Beach rock may be undermined and slabs tip seaward, attaining lower levels than previously. Alternatively they may be carried landward to higher levels by storm waves, where they may be cemented to other outcrops.

D. R. Stoddart and J. R. McCann (1965) have commented on Russell's views of beach rock formation, and have pointed out that in British Honduras in the Gulf of Mexico, Florida, the Bahamas, the Marshall Islands, the Persian Gulf and the Red Sea the cement of some beach rocks is aragonite in the primary fill and calcite in the secondary fill. The aragonite comes from sea water. Beach rock formed under these conditions is not dependent on the water table, which may not exist. The beach rock still occurs in the intertidal zone. Thus sea water and freshwater beach rock can be distinguished by the type of cement. The marine type occurs in arid areas, such as the Red Sea, where there is no water table.

An example of beach rock on the Ligurian coast of Italy is described by J. P. Bloch and J. Trichet (1966). This beach rock appears to form at the contact zone between fresh groundwater and the sea water. The beach rock outcrops on the foreshore and occurs in banks 15 to 20 cm thick at mean sea level, dipping gently seawards. At present it is being eroded. There is no aragonite in the cement, unlike the beach rock in the Society Islands. Some authorities have suggested that in time an aragonite cement becomes calcitic, where it is derived from coral beaches. If this were true of the Ligurian coast, then it argues for a considerable age for this example of beach rock.

R. F. McClean (1967) and E. M. Driscoll and D. Hopley (1969) comment on the occurrence of transverse furrows in outcrops of beach rock. The latter authors describe the beach rock of the north Queensland coast, which is characterized by a wide variety of different grades of material. The grooves are formed by erosion of the exposed beach rock. It occurs in different situations, as intertidal sand beach deposits, massive conglomerates at the base of boulder spits, and as conglomerate cemented onto rock abrasion platforms. Some of the beach rock occurrences are found in constructional features, such as beach ridges. The beach rock varies in age but does not appear to be forming at present. The lack of calcium carbonate may prevent cementation to form beach rock along part of this coast, which is mainly of siliceous material.

The ridges and furrows, which develop perpendicular to the beach rock outcrops in the intertidal zone of the beaches of Barbados (McClean, 1967), have a mean spacing of 60 cm, a mean furrow length of 5 m, and a mean width of 28 cm. The depth has a mean value of 18 cm.

The furrows are more or less regularly spaced. They may be initiated in incipient beach rock by backwash rill formation or by freshwater rills. The form of the furrows changes as they develop: at first deepening is greater than widening, but in time they become wider and the separating ridge becomes serated and eventually destroyed. The features are clearly erosional in origin. The form is probably initiated when the beach rock is only weakly cemented. The movement of water across the beach in parallel streams may help to initiate the furrows. It is not known, however, why groundwater should be channelled in this way.

Beach rock has also been described near Hong Kong by Tschang Hsi Lin (1962). The beach rock in this area is of recent origin. It appears to be associated with refuse from lime kilns in the vicinity, which provide the necessary calcium carbonate. As in other areas the beach rock is associated with coastal retreat. The beach rock occurs at mean sea level, forming small patches and detached slabs, with a maximum width of 20 m. The patches dip seaward between 6 and 13°, an angle smaller than that of the beach sediments.

It may be concluded that beach rock is a product of cementation in warm seas in which calcium carbonate is available either in groundwater or sea water. The deposit only occurs on retreating coasts and forms at or slightly above the mean water level in areas of moderate wave energy. It can form very quickly under suitable conditions and once formed is a resistant material.

b Coral reef shoreline features

Many beaches in the coral seas are formed of coral sand rather than quartz or basaltic sand. The latter is found on mineral sand beaches inside the Andesite line in the tropical Pacific, as well as in other tropical and extra-tropical areas. The main differences in the beach forms resulting from differences in sand type are due to the generally lower density of the coral sand, which is less dense than quartz sand. The high temperatures reduce the viscosity of the water. This reduces the amount of sediment that waves of a specific size can carry. It is a relatively minor effect in most areas. Coral reefs often exert a sheltering effect on tropical beaches when they occur some distance offshore.

Coral reef shoreline features have recently been reviewed by D. R. Stoddart (1969). Coral reefs are built mainly by anthozoan corals. The reef building members of this group have the ability to build massive calcium carbonate structures. The ecology of the reef system is an important aspect of coral coasts, but space does not permit this aspect to be considered. Some general points concerning the morphology of the reefs and their development will be mentioned briefly. The modern corals appear to form a thin veneer on older structures. It is useful to distinguish between structural coral reefs, in which corals are actively contributing to the topographic development of the reef, and coral communities, which are an assemblage of reef organisms growing on a substrate that is other than their own.

Darwin's theory of subsidence has been confirmed by deep boring in the Marshall Islands and Eniwetok Atoll, where 1405 m of reef limestone was penetrated before entering basement rock. All the limestone was shallow-water material. Three periods of emergence were indicated by aragonite layers, at 91 m, 335 m and 847 m. Rates of subsidence for the Eocene, Miocene and post-Miocene are 51·9, 39·6 and 15·2 m/million years respectively. The subsidence theory applies mainly to the open Pacific Ocean.

Elsewhere reefs are much thinner and do not suggest subsidence. At Bermuda bores entered lava at 171 m, 33 m and 43 m, and at 21–24 m. Other bores showed thicker limestone. In the Bahamas 4488 m of limestone and dolomite were penetrated on Andros Island. In the Caribbean coral formations were 959 m and 1219 m thick. The barrier reef of Queensland is not formed by subsidence, though its structure is complex and some subsidence has occurred. The reef lime-stones in this area have been recorded as 115 m, 154 m, 121 m, 547 m and 225 m thick at various sites. The sedimentation and reef growth was not, however, continuous in all the bores. Else-where reefs are also thin, as in Samoa, the New Hebrides and the Solomon Islands and many other places.

Some reefs have been affected by recent changes of sea level. Reefs exposed during low sea levels are resistant to erosion. Solution in the intertidal zone averages 1 mm/year, so that interglacial low sea levels would not have been long enough to bevel the reefs. Some karst features probably developed, such as reef knolls and 'blue holes' in the reef floor of lagoons.

Corals grow mainly above 25 m depth, and grow best at temperatures between 25°C and 29°C. The minimum they can tolerate is about 16°C. Other conditions such as salinity, exposure, sedimentation and occasional catastrophic mortality are important in the distribution and growth of corals. Depredation of living coral by invertebrates is causing concern at present. Coral reefs can be classified according to their morphology. The main classes are the fringing reef, barrier

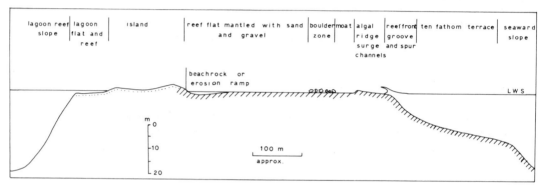

Figure 14-2 Schematic section through a windward Indo-Pacific atoll reef. Scales are only approximate and not all zones are necessarily found. (*After Stoddart, 1969.*)

reefs and atolls. The apron reef is an embryo fringing reef. A table reef is a small open-ocean reef, without central island or lagoon.

Reefs can be considered in terms of their zonation from sea to lagoon. The zones are shown in the diagrammatic cross-section in figure 14-2. Some reefs are distinguished by an algal ridge, while others do not have these features. An algal ridge is cuesta-like in form, with a steep sea-ward slope, rising 0·3 to 0·6 m above low tide. The algal reef is only found on windward seaward reefs. It is only poorly formed if present on leeward seaward reefs, and windward lagoon reefs, and never occurs on leeward lagoon reefs. The feature is wave-resistant and thus important in the more exposed parts of reefs. Their presence or absence may help to account for morphological differences between reefs.

One of the problems of reef analysis is to establish how much of the reef form is due to present-day reef building and how much is inherited from earlier reef structures. Some elevated reefs, at heights of up to 9 m above present sea level, have been dated at between 100,000 and 160,000 years old. This places them in the last major interglacial. The detailed origin of many of the features characteristic of different coral zones cannot yet be explained. Some, such as the groove and spur systems, may develop in different ways. The algal ridge appears to be an erosional feature in the Tuamotus at least. The algae veneer an older, higher reef surface. Reef sediments are sand and gravel sized mainly, and of skeletal origin. Large blocks also occur in places. In the lagoons the sediments are usually zoned, indicating little mixing and derivation from the immediate vicinity. The pattern is more complex where knolls and reef patches exist. Sediments are often poorly sorted, especially in quiet environments, consisting of coral sand and muds. Beaches are usually restricted in atoll environments and represent well-sorted sediments, the sands being organic in origin.

Over a long time scale the reef growth controls the reef morphology, but in the short time the relationships may be reversed. The modern reefs are affected by the relatively recent emergence. This has caused karst erosion of the older reefs. Reef growth began again on the old foundations, following the subsequent transgression. In places colony growth may be 1 to 10 cm/year and reef growth 1 to 2·5 cm/year. At these rates the forms reflect modern growth. In areas liable to frequent hurricane damage the reefs may be undergoing erosion and destruction. Modern growth can only have been taking place in the last 5000 years, so the morphological affect must be limited. Erosion of older forms is, however, also slow. It must be concluded that many features associated with coral reef morphology are not in equilibrium with inherited features. Features both recent and of older origin can be seen in present coral reefs.

5 Polar beach features

Arctic beaches have a variety of minor forms, some of which are characteristic of high latitudes generally, while others are not found in the Antarctic. The main feature that causes special polar beach forms is the presence of ice on the beach and along the coast for a large part of the year. This means that for much of the year the coasts are low energy. There is no change at all during the long season when sea ice is frozen to the beach. Even in late autumn, when the water is most open, floating ice offshore tends to reduce the effectiveness of waves in many polar areas. Another characteristic of many Arctic beaches, and one in which they differ from Antarctic beaches, is the isostatic recovery that many of them have undergone or are undergoing. This process is not limited to, or ubiquitous in, Arctic regions, but it is an important factor in many of them. Thus raised coastal features, such as those described in chapter 7, are characteristic of many Arctic coasts.

Not all Arctic shorelines are of low energy all the time. An example of an occasional catastrophic occurrence on the north coast of Alaska near Barrow has been described by J. D. Hulme and M. Schalk (1967). They have measured the average yearly transport along this Arctic coast under normal conditions, and found that between 1948 and 1952 west of Point Barrow 76,455 m^3 moved northeastwards. East of Point Barrow the movement was 7250 m^3 to the southeast. On 3 October 1963 a storm hit the coast with waves 3 m high and a surge raised sea level about 3·5 m above normal. This storm occurred during the time of most open water and, therefore, did the maximum damage. It was estimated to be of an intensity to be expected once every 200 years. It moved 152,950 m^3 of material, the equivalent of 20 years' normal movement. If the climate became warmer such storms would be more likely to be destructive, as they would exert a damaging effect for a greater period during the year, when now the sea is frozen.

One of the features characteristic of some polar beaches is due to ice rafting on the shoreline. E. de K. Leffingwell (1919) states that the beach in the Canning River region of North Alaska can be over-ridden 4·6 to 6·1 m by ice. Normally the ice is frozen to the bottom offshore, but during the break-up, rafts of ice can move inshore. A maximum movement of 61 m inland has been recorded at Point Barrow, but this was exceptional. Over most of the coast the inshore movement does not exceed 6·1 m. The ice raft pushes up ridges on the upper foreshore, but they seldom exceed a height of 1·52 to 1·83 m, when the ice within them has melted. These ridges rarely survive the summer, being destroyed by waves when the sea is open. Leffingwell only observed them at one point on the northern shore of Alaska in late summer. He states that waves in ½ hour of autumn gales can accomplish more work on the beach than shore ice in a period of 50 years. The grounding of heavy sea ice, however, can play a part in the formation of shoals in shallow water.

G. W. Moore (1966; 1968) states that gravel beaches are more common in the Arctic than elsewhere, but sand beaches also occur. One characteristic feature of these beaches is the Kaimoo. This is a shelf above the high-water level that is built in the autumn when air temperatures fall below freezing, but before extensive sea ice has formed. The advancing waves leave a thin layer of ice on the upper beach and these thin layers become interdigitated with layers of sediment. Together the ice and sediment form a flattish shelf at the limit of wave runup. The kaimoo deposits may be rafted out to sea during the summer ice break-up. Melting water from these

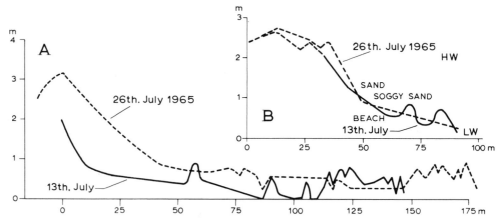

Figure 14-3 Arctic beach profiles at Butterfly Lake, west Baffin Island.

formations may cause a rough beach surface, which the small waves cannot smooth. Such microrelief can last until late August.

An example of the irregularity of an Arctic beach in mid-summer is shown in figure 14-3. The beach profile was surveyed on the west coast of Baffin Island in July. This is a very low-energy coast owing to the presence of 50% ice cover throughout the summer season, and to the very shallow water of Foxe Basin. The fetch is also limited. The foreshore was characterized by mounds of fine sand with intervening hollows with 0·4 to 0·55 m relief. The foreshore sediment was a mixture of fine sand, mud and boulders, and it was very soft and unconsolidated. Between the two surveys shown some break-up of the ice allowed slightly more effective waves to act on the beach. These waves were able to consolidate the steeper, upper part of the foreshore, but had little effect on the flatter, lower portion. The mounds appear to have formed around small icebergs that became stranded on the beach as the tide fell, but later floated off on the rising tide. A few small, anvil-shaped icebergs were seen on the beach at low tide. The sand on the upper foreshore had median diameters for three samples between 0·53 and 1·00 ϕ and relatively poor sorting values between 0·70 and 0·84, using the graphic measures of Folk and Ward. The skewness showed a negative value characteristic of the more energetic beach environment. A sample of sand from the lower, flatter part of the foreshore was finer, with a mean diameter of 1·73 ϕ and a positive skewness of +0·163. The positive skewness indicates a tail of fine grains, which would be likely to occur in such a very low-energy environment. This contrasts with the more energetic swash environment already mentioned.

W. P. Dillon and J. Towne Conover (1965) have drawn attention to the formation of ice-cemented blocks on a beach. Such blocks may become broken off and incorporated in the normal beach deposits so that when the ice melts zones in which the stratification suddenly varies will occur. They record the formation of such features on the coast of New England, when a sudden fall of temperature to −20°C was accompanied by strong wave action. This example shows that features normally associated with polar beaches can occur in the temperate zone where low winter temperatures are experienced.

R. L. Nichols (1961) lists 13 features associated with polar beaches, basing his observations mainly on Antarctic beaches. The features are the following:

1   Beaches resting on ice
2   Pitting of the beach
3   Ridges and mounds formed by ice push or deposition from stranded ice
4   Abruptly terminating beach ridges due to presence of ice during their formation
5   Ice-rafted fragments in the sediments
6   Poorly rounded beach stones
7   Frost cracks and mounds
8   Stone circles, polygons and solifluction activity
9   Meltwater streams may form gaps through beach ridges
10   Ice-contact features associated with proglacial deltas or other features
11   Ventifacts
12   Cold-water fossils
13   Soft parts of marine organisms

Pitting is one of the most characteristic and conspicuous minor features of polar beaches. It is common both in Antarctica and the Arctic. The pits are subcircular, less than 4·6 m in diameter and 0·3 to 0·61 m deep. Pits of this type were seen on the coast of East Baffin Island, where they were up to 50 to 80 cm deep and roughly aligned along the beach. They appeared to be left by the melting out of stranded and partially buried lumps of ice.

Ice-pushed ridges and mounds are formed by sea ice and growlers. They are common in both Arctic and Antarctic beaches. At Marble Point a ridge up to 2·74 m above sea level was found 30·5 m offshore. It was surrounded by water in summer and ice in winter. The ridge had a core of ice, and only a thin veneer of gravel about 30 to 60 cm thick. It may have taken several years to form as it included layers of sand, as well as the gravel capping. It probably represented a detached, rafted and stranded ice-foot, formed as a result of tidal fluctuations of sea level.

Summary

The most common minor beach features are the ripples caused by the oscillatory flow under wave action. Experimental studies of ripples indicate that two types exist, the rolling grain ripples forming at lower velocities and the vortex ripples at higher velocities. Vortex ripple length appeared to be independent of speed of oscillation but was affected by grain size. Observations made in shallower water showed that ripples moved seawards in deeper water and landwards in shallower water. The landward movement caused asymmetry of form to develop, with erosion on the upstream side and deposition on the downstream side. More energy is lost over a rippled bed than a smooth one. In nature larger ripples are associated with coarser material, and form with orbital velocities between 10 and 100 cm/sec. The ripples are larger in deeper water and in more exposed areas.

Beach cusps form on the upper foreshore in shingle, mixed and sand beaches. The coarser material accumulates on the promontories between the bays, in which finer material collects. The cusps are due to a cellular form of water flow, which may be initiated in the step zone below the swash zone. The sorting of material also causes variations in water movement through the beach sediment, and these variations are important in cusp formation. A relationship has been found between the cusp spacing and swash length. Cusps formed most readily where there was a vertical stratification of material. Wave direction does not have an important control on cusp formation. Some observers consider cusps form under destructive conditions, but others have seen them form as the summer berm is building out. The cellular type of flow, operating on poorly sorted beach material seems fundamental to cusp formation, while their size is controlled by the swash periodicity. Transverse bars are larger transverse features that develop in areas of low to moderate energy, with ample material and a shallow offshore zone. Cellular water movement is also important in their development due to energy concentration by wave refraction.

Features characteristic of warm seas include beach rock, which is a product of cementation by calcium carbonate. Retreating beaches are necessary for its formation and the deposit is closely tied to the mean sea level. Corals also grow in warm seas, building reefs that at present are adjusting to Pleistocene sea level changes. Of features found in polar beaches, the most characteristic are the mounds and hollows on the foreshore that form as a result of freezing of the beach sediments and grounding of ice. Ice-pushed ridges also occur at the limit of wave action during the short period of summer thaw. Polar beaches are low energy, due to the damping effect of offshore ice on wave action in summer and freezing of the sea in winter.

References

ALLEN, J. R. L. 1965: Sedimentation to the lee of small underwater sand waves: an experimental study. *J. Geol.* **73**(1), 95–116.

ALLEN, J. R. L. 1968: *Current ripples*. North Holland Pub. Co. (447 pp.)

BAGNOLD, R. A. 1940: Beach formation by waves: some model experiments in a wave tank. *J. Inst. Civ. Eng.* **15,** 27–52.

BAGNOLD, R. A. 1946: Motion of waves in shallow water, interaction between waves and sand bottom. *Proc. Roy. Soc.* A **187**(1008), 1–15.

BLOCH, J. P. and TRICHET, J. 1966: Un exemple de grès de plage (Côte Ligure italienne). *Mar. Geol.* **4**(5), 373–7.

CARSTENS, M. A., NEILSON, F. M. and ALTINBILEK, H. D. 1969: Bedforms generated in the laboratory under an oscillatory flow: analytical and experimental study. *C.E.R.C. Tech. Memo.* **28.** (39 pp.)

DAVIS, R. A. 1965: Beach pitting: an unusual beach sand structure. *J. Sed. Petrol.* **35**(1), 495–6.

DILLON, W. P. and TOWNE CONOVER, J. 1965: Formation of ice-cemented sand blocks on a beach with lithological implications. *J. Sed. Petrol.* **35**(1), 964–7.

DRISCOLL, E. M. and HOPLEY, D. 1969: Beachrock and conglomerate in the Townsville area. *Brit. Geomorph. Res. Gr. Occ. Pap.* **5,** 89–96.

EVANS, O. F. 1938: The classification and origin of beach cusps. *J. Geol.* **46,** 615–27.

FLEMMING, N. C. 1964: Tank experiments on the sorting of beach material during cusp formation. *J. Sed. Petrol.* **34,** 112–22.

GUILCHER, A. 1961: Le 'Beach-Rock' ou Grès de Plage. *Ann. de Geog.* **70**(378), 113–25.

HUME, J. D. and SCHALK, M. 1967: Shoreline processes near Barrow, Alaska: a comparison of the normal and the catastrophic. *Arctic* **20**(2), 86–103.

INMAN, D. L. 1957: Wave generated ripples in the nearshore sands. *B.E.B. Tech. Memo.* **100.**

JOHNSON, D. W. 1919: *Shore processes and shoreline development.* Facsimile edition, 1965, New York: Hafner. (584 pp.)

KENNEDY, J. P. 1963: The mechanisms of dunes and antidunes in erodible bed channels. *J. Fluid Mech.* **16,** 521–44.

KING, C. A. M. 1965: Some observations on the beaches of the west coast of County Donegal. *Irish. Geog.* **5**(2), 46–50.

KING, C. A. M. 1969: Some Arctic coastal features around Foxe Basin and in E. Baffin Island, N.W.T. Canada. *Geogr. Ann.* A **51**(4), 207–18.

KUENEN, P. H. 1948: The formation of beach cusps. *J. Geol.* **56,** 34–40.

LEFFINGWELL, E. DE K. 1919: The Canning River region, North Alaska. *U.S. Geol. Surv. Prof. Pap.* **109,** (251 pp.)

LONGUET-HIGGINS, M. S. and PARKIN, D. W. 1962: Sea waves and beach cusps. *Geog. J.* **128**(2), 194–200.

MANOHAR, M. 1955: Mechanics of bottom sediment movement due to wave action. *B.E.B. Tech. Memo.* **75.**

MCCLEAN, R. F. 1967: Origin and development of ridge-furrow systems in beachrock in Barbados. *Mar. Geol.* **5**(3), 181–94.

MII, H. 1958: Beach cusps on the Pacific coast of Japan. *Sci. Rep. of Tohoku Univ. Sendai, Japan, 2nd Series,* **29,** 77–107.

MOORE, G. W. 1966: Arctic beach sedimentation. Chapter 22 in Wilimovsky, N. J. and Wolfe, J. N. (Editors), *Environment of the Cape Thompson region, Alaska,* U.S. Atomic Energy Commission, 587–608.

MOORE, G. W. 1968: Arctic beaches. In Fairbridge, N. W. (Editor), *Encyclopedia of geomorphology,* New York: Reinhold, 21–2.

NICHOLS, R. L. 1961: Characteristics of beaches formed in Polar climates. *Am. J. Sci.* **259,** 694–708.

NIEDORODA, A. W. and TANNER, W. F. 1970: Preliminary study of transverse bars. *Marine Geol.* **9**(1), 41–62.

OTVOS, E. G. 1964a: Observations of rhomboid beach marks. *J. Sed. Petrol.* **34,** 683–7.

OTVOS, E. G. 1964b: Observations of beach cusps and beach ridge formation on the Long Island Sound. *J. Sed. Petrol.* **34**(3), 554–60.

PANIN, N. 1967: Structures des dépôts de plage sur la côte de la Mer Noir. *Mar. Geol.* **5**(3), 207–220.

RUSSELL, R. J. 1962: Origin of beach rock. *Zeits. für Geomorph.* **6,** 1–16.

RUSSELL, R. J. 1967: *River plains and sea coasts.* Berkeley and Los Angeles: Univ. California Press.

RUSSELL, R. J. and MCINTIRE, W. G. 1965a: Southern Hemisphere beach rock. *Geog. Rev.* **55,** 17–45.

RUSSELL, R. J. and MCINTIRE, W. G. 1965b: Beach cusps. *Bull. Geol. Soc. Am.* **76,** 307–20.

SCOTT, T. 1954: Sand movement by waves. *Inst. Eng. Res.* Univ. of Calif.: Wave Res. Lab.

STODDART, D. R. 1969: Ecology and morphology of recent coral reefs. *Biol. Rev.* **44,** 433–98.

STODDART, D. R. and MCCANN, J. R. 1965: Nature and origin of beachrock. *J. Sed. Petrol.* **35**(1), 243–7.

B C—S

TANNER, W. F. 1965: High index ripple marks in the swash zone. *J. Sed. Petrol.* **35,** 968.

TANNER, W. F. 1967: Finger bars on an ideal low wave, low-tide beach, Santa Catarina Island, Brazil. *Abs. Vol. Ann. Meeting Geol. Soc. Am.,* New Orleans, 219.

TIMMERMANS, P. D. 1935: Proeven ove den invloed van golven op een strand. *Leidische Geol. Med.* **6,** 231–386.

TSCHANG HSI LIN 1962: Beach rock observations on Ping Chau Island, Hong Kong. *Chung Chi J.* **1**(2), 117–22.

WORRALL, G. A. 1969: Present day and subfossil beach cusps on the West African coast. *J. Geol.* **77,** 484–7.

ZENKOVICH, V. P. 1946: On the study of shore dynamics. *Trudy. Inst. Okeanologie* **1,** 99–112.

Part IV

Coasts

15 Coastal classification

1 **D. W. Johnson**

2 **F. P. Shepard**

3 **C. A. Cotton**

4 **H. Valentin**

5 **A. L. Bloom**

6 **W. Armstrong Price**

7 **J. L. Davies**

Summary and conclusion

Some attempt to classify the very wide variety of different types of coast is of value in assessing the different controls that lead to the great variety. The fact that so many different classifications have been proposed indicates that any stretch of coast can be defined according to a wide range of criteria, all of which play a part in giving it its particular characteristics. The criteria for 13 systems of classification have been summarized in a table given by W. F. Tanner (1960b). Some of these are considered in more detail in this chapter. Tanner's table is given in table 15-1, where it has been modified to include one or two other classifications that have been proposed since he wrote. Two of these are of interest and will be discussed; these are the ideas of J. L. Davies and A. L. Bloom, who approach the problem of coastal classification from the dynamic point of view.

R. J. Russell (1967) considers that attempts to classify coasts are premature. He states that taxonomy should follow, and not precede, the acquisition of precise factual information concerning the variety of coasts. He points out that some of the older classifications have been shown to be unsatisfactory. This does not mean that none of the newer ones, and especially the attempts at dynamic classification, are not useful. Russell comes to the conclusion that a sound coastal classification may eventually be based on the lithology of the coast. Crystalline rock coasts exhibit striking similarities in a great range of environments. Sedimentary and poorly consolidated sediments might eventually make further subdivisions. Other possible criteria that he mentions include the amount of longshore drift, exposure to different types of waves, the width of the continental shelf, and the presence of organisms.

No completely satisfactory classification of coasts has yet been proposed. Some are purely descriptive, while others are genetic. Three main variables may be taken into account in devising any coastal classification. These are the form of the land–sea contact zone, the relative movement of sea level and the effect of marine processes. Two or more of these variables are used by all the proposed classifications. E. Suess (1888) used the first two variables. He proposed as the major groups of his classification the well-known 'Atlantic' and 'Pacific' coastal types. In the former

Table 15-1 Coastal classification criteria

	1*	2*	3*	4*	5*	6*	7*	8*	9*	10*	11*	12*	13*
1 Structure-type	×				×		×				×		×
2 Structure-stability						×			×				
3 Motion—horizontal								×					×
4 Motion—vertical		×	×	×		×	×	×					×
5 Agency—present					×		×	×	×				
6 Agency—former		×		×	×								×
7 Materials—bedrock									×	×			
8 Materials—in transit									×	×			
9 Energy-type									×	×		×	
10 Energy-level									×	×		×	
11 Geometric pattern	×	×	×	×					×	×	×		
12 Coastal equilibrium		×								×			
13 Transverse profile		×	×	×					×			×	
14 Erosion/deposition						×		×				×	×
15 Stage (or age)		×		×									
16 Climate									×	×		×	
17 Ecology													
18 Time									×				×

1* Suess 2* W. M. Davis 3* F. P. Gulliver 4* D. W. Johnson 5* F. P. Shepard
6* C. A. Cotton 7* R. H. Fleming and F. E. Elliott 8* H. Valentin 9* W. A. Price
10* W. F. Tanner 11* A. Guilcher 12* J. A. Davies 13* A. L. Bloom

the general trend of the land structures run normal to the coastal margin, while in the Pacific type the structures run parallel to the coast. The dichotomy is generalized, but the first category can be broadly applied to most of the Atlantic coasts, while the general trend of the west coast of North America and South America is parallel to the major folds of the Rocky Mountains and Andes. The classification is too generalized for use for small areas.

Some of the earlier coastal classifications were based on the relative movement of land and sea.

D. W. Johnson (1919) used this basis of classification, but he was not the first to put it forward. J. D. Dana (1849) was an early author to observe the effect of submergence on the coast. He recognized that the deeply embayed coast of Tahiti was the result of drowning the valleys by a rising sea level. W. M. Davis (1898) and F. P. Gulliver (1899) followed Suess (1888) and F. von Richthofen (1886) in using the distinction between submergence and emergence as the basis for their coastal classification. R. A. Daly (1934), in his work on the glacial control of sea level in relation to the formation of coral atolls, also drew attention to sea level oscillations resulting from recent glacier fluctuations. Some of the coastal classifications that have been proposed will be reviewed briefly.

1 D. W. Johnson

Perhaps the best-known classification is that proposed by D. W. Johnson (1919). He enlarged the dichotomy of coastal types put forward by earlier workers in his classification, still retaining, as his two major groups, coasts of submergence and emergence, but adding neutral and compound categories. Neutral coasts include those that are not mainly due to submergence or emergence, such as delta shorelines, alluvial and outwash plains and fault shorelines. Compound shorelines show features of two or more of the other three main categories, and include coasts showing features of both emergence and submergence. Parts of the eastern coast of the U.S.A. exemplify this type: the coast is characterized by a deeply embayed outline behind an offshore barrier, which Johnson

Table 15-2 D. W. Johnson's (1919) coastal classification

			Examples
1 SUBMERGENCE COASTS	i	Ria coasts	S.W. Ireland—Dingle Bay
	ii	Fjord coasts	West Norway—Sogne Fjord
2 EMERGENCE COASTS (WITH BARRIERS)			Baltic Sea
3 NEUTRAL COASTS	i	Delta coasts	Mississippi Delta
	ii	Alluvial plain coasts	Northwest India
	iii	Outwash plain coasts	Southeast Iceland
	iv	Volcano coasts	Hawaii Islands
	v	Coral reef coasts	Great Barrier Reef, northeast Australia
	vi	Fault coasts	North Island, New Zealand, Wellington
4 COMPOUND COASTS—any combination of the first three types			

considers is a feature typical of an emerged coast. Another example is the fjord coast of southwest New Zealand, which shows characteristics both of submerged glacial relief and the straightness and steepness of a typical fault coast, thus combining groups one and three. Each of Johnson's main coastal types can be further subdivided, giving the groups shown in table 15-2.

The classification is genetic in type. If it were to be applied strictly, however, many coasts would fall into the compound category. Most areas have been affected both by a rising and a falling sea level in the recent geological past. The recent date of the major mountain-building period of the Alpine orogeny has caused much crustal instability, resulting in the fairly recent uplift of considerable areas of the earth's crust. Some areas show a predominance of either submergence or uplift, thus placing them in one of the first two categories. The ria coast of southwest Ireland may be cited as an example. In the fjord coasts the evidence of submergence is often more doubtful,

405

as it is possible for glaciers to erode well below sea level so that fjord valleys would be drowned as the ice retreated even without a rise of sea level. Johnson did himself recognize this possibility.

The emergence group of Johnson's classification is the least satisfactory. In this category he recognizes only the emergence of a very flat sea floor, which would give rise to a straight coastline in plan. The criteria by which he recognized such coasts are the dune-covered barriers associated with coastal lagoons and salt marshes. Johnson did recognize that such features need not be entirely restricted to the type of coast of emergence that he envisaged. They may, for example, also form on a very flat coastal plain that has been slightly submerged. In this he anticipated a later criticism of this part of his classification.

Johnson did fail, however, to consider the possibility of the emergence of a steep coast. The inclusion of this type has been suggested by W. C. Putnam (1937), who has discussed the development of a steep coast of emergence. In the limited interpretation of the emergent coastal type Johnson was following W. M. Davis and other earlier workers. The straightness of emergent coasts has often been assumed, but they need not necessarily be so. Where submarine canyons approach close to the beach, emergence of the land would lead to a more intricate coastline than the present one. This applies to part of the coast of California.

2 F. P. Shepard

F. P. Shepard proposed a coastal classification in 1937 in which he abandoned the previous dichotomy of submergence and emergence. He considered that emergent coasts can be ignored. The basis of his classification is the distinction between coasts that have been shaped mainly by terrestrial agencies and those that have been modified by marine processes. His classification considers the function of marine processes to be of major significance. He has slightly modified the classes of his classification given in 1948 in the second edition of 'Submarine Geology' (1963). Table 15-3 gives the later classification.

The classification is comprehensive. It has much to recommend it, although the lack of a category for emergent coasts is a disadvantage. The criticism of the emergent category in Johnson's classification is no reason for entirely abandoning it. A major difficulty in the application of this coastal classification is to determine the moment when a coast has been sufficiently altered by marine agencies to allow it to be classified in the second major group. The classification cuts across the cyclic description of coasts. It uses the youthful stage of development for the second group of the classification. A coast that is put into the second group automatically loses any reference to the initial form of the coast, though this may be no disadvantage as far as the description of the coast is concerned. The coast of southeast Iceland, for example, is one which has been built out by rapid fluvioglacial deposition of outwash material. The outbuilding has been assisted by a fall in base level. A barrier beach has been built by the waves along the greater part of this coast. It could, therefore, be classified as a coast straightened by marine deposition, in the form of an offshore barrier. It could alternatively be placed in the class of coasts shaped by terrestrial deposition. Whichever category is used some of the essential features would be omitted.

Shepard's classification is valuable when the original form of a coast has been eliminated by marine processes. The coast can then be placed in the second group and no assumptions concerning its original state need be made. Owing to the instability of sea level in recent times such coasts are, however, likely to be rare. Defending the omission of the emergent category, Shepard points out that most coasts show evidence, in the form of raised terraces, of former higher sea levels. Coasts of emergence due to recent faulting would be difficult to delimit from map or chart

Table 15-3   F. P. Shepard's (1963) coastal classification

I PRIMARY (YOUTHFUL) COASTS

    A Land erosion coasts

        1 Ria coasts (drowned river valleys)   a Dendritic type

                                                  b Trellis type

        2 Drowned glacial erosion coasts   a Fjord coasts

                                                  b Glacial troughs

        3 Drowned karst topography

    B Subaerial deposition coasts

        1 River deposition coasts   a Deltaic coasts   i Digitate (birdfoot)

                                                                ii Lobate

                                                             iii Arcuate

                                                             iv Cuspate

                                            b Alluvial plain coasts

        2 Glacial deposition coasts   a Partially submerged moraines

                                                  b Partially submerged drumlins

                                                c Partially submerged drift features

        3 Wind deposition coasts   a Dunes

                                                 b Fossil dunes

                                                c sand flats

        4 Landslide coasts

    C Volcanic coasts

        1 Lava flow coasts

        2 Tephra coasts

        3 Volcanic collapse or explosion coasts

    D Shaped by diastrophic movements

        1 Fault coasts   a Fault scarp coast

                                               b Fault trough type

                                               c Overthrust type

        2 Fold coasts

        3 Sedimentary extrusions   a Salt domes

                                           b Mud lumps

II SECONDARY COASTS

    A Wave erosion coasts

        1 Wave straightened coasts   a Cut in homogeneous materials

                                             b Hogback strike coasts

                                             c Fault line coasts

        2 Made irregular by wave erosion   a Dip coasts

                                             b Heterogeneous formation coasts

    B Marine deposition coasts

        1 Barrier coasts   a Barrier beaches

                                           b Barrier islands

                                             c Barrier spits

                                             d Bay barriers

                                             e Overwash fans

        2 Cuspate forelands

        3 Beach plains

        4 Mud flats or salt marshes

    C Coasts built by organisms

        1 Coral reef coasts

        2 Serpulid reef coasts

        3 Oyster reef coasts

        4 Mangrove coasts

        5 Marsh grass coasts

evidence. Many of the coastal types enumerated in this comprehensive classification will be considered further in the following chapters.

3 C. A. Cotton

A different dichotomy has been suggested by C. A. Cotton (1952). His classification, which is given in table 15-4, is divided basically into coasts of stable regions and those of mobile regions. He does not feel that types dependent on submergence and emergence should be dropped entirely, but he does consider that this criterion should be relegated to second place. Many of his examples have been taken from New Zealand, which is a mobile area. Stable areas have only been affected by eustatic oscillations of sea level. In the mobile areas the coast itself has been uplifted, or depressed or warped. The major significance of the distinction is that all stable coasts have been affected by the recent rise of sea level. On the other hand mobile areas may have been elevated to an equal or greater extent. They may show direct evidence of uplift or emergence. Not all stable coasts will be coasts of submergence, nor will all mobile coasts have emerged. Other categories in both major classes need not show any indication of base level changes. The classification

Table 15-4 C. A. Cotton's (1952) coastal classification

A	COASTS OF STABLE REGIONS
	1 Dominated by features of the most recent submergence
	2 Dominated by features of an earlier emergence
	3 Miscellaneous—volcanic, fjord, etc.
B	COASTS OF MOBILE REGIONS
	1 Coasts on which the most recent change has been submergence however caused
	2 Coasts on which recent diastrophic movement have resulted in emergence
	3 Fault and monoclinal coasts
	4 Miscellaneous coasts—volcanic, fjord, etc.

may be considered partly as a subdivision of the all-embracing compound group of Johnson. The last major change of sea level is recognized as important in defining coastal types, but other features, such as faulting or flexure, must be allowed for in the coastal types.

Marginal flexure has been considered by J. Bourcart (1950). If the process can be shown to be widespread then it may have a significant bearing on coastal classification. The marginal flexure hypothesis suggests that the land tends to rise while the sea floor tends to subside. The inland area may show evidence of a falling base level in the development of features of rejuvenation, while the offshore zone will be deepening. The coastal type would depend on whether the hinge line is seaward or inland of the present position of the coast. If it lies inland, the coast would appear to be submerged. If it lies seaward, the coastline would appear to be emerged.

The problem of variation of base level is relevant to coastal classification and to the concept of a marine cycle of erosion. Davis and Johnson based their classifications on the initial form of the land surface against which the sea comes to rest at the beginning of a supposed cycle. Modification of the coastline is described by reference to stages in a cycle. Still-stands of sea level are essential to allow a cycle, or even a partial cycle, to run its course. The concept of a static base level alternating with periods of rapid change, has been questioned recently (Mercer, 1968). The classification of coasts put forward by H. Valentin (1952) attempts to get away from the cyclic concept.

4 H. Valentin

The recognition of non-equilibrium conditions along a coast led Valentin (1952) to suggest two related but slightly different coastal classifications. The first is a classification of coastal configuration of genetic type, where the coastline is defined in terms of past processes. This classification is given in table 15-5. The second classification is based on present coastal dynamics, and is expressed in the present tense, whereas the first is expressed in the past tense. The dual classification was found to be necessary because on some coasts present processes are not in harmony with the coastal configuration. The coast of Holderness illustrates the condition in which the processes of past and present are in harmony: the coast has suffered retrogression in the past and is still undergoing erosion. The disharmonious condition is illustrated, for example, by the east

Table 15-5   H. Valentin's (1952) coastal configuration types. (Translation of Valentin, 1955, p. 55.)

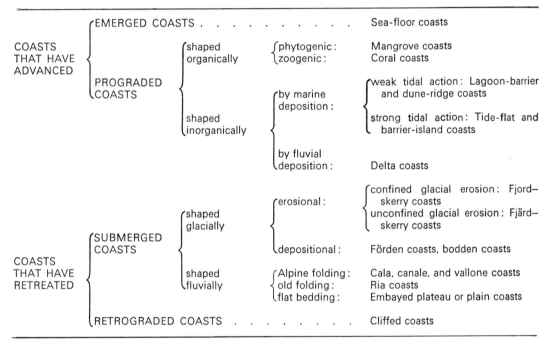

coast of Sweden, which is emerging at present, but at the same time exhibits features of submergence. In the first type of classification, its configuration is a submerged fjärd–skerry coast. The combination of both aspects of the two classifications determines the coastal condition, which can be defined as the sum of the coastal configuration and the present coastal dynamics. An important implication of this approach is the recognition that marine forces are continually active. They influence the coast even during changes in sea level. According to the older classifications, these changes should initiate a new cycle of erosion on a new coastal type. Valentin's classification allows for continuous changes of sea level.

Records of sea level show that changes are currently taking place. Still-stands are unlikely to have occurred during much of Pleistocene time, with the possible exception of the longer interglacial periods. Under some conditions sea level can be static for long enough for wave-cut platforms to be formed. Good examples of raised platforms are found along the western coast of

Scotland. W. B. Wright (1937) has suggested that some of these were cut during a period when both land and sea level were rising together. Sea level was rising eustatically, while the land was rising isostatically. An apparent stability of base level would be achieved when the two changes were acting together at the same rate.

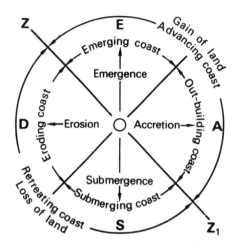

Figure 15-1 Valentin's theory of coastal classification. (*After Valentin, 1952.*)

Valentin's coastal dynamics classification is illustrated diagrammatically in figure 15-1. OA represents accumulation, increasing outwards from O; OE represents emergence as a result of a falling base level. OD represents coastal erosion and OS represents submergence. The line ZZ′, passing through O, indicates the line along which two forces balance one another. The position of the coast remains stationary in this situation. Erosion is counteracted by emergence in the quadrant ZEOD. In the opposite quadrant OAZ′S the rate of accumulation is counteracted by the rise of sea level. The two variables exactly balance along the lines OZ and OZ′ respectively. In the segment EAO both sea level is falling and the land is building out so that rapid progradation will result. In the opposite segment DOS sea level is rising, causing submergence, and erosion is taking place. A very rapid retrogression of the coast will, therefore, take place. Lines of equal advance or retreat of the coast can be drawn parallel to ZZ′, the change increasing away from ZZ′. Valentin (1952) has mapped the coasts of the world according to his classification.

C. A. Cotton (1954b) has applied Valentin's coastal configuration classification to the coast of New Zealand, where he finds examples of many of the categories. The recent changes in sea level, due to earth movements in this unstable zone, make it a good area in which to test the classification. The Motunau coast of North Canterbury is an example of coastal type IA, where a coastal plain, covered with recent shells, has been uplifted. It is now being cliffed by the sea and dissected by gullying. Coastal type IB is illustrated by the Eastbourne cuspate foreland in Port Nicholson. Here sand coming from inland has been moved alongshore to form a low sandy plain in front of the old cliff line. Type IIA is illustrated by the fjords of southwestern South Island, and the drowned valleys of the Marlborough Sounds. Cape Kidnappers on the east coast of the North Island illustrates the cliffed coasts of category IIB.

5 A. L. Bloom

A. L. Bloom (1965) adopts a somewhat similar approach to what he terms the explanatory description of coasts, in emphasizing the dynamic nature of coastal land forms and the necessity of appreciating their genetic development. He follows Valentin's description of coasts, but adds to it a third dimension, that of time. He illustrates the description by a diagram, shown in figure 15-2. The time dimension is added to the two axes that show erosion and deposition, and emergence and submergence, giving three mutually orthogonal axes. It is possible in this type of diagram both to illustrate the history of the coast and, as shown in Valentin's diagram, to indicate its present state.

The earlier explanatory schemes of Johnson and Shepard can be shown to be special cases,

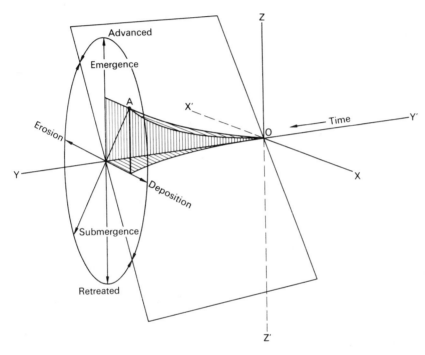

Figure 15-2 Bloom's theory of coastal classification. (*After Bloom, 1965.*)

which can be fitted into the general scheme. The advantages of this scheme are that it can accommodate the full range of coastal development, and it can be applied on any required scale, from large areas to small ones. It is a flexible scheme in that the scales of the different axes can be adapted to different situations. It can be represented graphically in a perspective diagram, and it can incorporate previous schemes. The scheme also has the advantage that it can deal with both submergence and emergence in one system. This is valuable as so many coasts at present show the effects of both these changes.

6 W. Armstrong Price

Another useful dynamic approach has been suggested by W. Armstrong Price (1955) and W. F. Tanner (1960a and b). Armstrong Price divides coasts according to the energy that they receive. He suggests that coasts may be classified as high-energy, moderate-energy or low-energy coasts.

The categories are based on ramp angles of $\leqslant$ 45·8 cm and $\geqslant$ 76·3 cm/1·6 km. These values separate the coasts into the three groups. Divisions can also be made in terms of the mean breaker heights. He gives the limiting values as $\leqslant$ 10 and $\geqslant$ 50 cm. Zero-energy coasts with no breakers or ones of only a few millimetres may also exist.

The ramp angles can be obtained if good charts are available. Breaker heights require some wave recording data. The value of the classification lies in the dynamic element of the basic subdivisions. Tanner applied the classification, as well as other more descriptive measures, to the coasts of Florida. He showed that high energy characterizes the southern beaches on the east side of the peninsula. The Gulf coast falls partly into the moderate-energy and partly the low-energy categories, with small stretches of zero energy. The low to moderate energy of many Arctic coasts has already been commented upon in section 14-5.

7 J. L. Davies

The world-wide dynamic classification proposed by J. L. Davies (1964) is based on the wave climate of the area. He defines four main types of wave climate—firstly the storm wave environment, secondly the west coast swell environment, thirdly the east coast swell environment and finally the low-energy environment. Each environment is affected by waves that cause different coastal features to form. Their distribution is shown in figure 15-3.

The storm wave environment occurs in high latitudes in the belt of strong and variable winds, in which storm waves are generated. In the southern hemisphere this belt is centred at 54° S in winter and 56° S in summer. This southern belt occurs in a latitude where ocean predominates. Therefore, the storm wave coasts are relatively restricted in the southern hemisphere, being limited to the extreme south of South America. The northern hemisphere storm belt is more varied in position with the seasons, lying at 46° N in winter and 62° N in summer. The frequency of storms is much greater in winter. The zone liable to storm wave activity, especially in winter, is greater in the northern hemisphere. It covers the coast of North America from northern California and New York northwards, the coast of Europe from north France to north Norway, and the Asian coast from Japan northwards. In low latitudes only the occasional hurricane upsets the normal wave pattern.

The swell environments occupy the low latitudes between the storm wave belts. The waves originate in the storm wave zone, but they move out as swell to reach all the low latitude coasts as long, low, generally constructive waves. The swell travels along great circle tracks, and this must be taken into account in considering its direction of approach. A swell that leaves the Cape of Good Hope in a southeasterly direction, having been generated by a northwesterly gale, will reach Tasmania from the southwest. The southwesterly swell is dominant in the southern hemisphere, and the northwesterly swell in the northern hemisphere. The west-facing coasts will, therefore, have stronger swells than the east-facing coasts. The mean period of the swell varies from 14 to 20 seconds, being 305 to 610 m long in deep water. The east coast swells are lower and less consistent.

The final groups are in the low-energy coastal type, which is protected from swells and storm waves by some barrier. The barrier may be land in enclosed seas, or seas with intricate outlines, or it may be ice in the polar seas. Each of the environments has its characteristic forms.

The storm wave environment has a minimum of depositional forms, especially where longshore movement of material does not replenish that lost alongshore. Shingle is common in constructional features, as this is built up into ridges by storm waves. Orientation, therefore, tends to be

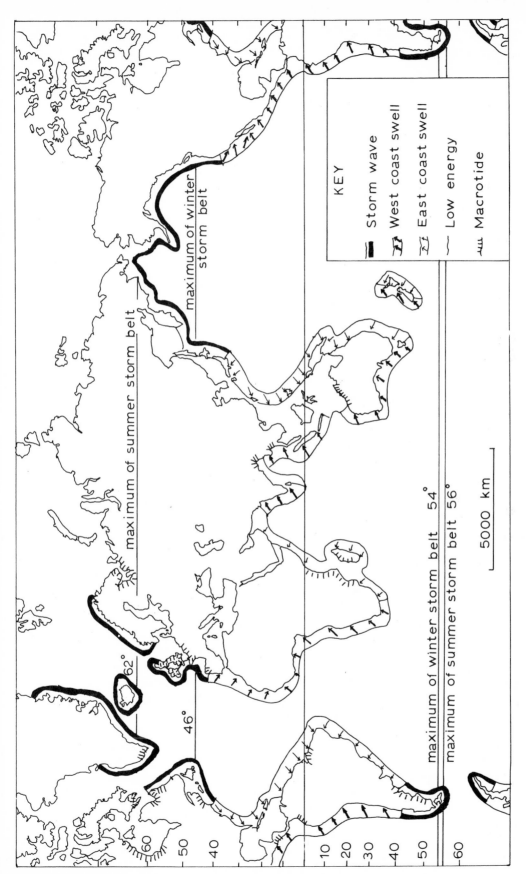

Figure 15-3 The world distribution of wave types. (*After J. L. Davies, 1964.*)

KEY

━━━ Storm wave

↗↗ West coast swell

↗↗ East coast swell

─ Low energy

⊥⊥ Macrotide

maximum of winter storm belt

maximum of summer storm belt

maximum of winter storm belt 54°

maximum of summer storm belt 56°

5000 km

62°

46°

60
50
40

10
20
30
40
50
60

related to the approach direction of the storm waves, and the local winds that generate them. Cliffing is important and shore platforms are well developed.

In the swell environment sand is the most common beach material. The coast often has a well-developed berm and orientation is determined by the direction of refracted swell approach. Weathering is more important than mechanical action in coastal retreat, partly owing to the warmer climate.

In the low-energy environment direction of wave approach is not uniform, and smaller more complex features tend to form. This is partly due to the limited refraction owing to the shortness of the waves, which is the result of the small available fetch. Waves tend to be flat, however, so small and intricate constructional features characterize these low-energy coasts. Local fetch is important in the orientation of the features.

The processes to which Davies draws attention will be important in determining the detailed outline of the coast and will also help to determine the nature of longshore movement. On coasts exposed to long constructive swells longshore movement is likely to be small, because the beach swings round to adjust to the direction of swell approach. On the storm wave coasts, on the other hand, longshore movement may be an important variable, although this depends also on the general configuration of the coast. Where the coast is made crenulate by erosion, longshore drift is not so continuous as on the softer coasts that form smoother, broader curves. The longshore movement is particularly important in explaining accretion and erosion, which are considered in the next chapter.

Summary and conclusion

Four of the different coastal classifications that have been mentioned are summarized in tables 15-2 to 15-5, while table 15-1 indicates possible criteria for coastal classification. The first three classifications tabulated are genetic in type, although they are based on different basic dichotomies. The most comprehensive of the three is F. P. Shepard's, which allows a descriptive classification of nearly any coast solely on map evidence in many instances. His major criteria of classification are the degree to which the coast has been modified by wave action and the nature of the processes that form the coastal character. Johnson uses changes of sea level and Cotton structural stability as major criteria. All these classifications imply a cyclic development, which is not an essential element of the other classifications discussed. This problem is developed further in chapter 21. It is worth bearing in mind, however, that all the coasts of the world have been affected by large and rapid fluctuations of sea level during the last 30,000 years, and indeed throughout the Pleistocene.

The newer approaches of Valentin and Bloom are valuable in that they are based essentially on the effect of sea level changes in conjunction with marine processes. They are, therefore, dynamic in character. One difficulty in the application of these classifications is the need to know how the coast has changed, whether it has suffered erosion or has been building outwards. This difficulty is intensified in Bloom's method, in that the history of the coast must be known over a considerable period of time if it is to be correctly portrayed according to his criteria. These two classifications are only suitable, therefore, for areas that have been studied sufficiently intensively to yield data on changes of sea level, both past and current, and also on the processes that have been operating on the coast for a considerable period of time. For this reason the more descriptive classification of Shepard is useful in discussing the distribution of certain coastal features.

The classifications of Armstrong Price and Davies are of a different type. They are based on the nature of the wave action that is reaching the coast. They are dynamic classifications that distinguish between features directly related to the processes that give the coast its character, rather than considering the nature of coastal outline and character. They cannot, therefore, be used to identify specific features, except in so far as these are directly produced by the type of process associated with the particular wave characteristics on which the classifications are based. Davies' classification does, however, provide a valuable link between the processes and form of the coast. It is particularly applicable to the form of the beach, which is more easily modified by, and more responsive to, different waves than the coast. His classification can be related to features such as coastal orientation and longshore movement of material, which are important in discussing the origin of coastal accretion and erosion and the resulting coastal features. These aspects are considered in following chapters. Both the descriptive, genetic classifications and the dynamic ones have their uses for different purposes, and each brings out some point of importance concerning the nature of the coast, and the processes that operated and are operating on it to give it its special character.

References

BLOOM, A. L. 1965: The explanatory description of coasts. *Zeits. für Geormorph.* NF **9**, 422–36.

BOURCART, J. 1950: La théorie de la flexure continentale. *C.R. Cong. Int. Geog. Lisbon*, 1949 **2**, 167–90.

COTTON, C. A. 1918: The outline of New Zealand. *Geog. Rev.* **6**, 320–40.

COTTON, C. A. 1952: Criteria for the classification of coasts. *17th Int. Geog. Cong. Abs. of Papers*, 15.

COTTON, C. A. 1954a: Deductive morphology and the genetic classification of coasts. *Sci. Monthly* **78**(3), 163–81.

COTTON, C. A. 1954b: Tests of a German non-cyclic theory and classification of coasts. *Geog. J.* **120**, 353–61.

DALY, R. A. 1934: *The changing world of the ice age.* Yale Univ. Press.

DANA, J. D. 1849: *Geology U.S. Exploring Expedition.* Philadelphia.

DAVIES, J. L. 1964: A morphogenetic approach to world shorelines. *Zeits. für Geomorph.* **8** (Sp. No.), 127*–42*.

DAVIES, W. M. 1898: *Physical Geography.*

GULLIVER, F. P. 1899: Shoreline topography. *Proc. Am. Acad. Arts and Sci.* **34**, 151–258.

JOHNSON, D. W. 1919: Shore processes and shoreline development. New York: Wiley. (584 pp.)

MARTONNE, E. DE 1909: *Traité de Géographie physique.* Paris.

MERCER, J. H. 1968: The discontinuous glacio-eustatic fall in Tertiary sea-level. *Paleogeog. Paleoclim. and Paleoecol.* **5**(1), 77–86.

PRICE, W. A. 1955: Correlation of shoreline types with offshore bottom conditions. *A. and M. College of Texas, Dept. of Oceanog., Proj.* **63**.

PUTNAM, W. C. 1937: The marine cycle of erosion for a steeply sloping shoreline of emergence. *J. Geol.* **45**, 844–50.

PUTNAM, W. C., AXELROD, D. I., BAILEY, H. P. and MCGILL, J. T. 1960: Natural coastal environments of the world. Los Angeles. *Off. Naval Res., Geog. Br., Con. No.* NR 388–013. (140 pp.)

RICHTHOFEN, F. VON 1886: *Führer für Forschungsreisende.* Hanover: Janecke.

RUSSELL, R. J. 1967: *River plains and sea coasts.* Univ. of California Press, 84–8.

SAVAGE, R. P. 1957: Sand bypassing at Port Hueneme. *B.E.B. Tech. Memo.* **92**.

SHEPARD, F. P. 1937: Revised classification of marine shorelines. *J. Geol.* **45**, 602–24.

SHEPARD, F. P. 1948: *Submarine geology*. New York: Harper & Row.

SHEPARD, F. P. 1963: *Submarine geology*. 2nd Edition. New York: Harper & Row. (557 pp.)

SUESS, E. 1888: *The face of the earth*, **II.** (English translation by H. B. C. Sollas, 1906.) Oxford University Press.

TANNER, W. F. 1960a: Florida coastal classification. *Trans. Gulf Coast Am. Geol. Soc.* **10,** 259–66.

TANNER, W. F. 1960b: Bases of coastal classification. *S.E. Geol.* **2**(1), 13–22.

VALENTIN, H. 1952: Die Küsten der Erde. *Petermanns Geog. Mitt.* Ergänzungsheft **246.**

VALENTIN, H. 1953: Present vertical movements of the British Isles. *Geog. J.* **119,** 299–305.

WRIGHT, W. B. 1937: *Quaternary ice age*. Chapter 22, 404–38. London: Macmillan.

16 Constructive wave action and coastal accretion

1 Constructive action in profile—the beach: a) Effect of material: (*i*) *Shingle beaches*; (*ii*) *Sand beaches*; b) Effect of waves, wind and other processes; c) The offshore zone; d) Summer beaches.

2 Forms of accretion: a) Shingle ridges; b) Sand features; c) Fine sediment accumulation —salt marsh growth.

3 An example of coastal accretion—south Lincolnshire

4 Coastal reclamation

Summary

In this chapter the processes which build out the beach and coast are considered. Some of these processes have already been mentioned in discussing the characteristics of water movement in waves, and in describing experimental work on sand transport in a wave tank. The forces that operate on the beach to cause a building up of material are summarized. These forces are rarely continuous in their operation and do not often lead to extensive or permanent coastal accretion. The special circumstances that result in a building out of the land at the expense of the sea are discussed and one example of coastal accretion is discussed in detail. Finally artificial gain of land by reclamation is considered briefly.

1 Constructive action in profile—the beach

a Effect of material

Coarser beach material is more mobile than fine. Accretion on a beach profile will be greater, under similar conditions, if the beach is composed of shingle rather than sand. The change in the form of the profile will differ between the two materials. Accretion on shingle beaches will be considered first.

(*i*) *Shingle beaches:* W. V. Lewis (1931) was one of the first authors to discuss in detail the reasons for, and the results of, constructive waves on shingle. He drew attention to the importance of the wave characteristics, as well as noting the changes in the profile. When constructive waves act on shingle they form a small ridge on the foreshore at the limit of the swash. A beach building up when the tides are rising from neap to spring level will show one ridge at the limit of the last high tide. When the tide is falling from spring to neap each tide is marked by a small ridge, pushed up by the waves at high water. These small ridges differ from the much larger features found on some sand beach profiles. They should also not be confused with the much higher backshore ridges on shingle beaches, which are built by storm waves above the limit of the normal high spring tides.

(*ii*) *Sand beaches:* Constructive action on a sandy beach builds up a berm, the chief characteristic of which is the marked break of slope at the seaward edge of a nearly horizontal platform. The break of slope is usually a little above the mean high water mark. The berms at Marsden Bay, County Durham, are shown in figure 16-1. The profiles demonstrate the effect

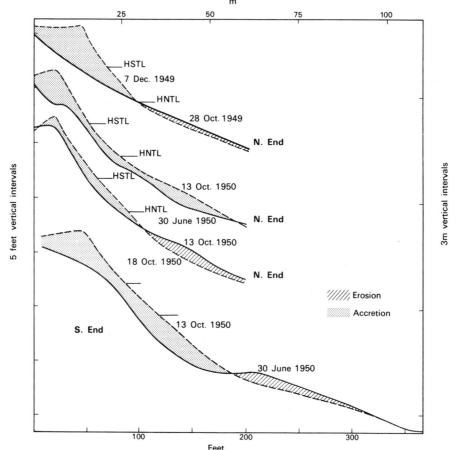

Figure 16-1 Profiles of Marsden Bay, Co. Durham, to show the formation of berms.

of constructive wave action. The sand is fairly coarse, having a median diameter of 0·37 mm at the north end of the bay and 0·35 mm at the south end. The maximum amount of accretion is about 1·22 m on one profile. This type of normal constructive berm must not be confused with a similar feature resulting from destructive wave action. A good example of the destructive type was surveyed on the Lincolnshire coast at Anderby Creek after the 1953 storm tide. The material forming the berm was eroded from the dunes and moved seawards onto the beach.

The berms mentioned above are on beaches of fairly coarse sand and show relatively large changes in level. On fine sand beaches the changes are smaller. The berm is often not so conspicuous on the profile after a period of constructive waves. On the smooth sand beach at Rhossili in south Wales, where daily observations of sand level were made over a period of variable weather, the changes recorded rarely exceeded 2·5 cm at any point on the profile. The beach profile was very similar in three consecutive annual surveys. The median diameter on this beach is 0·23 mm. Over a longer period and under more extreme conditions larger changes would probably occur.

On a ridged beach of fine sand, such as that at Blackpool, daily and weekly surveys show that the rate of accretion under the action of constructive waves is slow. The growth of ridge crests was measured at weekly intervals during periods from February 1943 to August 1943, and December 1943 to October 1944. During the first period ridge accretion greater than 30 cm only occurred on one occasion. During nearly every other week the change in level was less than 15 cm. Similar changes occurred during the second period.

Changes occurring on a coarse sand beach near Point Reyes, California, have been described by P. D. Trask (1956). The beach is composed of sand between 0·56 and 0·77 mm diameter. Between August and October 1955, a berm built up, resulting in accretion of over 2·13 m of sand in a small area. Between November and December over 1·83 m of sand accumulated on the berm.

b   Effect of waves, wind and other processes

Wave steepness has been shown to be the most significant factor on the foreshore. A flat wave will move material landwards and build up the profile, while a steep wave will produce the opposite effect. W. V. Lewis (1931) first drew attention to the importance of wave frequency in relation to shingle beaches. He stated that waves of low frequency were constructive on the beach, while those of high frequency were destructive. A variation of wave length was thus considered to be important. Variation in steepness, however, is probably the more important factor. Lewis considered that the swash of low-frequency waves was more effective than the backwash, thus moving material up the beach.

The critical steepness at which the waves change in character from constructive to destructive is important. The value varies from beach to beach according to the size of the material and other variables. Some values of the critical steepness, which apply also to observations in wave tanks, have already been given in section 9-2(a)(iii). The values for natural beaches seem to be lower than those established in tank experiments, although there are few precise values available. A short series of observations on Rhossili beach, south Wales, suggested that on this flat beach of fine sand the critical steepness was about 0·011. The value may have been affected, however, by the direction and strength of the wind. On a shingle beach, on the other hand, the critical steepness for a short series of surveys was found to be about 0·017. These figures indicate a tendency for the critical steepness to increase as the beach material becomes coarser.

The dimensions of the waves are also important because their energy depends on their height and length. E. C. Lafond (1939) has shown that the relatively long, low waves at La Jolla, California, are constructive on parts of the profile. More continuous fill occurred with low waves of shorter period. Because of their much lower energy, however, the shorter, low waves did not deposit as much in seven days as was removed by high waves in one day. Long, low waves also require much longer to build up a beach than the high, steep storm waves require to erode it. This factor is counterbalanced by the short duration of the high waves on most occasions.

The material moving alongshore must be taken into account in a consideration of constructive wave action. This material may in some instances be much more important than the material transported normal to the coast. The function of groynes is to trap material moving alongshore, encouraging beach accretion in areas where the natural supply of sand is small. Other obstructions may have less desirable results by trapping too much sand on the up-drift side of the barrier, thus causing erosion on the other side. Accretion of material on the beach is affected, therefore, not only by the steepness of the waves, but also by their direction of approach, which determines the direction of movement of beach material. F. P. Shepard (1950) has described a clear instance of accretion on a small beach being due to the lateral shift of beach material in a restricted bay. Boomer beach on the coast of California has been built up 2·44 m at one end during one day, while the beach was completely removed at the other end by waves approaching oblique to the shore. Changes are not normally as rapid and great as on this occasion. Accretion can take place under destructive conditions if more material is moved into the area alongshore than is being moved seaward by the destructive forces.

The wind is another factor which may reverse the movement to be expected from the wave characteristics. A strong onshore wind may more than counteract the effect of waves which would otherwise be constructive on the beach. This process has already been discussed. Tidal streams have a constructive effect in some areas. An example is described in section 16-3.

c   The offshore zone

Accretion on beaches with a considerable tidal range, such as Marsden Bay, where the spring tidal range is 4·3 m, often does not extend to low-water level. A fill on the upper beach is balanced by a cut lower down the foreshore. Where the tidal range is smaller the change in beach level often continues below the mean low-water level. The coast of California at La Jolla with a tidal range of 1·7 m, exemplifies this type. The seasonal changes on this beach have already been referred to (section 12-3 e(i)). The summer fill often extends to a depth of about 3·7 to 4·3 m below mean sea level. At this depth the change in level is over 1·52 m on some occasions, although it is usually about 1·2 m. During the winter period, when the foreshore is being eroded, the deeper water fill may amount to as much as 1·83 m in a depth of about 6 m of water. Usually the accretion in deep water under these conditions is nearer 1 m. This accretion is caused by seaward movement of material to deeper water by destructive waves.

Accretion of sand can occur to considerable depths, as has been considered in chapter 9. It is difficult to establish whether the material is brought by constructive waves, because its source is often in doubt. D. L. Inman and G. A. Rusnak (1956) made observations off the coast of California south of the Scripps Institution in depths of 9·15 m, 15·9 m and 21·3 m. They suggest that the changes in sand elevation at one depth correlate with those at another. This implies an onshore or offshore movement of sand. When the sand level fell at 21·3 m there was a rise at 9·15 m, indicating a landward or constructive wave action. Sand probably started to move in a depth of about 15·9 m. The reverse change was also noted. There was usually a positive correlation between the changes at depths of 21·3 m and 15·9 m, but little correlation between 9·15 m and 15·9 m. At a depth of 9·15 m the sand level tended to build up during the summer. This is part of the summer accretion often found on the foreshore. This summer accretion extends to considerable depths in some areas. The amount of change in level was very small at 9·15 m, amounting to a total change of 2·13 cm between the average summer and winter levels, although individual surveys showed greater changes. The maximum range at this depth was less than 9·15 cm.

d   Summer beaches

Constructive wave action on the beach results from the action of waves which move material towards the shore. Such waves are long relative to their height, and have a low steepness ratio.

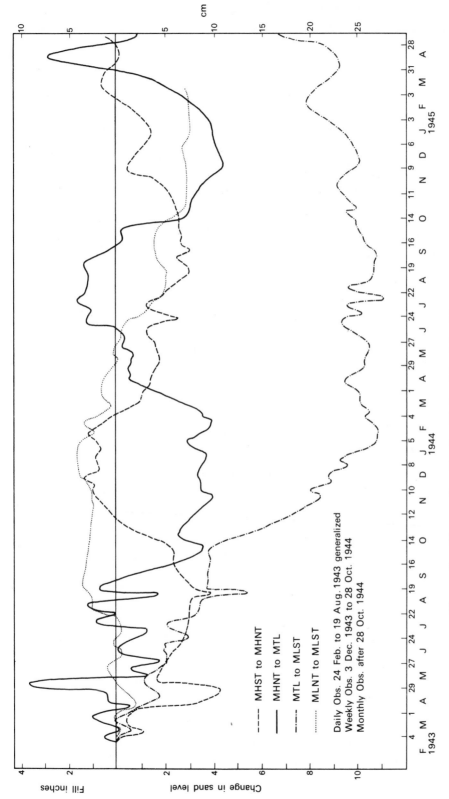

Figure 16-2 Changes of sand level on Blackpool beach for different parts of the foreshore.

Their constructive action is helped by the presence of offshore winds, and may be reversed by strong onshore winds. The building up of beaches is a seasonal process in some areas, as in parts of California. The variation of wave type with the seasons is marked in this area. The beach builds up during the summer to produce a summer profile. This profile has a wide berm at high-tide level and is relatively smooth offshore. The depth to which the summer fill extends offshore may reach about 9 m in some areas. Considerable changes of level are usually restricted to shallower water of about 3·65 m in depth. The changes are greater in volume where the beach material is coarser. The size of material also affects the depth to which fill extends.

On ridged tidal beaches, such as at Blackpool, the accretion of sand is largely achieved by additions to the ridge crests. On this beach, which has a tidal range of over 7·6 m at spring tide, seasonal changes in sand elevation have been recorded during the period 1943 to 1945. The changes are shown in figure 16-2. On this type of beach the ridges grow in height under the action of constructive waves. The summer season is a period of build-up on the beach, particularly between high neap tide and mean tide levels.

Other beaches do not show a seasonal change in character, but build up whenever suitable wave conditions allow. Continuous accretion on a beach often follows the action of a particularly severe storm. A good example of this type of accretion is shown in the gradual recovery of sand on the beach at Mablethorpe, Lincolnshire. The beach material was completely stripped off during the 1953 storm surge, leaving the clay base exposed (F. A. Barnes and C. A. M. King, 1955; see also figure 17-9). Beach accretion results from the action of waves that are more characteristic of the summer season in many areas. The steeper, storm waves, more often common in winter, are generally destructive on the beach.

2 Forms of accretion

The effect of waves on different materials was mentioned at the beginning of the chapter. In this section the form of features built up by waves and other processes in different types of material are mentioned. The processes by which shingle, sand and muddy sediments are built up into constructive features differ considerably. The part these features play in the modification of the coastal outline will be considered in chapters 19 and 20, dealing respectively with the modification of steep and flat coasts. The nature of the profile changes has already been discussed in chapter 12. In this section the form of the deposits are considered from a spatial point of view. The main emphasis is on salt marsh deposits, as the form of beaches and dunes have been considered already in chapters 12 and 6 respectively.

a Shingle ridges

Storm waves form the most permanent shingle ridges. They throw some shingle high onto the beach crest, well above the reach of normal waves. The pebbles are thrown upwards by the swash of the waves, and owing to the rapidity of percolation through the shingle, the backwash cannot remove those deposited at the upper limit of the swash. The rate of percolation is increased by the very well-sorted nature of beach shingle compared with other types of gravel, as pointed out by K. O. Emery (1955). Shingle can be thrown to considerable elevations above the mean sea level by storm waves. The height of Chesil Beach above high-water level of normal tides illustrates this, where pebbles are still sometimes thrown over the beach crest. It lies 7 m above normal high-tide level at Abbotsbury and 13·3 m at Portland, where the beach is composed of larger shingle about 5 to 7·3 cm in diameter.

The ridges which form the bulk of the large shingle structures of Dungeness and Orfordness have been built by storm waves. The material forming the ridges is brought to the vicinity by longshore movement of shingle under the influence of constructive waves, approaching the shore obliquely. It is the storm waves, however—which are generally destructive—that build the ridges to a height well above the normal high-water level. Two examples of shingle deposits will be described. The first represents an extensive spread of shingle involving a large area and great mass of material. The other represents intricate forms of shingle on an indented coast.

The beach-plain deposits of Dungeness have been studied by R. W. Hey (1967). The shingle structures have been exposed in excavations for the atomic power station made near the tip of the cuspate foreland. A considerable thickness of shingle, and shingle packed with sand, resting on pure sand at depths between 3·66 and 7·6 m below sea level were revealed. The shingle spread in this area is very extensive, stretching for up to 3·2 km inland from the present shore. Low parallel ridges mark the surface, representing ancient beach ridges, while shingle is still being added on the east side of the foreland. This area provides a very good example of an actively prograding shingle beach-plain. There were two excavations. The northern one extended from +5·5 m O.D. to −3·96 m O.D. and the southern one went down to −13·7 m O.D. In the former sand overlay shingle at −3·96 m, and in the southern side of the southern pit at −7·33 m. The uppermost layer of pure shingle was 0·915 to 1·53 m thick and was underlain by sandy gravel, which was in beds 7·6 to 91·3 cm thick. These beds dipped with remarkable uniformity to the south-southeast at 8 to 10°. There were few unconformities and all were at very low angles. The individual beds varied little in thickness, apart from a few which thinned in an up-dip direction. The strike of the bedding planes was slightly oblique to the modern coastline at its nearest point, but was exactly parallel to the strike of the beach ridges in the vicinity.

Most of the deposits must be shoreface ones. The loose shingle is more likely a backshore deposit. All the gravel must have been deposited in the last 350 years. The low dip suggests that a mixture of sand and shingle accumulated on the foreshore. The dip angle is similar to that on the present Dungeness beaches, where sand probably underlies the surface shingle. The sand reduces the permeability, so that the beach gradients are lower than those associated with pure shingle beaches.

The rate of accretion, averaged over the period between 1600 and 1800, indicates a progradation of 5·04 m/year. The mean rate of sedimentation normal to the bedding is 76 cm/year. Five to six beds would have been laid down on average each year, each bed being laid down relatively quickly in a short time interval. The beds in the northern section descend to lowest spring-tide level, and in the southern section to 2·4 to 3·4 m lower still. It is suggested that the deposits were laid down during period of spring tides that were accompanied by constructive wave action. This combination could well only occur during five or six periods each year.

The absence of unconformities in the sections suggests that the supply of material was such that little erosion took place during the accumulation of the deposits. There is still doubt as to the relationship between the surface ridges and the underlying structure. The mechanism whereby the ridges on the surface were formed is not fully established. The lack of erosion of the foreshore deposits would not confirm the storm origin of these ridges.

The shingle accumulations of the part of the coast of Brittany discussed by J.-P. Pinot (1963) are of two types. One is arranged parallel to the forces that form them, in the shelter of some feature: these are the 'comet's tails'. The others are arranged perpendicular to the direction of the forces forming them and are fixed at two points: these are the transverse ridges. Different controls determine the two types.

The comet's tails cannot develop in areas where the waves are too variable, while the transverse ridges cannot form where the points of attachment are too far apart. The coast is exposed to the north-northwest, but protected from the main waves coming from the southwest. The shingle formations are related to isolated outcrops of granite at the coast and on the foreshore. These outcrops form the points of attachment for the ridges. A good example of a simple comet's tail ridge is situated in the lee of the Roc'h Louet du, and is illustrated in figure 16-3A. A rocky platform surrounds the rock islet, beyond which is a sandy-muddy beach. The shingle extends about 100 m southeast from the rock outcrop and is separated from the shore by a further gap of a little over 100 m. The ridge is formed of small granite pebbles. The elongation of the comet's tail ridge is determined by the direction of the waves refracted round the rocky outcrop to seaward. Another comet's tail ridge, attached to the Enes Iec, has a blunted hammer-headed end, due to swell coming sometimes from the opposite direction. This feature, shown in figure 16-3B, is 200 m long. The island to which it is attached is 150 m wide and 700 m from the shore. It is protected from the Atlantic swell and is shaped by waves from 005°, and also by waves coming from the northeast. The action of these two sets of waves has resulted in a sinuous ridge. The strong southwest winds, blowing over only a small fetch, form the broad distal end of the spit. The form of the feature is a balance between the winds from opposing directions of different strengths and with different fetch.

An example of a relatively simple transverse ridge is that of Ziliec. The ridge lies behind a sandy beach. It is separated from the shore by a sandy-muddy strand and by a lagoon, surrounded by salt marsh, which has developed between it and the island of Balanec. The ridge is arcuate between the small rocks, to which it is attached at various points along its length. The base of the shingle lies at low water of mean spring tide and the crest lies above the highest tides. The width of the ridge varies between 80 and 190 m, and it is 1500 m long, in three arcs, the largest being 1000 m (see figure 16-3C). Swell can reach the arcs from two directions, the north-northwest and the northeast, with fetches of 190 and 130 km respectively. There are remnants of old comet's tails elongated to the southwest on the southwest side of the arcuate ridge, which faces north in the centre of the feature. Small rocks, now below high-water level, were the original points of attachment for the comet's tails, which were formed by the northeast waves. At this stage rocky obstacles prevented the approach of effective waves from north-northwest. These obstacles have now disappeared, and the swell from the north-northwest has played its part in forming the curved arcs of the ridge.

Other parts of this coast have more complex ridge patterns, including elements of both types of shingle structure. The complexity of the shingle accumulations of this area is due to the different directions of wave approach, the variations in fetch, and to the large number of isolated rocky islets close to the shore and separated from it by relatively shallow water. The abundance of granite pebbles provides the material that forms the shingle ridges. These features exemplify some of the points made concerning orientation in section 13-1(b)(i).

b Sand features

Sandy accretion features include beach ridges, which may become colonized, grow into coastal foredunes, and eventually become stabilized coastal dunes. The details of this process will be considered in section 16-3, which deals with the accretion at the southern end of the Lincolnshire coast. Both early and later stages are visible in the backshore area here. Sandy ridges can form as a berm at the back of a beach either where it abuts against a solid rock coast, or where it lies against a low drift coast, or on a barrier island where it is separated from the shore by a lagoon. In all these environments the berm can form into dunes, although they are best developed on a low coast and barrier islands. Sandy ridges of this type can be built by the waves to the

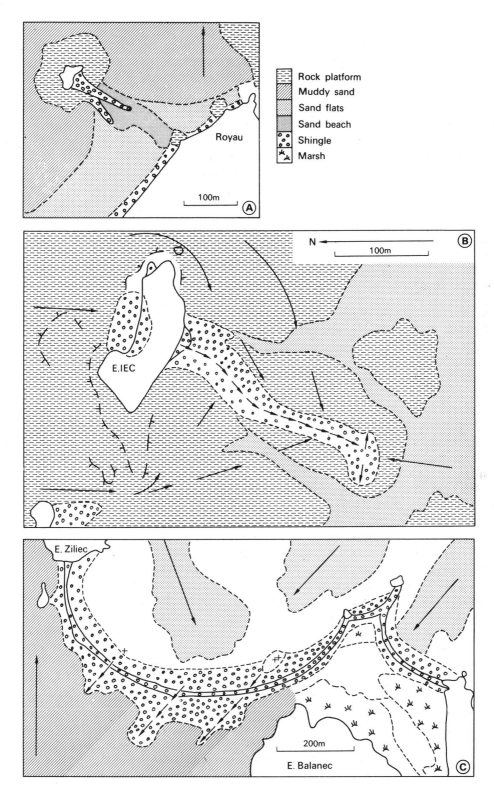

Figure 16-3 Examples of features of accumulation from the coast of Brittany. **A** and **B** show comet's tail spits, and **C** shows a beach ridge normal to the refracted wave crests. (*After Pinot, 1963.*)

limit of their swash. They are formed of sand moved up the beach under constructive conditions, as already indicated. Sand adding to their height by wind activity, is usually derived from the foreshore. Onshore winds are particularly effective on a wide tidal beach at low water, when the extent exposed is great.

The creation and stabilization of coastal dunes on sandy barriers have been discussed by R. P. Savage and W. W. Woodhouse (1968). Barrier island dunes form very effective protection to the coast. They should be encouraged by artificial means if necessary. They prevent over-topping and provide a reservoir of sand on which storm waves can expend their energy. Sand dunes are particularly important along low coasts such as the Netherlands. They are also being extensively encouraged along the barrier islands of the eastern U.S.A. as discussed in section 6-3 (d).

Field experiments have been carried out along the outer banks of North Carolina, using fences and dune grasses. The ordinary berm along these barriers is 1·22 to 1·83 m above the mean sea level, and the barrier islands are between 0·4 and 1·6 km in width. Salt is a particular problem in this area as it comes both from the open sea and the Sound, and storm damage can be severe. The conclusions of the study showed that suitable grasses, such as American beach grass, can trap sand in much greater amounts than are usually available, collecting up to 12·2 m³/30 cm (40 m³/m) of beach. An advantage is that growth of the grass increases the height continuously, and the growing accumulation also spreads with the spread of the plants. The spacing of the plants is important. The optimum appears to be closer in the centre of the area, to assist in the build-up of a ridge-shaped dune, higher in the centre with gently sloping flanks. The beach grass is the best early plant to use as its survival rate is high. A small admixture of sea oats, which is a better final grass, is advantageous, so that as the dune matures the sea oats can become dominant. Where dune grasses will not grow, or are not available, fences provide a possible alternative. Their porosity should be about 40%. With this value they trapped about 6·75 m³/m. Additional fences must be fixed as the first become buried by sand. The dune height is thus increased in stages and the dune crest can be placed in the optimum position on the dune to withstand storm wave activity (R. P. Savage and W. W. Woodhouse, 1968).

c Fine sediment accumulation—salt marsh growth

The deposition of fine sediment can only take place in sheltered areas. The situations where fine sediment is found in coastal locations are therefore within estuaries, where wave action cannot penetrate, and on low-energy coasts. In both areas vegetation, including mangroves in the tropics and salt marsh vegetation in all latitudes, can trap fine sediment. Such sediment can only occur on open beaches behind wave-formed barriers, such as beach ridges and offshore tidal sandbanks.

Estuarine siltation in the Mersey estuary has been studied in the field and by means of scale models by W. A. Price and M. P. Kendrick (1963). Siltation in the upper Mersey estuary has caused navigation problems. The material causing siltation comes from Liverpool Bay. The outer estuary contains extensive sand-banks, and a channel must be dredged to maintain access to Liverpool docks. Above the Narrows the upper tidal estuary opens out to a maximum width of 5500 m, stretching 41·6 km upstream. The salinity stratification causes a net inland movement along the bottom. This flow allows material to move upstream into the estuary where it settles. It was concluded as a result of model studies, and field observations on which the model studies were based, that the training walls in Liverpool Bay contributed to the upper estuary siltation by altering the circulation in the outer estuary. The stabilization of the low-water channel has also added to the siltation. Meandering, which is natural in such channels, is an erosional process and prevents accumulation of material. Works constructed in the upper estuary have reduced the movement of the channel and hence increased the siltation. The dumping of dredged material offshore may also be deleterious, as the material can more readily return up the channel. Price and Kendrick indicate the interrelation between processes operating throughout the whole estuary. There is a danger, for example, of causing a deleterious change in one part, as a result of improvement elsewhere in the channel. The study illustrates as well the value of model studies in elucidating the cause and possible cure of siltation problems in navigable channels.

Chesapeake Bay is also an area of siltation (J. R. Schubel, 1968). Some of the material accumulating in the head of the bay comes from coast erosion, amounting to a total volume of 0.2×10^6 tons/year of sand and silt sediment out of a total of 0.3×10^6 tons/year. The rivers, however, provide five times more sediment. The Susquehanna provides 90% of the fluvial sediment that comes into the bay. The material that settles in the upper part of the bay is the coarser fraction of the sediment. The rate of sedimentation is between 6·1 and 6·85 mm/year. The volume of the upper estuary is reduced by this amount.

Salt marshes will develop either in the shelter of some structure, or in areas where the force of the waves is diminished to such an extent that fine-grained silt can be deposited. An essential factor in the development of a salt marsh is the part played by vegetation. The development varies from place to place. In Britain different characteristics have been distinguished in the marshes of the west, south and east coasts. In each area there is a distinct sequence of vegetation communities, with changing environment as the marsh develops. Another essential factor for the growth of salt marshes is a supply of silt to build up the surface by deposition. Growth of salt marsh is accelerated by the tide, which brings the silt and seeds into the marsh.

The southern part of the Lincolnshire coast illustrates well the stages of salt marsh formation. The marsh is growing in the shelter of marine structures to seaward (F. A. Barnes and C. A. M. King, 1951; 1961). There are two main stages of salt marsh development, termed 'slob-land' and 'salting'. Both these are well illustrated at Gibraltar Point, Lincolnshire. The slob-land stage applies to areas where the tide ebbs and flows as a continuous sheet of water. In the salting stage the tide rises and falls along a series of intricate marsh creeks.

The first stage of marsh development is shown in the New Marsh, which is forming in the shelter of the spit prolonging the north–south coastline. The spit is probably less than 50 years old, having developed after 1922. Figure 16-4 shows the extent and some of the characteristics of this marsh area. Its elevation lies between 2·13 and 3·35 m O.D. Liverpool, where the mean high spring tide level is 3·32 m O.D. and mean high neap tide is 1·77 m O.D.; the heights of mean low neap tide and mean low spring tide are −1·13 m and −2·38 m respectively. The new marsh is, therefore, covered by high spring tide, but not by high neap tide. The gradient along the axis of the marsh slopes very gently at 1 : 350, and the surface is generally smooth, well-defined creeks being limited to the seaward margin. At a level around 2·44 m O.D. the surface is composed of soft, fluid mud; but above about 2·75 m O.D. the surface, particularly in the area nearer the sandy foreshore and the spit, is composed of mud layers interbedded with thin layers of sand. The sand layers are blown onto the marsh during periods of neap tide, when the mud dries and hardens and much dry sand is exposed on the spit and upper beach.

The zones of vegetation are closely related to the height of the marsh. In many marshes *Zostera* spp. (Eel Grass) is the first colonizer. In this area, however, in the early 1950s, clumps and shoots of *Spartina townsendii* (Rice Grass) were growing in the sloppy mud. This species of marsh grass has spread with characteristic rapidity in the last two decades. Another marsh plant, important in the early stages of development, is *Salicornia herbacea* (Annual Glasswort), which flourishes on the New Marsh at Gibraltar Point, as well as in many other areas. This plant requires more stable conditions than *Spartina* and grows best at levels which are above

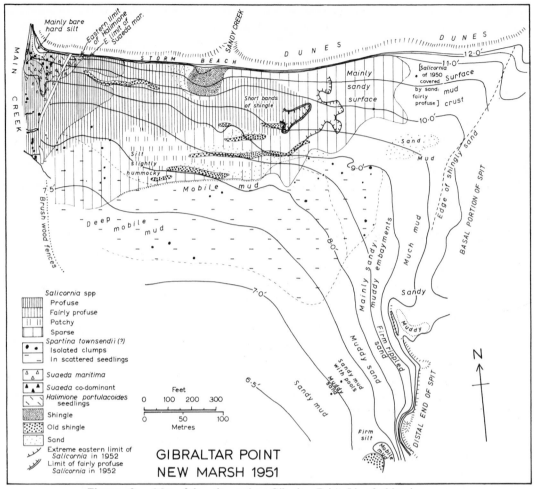

Figure 16-4 Map of the salt marsh at Gibraltar Point, Lincolnshire, in 1951.

the tide every day for a considerable period. On the New Marsh this plant has spread outwards from the Main Creek. It occurs at levels varying from 2·44 m to 3·35 m O.D. on muddy ground. *Salicornia* is an annual, so it does not trap silt so effectively as *Spartina*, and does not usually form a complete cover. *Suaeda maritima* (Annual Seablite) is closely associated with the *Salicornietum* zone, and is now co-dominant with *Spartina* over much of the higher parts of the New Marsh. In some areas *Aster tripolium* (Sea-aster) also grows at this stage.

Over the area of the New Marsh away from the marginal creeks, the tide ebbs and flows smoothly. As deposition proceeds the tide is gradually canalized into definite channels, as irregularities of deposition occur around the growing vegetation. This canalization in itself leads to further variation in deposition.

At the stage where tidal creeks are well developed the marsh may be termed a salting. The mature marsh at Gibraltar Point has reached this phase. It has developed in the shelter of the main eastern dune ridge, which formed during the middle part of the nineteenth century. In the development of marsh creeks natural levées are formed along the edge of the creek. As the rising tide overflows along the creek banks, its speed is slackened, and deposition takes place most rapidly along the edge of the creek. The greater height of the creek borders is well brought out by the distribution of the two major plants in the mature marsh. On the lower ground between the creeks and along their lower banks the dominant plant is *Halimione portulacoides* (Woody Sea-purslane). Other plants in the *Halimionetum* are *Limonium vulgare* (Sea-lavender), *Artemesia maritima* (Sea-mugwort), *Puccinellia maritima* (Sea-grass) and a variety of other plants. Spot heights surveyed in the *Halimionetum* show a very small height range between 3·44 and 3·54 m O.D., which indicates that this part of the marsh is only covered by the higher spring tides.

The higher borders of the creeks are covered by a dense growth of *Agropyron pungens* (Sea Couch-grass) which lies in a height range between 3·59 and 3·87 m O.D. These creek banks are now rarely flooded. The creeks overflow first at their heads during periods of high spring tides. Pans have formed at the heads of some of the creeks in the mature marsh. There are two types of pans. The primary pans are due to original irregularity of deposition, being small areas entirely surrounded by higher ground. The pan cannot drain freely. The soil becomes too saline by evaporation of the trapped salt water and the plants can no longer survive. The area becomes bare as a result. The secondary pan, which is well illustrated at the heads of some of the active creeks on the mature marsh, is caused by the blocking of an active creek near its head. The upper part cannot drain and concentration of salt prohibits plant growth.

Further growth in height will soon raise the mature marsh above the reach of the highest tides. A fresh-water marsh community will then take the place of the salt marsh plants. Eventually, providing sea level does not rise too fast, carr or woodland will form the vegetation climax of the sequence.

Salt marshes round the coasts of England and Wales fall into regional types. The east coast marshes are formed mainly of firm clay. They have a sequence of vegetation phases similar to that outlined above. The south coast marshes are mainly soft silt, and their vegetation is dominated by *Spartina townsendii*. The west coast marshes are predominantly sandy, and *Puccinellia maritima* is their dominant plant.

Measurements of the upward growth of salt marshes have been made in Norfolk by V. F. Chapman (1938a and b) and J. A. Steers (1938) on a marsh formed in the shelter of Scolt Head Island. It was found that the rate of sedimentation varied with the environment and plant cover. The rate was usually highest on the lowest marshes and on the edges of the larger creeks, where these had a good cover of *Halimione*. The higher areas, because of fewer inundations, grew up less rapidly. Over a period of 45 months deposition varied between 0·81 cm and 2·67 cm. The most rapid accretion occurred in the *Asteretum* zone at the rate of 0·98 cm/year. Chapman calculated that, to reach full maturity, a marsh similar to those of Norfolk would require a period of about two centuries and 1·28 m of silt would accumulate during this period. The sandy marshes of the west coast, such as those of the Dyfi estuary, develop at a greater rate.

Another survey of the salt marsh at Gibraltar Point was made in 1959. The change in vegetation and the amount of accretion is shown in figure 16-5. The section shows that the lower part of the marsh and the area bordering the main creek have grown up most. The rate of accretion was in excess of 30 cm in 8 years. Over much of the marsh the growth rate was between 1·9 cm and 2·8 cm/year. The major change in vegetation that took place between the two surveys was the rapid spread of *Spartina* across the marsh. It is now co-dominant with *Suaeda maritima* over much of the southern part of the marsh near the main creek. *Puccinellia* has also spread rapidly through the area bordering the storm beach along the western margin of the New Marsh. There has been little change in the mature marsh during the period, with the exception of the area around the head of Sandy Creek, which has become considerably deeper.

429

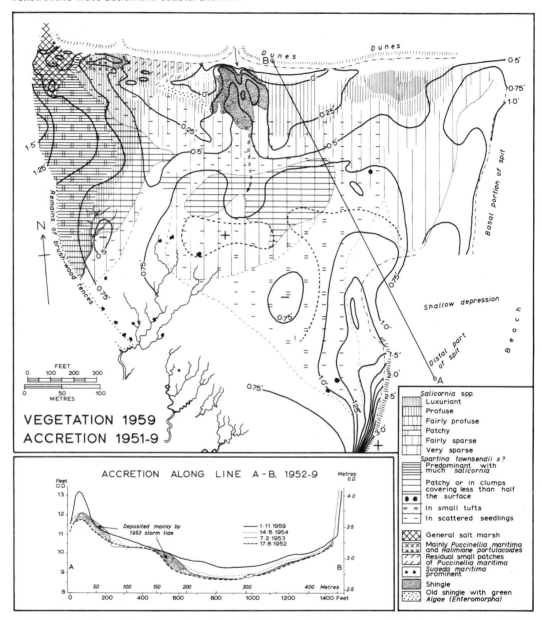

Figure 16-5 Map of the salt marsh at Gibraltar Point, Lincolnshire, in 1959. (*After Barnes and King, 1961.*)

One of the most important new elements in the salt marsh vegetation of British marshes in the twentieth century has been the rapid spread of *Spartina townsendii*. This plant is an extremely efficient trapper of material and hence is very important in marsh development. D. S. Ranwell (1964; 1967; 1968) and E. C. F. Bird and D. S. Ranwell (1964) have made very detailed studies of various aspects of *Spartina townsendii* in British salt marshes. This grass first appeared in the latter half of the nineteenth century, and was named *Spartina townsendii* at Hythe in Southampton Water in 1870. It was thought to be a natural hybrid of the American and British *Spartina*.

It normally grows on mud in the intertidal zone, from mean high water of ordinary tides to a level where the maximum continuous submergence is about six hours. It is a perennial of robust growth and it can spread up to 1 m radially in one year. It can cause accretion at a rate of 10 cm/year under optimum conditions. In Bridgwater Bay, where the tidal range is 12 m and the silt content of the water is high, a mean rate of 5 cm/year was recorded. In the much more mature marsh of Poole Harbour the rate was only 0·5 cm/year. The *Spartina* marsh in Poole Harbour is 50 years old.

Poole Harbour is a good example of estuarine salt marsh development now in a mature stage. The shape of the estuary results from submergence that reached its maximum in this area about 6000 years ago. Sand spits at the entrance provide shelter inside the estuary, the outlet being kept open by tidal currents up to 2·6 m/second. The tidal range in the area is small, being about 2 m. The pattern of tidal channels has been stable for the last 178 years, when it was first surveyed. *Spartina townsendii* first grew in the area about 1899. Since then the marsh level has been raised by as much as 70 cm, so that now it is only a few cm below high spring tide level. Most of the *Spartina* marsh in the estuary lies between +0·1 and +0·6 m O.D., and the plant is rare in the lower levels. The plant is still advancing in a few parts of the estuary, but elsewhere it is being eroded. Its extent is at a maximum under existing ecological conditions, and covers about 873 ha in the intertidal zone. *Phragmites* is growing in the higher parts, covering 251 ha. The intertidal zone occupies 82% of the estuary, and of this area 36% is occupied by *Spartina* and *Phragmites* combined.

Spartina is one of the most common marsh plants of the southern English salt marshes. Rates of accretion have been measured in Bridgwater Bay, Somerset, and Poole Harbour, Dorset, by Ranwell (1964). These two areas form an interesting contrast as the tidal range and silt content are at a maximum in Bridgwater Bay and near a minimum in Poole Harbour. The maximum rate of accretion in Bridgwater Bay was 8 to 10 cm/year in high-level, ungrazed marsh. The pattern of accretion is seasonal, with August to October providing about 75% of the total. The reasons for this are partly related to tidal levels, and probably partly to the stabilizing effect of microbiological activity on the mud surface in summer. By contrast the accumulation in Poole Harbour is about one fifth to one tenth that in Bridgwater Bay, where the marsh is still being actively colonized.

A statistical multiple regression analysis has been carried out to assess the importance of different variables in accounting for the mean annual accretion in the marshes. The significant variables include the height of the site (with a positive sign) the distance seaward (with a negative sign) and height, weight and density of vegetation (all with positive signs). The equation— accretion = 0·643 mean height + 0·0462 mean height of vegetation + 0·00135 weight of vegetation − 1·143—sums up the results of the analysis. The maximum accretion is at the upper levels of the marsh. This contrasts with the Dovey marshes, where the maximum build-up is at the lower levels.

The distribution of *Spartina townsendii* in Britain and in the world is shown in figure 16-6. The plant has gradually spread north from the south coast of England (J. C. E. Hubbard and R. E. Stebbings, 1967). Part of the spread has been natural, but in other areas it has been planted for reclamation purposes and for stabilization. The total area covered in Britain is estimated at 12,044 ha. On the south coast the *Spartina* marshes are mature and even degenerate, covering 3443 ha. On the west coast there are 2313 ha and on the east coast 6381 ha, where 80% is in the Wash and the Essex marshes. The English and Welsh coastal marshes represent a large proportion of the world distribution of *Spartina*.

At present the latitudinal spread of *Spartina* is very limited (D. S. Ranwell, 1967). In

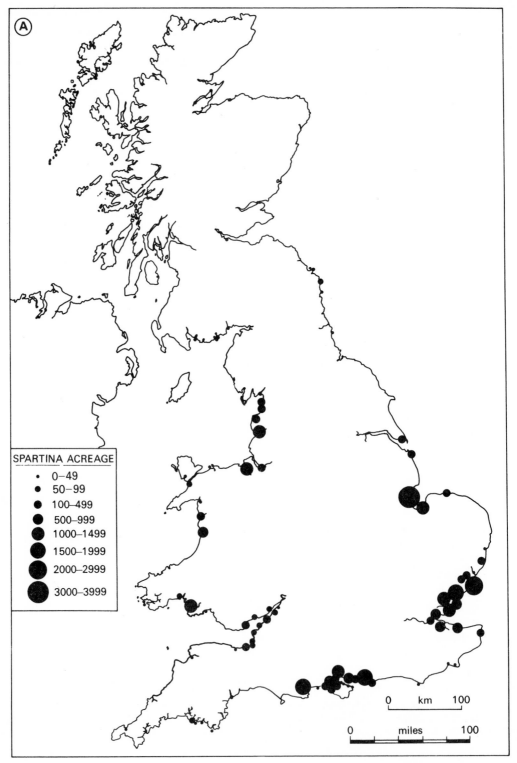

Figure 16-6 **A:** The distribution of *Spartina townsendii* in England and Wales. (*After Hubbard and Stebbings, 1967.*)

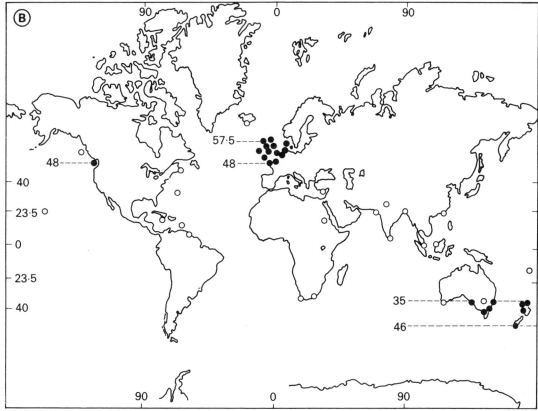

Figure 16-6   B: The world distribution of *Spartina townsendii*. (*After Ranwell, 1967.*)

the northern hemisphere it is restricted to between latitudes 48 and 57·5° N and in the southern hemisphere it grows only between 35 and 46° S in southeast Australia and New Zealand. There is one successful development on the west coast of the U.S.A. at 48° N, but attempts to introduce the plant on the east coast, which is much colder, have not been successful. Nor has the plant

Table 16-1   Distribution of *Spartina townsendii* and date of introduction

Great Britain	1870	12,000 ha	France	1930	4000–8000 ha
Ireland	1925	200–400	Australia	1930	10–20
Denmark	1931	500	Tasmania	1927	20–40
Germany	1927	400–800	New Zealand	1913	20–40
Netherlands	1924	4000–5800	United States	1960	less than 1
Total		21000–27700 ha			

taken successfully in subtropical and tropical areas. *Spartina* does grow well on European marshes in Holland and Denmark. Table 16-1 gives the dates of introduction and areas covered over the world. These figures indicate the spread of the plant from Britain where it originated only 100 years ago.

It has been estimated that about 270 miles (432 km, 9·8%) of the coast of England and Wales is bordered by salt marsh (D. S. Ranwell, 1968). The approximate area is about 80,970 ha in total. The northern and western marshes are characterized by short turf, including much *Puccinellia*, the southern marshes are muddier and have mainly tall grasses, of which *Spartina* is most important; while the eastern marshes have a high proportion of herbs in their flora and less grass. These marshlands are the most valuable potential land for reclamation and this aspect of their development is considered briefly in section 4 of this chapter. There are, however, many conflicting possible uses for the marshland areas.

3 An example of coastal accretion—south Lincolnshire

The coast of Lincolnshire south of Skegness has been accreting steadily for several centuries. The process is actively continuing, and has been recorded in some detail over the last two decades (C. A. M. King, 1970). The area consists of a number of distinct zones, some of which have already been described. The arrival of sediment at the coast is closely related to the pattern of offshore banks, and the tidal streams that are responsible for their formation and movement. These banks and associated tidal streams were considered in chapter 5. It was shown that residual tidal currents are responsible for the arrival of sediment on the coast at localities that change with time. At present the area most affected by the tidal-streams sediment supply lies just at the southern edge of Skegness. The record of the arrival of material is shown in the series of profiles surveyed along profile 4 (figure 16-8). The tidal processes are of considerable importance in this area in explaining the exact location of the major zone of accretion at any time.

The actual accretion takes place initially on the foreshore, and is therefore influenced by the waves, which are the major process operating in this zone. The foreshore on this stretch of coast is characterized by a series of beach ridges, which were described in chapter 12. The ridges are built by the waves and they diverge slightly from the coast southwards, probably due to the approach of the main constructive swells from the north. Waves from this direction would be refracted so as to reach the coast at a slight angle similar to that of the ridge alignment. Owing to the oblique approach of the dominant ridge-building waves, the material moves in general south along the foreshore, and the ridges move bodily southwards also. Thus on any one profile they appear to move steadily inland.

The pattern of inland movement of the ridges is shown in figure 16-7. The ridges on profile 4, at the southern edge of Skegness, develop about 244 m seaward of the dune foot or stabilized beach ridge. The trend lines on the figure indicate the rate of landward movement of the ridges, which is shown to be very regular, until the ridges slow down and become fixed as a new one grows to seaward. The older ridges moved landwards at about 45·8 m/year, although one moved at 103·5 m/year. As the ridges move towards the upper beach they become stabilized by the growth of other ridges to seaward. When this stage has been reached the force of the waves at high tide is reduced, so the ridge becomes static in position, but still continues to grow slowly in height. The plan form of the stabilized ridges is arcuate, with the convex side towards the sea. This is due to the swinging round of the distal end of the ridge towards the shore, after the proximal end at the top of the beach has become stabilized and ceased to move landwards.

The growth in ridge height is now brought about mainly by the establishment of sand-loving grasses and other plants on the ridge crest. The plants help to trap wind-blown sand, thus increasing the height of the ridge crest and stabilizing it still further. Meanwhile the runnel to landward of the ridge collects mud and salt marsh plants become established in it. Thus the depth of the runnel gradually decreases. On profile 4 the maximum depth of 2·13 m has been reduced to 1·2 to 1·5 m or less, according to the relative rates of runnel infilling and dune develop-

434

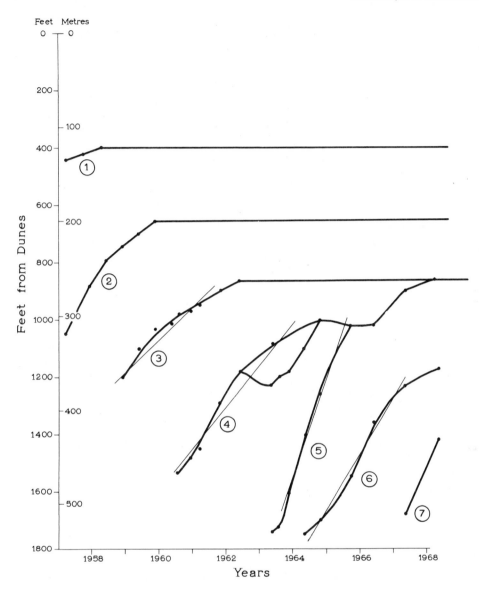

Figure 16-7 The movement of ridges on profile 4, south Skegness, Lincolnshire. *(After Doornkamp and King, 1971.)*

ment on the ridge crest. On the same profile the inner ridge crests have become stabilized since 1959, when vegetation first became established on the innermost ridge. The shoreline has effectively moved over 244 m offshore since this date.

The height of the ridges is partly a function of the amount of material available on the fore-shore. The ridges represent the building up by the waves of their equilibrium gradient on a slope that is too flat in overall gradient. Thus the more sand that is reaching the beach, the flatter the overall gradient will be, and the larger the ridges on the foreshore would be expected to grow. Another variable is the size of the sand. The coarser the sand, the higher the ridge is likely to be, since the coarse sand will require a steeper equilibrium slope.

To test these hypotheses the sizes of the ridges on three profiles have been related to the rate of accretion on the profiles. One profile is situated in the area of maximum accretion (profile 4) at the south end of Skegness. The second lies near the southern limit of accretion, just north of Gibraltar Point (profile 2). The last profile lies across the spit that prolongs the coast just south of profile 2, where the dunes turn inland (profile 1). The amount of accretion on the three profiles

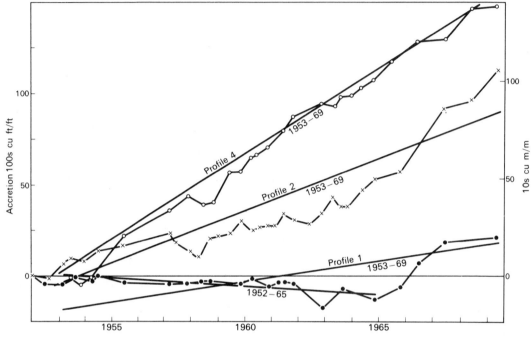

Figure 16-8   Accretion on profiles 1, 2 and 4 south of Skegness, Lincolnshire.

was estimated by measuring the area of cut and fill between successive surveyed profiles. The results are shown in figure 16-8, and the trend equations are as follows:

Profile 4	$Y = 1504 + 190.71\ X$
Profile 2	$Y = 826 + 114.68\ X$
Profile 1	$Y = -1 + 43.42\ X$

Y is the amount of accretion and X is the time in years. The results show that profile 4 has gained consistently more than the others, and that profile 1 has indeed gained a negligible amount. The sweep zones for the three profiles also illustrate the great growth on profile 4: these are shown in figure 16-9. The increasing width of the sweep zones of the profiles from 1, through 2 to 4 indicates that profile 4 has the highest ridges.

The relationship between ridge height and accretion is shown in figure 16-10. The regression lines indicate the relationship between the three profiles, which is highly significant for profiles 2 and 4, with $r = 0.747$ and 0.754 respectively. There is no significant relationship between ridge height and accretion on profile 1. The three sets of data have been combined by analysis of co-variance. This method, which controls for the variation in ridge size between the three profiles, raises the explanation from about 50% ($0.7^2 \times 100$) to about 80%. Thus the relationship between ridge height and amount of accretion is confirmed.

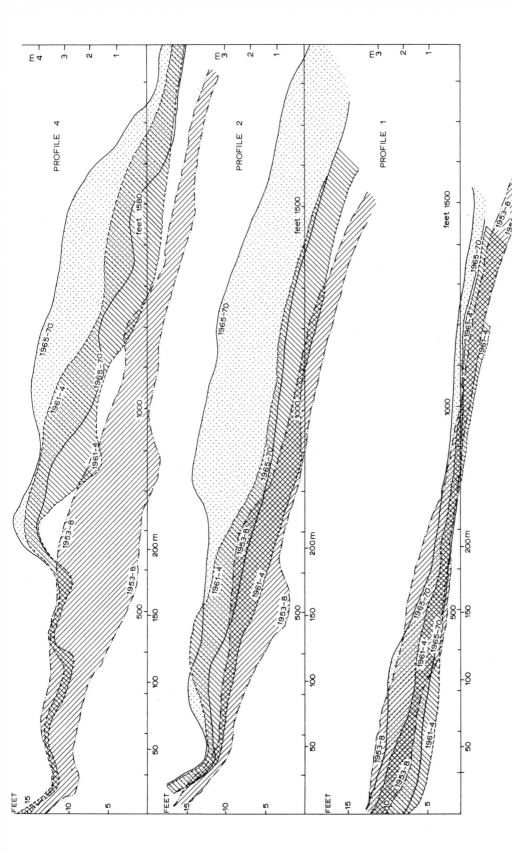

Figure 16-9 Sweep zones for profiles 1, 2 and 4 for the periods 1953–58, 1961–64 and 1965–70.

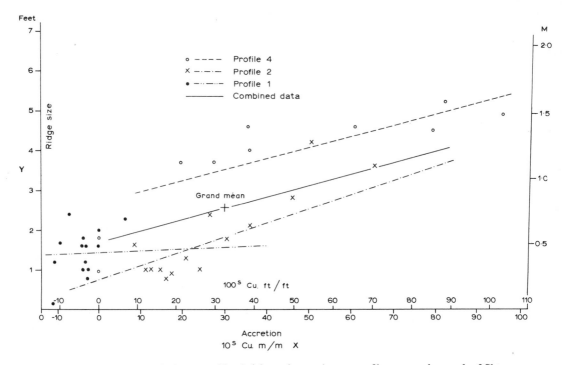

Figure 16-10 The relationship between ridge height and accretion on profiles 1, 2 and 4 south of Skegness.

The differences in ridge height is due to different sand size on the profiles. Profile 4 has a mean sand size of 1·35 ϕ compared with 2·27 ϕ on profile 2. Thus larger ridges are related to the rate of accretion on the foreshore. They are an essential preliminary to the development of foredunes in this area, as they provide their foundation. In this manner stable foredunes and strip saltings develop, and these cause the eastward progradation of the coast by accretion.

Some of the sand that passes south along the upper foreshore from profile 2 goes to build up the spit that is growing up steadily (C. A. M. King, 1970). There is a close correlation between the volume added to the spit and the accretion on profile 2 to the north, as shown in figure 16-11. The correlation coefficient is 0·90, explaining 80·8% of the variation in the spit volume. This relationship is probably caused by the southward transfer of material along the upper beach. The lack of correlation between the accretion on the spit and that on profile 1, across it, supports the view that movement takes place mainly on the upper beach. The waves at high tide are the force that causes the transfer of sand. At low tide wave action is very weak, owing to the exposure of offshore banks about 0·8 km offshore at this stage of the tide.

The spit is a small one, only about 600 m long. It is also relatively ephemeral. It started to grow after a storm in 1922 drove sand over the edge of the mature marsh and initiated the formation of the new marsh. The earlier dune ridges were truncated. Since this date the spit has extended southwards and has provided shelter for the new marsh development. This marsh has already been commented upon earlier in the chapter. The spit in its present position is a recent feature, but it was preceded by earlier spits, which were situated further west. Accretion on this coast is largely achieved by stabilization of beach ridges and by the development of dunes on them and salt marsh in the intervening runnels. At each stage of growth a small spit is likely to prolong the outermost dune ridge extending a short distance southwards. The spit will, however, decay as newer ridges develop to seaward. These ridges cut off the supply of sand that moves along the upper foreshore to feed the spit.

Accretion on this coast is, therefore, primarily due to the arrival of excess material on the foreshore by the residual tidal stream flow. This material is built up into ridges by wave action on the foreshore. It is then stabilized by dune and salt marsh development, on the ridges and in the runnels, respectively. Thus both sand, sandy shingle, as well as finer material are

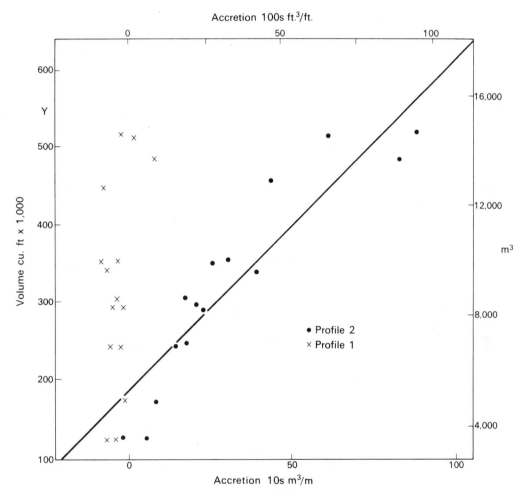

Figure 16-11 The relationship between the volume of material on the spit at Gibraltar Point and the accretion on the beach on profiles 1 and 2.

involved in the accretion on this coast. The bulk of the material is supplied from the north through coastal erosion and from inland. Further stabilization is produced by the maturing of the dunes, as they approach their climax vegetation and trap further sand, thus increasing their height. The salt marsh also grows relatively rapidly to maturity. *Spartina townsendii* is playing an important part in the rapid growth of the new marsh, but was not present in the stabilization and upgrowth of the mature marsh. It is also present in the strip saltings that are developing in the recently colonized runnels near profile 4.

4 Coastal reclamation

Coastal salt marsh provides the most useful land for reclamation for agriculture. Salt marsh silt, once the salt has been washed out, forms very fertile soil. One area of very exensive reclamation is around the Wash, where reclamation has been going on since Roman times. According to O. Borer (1939) 8660 ha were reclaimed in the Wash during the seventeenth century, 48 ha in the eighteenth century, increasing again to 2220 ha in the nineteenth century. The large amount reclaimed in the seventeenth century was made possible by taking advantage of all the natural accretion that had taken place since the Roman period. Of the land reclaimed 1975 ha were along the Norfolk coast and 9150 ha were in south Lincolnshire.

This type of reclamation cannot be made in large areas because the marsh must build up naturally to a certain height before successful reclamation can be achieved. When the marsh is built to such a height that only the highest tides inundate it walls can be built on the seaward side. Drains must be established to wash out the salt water and maintain the fertility. To facilitate this process a series of ditches are dug, running across the marsh to the sea, with a fall of 61 cm/ 1·6 km (38 cm/km) (2 feet/mile). The material from the ditch is placed on the side facing the flood tide so that material eroded from the pile is washed onto the marsh and can settle in the relatively quiet water. The ebbing tide is assisted by the ditches, which allow the newly deposited silt time to consolidate before the next high water covers the area.

An unsuccessful reclamation scheme was started in 1839 by Sir J. Rennie and the Norfolk Estuary Company. An attempt was made to enclose a large area at one time. By 1876, however, only 606 ha had been enclosed and reclaimed, while the remainder—12,100 ha—was bare sand. Of this area 963 ha were reclaimed by 1914 and 323 ha have been reclaimed since then. Reclamation is still proceeding slowly around the margins of the Wash and there are schemes for larger operations, both for reclamation and water storage.

Successful reclamation is now being carried out in the Lincolnshire part of the Wash. This follows unsuccessful schemes proposed in 1857 by the Lincolnshire Estuary Company, who hoped to reclaim a strip up to nearly 4·8 km in width at one operation. This failed because the width of the area prevented natural accretion taking place to a sufficient height throughout the zone. The width of active salt marsh growing in this area around Wainfleet is 0·8 to 1·2 km. The reclamation in this area has taken a strip 0·8 km wide. Reclamation in Morecambe Bay has also been extensive, but because sand rather than silt is deposited in this area, the reclaimed land is not of great value. The Royal Commission on Coast Erosion state in their report of 1911 that of the 405 ha gained in this area about half has since been abandoned.

Reclamation has been again increasing recently. D. S. Ranwell (1968) has estimated that natural siltation and reclamation have increased during the last 150 years at a rate 12 times that of the previous 6000 years. The rate of embankment in the Wash has been 32,400 ha since the seventeenth century and could continue at a rate of about 6,100 ha/century.

Reclamation in the Danish Wadden Sea has been aided by the use of *Puccinellia, Spartina,* and other plants. Their establishment is aided by digging shallow trenches across the marshland, increasing sedimentation. *Spartina* is helpful in this process as it grows at a lower level than the other plants, though, on the other hand, it tends to prevent even development and interferes with ditching. *Spartina* has also been used for reclamation in the Netherlands since the mid-1920s. Between 1924 and 1950 an area of 490 ha has been planted with *Spartina* in a successful reclamation programme. This area is now a settled agricultural district. A specially hardy species of *Spartina* had to be developed to withstand the winter frost in this area. *Spartina* marshland can be used for grazing, but only the older breeds of sheep will eat it. Thus where modern breeds predominate, as in Holland and Denmark, it is not so highly thought of as a pasture plant. The *Spartina* marsh gradually gives way to *Puccinellia* at the higher levels. This is also a useful grazing plant, as well as being valuable for turf.

Some large-scale reclamation schemes have been suggested, such as the building of barrages across the Wash, the Solway and Morecambe Bay, and feasibility studies initiated. These schemes are usually designed for several purposes, including water storage, improved routeways, and reclamation of land for agricultural, urban and industrial development. The only good agricultural land will be that previously in the form of fine-grained salt marsh deposits.

One of the most ambitious projects of coastal reclamation is that of the Zuiderzee in the Netherlands. The Zuiderzee occupies a large and old depression behind the outlying islands off the Dutch coast. It was once the estuary of the Meuse and Rhine, before they were deflected to their present outlets. Early reclamations probably date from Roman times, when dykes were built to protect the land from the sea (A. R. Orme, 1966). Draining of the reclaimed land has become increasingly difficult owing to the continued rise of sea level, which is partly due to subsidence in this area. Until drainage of the reclaimed land could be carried out effectively reclamation was limited. Windmills served this purpose in the seventeenth century; steam power was introduced in the eighteenth century; while at present diesel and electric power are used.

Between 1200 and 1919, when the Zuiderzee project was started, 380,000 ha of marine and fluvial land was gained, plus 139,000 ha of drained lake floor. During the same period 566,000 ha had been lost by erosion and inundation. The Zuiderzee before reclamation was about 3·05 to 4·9 m deep with some deeper channels cut by tidal streams. The main dyke was built between 1927 and 1932. The reclamation of the Polders was between 1927 and 1930 in the northwest, 1937, to 1942 in the northeast, 1950 to 1957 in the east central area and 1950 to 1968 in the south. Further land has been gained in the southwest, leaving a large water body in the extreme north, the Ijsselmeer, which is now a freshwater lake. The main barrier dam is 91·5 m wide at the water line, which is 7·0 to 7·6 m above mean sea level, and 3·66 m above the highest known tide. The conversion of the Ijsselmeer into a fresh-water lake has greatly improved the land around, as well as providing a valuable water supply. The lake occupies the deeper part of the area where the bottom sediments are sandy, and thus do not form good agricultural land. The clay areas on the margins have been reclaimed to form the five main polders. The latest reclamation has been of the Markerwaard Polder in the west. This will bring a further 59,800 ha under cultivation. Expense has restricted this plan to 44,000 ha in Southern Flevoland.

The reclaimed areas will remain as islands surrounded by narrow marginal lakes. They will be used for discharging water from the land, for navigation and eventually for recreation. Without the lakes the drainage of the polders would upset the groundwater table, to the detriment of adjacent areas. When the scheme is complete by the 1980s, about 226,000 ha of new land and the large fresh-water lake of the Ijsselmeer, covering 121,000 ha, behind the great barrier dam, will have been gained. The dam also greatly adds to the security of the whole area from flooding by storm surges, such as that of 1953, which caused so much damage along the low-lying coast of the Netherlands. The dam also acts as a useful communication link between the densely settled area to the west of the former Zuiderzee and northeast Holland. In 1953 162,000 ha of land were flooded, and 1800 people lost their lives as a result of the storm surge. With the barrier dam, as a first line of defence, such disasters should not recur in the future. The polder dykes provide a second line of defence (A. R. Orme, 1966).

The coastal works associated with land reclamation and sea defences in the Netherlands are in many respects unique. A recent description by K. P. Blumenthal (1967) divides the coastal

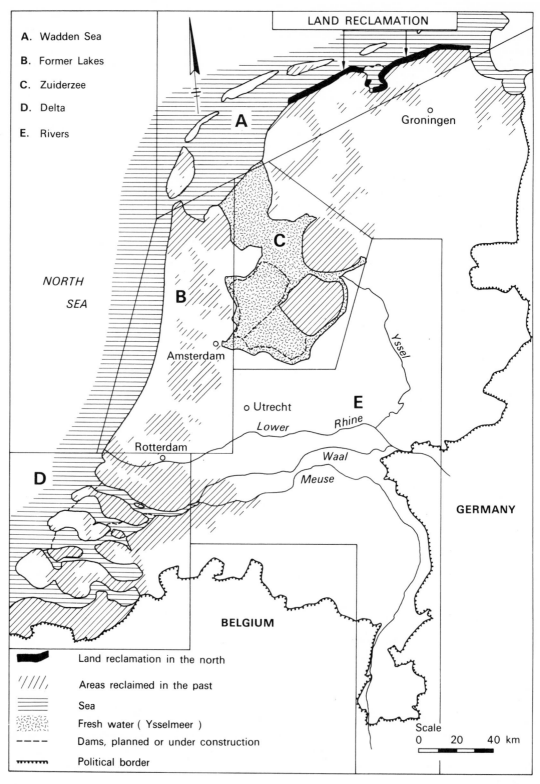

Figure 16-12 Land reclamation in the Netherlands, past and present. (*After Blumenthal, 1967.*)

zone into five areas, as shown on the map in figure 16-12. The Delta plan in the southwest was initiated following the disastrous storm surge of 1953. The sea defences around the low islands of the delta region are 900 km in length. By linking the islands and closing the branches of the delta, 25 km of dykes can provide good protection for the coast. This coastal defence plan is not associated with land reclamation, but it will provide fresh-water reservoirs, better communications and improved inland navigation. The Waddensee in the northern part of the area, around Friesland and Groningen, is of greater interest from the point of view of reclamation. Small portions of land in this area have been reclaimed for a long time, as shown in figure 16-13. The reclamations are long and narrow, thus incorporating the land raised naturally to the high salting level. The silt that accumulates in the Waddensee comes from the Rhine and Meuse, and is carried north along the coast. Only a small proportion settles out from suspension owing to its very low settling velocity. One method of increasing settling is the passing of the silt through mussels, cockles and other lamellibranches that feed by filtering the water. This process concentrates the silt, which is excreted as little balls. It is estimated that at least 1·3 million tons of pure clay is deposited annually by this means on the shallows north of Groningen alone.

Diatoms also play a part in the deposition process in that they cover the mud with a slimy coherent layer, which protects it from erosion to a certain extent. Sedimentation is most rapid in the sheltered waters in the watershed areas between the islands. The process is now accelerated by artificial procedures. Under natural conditions sand is deposited in deeper water and clay near the shore. The sand is more easily eroded and a clay cliff is often formed as a result. This feature is difficult to eradicate once it has formed, and its retreat leads to erosion of the salting. In order to increase the rate of sedimentation ditches are dug, with intervening dams about 200 m apart. The dams cause quieter water and silt settles out more rapidly.

A more recent method of speeding sedimentation has been the building of sedimentation fields, measuring 400 by 400 m. The boundaries are formed of brushwood dams extending 0·3 m above mean high tide. They are semi-pervious, as an aid to sedimentation. There are two main drainage channels, perpendicular to the dykes, and 100 m apart, with intervening earth dams. As they silt up, the ditches often have to be redug, for which special mechanical equipment can be used. The siltation amounts to between 2 and 7 cm each year under this scheme. Three or four sedimentation fields are reclaimed simultaneously stretching away from the shore. At present there are extensive works of this type in the north (figure 16-14). The Lauwerzee will have been completely reclaimed by 1969, involving a major dyke closing a gap with a tidal volume of 120 million m³. The land reclamation will amount to 1300 ha for cultivation.

Other possible projects include linking the island of Ameland to the mainland with dykes, a project which would provide an additional 3000 ha of cultivable land. In eastern Groningen 3900 ha could be reclaimed, although it will probably not be as it would depend on enclosing the whole Waddensee. The Wadden plan is several times the magnitude of the Delta plan. Even if it were executed, it would not be complete until 2025. It would take 46 years and could not be started until the Delta plan is complete. It seems that this plan is unlikely to be fulfilled.

Summary

Constructive wave action on the beach depends on the type of material. On sand beaches constructive waves build up a berm at or above high-tide level. The waves are usually flat and are more constructive when they are accompanied by an offshore wind. Accretion by constructive waves is caused by sand movement normal to the shore, but accretion can also result from

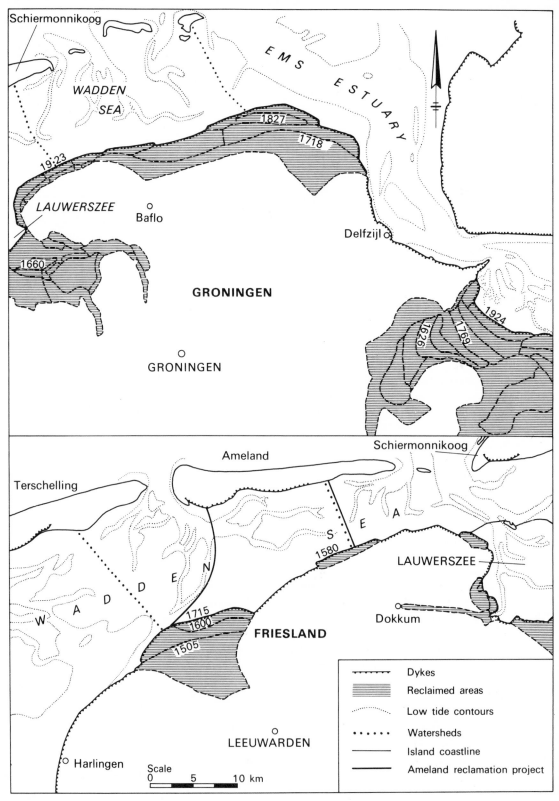

Figure 16-13 Land reclamation in the north of the Netherlands later than 1400 A.D. (*After Blumenthal, 1967.*)

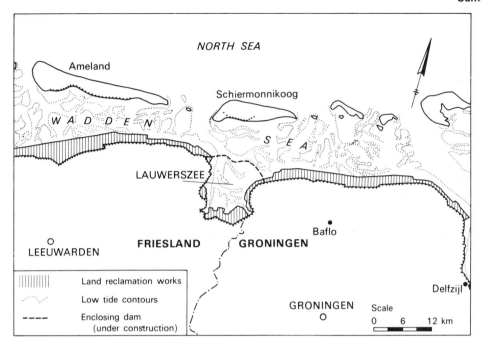

Figure 16-14   Land reclamation in Eastern Wadden Sea. (*After Blumenthal, 1967.*)

longshore movement of sand. Accretion is often seasonal in character, the beaches usually building up during the summer months, when waves are flatter and storms less common. The profiles typical of such constructive conditions are, therefore, often called summer profiles. These are usually fairly smooth below the berm on the upper foreshore. Summer fill may extend to a depth of about 10 m, but large changes of level are usually restricted to about 4 m.

The coastal forms typical of accretion depend again on the nature of the material. The most permanent features on shingle beaches are those built up by the swash of storm waves above the reach of normal calm-weather waves. These ridges are common in shingle structures, such as Chesil Beach, and Orfordness. The material is brought into the area often by longshore drift, and is built up by the storm waves. A study of the Dungeness shingle beach-plain indicates that shingle was added to the area about five to six times a year as shoreface deposits, dipping seaward at 8 to 10°, the deposits accumulating over the last 350 years. The deposits were probably laid down when constructive conditions were combined with specially high tides. In areas of intricate outline shingle features may be either elongated parallel to or normal to the direction of refracted wave approach. The first type consists of comet tails, which are attached to an offshore islet. The ridges that form normal to the wave approach direction are attached at both ends to rocky outcrops. Accretion on sandy coasts is in the form of beach ridges on the foreshore where conditions are suitable, or berms at the limit of the foreshore. In the backshore zone coastal dunes are common on low coasts and especially on barrier islands.

Where the sediments are fine, salt marsh growth facilitates and speeds up coastal accretion. The growth of salt marshes depends on the deposition of tidal silt in an area from which violent wave action is excluded. The development is in two stages, the slob-land stage occurs when the tide ebbs and floods evenly over the area. In the higher salting stage the tide is partially confined to marsh creeks, except at very high tide. Marsh growth is most rapid along the margins of the

445

creeks. *Spartina townsendii*, which first appeared in Britain in 1870, has spread rapidly on British and continental coasts and greatly speeds up salt marsh growth. A maximum of about 10 cm/year has been recorded. *Spartina* is restricted to a narrow latitudinal belt of 48 to 57° N and 35 to 46° S.

Coastal accretion in south Lincolnshire depends upon material brought into the area by the residual tidal streams. The material is built into beach ridges by the waves and these move inland until they are stabilized by the growth of another ridge to seaward. Ridge height has a high positive correlation with accretion on the foreshore, the ridges representing the attempt of the waves to build their equilibrium gradient on an overall gradient that is too flat owing to accretion. This coast is building out eastwards by the stabilization of the beach ridges to form dunes and of the runnels to form strip saltings.

Coastal reclamation for agricultural land has taken place around the Wash and in other estuaries since Roman times. Large-scale schemes are often not successful as only a narrow strip of salting can build up naturally. More extensive reclamation has taken place in Holland, where the Zuiderzee has been reclaimed to form both agricultural land and fresh-water reservoirs. Other even more ambitious schemes are under consideration in the Waddensee in Holland, and the Wash, Solway and Morecambe Bay in England.

References

BARNES, F. A. and KING, C. A. M. 1951: A preliminary survey at Gibraltar Point, Lincolnshire. *Bird Obs. and Field Res. St. Gib. Pt. Lincs. Rep.*, 41–59.

BARNES, F. A. and KING, C. A. M. 1955: Beach changes in Lincolnshire since the 1953 storm floods. *East Mid. Geogr.* **4,** 18–28,

BARNES, F. A. and KING, C. A. M. 1961: Salt marsh development at Gibraltar Point, Lincolnshire. *East Mid. Geogr.* **15,** 20–31.

BIRD, E. C. F. 1960: The formation of sand beach ridges. *Australian J. Sci.* **22**(8), 349–50.

BIRD, E. C. F. and RANWELL, D. S. 1964: *Spartina* salt marshes in south England, IV: the physiography of Poole Harbour, Dorset. *J. Ecol.* **52,** 355–66.

BLUMENTHAL, K. P. 1967: Some aspects of land reclamation in the Netherlands. Chapter 76 in *Proc. 10th Conf. Coastal Eng.*, 1331–59.

BORER, O. 1939: Changes in the Wash. *Geog. J.* **93,** 491–6.

CHAPMAN, V. J. 1938a: Marsh development in Norfolk. *Trans. Norfolk and Norwich Nat. Soc.* **14,** 394.

CHAPMAN, V. J. 1938b: Studies in salt marsh ecology, I, II, III. *J. Ecol.* **26,** 144–79.

CHAPMAN, V. J. 1960: *Salt marshes and salt deserts of the world.* London: Leonard Hill.

COMMISSION ON COAST EROSION 1911: *Final Report.*

EMERY, K. O. 1955: Grain size of marine beach gravel. *J. Geol.* **63,** 39–49.

HEY, R. W. 1967: Sections in the beach-plain deposits of Dungeness, Kent. *Geol. Mag.* **104**(4), 361–70.

HUBBARD, J. C. E. and STEBBINGS, R. E. 1967: Distribution, dates of origin and acreage of *Spartina townsendii* (s.l.) marshes in Great Britain. *Proc. Biol. Soc. Br. Is.* **7**(1), 1–7.

INMAN, D. L. and RUSNAK, G. A. 1956: Changes in sand level on the beach and shelf at La Jolla, California. *B.E.B. Tech. Memo.* **82.**

KING, C. A. M. 1970: Changes in the spit at Gibraltar Point, Lincolnshire, 1951–1969. *East Mid. Geog.* **5**(33 & 34), 19–30.

LAFOND, E. C. 1939: Sand movement near the beach in relation to tides and waves. *Proc. 6th Pacific Sci. Cong.* 795–9.

LEWIS, W. V. 1931: Effect of wave incidence on the configuration of a shingle beach. *Geog. J.* **78,** 131–48.

ORME, A. R. 1966: The reclamation of the Zuiderzee. *Geog. Viewpt.* **1**(3), 101–23.

PINOT, J. P. 1961: Les accumulations vaseuses littorales au sud de L'Île Grande, *Cahiers Oceanog.* **13**(7), 460–84.

PINOT, J. P. 1963: Quelques accumulations de gabets de la côte tregoroise. *Ann. de Geogr.* **72,** 13–31.

PRICE, W. A. and KENDRICK, M. P. 1963: Field and model investigations into the reasons for siltation in the Mersey Estuary. *J. Inst. Civ. Eng.*, Pap. **6669,** 473–517.

RANWELL, D. S. 1958: Movement of vegetated sand dunes at Newborough Warren, Anglesey. *J. Ecol.* **48,** 83–100.

RANWELL, D. S. 1964: *Spartina* salt marshes in south England, II: rate and seasonal pattern of sediment accretion. *J. Ecol.* **52,** 79–94.

RANWELL, D. S. 1967: World resources of *Spartina townsendii* (*sensu lato*) and economic uses of *Spartina* marshland. *J. Appl. Ecol.* **4,** 239–56.

RANWELL, D. S. 1968: Coastal marshes in perspective. *Reg. Stud. Gr. Bull.* **9.** (26 pp.)

SAVAGE, R. P. and WOODHOUSE, W. W. 1969: Location and stabilisation of coastal barrier dunes. Chapter 43 in *Proc. 11th Conf. Coast. Eng. London 1968*, Am. Soc. Civ. Eng., 671–700.

SCHUBEL, J. R. 1968: Shore erosion of the Northern Chesapeake Bay. *Shore and Beach* **36**(1), 22–6.

SHEPARD, F. P. 1950: Beach cycles in southern California. *B.E.B. Tech. Memo.* **20.**

SHEPARD, F. P. 1952: Revised nomenclature for depositional coastal features. *Bull. Am. Assoc. Petrol. Geol.* **36**(10), 1902–12.

STEERS, J. A. 1938: The rate of sedimentation on salt marshes on Scolt Head Island, Norfolk. *Geol. Mag.* **75,** 26–39.

TRASK, P. D. 1956: Changes in configuration of Point Reyes beach, California, 1955–1956. *B.E.B. Tech. Memo.* **91.**

17 Destructive wave action and coastal erosion

1 Destructive wave action in profile—the beach and cliff: a) Effect of waves, wind and other processes; b) Destructive wave action on the beach : (*i*) *Shingle*; (*ii*) *Sand.*

2 Erosion of solid rocks by the sea

3 Shore platforms and other erosional forms

4 Cliffs

5 Destructive marine action in plan—coastal erosion: a) Causes of coastal erosion : (*i*) *The part played by the beach*; (*ii*) *The character of the coast*; (*iii*) *Offshore relief*; (*iv*) *Sea level changes*; (*v*) *Man-made structures*; (*vi*) *Longshore movement of beach material*; b) Coast erosion—general points.

6 Examples of coast erosion: a) North Yorkshire; b) Holderness; c) East Anglia; d) Sumner, New Zealand.

7 Rates of coastal erosion

8 Coastal defences

Summary

The conditions under which destructive beach processes operate, and coastal erosion takes place, are usually more spectacular than the slower and less conspicuous changes which occur under constructive conditions. The latter, however, produce greater areal change in the amount of land and sea round the coasts of the British Isles, according to the report of the Royal Commission on Coastal Erosion (1911). The gain takes place largely in sheltered estuaries, while the losses occur mainly on the open coast. Some of the erosion now taking place is due to the effect of man-made structures. Before coastal erosion is considered, the nature of destructive wave action on beaches will be examined, and the processes by which waves attack sea cliffs and marine benches will be analysed.

1 Destructive wave action in profile—the beach and cliff

a Effect of waves, wind and other processes

Steep waves are normally destructive, lowering the level of the foreshore surface and transporting material seaward. The larger the waves are, provided they are above the critical steepness

448

for destructive action, the greater will be the removal of material from the beach, because of their greater energy. Destructive waves are normally associated with storms and high wind velocities. Strong winds, blowing onshore near the coast, generate steep seas, and the wind itself, as has already been demonstrated in laboratory experiments and field observations, has a marked effect on the destructive nature of the wave attack. A strong onshore wind may also assist the destructive tendency of the waves by raising the water level above its normal height. Thus the sea can attack zones normally beyond its reach. Strong winds, and the rapid changes in atmospheric pressure associated with them, can generate surges in some areas. These have been considered in chapter 4.

The recorded height of storm waves on the coast may be exaggerated on some occasions, but considerable wave heights can be attained. Waves near the coast are not normally so high as those in the open ocean. The waves in the North Sea that caused so much damage during the storm surge of 1953 were about 6 m high. These waves were generated by winds of exceptional force. C. K. M. Douglas (1953) calculated a geostrophic wind speed of 280 km/hour. The wind was blowing over a long fetch for a long time and, therefore, probably produced the maximum possible wave size for the North Sea.

Waves of this height are more common off coasts exposed to the open ocean. F. P. Shepard (1950) states that off Washington and Oregon waves of 6 m are fairly common, but off southern California waves are rarely higher than 3 m. Occasional records of waves up to 6 m in height have been obtained from the Atlantic coast of America, but in general waves are lower than 3 m here. Further data on observed wave heights are given in section 4-3.

b   Destructive wave action on the beach

(i) *Shingle:*   There is a significant difference between the effect of storm waves on shingle and on sand beaches. W. V. Lewis (1931) has described the action of destructive waves on a shingle beach. He noted the relative weakness of the swash compared with the backwash. Destructive waves can cause very rapid removal of shingle from the upper foreshore to a position just outside the break-point. On Chesil Beach at Abbotsbury the crest of the shingle beach was cut back over a width of 1·53 m within 3 hours on one occasion (20.9.49). The waves were short and steep, with a steepness ratio of 0·019. On the following day steep waves cut away a vertical thickness of 0·61 to 0·915 m of shingle in one hour. The shingle had a median diameter of 10·3 mm. In great storms very large volumes of shingle may be removed from the foreshore into deeper water, to be returned by the constructive waves after the storm.

(ii) *Sand:*   Steep storm waves attacking a sand beach are usually entirely destructive in their effect, moving sand to deeper water offshore. Exceptions occur when extra high-water levels allow waves to wash sand over the backshore zone into a lower area inland, such as a lagoon behind a barrier beach. The coarser the sand, the greater the amount removed seawards under similar wave conditions. During the period 2–12 December 1950, about 0·9 m depth of sand was removed from the entire width of the beach at the north end of Marsden Bay, while similar but lesser erosion occurred at the south end of the bay. In some instances a vertical scarp is left on the beach at the limit of the high tide. This feature was well developed on the profile for 28 October 1950, shown in figure 17-1.

In some areas the whole beach may be removed by storm waves. A good example of this was the removal of sand from some of the beaches of Lincolnshire as a result of the storm surge of January–February 1953, leaving the clay base of the beach exposed, as shown in figure 17-9. Similar removal of entire beaches is reported from California by F. P. Shepard (1950). Some of

449

these beaches, such as Boomer beach, which has already been mentioned in section 16-1 (b), and Windansea beach, lose their material by longshore transport due to oblique waves. Erosion can result in changes of beach level of over 1·83 m, taking place over periods as short as one day. On many of the Californian beaches marked erosion occurs on the upper beach during stormy winter

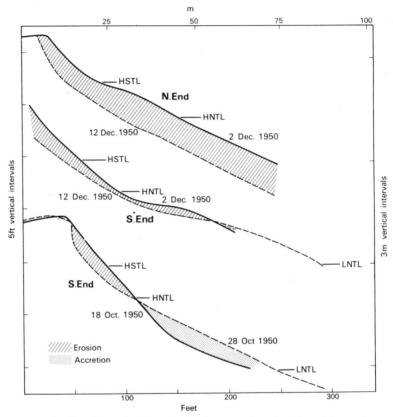

Figure 17-1   Profiles of Marsden Bay, Co. Durham, to show the effect of destructive waves.

periods. Erosion at this season has also been observed on the ridges of Blackpool beach, which are made of fine sand.

The most serious beach depletion and coastal erosion is usually associated with abnormal conditions of weather and water level. In some areas these are associated with the development of a storm surge, which may greatly raise the water level. Such events are important from the point of view of coastal defences and geomorphological changes.

2 Erosion of solid rocks by the sea

The sea does not only remove the loose material of the beach to deeper water when destructive conditions prevail, but may also attack the solid rocks of the coast. Cliffs are formed and wave-cut benches are eroded in front of the cliffs. The retreat of the cliffs is intimately linked with the cutting of the platform. Both depend on the ability of the waves to reach the rocks. These features can only develop where there is no protective beach, covering the rock platform and preventing the waves from attacking the cliffs. It has already been shown that the thickness of beach cover need not be great, unless it is entirely removed by destructive waves, because the depth of disturbance of sand is small.

The processes by which the sea attacks the rocks of the cliffs will be mentioned first. The four main processes are well known and need not be considered in detail. They are corrosion, corrasion, attrition and hydraulic action. The first is concerned with the chemical weathering of the rocks by contact with the sea water. This process is particularly effective on limestone. Corrasion implies the direct attack of the cliffs by waves laden with sand grains and pebbles. The rocks are gradually worn away and smoothed by this process. Attrition is the breaking up of pieces of rock derived from the cliff or elsewhere. The rocks become gradually rounder and can then be more easily moved away, or used as tools for corrasion, as their size is reduced.

The last process, hydraulic action, is probably the most effective agent of erosion. When waves break against a cliff air in the cracks is strongly compressed and later, as the wave recedes, the pressure is suddenly released. These sudden changes of pressure can enlarge the crack and loosen pieces of rock. This process is more effective in well-jointed rocks. The forces exerted directly by the waves are also important. Shock pressures are sometimes exerted by a wave as it breaks against a structure in such a way that a pocket of air is enclosed. This process was described in section 4-1(h). If the cliff descends straight into deep water, or if the waves break before they reach the cliff, no shock pressure will be induced. The pressure exerted by breaking waves has been recorded by dynamometers. The values agree quite well with the theoretical values derived from a formula of D. B. W. Gaillard (1904)

$$1 \cdot 31(C + V_{max})^2 \varrho/2g$$

where C is the wave velocity and V_{max} the orbital velocity at the crest of the wave. For a wave 3·05 m high and 45·8 m long the calculated pressure would be 1241 lbs/square foot (0·608 kg/cm²) while the observed value was 1210 lbs/square foot (0·593 kg/cm²). When the waves are long, and hence have a high velocity, the pressures generated are quite sufficient to cause very extensive damage to cliffs or structures. Only a very few waves, however, produce shock pressures, according to records taken at Dieppe. The maximum pressure recorded was 6·22 kg/cm², but the pressure only exceeded 2·94 kg/cm² for $\frac{1}{100}$ second. The deep water wave height was nearly 1·83 m and the length 40·3 m (A. de Rouville, 1938).

The very high pressures enable waves breaking against cliffs to dislodge fragments. As soon as the fallen debris causes the wave to break before it reaches the cliff, the rate of erosion will slow down as shock pressures will not be generated. Where there is a large tidal range the attack of the sea at high tide will probably continue to be effective for a longer period than in a tideless sea.

H. Mitsuyasu (1967) has recorded shock pressures of breaking waves experimentally and compared the results with analytical theory. The pressure gauges used had a very high-frequency response. A new air-cushion model was developed to account for the pattern, based on R. A. Bagnold's earlier air-cushion theory. The records of the shock pressures show them to be extremely short-lived, but with a magnitude much greater than the normal wave pressure. They last less than 0·01 second. Following the initial maximum pressure there is an oscillatory pattern, and the pressure is rapidly reduced logarithmically. The whole process only takes 40 microseconds. Owing to the irregularity in the wave front, shock pressures are extremely local as well as very short-lived. The air-cushion model is only concerned with the very high, brief shock pressures.

3 Shore platforms and other erosional forms

The process of shore platform formation has not yet been fully explained. The result of the process can be seen round many cliffed coasts, particularly near headlands, where beach material is less likely to accumulate. On tidal beaches an irregular surface of bare rock slopes gently seawards. It may terminate near low water in a secondary cliff. Figure 17-2 shows a

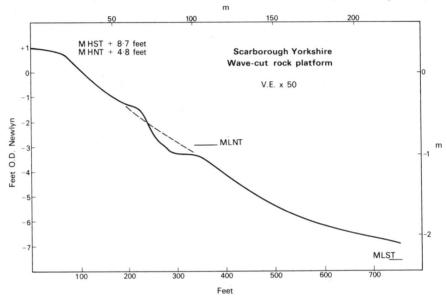

Figure 17-2 Rock platform on the foreshore at Scarborough, Yorkshire.

profile across a typical wave-cut platform near Scarborough. The platform has an overall gradient of 1 : 90, with a concave upward profile. The slight irregularity is caused by the outcrop of harder strata on the beach, showing that the surface does not coincide with any one bedding plane. It cuts across the dip of the relatively resistant Scarborough Limestone, which occurs within the Upper Estuarine Series of the Jurassic. The tidal range at spring tide is about 6 m, resulting in considerable width of rock coming under the influence of the swash and backwash of the waves.

C. K. Wentworth (1938), in his study of the wave-formed benches around the coast of Oahu in the Hawaii Islands, distinguished four processes: (1) water-level (water-layer) weathering, (2) solution benching, (3) ramp abrasion, and (4) wave quarrying. The tide had a maximum range of only 0·915 m. Some of the processes were helped by the presence of small amounts of sand and gravel, while others were hindered by it. Water-layer benching was observed to be most effective in weathered basalt with dykes, and in palagonite tuff. It occurred at any level up to about 6·1 m above sea level where pools of quiet water can remain and be replenished at fairly frequent intervals. At any one place a series of benches at different levels may form. They do not appear to be related to variations in sea level. The hollow that initiates the bench is gradually flattened as the parts that dry as the water evaporates are attacked. The margins and lip are lowered in the same way. Such benches may be 3·05 m wide and 6·1 to 9·15 m long. Some are smaller, but only a few larger. The bench is liable to destruction once the rampart holding in the water at its seaward edge is breached. This rampart is often very rugged, being eroded directly by the waves, owing to its exposed position.

The process of water-layer benching appears to be a form of physical weathering caused by the frequent wetting and drying of the rock. This exposes its structure very clearly. The process probably completes, and makes more perfect, the flattening of a bench already partially formed by wave quarrying and other means. There is often a very sharp break of slope at the landward side of the bench. Wave quarrying tends to produce a broadly rounded nip under the cliff instead of the flatter slope, and sharper break, associated with water-layer weathering.

A somewhat similar form is obtained by solution weathering on calcareous rocks, but this is restricted to levels about 1·22 to 1·53 m above sea level. The two processes are, however, quite distinct. The conditions necessary for the development of the solution forms are undrained hollows that are clear of debris. Much of the initial erosion on such a coast may be due to wave quarrying at a higher sea level.

J. A. Bartrum (1938), who has worked on the problem of marine benching in New Zealand, suggests that weathering is rapid down to the level of saturation. He and F. J. Turner (1928) also considered that weathering can flatten platforms originally formed by other agencies. D. W. Johnson (1938) considered that weathering may roughen rather than smooth the platforms.

E. S. Hills (1940) suggested that the term 'water-layer' weathering should be used instead of 'water-level' weathering, which Johnson had pointed out might be confused with sea level. Hills considered that water-layer weathering can only operate on rocks susceptible to weathering by alternate wetting and drying. The platforms formed by this process are best developed where the wave attack is only moderate in intensity. The ramp at the seaward side of the platform tends to be protected from weathering because it is always wet, and therefore below the level of saturation. It may be eliminated when the rest of the platform is reduced to saturation level. The features will probably not form so perfectly where the tidal range is great.

F. Nansen (1922) has shown that freezing is likely to prevent the formation of the platforms. On the other hand tropical or monsoonal conditions will accelerate their formation. Hills pointed out that wave action on a platform is more likely to produce a sloping surface rather than the plane surface typical of water-layer weathering. He favours this process, while minimizing the effect of wave action.

A. B. Edwards (1951) has, however, put forward arguments in favour of the wave-erosion theory of the development of the platforms. He takes his examples from the coast of Victoria, Australia. The platforms here are best developed in front of the cliffed headlands. The platforms are covered by over 30 cm of water at high tide and are exposed at low tide. Near the outer edge of the platform the level sometimes rises slightly and the surface becomes more irregular. Below the main cliff an inclined ramp forms and the platform is smoother in this zone. At low-tide level another small cliff forms, which can be attacked at all times. A layer of sand between 15 and 30 cm in thickness sometimes covers the platform. It is washed to and fro across the rocks by the waves at times, thus helping to abrade the platform. At spring tide the waves can attack the cliffs at the back of the ramp. It is mainly during the periods of storm that the main cliff is attacked and the platform most strongly abraded. The sea level is raised by the onshore winds and the main cliff is strongly attacked. Erosion is helped by the kelp that grows offshore. During storms the kelp is torn loose and is flung by the waves against the rocks and cliff. Rocks, weighing up to 9·1 kg, are attached to 90% of the kelp. These can do considerable damage to the cliff.

The shore platform will diminish in width if the main cliff is not cut back at a greater rate than the low tide cliff. The processes that operate to cut back the main cliff are, therefore, the most important in the growth and preservation of the platform. Storm erosion, which concentrates the maximum energy above a certain level, causes vigorous erosion at high-water level, resulting in the retreat of the main cliff. This is mainly responsible for the widening of the platform. The planation of the platform is the result of scouring by sand-laden waves. Water-layer weathering becomes more important as the platform becomes wider and more level.

Most authorities in the classical view of platform cutting, such as W. M. Davis (1910), D. W. Johnson (1919) and C. A. Cotton (1940), consider that sea level must be stationary during platform development. The main process by which the platform is widened, according to this view, must be by submarine abrasion as the cliff is cut back and driven inland to produce the platform. The width of the platform therefore depends largely on the depth to which it can be cut. W. C. Bradley (1958) has considered this problem in relation to observations made on the platform near Santa Cruz on the coast of California. The depth at which rocks can be abraded is less than that at which sediment can be moved. According to K. Rode (1930) sand cannot abrade unless it is greater than 1 mm in diameter and W. H. Twenhofel (1945) considers that sand grains less than 0·5 mm can accomplish no significant erosion. Rode calculated that abrasion was theoretically possible to a depth of 45·8 to 91·5 m. This estimate reduces considerably that of D. W. Johnson (1919), who set the limit of wave erosion at 183 m. It has since been further reduced and more modern views, including that of W. C. Bradley (1958), place it at about 10 m. This seems to be a more probable depth. The evidence on which Bradley bases his estimate is related to the rounding of pyroxene grains, which takes place in the area of vigorous wave action in the surf zone. He found that in depths below 9·15 m the pyroxene grains, derived from the land, are significantly less abraded than those in shallower water.

The modern platforms off California are about 484 m wide at a depth of 9·15 m, giving a gradient of about 1 : 53. This is steeper than the platform at Scarborough, and suggests that where the tidal range is greater the platform may be wider at that depth. Bradley considers that platforms wider than 500 m can only be cut during a rising sea level. The modern platforms are in places wider than this, and their concave profile suggests cutting during slow submergence. This point is considered more fully in chapter 21, and figure 21-2 illustrates the necessity for a rising sea level in cutting a wide abrasion platform.

L. W. Wright (1967) has compared the characteristics of shore platforms in the English Channel with those of New Zealand. The English Channel shore platforms are developed under a macrotidal storm wave environment. The distribution of shore platforms around Britain and New Zealand is shown in figure 17-3. Between Reculver and Land's End about 30% of the coast is fronted by a shore platform. The most continuous sections occur around the Isle of Thanet and between Start Point and the Helford River in Devon. The platforms differ in character and are cut on very different rock types, ranging from mobile silts off Selsey Bill, chalk in the Isle of Thanet and elsewhere, to granites in the southwest. The rocks vary in age, type, bedding and dip. The character of the platforms varies on either side of Hope's Nose, near Torquay. East of this headland the platform terminates in a cliff, at a point below the maximum level of marine action, often at mean high neap-tide level. The platforms are gently inclined and vary in width, sometimes having a concavity in the upper 3·05 m and a convexity in the lower part. When the rock dips between 8 and 10° the platform usually has the same gradient. A range of slopes between 1 : 14 and 1 : 90 has been recorded. In some places the platform is a multiple feature, reflecting changes in sea level. Parts of some of the platforms are of considerable antiquity.

On the east coast of New Zealand the platforms have developed in an east coast swell environment, with mesotidal conditions. On the west coast there is a west coast swell and macrotidal environment. The tidal range is not, however, very different and is mostly lower than round

Britain. Figure 17-3 shows the paucity of platforms on the west, because sand accumulations are characteristic of this coast. The platforms are cut across a variety of rocks and show some similarity to those in the English Channel in that some are inclined planes and others are stepped in form. The New Zealand ones tend to be wider and of gentler slope, approaching 1 : 100. The stepped platforms differ in some respects from the English type, there being a more pronounced low-tide cliff and gentler slope. Another common type in New Zealand, but not in England, is the steeply sloping platform leading up to a notch formed well above the tidal limit.

R. J. Russell (1963) has commented upon the recession of tropical cliffed coasts. He shows that all coasts have suffered submergence and many show negligible cliffing, citing Cape St Vincent

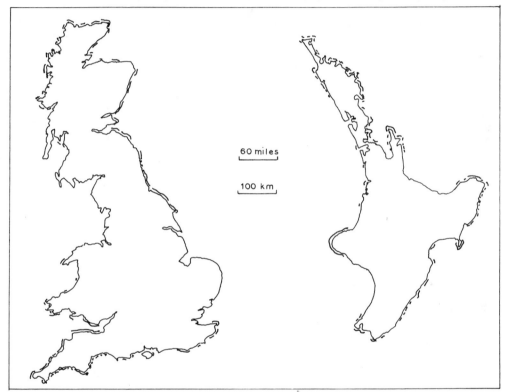

Figure 17-3 Distribution of shore platforms in England and Wales, and New Zealand, North Island. (*After Wright, 1967.*)

as an example that has not changed over 4000 years. Some of the most marked recent cliffing, developed in the Quaternary, is associated with tropical calcareous rocks. These rocks, such as calcareous eolianite, show well-marked notching between sea level and more than 1·52 m above, for example in Oahu. Other areas showing this feature include Puerto Rico, where limestone descends almost vertically into the sea. The notches here extend 3·05 m into the rock. A pitted zone extends up to 91·5 m above sea level in Victoria and Tasmania. The level at which benches form is very varied, ranging from low-tide level to high-tide level and above. These features are therefore of limited use for assessing past sea levels. Some of them are of recent origin, while others are of considerable age.

Other corrosion forms in volcanic rocks in a tropical climate are discussed by A. Guilcher *et al.* (1962). Volcanic rocks produce special features which are not related to mechanical erosion.

455

One type of platform, which occurs in the spray zone, is separated from the sea by an outer rampart higher than the platform. This is similar to the type described by Wentworth and occurs also near Dakar and on the islands northwest of Madagascar, in Sicily and New Caledonia. There are many minor features of interest formed by corrosion, including corrugations, small pinnacles, honeycomb patterns and notches. There are forms associated with the structures of the volcanic rocks—such as cells, circular or polygonal, with either lower or higher rims—some of which resemble the Giant's Causeway in Antrim. The variation of form can be partly accounted for by the petrological character of the rocks. The effect of temperature in accounting for the minor features is not yet known.

Corrosion forms in a colder climate have been described and classified by C. Dionne (1967) along the southern shore of the Saint Lawrence estuary. They occur in a variety of rock types—limestones, conglomerates, sandstones, schist and crystalline rocks—and include lapiés, vermiculations, cupules, pitting, notches and rainures. Both biochemical and biomechanical action take place, as well as corrosion, despite the low salinity and freezing air temperatures in winter and low water temperatures at all times. Many different processes are responsible for the detailed forms as well as the general erosional processes.

Coastal corrosion forms are very well developed in limestone. Examples found around the Bay of Biscay have been described by A. Guilcher (1958): these are superficial and develop in different zones relative to sea level. In the storm wave and spray zones large pinnacles form in exposed areas. At the high-tide zone an overhanging visor 1·22 to 1·52 m wide develops, often broken with lapiés. Below the visor and extending down to low-tide level is a bench 1·52 to 4·57 m wide, with a steep seaward slope, often between 15 and 20°. This bench ends in a very steep or vertical slope, the upper part of which is exposed at low spring tide. It contains rounded ponds and grooves and there are surge caverns below it in places. This zonation found on the east Asturian coast is somewhat similar to that of subtropical waters, owing to the visor. In Brittany corrosion forms are best developed on the exposed parts of the coast and little developed in sheltered waters. In Britain the zonation on limestone coasts consists of very small honeycomb corrugations in the spray zone. Below are very jagged lapiés, 7·5 to 30 cm in size, extending down to low-water level. Shallow, flat-bottomed ponds with overhanging sides develop at both levels.

Erosional features on the coast of Japan have been described by H. Mii (1960; 1962). There are four major features, the offshore platform, shore and coast platforms and the sea cliff. The offshore platform is permanently covered by water and has a seaward slope of about 5°. The depth of the seaward margin varies with exposure, being about 10 m in open water, decreasing to 5 m off sheltered coasts. The platform is thought to be cut by the waves, and so is called a wave-cut platform. The shore platform is intertidal and has a nearly horizontal surface with a steep slope at the low-tide level. The level only varies slightly with exposure, being slightly higher on exposed coasts. Wave planation, exposing the lowest limit of active subaerial weathering, is thought to cause the platform. It is called a sea level platform. The coast platform occurs at various levels above the highest high water and usually slopes seawards. Some levels, at 2 and 6 m, may represent earlier, higher sea levels. Other features at inconsistent heights are probably formed by storm waves or subaerial processes. The steep cliffs fall into two classes—active cliffs which are well developed on the open coasts, and dead cliffs occurring in sheltered areas.

Minor features include wave-cut notches, caves and tunnels, wind-blasted notches, potholes, solution pools, honeycomb structure and miniature valleys and channels. The rock type determines the detail of the features in any one area. In limestone the higher benches often have a higher rampart on the seaward side. Mushroom rocks, representing a higher level that is being eroded, are sometimes found projecting above a bench forming at a lower level. The limestone surfaces are wider and usually deeply pitted on the higher benches. In slates the surfaces are narrower and angular, sloping slightly seaward or horizontal. On the lower benches, in the intertidal zone, the slate platforms are wider than the limestone on both open and sheltered coasts. Both rock types develop a gentle seaward slope in this zone. Abrasion is the major process, with solution adding to the variety of forms on the limestone. The greater width of the upper limestone platforms in exposed situations is due to the greater resistance of the limestone to wave attack and partly to the saturated water inhibiting solutional activity.

4 Cliffs

The erosion of cliffs and the development of cliff profiles is one of the aspects of coastal geomorphology in which there has been relatively little definitive research or theory. It is generally agreed that the cliff profile is dependent on the rock type, and on the exposure and the geomorphological history of the area.

A. Wood (1959), in discussing the cliffs around Aberystwyth, notes three points of importance. The coastal bevels or hog's back cliffs are the remnants of cliffs cut by marine erosion and degraded by subaerial activity in several stages; raised beaches are backed by degraded cliffs, which merge laterally into the coastal bevel, and thirdly there are also fossil cliffs, cut possibly during two phases of lower sea level, and then buried by solifluction of drift material. At places the fossil cliffs run inland to be replaced by the drift deposits banked against them. Elsewhere they are overlain by till in the upper part of the cliff section. The prolongation of the fossil cliffs meets the present day rock platform on the foreshore where it is exposed. The coastal bevel is a degraded cliff, originally cut at different times, and extending nearly to present sea level where it is not interrupted by benches. Its base is often rejuvenated by current marine activity. The upper slope of 32° to 33° is due to subaerial modification of the marine slope.

Post-glacial marine erosion has been responsible for removing much till that formerly covered the coastline beyond the bevel and the fossil cliffs. The coastal outline was probably strongly digitate. The rising post-glacial sea allowed continuous attack on this material. Erosion combined with submergence caused the coast to retreat but only by a few hundred metres during the last 5000 to 6000 years of relatively static sea level, on the evidence of the downward projection of present boulder clay slopes. The width of the rocky platform indicates the amount of erosion in the solid rock. It amounts to about 76·2 m on average. Solid rock is therefore being eroded at no more than about 1·25 cm/year, and the volume is small, as only a wedge of material has been removed owing to the coastal bevel.

The abandoned and composite sea cliffs around southwest Britain and Ireland have been considered by A. R. Orme (1962). Cliff profiles are the result of a complex history of development. Some are abandoned by the sea, and lie wholly inland of the modern coast. Others are composite and have an upper older portion and a lower portion that is being actively developed at present by marine processes. Some sea cliffs are abandoned through progradation, such as those discussed by R. A. G. Savigear in South Wales, others by falls of sea level. The lowest parts of abandoned cliffs are usually preserved beneath a growing accumulation of cliff-foot debris and thus the buried rock slope maintains its steep gradient. These fossil cliffs merge upwards into the subaerially modified coastal bevel.

Since sea level returned to its present height about 5000 to 6000 years ago, the fossil cliffs and coastal bevel have been re-exposed or reworked to varying degrees. All stages in the removal of the fossil elements can be seen around the coast of Devon and south Ireland. At Start Point the fossil cliff dominates. In softer rocks, or in the more exposed sites, the present sea has removed most of the fossil elements of the cliff profile. Along much of the coastline, however, there is still evidence of the complex development the cliffs underwent during the Pleistocene period of large-scale rapid changes of sea level.

In the west of Ireland some of the cliffs reach very great heights. These have been discussed by A. Guilcher (1966), who defines high cliffs as those with heights of 100 to 500 m, and mega-cliffs as those exceeding 500 m. The cliff of Croaghaun in Achill Island exceeds 666 m. In Kerry the highest cliffs occur in the Dingle Peninsula, reaching 300 to 400 m on the north side, where they face northwest. The hog's back form predominates in this area. The slopes are very steep, between 60° and 75°, with heights of 90 to 150 m, increasing near Brandon to 375 m.

Marine processes appear to influence the cliff to an elevation of 395 m. Landslides induced by marine erosion are effective, and periglacial processes may have been important in preparing the material near the surface. They cannot be effective in the present mild climate. Another possibility is the development of joints in the rock owing to stresses set up within the face on the high, exposed slope facing the sea. As soon as the sea has created a vertical slope the process could begin. Jointing would facilitate further marine activity, and so the process would be self-generating, due to positive feedback. Such jointing would facilitate rockfalls and landslides. The speed of development of the Kerry cliffs is very variable.

The same process seems to have operated to produce the 666 m cliffs on Croaghaun, Achill Island, which are formed of quartzite. Very large scree deposits occur on the cliff slope. The formation of this cliff has resulted in a retreat of 1200 m at a level of 300 m. The northwest orientation of these two high cliffs indicates the direction of maximum wave attack when they were formed. At present the most effective waves come from the southwest. Only Slieve League cliff, which is 600 m high, faces in this direction. This may be due to a change in the direction of maximum wave attack since the cliffs were formed. It is suggested, therefore, that the cliffs have been forming over a very long interval of time. They may have been initiated during the high sea levels of the Pleistocene, or even in the later Tertiary. The cliffs are cut in hard rocks, Old Red Sandstone in Kerry and Dalradian quartzites in Donegal.

The work of non-marine forces must be stressed in the retreat of soft rock cliffs, where slumping, weathering and other processes of mass movement are the most important. The sea acts mainly as the transporting agent, maintaining the steepness of the slope by removing the material brought onto the beach by mass movement. Storm waves are effective at times, however, as shown by the retreat caused on some cliffs by the storm surge of 1953. W. H. Ward (in E. G. Irving, 1962) stresses the importance of landslides in the retreat of some cliffs. Landslides cause intermittent retreat and in suitable strata take place along rotational shear planes, for example at the Folkestone Warren.

Other types of landslide failure include rockfalls, shallow surface slides in clays, tills, sands and gravels, and slips due to internal water erosion of fine sands interbedded with clays. Some of the most active areas of coastal landslide activity occur at Christchurch Bay, where the maximum average rate of retreat is 0·915 m/year. The Norfolk cliffs between Happisburgh and Sheringham are 15·25 to 61 m high, and consist of drift. Inland drainage, however, gives them more stability than the Christchurch cliffs. Slipping in Norfolk is superficial, but between Trimingham and Cromer the water drains seaward, and sand layers are eroded, causing cliff flows and a lower cliff angle of only 20°. Rotational slips occur in the Isle of Wight at Seagrove Bay in Oligocene clays, overlain by limestone, marls and gravel. Slips occur when the water pressure is increased.

Cliffs and marine benches are an indication of marine erosion in solid rocks or drift. Destructive processes of this type cause the permanent landward retreat of a coast. Destructive wave action on the beach, on the other hand, is usually only temporary in its effect. The eroded material is carried seawards, but can return to the beach when conditions become constructive again. Once the solid rock or drift material has been carried away by the sea, however, it cannot be replaced, and a permanent modification of the coastal outline has occurred. In the next section the causes of coast erosion will be considered and some examples will be described.

5 Destructive marine action in plan—coastal erosion

The Royal Commission on Coast Erosion (1911) gave figures that indicate the extent of erosion and accretion on the coasts and in the tidal rivers of the United Kingdom. The evidence is derived from a comparison of the various editions of the 6 inch to 1 mile Ordance Survey maps. The results show that over an average period of 35 years in England and Wales 1900 ha were lost, while 14,320 ha were gained, giving a net gain of 12,420 ha. For Scotland the figures are 330 ha lost, 1905 ha gained, resulting in a net gain of 1575 ha. The interpretation of the maps was difficult because of a change of datum from ordinary spring tide to ordinary tide level.

The area of foreshore lost is given as 18,150 ha, and that gained as 5415 ha, in England and Wales. In Scotland the loss was 5400 ha and the gain 1645 ha. The net loss must imply a general steepening of the foreshore. The reduced area of the foreshore is partly the result of reclamation. Evidence derived from the comparison of maps is not always reliable. One witness from Ireland pointed out that the maps of Clew Bay, Co. Mayo, show accretion between 1839 and 1898, but he knew that partially submerged drumlins had been eroded during the period under consideration. Although the figures in detail may not be completely accurate, they do show that more land was gained in the British Isles from the sea than was lost to it during the period of the survey. Nevertheless coastal erosion remains a serious problem in many areas.

a   Causes of coastal erosion

(i) *The part played by the beach:*   A wide beach, which prevents the waves reaching the solid rock at the back of the beach or beneath it, will form an effective protection to the coast, and will prevent coastal erosion. If, however, the beach is thin enough to be removed by storm waves, the cliffs can be attacked by these waves, which are the only ones capable of effective erosion. Where there is a considerable tidal range the vertical extent of the beach must be greater to afford a protection to the coast. This applies particularly in areas where the sea level is liable to be raised abnormally.

The effects of the 1953 storm surge on the Lincolnshire coast illustrate well the part played by the beach in coast protection. As soon as possible after the floods a series of 23 profiles were surveyed at different positions on the coast between Gibraltar Point in the south and Theddlethorpe in the north. They are shown in figure 17·4. They cover areas where the damage ranged from minor dune cliffing to complete destruction of massive concrete defences. The nature and amount of damage was closely related to the character and height of the beach. The profiles can be divided into eight different groups according to the beach characteristics and the nature of the damage (F. A. Barnes and C. A. M. King, 1953):

Group I: Profiles 1 to 4 to the south of Skegness showed a wide beach, a considerable part of which was above 2·44 m O.D. It protected a wide, high and well-vegetated dune system. This part of the coast needs no artificial protection, and damage was restricted to minor

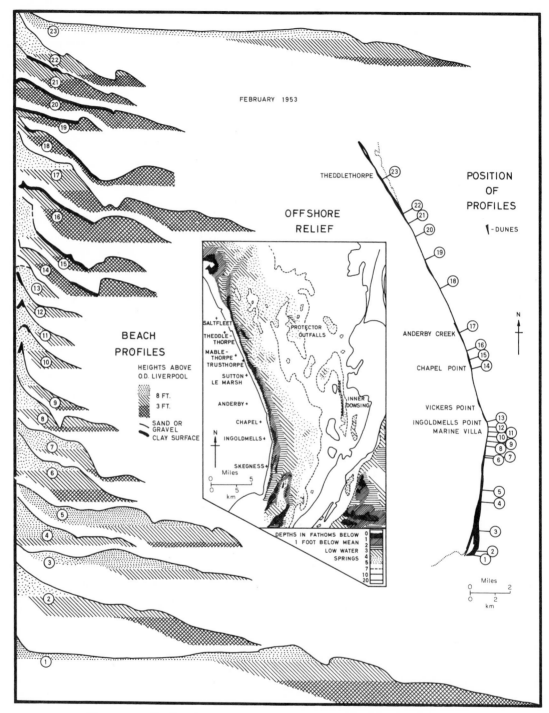

Figure 17-4 Profiles of the Lincolnshire beaches surveyed after the surge of 1953.

dune erosion, resulting in sand cliffs up to 3 m high. There was a close relationship between the width of the beach and the amount of dune erosion.

Group II: The next profile, 5, was surveyed from the centre of Skegness. This profile showed a particularly wide beach, and, although dunes are no longer able to form on it, the wide, high beach, absorbed the wave energy sufficiently to prevent serious damage in the town. The height of the pullover (5·58 m O.D.), however, was dangerously near the surge high-water level (5·37 m O.D.). Minor flooding of reclaimed dune slacks was the only damage.

Group III: Profiles 6 and 7, surveyed at the north end of Skegness, were transitional in character. The beach was much narrower, but still fairly high, probably partially due to combing down of sand onto the beach. This prevented serious erosion.

Group IV: The next series of profiles, 8 to 13, covered the area between the south end of Butlin's Holiday Camp and Ingoldmells Point. The most southerly of the major breaches of the sea defences occurred in this stretch. All the profiles of this group were much lower and narrower than the others. The dunes at the back of the beach were attenuated and offered little resistance to the waves. At high water the waves could break close inshore and concentrate their energy on the artificial defences, which were needed to protect the northern part of this stretch of coast. The concrete defences of the artificial points of Marine Villa and Ingoldmells suffered very severe damage and were completely destroyed over some distance.

Group V: Profiles 14, 15 and 16 covered the area near Chapel Point. This was another area of severe damage to the coast defences and houses built on the relics of the dunes behind the rather flimsy concrete wall were destroyed. This area has suffered from erosion for some time. The lack of dune sand resulted in an absence of material on which the waves could expend their energy. The small amount of beach material was completely stripped from the beach along most of profile 16, exposing the impermeable clay base.

Group VI: At Anderby Creek, where profile 17 was surveyed, the beach again showed a wide berm of sand. This was formed of sand eroded from the dunes by the storm waves. The dunes were fairly high, but were very severely cut back to form cliffs about 6 m high. This sand absorbed the wave energy to a sufficient extent to prevent a complete breach and raised the foreshore to a considerable height.

Group VII: The profiles 18 to 21 covered the area of most severe damage along the coast between Sandilands, Sutton-on-Sea and Mablethorpe. The beach on these four profiles was very low and narrow. Even neap high tides reached up to the sea walls, which provided an essential defence for this coast in the absence of effective dunes. The lack of a reserve supply of sand in the form of dunes at the back of the beach caused very extensive damage by waves. The coastal defences were completely breached over a considerable stretch of coast. The small amount of beach material on the foreshore was removed by destructive storm waves, which washed some inland through the breaches and exposed the clay base of the beach. The deep water immediately adjacent to the defences and the absence of beach material enabled all the wave energy to be concentrated on the destruction of the sea walls. These were over-topped owing to the high water level and so were undermined from the rear as well as being attacked from the front.

Group VIII: North of Mablethorpe profiles 22 and 23 showed a return to conditions similar to those obtaining in the first 5 profiles south of Skegness. The dunes were wide and high, making artificial sea defences unnecessary. At Theddlethorpe the beach becomes very wide above 2·44 m O.D. and the wave energy was spent over a wide area and only very minor dune cliffing resulted.

These profiles show clearly the value of a wide, high beach in protecting a coast from erosion. The reserve of sand held in the dunes provides a good safeguard against erosion on a coast of this type. The presence of a thick beach absorbs the wave energy and prevents it being used against the structures at the back of and under the beach. The permeability of the beach material is important as it reduces the power of the backwash, which can act with much greater force when none of the swash can percolate to lower levels, a state that occurs where waves break on an impermeable clay bench or on concrete sea defences.

(*ii*) *The character of the coast:* The liability of coasts to erosion varies greatly. It depends on a number of factors which are listed below:

Exposure	a)	Form of coastline in plan
	b)	Exposure to wave attack—dominant wind direction and fetch
Coastal type	a)	Low coast with dunes etc.
	b)	Rocky coast, generally with cliffs

Rock type (where relevant)
Offshore relief
Sea-level changes
Man-made structures
Longshore movement of beach material

Exposure: Where the coastline is irregular the attack of the sea will tend to be concentrated on the headlands. This is partly due to the concentration of wave energy on the headlands by refraction, and beaches are often absent on headlands. On the other hand they are frequently composed of harder rock, which has already resisted erosion to a greater extent than the neighbouring bays, and which will continue to do so.

Coasts exposed to the prevailing winds would be expected to suffer more rapid erosion than sheltered coasts. This is not always true, however, as exemplified by the east coast of England, which is being eroded at a greater rate than the exposed parts of the west coast. In this instance other factors more than compensate for the greater exposure of the west coast.

Coastal type: From the point of view of their susceptibility to erosion, coasts may be divided broadly into low coasts and cliffed, rocky coasts. Low coasts are only protected by superficial deposits. They include sand dune coasts, which have already been shown to stand up well to wave attack, especially if the dunes are high and well vegetated. Some low coasts in sheltered areas are protected by growing salt marsh. They are unlikely to be seriously affected by storm waves as they can only grow in sheltered areas. In other climates low coasts may be protected by the growth of mangroves or corals in warmer waters, or by ice in very cold areas. In all these types the coastal protection is related to their marine environment and low nature. Should conditions change, such as a change of climate or sea level, these coasts may become liable to rapid modification. Human interference may also have serious results. Not all low coasts are adequately protected by nature. The continuous erosion along part of the Lincolnshire coast is an example.

Rocky, cliffed coasts can be attacked by the sea if a protective beach is lacking. The susceptibility of these coasts to erosion will then depend largely on the nature of the material forming the cliff and platform. This may range from glacial sands and gravels, as in part of the cliffs of Suffolk, to the extremely resistant rocks forming some of the Cornish cliffs. Exposure to wave attack and longshore movement of material will be secondary considerations. These factors will determine whether a protective beach is present or not.

(*iii*) *Offshore relief:* The offshore relief is important in a consideration of coastal erosion for several reasons. The effect of offshore relief on wave refraction was discussed in chapter 4. It may explain the concentration of wave energy at particular places, with subsequent variation in erosion along the coast. A wide shallow continental shelf will render waves less erosive than where the water is deep close offshore. Changes in offshore relief near the beach may be important in determining the location of areas suffering from erosion at different periods. On the Lincolnshire coast, for example, there are offshore sand-banks which migrate slowly in position. They are exposed at low water and, therefore, provide a measure of protection to the beaches in the immediate vicinity. The gradual movement of these offshore banks may account for the change from erosion to deposition near Skegness during the last few centuries. A similar movement of offshore banks has been suggested as a possible cause of the northward movement of Benacre Ness on the Suffolk coast. Here also the areas suffering from erosion have temporarily become areas of accretion.

(*iv*) *Sea level changes:* Changes in sea level also affect coastal erosion. A falling sea level, by causing withdrawal of the sea, will probably result in reduced erosion. The depth of water offshore will be reduced and the attack of storm waves diminished in efficiency. A rising sea level, on the other hand, will deepen the water offshore, allowing waves to break closer inshore. It will increase their erosive capacity, hence leading to an acceleration of coast erosion in areas already affected, and perhaps starting it in areas previously immune.

(*v*) *Man-made structures:* Coastal erosion in some areas is initiated by man-made structures, of several types. One of the more common types is the jetty or breakwater built out from the coast. These structures, if they are built in an area where there is a strong longshore movement of material, will interfere with this transport. Erosion will occur on the down-drift side of the structure. Several examples of this were mentioned in chapter 9.

Erosion in other instances has been caused by the artificial cutting of a passage through a coastal barrier. A detailed study of an example of this type of artificially induced coast erosion is discussed by P. Bruun (1954). The coast in the area studied, which is in west Jutland near Thyboroen, is low and consists of a series of barriers, separated by lagoons from the mainland. This coast has been surveyed in detail since 1695. In 1791 there was a continuous barrier across Lime Bay. In 1825 a channel was cut through the barrier. Between 1874 and 1950, 22 surveys of the coast have been made, at approximately two year intervals during the present century. The 17 profiles extend into water between 9·15 and 12·2 m deep, over a 48 km stretch of coast.

The profiles show a gradual inland shift, indicating retreat of the coast, increasing in amount as the edge of the channel is approached. Analysis of the profiles shows that the movement of the shorelines was of three types: (1) migrating waves, (2) seasonal fluctuation, and (3) long-period changes due to erosion. The first need not be considered. The second illustrated the retreat of the coast under the action of strong onshore winds. The third showed a maximum annual recession since 1921 of 4·77 m on the northern barrier and 2·74 m on the southern barrier, despite the building of groynes to help stabilize the coast. The changes are shown in figure 17-5. During the retreat the beach has tended to become steeper, though the median diameter of the sand, which is about 0·26 mm, has remained more or less constant.

(*vi*) *Longshore movement of beach material:* The movement of material alongshore is responsible for nearly all coastal erosion, directly or indirectly. R. R. Minikin (1952) stresses the importance of alongshore movement of material in the protection of coasts. Destructive waves, acting normal to the shore, can only move the beach material a relatively short distance offshore, from where most of it can be returned to the beach by constructive waves acting during periods of normal weather. The permanent absence of a beach, however, can usually be explained by longshore movement, unless the water is so deep offshore that this prevents a beach forming.

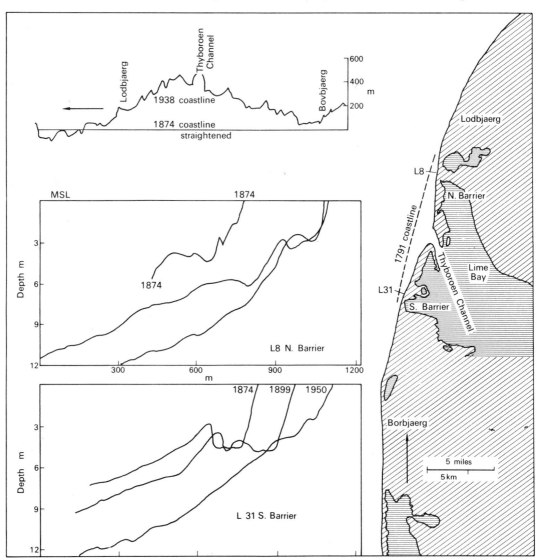

Figure 17-5 Map and profiles of the west coast of Jutland to illustrate the erosion since the cutting of the Thyboroen channel. (*After Bruun, 1954.*)

Coast erosion is most likely to take place, therefore, where more material is moved alongshore out of the area than is being moved into it from the up-drift direction. This situation is likely to occur on headlands, where the movement of material is away from the headland. Selsey Bill provides a good example of this. A coast with a smooth outline is also liable to erosion because there is no obstruction to hold up the movement of material along the beach. This process will be particularly effective where a headland prevents the free passage of material from the up-drift direction. Examples of coast erosion due to this cause will be described.

b Coast erosion—general points

Some of the causes of coastal erosion have been mentioned and examples of their operation will be described. There are, however, some general points concerning the scale and tempo of coastal erosion that should be made.

M. L. Schwartz (1968) has considered the scale of shore erosion in relation to the time scale. He defines his terms on the basis of Bruun's theory of sea level rise as a cause of shore erosion. A similar point is made by R. C. H. Russell (in Irving, 1962). The theory of Bruun (M. L. Schwartz, 1967) states that, if a profile of equilibrium is assumed, as sea level rises, material eroded from the upper beach is deposited on the nearshore bottom down to the depth at which waves can act. The upper beach will be displaced shoreward as material moves seaward. The volume moving seaward will equal the volume eroded. The rise of sea level will equal the amount of deposition on the offshore bottom, thus maintaining the depth.

The theory was tested in model experiments and by short-term profile changes due to variation in tide level (M. L. Schwartz, 1967). The model experiments showed that with a rise in water level the equilibrium profile was moved upwards and landwards. The outer edge of the pre-rise offshore shelf was found to remain lower than that developed at the higher level. The results showed a mean deviation in the change in water depth of 4% but the deviation of the rise in profile was only 0.4%. Thus the experiments confirmed that a rise of water level results in a constant change in water depth on the shelf edge. The rise in level of shelf sediment was equal to the rise of water level, hence confirming Bruun's theory experimentally.

The field experiments were carried out on Cape Cod on two dissimilar beaches, one on the exposed side, the other in a more sheltered locality. Profiles taken over the spring and neap tide intervals were compared. The results confirmed that there was a shoreward displacement of the profile as the upper beach was eroded at spring tide. The material eroded at spring tide was deposited predominantly within the zone bounded by the 1.83 m mark. There was a rise in beach level at 1.83 m which accompanied the rise in water level. Thus both laboratory and field work confirmed the accuracy of the Bruun theory of sea level rise in association with coastal retreat.

The scale at which the process takes place has been demonstrated to apply both to laboratory conditions and full-scale changes of short duration and small amount. M. L. Schwartz (1968) considers this effect on a micro-, macro- and megascale. The microscale represents the swash–backwash zone covering 10^1 cm and mean periods of 10^1 minutes. The macroscale represents neap–spring cycles or seasonal cycles, on a scale of 10^4 to 10^5 minutes and covering a vertical range of the order of 10^2 cm. The megascale represents long-term changes, covering periods of 10^9 and 10^{10} minutes, or 10,000 to 20,000 years. These represent major changes of sea level, with a vertical range of the order of 10^3 to 10^4 cm (10 m to 100–150 m), covering the post-glacial rise of sea level.

The microscale operates within the swash–backwash zone and represents the equilibrium between sediment moved up by the swash and brought down by the backwash, when conditions are stable. A change takes place within this scale over the tidal rise and fall each tidal cycle. The magnitude of scour at this scale is of the order of 12 cm.

The macroscale applies to the neap–spring cycles at one end and the seasonal cycles at the other. Examples have already been given in chapter 12 of such changes. The magnitude of the spring-neap changes is about 1.2 to 1.5 m at Virginia Beach, 0.6 to 0.9 m in the Bay of Bengal, and 0·3 to 0·6 m on Cape Cod. A mean of 1 m gives a reasonable estimate. The seasonal changes vary from 1 m to about 3 m. These two scales are sufficiently similar to be grouped together when contrasted with the megascale group, which is the most important as far as coast erosion is concerned. The first two apply to the beach, while the latter applies to the coast.

The theoretical model consists of a significant rise of sea level, followed by a stillstand. This is approximately the nature of the post-glacial change of sea level, as indicated in chapter 7. There has not been long enough during the last 5000 to 6000 years for an equilibrium state to be achieved. The surf base is important in this respect and may be considered to lie at a depth of about 10 m. There is evidence that an equilibrium profile will become established on rapidly evolving coasts.

It is assumed that the outer edge of the continental shelf at Cape Cod was at the surf-base of 10 m when it was formed. Erosion products of the rising sea level would be spread out on the inner shelf, forming the paralic wedge. The upper surface of the wedge may be considered the equilibrium profile. The span of time required to produce the equilibrium slope will vary greatly, according to the character of the coast and the wave climate. Probably 10,000 to 20,000 years is a reasonable estimate. The amount of shoreline displacement will depend on the slope

Table 17-1 Frequency and damage of coastal storms on east coast of U.S.A.

Class of storm	Frequency total number	Damage estimate	
1	56	2·05	
2	9	2·44	
3	23	2·09	
4	22	1·91	1 = low, 2 = moderate, 3 = severe
5	14	1·69	for the period 1921–1962
6	25	1·75	
7	14	1·54	
8	7	1·00	

of the coast and the magnitude of sea-level rise. It is therefore reasonable to expect that, until equilibrium is reached, many coasts will undergo landwards retreat while the new profile of equilibrium is becoming established.

Erosion and damage that cause coastal retreat are intermittent in character, occurring when wave conditions are especially destructive during time of storm. It is useful to have some indication of the frequency of occurrence of damaging storm conditions. A study has been made by J. R. Mather et al. (1965) for the eastern U.S.A. They define eight weather conditions that give rise to damaging storm waves. These are as follows:

1   Hurricanes and severe tropical storms.
2   Frontal wave developments forming well east of the U.S.A. or near Cuba.
3   Wave developments along cold fronts over southeast coastal states or in the Atlantic just off the southeast coast.
4   Wave developments along cold or stationary fronts in the Gulf of Mexico.
5   Depressions moving across the southern U.S.A. that intensify on reaching the coast.
6   Depressions developing as secondary cyclonic disturbances along the coast.
7   Intense cyclonic storms over the land.
8   Strong cold fronts accompanied by squall lines and severe local weather.

The frequency and damage of these storms is given in table 17-1. Tables are also given for seasonal occurrence and damage by states for the 8 types of storm. Massachusetts has the highest number of 78, and Georgia the lowest of 15. The mean recurrence intervals range from 0·8 years for Massachusetts to 4·2 years for Georgia, and is 1·4 years for New York and New Jersey. The physical nature of the coast has not yet been considered in the study. Some areas are more prone to damage than others. In a state as a whole there is considerable variation in the intensity of local damage.

6 Examples of coast erosion

a North Yorkshire

A study of long-term coast erosion by R. Agar (1960) deals with the north Yorkshire coast between the Tees and Ravenscar. This stretch of coast is 56 km long and consists of high cliffs, exceeding 91 m at Ravenscar in the south, but decreasing to the north. Drift reaches sea level in parts of Robin Hood's Bay, around Whitby and north of Saltburn. Figure 17-6 illustrates the nature of the cliff profile and the amount of erosion that is going on at present. The cliff is fronted by a wave-cut platform, which has had a complex development. Surveys show that the average rate of cliff recession is 9·15 m/century where the cliff and foreshore is of bare shale. The presence of till in the bays, however, complicates the pattern.

The offshore slope gradually steepens to reach a gradient of 1 : 100 near the shore on the softer rocks, but it is 1 : 30 on the harder Middle Lias. The foreshore continues without a break from the offshore zone, it consists of shale scars, with only small amounts of loose beach

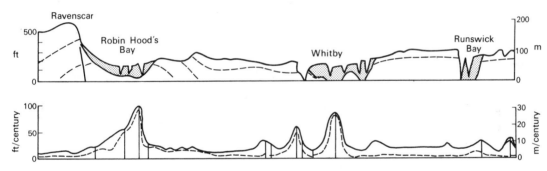

Figure 17-6   Profile of the cliffs along the north Yorkshire coast, showing the distribution of glacial deposits stippled. The amount of erosion along the coast is shown below. (*After Agar, 1960.*)

material and odd boulders, and is about 152 m wide, increasing to 305 m where it is bare shale. It forms two zones, the lower averaging 122 m wide and sloping at 1 : 80, and the upper, which is about 30·5 m wide and starts at mid-tide level, curving up steeply with a gradient of 1 : 8 at the cliff foot.

At some points perched blocks and beach conglomerate rest on pedestals on the upper part of the lower foreshore. The blocks provide evidence that about 21·3 m of cliff recession has taken place. A wave-cut notch at high water of medium to spring-tide level, separates the cliff from the wave-cut platform. It is situated at 2·13 m O.D. A vertical section then follows about 1·53 m high, which shows evidence of wave action. The slope above the vertical section depends on the rock type. Major landslips have occurred at some places along the coast.

The post-glacial development has been affected by sea level changes. Along this coast sea level rose rapidly until 5000 B.C. Then, owing to isostatic recovery, it is thought that sea level rose to 9·15 m above the present level, and only returned to the present level about 1000 A.D. The general sequence of events suggested by Agar (1960) for this coast may be summarized as follows: during the Eemian interglacial the cliff line receded from the present low-water level to 21·3 m from its present position, and the lower foreshore platform was cut. During the last glaciation sea level was lower: the cliff top weathered back, landslips occurred and the cliff-foot notch was hidden under debris, glacial drift was deposited, but there was little erosional activity. In the post-glacial period sea level rose rapidly to −4·88 m O.D., removing most of the drift and the submerged forest from the shale platform, gravel and sand were left on the sea bed, and the solid rock was not appreciably altered. As sea level rose further weathered shale and drift was cleared off the lower foreshore zone, leaving the sandstone and conglomerate boulders perched on the platform surface. Sea level continued to rise rapidly, passing the present level. Debris was cleared from the old cliff-foot notch, and erosion of the solid cliff face started. The sea then reached its maximum level and gradually receded to its present height. During this time slow erosion of the solid cliff took place, and the present upper foreshore zone landward of the perched blocks was eroded. Since 1000 A.D. sea level has been static and slow downward erosion has continued, increasing the height of the boulder perches. The cliff-foot notch has continued to retreat, while erosion has also affected the lower vertical cliff section. Actual current rates of erosion are considered in section 17-7.

b   Holderness

One of the best-known areas of coast erosion in the British Isles is the Holderness coast of east Yorkshire. A detailed study of erosion along this coast has been carried out by H. Valentin (1954) for the period 1852 to 1952. Erosion has, however, been going on at least since Roman times (T. Sheppard, 1912). The Holderness coast forms a smooth sweeping curve between the chalk cliffs of Flamborough Head in the north and the sandy spit of Spurn Head to the south. Flamborough Head is one of the boldest headlands on the east coast. It is composed of the resistant Upper Chalk with few flints. Very little beach material passes south round this headland on the foreshore to supply the beaches to the south. The Holderness cliffs are 3 to 10 m in height, but reach a maximum of 30·5 m at Dimlington, in the south. They are composed entirely of easily eroded glacial drift south of Sewerby for a distance of 61 km. The glacial drift in the cliffs is not uniform in type. Valentin has shown that the variations in height and material are probably only of secondary importance in explaining the erosion on this coast. The fundamental cause of the erosion is the inadequate protection of the coast by a beach. The material on the shore is transported south by the dominant northerly waves. The beach at Sewerby, where the chalk runs inland, is composed largely of rounded chalk pebbles. These decrease very rapidly in quantity southwards, owing to the relative ease with which the sea can destroy them, both by solution and mechanical erosion. The sea in its attempt to build up an equilibrium gradient must make good the lack of beach material by erosion of the relatively soft cliffs behind the beach to which the waves have easy access.

On the whole the rate of erosion increases towards the southeast, probably due to increasing exposure in this direction. Erosion is particularly severe immediately to the south of coastal protection works, for example just south of Withernsea. At this point the normal supply of material eroded from the cliffs is lacking. It is compensated for by increased erosion in a down-drift direction. The immediate cause of erosion is the action of storm waves, combined with processes of mass movement acting on the weakly consolidated and inadequately protected cliffs. Only 3% of the volume of material eroded from the cliffs goes to build up the sand spit of Spurn Head. The remainder must be moved into deeper water offshore, while some travels south across the Humber estuary with the residual of the tidal streams.

Valentin (1954) estimated that about 76,450,000 m³ of material has been lost from the Holderness coast in 100 years. This amount spread out over the sea bed in an area 64 km long and 1·6 km wide would only represent a thickness of 8·6 mm/year. The erosion will be aggravated by a rising sea level. Valentin has suggested a relationship between the average rates of erosion and variation of sea level during the century 1852 to 1952. High sea level is accompanied by more rapid erosion. He gives the following averages for coastal retreat at 30 points that have erosion rates in excess of 1·5 m/year:

1852–1889	Low sea level	1·53 m/year
1889–1908	Rising sea level	1·77 m/year
1908–1926	High sea level	1·89 m/year
1926–1952	Slowly falling	1·71 m/year

c East Anglia

The area extending south from Cromer along much of the coast of Norfolk and Suffolk has suffered severe erosion. The cliffs in this area are also composed of unresistant glacial deposits and other unconsolidated and easily eroded strata. One reason for the serious erosion at Cromer is the amount and direction of beach drifting. To the west, material moves west with easterly winds towards the Wash where it forms the complex features of Blakeney Point and Scolt Head Island which is a barrier island. South of Cromer there is a general tendency for southerly movement of material under the influence of westerly or northerly waves. The overall pattern

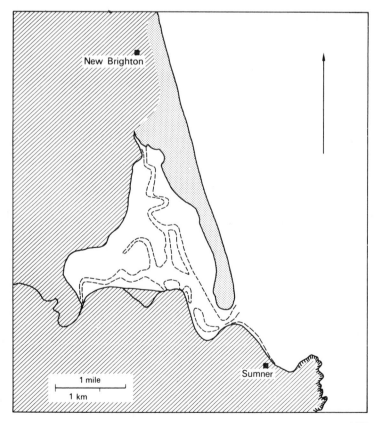

Figure 17-7 Map of the Sumner area near Christchurch, South Island, New Zealand.

of longshore drift causes a deficit of material in this area, although a well-defined drift parting does not exist near Cromer. The material that has drifted south is built into the constructive shore features further south, such as Yarmouth Spit. Still further south the shingle structure of Orfordness indicates the dominant southerly movement of beach material. Between these two features erosion occurs when storms attack the coast, aided by mass movement.

d Sumner, New Zealand

An example of very local erosion has been described by W. H. Scott (1955) at Sumner near Christchurch. The beach only started to erode in 1946, but erosion has continued since then with serious results to the foreshore in the bay. The beach is illustrated in figure 17-7. It lies in a fairly sheltered bay in an area which is, in general, building out. The spit at New Brighton has built out considerably by about 49 to 61 m in the last 50 years, due to transport of material south alongshore from the rivers to the north.

The sudden absence of material reaching the foreshore at Sumner, on the south side of the estuary, is considered by Scott to be due to a change in position of the channel in the estuary. In 1940 the channel moved over to near the distal end of the New Brighton spit, causing erosion on its landward side. This resulted in the northward migration of the submarine bar associated with the distal end of the spit. The replenishment of the foreshore at Sumner had been by longshore movement along the bar. Its northward movement diverted the material away from the beach in Sumner Bay. The erosion here will not cease until the channel regains its former position and the bar can move southwards again. Then material moving along it will once more reach the beach in the bay. The erosion here is thus due to the interruption of the normal pattern of longshore movement offshore by changes in the estuary channel.

7 Rates of coastal erosion

Examples of extremely rapid erosion were reported by W. W. Williams (1953) on the coast of Suffolk, as a result of the storm surge of 1953. He states that on the coast south of Lowestoft a cliff of glacial sand 12·2 m high was cut back 12·2 m overnight. Where the cliff was only 1·82 m high it was driven back 27·4 m. This is an extreme example of very destructive waves, with an abnormally high water level, acting on unconsolidated cliffs.

The soft cliffs of Suffolk suffer considerable erosion even under more normal circumstances. J. A. Steers (1951) has made measurements from different editions of the 6 inch to 1 mile Ordnance Survey maps. At Hopton erosion has been at the average rate of 0·76 to 0·915 m/year over the period 1925 to 1950. At Covehithe it has been much greater, averaging 5·2 m/year from 1925 to 1950. South of Southwold it averaged 3·05 to 3·36 m/year. In some areas, due to shore protection works, the coast has been static, as for example at Southwold Pier and near the north end of Dunwich cliffs. There has been erosion both to the north and south of Dunwich, but Dunwich itself has escaped.

H. Valentin's work (1954) in Holderness shows that here too, although erosion has been going on for a very long time, it has not done so at an equal rate along the whole coast, and some small areas have escaped. The average rate of erosion along this coast over the last century has been about 1·8 m/year. The detailed work of Valentin, illustrated in figure 17-8, has shown the great variation of rates of erosion along this coast. In two areas there have been small gains, between Bridlington and Sewerby and just south of Carnaby. Elsewhere during the 100 year period erosion has taken place at varying rates. It has been most rapid between Barm-

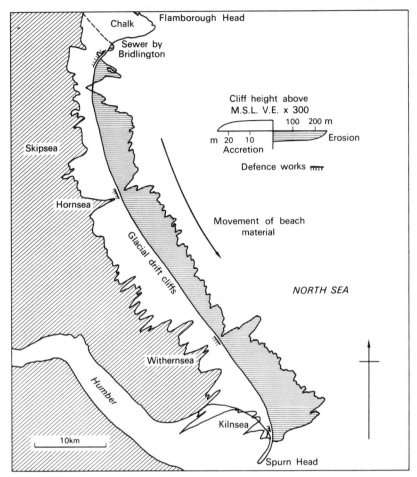

Figure 17-8 The erosion of the Holderness coast between 1852 and 1952 showing the cliff profile. (*After Valentin, 1954.*)

ston and Skipsea at about 1·5 m/year, while near and to the north of Easington it has been over 2·5 m/year, with a maximum of 2·75 m/year.

The erosion has not been constant in time or place during the century. For example, just north of Barmston the coast shows a net gain for the whole century in an area that suffered severe erosion between 1941 and 1952. The change may be related to the building of coast defences. On the whole it may be said that the amount of erosion increases from north to south, as shown by the average rates in four sections as follows:

1	Sewerby to Earl's Dyke	0·29 m/year
2	Earl's Dyke to Hornsea	1·10 m/year
3	Hornsea to Withernsea	1·12 m/year
4	Withernsea to Kilnsea Warren	1·75 m/year

There seems to be little relationship between the cliff height and the rate of erosion. Variations in the type of drift forming the cliffs is one factor affecting the rate of cliff retreat. The position of coastal defences also affects the rate of erosion. A considerable increase takes place immediately south of the defences. Much of the irregularity in the erosion along the coast is a modern phenomenon, related to the building of coastal protection works. The increase of erosion southwards from Bridlington is partly due to the decrease in effectiveness of the shelter provided by Flamborough Head for waves approaching from the north. The 10 m depth contour approaches to within 600 m of the shore at Dimlington. The wave energy can, therefore, be used more effectively on the coast in this area.

The form of the whole coast is S-shaped, with Flamborough Head forming the northern promontory and the high cliffs of Dimlington the southern bulge. The sea is attempting to straighten the curve by concentrating erosion on the hard chalk headland, which yields very slowly, and on the southern bulge, which is much more susceptible. The whole coast is tending to swing around the hinge of Flamborough Head.

In contrast to these areas of soft rocks, where coastal erosion is rapid, the erosion of part of the coast of southwest England is of interest. This coast is exposed to the full force of the Atlantic waves. Erosion here, however, has been very slow during the last 10,000 years or more. Evidence for this slow tempo of erosion is found in the nature of the cliff profile. C. A. Cotton (1951) states that some of the features on the Cornish cliff profiles probably date back to an interglacial, about 100,000 years ago. The sea has not attacked the cliffs, however, during all this period, owing to lower sea level in the glacial periods, but has probably been modifying the cliff during the last 5000 to 6000 years. Only the lower part of these two-cycle cliffs is being actively freshened by the sea at present.

On some rejuvenated cliffs of this type remains of raised beach deposits occur at a height of about 3 m above sea level. The sea cliff must, therefore, have been cut before the beach deposits were laid down. The only subsequent erosion is the very small amount of freshening of the cliff profile in the short section of steeper cliff just above sea level. The rocks of this area are extremely resistant to marine erosion. This accounts largely for the small amount of change recorded over such a long time period.

The cliffs of the Gower peninsula in South Wales also show an extremely slow rate of marine erosion. Caves, cut at a slightly higher sea level, can still be seen on the cliff face. They are now about 3 m above the sea. They contain archaeological remains, which date from an interglacial period. The cliff has not retreated measurably since then.

The present rates of erosion along the north Yorkshire coast have been measured by R. Agar (1960) and are summarized in table 17-2. They were established by comparison of the 1892 1 : 2500 Ordnance Survey map with special resurveys at selected points. The average cliff foot rate is 9·15 m/century, and the average glacial drift rate is 28·0 m/century. The following averages were calculated for the whole coast:

cliff top	2·13 m/century
cliff foot	4·88 m/century

For headlands the values were

cliff top	1·22 m/century
cliff foot	3·66 m/century

For the bays the values were

cliff top	3·96 m/century
cliff foot	6·70 m/century

The coast is thus becoming more irregular. The greater values for the cliff foot indicate a steepening of the cliffs. This rate has been going on for about eight centuries on the evidence of the Roman Signal station at Huntcliff, which has half fallen away, indicating a total erosion of about 30·5 m during the 800 years. The results show how much more rapid the erosion is on the glacial drift than in the solid rock, although not all the drift cliffs are receding. Those at Redcar are protected by a good beach and at Runswick Bay shelter is provided by headlands. In both places erosion is negligible, and only occurs during exceptional storms. Rain-wash on the exposed drift is the only effective method of cliff retreat.

Some rates of coastal cliff retreat are given by J. A. Steers (in E. G. Irving, 1962), for areas of differing resistance. Loss along the East Anglian coast at Dunwich has a long-term average of 3·96 to 4·28 m/year over 108 years. Chalk cliffs in north France are generally retreating at 0·25 m/year. The value at Dieppe is 40 cm/year, where the chalk is more marly. The rates are, however, greater between Yport and Fécamp.

Detailed measurements of marine erosion have been recorded by A. F. Richards (1960).

Table 17-2 Rates of cliff erosion in north Yorkshire

Grid reference	Location	Cliff-top erosion m/year (× 100)	Cliff-foot erosion m/year (× 100)	Cliff-foot rock
687220	Huntcliff, Roman Signal St.	3·96	3·96	Lower Lias
783191	Staithes Cowbar Nab	4·88	4·88	Middle Lias
788189	Staithes Penny Nab		10·04	Middle Lias
799175	Port Musgrave		10·04	Upper Lias
811162	Runswick Gt Ship Rock		9·75	Upper Lias
881120	Upgang	25·90	25·90	Glacial drift
896115	Whitby west cliff		3·05	Deltaic series
901114	Whitby east cliff		8·55	Upper Lias
903115	Whitby east cliff	18·90	18·90	Upper Lias
921107	Near Black Nab		5·48	Upper Lias
922107	Near Black Nab		11·00	Upper Lias
953050	Robin Hood's Bay		6·70	Lower Lias
953046	Robin Hood's Bay to Mill Beach	30·5	30·50	Glacial drift
957037	Robin Hood's Bay Tinkler's Stone		15·85	Lower Lias
973024	Low Peak, The Dock		4·57	Lower Lias

The volcanic island of San Benedicto, which lies off the Pacific coast of Mexico at 110° W 20° N, was extended by 900 m when the Volcan Barcena erupted tephra between 1952 and 1953. The tephra, which had a grain size of 38·5 microns, was extruded on the southeast side of the island. The marine erosion of the newly extruded material was measured from 1952 to 1957. It is estimated that 7×10^5 m³ (about 17,000 m³/day) of tephra was eroded by wave action between 11 August and 20 September 1952. The linear rate of retreat of the bulge of material was slightly less than 1 m/day.

More resistant lava reached the sea between December and March 1952–1953, and extended about 650 m offshore. The seaward 18 m of these lava tongues were eroded in the summer storms between 16 April and 21 September 1953, representing an average rate of retreat of 11 cm/day. The erosion produced a vertical cliff. Subsequently the rate of retreat slowed down considerably. The erosion was probably intermittent, occurring during storm wave activity. The results show the difference in rates of erosion of unconsolidated tephra and the much more solid and resistant lava.

Coastal erosion is severe in the southern part of the Ishikawa coast of Japan (M. Aramaki and

S. Takayama, 1967). The coast has retreated 2 km in 1800 years. Local storms cause drastic erosion, amounting to 16 m in one storm. Erosion took place when the wave steepness exceeded 0·020. The largest waves to attack the coast had a height of 2 m and a period of 8·5 seconds.

J. M. Zeigler, S. D. Tuttle, G. S. Geise and H. J. Tasha (1964) have compared the position of the coastline along outer Cape Cod between Nauset and Highland in 1958–1959 with detailed surveys made in 1887–1889 by H. Marindin. The latter compared his results with earlier surveys made in 1848, 1856 and 1868, and estimated the average rate of erosion along the 26·85 km stretch of coast to be 0·98 m/year. The comparison of the 1887 profiles with those of 1958 and 1959 suggests an erosion rate along the glacial drift cliffs of 0·793 m/year. The rate decreases to nil and becomes accretion to the north of Highland, but increases on Nauset spit to the south. The material on the beach has not increased. It is carried out of the area by longshore drift both to north and south. Zeigler *et al.* computed the volume of sediment supplied to the beach and bars in front of the cliff, both by cliff erosion and by loss of material from the sea floor under the beach and bars. The sea floor is composed of glacial sediments, which outcrop frequently in the troughs on either side of the nearshore bar. This material is eroded as the equilibrium barless beach profile is transferred inland as the cliffs retreat. The equilibrium barless beach profile is called the profile of erosion. The estimate of cliff erosion volume was 312,500 m³/year from above higher high water at +4·3 m elevation, and the volume eroded between this elevation and −12·2 m from the erosion profile was estimated at 334,200 m³/year, making a total of 647,000 m³/year for the whole stretch of coast under consideration.

In order to calculate the residence time of the sand in the two submarine bars and the beach, Zeigler *et al.* estimated their volumes, which they give as beach 4,380,000 m³, nearshore bar 6,350,000 m³ and offshore bar 13,420,000 m³. The residence time is given by the ratio of the volume of the features to the amount of new material added, and the material apportioned between the beach and the two bars according to the size characteristics. They concluded that the residence time on the beach and inner bar is 38·2 years and for the offshore bar 57·2 years. The beach and inner bar both contain coarser sediment than the outer bar. Some of the finer glacial material, estimated at about 20%, is lost from the nearshore area altogether, being blown onto the dunes or carried to deeper water. The proportion going to the different beach zones is estimated as follows: beach and inner bar 43·3%, offshore bar 36·3%, lost mainly offshore 20·5%. The results indicate that if the cliff erosion were stopped by defence works, thus reducing the sand supply by half, the beach would completely disappear in 86 years or sooner. The offshore supply would also be cut off because the profile retreat would no longer occur as at present. The data can also be used to estimate longshore drift volume—calculated to be 519,000 m³/year. This area is well suited to this type of analysis as the beach and nearshore bar zone is in approximate stability. The supply of material can also be readily measured, because no other source than coastal erosion is available in the immediate area.

8 Coastal defences

Coastal defence is only necessary on those coasts liable to erosion. Coasts in areas of hard rock do not require further protection. Where the coast is potentially erodible, as a result of either its low character or non-resistant cliff and foundation, its natural defence against marine erosion is an adequate beach. The beach absorbs the wave energy and prevents the sea having direct access to the cliffs or wave-cut platform beneath the beach. A low coast is best defended by sand dunes, consolidated by the roots of sand-loving plants, such as Marram grass. The effectiveness of such a protection against very violent attack by the sea has been indicated in the account of the effect of the storm surge on the low coast of Lincolnshire. The report (1954) of the Waverley Committee, set up to investigate the coastal flooding in 1953, also stresses the importance of the beach and dunes as a natural defence against erosion. The reserve supply of sand held in the dune is a valuable safeguard against erosion.

Any artificial method that helps maintain a wide, high beach is desirable. A beach can be built up artificially by means of groynes. Such structures are, however, not without danger on a beach. The aim of a groyne, which is usually built approximately at right-angles to the beach, is to trap material moving alongshore to build up the level of the beach. The danger of groynes,

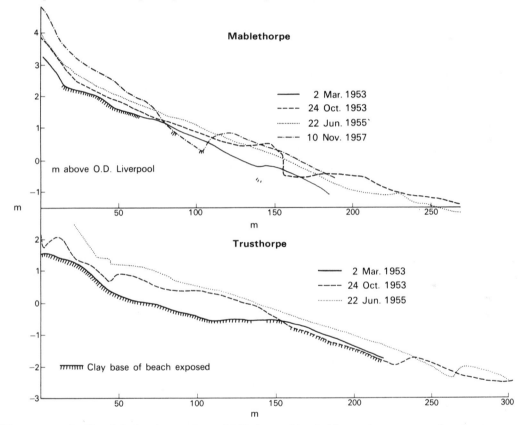

Figure 17-9   Profiles of the beach at and near Mablethorpe, Lincolnshire, to show recovery after the 1953 surge.

like that of breakwaters and other structures, is that the down-drift area is starved of beach material and erosion may be accelerated in this area. The Committee on Coastal Flooding suggests that while research on the movement of beach material, offshore bank movement and other coastal problems is being carried out, groynes should be used in areas where they are known to help to stabilize the beach. Groynes have been built or renewed along much of the badly damaged part of the Lincolnshire coast since the storm surge. Repeated surveys of the same profiles, which were first surveyed soon after the floods, show that the beaches have built up steadily since the storm, when they had very little material. The beach had an almost complete cover by 1955, the groynes being built between 1954 and 1955 along this stretch of coast. The profiles are shown in figure 17-9.

R. R. Minikin (1952), in his discussion of groynes, suggests that their arrangement and character must be suited to the beach concerned, so that generalization is of limited value. Their length should be related to the amount of littoral drift. When it is small the groynes should usually be shorter, so that the small available supply of material is accumulated at the top of the foreshore where it is required. Shingle beaches should only have short groynes, ending a few metres from where the beach becomes sandy. Minikin considers that groynes should not exceed the maximum height to which the beach may be expected to accrete. They should dip slowly down to below beach level at their lower end, conforming in general to the slope of the beach. Short groynes should be spaced a distance equal to their length, while longer ones may be spaced $1\frac{1}{2}$ lengths apart.

A model study of the effect of groynes made by the Hydraulics Research Board (1958) has shown that high groynes, the equivalent of 0·915 m on the prototype, and spaced at the equivalent of 55 m apart and having a length equivalent to 55 m, reduced the littoral drift to one eighth of its value without groynes. Where the groynes were high and closely spaced, however, the beach material was often unable to build up to the top of the groyne on the up-drift side. This resulted in loss of beach material normal to the shore. It was concluded, therefore, that low, widely spaced groynes are more beneficial to the beach. They do not trap so much of the longshore drift, but they can be built up to the top on the up-drift side. Groynes of this type did not lead to a general loss of beach material from the foreshore, as occurred with the high, closely spaced groynes under the conditions of the experiment.

P. H. Kemp (1962) has studied the behaviour of beaches and groynes in a model wave tank. He used light pumice sand in the model tank, which was 4·6 m by 2·73 m, to overcome scale problems. Each groyne type was tested at three angles, normal to the beach, 30° up-drift, and 20° down-drift. The groynes tested were low and high long ones, and high short ones, all of which were exposed to steep and flat waves. The results showed that the groyne type played a part in determining the shoreline orientation and the rate of littoral drift. The accumulation increased when the groynes pointed up-drift, but there was more even accumulation on either side of the groynes when they pointed down-drift. The reorientation of the shoreline due to the groynes can reduce scour caused by the return flow and the longshore current, and the height of the groynes was found to have an effect on the longshore current velocity, which was reduced to 40% of the value to seaward with high groynes and to 60% with low groynes. The low groynes had the advantage of eliminating eddies. When the groynes were high enough to impede the movement of material the shoreline swung round to face normal to the wave approach. The optimum pattern depends on the local situation, including such factors as the direction of approach of storm waves relative to normal waves. The groynes should be so arranged that the storm waves approach the beach normal to the contours at the water line.

W. A. Price and K. W. Tomlinson (1969) have shown by laboratory wave tank tests that groynes have relatively little effect on an equilibrium beach. Permeable groynes had little effect either onshore or offshore, while impermeable groynes produced some build up on the lower beach below the groynes. The tests were carried out in a wave basin 58 m by 23 m, in which the beach was stabilized before model groynes were inserted. Waves at angles of 5° and 20° to the beach were tested and both yielded similar results.

N. Pallett (1969), in considering the effectiveness of groynes, cites West Wittering in Sussex where groynes succeeded in halting erosion that previously had taken place at the rate of 5 m/year. Pallett also cites Aberdeen where the face of sand dunes had suffered erosion by 2 m/year between 1868 and 1962: after groynes were installed in 1962 accretion took place between high and low water and much sand accumulated below low water. The groynes can only be effective, however, where material is available to drift alongshore. If material is not available, artificial refill is necessary, as has been carried out on the Pett foreshore near Rye. 30,000 m³ were taken from Rye Harbour and distributed along the foreshore to the west from where it was derived by natural beach drift. An example of erosion beyond terminal sea defence works is provided at Hastings in Sussex where sea walls, groynes and an old harbour arm have caused one million m³ to accumulate in the old harbour in 60 years. Erosion has taken place on the 100 m high cliffs down drift of the old harbour.

On a low coast another safeguard against serious flooding is the existence of a strong second line of defence, in the form of an inner sea bank. Along most of the southern part of the Lincolnshire coast the so-called 'Roman Bank', a medieval structure, lies inland of the outer sea defences, and forms a good second line of defence. In the northern part of the coast this extra defence is lacking because earlier erosion has removed the bank. The Committee on Coastal Flooding (1954) also drew attention to the desirability of a second line of defence in areas where the land behind the coast is below high-tide level.

Measures to strengthen or initiate sand dunes have already been considered in chapter 6. This is an important coastal protection measure in suitable areas, but along some coasts the only possible method of protecting land and property is to build sea-walls. Walls can be built to protect land from erosion or to provide facilities for holiday-makers, including promenades. In other areas walls are necessary to protect low-lying land from flooding at high tides. These defences can be earthen banks, such as those built along many tidal rivers and in areas not liable to very destructive wave action. Banks of this type protected much of the coast of Essex before the 1953 storm surge. They were over-topped and breached by the storm waves on this occasion.

On more exposed coasts more solid masonry walls are usually built. Many of those protecting the coast of Lincolnshire, where the beaches were very low and narrow, were completely destroyed. This was caused in many areas by the undermining of the back of the wall by the water over-topping it. Once the wall had been undermined from the rear its collapse was rapid and complete. The new defences built since the floods are much higher and have greater strength in depth and at the rear.

The problem of sea-walls in connection with the maintenance of sand dunes is that they provide an obstacle to the movement of sand by wind from the foreshore to the dunes. A concrete or masonry wall is a very inflexible structure, which will return all the water thrown on it by the swash. The backwash will be powerful, because none is lost by percolation. This seaward movement, which will be strengthened during periods of strong onshore winds, will help to remove the beach material immediately in front of the wall. No reserves of sand are available to help cushion and stabilize the upper beach. The reduction in height of the beach in front of the wall will allow deeper water to penetrate closer inshore, and the energy of the waves becomes concentrated over a shorter distance and their destructive effect is intensified. On the Lincolnshire coast the small amount of beach material may be stripped entirely away, leaving only the clay foundation of the beach. The storm waves can then attack the clay, which shows signs of erosion in places. The beach is then permanently lowered, because, even if the same amount of sand does come back to the beach after the storm, it will lie at a lower level.

It is very likely that the deterioration of the beach during periods of destructive wave activity will be transmitted in a down-drift direction. The danger of the transmission of wave energy from the areas protected by walls to adjacent areas protected by dunes was illustrated by the position of the breaches during the 1953 storm surge. Many of these occurred at points immediately south of the end of the concrete walls (F. A. Barnes and C. A. M. King, 1953).

L. D. Stamp (1939) drew attention to a similar instance of especially severe erosion at the end of a sea-wall, at Hampton in Herne Bay. An example of the difficulty of maintaining a beach in front of a sea-wall is described by V. P. Zenkovich (1958). Between Tuapse and Adler, on the northeast coast of the Black Sea, the coast is backed by the Caucasus Mountains and the railway is forced to run immediately behind the beach, which is narrow and shingly. An almost vertical stone wall was built to protect the railway. The wall caused the backwash of the waves to remove much of the beach material, establishing a new beach profile, which was narrower and lower than before. The waves were now able to break directly onto the wall. Water velocities of 8 m/sec had been recorded. Shingle thrown at the wall by the breaking waves, which could attack the wall continuously owing to the reduction in beach level, have undercut the base of the wall to a depth of 3 to 4 m at a rate of about 30 cm/year.

On the Lincolnshire coast artificial 'points' have been established where the main outfalls of the drains and streams reach the sea, to prevent silting up of these channels. The promontories, some of which may be sited on natural till hummocks, affect the movement of beach material in such a way that the beach, particularly on the down-drift southern side, is lowered in relation to the level of the beach on the straighter sections of the coast. Deflection of the waves round the sharp point may prevent beach material collecting in their lee. The lowering of the beach in the vicinity of the points helped to weaken these areas and breaches occurred near the points in many instances. This was well shown in the vicinity of Ingoldmells Point, where the damage was very severe (F. A. Barnes and C. A. M. King, 1953).

The artificial replacement of eroded beach material is becoming a more common method of shore protection. This technique has been employed in the U.S.A. by a variety of methods. The sand by-passing at Port Hueneme in California is a good example, which illustrates also the danger of interfering with the natural drift of beach material, which made the project necessary (R. P. Savage, 1957). Two jetties were built during the period 1938 to 1940. These caused accretion on the up-drift side and serious erosion on the down-drift side of the structures. The sand from the zone of accretion was transferred to the depleted beaches by dredging with a floating dredge, which operated behind a narrow barrier and in the surf zone. Much time was lost during dredging in the surf zone, owing to the necessity for the floating dredge to retreat behind the barrier during rough weather. The recorded wave heights during the period of dredging rarely exceeded 1·22 m, and were never greater than 1·83 m.

The fill used to replenish depleted beaches may be derived from the same coast up-drift of the obstruction causing erosion, as at Port Hueneme. Alternatively it may be derived from a completely different source. If the former situation applies, the sand fill will have the same general character as that lost by erosion, and the beach should maintain its stability. If, however, the beach fill is from a different source care must be taken if the process is to result in a stable beach. This problem has been considered in section 9-6. W. C. Krumbein (1957) points out that an eroding beach will tend to become coarser, a consideration that must be taken into account in supplying material to stabilize it. For optimum results the fill should be rather coarser than the normal beach material and also better sorted.

Where sand is not available from adjacent accreting beaches another suitable source must be sought, and then there is the problem of moving the sand to the required place. The feasibility of a wave-powered device to move sand has been tested and reported by F. F. Monroe (1967). The machine was designed to exploit offshore sand sources and one of its advantages would be the use of readily available wave power. The model consisted of two flotation pads attached to two laterally located horizontal beams. The device was adjusted to operate in variable depths. Theoretically it works seaward of the breakers. As the wave crest passes the water current is allowed to pass uninterrupted, but when the trough passes a strong downward-directed current is developed to stir up the sand into suspension. Then when the next crest passes this sand should move landwards with the current through the opened valves of the instrument. Thus material should be removed from under the machine and transferred landward. As the machine moves landwards so the sand should also be transported shorewards. After a considerable amount of testing it was found that the device was not suitable for moving sand shoreward from offshore sources. Only 2 out of 16 runs showed any landward movement of material. The device could prove useful if the sand raised into suspension could be carried far enough on the wave crest to prevent it being carried back again with the next trough, but at present the device has not been found satisfactory.

J. M. Caldwell (1966) shows that the problem of beach maintenance is associated with the fact that streams add little material to the beach systems, and that any material lost from the beach is a permanent loss. He considers that temporary solutions to the maintenance problems of the east coast beaches of the U.S.A. involve the placing of new sand on the beach. The maintenance of this material by means of groynes should provide an additional defence where necessary. The long-term solution involves the control of the tidal inlets with jetties of improved design, and better arrangements for sand by-passing. The problem is seen to be very closely

Table 17-3   Beach material drift deficit along part of the New Jersey coast

	Mantoloking to Manasquan	Manasquan to Asbury Park	Asbury Park to Sandy Hook	Along Sandy Hook m³/year
Net drift entering	0	56,500	244,000	376,000
Net drift leaving	56,500	244,000	376,000	—
Deficit of drift	56,500	187,000	133,000	—
Average shore erosion including silt and clay	83,300	278,000	195,000	376,000 accumulation
Sand erosion	56,500	187,000	133,000	376,000 accumulation

associated with the longshore transport of sediment, as has already been indicated. Table 17-3 indicates the deficit of sand that must be made good on some stretches of coast. Erosion is inevitable where each successive sector shows increasing littoral drift, as occurs along this stretch of the New Jersey coast.

The problem is aggravated on the southern part of the New Jersey shoreline, where in contrast to the northern part just considered, there are eight large tidal inlets. The net loss of beach material by erosion along this stretch of coast amounts to 1,345,000 m³/year over a distance of 136 km. This material is not carried offshore, but a large part of it is carried into the interior bays by the tidal and wave currents. The ebb tide cannot carry it all out again, as it is opposed and not assisted by the waves. The amount of material passing the inlets during the year amounts to 5,930,000 m³/year, and about 23% of this is permanently lost into the lagoons through the tidal inlets. This has resulted in a retreat over 120 km of the coast of 152·5 m or more during the last 100 years. Efficient by-passing will be necessary to prevent such loss in future, although temporary beach fill is needed as a short-term amelioration of the situation.

D. B. Duane (1969) has assessed the availability of sand for beach replenishment on the New Jersey and northern New England coast from offshore sources. Experiments have shown the feasibility of using offshore sources for beach replenishment by means of a hopper dredge. Recent advances in dredging technique indicate that submersible dredging equipment could exploit offshore sand sources soon. The estimated initial fill requirements for the New Jersey coast is 16·8 million m³, with an annual maintenance of nearly 1 million m³, which over a period of 50 years would amount to a total of nearly 50 million m³. In order to assess the offshore potential supply of sand 2660 km of continuous seismic soundings were carried out and 198 cores of sediment obtained. The analysis of these data suggests that about 2·3 billion (1000 million) m³ of sand are available off the New Jersey coast within 16 km of the shore and within a depth range of 18·3 m. The sediments are mostly medium grade of about 0·5 mm diameter. The sources of supply so far delimited are adequate to provide the necessary beach fill.

A similar inventory has also been carried out along the coast of Florida by D. B. Duane (1968). Surveys show that an initial fill of 19·1 million m³ is required to stabilize the coast. An annual replenishment of 84·2 million m³ is also required. In order to assess the offshore sand supplies to fulfil these needs 4160 km of survey have been run offshore in depths of 4·58 to 30·5 m. Six areas have been located with 458 million m³ of sand of suitable size. One problem is the distance between the areas requiring nourishment and the sources of suitable sand. Other suitable deposits of sand must be sought for this reason. These figures give some measure of the magnitude of the beach nourishment problem along this coast.

A similar study is being undertaken in California, where the coastal setting is very different. A study is under way to establish sediment sources from both inland and offshore in relation to the requirements (A. J. Bowen and D. L. Inman, 1966).

Some of the problems of tidal inlets are discussed by C. E. Lee (1968). From the point of view of navigation, the shoal that develops at the entrance to the inlet is a problem. On the other hand, it does allow some sand to pass across the inlet and hence improves the down-drift beaches. In order to study problems associated with tidal inlets three new wave tanks are being designed. The first two have dimensions of 15·2 by 45·8 m and the third 45·8 by 99 m. Sand by-passing methods will be studied in the larger tank.

Other methods of trapping additional sand on the foreshore have been used experimentally. One such experiment was carried out by I.C.I. on the beach near Bournemouth. Artificial seaweed was placed offshore 97·6 to 146 m from the promenade over a distance of 152·5 m along the shore. The depth at the site was originally 2·74 to 3·05 m. Sand accumulated at the landward margin of the strip and offshore. A maximum gain of 1·83 m occurred on the windward inner side of the strip of seaweed.

W. A. Price, K. W. Tomlinson and J. N. Hunt (1969) have experimented with artificial seaweed in beach improvement projects. Tests in a wave tank were conducted to find out whether seaweed placed offshore would result in a build up of the beach. The tests showed that under certain waves the beach did in fact build up. The seaweed reduced wave heights shoreward of its position by 4%, and induced higher viscosity near the bed which produced higher mass transport shoreward near the bottom. Shorter, thicker fibres should enhance this effect. Field trials at Bournemouth were also successful, where the beach built up despite destructive wave action. The storms did, however, damage the artificial seaweed.

Summary

Steep storm waves, accompanied by strong onshore winds, are destructive on the foreshore. On shingle beaches such waves cause rapid seaward transfer of shingle, although some is thrown above the reach of ordinary waves to form long-lasting shingle ridges. On sand beaches storm waves are entirely destructive in character and take the sand out to deeper water. Solid rocks are eroded by corrosion, corrasion, attrition and hydraulic action. Shock pressures set up by breaking waves are particularly effective in jointed rocks. Shore platforms are eroded partly by wave scour in the intertidal zone, water-layer weathering is effective in forming small platforms above high-water level. Effective wave abrasion is limited to a depth of about 10 m. Small-scale corrosion forms occur on most rocks, but are best developed on limestones. Many cliffs show a two-stage development with modern erosion forming the steeper lower cliff section. In soft rocks mass movement combines with marine action to cause cliff retreat.

The beach plays an important part in determining areas susceptible to erosion. The best defence of any coast is a wide, stable beach, while sand dunes serve a valuable function in the protection of low coasts. Where it is necessary to build sea walls they are liable to enhance the destructive effect of storm waves, owing to their impermeability. This was demonstrated in the effects of the 1953 storm surge on the Lincolnshire coast. Longshore transport of beach material is very important in coast erosion. Examples of erosion due to this cause occur along the Holderness coast, where Flamborough Head cuts off the southerly movement of material into the area. The soft drift cliffs are cut back about 2 m/year as a result. Groynes may help to hold material moving alongshore, but the down-drift beaches may suffer. The post-glacial rise of sea level has been responsible for the general retreat of some coasts. Rates of coastal erosion are largest on unconsolidated coasts and are usually very slow in hard rocks. The best means of coastal defence is to provide a wide, high beach. Modern methods include the placement of large volumes of beach fill, sometimes obtained from offshore areas, on the foreshore. Surveys are being carried out around the U.S.A. to assess the availability of offshore sand supplies as well as studies to improve the design of tidal inlets.

References

AGAR R. 1960: The post-glacial erosion of the north Yorkshire coast from the Tees Estuary to Ravenscar. *Proc. Yorks. Geol. Soc.* **32**(4), 409–27.

ARAMAKI, M. and TAKAYAMA, S. 1967: A petrological study on littoral drift along the Ishikawa coast, Japan. Chapter 36 in *Proc. 10th Conf. Coast. Eng.*, 615–31.

ARBER, M. A. 1949: Cliff profiles in Devon and Cornwall. *Geog. J.* **114**, 191–7.

BARNES, F. A. and KING, C. A. M. 1953: The Lincolnshire coastline and the 1953 storm-flood. *Geogr.* **38**, 141–60.

BARTRUM, J. A. 1938: Shore platforms. *J. Geomorph.* **1**, 266–8.

BARTRUM, J. A. and TURNER, F. J. 1928: Pillow lavas, peridotites and associated rocks of north west New Zealand. *N.Z. Inst. Trans.* **59**, 98–138.

BORGMAN, L. E. 1965: The statistical distribution of ocean wave forces on vertical piling. *C.E.R.C. Tech. Memo.* **13.** (31 pp.)

BOWEN, A. J. and INMAN, D. L. 1966: Budget of littoral sands in the vicinity of Point Arguello, California. *C.E.R.C. Tech. Memo* **19.** (41 pp.)

BRADLEY, W. C. 1958: Submarine abrasion and wave-cut platforms. *Bull. Geol. Soc. Am.* **69**, 967–74.

BRUUN, P. 1954: Coast erosion and the development of beach profiles. *B.E.B. Tech. Memo.* **44.**

CALDWELL, J. M. 1966: Coastal processes and beach erosion. *J. Soc. Civ. Eng.* **53**(2), 142–57.

CORKAN, R. H. 1950: The levels in the North Sea associated with the storm disturbance of 8 Jan., 1949. *Phil. Trans. Roy. Soc.* A **242**, 493–525.

COTTON, C. A. 1922: *Geomorphology of New Zealand. Part I: Systematic.* N.Z. Board of Sci. and Art. Man. No. **3,** Wellington: Dominion Museum.

COTTON, C. A. 1951: Atlantic gulfs, estuaries and cliffs. *Geol. Mag.* **88,** 113–28.

COTTON, C. A. 1963: Levels of plantation and marine benches. *Zeits. für Geomorph.* NF **7**(2), 97–111.

DAVIS, W. M. 1909: *Geographical Essays* (Johnson, D. W., Editor), Boston.

DEPARTMENTAL COMMITTEE ON COASTAL FLOODING 1954: *Report.* Cmd. 9165, London: H.M.S.O.

DIONNE, C. 1967: Formes de corrosion littorale, côte sud du Saint-Laurent. *Cah. Geog. Quebec* **11**(23), 379–95.

DOUGLAS, C. K. M. 1953: The gale of 31 Jan., 1953. *Met. Mag.* **82,** 97–100.

DUANE, D. B. 1968: Sand inventory program in Florida. *Shore and Beach* **36**(1), 12–15.

DUANE, D. B. 1969: Sand inventory program. A study of New Jersey and North New England coastal waters. *Shore and Beach*, Oct. 1969, and *C.E.R.C.* **R–2–70.**

EDWARDS, A. B. 1951: Wave action in shore platform formation. *Geol. Mag.* **88,** 41–9.

GAILLARD, D. B. W. 1904: *Wave action.* Washington D.C.: Corps of Eng., U.S. Army.

GUILCHER, A. 1958: Coastal corrasion forms in limestone around the Bay of Biscay. *Scot. Geog. Mag.* **74**(3), 137–49.

GUILCHER, A. 1966: Les grandes falaise et megafalaise des côtes sud-ouest et ouest de l'Irlande. *Ann. de Geogr.* **75,** 26–38:

GUILCHER, A., BERTHOIS, L. and BATTASTINI, R. 1962: Formes de corrosion littorale dans les roches volcaniques, particulièrement à Madagascar et au Cap Vert (Senegal). *Cah. Oceanog.* **14**(4), 208–40.

HILL, E. S. 1949: Shore platforms. *Geol. Mag.* **86,** 137–52.

HYDRAULICS RESEARCH BOARD 1958: *Report: hydraulics research 1957.* D.S.I.R., London: H.M.S.O., 52–4.

IRVING, E. G. (Chairman) 1962: Coastal cliffs: report of a symposium. *Geog. J.* **128**(3), 303–20.

JOHNSON, D. W. 1919: *Shore processes and shoreline development.* New York: Wiley. (584 pp.) Facsimile edition, 1965, New York: Hafner.

JOHNSON, D. W. 1938: Shore platforms. *J. Geomorph.* **1,** 268–72.

KEMP, P. H. 1962: A model study of the behaviour of beaches and groynes. *J. Inst. Civ. Eng.* **22,** 191–217.

KRUMBEIN, W. C. 1957: A method of specification of sand for beach fills. *B.E.B. Tech. Memo.* **102.**

LEE, C. E. 1968: Tidal navigation inlets. *Shore and Beach* **36**(1), 27–30.

LEWIS, W. V. 1931: The effect of wave incidence on the configuration of a shingle beach. *Geog. J.* **78,** 129–48.

MATHER, J. R., ADAMS, H. and YOSHIOKA, G. A. 1965: Coastal storms of the Eastern United States. *J. Appl. Met.* **3**(6), 693–706.

MII, H. 1960: Erosive features along the rocky coast of Iwaizaki, Miyagi prefecture. *Saito Ho-on Kai Museam Res. Bull.* **29.** (16 pp.)

MII, H. 1962: Some ancient shore features. *Sci. Rep. Tohuku Univ. Japan.* sp. vol. **5** *2nd Ser.,* 361–71.

MINIKIN, R. R. 1952: *Coast erosion and protection.* London: Chapman & Hall.

MITSUYASU, H. 1967: Shock pressures of breaking waves. Chapter 18 in *Proc. 10th Conf. Coast. Eng.,* 268–83.

MONROE, F. F. 1967: A feasibility study of a wave-powered device for moving sand. *C.E.R.C.* **MP 3–67.** (39 pp.)

MURAKI, Y. 1967: Field observations of wave pressure, wave run-up and oscillation of break-waters. Chapter 20 in *10th Conf. Coast. Eng. Proc..* 302–21.

NANSEN, F. 1922: *The strandflat and isostasy.*

ORME, A. R. 1962: Abandoned and composite sea cliffs in Britain and Ireland. *Irish Geogr.* **4**(4), 279–91.

PALLETT, N. 1969: The terminal problem in coastal protection. Chapter 34 in *Coastal engineering* **1**; *Proc. 11th Conf. Coast. Eng., London, 1968,* New York: Am. Soc. Civ. Eng., 549–57.

PRICE, W. A. and TOMLINSON, K. W. 1969: The effect of groynes on stable beaches. Chapter 32 in *Coastal engineering* **1**; *Proc. 11th Conf. Coast. Eng., London, 1968,* New York: Am. Soc. Civ. Eng., 518–25.

PRICE, W. A., TOMLINSON, K. W. and HUNT, J. N. 1969: The effect of artificial seaweed in promoting the build-up of beaches. Chapter 36 in *Coastal engineering* **1**; *Proc. 11th Conf. Coast. Eng., London, 1968,* New York: Am. Soc. Civ. Eng., 570–8.

RAISON, J-P. 1961: La falaise et l'estran rocheux du Cap D'Alprech (Pas-de-Calais). *Cah. Oceanog.* **13**(9), 636–51.

RICHARDS, A. F. 1960: Rates of marine erosion of Tephra and lava at Isla San Benedicto, Mexico, *Rep. of Int. Geog. Cong.* **21,** Norden. Pt X Sub. Geol., 59–64.

ROBINSON, A. H. W. 1953: The storm surge of 31 Jan.–1 Feb., 1953. *Geog.* **38,** 134–41.

RODE, K. 1930: Geomorphogenie des Ben Lomond (Kalifornien) eine Studie über Terrasenbildung durch Marine Abrasion. *Zeits. für Geomorph.* **5,** 16–78.

ROSSITER, J. R. 1954: The North Sea storm surge of 31 Jan. and 1 Feb., 1953. *Phil. Trans. Roy. Soc.* A **246,** 371–99.

ROUVILLE, A. DE 1938: *Annale des Ponts et Chaussées.*

ROYAL COMMISSION ON COASTAL EROSION 1911: *Report.* London: H.M.S.O.

RUSSELL, R. J. 1963: Recent recession of tropical cliffy coasts. *Science* **139**(3549), 9–15.

SAVAGE, R. P. 1957: Sand bypassing at Port Hueneme, California. *B.E.B. Tech. Memo.* **92.**

SAVAGE, R. P. 1959: Laboratory study of the effect of groins on the rate of littoral transport. Equipment development and initial tests. *B.E.B. Tech. Memo.* **114.** (56 pp.)

SAVILLE, T. GARCIA, W. J. and LEE, C. E. 1966: Breakwaters with vertical and sloping faces. *Int. Geog. Cong.* **21,** Section II: *Ocean. Navig. C.E.R.C.* **R–2–66.**

SCHWARTZ, M. L. 1967: The Bruun theory of sea-level rise as a cause of shore erosion. *J. Geol.* **75**(1), 76–92.

SCHWARTZ, M. L. 1968: The scale of shore erosion. *J. Geol.* **76,** 508–17.

SCOTT, W. H. 1955: Sea erosion and coast protection at Sumner, New Zealand. *N.Z. Eng.* **10,** 438–47.

SHEPARD, F. P. 1950: Longshore bars and longshore troughs. *B.E.B. Tech. Memo.* **20.**

SHEPPARD, T. 1912: *The lost towns of the Yorkshire coast.* London. (329 pp.)

SO, C. L. 1965: Coastal platforms of the Isle of Thanet. *Trans. Inst. Brit. Geogr.* **37,** 147–56.

STAMP, D. L. 1939: Some economic aspects of coastal loss and gain. *Geog. J.* **93,** 496–503.

STEERS, J. A. 1951: Notes on the erosion along the coast of Suffolk. *Geol. Mag.* **88,** 435–9.

THORN, R. B. 1960: *The design of sea defence works.* London: Butterworths.

TWENHOFEL, W. H. 1945: The rounding of sand grains. *J. Sed. Petrol.* **15,** 59–71.

VALENTIN, H. 1954: Der Landverlust in Holderness, Ostengland von 1852 bis 1952. *Die Erde* **6**(3-4), 296–315.

WENTWORTH, C. K. 1938: Marine bench formation: water level weathering. *J. Geomorph.* **1,** 6–32.

WILLIAMS, W. W. 1953: La Tempète des 31 Jan. et 1 Fev., 1953. *Bull. Inform. C.O.E.C.* **5,** 206–10.

WILLIAMS, W. W. 1956: An east coast survey. *Geog. J.* **122,** 317–34. (Discussion.)

WOOD, A. 1959: The erosional history of the cliffs around Aberystwyth. *Liverpool and Manchester Geol. J.* **2**(2), 271–87.

WOOD, A. 1968: Beach platforms in the Chalk of Kent, England. *Zeits. für Geomorph.* NF **12**(1), 107–13.

WRIGHT, L. W. 1967: Some characteristics of the shore platforms of the English Channel and the northern part of North Island, New Zealand. *Zeits. für Geomorph.* NF **11**(1), 34–46.

ZEIGLER, J. M., TUTTLE, S. D., GIESE, G. S. and TASHA, H. J. 1964: Residence time of sand composing beaches and bars of Outer Cape Cod. *Proc. 9th Conf. Coast. Eng.* **26,** 403–16.

ZENKOVICH, V. P. 1958: *Berega Chernovo i Azovskovo morey.* (Coasts of the Black Sea and the Sea of Azov.) Moscow: Geografgoz. (292 pp.)

18 Historical data on coastal change

1 Evidence of maps

Maps provide useful evidence of coastal change, although they have drawbacks, one of which is the inaccuracy of many early maps. Few can be relied on before the Ordnance Survey maps were published at the beginning of the nineteenth century, and even these maps, on the scale of 1 inch to 1 mile, are of limited value unless coastal changes are large in amount. The 6 inch to 1 mile maps can be used to give accurate values for cliff recession, and the tide lines often provide useful evidence. Frequently the exact state of the tide shown on the map is not made sufficiently clear for comparison with modern maps. Maps, of course, only give evidence of the state of the coast at the date of survey. They cannot give a continuous picture of coastal development. Important steps may be omitted in the cartographic evidence of coastal change, if the surveys are few.

It must not be assumed that all cartographic evidence before the Ordnance Survey is useless, but early maps must be treated with caution. During the seventeenth and eighteenth centuries many excellent county surveys were made by such well-known surveyors as Saxton and Speed. Their maps can, however, be misleading. Some of Norden's early work which was specifically surveyed to give an accurate map of some coastal areas such as Orford, is of considerable value. The hydrographic surveys of the coast also provide valuable evidence of coastal and offshore changes.

The analysis of the development of the spits across the harbour mouths of Poole, Christchurch and Pagham on the south coast of England by A. H. W. Robinson (1955) illustrates the use to which information from surveys of different kinds can be put in the elucidation of coastal change. The maps and charts used for the study of Poole harbour area include an early undated and unsigned map, which probably dates from about 1585 to 1586. It is on a scale of 0·78 inches to 1 mile. Another map, drawn by Robert Adams, is dated 1597 and covers all Poole Harbour. About 100 years later in 1698 naval commanders produced a chart of the ports of the south coast, including Poole. A small-scale map was produced of the area in 1720, and a 6 inch to 1 mile map of Poole Harbour, surveyed by Lieut. Mackenzie, is dated 1785. Further hydrographic surveys were produced in 1849, 1878, 1891, 1910, 1924 and 1934. The Ordnance Survey maps of the area include the first edition 1 inch to 1 mile. A 25 inch to 1 mile plan was produced in 1886, and revised in 1900 and 1924. The Ordnance Survey produced an air photograph mosaic of the area, flown in 1947. This area has, therefore, been surveyed at least 16 times since the end of the sixteenth century at increasingly frequent intervals.

A similar number of surveys of the other two harbours studied by Robinson are also available. He could, therefore, trace with fair accuracy the evolution of the spits at the entrances to the harbours from the beginning of the eighteenth century to the present day. These areas include harbour entrances that are important for navigation and which are subject to fairly rapid changes. Accurate information of the coastal area was, therefore, essential. It is not likely that such a complete cartographic record of coastal change would be available for more open coasts.

Mention was made in section 2-4 of the use of maps in tracing coastal change. The contributions of G. de Boer (1963; 1964) and de Boer and A. P. Carr (1969) are useful in this field. The findings of de Boer will be considered in the next section, dealing with the historical evidence for the different stages of development of Spurn Head.

A. P. Carr's study deals with Orfordness in Suffolk (G. de Boer and A. P. Carr, 1969). This spit has varied greatly throughout the historical period. The cartographic evidence for its growth up to 1650 A.D. begins with a chart dating from the reign of Henry VIII. The chart, which is crude and undated, shows the mouth of the River Ore opposite the castle. The next chart dates from 1584. It is good but on a small scale. Norden produced an estate map of Orford and Sudbourne parishes in 1601. Norden's map is of variable accuracy, but it is the most reliable early map available. At this time the distal point of the spit was situated 1·6 km south of the southern tip of Havergate. The cartographic evidence for the sixteenth century suggests relative stability during this period.

There is earlier written evidence concerning the nature of Orfordness. The King's Marshes were recorded in the Pipe Rolls as having been reclaimed in about 1166 A.D. with the help of engineers from Normandy. The historical evidence indicates both from written and cartographic sources that the marshes reached their present configuration and character early. There is little cartographic evidence of changes in the spit in the second half of the seventeenth and the whole of the eighteenth centuries. There are maps in 1671, 1682 and 1693, and small-scale maps for 1736 and 1783. These maps do not give any very detailed or accurate information concerning the development of the spit.

The nineteenth century produced more maps than the first half of the twentieth. Eleven maps date from the last century and show widely fluctuating distal points of the spit, which appear to be almost randomly distributed. The maps of this period are of acceptable accuracy and the dates of survey are given reliably. Some of the maps of this period are marine charts, others are land surveys.

The maps and charts indicate that the spit reached its maximum length between 1811 and 1813. Subsequently it was reduced in length by over 1525 m by 1820. It had almost the same distal position in 1804, 1838, 1867, 1902 and 1967, but between these dates it was as much as 1370 m shorter and 1525 m longer. The great variability of the positions of the distal point indicates one of the problems of using maps to study the changing form of the spit. The maps are produced at irregular intervals and they may well not record the maxima and minima of the movements of the tip. From 1880 there have been 6-inch Ordnance Survey maps of the area, so that accuracy is good from this time in the land maps, but the dates of survey are not very frequent. No Ordnance Survey of the distal point was made between 1902 and 1945, when the first air photograph cover became available. Only one hydrographic survey was carried out during this period, and it does not give a direct position of the tip of the spit.

Owing to the great variability of position of the distal tip, shown by the cartographic evidence, a mean value for the growth of the spit is of little value. The maximum rate is about 183 m/year.

An account of the art of marine cartography and a history of the development of marine cartography has been published by A. H. W. Robinson (1962). This book is useful as a guide to the marine cartographic data on coastal change, as it deals with surveys made at sea. These concentrate on offshore and coastal changes, which are often closely associated with each other. Data also tend to be particularly numerous and accurate at harbour entrances and other areas where there are often features of geomorphological interest, such as offshore banks, spits and barriers. During the last few decades the rapid increase in the availability of aerial photographs has also provided a valuable means of studying coastal development of various types.

2 Examples of the use of historic evidence

Sources other than maps may provide evidence of coastal change. The nature of the evidence will vary with the type of coast. On a coast where erosion is dominant records of the loss of land and buildings may be available, which will often give information concerning the time and place of erosion. On coasts which are building out by accretion, evidence may refer to silting up of ports and similar events. The type of evidence available for coasts of erosion and accretion, taking Lincolnshire and Dungeness as examples respectively, will be considered. An example of cyclic change will also be given, by describing the development and decay of Spurn Head and its predecessors.

a Erosion coast—Lincolnshire

The loss of land on the Lincolnshire coast is not as well known or conspicuous as that of the Holderness area. It is nevertheless quite extensive, and the type of coast renders the erosion more dangerous to life and property, because it is often associated with coastal flooding. A. E. B. Owen (1952) has assembled much relevant information. The earlier development of the coast of

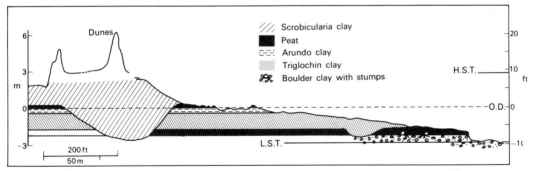

Figure 18-1 Diagrammatic section through the post-glacial deposits of the Lincolnshire coast at the beach north of Chapel Point. (*After Swinnerton, 1931; 1936.*)

Lincolnshire during the post-glacial period before the erosion started in the fourteenth century has been worked out by H. H. Swinnerton (1931) and (1936) and is illustrated in figure 18-1. During the post-glacial period silt and salt marsh clay, with layers of peat, accumulated on the till, which formed the shore in immediate post-glacial times. Tree stumps are incorporated in the lower of the two peat layers. The trees grew on the till surface, which was exposed during the period of low sea level, following the ice retreat in late and post-glacial times. These stumps are now exposed at extreme low tide level on the beach. The upper layer of peat occurs at about 30 cm O.D. and is of later bronze and iron age. Between the two peat layers are thick deposits of tidal salt marsh clay. These were deposited with a rising sea level behind a barrier to seaward, which cut off direct wave action from the area of clay accumulation. Since the deposition of the upper peat, sea level must have risen about 2·74 m in this area.

During the late-bronze–early-iron age the coastal zone was used for salt extraction. The industry had ceased before the area was occupied by the Romans. It seems likely, from the position of the Roman remains, that sea level started to rise before the end of the period of Roman occupation. After the Roman period sea level continued to rise and a layer of salt-water clay was deposited on the upper peat. The gradually rising sea level and the stormy years of the thirteenth century probably destroyed the coastal barrier, behind which the salt marsh deposits had been accumulating. Frequent flooding is recorded in the area after the close of the thirteenth century.

Since the end of the thirteenth century erosion by the sea has been serious on the Lincolnshire coast and Owen states that five parishes have been lost to the sea. During the last four centuries the sea has advanced between 0·4 and 0·8 km in the Mablethorpe, Trusthorpe and Sutton-on-Sea areas (see figure 18-2). Some of the earliest evidence of loss of land and buildings in the Mablethorpe area, given by Owen, refers to the stormy thirteenth century. In the year 1287 the Louth Park Chronicle records that St Peter's church in Mablethorpe was 'rent asunder by the waves of the sea'. In 1335, according to the records, the waves breached the sea-banks and flooded the land behind, causing loss of stock and crops. By 1430 the sea-walls again needed repair. A statement records that the parson of St Mary's Mablethorpe was required to furnish an account of the use of money and goods received for the repair of the sea-walls, which were necessary for the protection of the parish. The lord of Mablethorpe manor in 1443 was exempted from certain duties, which would have entailed expense, on account of loss of revenue resulting from inroads by the sea and cost of repairs to the sea defences. The duties included appointment to various public offices and acceptance of the honour of knighthood.

A survey of 1503 states that Mablethorpe was 'in very great danger of the sea'. Evidence of erosion is found in the Alford and Spilsby Courts of Sewers records, which begin in the middle of the sixteenth century and provide useful information on the problem of erosion. In 1540 or thereabouts the church of St Peter's was finally destroyed and an account of 1602 tells that 'both church and chancel were swallowed up with the sea above 50 or 60 years past'. The number of communicants of the parish dwindled from 67 in 1603 to only 4 families in 1722. In 1745 the parish was joined to that of Theddlethorpe St Helen. The tax imposed by parliament in 1645 on Lincolnshire, for defence of the county, was demanded from Mablethorpe, amongst other places, on account of the severe losses recently sustained by sea erosion. The loss was partly due to the bad state of repair of the sea-banks, necessary to the safety of the coast then as now.

There are also records of damage and danger from the sea at Sutton, just south of Mablethorpe. The records of the Commissioners of Sewers show that in 1631 the sea-banks at Sutton were in a very bad state of repair. The sea came over the old bank at every high spring tide, while a new one was being built landward of it. In 1637 the inhabitants of Sutton sent a petition to the Privy Council. In this they complained of the failure of the Commissioners to provide a new bank, stating that 'the town hath been divers years and yet is in great danger to be destroyed by the rage and violence of the sea'. They pointed out that 'our ancient parish church, some houses inhabited, and very much of the best grounds in our said town was destroyed by the sea and now is sea'. Sutton is still very much in danger of the sea, as the serious flooding showed in 1953.

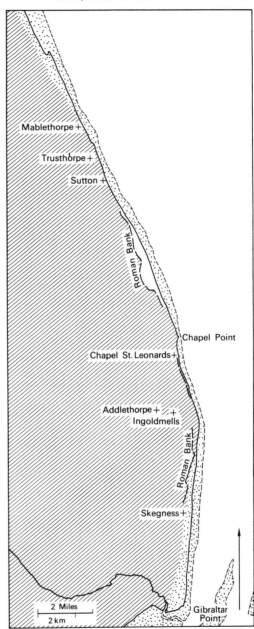

Figure 18-2 Map of the Lincolnshire coast.

This recent disaster can be seen in its historical perspective as only one event of a long-continued process of incursion by the sea.

In areas further south along the coast there is more evidence of the inroads of the sea. For example as early as 1272 it was a customary service for tenants to do sea-walling at Ingoldmells. During the fifteenth century there are plenty of records of inundation of land by the sea. A particularly interesting account is quoted by Owen from an earlier source (E. Oldfield, 1829). This illustrates the occurrence of a disaster very similar to that of 1953 about 200 years earlier, when serious flooding occurred on 16 February 1735. 'From five to eight in the morning, the day after full moon and a boisterous wind blowing northwest the sea for some hours before and after the time of high water overflowed Ingoldmells Bank for above a mile together, and laid the greatest part of the lands on this side of Dydick Bank in this parish and in Addlethorpe under water. There was so much salt water in the Parishes that it was near three weeks in running off. So great a tide has not been known in the memory of man.' This flood was the result of a North Sea surge due to strong northerly winds coinciding with a period of spring tides.

These few examples show that this low-lying coast has been suffering from erosion for at least 400 years. The fact that the land behind the thin line of natural dunes has been increasingly lowered relative to high-tide level by the rise of sea level means that breaching of the banks and dunes leads to increasingly serious flooding of the land. This leads to public demands for security. Other historical evidence of the encroaching sea is also available.

A. E. B. Owen (1961) has collected useful information concerning the sea defence scheme of the Lincolnshire coast from *The Levy Book of the Sea, and Towns in Great Danger*. This book first appeared in about 1600, and subsequently in several editions, dating from the seventeenth and early eighteenth centuries. It is reprinted in Owen. The flooding in Lincolnshire in 1499 to 1500 is not mentioned by P. Thompson in his *History of Boston* (1856), but it is the subject of a letter from the King dated 21 February 1500. The letter is concerned with the making of a sluice at Boston and other remedial measures. The Levy Book is concerned with acreages of reclaimed marshland and the sea defences needed to preserve them from flooding. It reveals that drainage and sea defence organization had a great continuity. A scheme was promulgated by the Commissioners of Seres in or before 1345, and was probably based on more ancient local agreements. The scheme was modified, but continued almost unchanged until 1500, and formed the basis for arrangements up until the recent past. Some of the measures in the Levy Book are of importance in a study of the coastal development, and these will be quoted:

(1) The first measure taken and tried by the said Commissioners with the 24 sworn men and the levellers was the sea dyke or bank at Skegness and so even along by the water of the Lym to the utmost part of the Wold edge. . . .
(3) The third measure taken from a place in Sutton sea bank called Well Howes and so the border of the Wold edge. . . .

There follows a list of the towns on the coast called 'frontagers', and the acreage for which they were responsible. The towns are described as being in 'great' or 'very great' danger of the sea. Those in very great danger of the sea were Skegness, Mumby cum Chapel, Sutton, Trusthorpe, Mablethorpe and Theddlethorpe. Those in great danger are Croft, Huttoft and Anderby. Saltfleetby is described as being only in 'danger' of the sea. Another list of inland towns is given, these being the levy towns required to help with the coastal towns' sea defences. The second list includes Winthorpe, Burgh, Orby, Hogsthorpe, Alford and others to a total of 42.

The list of coast towns in danger is of particular interest in that, apart from Skegness, the degree to which they apparently suffered from the sea, at the time of the Levy Book and before, is very similar to the degree of damage that they sustained during the 1953 storm surge. The account of the damage given in chapter 17 agrees closely with the list given above. Only Skegness has now come within the zone of accretion at the southern end of the coast. Croft, still further south, is another place that is now no longer threatened by the sea. The coast from the northern limits of Skegness towards Mablethorpe in the north is still in potential danger.

b Coast of accretion—Dungeness

During the early stages of development of the large shingle structure of Dungeness the shingle probably formed a fairly simple spit across the mouth of a wide shallow bay, running from

490

Hythe in the north via Appledore to Rye and Winchelsea in the south, as shown in figure 18-3. The development of this coastal area is bound up with the draining of the marsh, the changing courses of the rivers across the area, and the silting up of former ports due to marine accretion.

The reclaiming of Romney Marsh may have been achieved in the Roman period. This would have been facilitated by the relatively low sea level at this time. Evidence for this is given by W. V. Lewis and W. G. V. Balchin (1940), who state that the sea level was probably 1·52 to 1·83 m lower during the Roman period than it is now. This result was obtained from an accurate survey of the heights of the shingle ridges of Dungeness foreland. It supports the historical evidence of draining of Romney Marsh during the Roman period, according to T. Rice-Holmes's (1907) deduction of a Roman date for the Rhee wall. G. Ward (1933), on the other hand, does not accept the Roman date for the Rhee wall, and in discussing Lewis and Balchin's work he raises several historical arguments against it. He points out that if the wall were Roman the marsh to the south would be expected to differ from that to the north: it would probably be flooded by the high tide, whereas good arable land would be expected to the north. The Roman date of the wall is now, however, generally accepted and is supported by the evidence of the Saxon charters. These mention no difference at all between the area to the north and south of the wall. In fact a wall is never mentioned in them. The place names do not differ on either side of the wall. The oldest ones, which end in -ham, are found equally on either side of the wall. There is also positive evidence in the possible reference to the building of the wall during the fourteenth century. The wall appears to consist of banks on either side of a channel. In 1324 the King appointed a commission to enquire into damage caused by a trench cut across the marsh, which may refer to the Rhee wall channel. This was cut for drainage and periodic deepening to keep it clear would lead to an increase in the height of the banks.

The controversy over the date of the Rhee wall is related to the former course of the Rother, or Limen as some think it was called. Ward considers that the Rother flowed to the sea at or near Hythe, but most other authorities suggest that it reached the sea nearer to Appledore. This contradiction may have arisen over confusing the Portus Lemanis, where Caesar landed near Hythe, with the Limen or Rother (T. Lewin, 1862). These doubts illustrate the possible danger of relying too much on the interpretation of rather vague historical material.

There is more definite historical evidence of the growth of the shingle ridges and the development of the marsh strips between them in the eighth century. There are two charters, Eadbriht's of 741 and Offa's of 774, which make grants of land in the marsh near Lydd to the Church of Christ at Canterbury. This indicates the growth of Dungeness towards the east. At the same time there is evidence of sea to the east and north of Lydd. In 893 Danes sailed past Lydd to Appledore with a fleet of 250 vessels.

The outgrowth of Dungeness to the east held up shingle travelling from the southwest and prevented it from reaching the area to the north near Dymchurch. This necessitated the building of the Dymchurch wall by Rennie in 1803 to 1804. The lack of shingle was causing danger of coast erosion here (J. Elliott, 1847).

Another major change, for which there is also historical evidence (W. V. Lewis, 1932), had a marked effect on the development of the coast. In the thirteenth century the Rother was diverted from its old outlet near New Romney to Rye. The change was accompanied by the destruction of Old Winchelsea and Promehill. The probable site of Old Winchelsea was about 9·6 km northeast of Fairlight cliff and 3·2 km south-southeast of the present site of Rye. These settlements were probably situated on a shingle spit that formed a link across the bay, allowing communication between Winchelsea and a part of its parish which is now on the Rye side of the estuary. The gradual erosion of this spit, which culminated in the break-through of the

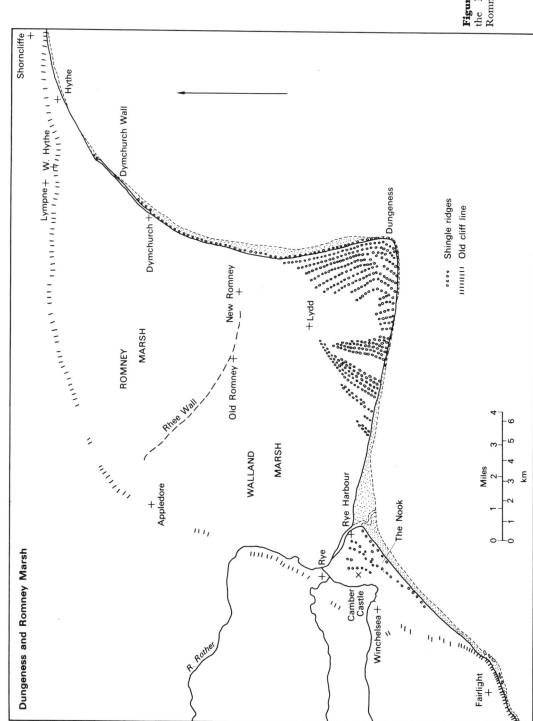

Dungeness and Romney Marsh

Shorncliffe

Hythe

Lympne W. Hythe

Dymchurch Wall

Dymchurch

New Romney

ROMNEY

MARSH

Rhee Wall

Old Romney

Lydd

Dungeness

Appledore

WALLAND

MARSH

Rye

Rye Harbour

The Nook

Camber Castle

Winchelsea

R. Rother

Fairlight

Shingle ridges
Old cliff line

Miles
0   1   2   3   4
0 1 2 3 4 5 6
km

Figure 18-3 Map of the Dungeness and Romney Marsh area.

Rother in 1287, is shown by references to the half-ruined state of the town of Old Winchelsea from 1236 to 1276. The King himself visited the town in 1276 and planned its removal, but it was almost entirely swept away in the catastrophe of 1287. The early chroniclers, quoted by W. MacL. Homan (1938) give evidence of these facts. New Winchelsea was built by Edward I to be used as the headquarters of the Cinque Ports, and in 1292 the inhabitants moved to the new town. Before long, however, another change in the marine processes defeated the King's purpose: the old Winchelsea had been destroyed by the destructive action of the sea—the new one was ruined by its constructive action. It was not long before deposition isolated the new Winchelsea from the open coast and its days as a port were over. This growth of the coast outwards in the region of Rye and Winchelsea may also be connected with the break-through of the river, which completed the destruction of Old Winchelsea. The drifting of material along the developing southern side of Dungeness, which was now beginning to turn further and further to face the dominant waves from the south-southwest, was reduced. The increasing eastward projection of the ness helped to trap beach material in this angle, thus cutting these places off from the sea.

Winchelsea had become useless for defence from the sea during the sixteenth century. Henry VIII, therefore, built Camber Castle to take its place. This fortification was sited near enough to the sea to act as a substitute for Winchelsea. The sea again spoilt the plans. The continued withdrawal of the sea, as shingle ridges were built out from the shore, soon isolated the castle from the sea, which now stands as a ruin, a monument to coastal change. The alignment of the Camber Castle shingle ridges and the date at which they were built have been analysed by H. Lovegrove (1953). The earliest ridges that he mentions are related to the destruction, in 1287, of an old sea-wall extending north-northeast to protect the marshes east of Winchelsea. Between this date and 1594 a complex series of ridges was formed. These extended the coast northwards to beyond Camber Castle. The fortification was at this time about 244 m from the sea. The evidence for the position of the coastline at this date is derived from Philip Symonson's map, which agrees very well with the evidence provided by the alignment of the shingle ridges. An undated and unsigned map, which Lovegrove considers to date from about 1695, illustrates the rapid growth of the coast outwards during the seventeenth century. This growth included the development of salt marshes, which were sheltered behind the Nook beach ridges. In the neighbourhood of Camber Castle the coast built out over 610 m during this century. The accretion also extended further north to within 381 m of the present position of the River Rother. The outgrowth was only about 61 m about 3.2 km to the southeast.

Surveys during the nineteenth century showed the development of the ridges to the southeast of the Nook, which first formed as a salt marsh in their shelter and was reclaimed by 1845. This series of surveys, with supporting historical evidence, gives a fairly complete picture of the outward growth of this part of the coast. The evidence can be confirmed and supported by a geomorphological study of the distribution of the shingle ridges and strips of salt marsh on the ground.

c Cyclic development—Spurn Point

The examples considered so far illustrate a coast of erosion and a coast of more or less continuous accretion. The third example is of a feature that has had a cyclic development. It is also one for which a great deal of historical evidence has been collected by G. de Boer (1963; 1964). The historical evidence for the development of Spurn Point is summarized in the diagrams shown in figure 18-4. It illustrates the cyclic nature of the development and shows how erosion to the north along the Holderness coast is intimately linked with the development and decay of successive spits. Each new spit grows to the northwest of the earlier one as the coast to the north is

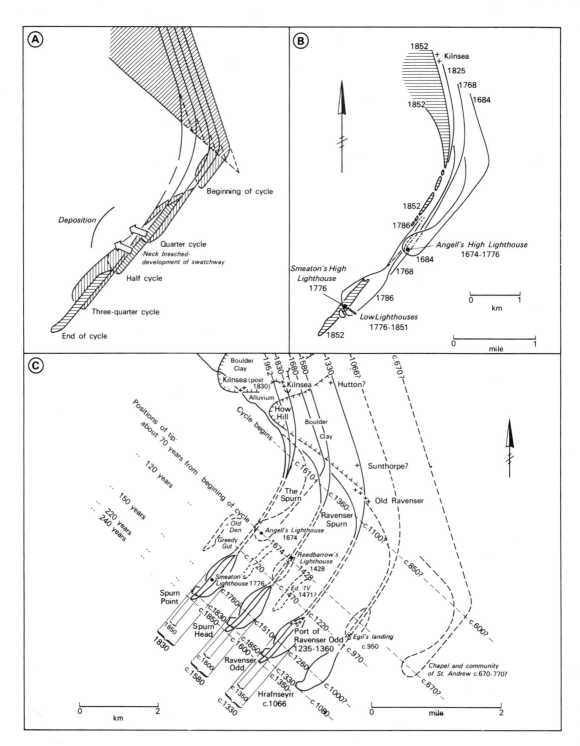

Figure 18-4   **A:** Hypothetical evolution of Spurn Point; **B:** Spurn Point between 1684 and 1852. **C:** Spurn Point and its predecessors. (*A, B, C after De Boer, 1963.*)

cut back by erosion. The erosion at the neck of the spit causes it to be more and more exposed to the destructive effect of strong north to northwest winds, which are the most damaging along the spit. In time the spit is breached at its neck and the distal end disperses, moving across the Humber estuary to build up the marshes of north Lincolnshire. The cycle runs its course in about 250 years. The new spit gradually grows southwestwards across the mouth of the Humber, until its neck again becomes vulnerable to wave attack, as the coast to the north continues to retreat. The position of the spit in the Humber is one reason for the wealth of historical evidence that de Boer has used. He has elucidated the growth and decay cycles of five separate Spurn Points during the period between about 670 A.D. and the present.

At the beginning of the cycle a small spit extends southwest from the tip of the glacial drift coast. The spit gradually grows, moving slightly inland northwestwards as it develops, and elongating to the southwest. At the end of the cycle the distal part becomes narrow and elongated, and a breach occurs about half way along the spit, where it develops a very narrow neck. The widening of the distal end of the spit during the cycle is due to the transport of material around the distal end into the shallow marsh area between the spit and north Humber shore. The material washed through the breach forms a gravelly deposit in this shallow area, known as the Old Den.

The historical evidence is useful in establishing the date of the breaches, which bring the cycle to a close. The clearest evidence for a breach was found in a course of lectures on the Statute of Sewers by Robert Callis in 1622. Other confirmation comes through litigation occasioned by the disagreement of the Angell family, who built lighthouses on Spurn Point, and another family who claimed the land on which they were built. Actions in about 1684 and 1695 indicated that the Ravensey Spurn had been swept into the Humber about 80 years previously.

There is less information for the early period and the first really useful evidence is a reference to the appearance of the port of Ravenser Odd in about 1235. It is difficult, however, to establish the position of the place referred to. It seems likely that it was situated on a spit, a forerunner of the present Spurn Point. There is some reference to an island suggesting that the sea occasionally overflowed the neck of the spit. The position of Ravenser Odd also fits in with the evidence that states that it lay 4 miles (6·4 km) south of Easington. By about 1330 the site of Ravenser Odd should have been becoming difficult to maintain. Mention of damage to the town first appears in 1310. Between 1327 and 1343 the references become more numerous, and by 1346 two-thirds of the town had been destroyed. Damage and destruction continued during 1350 to 1355, when there is reference to the destruction of the chapel of St Mary and damage to the graveyard. By 1362 the port was derelict.

The new feature that replaced the old spit is called Ravenser Spurn or Ravenspurn. The change in name is given in the Meaux Chronicle. It refers to a spit, not to a town. The next reference to the spit was in 1406. By 1428 there is reference to a hermit, who built the first lighthouse on the spit. This date is within a year or two of being 250 years earlier than Angell's lighthouse on the spit. A description of 1567 states that 'Ravensey Spurn is a sandy hill environed and compassed about upon the sea side with the sea and on the other side with the Humber.' The later stages of this cycle are shown on the earliest maps to show any reliable detail of the area. They are somewhat crude, dating from 1540 and 1580 approximately. Nevertheless the shape of the spit they indicate agrees with the corresponding stage of the next cycle, as shown in Tuke's map of Yorkshire in 1787 and the 1 inch to 1 mile Ordnance Survey map of 1824. The approaching breach is suggested by a survey of 1602, which refers to the 'wasting and the great Dekay of Ravinspourne'.

The spit that followed the seventeenth-century breach can be traced by reference to the succession of lighthouses that were built upon it. Lighthouses stood on Kilnsea Common or Point. The evidence given by seamen in the cases dealing with arguments over the lighthouses, indicates that in 1695 the spit did not extend as far south as the Den. The spit had by then been shortened by the breach. A chart accompanying sailing directions for entering the Humber, published in 1625, shows a short Spurn spit and a little island. Another chart of 1671 shows the tip of Spurn well short of the island, which is now called the Denn. A later publication, probably in 1675, shows the lighthouse built by Angell in 1673 to 1674 on the tip of the spit, indicating the stage to which the cycle had reached by this date. Spurn continued to grow longer in the following years, as testified by a variety of evidence. Smeaton's high lighthouse, built in 1776, lies just about 1680 m south of Angell's lighthouse. The need for a new lighthouse was recognized by 1760 as the old one was so far from the tip. The new lighthouse was 393 m from high-water mark by 1786. Growth continued into the nineteenth century.

There is also evidence of the westward retreat of the spit as a whole. Angell's lighthouse had to be resited in 1735, 1763 and 1776, and Smeaton's low lights were also affected, new ones being required in 1772, 1778, 1816, 1831 and 1851. The neck was also changing during the period. In 1789 a storm broke over the spit. This occurred with increasing frequency. The tip was also attacked from both sides, and dwindled in size markedly after about 1825. It was also increasingly referred to as the island of Spurn. The breach was eventually completed in a northwesterly gale of 28 December 1849, and was widened in 1850 to about 293 m at ordinary high tide. In 1851 it was 458 m wide and 4·88 m deep at high water. Other breaches occurred to the north in 1851 and 1856.

During the years 1852 to 1856 these breaches were closed artificially with considerable difficulty. The neck was strengthened by groynes and has been maintained artificially ever since. This new aspect in the situation has broken the cycle of development that caused a new Spurn Point to develop, grow and decay during a period of 240 to 250 years. Since the breach was artificially healed in the middle of last century erosion has continued to the north. The spit has continued to grow southwards, and has redeveloped its spatulate form, as material continues to move southwards along the seaward side of the spit. The dunes on the spit have also increased in height, owing to the increase of material on the beach resulting from the building of the groynes.

The historical evidence on which the cyclic development of the feature has been based is particularly full in this instance, owing to the importance of the Humber to shipping and for port facilities. From the geomorphological point of view the spit is of considerable interest in that it is situated adjacent to a coast of long-continued and severe erosion. The intimate relationship between the two different coastal processes indicates the necessity of studying the whole situation in attempting to explain the growth and development of coastal features. The cyclic nature of the spit development can be matched to a certain extent at the southern end of the Lincolnshire coast. Accretion on the coast south of Skegness has already been described. The spit in this area has been shown to undergo a cyclic development of a less regular kind than that taking place at Spurn Point. It is, however, one in which a succession of spits can be identified on the evidence of old maps and other historical and geomorphological evidence.

Summary

Historical evidence gives a consistent picture of the incursion of the sea along the Lincolnshire coast, since the stormy thirteenth century. Reference is made to loss of land and damage to the sea-banks, which have been a necessary defence. Clear descriptions of flooding due to surges is given for 1735, similar to that of 1953.

The Dungeness area has built out mainly since Neolithic times. The evidence is found in records of land reclamation, or inning, dating from the eighth century onwards. There is evidence of Roman activity in the marsh area, as the Rhee wall drainage ditch is probably Roman. Erosion has taken place locally, including the destruction of Winchelsea in 1287, but from this time on New Winchelsea has been isolated from the sea by accretion. The outgrowth is indicated by cartographic evidence as well as that of buildings, of which Camber Castle is the most conspicuous.

Spurn Point has undergone a cyclic development of growth and subsequent decay, the period of the cycle being about 250 years. The new spit, which grows south from the erosion coast of Holderness, lies northwest of its predecessor. It becomes gradually longer until its neck is weakened by exposure to wave action, which increases as the coast to the north is cut back by erosion. A breach in the neck of the spit isolates the distal portion to form an island, which is gradually eroded away as a new spit develops to the north. Evidence for the cyclic development is found in various forms, such as maps and litigation over the positions of the various lighthouses that have been built on the spit.

References

BOER, G. DE 1963: Spurn Point and its predecessors. *The Naturalist* **887,** 113–20 (Hull).

BOER, G. DE 1964: Spurn Head: its history and evolution. *Trans. Inst. Brit. Geogr.* **34,** 71–89.

BOER, G. DE and CARR, A. P. 1969: Early maps as historical evidence for coastal change. *Geog. J.* **135**(1), 17–39.

ELLIOTT, J. 1847: Account of the Dymchurch Wall. *Mins. Proc. Inst. Civ. Eng.* **6,** 486.

HOMAN, W. MACL. 1938: The marshes between Hythe and Pett. *Sussex Arch. Coll.* **79.**

LEWIN, T. 1862: *The invasion of Britain by Julius Caesar.* 2nd edition. London.

LEWIS, W. V. 1932: The formation of Dungeness foreland. *Geog. J.* **80,** 309–24.

LEWIS, W. V. and BALCHIN, W. G. V. 1940: Past sea-levels at Dungeness. *Geog. J.* **96,** 258–85.

LOVEGROVE, H. 1953: Old shorelines near Camber Castle. *Geog. J.* **119,** 200–207.

OLDFIELD, E. 1829: *History of Wainfleet and the Wapentake of Candleshore,* 366. London.

OWEN, A. E. B. 1952: Coast erosion in east Lincolnshire. *Lincs. Hist.* **9,** 330–39.

OWEN, A. E. B. 1961: The Levy Book of the Sea: the organisation of the Lindsey sea defences in 1500. *Lincs. Archit. and Archaeol. Soc. Rep. and Pap.* **9**(1), 35–48.

RICE-HOLMES, T. 1907: *Ancient Britain and the invasions of Julius Caesar.*

ROBINSON, A. H. W. 1955: The harbour entrances of Poole, Christchurch and Pagham. *Geog. J.* **121,** 33–50.

ROBINSON, A. H. W. 1962: *Marine Cartography in Britain.* Univ. of Leicester.

SWINNERTON, H. H. 1931: The post-glacial deposits of the Lincolnshire coast. *Quart. J. Geol. Soc.* **87,** 360–75.

SWINNERTON, H. H. 1936: The physical history of east Lincolnshire. *Trans. Lincs. Nat. Trust Pres. Add.,* 91–100.

WARD, G. 1933: The River Limen at Ruckinge. *Arch. Cant.* **45,** 129.

19 Features characteristic of steep, indented coasts

1 **The initial form and modifying processes**

2 **Modifications produced:** a) By erosion; b) By deposition.

3 **Classification of depositional forms**

4 **Processes related to accumulation forms**

5 **Examples of accumulation features:** a) Spits: (*i*) *Complex initial form—Clew Bay*; (*ii*) *Importance of exposure and material—Dingle Bay*; (*iii*) *Spit structure and development—Derrymore spit*; (*iv*) *Unusual events—Godivari spit*; b) Tombolos; c) Barriers; d) Cuspate forelands.

Summary

From the point of view of description and explanation of the origin and development of coastal features it is necessary to classify the wide variety of coasts into a few groups. In this chapter the features characteristic of steep, indented coasts will be considered. The reason for selecting this particular type of coast is that all coasts in this category have certain characteristics in common. These include:

1   A complex pattern of longshore drift.
2   A variety of beach type, ranging from rocky coasts with only a few large rocks on a rock platform, through pocket beaches of boulders, shingle, sand or a mixture of these materials, to wide sandy beaches or shingle structures.
3   A complex, irregular outline.

On a coastline of this type erosion and accumulation forms are both important, and the variety of the latter is particularly great. The sections of this chapter, therefore, deal first with modification of this type of coast by (a) erosion and (b) deposition. The types of deposition are classified and the processes relating to the formation of the various features are analysed, with particular reference to spit formation. Then examples of different types of feature will be discussed.

The result of the changes taking place along the coast is in general to straighten its outline. Not all the processes, however, produce this result. Some features that make the coast more irregular will be mentioned. One of the most important processes bringing about these changes is the alongshore movement of material. The importance of longshore drift has been stressed in the discussion of coastal erosion, and its importance in coastal accretion has also been indicated.

1 The initial form and modifying processes

The initial form is theoretically one which has not been altered at all by marine agencies. The sea comes to rest against an area of diverse relief with fairly steep slopes. This form is well shown in the Marlborough Sound area off the northern South Island of New Zealand (C. A. Cotton, 1954). This mountainous area has been submerged recently and even the headlands are not yet cliffed. This coastal type is most often formed as the result of submergence, but need not necessarily be initiated in this way. It is what D. W. Johnson (1919) considered to be the typical shoreline of submergence.

The most important modifying process on such a coast is wave action. The effect of the outline of the coast on the pattern of wave attack is significant. Wave attack will be very uneven in intensity on an indented coast. Refraction will concentrate the energy of the longer waves on the headlands and dissipate it in the bays. Waves will approach parts of the coast obliquely, causing longshore movement of beach material, which will tend to move towards the bays. The direction of movement of beach material will not necessarily be in a uniform direction along large stretches of coastline. Headlands still hamper the free movement of material alongshore.

On an indented coast of this type it is likely that the tidal range will vary from place to place and that tidal streams will be locally strong, particularly where there are narrow straits through which the tide flows. Tidal streams may be locally important in the movement of material. On the whole, however, the direction of wave approach is the fundamental factor on which the direction of movement depends in the early stage of development. The direct influence of the wind in the early stage is very small. There is little loose beach material available, and the steep slope of the land prevents deposition of wind-blown sand. The wind is largely important in its effect on the waves. The absence of beach material is important at first, in that waves have access to the rocks of the headlands at least, allowing these to be cliffed. This process, however, provides material that can initiate the formation of beaches. In the bays, however, rivers will provide the bulk of the material forming the bay-head beaches. The character of the cliffs and the type of material brought down by the rivers will determine the size of the beach material. The resultant shore forms will vary according to whether sand or shingle predominates in the beach material.

The modification of a coast of this type is likely to be delayed if the sea level is rising, because the waves cannot attack the cliffs at the same position for long enough to erode them. A static sea level will allow a more effective attack on the rocks along the coast, at first at least. In the later stages, when the offshore zone has been shallowed, a rising sea level will help to prolong the stage of active erosion.

2 Modifications produced

a By erosion

The absence of beaches allows the waves to attack the rocks. Their attack is most effective where their energy is concentrated on the headlands. In general this has the effect of straightening the coastline, which is the ultimate aim of the marine forces. In detail, however, the initial result may be the reverse. If the rocks are of uneven resistance to marine erosion, the softer ones will be worn away more quickly and the coast will become more irregular. The initial increase in the detailed complexity of the coastal outline produces a 'crenulate' coast. It is well illustrated in the coasts of southwest Wales and parts of the southwest peninsula of Devon and Cornwall, shown in figure 19-1.

Coastal irregularity due to differences of rock resistance is very clearly shown in the part of the coast of Dorset where the strike of the rocks trends parallel to the coast. The resistant Portland and Purbeck rocks have been narrowly breached at Lulworth Cove, and the wider bay behind has been scooped out in the soft Wealden clay inland of the limestone. Stair Hole to the west of the Cove illustrates an earlier stage of development, where the hard rock has only just been breached by a tunnel. The sea is starting to remove the softer rock from behind, in which it is assisted by much slumping and mudflow activity in the clays (G. M. Davies, 1935). The various stages, including the more open Worbarrow Bay to the east, are shown in figure 19-2.

b By deposition

During the early stage of modification of a steep indented coast the features formed by deposition are many and varied. Their form depends mainly on the type of material available and on the

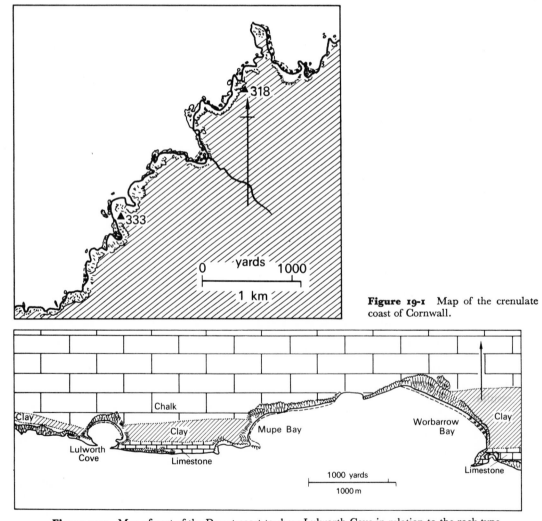

Figure 19-1 Map of the crenulate coast of Cornwall.

Figure 19-2 Map of part of the Dorset coast to show Lulworth Cove in relation to the rock type.

relationship between the coastal outline and the incidence of wave forces. In considering the form of the depositional features there are two tendencies to be taken into account. Firstly, the movement of material along the shore tends to prolong the direction of the solid coastline at points where there is an abrupt change in direction of the rocky shore. Secondly, there is the tendency for wave-built structures to turn to face the direction from which the dominant waves are approaching. The former process depends on the movement of material alongshore, either under the influence of short, and therefore, less refracted, waves with an oblique approach, or under the influence of long, greatly refracted waves. The long refracted waves develop convergences or divergences of energy. Longshore movement takes place from zones of high energy to zones of low energy.

Which type of wave is dominant on beaches depends on the material. Storm waves, which can form beach ridges at the limit of the swash, are dominant on shingle beaches. These ridges are relatively permanent features. The importance of the material in the reaction of shore features to storm waves is mentioned by S. Ting (1937), who considered that storm waves are responsible for the formation of shingle features at great heights above sea level. Such features as Brodrick Bar (barrier), which is a bay-head barrier, on the other hand, are composed entirely of fine sand. This feature is formed by the action of normal swell waves.

The process causing prolongation of the direction of the solid coast operates equally well on sand or shingle. The spit at Gibraltar Point is predominantly sand. It prolongs the north–south coast of Lincolnshire where this turns sharply west. Spurn Head, which is a mixture of sand and shingle, also prolongs the direction of the Holderness coast. The orientation of wave-built features was considered in more detail in chapter 13. Longshore movement of material generally tends to straighten the coastline. The tendency of structures to face the dominant waves can produce greater irregularity of outline. The two processes are linked by the fact that longshore movement of material is necessary in reorientating structures to become aligned normal to the direction from which the dominant waves come. The realignment may be achieved entirely by deposition, or by erosion, or a combination of the two processes. The outbuilding of False Cape on the east coast of Florida is depositional, while the form of Dungeness is due to both erosion and deposition, the south side showing the effects of erosion, and the east of deposition. Other examples of somewhat similar types are illustrated and discussed by A. Schou (1945) with reference to the coast of Denmark.

If the prevalent and dominant waves come from the same direction, both processes will tend to favour the development of a shoreline perpendicular to the approach of the dominant waves, as pointed out by W. V. Lewis (1938). If the supply of beach material is restricted by headlands, then the dominant waves will the more readily be able to turn the coastline to face their direction of approach. The material can be moved to the down-drift end of the bay, until longshore movement is stopped. The beach will now face the direction from which the waves come. W. V. Lewis (1938) considered that if the bay is fairly restricted, the shore will tend to form an almost circular arc. Lines drawn normal to the shore will meet near the centre of the bay. He did not, however, take into account the effect of wave refraction, and this will account for the form of the bay.

Where the direction of approach of the waves is very oblique to the shore, as along parts of the east coast of England, longshore movement will be the predominant process. As a result, spits may be expected to form, particularly where the coastline is open in nature, as in east Yorkshire, Lincolnshire and east Norfolk and Suffolk. These features will form where the coast makes a sudden change in orientation, or where rivers and estuaries enter the sea. Examples of such features are the spits of Spurn Head, Gibraltar Point, Yarmouth spit and the more complex feature of Orfordness in Suffolk.

3 Classification of depositional forms

A classification of the very diverse forms of accumulation can best be made on the basis of the processes responsible for their formation and character. The main categories of features are the following—(1) beaches, (2) spits, (3) tombolos, (4) barriers and (5) forelands. The characteristics that differentiate these groups are as follows:

Beaches— are attached along their whole length to the mainland coast
Spits— are attached at one end to the mainland
Tombolos—are attached at both ends, one end being an island
Barriers— are attached at both ends, both ends being on the mainland, although they may
have tidal or river inlets through them
Forelands—project out from the coast usually rendering the outline more irregular. The full
classification is given in table 19-1 and illustrated in figure 19-3.

Table 19-1   Classification of accumulation forms on a steep, indented coast

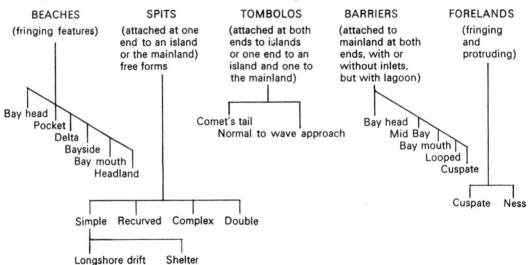

Note: The forms characteristic of a steep, indented coast can be of either sand, shingle or mixed, or boulders.

The second criterion for subdivision consists of the position of the feature relative to the coastal indentations. The third criterion is the nature of the material forming the feature. This classification is similar to that suggested by V. P. Zenkovich (1967), in which he differentiates the following classes: Attached forms, free forms, hooked forms, fringing forms, detached forms. His classification is given in table 19-2. He emphasizes the importance of the method of supply of material and its source, by separating features fed from only one direction from those fed from both alongshore directions and those fed from the bottom. His description does not restrict the term 'spit' to a free form, attached only at one end. In the previous scheme the term 'spit' is reserved for features of this type, and the term 'barrier' for features attached to the mainland at both ends, with a lagoon between the barrier and the shore. Some confusion may arise in the use of the term 'barrier', since in the next chapter it is used for features that can be free at both ends. In an attempt to avoid ambiguity, the feature discussed in the next chapter will be

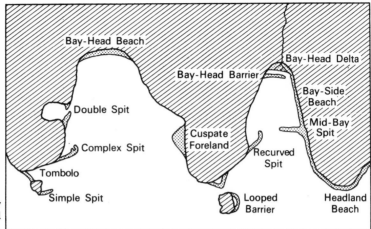

Figure 19-3 Diagram to show different types of depositional features on a steep indented coast.

Table 19-2 Classification of coastal accumulation forms. *After V. P. Zenkovich* (1967)

I   ATTACHED FORMS
      1 *Beaches*
      2 *Above-water terraces (berms):*
          a) On smooth and projecting sectors of coast
          b) Filling indentations: Simple (unilateral), or double
      3 *Forelands, relative length to width less than unity:*
          a) Simple (unilateral, symmetrical*)*, rounded, cuspate
          b) Double (symmetrical), rounded, cuspate

II   FREE FORMS (relative length greater than unity)
      4 *Spits (simple forms fed from one direction only):*
          a) Continuing line of the original coast or curving into bays
          b) Trending seawards from the coast
      5 *Spits (fed from both sides, usually symmetrical relative to the original coast)*

III   BARRIERS (extending from the original coast and enclosing a lagoon)
      6 *Looped barrier (symmetrical rounded form)*
      7 *Double fringing barrier*
      8 *Bracket-shaped barrier*
      9 *Double fringing spit*

IV   LOOPED FORMS (both ends connected to the shore)
      10 *Barrier beaches (enclosing a bay)*
      11 *Tombolos linking island to mainland:*
          a) Asymmetrical
          b) Symmetrical
      12 *Tombolos between islands*

V   DETACHED FORMS
      13 *Barrier beaches (not in contact with the coast for long distances)*
      14 *Accumulation islands:*
          a) Relict forms
          b) In the course of formation

referred to as a barrier island. It has a lagoon, but need not be attached at either end, and usually is broken by tidal inlets. Zenkovich's recognition of the importance of longshore movement of material in the formation of depositional features confirms the importance of this process, which has already been stressed.

4 Processes related to accumulation forms

V. P. Zenkovich has made a theoretical analysis of the development of accumulation forms. He considers a re-entrant along a coast on which material is moving alongshore. The wave resultant lies normal to the inset part of the coast, as shown in figure 19-4A. The material will accumulate until the re-entrant has been filled and will then extend upcoast as long as the supply continues. If it is cut off the material will move around the indentation until the beach has been built up to fit the refracted wave fronts in the embayment. The final form will depend on the relative rates of longshore movement along the different sectors of the coast, in terms

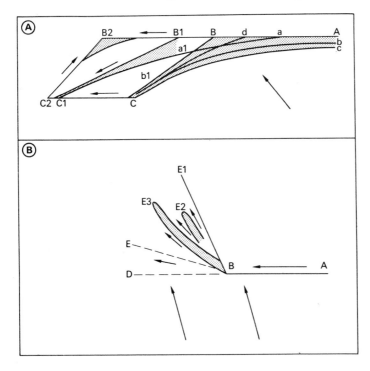

Figure 19-4 Diagrams to illustrate **A:** the theoretical filling of a coastal angle; **B:** the alignment of a spit relative to the amount of longshore drift. (*A, B after Zenkovich, 1967.*)

of the refracted wave energy. Only where there is a decrease in movement alongshore will accumulation result in the development of a stable form. This will only be maintained as long as the longshore drift is consistent and unchanged in amount or direction.

Zenkovich has also considered the alignment of a spit resulting from longshore drift moving material past an abrupt change in coastal direction, as shown in figure 19-4B. The resulting direction will depend on the relationship between the angle of wave approach and the line of the coast. The capacity of the longshore drift will increase at the point B as the angle between the wave resultant and the coastline increases. Wave refraction will lead to a reduction of wave energy in the portion BE. The more oblique the waves in the section BE, the lower will be their energy, but the higher will be the rate of longshore movement. If there is a decrease in the capacity of flow at B, then deposition will occur at this point. The material will begin to form a spit, because it cannot move past the initial deposit towards E. The angle of the spit will divide the angle E_1BD into two sectors, with a larger capacity of flow towards BD than along AB. The capacity will be smaller in the sector E_2BE_1. As the form is free it will lie along E_3, the line along which the capacity of flow is the same as along AB. If it lay near BD the movement along it would be greater than along AB so its face would be eroded and it would retreat towards BE_1. If the spit lay along the line BE_2, where the longshore movement is less than along AB, material would be added to the face until it lay along the line BE_3. The flow would then be uniform along the whole stretch, including the spit.

The argument assumes a balance between the increase of longshore drift due to the greater angle to the wave resultant and the decrease due to the reduction of wave energy. The reduction of energy is due to refraction, because the angle between the waves and the coast increases. The argument would account for the change in angle where a spit leaves the mainland, in terms of the wave direction resultant and the amount of longshore drift. There are examples, however, where a spit turns seaward from the mainland coast. Hurst Castle spit in Hampshire can be cited as one instance. The reason for this has already been considered in chapter 13, in dealing with the orientation of beach features. In this connection it is important to take into account the material of which the feature is formed, a factor also considered in chapter 13. It is one of the criteria used for subdivision of the depositional forms indicated in table 19-1. Sand features will be more affected in their orientation by the refracted swells, which are most important in building them up. Shingle features will respond more to the direction from which the storm waves come. These waves form the most permanent features in shingle. Zenkovich's analysis is a rather drastic over-simplification of the real situation, in that he does not differentiate between the waves that bring the material to the spit, and the waves that build it up. These may be the same in some instances, but often they are not.

Another important point concerning the pattern of accumulation forms was made in the description of forms in chapter 16. This is the distinction between forms that are primarily aligned normal to the wave approach, and those that lie parallel to it. The former represent those features that formed to fit the wave fronts. They include features that are fringing, free at one end or tied at both ends. The latter represent features that are dependent upon the shelter provided by a solid outcrop. They include several types of tombolos and some spits, such as the comet's tail type. The existence of shelter can also account for many cuspate forms, particularly when combined with the effects of wave refraction. The cuspate features grow towards the sheltering object rather than forming behind it.

The practical importance of shelter in promoting accumulation is clearly seen in the work carried out to prevent erosion at Port Hueneme in California. The normal flow of material alongshore was interrupted in this area by the building of the port breakwater in 1940, leading to erosion of 917,000 m^3/year down-drift of the breakwater. W. J. Herron and R. L. Harris (1967) describe the sand by-passing plant built to overcome this problem. The scheme was started in 1960 to 1961 by constructing a harbour up-drift and an offshore breakwater 700 m long at a depth of 9·15 m. The breakwater provides shelter for the harbour and served as a sand trap. Three cycles of biennial sand by-passing have been successfully completed and have supplied 8,410,000 m^3 to the eroding shoreline at an average cost of 0·3 dollars/m^3. The sand trap dimensions are related to the diffraction patterns of the prevailing wave trains at both ends of the offshore breakwater. The rate of impoundment is equal to the rate of littoral drift in the area. It was concluded that the offshore breakwater aligned parallel to the coast provides the most positive method of trapping littoral sand known at present. It will trap sand moving either up- or down-drift and is nearly 100% effective if its length is suitably related to its distance offshore. The standard diffraction pattern for the prevailing waves provides a method of establishing the optimum size of the structure in relation to the required amount of sand and the dimensions of the sand trap.

One of the positions in which spits and other forms are most likely to occur is at the mouth of a river or estuary. The forces important in the formation of features in this situation have been considered by C. Kidson (1963). The presence of the estuary interrupts the movement of material along the coast, and on tidal coasts the diurnal ebb and flow of the tide into the estuary is also important. The tidal streams frequently cut across the direction of longshore drift: rivers and estuaries are not necessarily barriers to the flow of material along the coast, and several studies, such as that of P. Bruun and F. Gerritson (1959), show that material can move across estuaries. The movement may take place around a bar at the mouth of the estuary, despite very strong tidal streams. This process has been demonstrated by studies with radio-active tracers off the River Ore at the tip of Orfordness.

Often a large amount of material is deposited in estuaries to form various types of spits and barriers. Some estuaries are completely closed in this way. Loe barrier on the coast of Cornwall exemplifies this situation. It can only occur where the amount of water draining out of the estuary is very small, or where the barrier is very permeable.

Differing views have been expressed concerning the formation of features in bays and estuaries. A. H. W. Robinson (1955), for example, has discussed the formation of double spits. He produced cartographic evidence to suggest a method by which two spits trending in opposite directions could almost close a bay. The examples he cites are on the south coast of England at Poole, Christchurch and Pagham. The latter harbour, shown in figure 19-5, is almost closed by two spits. One trends northeast from the southern headland of Selsey Bill, continuing the line of the coast, while the other trends southwest from the opposite shore, near the Pagham beach estate. The cartographic evidence points to this pattern being due to the breaching of a spit, which had grown from southwest to northeast across the bay. An earlier spit is shown on a map of 1909 extending right across the harbour entrance. The material of which the spits are formed is derived from the rapid erosion that is taking place in the weak deposits of Selsey Bill to the southwest. During 1910 the continuous spit was breached by storm waves at a point about half way along its length. Two spits were then left trending in opposite directions, giving the double spit feature. Periodic changes in the position of the harbour outlet made the spits of different lengths at different times. The double spit form is, in this instance, the result of breaching by storm waves or flood waters of an originally single shingle bank. Robinson's hypothesis for this particular feature seems more satisfactory than other theories, one of which suggests that the spit is due to local counter-drift resulting from irregularities along the coast.

C. Kidson (1963) does not, however, believe that Robinson's explanation is always applicable. There are situations in which spits grow in opposite directions in neighbouring estuaries. In these instances it is not possible to account for the pattern by breaching. An important point, which is stressed by Kidson, is that longshore drift is rarely only in one direction all the time on any stretch of coast, even if there is a predominant net direction of drift along the coast. The importance of drift from both directions is illustrated by reference to other examples of double spits. In Bridgwater Bay a breach occurred in 1783 in a spit at the mouth of the River Parrett, isolating its distal end to form Stert Island. Between 1783 and 1840 the breach widened, but subsequently two spits grew, one from the mainland and one from the island. In the twentieth century the breach was reduced as the two spits grew towards each other, decreasing the gap to a third of its maximum size. Studies on the movement of shingle at Stert Point on the mainland showed conclusively that material is moving eastwards. It was also demonstrated that material from the island moves south.

Another instance of a double spit, discussed by Kidson, is found in the Taw–Torridge estuary, which is partially closed by the sand-dune-covered spit of Braunton Burrows and the pebble ridge of Westward Ho. These spits extend across the mouth of the estuary from north and south respectively. They appear to have been built independently from opposite directions. The spits

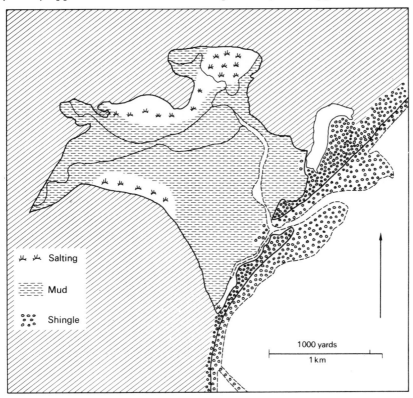

Figure 19-5 Map of the double spits of Pagham Harbour, Sussex.

seem to have been essentially stable since 1575, according to Saxton's map. Drift on the Westward Ho ridge is to the north, a direction confirmed by mineral evidence in the sand. On Braunton Burrows the drift is in the opposite direction.

In the Exe estuary there are two spits on either side of the estuary. Dawlish Warren extends northeast from the western side, and Exmouth Point extends from the eastern side. These spits are liable to breaching, but there is no evidence to suggest that the breach in one is related to changes in the other. Warren Point was breached in 1809. It had healed by 1839, but by 1851 its distal tip had been eroded. By 1950 it had again grown longer than before. The eastern end is thus very unstable and frequent breaching occurs with equally rapid rebuilding. During all these changes the Exmouth spit opposite has been very stable. Material from one spit does not appear to reach the other.

On intricate coastlines, such as those studied by Kidson, the dominant direction of drift can vary over short distances. At any one point it can vary with time, as the direction of wave approach varies. The direction of drift is determined by wave refraction, which is affected by the bottom contours and by variations in direction of wave approach in deep water. The approach direction will be particularly variable in the storm wave environment characteristic of the British coasts. The British Isles are situated, especially in winter, at the junction of major climatic influences. Winds from all directions may be experienced.

One characteristic of the accumulation forms typical of a steep indented coast is that they show great variety. Many of them are unstable, showing rapid changes and a geologically rapid evolution. It is impossible to describe all the wide variety of features, but in the next section some examples will be discussed. The form of the features often provides evidence of their earlier phases of growth, and this aspect will be considered also. The variety of form is partly related to the variety of drift direction, with opposite movements often in close proximity. A situation where movement in opposite directions along a beach will occur has been mentioned in discussing J. L. Davies's hypothesis of sand beach orientation. He shows that where a beach in a bay is not yet adjusted to the refracted waves it will have a sharper curvature than the wave crests. The curvatures will be reduced by the material from both sides moving towards the centre of the bay. The same process can operate in the formation of spits, and an example from Dingle Bay will be considered in the next section.

5 Examples of accumulation features

The criteria by which accumulation forms may be classified are divided by V. P. Zenkovich (1967) into morphological, dynamic and genetic. In the first category he lists 5 criteria:

  1   Shape
  2   Orientation (whether symmetric or asymmetric relative to the coast)
  3   Position (whether on the open coast, in bays on islands, behind islands, at the mouth, middle or head of a bay, on a cape, or strait or whether paired)
  4   Secondary morphological criteria (curvature, presence of hooks or secondary forms on the rear side)
  5   Size and numerical index of shape (ratio of length to width).

The dynamic category includes 8 criteria:

  1   Stable and mobile forms
  2   Growth mechanism
  3   Degree of mobility, autochthonous or subject to displacement
  4   Position, whether coastal, bottom or mixed
  5   Level of development
  6   Relative vertical movements
  7   Contemporary activity
  8   Direction from which material is supplied.

The genetic category has 6 subdivisions as follows:

  1   The main process in the supply of material
  2   Sources of supply, coastal erosion, alluvium, marine organic matter, wind-borne material

3 Causes of accumulation
   a) Upward and downward displacement
   b) Lateral displacement, filling an angle, passage of material around a projection, external shelter, decline in the wave energy field
4 Dependence of forms, primary, secondary and induced
5 Conditions of the wave regime
6 Stage of development, rudimentary, completely developed, relict or regenerated.

This very comprehensive classification allows features to be described in some detail, both in terms of their morphology and the processes that are important in their evolution. Not all possible combinations given in the classification can be described, but some of the most important aspects will be considered.

a Spits

Spits are free forms, and because they are only attached to the coast or an island at one point they develop a wide variety of types. Some spits are simple, others are recurved, and yet others are complex in various degrees. They can be of sand or shingle or a mixture of both. Some examples have already been considered to illustrate various points. In chapter 13 Hurst Castle spit was used as an example to illustrate the importance of waves coming from several distinct sources in the building of a shingle structure. It was also the model for computer simulation, discussed in chapter 2.

The cyclic growth of Spurn Head was described in chapter 18. It provided an example of the value of historical material in elucidating coastal development. This spit also demonstrates well the influence of longshore movement of material and the importance of a stable point of attachment in the prolonged stability of a spit. The retreat of the point of attachment is basically responsible for the cyclic nature of its development.

In chapter 16 the spit at Gibraltar Point in Lincolnshire was considered as part of the zone of accretion south of Skegness. It was shown that this spit also has a cyclic element. New spits form as the coast grows out eastwards, cutting off the supply of material to the old spit, thus preventing its further growth. In this situation it is more likely to be lost by later burial under marsh deposits than to be lost by erosion as happens to Spurn Head.

Complex spits that owe their form to rapidly shallowing seas in areas of isostatic falling sea level have been described in chapter 7. Examples on Foley Island off Baffin Island were cited. The chevron pattern of spits was described in chapter 13. Both these complex forms owe some of their characteristics to changes in level. The importance of the direction of longshore drift was stressed in the last section in considering double spits. In this section the examples will be chosen to illustrate other important features of spits. (i) In Clew Bay there are all stages in the formation of spits under unusual conditions related to the drowning of a drumlin field. This provides an intricate initial coastal form. (ii) A series of mid-bay spits in Dingle Bay illustrates the importance of exposure and availability of material. (iii) The stages of development of Derrymore spit in Tralee Bay can be deciphered by a study of its structure. (iv) An example, taken from the Indian coast, illustrates the importance of unusual events in the formation of a spit.

(i) Complex initial form—Clew Bay: Clew Bay is a deep indentation on the west coast of Ireland. At its head are numerous drowned and partially drowned drumlins. A. Guilcher (1962) has described the many spits that have developed as the drumlins have been attacked by the waves.

The forms depend on the direction of wave approach. If waves can attack the drumlin from two sides it is theoretically likely that spits will grow out on both flanks. They will form wings at either side. Eventually when all the drumlin has been eroded they could form an isolated ridge, which would soon disappear. If the waves can only approach from one direction then a comet's tail type of spit is likely to form in the lee of the drumlin. Material would be washed around it from the exposed side to the lee.

The shape of Clew Bay ensures that waves cannot come from a very wide range of angles, the major direction of wave approach being from the west. Three zones can be distinguished. In the centre and south-centre marine erosion is at a maximum. Large shingle spits have been built from the material eroded from the drumlins. Many of these are linked by the spits, which then strictly become tombolos, as they are attached to islands at both ends.

The pattern of the spits cannot be interpreted in the light of the present distribution of drumlins. Allowance must be made for some which have already been completely eroded away seawards of the remaining ones. Their foundations still support the spits elongated eastwards of their former sites. There are very good examples of the winged form deduced theoretically. Inishoo, Inishbee and Rabbit Island, for example, have a similar form. Cloghcormick illustrates the simple linear form: its drumlin is now only an eroded foundation. These forms are shown in figure 19-6. In places the wings from individual drumlins have become linked, as in the feature joining Dorinishmore and Dorinishbeg.

In the north of Clew Bay the process has not progressed so far. The drumlins are not yet linked and in many instances the formation of wings is in a very early stage. The wave attack is less strong here and the waves come more from the southwest. They attack the broad side of the drumlin, rather than the narrow side. At the southern side of the bay the wave attack is even less vigorous, and the drumlins are being linked by dune formation rather than by spits. The variations in the pattern of spit development as the drumlins are eroded can be seen to vary according to the nature of the wave attack. Its direction and intensity relative to the form of the drumlins determine whether the spit formation will be in the form of two wings, or one elongated spit. The maximum development has occurred where the wave intensity is greatest. In this zone the spits have become so long that in some instances they have linked separate drumlins to form tombolos.

(ii) *Importance of exposure and material—Dingle Bay:* Dingle Bay in County Kerry illustrates a number of points concerning the development of spits (A. Guilcher and C. A. M. King, 1961). This long bay, which is illustrated in figure 19-7, is open to the southwest, from which direction the long Atlantic swells can travel straight up it. There are three spits, which may be described as mid-bay spits, although they occur in the inner one third of the bay. They leave the land at an angle of almost 90°, extending towards the centre of the bay.

Conditions in the bay have been conducive to spit formation for a number of reasons. During the later stages of glaciation an ice front extended into the upper part of the bay, forming a moraine at the position of the innermost spit. The ice discharged a considerable amount of sandy outwash into the bay, thus providing the material for spit formation. Sea level was lower when the ice retreated and the floor of the bay would have been flat near the outer margin where the material was fine sand. The 9·15 m (5 fathom) line is 14·4 km from the head of the bay. The gradient from the water line of the outer spits to the 9·15 m line is 1 : 352, falling to about 1 : 440 between the 9·15 m and 18·3 m (10 fathom) lines. This slope is considerably flatter than the equilibrium gradient characteristic of the beaches on the seaward face of the outer spits, where the measured slope was 1 : 80. The outer spits, therefore, appear to have been formed

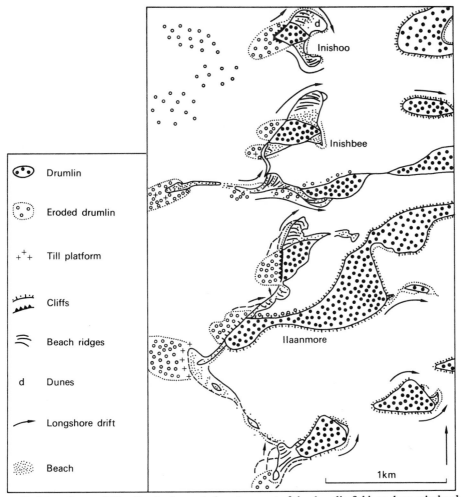

Drumlin

Eroded drumlin

Till platform

Cliffs

Beach ridges

d Dunes

Longshore drift

Beach

Inishoo

Inishbee

Ilaanmore

1km

Figure 19-6 Map of part of Clew Bay in the central western part of the drumlin field, to show spit development. (*After Guilcher, 1962.*)

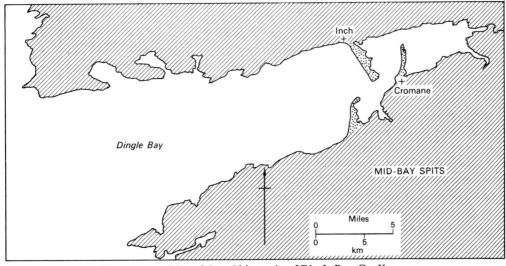

Inch

Cromane

Dingle Bay

MID-BAY SPITS

Miles
0   5
0   5
km

Figure 19-7 Map of the mid-bay spits of Dingle Bay, Co. Kerry.

by constructive wave action. The long southwesterly swells have built up their equilibrium gradient on a slope that was initially considerably too flat.

The two outermost spits (figure 19-8) are Rossbehy spit on the south side of the bay, and Inch spit on the north side. The position of Rossbehy spit does not appear to be related to the character of the mainland coast. It seems to have formed where the shallowing water allowed the waves to deposit their material and build up the spit. On the north side there is a slight indentation in the coast and this may account for the precise site of Inch spit. It is slightly further up the bay than Rossbehy spit.

Both spits narrow near their proximal ends, where they join the mainland. This feature could result from a poorer supply of sand to build dunes near the coast, but is more likely to be due

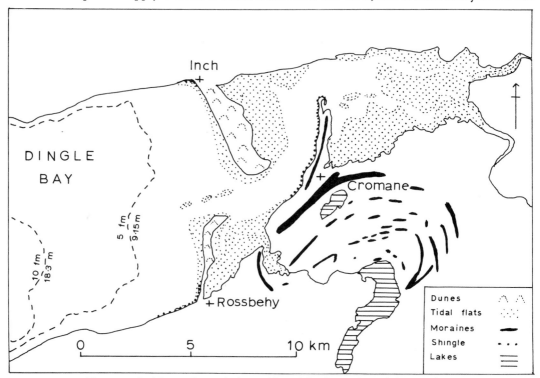

Figure 19-8 Map to show relative position of the three spits and the moraines.

to the tendency of the spit alignment to turn more towards the direction from which the swell comes up the bay. The distal ends of the spits are tending to move out towards the sea. Such a change of orientation would tend to cause erosion of the inner part of the spit, because material would move along the spits towards their distal ends as they swing round.

The same tendency has been noted in the way in which a bayhead beach tends to adjust its alignment to the swells (section 13-1(a)(iii)). It also applies to many other spits. Among these are included small spits in the Rade de Brest in Brittany, Spurn Head, for somewhat different reasons, the spit at Punta de Marca, which is 37 km long, closing Baia dos Tigres in South Angola. The tendency to proximal narrowing does not only apply to dune-covered spits, but also to shingle spits, such as Orfordness, Ero ar Saozon and Le Faou spit in the Rade de Brest. Narrowing at the root of the spit can develop so far that breaches occur at this position. They are often only at the high-water level, so that the spit can continue to grow, and the breaches are usually healed subsequently. Rossbehy spit illustrates this type of breaching. It is 3·6 km long, composed of shingle above mean high neap-tide level at its southern end, where it leaves the steep hillside. The sea can still pass over this low portion during storms, and the shingle at this end is in the form of a storm beach, reaching 2·74 m above high spring-tide level. The material comes from the coast seaward of the root of the spit. The increase in roundness and decrease in size indicate that the shingle moves along the spit towards its distal end. The shingle disappears about 800 m along the spit and the beach becomes sandy. Pebbles occur again near the distal end and on the landward side of the spit. The beach is backed by dunes where it is sandy. The dune belt is about 400 m wide and up to 15·25 m high. The beach profile has a gradient of 1 : 71 and forms a nearly straight line. It increases slightly in width towards the distal end of the spit, again suggesting movement of material to the north. A slight realignment of the spit is still in progress. The increasing amount of sand at the distal end is indicated by the formation of low ridges and runnels, which show up clearly on aerial photographs.

The Inch spit is longer and wider than the Rossbehy spit. It is about 4·8 km long and 1·2 km wide, and is almost entirely formed of sand, although a narrow belt of shingle exists at the northern end near the root. The flat gradient of 1 : 88 in the centre of the spit is due to the fine sand, which has a median diameter of 0·164 mm. The spit is also probably swinging slowly round about its root, as material moves along it. This movement is less marked than in Rossbehy spit and its width is more uniform. The greater width of Inch spit is due to the growth of sand dunes, which exceed 15·25 m in places. The dune form has suffered considerable destruction and the dunes are intensely eroded. The orientation of the large blow-outs is almost perpendicular to the beach alignment, indicating that the beach is orientated normal to the dominant wind. The eroded sand from the seaward side of the spit forms tongues of sand on the lee side. These tongue-shaped dunes are extending onto the sandy marsh. The spit is not being destroyed by this process, but is becoming wider, as there is a plentiful supply from the beach.

The innermost spit at Cromane is of a very different nature. The outer two spits are wave-formed features. Cromane spit, on the other hand, has been little modified by marine agencies, and is essentially a morainic structure. It is 2·4 km long and 460 to 550 m wide. It is sheltered from the open sea by the other two spits. The western beach consists mainly of shingle and there is a hooked bar of shingle at the northern distal end. The beach only extends 0·76 m above high spring tide at this point, in strong contrast to Rossbehy spit. The hooked bar has grown between 1842 and 1894, for which dates maps are available. It must have formed, therefore, under existing sheltered conditions. The central part of the spit is a mound 3 to 3·7 m high. It is a mixture of pebbles, sand, silt and clay. The stones have a low roundness value of 275, using Cailleux's index, compared with 325 at the northern end of the spit and 425 on the western beach at the south end. The central mound is part of the morainic ridge that marked the limit of the last ice advance.

The spit owes its form to erosion on the western side and to linking with the mainland by tombolo formation. It has not been affected by vigorous waves, suggesting that the outer spits formed at least as soon as Cromane spit. The difference is indicated by the higher roundness value of the Rossbehy shingle, which reaches 575, compared with 425 on the most exposed part of Cromane spit. The gradient of Cromane spit sand beach is steeper, owing to the restricted fetch. Only short waves can, therefore, be generated.

(iii) *Spit structure and development—Derrymore spit:* Derrymore spit is located on the northern side of the Dingle Peninsula in Tralee Bay. It is to the east of, and sheltered by, Castlegregory tombolo. Derrymore spit illustrates how the history of its growth can be established by a study of its form. It consists of a complex pattern of ridges, and can be called a complex recurved spit. (It is shown in figure 19-9.) It is situated in front of the Derrymore alluvial fan, which built a promontory at the coastline and determined the exact location of the spit. The spit is formed of pebbles. Old beach ridges are well preserved, and in places they are numerous and close together. The pattern shown in the figure is simplified. The only part of the spit where ridges do not occur is in the northwest, where they are buried by sand dunes, trending northeast to southwest, sand from the lower foreshore having reached them from the southwest. The upper foreshore consists only of pebbles.

Derrymore spit consists of three main sections of distinctly different ages. The older ridges have been subsequently truncated and now lie at right angles to the western shore. The truncation means that the western shore has retreated, and changed orientation considerably since

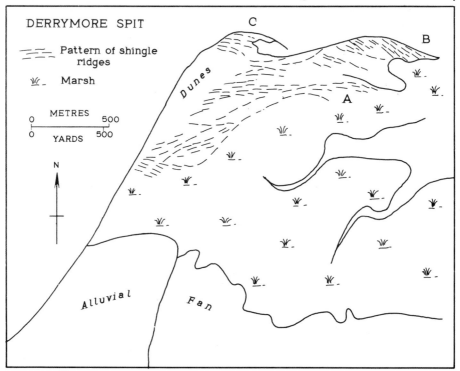

Figure 19-9 Map of Derrymore foreland. (*After Guilcher and King, 1961.*)

the early ridges were formed. The fulcrum of the spit has migrated in the process. The pattern of ridges is complex and there are some intervening swales. Beyond the old ridges, the outer part of the spit consists of three individual complexes each built successively beyond the earlier set. The eldest, marked A, lies to the east-southeast, the second, B, to the east-northeast and the youngest, C, lies to the northwest, where the modern beach drifting carries pebbles at present. Comparison of a map dated 1841 and the air photograph of 1949 shows that the development of the third ridge complex is still active. Between these dates the high-water mark retreated nearly 46 m eastwards along the western side. Nearly all the ridges of complex C formed during this interval. The alignment of these ridges illustrates the curvature of the wave crests due to refraction around the distal tip of the spit.

The pebbles on the northern and northeastern part of the spit also appear to be moving slowly along the outer edge of the spit towards B. They show a high degree of rounding. On the west side they have a mean roundness of 575 and at the eastern point B the value is 600. They cannot have come from the Derrymore fan, as the root of the spit lies to the west of the fan. They must have come from the drift deposits which form low cliffs between Derrymore spit and Castlegregory tombolo. The roundness of the pebbles in the drift is 275, indicating very efficient rounding by marine action in a short distance.

At present Derrymore spit is relatively sheltered, as it lies in the lee of the Castlegregory tombolo. The beach to the west of the spit is sandy, and there is no evidence of pebble movement along it at present. The situation can be explained, however, if Derrymore spit was formed before Castlegregory tombolo developed. In the absence of the tombolo, wave action would be much more vigorous: the erosion of the low cliffs could have supplied the shingle that makes Derrymore spit, and the previously more effective waves could round the Old Red Sandstone pebbles much more rapidly. Since Castlegregory tombolo has formed the material moving along the shore has been mainly sand. The sand has hidden the pebbles, and formed the dunes that bury some of the ridges.

The spit is, therefore, a fairly old feature. The changes in alignment of the several series of ridges indicate how the spit is becoming adapted to the cutting off of its source of supply of pebbles following the growth of the tombolo to the west. The pebbles on the spit are becoming redeposited to the north and east, as they are eroded from the western side. The whole feature is tending to migrate slowly by swinging around its root and moving bodily northeastwards.

(iv) *Unusual events—Godivari spit:* The changes in Derrymore spit were due to the cutting off of the pebble supply. The final example of a spit results from the sudden increase in material supply, and is the one formed north of the Godivari river mouth on the coast of India, which has been described by C. Mahadevan and R. Prasada Rao (1958). The spit has caused navigation problems as it extended northwards from Godivari Point, as shown on the series of outlines in figure 19-10. These maps are for dates between 1851 and 1929 and they illustrate the development and growth of the spit. It consists of sand and lies on the east side of Kakinada Bay, which is 77 km² in extent and has deep water. The Godivari delta lies on the southwestern side of the bay. The spit is on the eastern side of the delta where it extends north for about 16 km. It has an average width of 600 m and rises 1·52 to 2·44 m above sea level. It is washed over during spring tides and storms. The slopes on both the bay and the sea sides are steep.

The sand spit started to form between 1864 and 1878, and has continued to grow northwards since the latter date. The relatively sudden growth of the spit is due to a disturbance of the equilibrium situation, resulting from either marine causes or changes in the river. The spit could not have been caused by a shore structure as none had been built near enough to affect it. The cause of the spit is likely to be changes in the river basin, owing to floods or man-made disturbances causing excessive fluvial erosion. Cultivation, following deforestation, which took place particularly since 1874, resulted in an increase in soil erosion. The amount of sediment reaching the sea also increased. This material was built into the spit by the northern longshore drift. The tip of the spit later turned northwestwards.

The growth of the spit has disturbed the sediment circulation in the bay, and is resulting in erosion at Uppada. The erosion here may be the result of shelter provided by the spit. Waves are prevented from carrying material from the river to this part of the coast. The drift of material along the coast is not being replaced by material coming from further south.

This example provides evidence of the danger of disturbing the natural state of equilibrium. It shows how changes can have effects far beyond the immediate and obvious. It also illustrates

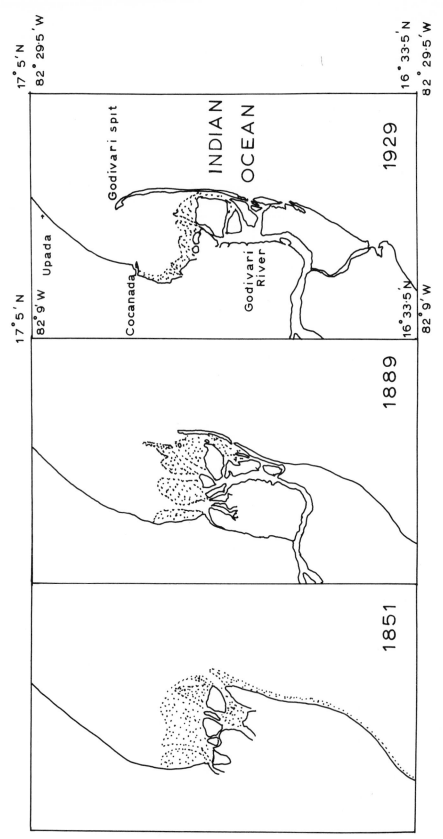

Figure 19-10 Maps to show the development of the Godivari spit on the coast of India. (*After Mahadevan and Prasada Rao, 1958.*)

how deposition in one area may cause erosion in an adjacent area. There are some points of similarity in the last two examples: in both instances deposition in one area was responsible for erosion elsewhere.

b Tombolos

The intricate outlines of southwest Ireland and Brittany provide many good examples of tombolos. Castlegregory tombolo, which was mentioned in the previous section, will be taken as an example of one type. Other examples have already been cited in chapter 16, in dealing with forms of accretion. Castlegregory tombolo is broad and sandy. At its root it divides into two ridges around the shallow lagoon of Lough Gill. Its width is increased by the spread of sand dunes

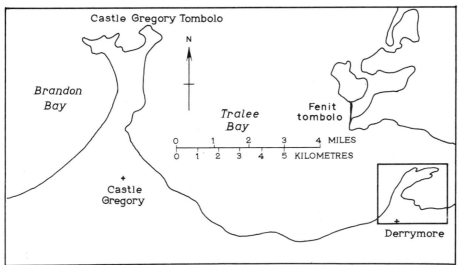

Figure 19-11 Map of Tralee Bay to show Castlegregory tombolo in relation to Derrymore spit. (*After Guilcher and King, 1961.*)

northeastwards. Its sandy beaches are shaped to fit the refracted swells, which reach the western side from the northwest. The distribution of pebbles shows that material moves northeastwards along the southern part of the west shore. Sometimes movement is southwards along the northern part of this coast, so that the tombolo is fed by drift material coming from both directions. On the east shore the drift is less easily determined, but it is probably southwards under the influence of westerly waves. The drift is certainly southwards at the mouth of Lough Gill, as the outlet of the lake is diverted south by the formation of a narrow spit.

There is a much narrower tombolo on the eastern side of Tralee Bay, linking Fenit Island to the mainland. This tombolo links the outer side of the island to the mainland. A marsh has formed in the shelter behind it. This is an example of the type of tombolo that faces the waves, and is curved to face the refracted swell coming into the bay from the west. Both tombolos are shown in figure 19-11 (A. Guilcher and C. A. M. King, 1961).

The tombolo shown in figure 19-12 forms a contrast. This tombolo is in the South Island of New Zealand. It is built of large shingle, and unlike the Fenit tombolo it is set back from the line of the coast. This position may be due to excessive depth of water at the entrance to Cable Bay. The tombolo faces the open sea in the same way, but at a position where the water is shallow enough for the waves to break. The landward side of the tombolo is shallow and the area is being silted up by deposits brought into the bay by the river. Marine action in this area is

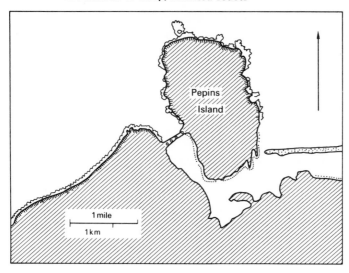

Figure 19-12 Map of the tombolo near Nelson, South Island, New Zealand.

excluded by the spit which almost closes the bay. The direction of longshore movement east of Pepin's Island is to the west. The tombolo is straight and, being formed of large shingle, is probably the product of storm waves. The shores of Cable Bay are steep, so the waves are little refracted in moving up the bay.

The tombolo at Roundstone in County Galway is a good example of a tombolo formed in the lee of an island. This sandy feature links a small island to the mainland. There are three beaches in the area. South Bay is situated at the seaward side of the island. Dog's Bay and Gorteen Bay lie on the west and east of the tombolo respectively. The beaches in the three bays are formed of white calcareous sand, consisting mainly of foraminifera. Although the beaches are similar in material size, their gradients differ. The difference can be explained in terms of their varying exposure. The outlines of the beaches are shaped by the waves, but these undergo a very different amount of refraction. Each beach conforms to the refracted direction of wave approach. The gradients of the three bays and their sand size and amount of refraction are shown below:

	Sand size mm	L.S.T.–H.S.T. Gradient 1:	L.N.T.–H.N.T. Gradient 1:	Orientation	Difference in orientation from 225°
Dog's Bay	0·152	21·6	23·4	121°	104°
Gorteen Bay	0·150	14·6	16·9	194°	31°
South Bay	0·200	17·3	18·7	291°	66°

The effect of differing exposure, resulting in much greater refraction on the tombolo beaches, can be seen in several variables. The sand size varies, the most exposed beach having the coarsest sand. On the other hand the gradient of the sheltered bays is flatter than those less sheltered, owing to the lower wave steepness of the waves. In the sheltered bays vegetation grows at a lower level relative to high-water level. It grows only 0·58 m above high water in Gorteen Bay, the most sheltered, 1·34 m in Dog's Bay and 1·86 m in the most exposed, South Bay. All the gradients are abnormally steep owing to the low density of the foraminiferal sand.

Other examples of tombolos formed in the shelter of islands do not necessarily show the effects of the refracted swells in the alignment of the bays on either side of the tombolo. This is so at Roundstone because the island is wide, relative to its distance from the shore. Where the island is narrow, as in the drumlins in central Clew Bay, or the small rocky islets described off the Brittany coast in chapter 16, then the tombolo is only a narrow ridge. This type grows out of the comet's tail spits already discussed. A tombolo forms as soon as the comet's tail reaches the coast or another island. The comet's tail spit elongates in the lee of the island. Deposits also grow out from the land, in a cuspate form, in the shelter of the offshore feature. The cuspate form often links with the comet's tail spit to form the tombolo. The features can be seen in all stages of development in the shoal area off northern Brittany (A. Guilcher *et al.*, 1959; M. Jussy and A. Guilcher, 1962).

Mention should also be made of the classic tombolo, which gave its name to these features, at Orbetello in Italy. This is a complex feature, being a double tombolo that links both sides of an island to the mainland. There is also a tombolo linking a small islet to the mainland between the two major tombolos; the tideless nature of the Mediterranean may have assisted in its formation. The single ridge in the centre is the shelter type of tombolo, while the other two face the approaching waves on either side of the larger island.

c Barriers

Barriers along steep coasts are usually shingle features. They often form complete barrages across the mouths of small estuaries. There are good examples on the south coast of England. At Loe Bar in Cornwall a barrier has formed of unusual material, which is intermediate between sand and shingle in size. This type of barrier is different from the sandy barrier islands. The barriers of steep coasts are usually smaller and shorter. Sandy barriers, which are discussed in the next chapter, are characteristic of flat coasts. The steep coast barriers are always attached to the land at both ends, although they are breached at times.

d Cuspate forelands

Nearly all the features that have been considered so far tend to straighten the coastal outline. There are some features, however, that create irregularities along the coast. The most important of these are the cuspate features. They are called forelands if they have no lagoon, but cuspate barriers if they enclose a lagoon. Cuspate features can form along coasts under two main conditions. Firstly, they may form in the shelter of offshore islands, as already mentioned. Alternatively, they may result from the restriction of wave approach direction, due to an intricate coastal outline.

J. N. Jennings (1955) has described a cuspate barrier foreland of the first type—Moila Point, shown in figure 19-13, which has grown out in the shelter of Shortland Island off Bougainville Island in the Solomon Islands. The sharp salient at the tip of the cuspate form is due to the island offshore, which prevents wave energy reaching the coast in its lee. Waves can be refracted to approach the two faces that are built of ridges parallel to the present shore.

Dungeness forms the best-known cuspate foreland in Britain. Its historical development has already been described in chapter 18. The sharp point of this feature is due to the proximity of France, which prevents waves approaching from the southeast. At the present time shingle is being eroded from the western side, while ridges are being built by waves coming from the northeast across the southern North Sea on the eastern side. The ridges on the western side are abruptly truncated by the present shoreline. Morfa Dyffryn in Cardigan Bay is another example of a cuspate feature built out into a bay. The feature is built out at a slight angle to the coast, owing to its tendency to face the direction of approach of the dominant waves coming up the Irish sea. These two features are relatively stable, and owe their form to the nature of the coastal outline. This restricts the directions from which waves can approach.

Features characteristic of steep, indented coasts

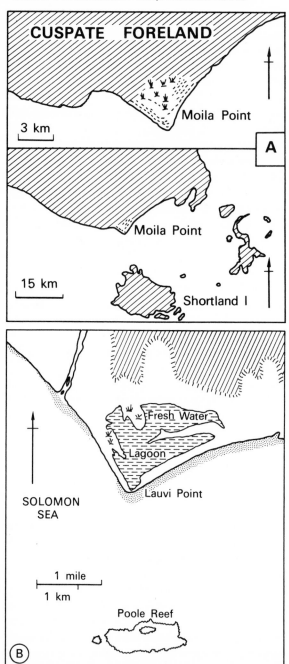

Figure 19-13 Cuspate forelands. **A:** Moila Point, Solomon Islands. **B:** Cuspate barrier at Lauvi Point, Guadalcanal. (*A after Jennings, 1955.*)

There are some features that are not stable in form or position. They move as cuspate irregularities along the coast. An example of such a feature is Benacre Ness on the coast of Suffolk, which has been studied by W. W. Williams and D. H. Fryer (1953) and W. W. Williams (1956). It is a smooth area of accretion, which has moved steadily northwards along the coast, from a position just north of Southwold. It was shown in this position in a survey by Saxton in 1575.

Bryant plotted it opposite Benacre Broad in 1826. On the Admiralty chart of 1940 it was shown over 1·2 km further north than its 1826 position, and it had moved another 400 m by 1955. By this date it lay within 1·6 km of Kessingland. The ness is formed of material derived from the soft cliffs of glacial sand and gravel, the former being much more plentiful. The material forming the ness, despite a superficial abundance of shingle, is largely sand. Many surveys have been carried out on the foreshore and extended offshore, and current observations have been made. No fully satisfactory reason for the northward movement of this zone of accretion was found, particularly as the general movement of material is south along this part of the coast. The northward movement need not be due to northward movement of material. If the sand moving from the north were deposited on the northern side of the ness, and the same amount of material eroded from the southern side, the feature would move north. This particular feature is of interest, because it is the only zone of accretion on a stretch of coast that is generally suffering severely from erosion. A possible reason for the unusual movement was suggested earlier in chapter 5, when tidal processes were considered. The movement of similar nesses of accretion on the East Anglian coast was shown to be related to the pattern of residual tidal streams. In this instance, therefore, it is the offshore relief and tidal streams, and not the outline of the coast and the waves, that are important in explaining the coastal outline.

The examples that have been cited in this chapter have drawn attention to the very great variety of forms of deposition on a steep, intricate coastline. Many further examples of complex features are described and illustrated by V. P. Zenkovich (1967), including many from the coasts of the U.S.S.R. In explaining the origin of these features, he rightly stresses the importance of the longshore movement of material. This process is responsible for the great variety of forms. Its variability on an intricate coast causes the complexity of the accumulation forms. Stability will not be reached in these conditions until the waves have adjusted the form of the coast in such a way that longshore transport is reduced to a minimum. The coastal outline will then fit the waves. A static state will not be reached even then. As long as the headlands are liable to erosion the form of the coast will continually be modified. The wave pattern in turn will also be modified.

Summary

Where the sea comes to rest against a steep indented land mass the coastal outline will be intricate, with bays and headlands. Longshore movement will be complex in pattern. The beach material will be variable along the coast and so also will be the incidence of wave attack. Modifying processes include cliffing at the headlands, where wave energy is concentrated. Where rocks are of uneven resistance, erosion of the softer strata will lead to a crenulate coastline developing. Depositional forms are varied, depending on the material available and the coastal outline. Features tend to prolong the direction of the mainland coast, and to turn to face the dominant waves, which will be storm waves on shingle beaches and long swells on sand features. Longshore movement tends to make the coast more regular, and is necessary in the realignment of the coast as it adjusts to the wave pattern.

The wide variety of depositional forms can be grouped into five main categories; these are beaches, spits, tombolos, barriers and forelands. Classifications are given of these forms in two slightly different ways in tables 19-1 and 19-2, the latter according to Zenkovich (1967). The theoretical orientation of free forms can be assessed in terms of the efficiency of longshore transport of sediment. The formation of double spits may in some instances be the result of breaching of a single continuous feature, but in others is due to drift from opposing directions. Accumulation forms can be classified according to morphological, dynamic or genetic criteria. Spits are free forms, and four different types of controls are discussed. The complex initial outline of the drowned drumlins in Clew Bay has given rise to winged islands and other complex forms. In Dingle Bay the exposure and type of material are important features in explaining the foundation of the three mid-bay spits. The outer two are wave-formed, while the inner one is a modified morainic deposit. The former illustrate the narrow root found in spits that are still adjusting their alignment to fit the swell. Derrymore spit on the north of Dingle Peninsula illustrates in its complex ridge structure the stages by which it has grown. It has been influenced by the cutting off of material supply by the growth of Castlegregory tombolo to the west. Godivari spit off the coast of India grew as a result of excessive erosion inland which caused an excess of material reaching the coast via the Godivari river. The spit grew during the nineteenth century. Tombolos form either normal or perpendicular to the wave approach direction. Barriers are not common, and forelands form where wave approach directions are limited.

References

BRUNN, P. and GERRITSEN, F. 1959: Natural bypassing of sand at coastal inlets. *J. Waterways and Harb. Div. Proc. Am. Soc. Civ. Eng.* **85,** 75–107.

CARR, A. P. 1965a: Shingle spit and river mouth: short term dynamics. *Trans. Inst. Brit. Geogr.* **36,** 117–29.

CARR, A. P. 1965b: Coastal changes at Bridgwater Bay 1956–64. *Proc. Bristol Nat. Soc.* **31**(1), 91–100.

COTTON, C. A. 1954: Deductive morphology and the genetic classification of coasts. *Sci. Month.* **78,** 163–81.

DAVIES, G. M. 1935: *The Dorset coast: a geological guide.* London: Murby.

EVANS, O. F. 1942: The origins of spits, bars and related structures. *J. Geol.* **50,** 846–65.

GUILCHER, A. 1962: Morphologie de la Baie de Clew (Compte de Mayo, Irlande). *Bull. Ass. Geog. France* **303–4,** 53–65.

GUILCHER, A. 1965: Drumlin and spit structures in the Kenmare River, southwest Ireland. *Irish Geogr.* **5**(2), 7–19.

GUILCHER, A., ADRIAN, B. and BLANQUART, A. 1959: Les queues de comète de galets et de blocs derrière des roches isolées sur les côtes nord-ouest et ouest de la Bretagne. *Norois* **22,** 125–45.

GUILCHER, A. and KING, C. A. M. 1961: Spits, tombolos and tidal marshes in Connemara and West Kerry, Ireland. *Proc. Roy. Irish. Acad.* **61** B **17,** 283–338.

GULLIVER, F. P. 1887: Dungeness Foreland. *Geog. J.* **9,** 636.

HERRON, W. J. and HARRIS, R. L. 1967: Littoral bypassing and beach restoration. Chapter 38 in *Proc. 10th Conf. Coast. Eng.,* 651–75.

HODGSON, W. A. 1966: Coastal processes around the Otago Peninsula. *N.Z.J. Geol. Geophys.* **9**(1–2), 76–90.

JENNINGS, J. N. 1955: The influence of wave action on the coastal outline in plan. *Australian Geogr.* **6**(4), 36–44.

JOHNSON, D. W. 1919: *Shore processes and shoreline development.* New York: Wiley.

JUSSY, M. and GUILCHER, A. 1962: Les cordons littoraux entre la Presqu'île de Quiberon et l'estuaire de la Vilaine. *Cah. Oceanog.* **14**(8), 543–72.

KIDSON, C. 1960: The shingle complexes of Bridgwater Bay. *Trans. Inst. Brit. Geogr.* **28,** 75–87.

KIDSON, C. 1963: The growth of sand and shingle spits across estuaries. *Zeits. für Geomorph.* NF **7**(1), 1–22.

KIDSON, C. 1964: Dawlish Warren, Devon: late stages in sand spit evolution. *Proc. Geol. Assoc.* **75**(2), 167–84.

LEWIS, W. V. 1932: The formation of Dungeness Foreland. *Geog. J.* **80**(4), 309–24.

LEWIS, W. V. 1938: The evolution of shoreline curves. *Proc. Geol. Assoc.* **49**, 107–27.

LEWIS, W. V. and BALCHIN, W. G. V. 1940: Past sea levels at Dungeness. *Geog. J.* **106**, 258–85.

MAHADEVAN, C. and PRASADA RAO, R. 1958: Causes of the growth of a sand spit north of the Godivari confluence. *Andhra Univ. Mem. Oceanog.* **62**(2), 69–74.

MII, H. 1956: Cuspate deposits within wave shadows along the coast of the Natsudomaii Peninsula, Aomori prefecture. *Saito Ho-on Kai Mus. Res. Bull.* **25**, 27–33.

OGILVIE, A. G. 1914: The physical geography of the entrance to Inverness Firth. *Scot. Geog. Mag.* **30**, 21–35.

ROBINSON, A. H. W. 1955: The harbour entrances of Poole, Christchurch and Pagham. *Geog. J.* **121**, 33–50.

SCHOU, A. 1945: Det Marine forland. *Folia Geogr. Danica* **4**, 1–236.

SPEIGHT, R. 1930: Lake Ellesmere Spit. *Trans. N.Z. Roy. Soc.* **61**, 147–69.

STEERS, J. A. (Editor) 1934: *Scolt Head Island.* (2nd edition, 1960.) Cambridge: Heffer. (269 pp.)

STEERS, J. A. 1964: *The coastline of England and Wales.* 2nd edition, Cambridge University Press.

TING, S. 1937: Shore forms in southwest Scotland. *Geol. Mag.* **74**, 132–41.

WILLIAMS, W. W. 1956: An east coast survey: some recent changes in the coast of East Anglia. *Geog. J.* **122**, 317–34.

WILLIAMS, W. W. and FRYER, D. H. 1953: Benacre Ness: an east coast erosion problem. *J. Inst. Chart. Surv.* **32**, 772–81.

ZENKOVICH, V. P. 1967: *Processes of coastal development.* (Steers, J. A., Editor), Edinburgh: Oliver and Boyd, chapters 7 and 8, 383–493.

20 Features characteristic of flat coasts

1 Origin

The essential characteristic of flat coasts is a low gradient, both offshore in the shallow marine environment, and onshore in the landward direction. Low-gradient coasts may be produced in a number of ways. D. W. Johnson (1919) considered that a flat coast would be likely to result from coastal emergence, but this can only occur where the offshore gradient is gentle. Against this view must be set the fact that sea level has risen over the whole world in the great post-glacial eustatic rise of sea level. Only in a few areas has the isostatic recovery more than compensated for this eustatic sea level rise, to produce emergent coasts. These areas are mainly restricted to high latitudes. Coasts showing the characteristics associated with a low gradient are most widespread in middle and low latitudes. Thus the cause that is responsible for the low-gradient coast must be sought elsewhere.

In suitable areas subsidence can produce a flat coast. If subaerial denudation has reduced an area adjacent to the coast to a very low gradient, typical of a peneplane, a rise of sea level will partially submerge this almost flat plain to produce a low coast. A peneplane will be likely to be covered by fine sediments. Weak materials of this type will assist the development of forms typical of a flat coast. The resultant coastline may initially be highly intricate in outline.

Another method whereby a low gradient can form a coastline is by the rapid outbuilding of fine materials from the land to form a low-lying plain of considerable extent. Such a plain can be of fluvial origin, often in the form of a delta. It can be formed by glacial meltwaters in the form of glacifluvial outwash deposits. The coast of southeast Iceland provides a good example of the latter, while the Mississippi delta region does of the former type.

In this chapter the essential characteristics of low coasts are first considered, and the conditions necessary for these characteristics to develop are enumerated. Then the distribution of the features is described, and some examples are considered, leading to a discussion of the formation of the features.

2 Characteristic features of low coasts and necessary conditions

Low coasts are often characterized by the presence of offshore barriers and the features associated with them. These include lagoons, in the shelter of the barrier islands, tidal inlets through them and sand dunes on them. The essential character that differentiates an offshore barrier island from the type of barrier considered in the last chapter is that it can be an entirely free form, unattached to the coast at either end. This is not, however, a necessary condition, and many barrier islands are in fact attached to the coast at one or both ends. Nearly all of them, however, are broken by inlets, which allow river water to flow out, and the tidal prism to flow in and out. The inlets normally separate the offshore barrier into a series of offshore islands, elongated along the coast. They often stretch for very great distances along the coast. The beach in front of the barrier island is frequently barred. Various patterns of submarine bars have already been mentioned, for example in chapter 13. Such features are not, however, always present and are often ephemeral at any one point, depending on the local wave conditions.

The low coasts considered in this chapter are characterized by an abundance of sediment in the coastal zone. Low coasts that are undergoing erosion and that have to be defended by artificial barriers against the sea are not included, nor are low coasts undergoing retreat by cliffing. An example of the first situation is found in central Lincolnshire, between Skegness and Mablethorpe. Low parts of Holderness and East Anglia exemplify the second area. Scolt Head Island, in north Norfolk, on the other hand, is included in the barrier island type of coast.

Barrier islands have been taken to be characteristic of the type of low coast under discussion. Such coasts are restricted to areas where there is sufficient material to form the barriers. This condition is likely to be fulfilled where a large amount of material is reaching the coast from inland, either via rivers or glaciers. Enough material will also be available where the sea has been rising over a gently sloping former sea bed, covered with an abundance of loose sediment. The material has been swept shoreward by wave action as the sea has risen during the Flandrian transgression. As long as the bottom gradient is gentle and sea level is rising, sandy material will be available to build into barriers.

As soon as sea level ceases to rise, however, then the available supply of material is likely to be reduced, at least in areas where longshore drift removes more than it brings into the area. In these areas the barriers will begin to suffer erosion and would eventually be destroyed. This has occurred in some areas during the still-stand of sea level that has been going on for the last 5000 to 6000 years. Thus a continued supply of material, mainly sandy in character, is essential to the formation and maintenance of barrier islands.

Barrier islands are usually well developed on coasts with a small tidal range. This characteristic probably helps in their formation. It is not, however, an essential condition, because barrier islands also occur in areas where the tidal range is large, if the other necessary conditions are fulfilled. They occur on the Pacific coast of Central America and in the Bay of Biscay, where the tidal range is between 2 and 5 m. The tidal range determines the number of tidal inlets through the barrier and the nature of the flow in and out of the lagoons (H. G. Gierloff-Emden, 1961).

Barrier islands are formed essentially by wave action. They are commonest in areas of swell wave activity of low to moderate intensity. They are not excluded, however, from the storm wave

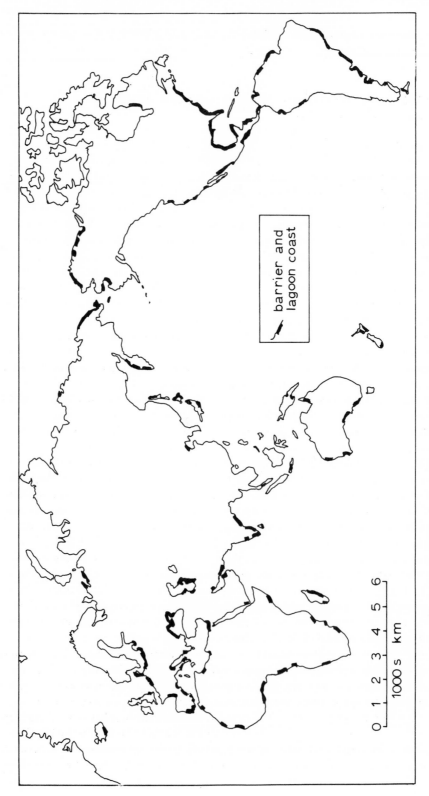

barrier and
lagoon coast

Figure 20-1 World map of the distribution of barrier island coastlines. (*After Gierloff-Emden, 1961.*)

0 1 2 3 4 5 6

1000 s km

environment of enclosed seas. In fact they are very common in enclosed seas, partly on account of the low tidal range in many of these situations. Wind also plays a part in barrier island development. It is responsible for the formation of the dunes that raise the height of the barrier and help to maintain it.

The essential conditions may be summed up to include: (a) an abundance of sand to form the barrier, and (b) a suitably low gradient on which it can be formed. The constructive conditions characteristic of swell environments are particularly suitable for the building of barrier islands on open coasts.

3 Distribution of barrier island coasts

The world-wide distribution of barrier island and lagoon coasts is shown in figure 20-1, taken from the work of H. G. Gierloff-Emden (1961). The relationship between the tidal range and the distribution of barrier islands is also shown. The map shows that while barriers are of world-wide distribution in all types of climate and tidal conditions, the most continuous and best-developed barriers are in lower latitudes and zones of low to moderate tidal range. It has been estimated that barrier coasts of this type cover 13% of the world coastline.

The longest stretch of barrier island coastline is that along the eastern coast of the U.S.A. and in the Gulf of Mexico. In the former area the offshore barrier islands allow 4500 km of navigation in sheltered lagoon waters, with only occasional breaks, while the Gulf of Mexico has 1000 km of coastal lagoons behind the barriers. They are common on the coasts of the Baltic, Mediterranean, Black and Caspian Seas, all of which have a negligible tidal range. They occur along considerable stretches of the African coast, for example on the Ivory coast, Togo, Dahomey and Nigeria, as well as shorter barriers on the Ghana coast. Barriers are common on the coast of India, parts of Australia and much of eastern South America. There are also barriers on the Arctic coasts of northeast Siberia and northern Alaska. They range from the equatorial zone to the polar zone. One of the major differences associated with this great latitudinal extent is in the nature of the lagoonal deposits and vegetation. This ranges from mangroves in the warmer seas with plenty of fine sediment, to salt marshes or bare lagoons in the temperate and colder seas respectively. Even in the Arctic, however, there are some salt marsh plants in coastal lagoons. The nature of the dunes and their vegetation on the barrier islands also changes with varying climatic conditions, and some northern barriers do not support dunes or dune vegetation. The paucity of tropical dunes was considered in chapter 6.

4 Examples of barrier island and similar features

Some specific examples of barrier island features will be described from differing areas. The features considered include: barriers off the coast of Iceland, the Netherlands, Ghana and other tropical areas, in southeast Australia, along the eastern coast of the U.S.A. and, finally, the chenier plains of northern South America, the Gulf of Mexico and Essex. These examples cover a wide range of latitudes and barrier types.

a Iceland

A good example of a relatively simple barrier beach is the one extending along the south coast of Iceland for 214 km from Vik in the west to Hornafjordur in the east (C. A. M. King, 1956).

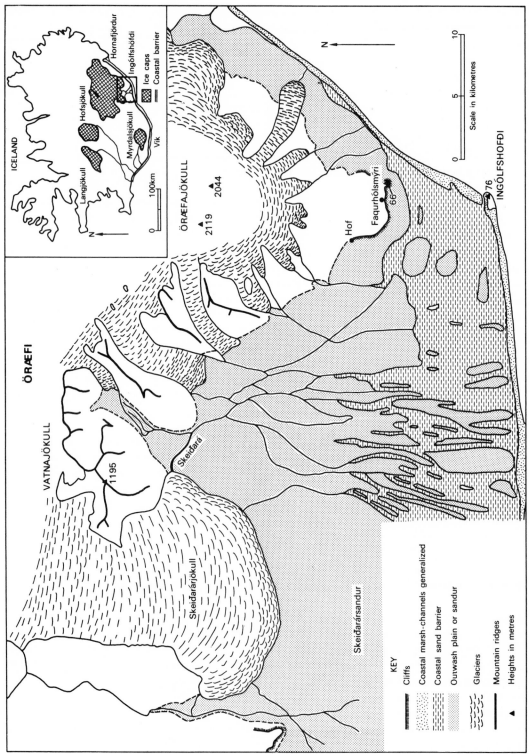

Figure 20-2 Map of the coastal barrier of southeast Iceland.

The island of Ingolfshöfði forms one of the major hinge-points along the barrier. This island is separated from the mainland by a shallow lagoon nearly 6½ km wide but only 30 to 60 cm deep. Its sandy bottom gradually rises above water level to the foot of a recently abandoned cliff about 8 km from the island. Figure 20-2 illustrates the character of the coast. The lagoon is floored with black, basaltic sand, which becomes finer towards the open sea. The coast is being rapidly built out by the deposition of a large amount of fluvioglacial material, brought down by the glaciers onto the outwash plain, which slopes gradually down to become the lagoon at its seaward edge. In some places the lagoon becomes very narrow and the outwash reaches right to the coast in others. The easily weathered nature of the volcanic rocks of the area and the active glaciers ensure an abundance of beach material. The material washed out of the glaciers is of all grades, but the sand-sized material is the most important in the building of the barrier along the coast. The large volume of sand available is an important factor in the development of the barrier.

Immediately to the west of the island of Ingolfshöfði there are two barriers. The inner, northerly one, is much the most conspicuous feature. It is much higher than the more continuous, but lower feature, seaward of it, which extends much further along the coast. Figure 20-3 illustrates the character of the two features. Both are formed of sand. The inner high one is built of sand of median diameter 0·39 mm, while the median diameter of the sand of the outer barrier is 0·42 mm. The inner feature reaches 24·4 m above mean sea level. It is a wind-formed barrier, which is tied to the island in whose shelter it has developed. It is nearly 1220 m long, gradually declining in elevation away from the island.

The feature seaward of the wind-formed bar is a true wave-built barrier. It is not very high, but it extends for a long way along the coast, apart from occasional inlets, through which the distributaries of the large meltwater rivers reach the sea, and the tide ebbs and flows. The tidal flow of water is not very important, as the range is small. The mean range is only about 1·2 m, increasing at spring tide to about 1·7 m. The small tidal range helps to explain the presence and character of the barrier.

The profile surveyed across the barrier shows that it extends only approximately 1·52 m above the high-water level. At high tide the swash of the larger waves could reach the crest of the beach and wash over it towards the lagoon behind. The low height of the barrier is due to the fact that it is made of sand. The barrier must have been built by the long, low constructive swells, as the steep, high destructive waves are normally entirely destructive on sand. No dunes have formed to raise and consolidate the barrier in this exposed and cool environment in which dune vegetation cannot flourish (C. A. M. King, 1956).

b   The coast of Holland

The barrier coast of Holland has been studied in detail by L. M. J. U. Van Stratten (1961; 1965). The barrier is very important in the protection of the low-lying hinterland from the sea. The barriers of this coast are of late-Atlantic and sub-Boreal age. They were formed in a period of 2000 years. They occupy the central part of the coast, stretching from just south of the Hague nearly to the island of Texel, which is itself a barrier. The islands to the north of it are also barriers. They separate the Wadden tidal flats from the open North Sea. Younger dunes are present seaward of the sub-Boreal barriers, and also on the Wadden Islands.

The development and character of the barriers are closely related to changes in sea level occurring during the period of their formation. Sea level in this area rose from −20 m in about 8150 B.P. at a steadily decreasing rate until the present. It was 2 m below present in about 2800 B.P. The stages of barrier development are summarized in the diagram shown in figure 20-4. The existence of the first barrier is surmised by the necessity for shelter, in which the earliest lagoon

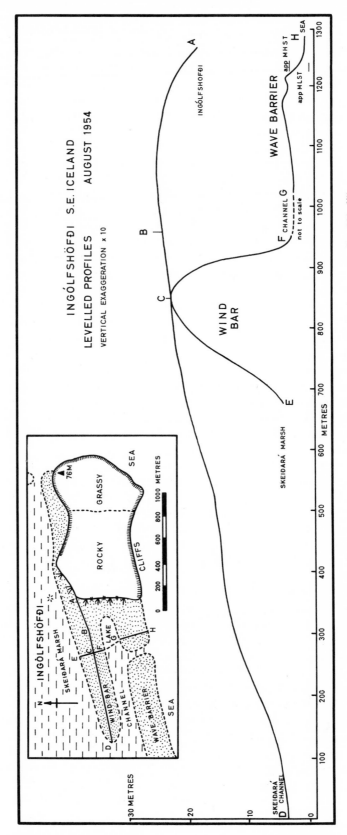

Figure 20-3 Profiles across the wind and wave barriers on the Iceland coast near Ingólfshöfði.

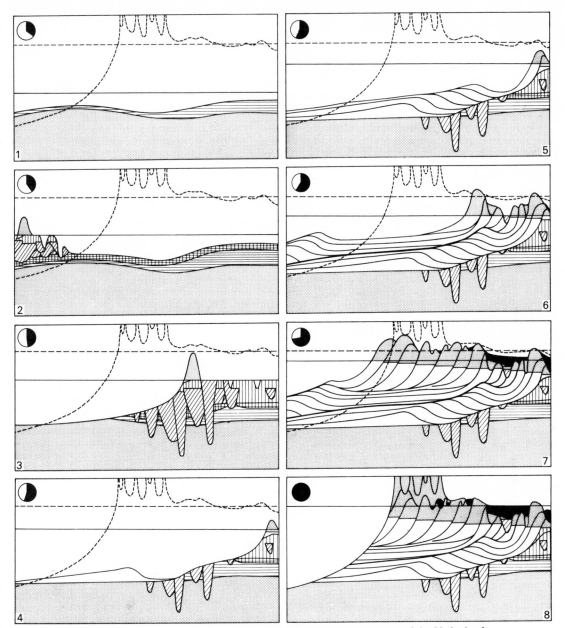

Figure 20-4 Reconstruction of the coastal barrier evolution of the coast of the Netherlands.

Approx. depth of sea level below N.A.P.		*Approx. time*	
1	10·0 m	4750 B.C.	Lake stage
2	8·0 m	4200 B.C.	Lagoon stage
3	6·0 m	3400 B.C.	Tidal flat stage
4	4·8 m	2800 B.C.	Inner barrier complete
5	4·3 m	2500 B.C.	Barrier depression formed between ridges
6	3·8 m	2200 B.C.	Second barrier ridge
7	2·2 m	850 B.C.	Maximum coast advance
8	sea level at N.A.P.	Present situation	

Vertical dimensions of diagrams 29 m; horizontal dimensions 14 km.
Lower stippling—Pleistocene. Upper stippling—dunes and beach deposits formed above mean sea level. Black—peat.
Vertical lines—tidal flat deposits. Diagonal lines—channel deposits. Cross hatching—Lagoon clays. Horizontal lines
—Lake clays. White with stratification—open sea deposits. (*After Van Straaten, 1965.*)

deposits accumulated. No other evidence of this barrier exists. The innermost barrier was complete around 2800 B.C. (4750 B.P.), when sea level was 4·8 m below present. A depression then formed between the barrier ridges before the second major barrier was built about 2200 B.C. (4150 B.P.). The coastal barriers built to their most advanced position by 850 B.C. (2800 B.P.), when sea level was 2·2 m lower than at present. Since this date the coast has been cut back somewhat. The seaward dunes have gained in height as sea level has risen to its present height (S. Jelgersma *et al.*, 1970). During this phase the sea floor has been lowered by at least 16 m. The exposure of the beach has increased and this has allowed the waves to erode it back. Much of the sand so released has been blown landwards to form the new dunes. The main cause of the coastal retreat has probably been the gradual exhaustion of the sand supply. This confirms that an adequate supply of sandy material is one of the essential conditions for barrier formation.

An important factor in considering the formation of this barrier system is the supply and movement of sand. Silt and clay are minor constituents of the barrier system, and are mainly brought into the sheltered areas via the rivers from inland. Sand can be supplied either by wave action transverse to or parallel to the coast. Where the transverse source is important the offshore gradient must steepen with time. This counteracts the process by making it more difficult for the waves to move sand onshore, by reducing the zone in which they are effective. This is a good example of negative feedback in coastal phenomena.

At the end of the Atlantic period the offshore gradient was very gentle, the slope being estimated at 1 : 450 from 0 to 10 m. It is now 1 : 150. Beyond 10 m the slope was even less. The low gradient may have been due to the very rapid rise of sea level, which did not give time for the establishment of the equilibrium profile. This profile is being increasingly achieved since the rise of sea level slowed down, and the gradient offshore is steepening. During the operation of this process a large amount of material was available. It is this material that was built into the barrier islands.

As the sand was moving landwards submarine bars formed offshore, and finer sediment was trapped on their landward side. Their presence facilitated the longshore transport of sand into the area. Thus the barriers were built up partly of the sand moving onshore, because the gradient was below the equilibrium value. Sand moving alongshore on the submarine bars in the offshore zone also added to the barriers.

The source of longshore sand lay to the southwest. Some of this material was reworked deltaic sediments from the rivers Rhine and Meuse, and some probably came directly from the rivers. More than half the sand forming the barriers probably came from alongshore. The supply from the transverse source was nevertheless not negligible. In particular the coarse sand at the base of the barriers was probably supplied from offshore, being the lower part of the large submarine bars. The dual source of supply would explain the pattern of barriers better, and account for the large depression between them. The uniformity of ridge pattern is difficult to reconcile with a longshore source of sand forming spits. The supply of material from both sources must have been large as the whole complex formed in 2000 years or less. The mean area of the barrier formation at Scheveningen is a minimum of 150,000 m², giving an average annual accretion of 75 m² or 86 cm²/hour. If half the accretion were due to transverse supply, in the form of asymmetrical ripples, then these would have had to move from the source area at 43 cm/hour. With reasonable wave dimensions, the transport would be smaller than the required amount. It is, therefore, suggested that probably less than half the total sand supply came from offshore.

The volume needed to build the barrier between Scheveningen and Leiden, a distance of 55 km, is $5 \cdot 5 \times 10^9$ m³. If half of this had been supplied by longshore drift in 2000 years the annual average is $2 \cdot 75 \times 10^6$ m³. It must, however, have been greater, as some material moved on up the coast. The present estimate of longshore movement is $1 \cdot 10 \times 10^6$ m³/year, which is only about $\frac{1}{3}$ of that needed to build the barriers. A possible source to make up the difference is wind-blown sand, passing along the coast under the prevailing southwesterly winds. In the sub-Boreal winds may have been more nearly parallel to the coast than the winds at present. The distribution of old dunes lends some support to this hypothesis, as they differ from the pattern of more recent dunes.

The evolution of the barriers along the coast of the Netherlands confirms, therefore, the great importance of an abundant supply of material in the building of barrier islands. The importance of the rising sea level and gentle offshore gradient is also shown.

c   Tropical barriers

H. G. Von Gierloff-Emden (1959b) has described an offshore barrier on the coast of El Salvador. This is differentiated from similar features elsewhere by the presence of mangroves in the lagoon behind the barrier islands. The beach ridges on the barrier indicate the stages by which the feature has developed. Dunes occur on some of them. The pattern of ridges suggests fairly strong longshore transport in the area, although numerous tidal inlets interrupt the barrier. Accumulation and erosion seem to balance in the estuary and the coast at present seems to be more or less in equilibrium.

The barrier coast of Ghana has been described by P. Galliers (1969). The barriers are fairly short, rarely exceeding 15 km in length, and often being less than 200 m long. They are single elongate sand ridges, rising slightly above the high-tide level. The longest ones include stable forms with settlements and mature vegetation. These rise about 8 to 10 m above sea level. The tidal range is less than 1 m. The barriers are all aligned east to west. They are formed of 90 to 95% quartz sand, with only a small percentage of shell sand. The foreshore and barrier sands are very similar. There are rather more shells in the barrier sands, and the sorting is rather poorer. The character of the barrier sands suggests that the barriers are built up by wave action, and that wind action plays a fairly small part in their construction. This conclusion supports the comments made in chapter 6, concerning the paucity of coastal dunes in tropical conditions. This is a significant point of difference between tropical barrier islands and those of temperate areas.

The barriers vary with seasonal change in wave type in Ghana. During the rainy season storm waves tend to cut into them, and the lagoons become filled by the greater runoff from inland. Breaches through the lagoons, initiated by the destructive wave action, which is aided by the saturated nature of the beach sand, are widened at this season. The barrier is built up again when calmer conditions return, and the breaches are healed. The second less intense rainy season is not sufficient to cause breaching in the smaller lagoons. The pattern supports the view that constructive waves are important in the formation of barrier islands. The alignment of the barriers suggests that they are built by the refracted long, low swells that come initially from the south-southeast, but reach the coast from the south.

d   Southeast Australia

The submerged coastal plain of southeast Australia has some very well-developed barrier island coasts. They have been described in detail by E. C. F. Bird (1961; 1965a and b) and J. R. Hails (1964). The coast of southeast Queensland consists of a series of barrier islands, spits and beaches. The barrier islands are mostly arcuate, forming zeta curves between headlands. The barriers form on the seaward side of a narrow coastal plain, which consists of estuarine deposits, coastal marshes and sand ridges. A scarp on the landward side marks the pre-Pleistocene shore. The plain has built seaward by land and marine deposition in an area formerly characterized by headlands and bays.

The growth of the barriers is probably due to two main causes. Firstly, a large volume of material was available in the offshore zone, and pluvial periods provided extra material from the land as well. Secondly, a decrease of discharge from the rivers promoted rapid deposition. During the early stages of development, features associated with a steep coast were common. Spits, growing from opposite headlands, often formed double features. Some of these were the result of breaching. Since this early stage barrier islands have developed, forming the outer barrier system. The outer barriers now form an almost continuous chain, following the trend of the zeta-curved coastline. They are separated from the mainland by Moreton Bay, and are covered by transgressive dunes, which trend northwest to southeast at an angle to the generally north to south coast. The barrier islands are probably Pleistocene in age, and a series of beach ridges has grown on their seaward side.

The outer part of the coastal plain was submerged before the barriers formed. Moreton Bay is a relic of the submerged zone, although much infilling has taken place since. Erosion on the outer coast of the barrier islands is indicated by active transgressive dunes on the eastern part of the islands. The first dunes are parabolic, and sand transported inland from them has gradually hidden the older beach ridges. Older transgressive dunes, which rise to heights of 152·5 m and in one instance to over 274 m, indicate earlier stages of erosion in the development of the barrier islands. These changes may have been due to fluctuations of sea level. These appear to have been complex in this part of southeast Queensland. Some of the older dunes appear to date from about 40,000 years ago.

E. C. F. Bird (1961 and 1965a) has studied the barriers of the East Gippsland coast, which provides a good example of a sandy barrier coast. The system consists of an outer barrier, which extends the whole length of the Ninety Mile beach. It is backed by a narrow zone of lagoons and swamps. Along part of the coast there is also an inner barrier, enclosing Lakes Wellington, Victoria and King. A still earlier barrier forms the landward side of the greater length of these lakes.

The three barrier systems developed successively on a coast of submergence produced by the post-glacial marine transgression. They are, therefore, of recent date. The earliest inner barrier developed as the transgression came to an end. It was followed by the second barrier, while the outer one formed about 1·6 km seaward of the second barrier shoreline. It has been attributed to a period of recent emergence.

More recent evidence has suggested some modification of the time scale, and it is now thought that the inner barrier formed during the late Pleistocene when sea level was at or a little above its present level (E. C. F. Bird, 1965b). The area was then dissected and the material partially rearranged by the wind during a period of low sea level in the late glacial. The outer barrier and part of the middle barrier formed when sea level had returned to its present height in recent times.

The sandy barriers of the east Australian coast are surmounted by beach ridges, built up as berms parallel to the shoreline of the time by progradation. The berms become colonized by foredune vegetation as sand collects. The form of the barrier is dependent on the direction of approach of the refracted swell waves. The barriers of the East Gippsland coast consist of mainly quartz sand. Carbonates on the Ninety Mile beach rarely exceed 10%. The main growth of the ridges depends on sand dune formation, aided by suitable vegetation. The middle barrier is complex and has had a complex history. It has been much modified since its formation. The pattern of ridges has been partly modified by the formation of parabolic dunes, some of which are now stabilized. Some of them are more than 27·4 m high.

The general plan of the different barriers is shown in figure 20-5. The outer barrier is separated from the middle one by Lake Reeve. Its seaward margin is the Ninety Mile beach. Its crest consists of closely spaced high dunes 6 to 24 m high and 27 to 46 m apart. The barrier island

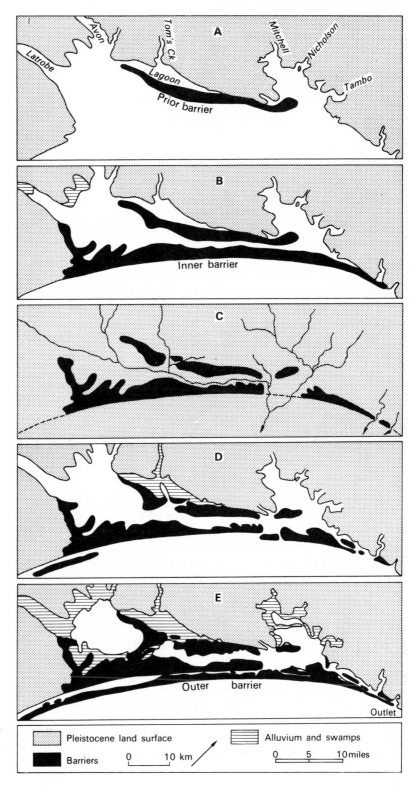

Figure 20-5 Evolution of the barrier islands in the Gippsland Lakes region. (*After Bird, 1965b.*)

appears to have been initiated offshore as Letts Beach was elongated to northeast and southwest, gradually prograding to take up its present seaward curve. Its northeastward growth was irregular as a series of old channels curve into Lake Reeve. Eventually the outer barrier was continued as far as Red Bluff where it linked to the mainland. An artificial gap was cut through it near the northern end at Lakes Entrance in 1889, and the natural outlet further east became sealed. An exceptional abundance of sand in the nearshore zone near Letts Beach may have initiated barrier formation. A possible alternative explanation is that local uplift initiated barrier formation at this point, because it lies on the seaward continuation of the Deadman's Hill ridge, which has been subject to uplift in the Quaternary. This uplift may also be responsible for the tilt in the middle barrier. There is no evidence of eustatic emergence along this coast.

The long-continued progradation along the shore appears to have come to an end at present. Cut has exceeded fill along the Ninety Mile beach during the last few decades. New dunes have not formed recently, truncation of the older dunes is taking place on their seaward side, and blowouts have occurred. This change has been attributed to a renewed eustatic rise of sea level, possibly accompanied by increased storminess. A reduction of sand supply is an alternative cause. This could be caused by a steepening of the offshore gradient, allowing more powerful wave attack. It is likely that both factors have played a part.

The main movement of sand along the Ninety Mile beach is to the northeast when waves come from the southwest, but in the opposite direction when waves come from the east. It is likely that the former movement is dominant, although the balance is fairly even. The southwestern part of the barrier has grown towards Wilson's Promontory. The origin of the barriers seems to be more closely related to the onshore movement of sand, and to the refraction of swell waves, which determine the coastal outline. The bulk of the material has been derived from offshore, swept landwards by the waves. This is particularly evident in the outer barrier: this developed seawards of possible land sources, which were situated behind the middle barrier. The sand was probably formerly in the form of barriers and dunes, abandoned by the falling sea level during the last glacial period. Off Flinders Island there are relics of submerged ridges, which could be drowned barriers or dune systems that survived destruction by the rising sea.

e Eastern U.S.A.

The barrier island coast of the eastern U.S.A. has already been mentioned in many connections. The coast is flanked by barrier islands for a very great distance, stretching from Cape Cod in the north to Florida in the south. It includes the Outer Banks of Carolina, lying a long distance offshore, and the other barrier islands situated closer inshore.

Plum Island may be taken as an example of a barrier island along this coast. It is 13·4 km long and mostly 0·8 to 1·6 km wide, and is attached to a drowned drumlin complex at its southern end. It formed between 6000 and 7000 years B.P. The northern tip has changed considerably in the last 150 years. A period of retrogression was followed by one of spit formation on the eastern side of the island. The spit grew over 1·6 km in length between 1827 and 1850. The area of the accretion has greatly extended since then. At present the northern end of the island is being eroded once more.

Beach profiles have been surveyed across the ocean beaches to study changes brought about by different wave types. After storm activity the profiles are flat and smooth. Sand comes back in the form of ridges and runnels, which move landwards and weld onto the backshore, followed by the growth of a wide berm, which progrades seawards. The same pattern was followed in the post-1953 storm surge profiles on the Lincolnshire coast. Cusps are common at the north end of the island, where the sand is coarser. In the shallow offshore zone there are submarine bars. Their positions may determine the zones of maximum erosion on the foreshore. There is some evidence that the bars are largest in the stormy winter months, when the beaches are undergoing a net loss of sand. This observation is in agreement with the views on submarine bar formation discussed in chapter 12.

The crest of the barrier is dune-covered. These dunes have already been considered in chapter 6. They consist of a foredune ridge, an interdune area, a backdune ridge and a wooded area with low, stabilized dunes, leading down to salt marsh. The foredunes are 9 to 11 m high. There are blow-outs, slip faces and new dunes. The backdune ridge is over 15 m high in places. In the interdune hollow there is a strong northwest to southeast lineation. This area is due to deflation by northwest winds. The backdune ridge has an active slip face, moving towards the forested area. The dunes are covered by bushes and trees, but there are some erosional forms.

f Chenier plains

The chenier plain coastal type is a rather different form of low coast. It is, however, similar in many respects to the offshore barrier island coast. The major difference is that in a chenier plain the sandy ridges are separated by silt- or clay-filled hollows rather than lagoons.

An example of a chenier plain is found along much of the coast of South America between north Brazil and Venezuela, in association with the mouths of the Amazon and Orinoco (W. Armstrong Price, 1954). It is composed of a series of sandy barriers separated by strips of marsh and swamp, which have a large clay content in their deposits. The coast of Surinam is typical of a chenier plain. The slope is gentle and sandy ridges are perched at intervals within or on the clay. The plain is 2240 km long and up to 32 km wide. The sandy ridges are between 1 and 2·7 m high and 76 to 107 m broad. The tidal range is 2·13 to 2·74 m. Heavy surf occurs at times, coming from the northeast. The surf waves build up the sandy ridges on this generally prograding coast. Where the wave energy is greater or the slope steeper the chenier plain is replaced by barrier islands.

The name 'chenier' was introduced by R. J. Russell (1967). He adopted the term used for these features in the Mississippi delta region, where the ridges supported evergreen oaks. A new chenier started to grow in this area in 1945. The main distributary of the lower Mississippi filled a large lake that once covered much of its basin with sediment. The fine sediments then began to reach the sea, moving westwards with the longshore currents. The deposits formed a mudflat in front of the beach, and the mud became colonized by Salicornia. By 1953 it was a typical salt marsh extending 65 km westwards. In the process of further extension the pre-1945 salt marsh has become a chenier. During a hurricane in 1957 large sections of the marsh were lifted up and carried over the area behind and deposited, essentially intact. The area moved was 2 km long and 370 m wide.

Another example of a chenier in this area has been described by A. Schou (1967): Pecan Island is a sand ridge surrounded by marshland. It is an element of a chenier system stretching over a distance of 100 km, and the whole system is only one of a series of such systems. Pecan Island is 400 m long and reaches a maximum height of 3 m above mean sea level, dimensions typical of Louisiana cheniers. The ridge is not an island as it is surrounded by grass-covered marshland. It is covered by evergreen oaks. The ridge was initially a sandy beach along the seaward side of a marsh plain. The ridges are built up by wave action. They cover the marsh surface as the sand is transferred inland, indicating a period of wave activity when the shoreline retreats. Between attacks by effective waves mud is deposited seaward of the beach, and a marsh builds up, isolating the old beach ridge from the sea so that it develops into a chenier. The chenier ridges are fairly regularly spaced along the Louisiana coast, indicating fairly regular ridge formation by alternating erosion and accretion. The regular cycle is explained by cyclic shifting of the direction of discharge of the Mississippi.

The pattern of ridges on Pecan Island is complex, indicating phases of marine erosion during the growth of the ridges. They vary in orientation, probably because they were part of a recurved spit. Further east subsidence has allowed the sandy ridges to be buried by marsh deposits, so cheniers do not exist in this area. The effect of hurricanes in the formation of the cheniers is seen in the presence of mud lumps or mud arcs, an example of which has already been cited. Thus both normal and catastrophic processes play a part in the development of cheniers.

A chenier type of sedimentation has been described by J. T. Greensmith and E. V. Tucker (1969) in Essex. The chenier plain deposits of this low coast extend 20 km north from the Thames estuary. They include shell concentrations in the form of offshore banks and sheets, with a maximum relief of 4 m, marsh edge sheets, and ridges of lower relief. There are also shallow channels and pockets, filled by more recent deposits. The ridges form the cheniers in this sequence. There are also degraded cheniers a little further inland, forming a narrow zone 0·1 to 1 km wide. They consist mostly of shells, but they have lost their relief.

The modern cheniers occur at the edge of the marsh deposits and the upper tidal flats. They are only overtopped during storm conditions. Some of these deposits are isolated marsh bars. They have the characteristics of cheniers in that they have a shallow base, being perched and sandy. They rest on clay, along a marshy seaward-facing tidal shore, and vary in height between 0·5 and 3·0 m above the tidal flats. Their transverse profile has a steep seaward face, with a gradient of 20° and a width up to 25 m. The upper surface slopes gently landwards at 2 to 5° and is up to 30 m wide. The back slope is steep, having a gradient of up to 30°, and is up to 3 m wide. The material consists of 51% shells, 47% sand and the rest silty mud, plant debris and flint pebbles. They are, therefore, much shellier than the Louisiana chenier and have less sand.

During storms minor ridges may be built to form storm ridges on the seaward faces. Storm waves also cause landward migration. At Sales Point air photographs indicate a landward movement of about 8 m/year on average for the last 22 years. A movement of 7 m was recorded after one storm. Marsh creeks become filled with shells during these movements. Shell beds up to 0·5 m thick occur within the marsh deposits, indicating the passage of earlier cheniers over the area. The initiation of a chenier at the marsh edge usually follows mass mortality of shells in the neighbouring tidal areas. Once established further material can be added mainly from offshore. Migration is the result of storm activity, and is favoured also by growth of marsh to seaward. Longshore movement can cause the elongation of the chenier ridges. Large masses of shells reached the coast following the heavy mortality due to the very severe winter of 1963. On the whole, however, the balance between erosion and accretion is delicate and ridge degradation has also occurred.

5 Formation of barrier islands

In the descriptions of the barrier island in different areas some mention has already been made of possible methods of formation. Different processes have been suggested by different authorities. One of the early authors to describe barrier islands was L. Elie de Beaumont in 1845. He considered that the barriers were built up by the landward movement of material from offshore. D. W. Johnson (1919) argued that as a result of the onshore movement of material the offshore profile seaward of the barrier should become flatter. A line continuing this offshore gradient should, therefore, cut the coast inland of the inner margin of the lagoon, unless the offshore gradient is very flat, in which case the lagoon would be exceptionally wide. Another theory which Johnson tested was that of G. K. Gilbert (1890), who considered that the barrier was entirely constructive, the material being derived from alongshore, leaving the offshore zone uneroded. A line continuing the offshore gradient should cut the coastline either at the inner edge of the lagoon or within the lagoon. Johnson found the 15 out of 18 profiles supported Elie de Beaumont's theory. The result could be incorrect, however, as it is unlikely that the original slope was uniform. If it were the normal concave curve, a continuation of the flatter offshore slope would in any case cut the original coast inland of the inner lagoon edge. Moreover, as movement of material takes place shorewards the slope becomes steeper and not flatter.

The theory put forward by Elie de Beaumont over 100 years ago is probably essentially correct, although the details of the wave processes were not known at that time. It is also true, however, that longshore drift plays an important part in the formation and growth of many offshore barrier islands.

The history of development of barrier islands can often be interpreted by means of a study in their sediments. This is sometimes exposed by the migration of the barrier along the coast. The occurrence of longshore migration itself indicates the importance of longshore movement in their formation. J. H. Hoyt and V. J. Henry (1967) have considered this aspect of barrier island formation. An example of a migrating barrier island is Sapelo Island in Georgia. This island is largely Pleistocene in age. The sea floor in front of it slopes at 76 cm/km for the first 16 km offshore, decreasing still further to 30·6 cm/km beyond this. The tidal range is 2·13 m, increasing to 2·74 m at spring tides. The barriers are 11·2 to 29 km long, 3·2 to 6·4 km wide and separated from the shore by 6·4 to 9·6 km of salt marsh. Inlets occur on average every 16 km. These are 1·6 to 6·4 km wide and 12·2 to 24·4 m deep.

Sapelo Island migrates southwards with the dominant littoral drift. Dunes and ridges are truncated on the north side and new ridges form at the southern end. The littoral and nearshore sediments are fine-grained, well-sorted sands with many shell layers. Finer sediments occur in the offshore zone and particularly in the marsh deposits of the lagoons. Sections through the barrier islands show an interdigitation of sandy sediments within the silt and clays of the lagoon sediments. As the sediments migrate with the barrier their structures are modified. Steep dips are associated with migrating channel sediments, while those of the seaward side of the barrier island dip gently seaward, at not more than 6°. On a large scale the migration of the islands leaves bodies of sand that are elongated parallel to the drift direction, but lense-shaped perpendicular to the drift direction. They are 9·6 km to 12·8 km wide.

A discussion of barrier island formation by J. H. Hoyt (1967) draws attention to the difficulties in the view that barrier islands were formed from submarine bars, as proposed by Leontyev and Mikiforov in 1966. They suggested that barriers were formed when submarine bars were exposed by the general lowering of sea level in the Holocene. There seem, however, to be no examples of such a process actually taking place. There may be small examples, but this method of formation can hardly account for the large barriers that have been described. The point that is most significant in refuting this theory is the absence of neritic and beach deposits landwards of the barrier islands. If they developed from submarine bars then there should be beach deposits on their landward side. Nowhere along the Georgia coast, where barrier islands of several ages occur, do beach deposits extend landwards of the barrier islands.

Coring in Padre Island lagoon showed that at no time did open-marine conditions occur in the lagoon while Padre Island was forming. Similar results have been obtained in Texan barrier areas (R. F. Le Blanc and W. D. Hodgson, 1959), along the Dutch coast (L. M. J. U. Van Straaten, 1965), and elsewhere in the world. The evidence strongly suggests that barrier islands have not developed from submarine bars. The section through Laguna Madre and Padre Island in Texas, shown in figure 20-6, shows the absence of barrier island facies in the lagoon.

In some areas it can be shown that much of the material forming the barrier islands comes from alongshore. This is true, for example, of the coast of Holland. Barrier islands may under these circumstances develop from spits. These become very elongated and break up into separate barrier islands, which may then migrate along the shore.

The conditions that a theory of barrier island formation must incorporate are:

1   The absence of marine sediments or shallow-water neritic sediments on the landward side of the lagoon.
2   The ability of barrier island systems to reform after their growth has been terminated by an emergence.
3   The absence of world-wide higher than present sea levels during the Holocene.
4   Development and maintenance of a barrier island system during a slow submergence (J. H. Hoyt, 1967).

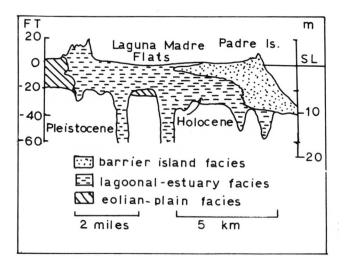

Figure 20-6   Cross-sections of the Laguna Madre and Padre Island, Texas. (*After Hoyt, 1967.*)

The rapid submergence taking place between 18,000 and about 5000 years ago must also be taken into account.

Hoyt's theory suggests that wherever the sea comes to rest against a sandy floor dunes will form at the back of the beach, or if the material is too coarse, shingle will be thrown up to form a ridge up to 6 m above sea level. Dunes may raise the level to 30 m or more. If sea level rises the ground behind the ridge will be flooded to form a làgoon, and the ridge becomes a barrier island. The width of the island will depend on the amount of progradation, which is related to the sediment supply. The lagoon depth will depend on the amount of submergence, and its width on the land slope. Both will be affected by subsequent infilling and marsh development. If the rate of submergence is too rapid the barrier may be drowned. If it is too slow the lagoon will become filled. In either event the barrier ceases to be an island. This theory is based on a rate of submergence within certain critical limits.

In areas where emergence followed the submergence a series of barriers may occur, the youngest being lowest and nearest the open sea. This situation occurs along the coast of Georgia, where Hoyt and J. R. Hails (1967) have located six barriers of Pleistocene and Holocene age. The six previous shorelines are marked by barriers, backed by salt marsh deposits. The older ones are progressively higher in elevation. This pattern suggests slow elevation of the land in this area, as the oldest barriers are 27 to 30 m above present sea level. This example shows that not all barriers are to be explained by submergence.

C. W. Cooke (1968) has criticized Hoyt's views of barrier island formation. He has suggested that barriers can form without a change of sea level, citing the Hatteras Banks as an example. In defending his views, Hoyt (1968) stresses the significance of the lack of open water deposits on the landward side of the barrier lagoons. He uses the same argument to refute the criticism of J. J. Fisher (1968). Fisher advocates barrier formation by modification of complex spits, formed on a shoreline of submergence. Both Fisher and Hoyt agree on the importance of submergence in barrier formation. Fisher criticizes Hoyt's view that barriers are formed from beach and dune ridges, suggesting that a stable shore is necessary for dune formation. Hoyt (1968) points out that dune ridges can form very rapidly under present conditions, so that this is not a strong argument against this theory.

E. G. Otvos (1970) has suggested that barrier islands form by the upward aggradation of submerged shoal areas. He considers that migration can take place parallel to, perpendicular to, or oblique to the mainland shore. Movement is most rapid when migration is parallel to the coast. He found no evidence to suggest that barrier islands form from engulfed beach and dune ridges during the early stages of transgression, as suggested by Hoyt. Most of the barriers of the Gulf of Mexico started to form about 3500 to 5000 years B.P., when the rate of transgression had slowed down or stopped. The lack of open sea sediments is not considered to be necessarily due to barrier formation during transgression. Evidence is cited of the formation of barriers from underwater shoals in historic times. The Grand Gosier Island, which is 7·5 km long, developed since 1869, by the amalgamation of small islands that had developed on the shallow sea floor. The migratory movement of barriers can be either seaward or shoreward. The former movement takes place by frontal migration. Often both frontal and lateral migration are combined.

D. J. P. Swift (1968) has suggested that these various ideas of barrier formation are not mutually exclusive. He believes that both longshore movement and shoreward movement play a part in barrier formation. They do indicate, however, different sources of sediment. Barriers will form wherever there is more sediment arriving in the area than is leaving it, whether sea level is rising, stationary or falling, if other conditions are also suitable. Shepard (1963, p. 90) attributes barrier formation to a slowing down of the rate of sea level rise after the climatic optimum, a view supported by Jelgersma (1961, p. 90) for barrier formation on the coast of Holland. J. R. Curray (1964) concluded that barriers grow upward during transgressions until their lagoons trap so much of the river-derived sediment that a barrier dependent on this source is starved, and overstepped by the sea. Swift agrees with Hoyt's view of barrier formation in some instances, such as where more sand is reaching the foreshore than is leaving it. He notes, however, that under these conditions outward growth takes place as well as upward growth, citing Galveston Island barrier as an example. Hoyt's theory can be linked with the river-mouth drowning mechanism, whereby the rivers supply the sand during the early stages. Spits tied to eroding headlands can also be incorporated as they will become periodically detached by inlet formation and migration. This is an important process in the re-sorting of the sediments of which the barriers are formed. The eroding headlands also supply sediment, for example in New Jersey.

The formation of barrier islands requires first of all a large amount of available sediment, either from an offshore source or an alongshore source. Another necessity is a suitably low gradient that allows waves to build up a feature above water level by their constructive action. The submarine bars that often lie seaward of the barrier are formed by a quite different process. They are caused by the reduction of sand transport at the breaker line. They tend to grow in size when the seaward face of the barrier is being eroded. The examples cited have shown that some barriers are fed mainly from offshore, while others have a predominant longshore component of supply. An important reason for their widespread present occurrence is the rise of sea level over a gently sloping sandy sea bed in the post-glacial transgression. This process has supplied the plentiful sediment and the gentle slopes necessary for barrier formation. As sea level becomes more stable the supply of sand is likely to be reduced, and some barriers are liable to undergo erosion. Some barriers have been shown to have already entered this phase of development.

W. P. Dillon (1970) has described the barrier island off Rhode Island, which is formed of reworked glacial sediments. The Charlestown barrier beach was formed at a lower sea level and has moved landwards as the sea transgressed. The seaward side is periodically eroded by storm waves and sand is carried over the barrier into the lagoon by storm waves. The lack of sand supply has meant that the barrier has remained small and this has also allowed it to move landwards. The barrier sands overlie lagoonal deposits, showing this landward migration. Virtually no sand is now supplied to the barrier front and little sediment reaches the lagoon, except that washed over the barrier. The base of the barrier is shallow, lying at 13 m below sea level. Lack of sediment is important in allowing the landward migration, and in preventing the drowning of the barrier during the period of rising sea level. The migration has also allowed the lagoon to be preserved. Thus the small size of the barrier has facilitated its preservation through migration.

6 Tidal inlets

J. W. Pierce (1970) has shown that washover fans and tidal inlets are genetically related, both being caused by barrier breaching under storm conditions. The breach can be made either from the lagoon side or the sea side, according to the nature of the storm. Breaching by attack from the sea side is only effective when the water is concentrated at specific points. Overtopping by storm waves can cause breaching if the water becomes channelled on the lagoon side. Overwash fans will form best where the barrier is wide, and where large tidal flats are present on the lagoon side. Inlets are most likely to form where the barrier is narrow and no extensive flats are present. In a wide lagoon a sudden reversal of wind direction from onshore to offshore as a storm centre passes can cause much water to pile up on the lagoon side of the barrier. If creeks allow channelling the water may break through the barrier to the sea. Inlets are breached through wide barriers mainly by this process taking place from the lagoon side.

The formation and early development of a tidal delta and inlet breach has been described by M. T. El-Ashry and H. R. Wanless (1965). The new inlet was opened 7·2 km north of Cape Hatteras during a great storm in 1962. The storm washed away the sand dunes where the barrier was ½ km wide and formed a breach 122 m wide. After five days a tidal delta in the lagoon had formed and had an area of 0·275 km². After a further two months the delta had grown to 0·52 km², increasing to 0·91 km² after 10 months. The inlet widened by 46 m during the first two months, and then it shifted south. After 10 months the inlet was 244 m wide.

From the point of view of coastal defence one of the problems associated with barrier islands is their migration along the shore, owing to the instability of the inlets. This causes erosion at one end of the barrier and accretion at the other, with attendant difficulties in the tidal inlets through the barriers. Problems associated with the stability of coastal inlets have been studied by P. Bruun and F. Gerritsen (1960), and some mention of them was made in chapter 17. The model study by T. Saville and J. M. Caldwell (1957) shows that arcuate bars form at both the sea side and the lagoon side of the inlet, with the deepest part of the channel in the centre. These bars are caused by the loss of velocity of the flood and ebb tides as they pass in and out through the inlet, respectively. In the experimental situation it was found that the inlet could only be maintained, in the face of obliquely approaching wave action, by the action of simulated storm tides. The closing of the inlet was greatly accelerated when the tidal prism was small, compared to the tests made when it was much larger.

Bruun and Gerritsen (1960), on the other hand, found that the maximum speed of flow through the inlet correlated more closely with other variables. The ratio of tidal prism to longshore drift is necessary to define inlet stability. If this ratio exceeds 200 the inlet is likely to be stable, but if it is less than 100 then problems are likely to occur. The closure of inlets can be due to several causes. These include the elongation of the inlet channel by longshore drift, overwhelming of the inlet during storms by littoral drift, splitting of the inlet into two channels and change of the area of the bay, which changes the tidal prism.

M. P. O'Brien (1967) has investigated the equilibrium flow areas of tidal inlets on sandy coasts and has concluded that the flow area is a unique function of the tidal prism. The size of material, presence of jetties and the magnitude of littoral drift do not appear to affect the equilibrium flow area. This relationship is given by

$$A = 4 \cdot 69 \times 10^{-4} P^{0 \cdot 85}$$

where A square feet is the minimum flow cross-section and P cubic feet is the tidal prism measured below mean sea level.

Problems associated with the artificial maintenance of tidal inlets across barriers, by the building of breakwaters to maintain the passage through the barrier, are aggravated in areas of strong longshore transport of sediment. The breakwaters lead to erosion on the down-drift side and accretion on the up-drift side. Such problems can be overcome by sand by-passing schemes, some of which have been mentioned already (section 19-4).

Barrier coasts are usually subject to considerable change, because they are mostly young features, which are either still actively growing or have reached a stage of erosion. The latter applies when they are dependent upon a source of sediment from offshore, and this has been cut off or reduced through a steepening of the offshore gradient. In both instances longshore movement of sediment can cause inlets to migrate, even if the barrier is otherwise stable.

Summary

Barrier coasts can form either through emergence, submergence or with a static sea level provided that there is an ample supply of sand and that the coast is low, with a very gentle offshore gradient. The large rise of sea level during the post-glacial Flandrian transgression, where the sea rose over a gently sloping sandy area, has provided many suitable conditions for barrier island formation. When sea level becomes static barriers may suffer erosion if their only source of supply is from offshore. A continued supply of material is essential to barrier stability and growth. Barrier islands usually occur on coasts with a low tidal range and develop best in the swell environment. They are, however, very widespread in occurrence and are found in all latitudes. They occur on 13% of the world's coasts.

The barrier along part of the south coast of Iceland is formed at the seaward margin of a sandy outwash plain. The barrier is low, only extending 1·5 m above high-water level, as it has no dunes on it. Barriers along the coast of Holland formed during a 2000 year period and consist of an outer and inner system, both with extensive sand dunes. Part of the material, probably less than half, was supplied from offshore and the rest from the Rhine and Meuse moved north along the coast to build the barriers. Wind-blown sand also added to the bulk of the barrier system. Tropical barriers tend to be narrow, owing to the paucity of dune formation in this area. They show seasonal changes with varying wave conditions and with the rainy season. Barriers on the east coast of Australia are well developed. They were built up of sand left on the offshore slope as sea level fell during the last glacial advance. This sand was formed into barriers by the waves of the advancing Flandrian sea. The earliest of the three barrier systems is Pleistocene in date, but the outer barrier at least is post-glacial in age. Dunes on the barrier systems rise to heights in excess of 150 m in places, although some of these are more than 40,000 years old. Since sea level reached its present height the barriers are beginning to erode. Barriers are common on the east coast of the U.S.A. and chenier plains occur in the Gulf of Mexico. The chenier plain consists of salt marsh deposits with occasional sand ridges, which were formed by more vigorous wave action during storm activity. A somewhat similar feature is found on the coast of Essex, where shells are more common in the ridges.

Barrier islands are formed by wave action. They are formed of sand which may be supplied from offshore or alongshore, or from a combination of sources. Where the material comes from alongshore the barrier may start as a spit, but it becomes elongated and broken by tidal inlets. Such barriers can then migrate along the coast. A rising sea level is indicated by the lack of open sea sediments in the lagoon deposits. The stability of tidal inlets depends on the relation between the tidal prism and longshore drift.

References

BIRD, E. C. F. 1961: The coastal barriers of East Gippsland, Australia. *Geog. J.* **127,** 460–80.

BIRD, E. C. F. 1965a: A geomorphological study of the Gippsland Lakes. *Res. Sch. Pac. Stud. Dept. Geog. Pub.* **G/1.** (101 pp.)

BIRD, E. C. F. 1965b: The evolution of sand barrier formations on the East Gippsland coast. *Proc. Roy. Soc. Victoria* **79**(1), 75–88.

BRUUN, P. and GERRITSEN, F. 1960: *Stability of coastal inlets.* Amsterdam: North Holland Pub. Co.

COOKE, C. W. 1968: Barrier Island formation: discussion. *Bull. Geol. Soc. Am.* **79**(7), 945–6.

CURRAY, J. R. 1964: Transgressions and regressions. In Miller, R. L. (Editor), *Papers in marine geology: Shepard commemorative volume,* New York: Macmillan, 175–203.

DILLON, W. P. 1970: Submergence effects on Rhode Island barrier and lagoon and inferences on migration of barriers. *J. Geol.* **78**(1), 94–106.

EL-ASHRY, M. T. and WANLESS, H. R. 1965: Birth and early growth of a tidal delta. *J. Geol.* **73**(2), 404–6.

ELIE DE BEAUMONT, L. 1845: *Leçons de Geologie pratique.* 7me leçon—Levées de sables et galets. Paris.

FISHER, J. J. 1968: Barrier Island formation: discussion. *Bull. Geol. Soc. Am.* **76**(4), 1421–6.

GALLIERS, J. A. 1969: Barrier beaches and lagoons of the Ghana coasts. *Brit. Geomorph. Res. Gr. Occ. Pap.* **5,** 77–87.

GIERLOFF-EMDEN, H. G. 1959a: Lagunen, Nehrungen, Strandwälle und Flussmündungen in Geschehen tropischer Flachlandküsten. *Zeits. für Geomorph.* **3**(1), 29–46.

GIERLOFF-EMDEN, H. G. 1959b: Die Küste von El Salvador. *Deutsche Hydrog. Zeits.* **12**(1), 14–24.

GIERLOFF-EMDEN, H. G. 1961: Nehrungen und Lagunen. *Petermanns Geog. Mitt.* **105**(2), 81–92; **105**(3), 161–76.

GILBERT, G. K. 1890: *Lake Bonneville*. U.S. Geol. Surv. monograph.

GREENSMITH, J. T. and TUCKER, E. V. 1969: The origin of Holocene shell deposits in the Chenier Plain facies of Essex (G.B.). *Mar. Geol.* **7,** 403–25.

HAILS, J. R. 1964: The coastal depositional features of southeast Queensland. *Australian Geogr.* **9,** 207–17.

HAILS, J. R. and HOYT, J. H. 1969: An appraisal of the evolution of the Lower Atlantic coastal plains of Georgia, U.S.A. *Trans. Inst. Brit. Geogr.* **46,** 53–68.

HAYES, M. O. 1969: In *Coastal environments N.E. Massachusetts and New Hampshire*. Dept. Geol., Univ. Mass., 36–58.

HOYT, J. H. 1967: Barrier Island formation. *Bull. Geol. Soc. Am.* **78,** 1125–36.

HOYT, J. H. 1968: Barrier Island formation: reply. *Bull. Geol. Soc. Am.* **79**(7), 947; **79**(10), 1427–32.

HOYT, J. H. and HAILS, J. R. 1967: Pleistocene shoreline sediments in coastal Georgia: Deposition and modification. *Science* **155**(3769), 1541–3.

HOYT, J. H. and HENRY, V. J. 1967: Influence of island migration on barrier island sedimentation. *Bull. Geol. Soc. Am.* **78,** 77–86.

JELGERSMA, S. 1961: *Holocene sea level changes in the Netherlands*. Maastricht. (101 pp.)

JELGERSMA, S., DE JONG, J., ZAGWIJN, W. H. and VAN REGTEREN ALTENA, J. F. 1970: The coastal dunes of the western Netherlands; geology, vegetational history and archaeology. *Med. Rijks Geol. Dienst* Nieuwe Serie **21,** 93–166.

JOHNSON, D. W. 1919: Shore processes and shoreline development. New York: Wiley.

JONG, J. D. DE 1960: The morphological evolution of the Dutch coast. *Geol. en Mijnbouw* **39,** 638–43.

KESTNER, F. J. T. 1962: The old coastline of the Wash. *Geog. J.* **128**(4), 457–78.

KING, C. A. M. 1956: The coast of southeast Iceland near Ingolfshöfði. *Geog. J.* **122,** 241–6.

LE BLANC, R. F. and HODGSON, W. D. 1959: Origin and development of the Texas shoreline. *Gulf Coast Assoc. Geol. Soc. Trans.* **9,** 197–220.

O'BRIEN, M. P. 1967: Equilibrium flow areas of tidal inlets on sandy coasts. Chapter 39 in *Proc. 10th Conf. Coast. Eng.*, 676–86.

OTVOS, E. G. 1970: Development and migration of barrier islands, northern Gulf of Mexico. *Bull. Geol. Soc. Am.* **81,** 241–6.

PIERCE, J. W. 1970: Tidal inlets and washover fans. *J. Geol.* **78**(2), 230–34.

PRICE, A. W. 1954: Environment and formation of the chenier plain. *A. and M. Project* **63.**

RUSSELL, R. J. 1967: Aspects of coastal morphology. *Geogr. Ann.* **49**A(2–4), 299–309.

SAVILLE, T. and CALDWELL, J. M. 1957: Preliminary Report of a laboratory study of the effect of uncontrolled inlets on the adjacent beach. *B.E.B. Tech. Memo.* **94.** (19 pp.)

SCHOU, A. 1967: Pecan Island: A chenier ridge in the Mississippi marginal delta plain. *Geogr. Ann.* **49**A(2–4), 321–6.

SCHROEDER-LANZ, H., WIENEKE, F. and SCHMIDT, W. 1967: Die Mündung der Lagune von Melides (Portugal). *Mitt. Geog. Gesell. München* **52,** 267–79.

SHEPARD, F. P. 1963. *Submarine geology*, 2nd edition. New York: Harper & Row. (557 pp.)

SWIFT, D. J. P. 1968: Coastal erosion and transgressional stratigraphy. *J. Geol.* **76**(4), 444–56.

VAN STRAATEN, L. M. J. U. 1961: Directional effects of winds, waves and currents along the Dutch North Sea coast. *Geol. en Mijnbouw* **40,** 333–46.

VAN STRAATEN, L. M. J. U. 1965: Coastal barrier deposits in south and north Holland in particular in the area around Scheveningen and Ijmuiden. *Meded. Geol. Sticht.* NS **17,** 41–75.

ZENKOVICH, V. P. 1959: On the genesis of cuspate spits along lagoon shores. *J. Geol.* **67**(3), 269–77.

21 The marine cycle—conclusion

1 **Tempo of marine change**

2 **The cycle concept—changes of sea level**

3 **The penultimate stage of a theoretical cycle**

4 **The ultimate stage**

5 **Conclusions**

Summary

In this final chapter some general problems concerning beach and coastal phenomena are commented upon briefly. One point that should have become apparent is the great variability of beaches and the great variety of beach and coastal types. Coasts are among the most rapidly changing of geomorphological phenomena, yet there is considerable variation in the speed with which different forms change and evolve. This matter is touched upon first and it leads on to the consideration of the concept of a cycle of coastal development. A cycle implies continued development, so that it is useful to consider the characteristics that beaches and coasts would be expected to have if they were given sufficient time to evolve to a late stage of development. Thus the penultimate and ultimate states of the coast are briefly speculated upon, leading to the final conclusions concerning the present nature of the beaches and coasts around the world.

1 Tempo of marine change

Some comments have already been made in various connections concerning the rate at which marine processes operate. Relaxation time was mentioned in the first chapter, and the scales of shoreline change suggested by M. L. Schwartz (1967) were discussed in chapter 17. Schwartz suggested three important tempos of change, the swash–backwash changes, covering periods of about a minute, tidal cycles and seasonal cycles occurring over a period of a few weeks to a few months, and long-term changes related to major change of sea level, covering periods of several thousand years. The former two periods are important on beaches, while the latter is relevant to coastal change and development.

Beaches, therefore, may be considered as working to a dynamic equilibrium over the short term, while coasts develop continuously over a much longer period. There is, however, considerable variety in the rate at which coasts develop. Examples of the rates of coastal erosion were given in chapter 17. Some areas were shown to retreat at considerable rates, such as Holderness, where erosion occurs at about 1 m/year. Others, such as the hard rock coasts of Devon and Cornwall, show negligible changes over the period of human occupance.

A large number of variables determine the rate of coastal erosion in these two contrasting areas. The nature of the rock is particularly important in determining the rate of erosion, because exposure favours the west coast rather than the east coast for erosion. Another variable that is of vital importance in explaining the tempo of coastal erosion and accretion in many areas is the amount and constancy of longshore drift along the coast. Only where material is being gained or lost from alongshore will permanent accretion or continuous loss occur. In determining the amount and direction of longshore drift the coastal outline and the exposure are important factors. Where the coast is in equilibrium with the waves shaping it changes will be slow and will rarely be continuous in one direction, as long as the controlling variables remain constant.

In the short term variability depends on changing wave conditions, but relative stability may be established around a dynamic equilibrium state. It is very unlikely in the longer term, however, that the other controlling variables will remain constant. The one that has varied most in the recent geological past, and especially during the post-glacial period, is the level of the sea. The position of the coastline depends on this variable to a large extent. At present all coasts can be considered to be undergoing some change, although not all changes are measurable on the human time scale.

Coastal changes have been shown to be continuous in some areas. The long-continued erosion in Holderness and the prolonged accretion on Dungeness are examples. In the latter area the actual extent of accretion has not been constant, owing to erosion partly compensating for deposition in the later stages. In some instances, however, coastal developments have been shown to be cyclic in character. Spurn Head is a good example of regular growth and decay. A somewhat similar but less regular cycle of spit development takes place at Gibraltar Point in Lincolnshire. In both instances, but particularly in the Spurn Head spit, evidence of the cycle can be derived from historical material. The active and dynamic nature of the beach and coast environment is readily apparent when the tempo of change is compared to that of many other geomorphological processes.

2 The cycle concept—changes of sea level

One of the basic assumptions of the cycle concept is that of a stable base level. Only if the base level is stable can a cycle run its course, whether it be on land or at the coast. This basic requirement has not been fulfilled during the development of any of the world's present coastlines. Thus the concept of a coastal cycle of erosion must be largely theoretical. There is not enough evidence in the geological record to study fully the possible character of coasts at different stages of a possible past coastal cycle of erosion. This is inevitably so, because much of the cycle must be erosional and erosional forms cannot be studied after they have been destroyed by subsequent erosion. The difficulties of a cycle concept are made apparent in the problems of coastal classification. Classifications that are not based on a cycle concept are the most useful. This is an indication of the difficulties inherent in a consideration of a marine cycle. The classifications that stress present changes and include a time element are the most valuable, but may be difficult to apply, in that they demand a knowledge of the changes the coast has undergone and is undergoing.

Rather than consider a theoretical cycle, it is more useful to analyse coastal features in terms of transgressions and regressions of the sea. These processes are fundamental in geology in that marine sedimentary record is closely linked with variations in sea level. This approach to present world shorelines is especially necessary in view of the recent and large-scale fluctuations of sea level brought about through the alternating growth and melting of large ice sheets.

The variations in sea level in the late and post-glacial periods were discussed in chapter 7. In this section some broad results of these changes will be considered. The late and post-glacial eustatic fluctuations of sea level consist of a phase of rapid rise between 20,000 and about 7000 years ago, a phase of slower rise between 7000 and 3000 years ago, and a final short phase of relative stability lasting since then. The effect of these changes has been considered for various areas by J. R. Curray (1964). Basing his views on a scheme similar to those suggested by H. Valentin (1952) and later by M. L. Schwartz (1967), he considers the combined effects of varying phases of transgression and the net rate of erosion and deposition along the coast. The resulting changes along any coastline can be illustrated on a diagram, such as in figure 21-1, which divides the possible effects into eight classes. Individual areas can be indicated by points on the diagram as indicated in the smaller insets in the figure. A few examples will be described to illustrate the coastal types that result under different combinations of sedimentation with the three standard phases of transgression. Although regression must have preceded the last transgression, it has not left sufficient evidence for a detailed analysis. Its general significance in coastal morphology will be mentioned in the last section.

The effect of transgression, such as has occurred in the last 20,000 years, depends on the nature of the slope over which the sea has risen. It also depends on the nature of sedimentation that accompanied the rising sea level. For the sake of simplicity the situations have been confined to three phases of sea level change, an initial rapid rise, followed by a period of slower rise, and finally one of stability. Three types of sedimentation are considered, a high rate of deposition, a low rate of deposition, and erosion. The divisions are entirely arbitrary, as both variables are continuous. The diagonal line in the diagram indicates a static shoreline. To the right transgression occurs, to the left regression of the shoreline takes place. The situation for each phase of sea level change can be shown.

The continental shelf off Rockport in Texas shows moderate to low deposition in the first two phases, becoming zero in the third phase. During the first two phases transgressive basal sand facies were deposited on the shelf as sea level rose, consisting of beach, dune and nearshore sands. Finer bay facies were deposited behind the barrier islands when sea level reached phase two. The wide shelf in this area would ensure a very rapid movement of the shoreline up the shelf. The barrier islands were probably built up during phase two, when deposition balanced the rise of sea level. The present shoreline is stationary, indicating little erosion or deposition since the sea reached its present level. Shelf muds are, however, gradually thickening by slow deposition on the outer shelf and covering the sandy facies, as shown in figure 21-1B.

The Mississippi delta provides an interesting contrast as it is an area of very high sedimentation rate. Sea level changes have been enhanced in this area by subsidence due to compaction of the thick sediments. Sedimentation is, however, localized, with different distributaries providing a variable amount of sediment in different areas at various times. Occasionally some areas receive no sediment and undergo transgression as a result. This state is indicated by the point marked IIIb in figure 21-1A. Transgression occurred during the rapid rise of sea level when the sedimentation could not keep pace with the rising sea level. The sediments of this phase include transgressive littoral and alluvial sands and muds. Bottomset muds overlie these sandier deposits. The deposits of phases IIa and IIIa may be described as ones of depositional regression, while phase IIIb is one of erosional transgression. This represents a phase when deposition ceased and erosion occurred, assisted by local subsidence. During phase IIIb some destructive sands were deposited over the deltaic beds. The section shown in figure 21-1 is hypothetical and composite, but it illustrates the type of sedimentation taking place under these conditions. A similar pattern applies to the other chenier marshlands of Louisiana.

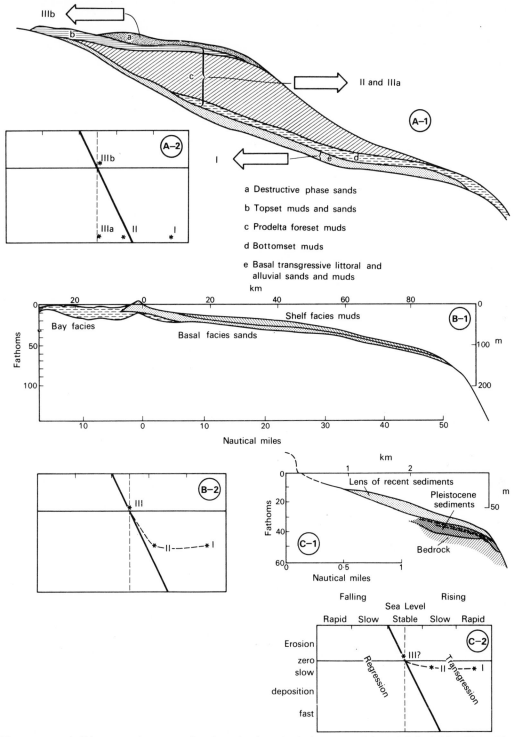

IIIb

II and IIIa

I

(A–1)

(A–2)

a Destructive phase sands

b Topset muds and sands

c Prodelta foreset muds

d Bottomset muds

e Basal transgressive littoral and
   alluvial sands and muds

km

Bay facies

Shelf facies muds

Basal facies sands

Fathoms

Nautical miles

(B–1)

(B–2)

km

Lens of recent sediments

Pleistocene
sediments

Bedrock

Fathoms

Nautical miles

(C–1)

Falling   Rising
Sea Level

Rapid Slow Stable Slow Rapid

Erosion

zero

slow

deposition

fast

Regression

Transgression

(C–2)

Figure 21-1 A: Diagrammatic cross-section through a hypothetical subdelta of the Mississippi delta. Phase I basal transgression deposits laid down. Phases II and IIIa show progradation of subdelta across shelf in depositional regression. Phase IIIb subdelta abandoned, leading to compaction and erosion and transgression. **B:** Section through late Quaternary sediments near Rockport, Texas, showing basal transgressive sandy sediments in phases I and II. Barrier island deposits and bay facies and inner shelf muds laid down during phases II and III. **C:** Generalized section off Palos Verdes, California. (*After Curray, 1964.*)

The Pacific coast of North America is one of less rapid deposition. Off Palos Verdes, California, slow deposition took place in phases I and II, as shown in figure 21-1C. One of the contrasts between this area and the Gulf of Mexico is the narrow shelf in the Pacific area. Thus a given rise of sea level will cause only a small migration of the shoreline. The shelf in this area is only 2·4 km wide compared with 80 km off Texas. Sediment thicknesses are greater on a narrow shelf with the same rate of sediment supply, owing to the very slow rate at which sea level advances across a steep, narrow shelf, and the fact that sediment can reach the whole shelf area. A lense of sediment, which is thickest in the centre of the shelf, collects. It thins at the outer edge and at about 22 m, on the inner margin. Deposition was greater in the first two phases than in the last. The strata probably represent shelf rather than beach facies. At La Jolla, where the rate of sediment supply was low owing to the presence of canyons offshore, only a thin veneer of sediment occurs on part of the narrow shelf, which is about 4 km wide here. Erosion has probably exceeded deposition in this area.

It seems likely that the rates of sea level transgression considered in this section, which apply to the late and post-glacial phases, were very rapid compared to those of earlier geological periods. It is possible that in the more quiescent geological eras the sea did in fact reach a measure of stability. If this were so, then the evidence on the modern coast is non-existent. The geological evidence, moreover, is not suitable for the reconstruction of various stages of possible past cycles of coastal land forms.

D. J. P. Swift (1968) has revived L. D. Stamp's term 'ravinement' in his discussion of the effects of transgression on coastal erosion and stratigraphy. The term is applied to disconformities in a transgressional sequence of deposits. The disconformities are caused by bevelling of former marginal, coastal deposits of the same contemporaneous cycle by the surf zone processes. P. Bruun's (1962) theory of shore erosion in relation to sea level rise provides the theoretical explanation of the process leading to ravinement, and M. L. Schwartz (1967) has justified it experimentally and by field tests.

Ravinement can take different forms. Where the wave energy is greater than the sediment supply, spits are moved shoreward over marsh deposits, which are exposed on the seaward side of the spit. Where the sediment supply is greater barriers form, but do not shift landwards. They grow upwards until they are abandoned by the shift of sea level. Examples of these processes are seen on the coast of the Bay of Fundy. Ravinement is the consequence of the shoreward migration of various beach zones and their associated facies. Shoreface erosion is an important factor in the ravinement process. Not all transgressional facies, however, include erosional elements. Transgressions can produce either erosional or depositional results according to the relative net deposition in relation to the rate of rise of sea level. The ravinement process is most important in the erosional transgressions.

A good example of rapid erosional transgression is seen in the flooding of the New England coast by the quick eustatic sea level rise between 12,000 and 11,000 B.P. Erosional transgression is now occurring on the south coast of Florida, where mangrove peat is emerging on the lower beach. A similar process is taking place in east Lincolnshire, where post-glacial sediments are often exposed to the lower foreshore. Ravinement can also take place during depositional transgression. The depth of reworking of sediment is an important consideration. Ravinement can only fail to operate when the shore face becomes mantled with lag deposits. This will protect the underlying deposits from erosion during the transgression. Thus ravinement depends more on the factors that determine the depth of reworking. These include the tide range, the intensity and direction of wave attack, amount and type of sediment supply and the relative rate of sea level rise.

Modern sedimentation is the result of the balance of sea level change and the supply of material. Sands brought to the coast at present do not come to rest further than 4·8 km from the shore off the Rhone delta, the Texas coast and most others, where depths are 9 to 18 m. Sand is distributed by the waves and tides on the beaches and the nearshore zone. Mud is carried further offshore, but probably rarely beyond about 32 km. Widespread marine coastal deposits can only have been laid down during periods of migration of the water line through transgression or regression. An exception to this generalization is provided by submarine canyons, through which material can be widely disseminated from the shallow-water zone into the deep ocean basins.

3 The penultimate stage of a theoretical cycle

As coastal modification takes place there is a tendency for the coastal outline to be simplified. The process is partly achieved by the concentration of wave attack on the headlands by wave refraction, and the filling of the indentations by deposits. The deposits gradually adjust themselves to the waves that built them. Eventually they become aligned parallel to the refracted dominant wave crests. As the bottom contours become smoother, the forms will tend to become simpler as they adjust to the more regular pattern of waves. Thus both erosion and deposition will help to achieve a general simplification or straightening of the coast.

The extent to which this process can continue is dependent on the depth of the surf-base. This point was mentioned in chapter 9, mainly from the point of view of sediment movement. It is also relevant in connection with wave erosion, which is important in considering the penultimate stage of marine erosion, and to the eventual planation of large areas.

A simple model of the theoretical effect of both rising and falling sea levels on the cutting of a platform by wave erosion will be considered. Certain assumptions are made in the model (C. A. M. King, 1963). It is assumed that the original coast was steeper than the equilibrium profile on the wave-cut platform, that there is a maximum depth below which wave erosion will not be effective in solid rock—the surf-base—and that there is a minimum slope below which the waves cannot flatten the rock slope. The effects of both a rising and a falling sea level are considered. The theoretical results based on this model are shown in figure 21-2. They show that with a falling sea level the resultant slope will be parallel to the original slope and only very narrow benches will occur if the sea level falls in small steps. A sea level rising in similar small steps, on the other hand, can produce a wide, gently sloping surface, the gradient of which is at the minimum angle that the waves can erode the rock. If the minimum gradient is taken to be about 1 : 100, which is the measured gradient of some surf-cut platforms, then a stable sea level could not form a platform wider than 1220 m, assuming a surf-base of 12·2 m. This value is in excess of some estimates (N. C. Flemming, 1965) and probably represents the maximum width of a surf-cut platform likely to occur with a stable sea level.

The result is difficult to reconcile with the views of D. W. Johnson, who claimed that the whole land surface could be reduced to what he termed 'wave-base' at a depth of 183 m. It is, therefore, concluded that only during a prolonged transgression could a wide surf-abraded surface be formed. This point is also made by R. S. Dietz (1963). He cites the shelf off part of California as a rock-cut surface on which thin modern sediments rest. The penultimate stage of the cycle, given a stable base level, would not be likely to progress very far in producing a wide zone of erosion.

Dietz points out that only in relatively shallow water are waves effective agents of erosion and deposition. The maximum depth of effective wave action he terms the 'surf-base'. This term is

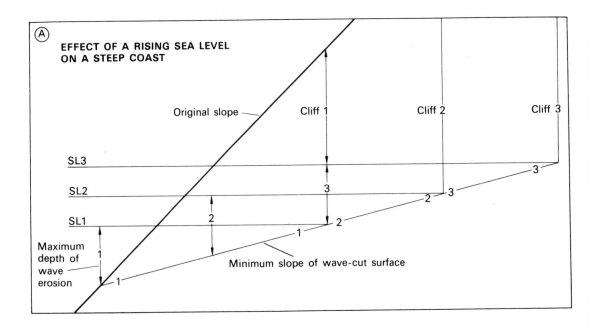

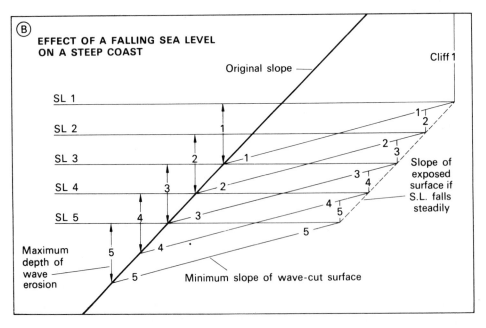

Figure 21-2 The theoretical formation of wave-cut surfaces on a steeply sloping coast **A:** with a rising sea level; **B:** with a falling sea level. Three basic assumptions are made: (1) the initial coast is steeper than the wave-cut platform; (2) there is a maximum depth below which waves cannot erode; (3) there is a minimum gradient below which waves cannot flatten the platform, but to which they will reduce it.

used in preference to 'wave-base', which has been used by different people to refer to different things. Surf-base is the maximum depth to which waves can erode solid rock and move substantial amounts of sand. It is probably about 10 m deep or less according to the length of the waves to which the coast is exposed. All significant wave action is confined with the area between surf-base and the backshore zone. Tidal processes may operate effectively in deeper water and these should not be ignored. Some of the tidal processes were considered in chapter 5.

R. M. Sorensen (1969) has discussed the concept of wave base with reference to the formation of marine terraces along part of the coast of California. His results conflict with suggested levels of wave base or surf base. The coast he studied is tectonically active and has been tilting seawards; the continental shelf is narrow, and the offshore zone is a modern wave-cut platform at least $\frac{1}{2}$ mile (800 m) wide. It is probably continuous for $1\frac{1}{2}$ miles (2·4 km), where the depth is 75 feet (23 m). The slope is about 1° near the shore, flattening to $\frac{1}{2}$° further offshore. The expected surf base in this area would be about 10 m. The average rate of cliff recession over a period of 80 years was measured at 0·4 m/year from surveys carried out between 1851 and 1860, and between 1932 and 1933. The actual depths recorded offshore are deeper than would be expected if sea level had been at its present height for about the last 5000 years. Sorensen argues that the greater depth throws doubt on the concept of a surf base at about 10 m. Because, however, the area in which he made his observations is tectonically very unstable, it is not certain that the world-wide eustatic sea level changes are applicable in this area. Alternatively the relatively low offshore platform could have been cut during a lower glacial sea level.

Within the zone of significant wave action material moves mainly shoreward. The reasons for this movement were examined in chapters 4 and 9. This conclusion raises the problem of wave-built terraces, which are generally shown as developing during the later stages of the theoretical marine cycle, for example by D. W. Johnson (1919). It seems reasonable to agree with Dietz that this concept is wrong, and that a wave-built terrace of the type advocated by Johnson does not in fact exist. There is no known process by which waves can transport large amounts of sediment seawards to the area beyond the surf-base. All evidence points to a predominant landward movement from the surf-base to the break-point of the waves. Even destructive waves cannot carry sand far offshore beyond the surf-base.

The only feature that would merit the name of wave-built terrace is the berm built up by the swash of the waves at the upper limit of their action. This process builds the massive berms and offshore barrier islands that characterize a prograding shore. It was to this type of feature, on a much smaller scale, that G. K. Gilbert referred when he introduced the term 'wave-built terrace' in his work on Lake Bonneville. The term has since been applied to the supposed wave deposited wedge of sediment that is shown as forming the continental shelf. In fact a wave-built terrace of this type does not appear to exist, so it is recommended that the term be no longer used.

The form of the continental shelf is reflected in the coastal morphology. It determines the way in which waves will be modified and refracted before they reach the coast, especially where long swells feel the bottom in depths of 150 m or more. D. S. Gorsline (1963) has shown that the sediments of the Atlantic shelf off the U.S.A. represent several periods of sedimentation. Only the nearshore zone consists of deposits related to present wave activity. These sediments are derived via the rivers from the coastal plain deposits. Much of this material, however, is trapped between the barrier islands and the mainland in the coastal marshes. The sediments of the central shelf are relics of lower stands of sea level and are now areas of non-deposition, beyond the area where silty sands are being deposited at present.

D. G. Moore and J. R. Curray (1964), in commenting upon Dietz's paper, suggest that the term 'wave-base' be retained, but that it be related to processes operating on the shelf in a more realistic manner. Problems associated with the term 'wave-base' are associated with different usages of the term. Some workers use it to denote the limit of wave erosion, others the limit of wave deposition, and still others suggest that it is related to the depth of the shelf edge. The latter is not suitable, as it is generally agreed that the shelf edge is a relict feature of low glacial sea level. The coarse sediments on the outer shelf are also relict from these times.

It is more realistic to consider wave-base in terms of particle size. As indicated in chapter 11 different-sized particles begin to move under wave action at different depths. There is, therefore, a zone of wave-base and not a line. Moore and Curray suggest that it is most useful to consider wave-base in the context of a cyclic period of the order of 100 years. During this period at least one severe storm may be expected to occur that can cause major changes that affect the processes operating during the remainder of the time. The whole of the period should be integrated to produce a sum of the effects of both normal quiet conditions and the occasional severe storm. The profile of equilibrium would become adjusted to the integrated processes that have operated over the whole of the cyclic period. Wave-base can then be defined as the depth over which the cyclic period processes have an effect.

Surf-base, on the other hand, marks the lower limit of the major changes that occur within the zone of active wave processes related to the breaking of the wave, and changes in its movement leading up to the breaking. There has not been sufficient time since the recent changes of sea level for the shelves to become adjusted to the new wave-base, as defined by Moore and Curray.

The return to grade of the continental shelves has been discussed by D. J. P. Swift (1970). He points to the presence of the nearshore modern sand prism, based on the null line mechanism, which is related to the surf-base as defined by Dietz. It is this zone that has been considered in this book. The zone further offshore is, however, relevant to the eventual result of prolonged marine action at one sea level.

In the zone seaward of the modern nearshore sand prism the cyclic period of Moore and Curray is effective. Wave-drift currents may be a dominant control in this zone. Sedimentation on the central shelf will only occur during storms. Movement in this zone is, therefore, likely to be random. The sediment surface will rise slowly due to the periodic sedimentation during storm activity. The source of sediment is the nearshore sand prism, and the sink is the shelf edge. There would be a net seaward movement on the central shelf. Tides and other agents would also be effective in this zone.

The first stage in establishing grade after a change of level is sorting of material on the shelf by size. Some of the material in the nearshore sand prism is derived from winnowing of the central shelf sediment at this stage. The second stage is the by-passing of the over-deepened estuaries by fine material in suspension. These sediments eventually accumulate as muds on the quieter parts of the shelf. Blankets of mud, prograding seaward, form as a result. The climax occurs when sand is also by-passed. Deposition of sand then takes place across the whole shelf. This is an ideal rather than a normative process of shelf equilibrium. At present the shelves are still in the early stage of the return to grade. Modern sedimentation of fine material is limited to certain parts of the shelf and much is still trapped in the estuaries. Eventually erosion must occur at the water line if the cycle is to progress once grade has been re-established.

The form of erosional platforms has been considered by N. C. Flemming (1965) in relation to past sea levels, both above and below the present. He has worked out an equation for the rate of development of a shore platform in terms of E, the rate of energy expenditure, and T, the time of erosion. The equation is

$$ET = R(x^2 \tan \alpha/2 - Dx/2) + F(x^3 \tan \alpha/3D - x^2/4)$$

where R is one unit of rock, F is a frictional resistance factor, D is the maximum depth of erosion or the surf-base, x is the width of the platform, and α is the slope of the original surface into which the platform is cut. The equation implies rapid erosion at first, slowing rapidly with time, but not reaching zero. Flemming assumes, following Bradley (1958), that D is equal to 9·15 m and that the probable minimum slope is 1 : 100, with a slightly concave profile. The conditions agree with those stated earlier as the assumptions on which the model of coastal platform erosion was built.

The penultimate stage of the theoretical cycle of erosion is frequently considered to be the state of maturity. The coastal outline has been theoretically smoothed and simplified, and the cliffs have been substantially cut back to produce wide abrasion platforms, with long beaches, occupying intervening stretches. Owing to the short period—not exceeding 3000 years—since sea level reached its present height, only where coastal change is rapid is it likely that such a stage could have been reached. Most coasts of the world are still in a state of immature development. Those small portions that could be described as mature are set amongst long stretches of immature coast. Conditions are not ideal for the further development beyond maturity.

Even in rapidly retreating coasts, such as Holderness, the amount of modification that is possible in 3000 years is limited. This coast is retreating at about 1 m/year, giving 3 km retreat in 3000 years, a value agreeing closely with other estimates. A retreat of 3 km would not allow a great deal of simplification to take place along an indented coast. It is thus concluded that only very limited stretches of the present coastline could even theoretically be considered as reaching the penultimate stage of the cycle of coastal erosion. The concept of such a cycle must, therefore, remain theoretical. There is, however, some evidence to be found in the geological record of possible conditions during periods of prolonged stability. This state may have been more common in the geologically quiet periods of the past.

4 The ultimate stage

According to D. W. Johnson (1919), during the old age stage of the cycle, the coastal abrasion platform increases greatly in width and is extended seaward by a wide continental terrace, while on its landward side a low, degraded cliff may be found. This feature will become imperceptible in time as the wave energy is almost completely expended in crossing the wide shelf. At the same time subaerial denudation will have reduced the height of the land to a small value. As the land is reduced in height so the supply of material to the sea would also be reduced to small quantities of fine debris. The landward part of the shelf would be almost bare rock as the fine material would more easily be carried to the offshore zone in suspension. This would not speed up the erosion of the platform, however, as it has been shown that material must be larger than about 0·5 mm diameter before it can cause appreciable erosion.

Johnson cites the strandflat off the west coast of Norway and part of the east coast of India as examples of very wide wave-cut platforms. Neither of these areas, however, show features corresponding to Johnson's theoretical old age stage, when degraded cliffs should be very low inconspicuous features. C. A. Cotton (1955) points out that features of both these areas can be more reasonably explained as the result of quite different denudational processes.

The Norwegian strandflat has been discussed in detail by F. Nansen (1922), who considers it to be the result of glacial sapping by ice-foot glaciers. It is about 50 to 65 km wide and is backed by steeply rising ground. The whole area has undergone rapid vertical movements in the recent geological past. The example from India consists of a low-lying plain up to 80 km wide in places.

It is backed by steep cliffs and there are on it very steep-sided residuals. Cotton explains this feature as an example of subaerial weathering and erosion under climatic conditions conducive to the formation of inselbergs, rising from a flat surface.

Cotton reached the conclusion, which is quite justified, that the theoretical concept of Johnson (1933) regarding marine planation is not proven. He considers, however, that it remains a highly probable theory. The problem of marine planation, in the way envisaged by Johnson, is related to the problem of the constancy of sea level. He considered that the ultimate stage could be reached without subsidence of the land. Other workers, however, have suggested that a slowly rising sea level will greatly assist the completion of the cycle. Among these are W. M. Davis (1896) and F. von Richthofen (1886). The latter considers a rising base level essential for planation, and owing to the relatively small depth to which waves can abrade rock surfaces, this conclusion is justified.

It is difficult to imagine the conditions under which sea level could remain constant for periods long enough to effect complete marine planation of an area of considerable extent. In the 500 million years since the pre-Cambrian, however, only two relatively short periods of glaciation have occurred.

The speed with which land masses may be reduced to peneplanes has been discussed by D. L. Linton (1957). He suggests that peneplanation of a continental margin could be achieved in 20 to 40 million years according to the range of initial relief. The erosion would mainly be carried out by subaerial agencies, while the sea was cutting a bench round the edge of the land. The effect of changing sea level on marine and subaerial denudation varies. A slight change of sea level of about 3 to 6 m will not have a marked result on the denudation of the inland area. A similar fall of sea level on the coast will cause the sea to start afresh on its work of altering the coastline. This is illustrated on parts of the west coast of Scotland. A raised beach at about 4·5 m has been stranded above the level of the waves, which have started to cliff the rocks again at a lower level. A similar fall in sea level accelerates subaerial erosion, except in the rather unusual case where the gradient across the newly exposed land is flatter than that of the lower reaches of the pre-existing river.

The evidence of the great geological transgressions of the past indicates that very extensive areas have been reduced to an almost plane surface. These surfaces are covered by marine sediments. The main work of reducing the surface to a peneplane was probably largely the result of subaerial processes. The fact that the overlying strata are marine is not proof that the surface on which they rest is the result of marine planation. The final trimming of the surface before the deposition of the marine sediments was, however, done by the waves. Evidence for this is shown by the fact that the marine sediments normally rest on the eroded edges of the older rocks. There is no sign of subaerial weathering or any intervening subaerial deposits.

The Cretaceous period in Europe is one in which a great transgression of the sea gradually spread marine deposits over old, worn-down land masses. The transgression took many millions of years to complete. The gradually expanding sea spread more and more widely as time went on, as the later strata covered the maximum area. The transgression, which spread from restricted Jurassic basins, finally covered nearly all Europe north of the Alpine geosyncline. Sea level must have been rising slowly and steadily throughout this long period. The rising sea would have facilitated the trimming of the underlying rocks by the waves over such a wide area.

5 Conclusions

The coasts of the world at present offer greater variety than probably existed throughout the greater part of geological time. The present variety is due to the rapid fluctuations of sea level during the last few million years, resulting from glacio-eustatic effects. Coastal forms at present are strongly affected by the most recent of these major oscillations of sea level. During the last major ice advance, which reached its maximum about 20,000 years ago, sea level was about 100 m lower than present. While sea level was low rivers cut down. The major valleys so formed were subsequently drowned to form deep embayments that are common along many coasts of the world.

The glaciers and ice sheets, as well as causing the lowering of sea level, also brought down to the sea large volumes of material of all grades, including boulders, shingle, sand and finer sediments. These glacial and fluvioglacial deposits have provided much beach material in higher latitudes. The frequent occurrence of shingle beaches in previously glaciated areas is probably largely due to the availability of these coarse, glacially-derived materials.

The most recent movement of sea level has been the late and post-glacial rise. This transgression has drowned the previously eroded landscape to produce many indentations. The intricate outline, in its turn, is responsible for the many complex depositional forms that were described in chapter 19. The transgression also played an important part in producing the barrier island shorelines, which were discussed in chapter 20, and which occupy 13% of the world's coastline. Much of the sandy material forming these massive structures was derived from that left exposed on the continental shelves when sea level fell, due to the growth of ice sheets. This material has been swept up by the transgressing sea and built by the waves into barrier islands, where the coast is low and has a gentle gradient. On the steeper, indented coasts the material has formed many complex spits, tombolos and barriers.

It is only in the last 3000 years that sea level has been more or less constant in some areas at least. This is too short a time for coastal features to reach stability. Thus changes are still taking place at a fairly rapid rate along many coastlines. It is interesting to speculate on the possible future state of the beaches if sea level maintains its present stand for an appreciable time. R. J. Russell (1967) argues that the supply of sediment reaching the sea from inland is likely to be reduced. This is the main source of supply, once the waves have steepened the offshore slope to such an extent that little more can be brought up from offshore. Factors causing the reduction of sediment from inland include the increasing use being made of dams across rivers, and reduction of river discharge due to increased water use. Both factors would allow more material to remain in the river valleys. Slope conservation measures would also cut down the load reaching the sea.

When the sediment supply is reduced coastal erosion is more likely to become severe, because the best protection for a coast is a wide, high beach. There may, therefore, be an increasing need to supply beaches artificially. Permanent loss of beach material occurs when material is carried offshore in rip currents, and along submarine canyons, into depths below those at which it can be transferred inland by wave action.

The opposite view is put forward by J. R. Curray (1964). He considers that, if sea level remained constant for a long period, some of the coastlines of the world would tend to prograde seaward, as a result of depositional regression. He states that marine deposition is now slow. Much material is deposited in the deeply eroded Pleistocene bays and estuaries, which are as yet unfilled, rather than on open ocean beaches and shelves. When the bays are filled there will be more material available for shelf sedimentation. Much of this would be deposited on the beaches and inner shelf. Relict sediments would in time be covered by sediments in equilibrium with their new environment. The time would be long, however, by Pleistocene standards, although short by geological ones. Shelf sedimentation would be counteracted by the trapping of material inland by dams across rivers and other factors. He agrees with Russell in suggesting that the filling of the estuaries will be slowed down and there may be a loss of sand along the coasts, before progradation can become general.

The problem is to a certain extent a theoretical one, because it is most unlikely that sea level will remain static for long enough to enable either possibility to be fulfilled. The melting of the present ice masses should lead to a further rise of sea level of the order of 30 m. On the other hand it is equally possible that further ice advances may take place, causing a renewed lowering of sea level.

At present the coastal scene is far from stable. A wealth of different features are available for study along both the smooth, low coastlines and the highly intricate steep coasts, which have been inherited from the complex sequence of events that took place during the Pleistocene and recent periods. These features provide the raw material of coastal geomorphology. Their characteristics and the processes operating upon them have been examined in this book.

Summary

Beaches can reach a dynamic equilibrium over a short period of about 1 to 10 minutes in the swash–backwash zone, and over a period of weeks or months in the zone between surf-base and the backshore. Coasts develop continuously over much longer periods. The cycle concept of coastal development implies the long-continued stability of sea level. As sea level has varied rapidly and greatly during the Pleistocene and recent periods the cycle concept can only be considered theoretically. It is more useful to consider the effects of regressions and transgressions. During the last 20,000 years sea level first rose rapidly, then more slowly and has been static during the last 3000 years. The effect of these three phases depends on the nature of the coast and shelf and the supply of sediment. Where sediment supply is large, depositional regression has been followed by erosional transgression. A simple model of the formation of wave-cut surfaces indicates that a wide, gently sloping surface can only form when sea level is rising. Waves cannot erode rocks below surf-base, which is about 10 m depth. Because material tends to move shorewards in the zone landward of surf-base a wave-built terrace, as suggested by D. W. Johnson, cannot form. At present coasts are immature and the shelf is still returning towards a graded condition. The only evidence of the ultimate stage of marine erosion is found in the plane surfaces beneath major marine transgressions, such as the Cretaceous transgression in Europe. The immature stage of development of present coasts accounts for the great variety and variability of present coastal features.

References

BRADLEY, W. C. 1958: Submarine abrasion and wave cut platforms. *Bull. Geol. Soc. Am.* **69**, 967–74.
BRUUN, P. 1962: Sea level rise as a cause of shore erosion. *J. Waterways and Harbours Div. Am. Soc. Civ. Eng. Proc.* **88**, 117–30.
COTTON, C. A. 1955: The theory of secular marine planation. *Am. J. Sci.* **253**, 580–89.

CURRAY, J. R. 1964: Transgressions and regressions. In Miller, R. L. (Editor), *Papers in marine geology: Shepard commemorative volume*, New York: Macmillan, 175–203.

DAVIS, W. M. 1896: Plains of marine and subaerial denudation. *Bull. Geol. Soc. Am.* **7,** 377–98.

DIETZ, R. S. 1963: Wave-base, marine profile of equilibrium and wave built terraces: a critical appraisal. *Bull. Geol. Soc. Am.* **74,** 971–90; A reply, **74,** 1275–81.

FLEMMING, N. C. 1965: Form and relation to present sea level of Pleistocene marine erosion features. *J. Geol.* **73,** 799–811.

GORSLINE, D. S. 1963: Bottom sediments of the Atlantic shelf and slope off the southern United States. *J. Geol.* **71,** 422–40.

GULLIVER, F. P. 1899: Shoreline topography. *Proc. Am. Acad. Arts and Sci.* **34,** 189.

JOHNSON, D. W. 1919: Shore processes and shoreline development. New York: Wiley. (584 pp.)

JOHNSON, D. W. 1933: Role of analysis in scientific investigations. *Geol. Soc. Am. Bull.* **44,** 461–94.

KING, C. A. M. 1963: Some problems concerning marine planation and the formation of erosion surfaces. *Trans. Int. Brit. Geogr.* **33,** 29–43.

LINTON, D. L. 1957: The everlasting hills. *Adv. of Sci.* **14,** 58–67.

MOORE, D. G. and CURRAY, J. R. 1964: Wave-base, marine profile of equilibrium and wave built terraces: Discussion. *Bull. Geol. Soc. Am.* **74,** 1267–73.

NANSEN, F. 1922: Strandflat and isostasy. *Vidensk Skr. M. N. kl.* **11.**

PRICE, W. A. 1954: Dynamic environments. *Trans. Gulf. Coast Assoc. Geol. Soc.* **4,** 75–107.

RICHTHOFEN, F. VON 1886: *Führer fur Forschungsreisende.* Hanover.

RUSSELL, R. J. 1967: Aspects of coastal morphology. *Geogr. Ann.* **49**A(2–4), 299–309.

SCHWARTZ, M. L. 1967: The Bruun theory of sea level rise as a cause of shore erosion. *J. Geol.* **75,** 76–91.

SORENSEN, R. M. 1969: Recession of marine terraces—with special reference to the coastal area north of Santa Cruz, California. Chapter 42 in *Coastal engineering* **1;** *Proc. 11th Conf. Coast. Eng. London, 1968,* New York: Am. Soc. Civ. Eng., 653–69.

STAMP, L. D. 1922: An outline of the Tertiary geology of Burma. *Geol. Mag.* **59,** 481–501.

SWIFT, D. J. P. 1968: Coastal erosion and transgressive stratigraphy. *J. Geol.* **76**(4), 444–56.

SWIFT, D. J. P. 1970: Quaternary shelves and the return to grade. *Mar. Geol.* **8**(1), 5–30.

SYNGE, F. M. and STEPHENS, N. 1966: Late and post-glacial shorelines and ice-limits in Argyll and northeast Ulster. *Trans. Inst. Brit. Geog.* **39,** 101–25.

VALENTIN, H. 1952: Die Küsten der Erde. *Petermanns Geog. Mitt.* Erganzungsheft **246.**

General index

Locational index